ROADS TO ROME

This then, brought our new making. Much emotional stress –
Call it conversion; but the word can't cover such good.
It was like being in love with ambient blessedness –
In love with life transformed – life breathed afresh,
though yet half understood.
There had been many byways for the frustrate brain,
All leading to illusions lost and shrines forsaken …
Our road before us now – one guidance for our gain –
One morning light – whatever the world's weather –
wherein wide-eyed to waken.

Siegfried Sassoon

The publisher wishes to acknowledge the generous aid from
The Stella Maris Fund
toward the publication of
Roads to Rome.

ROADS TO ROME

A GUIDE TO NOTABLE CONVERTS FROM BRITAIN AND IRELAND FROM THE REFORMATION TO THE PRESENT DAY

John Beaumont

Introduction by Joseph Pearce
Foreword by Marcus Grodi

ST. AUGUSTINE'S PRESS
South Bend, Indiana

Manufactured in the United States of America

1 2 3 4 5 6   15 14 13 12 11 10

Library of Congress Cataloging in Publication Data
Beaumont, John.
Roads to Rome: a guide to notable converts from Britain and Ireland
from the Reformation to the present day / John Beaumont:
introduction by Joseph Pearce; preface by Marcus Grodi.
p cm.
Includes bibliographical references.
ISBN 978-1-58731-720-0 (clothbound: alk. paper)
ISBN 978-1-58731-721-7 (limited edition clothbound: alk. paper)
1. Catholic converts – Great Britain – Dictionaries. 2. Catholic converts –
Ireland – Dictionaries. I. Title.
BX4668.A1B385 2010
248.2'42092241 – dc22
[B]   2010024859

∞ The paper used in this publication meets the minimum requirements of the
American National Standard for Information Sciences - Permanence of Paper
for Printed Materials, ANSI Z39.48-1984.

ST. AUGUSTINE'S PRESS
www.staugustine.net

Contents

Acknowledgments

During the preparation of this book I have been very fortunate to have had assistance from many people. There are too many to mention all of them individually, but I would single out Michael Dolan, the librarian of the wonderful Talbot Library in Preston, England, whose generous support is much appreciated, together with that of his staff, in particular John Shaw and the late Charles Miller. I am very grateful to Bruce Fingerhut of St. Augustine's Press for his patience, courtesy, and efficiency. In addition, I owe much to the encouragement and assistance of Bill Wendt, a great American supporter of Catholic causes. Another debt of gratitude is owed to the help and friendship of Anthony Cornwell, whose knowledge of Catholic history is remarkable. I appreciate also the assistance given to me at different times by John Walsh, Brian Morris, Fiona Mercey, and Fr. Michael O'Halloran, SJ. In addition, I have been helped on many occasions by the staff of the Brotherton Library, Leeds University, and the Lancashire County Library Service. Any omissions and errors remain my responsibility.

Finally, in a very real sense I would like to acknowledge a great personal debt to many of the characters included in this book, since it is due in part to them that under God's grace I owe my own conversion to the Catholic faith and reception into the one true fold of Christ on 5th March 1980.

Foreword

For the first forty years of my life, a staunch Protestant from baptism to ordained ministry, I never considered the possibility of becoming a Catholic. No Catholic ever talked to me about the faith and it never crossed my mind that there was any reason whatsoever even to consider the Catholic Church. During those forty years, I had moved between different Protestant churches, but the Catholic Church was never an option.

One piece of disinformation that reinforced my disinterest was that I had never heard of any Protestant minister or otherwise educated Protestant becoming Catholic. I was aware of Catholics becoming Protestant – a third of my congregations were ex-Catholic – and I had heard of priests and nuns as well as laity being "rescued from the whore of Babylon." I also was aware of Protestant laity becoming Catholic through marriage, but I assumed they could do this only because they either had not understood their Protestant faith or merely lacked convictions. But the idea that a well informed sincerely convinced evangelical Protestant could become Roman Catholic was far beyond the pale. Absurd! And I have found that this similar lack of information was shared by most of my friends.

Then through the grapevine I heard a rumor that an old seminary classmate, Dr. Scott Hahn, who upon graduation had also become a Presbyterian minister, had "poped." Because this didn't fit into any of my mental categories, I gave the rumor no heed. I waved it off and moved on.

Then I discovered that there were many others, both those who had converted or were presently on the journey. The fact that there was this steady stream of men and women clergy on the road to Rome – many of whom were like I was, unaware of others on the journey – eventually led to the formation of the *Coming Home Network International*, a lay apostolate established to help non-Catholic ministers and laity "come home" to the Catholic Church.

Is this steady stream of highly informed non-Catholic intellectuals into the Church only a modern phenomenon? Is it merely the result of the modern crisis within Protestantism teamed with the increased accessibility of truth about the Catholic Church through technical media?

Many of us only became aware of conversions to the Catholic Church through contemporary collections of conversion stories, like *Surprised by Truth*, *Spiritual Journeys*, or my own book *Journeys Home*. The truth is, however, that throughout the twentieth century there was a continuous stream of these books. Moreover, books like Joseph Pearce's *Literary Converts* and Patrick Allitt's *Catholic Converts: British and American Intellectuals Turn to Rome* indicate that there have always been clergy and lay converts to the Catholic Church.

In 1907, a D. J. Scannell-O'Neill published a book entitled *Distinguished Converts to Rome in America*. This 180–page book contained nothing less than an amazing annotated alphabetical list of 3000 American converts since the discovery of America! This list included a bishop, 372 clergymen, 3 Rabbis, 115 doctors, 126 lawyers, 45 U.S. Senators and Congressmen, 12 governors, and 180 military officers, from over fifteen different Protestant groups.

What Scannell-O'Neill did for American converts, John Beaumont has now done for the British Isles. Certainly most Brits are familiar with a dozen or so notable British Catholic converts, such as John Henry Newman, Ronald Knox, G. K. Chesterton, or Graham Greene, but Beaumont demonstrates that there has truly been a constant even flow of individuals into the Church, from all walks of life. I dare say almost any of us can look into this list and find an ancestor who was led by the Spirit to come home to the Church.

May this exhaustive list of men and women, who braved the resistance from their old worlds to follow truth and find that pearl of great price, be an encouragement to your own journey of faith.

Marcus C. Grodi
President, Coming Home Network International
Host, *The Journey Home,* EWTN

Preface

This book would never have been written but for the encouragement and support of the late Fr. Stanley Jaki (1924–2009), with whom I had the great privilege of working for the last five years of his life. It was the opinion of Fr. Jaki that the Church had in recent years rather neglected converts. He deplored this and welcomed any attempts to publicize the role played by them in the course of the Church's history. The present volume attempts to do this. Its aim is to draw attention to notable converts in Great Britain and Ireland since the Reformation. Of course, all converts are notable in one important sense. They all add to the life of the Church. They do so in many ways and the greatest of them may be completely unknown to their fellow human beings and known only to God. Almost inevitably the present book selects for consideration those who have a public element in their lives. Some, such as Newman, Campion and Chesterton, are celebrated throughout the world. Others are worthy of note for the different ways in which they have highlighted the Catholic faith. In a few cases this is so even though they sadly lapsed from that faith before their death. The main purpose is to give emphasis to those who set out reasons, usually in print, for taking the "Road to Rome" and making the final move into the One, Holy, Catholic and Apostolic Church. Of course, the list from which one has to choose is enormous. Many others could have been included as being notable in this context. The final choice, though based on the above criteria, was a very difficult one to make.

Each entry gives the date and place of birth, and the date of conversion, where these things are known. In the case of those deceased, the date and place of death is also given, where known. There is then a summary of the person's life and achievements. This may be quite detailed, but, since some converts wrote only about their "journey home" and left very little further information about themselves, it is the case that sometimes little is known about them.

In many cases extracts from writings are then set out. These texts are generally chronological for convenience and are taken from the person in question's own writings, supplemented on occasion by comments of third parties about that person. They are inevitably selective and cannot cover all the issues raised by those who wrote a considerable amount, as is most notably so in the case of such as Cardinal Newman. A list of the more significant written works by or about the person listed is also given (latest editions are generally cited in this respect). In addition, works dealing with converts from a general perspective are cited at the end of the entry, together with a reference to Gillow's *Dictionary of English Catholics*, the *Catholic Encyclopedia*, and the *Dictionary of National Biography*, where these are relevant.

One further aspect of the book's approach should be mentioned. Perhaps the greatest of these converts is John Henry Cardinal Newman and not the least of his achievements is the number of converts he himself brought into the Church. A very fine study of Newman's relationship to converts is that of Fr. Jaki himself in his book,

Newman to Converts, published in 2001. In view of the high quality of argument used by Newman in his correspondence with prospective converts, extracts from his letters to them, as set out in Fr. Jaki's book, have been used frequently during the course of this book. In addition, the introductions written by Fr. Jaki to three earlier booklets on converts written by myself are reproduced as Appendices One to Three to this book.

Appendix Four relates to a matter more controversial. There have been many rumors over the years of royal converts to the Catholic faith further to those noted as definite converts in this book. The most notable relate to King Edward VII and King George V. Whilst the evidence is not conclusive on these two figures, and therefore they are not included in the main text of the book, there is some quite persuasive material supporting the case for their conversion (and for that of George V's wife, Queen Mary). Appendix Four consists of an article co-written with Fr. Mark Elvins, OFM. Cap, on this subject.

Finally, the emphasis placed on Newman, referred to above, explains Appendix Five. This is an attempt to bring home the life-changing nature of conversion, the importance attributed by Newman to the Church as the one true guardian of Revelation, and the crucial importance of the decision to join that body. This is as important now as it ever was.

John Beaumont
5th March 2010

Introduction

One of the biggest problems afflicting modern England is her lack of knowledge of herself. Due to what Hilaire Belloc called the "ignorant wickedness" of the "tomfool Protestant history"[1] with which she has blinded herself, England gropes and flails in the darkness of her self-constructed materialist dungeon. She finds herself in this sorry position because she has lost sight of who she truly is. And she has lost sight of who she truly is because she has forgotten who she truly was. Her problem is one of amnesia.

For more than a thousand years, from her Roman infancy as Albion, and her first martyr, St. Alban, through to the treachery of Henry VIII and his cohorts, England was inseparably united with Christ and His Catholic Church. In her Anglo-Saxon youth she gave us sublime poetry, such as *Beowulf* and "The Dream of the Rood", and a holy host of saints too numerous to mention, whose names emblazon the countless churches dedicated to them which are strewn like manna across her landscape.

In the eleventh century, England was ruled by St Edward the Confessor, a veritable paragon of Christian kingship, and it was during his reign, in 1061, that the Blessed Virgin appeared to a noblewoman at Walsingham in Norfolk, an apparition that is the crowning moment in all of England's history and the greatest blessing that she has ever received. The heavenly apparition and the reign of the saintly king served as the pyrotechnic climax to Anglo-Saxondom, a super nova that burned at its brightest as it passed away. Five years after the apparition and in the same year as Edward's death, England was conquered by the Normans, heralding the setting of the sun on England's Anglo-Saxon ascendency.

For some, such as J. R. R. Tolkien, the Norman Conquest was an unmitigated disaster that destroyed something beautiful and irreplaceable; for others, such as Hilaire Belloc, the Conquest was a glorious rebirth that enabled England to grow into the fullness of her mediaeval splendor. Either way, England was as Catholic and as devoted to her faith after the Conquest as she had been before it. England became known as Our Lady's Dowry, and Walsingham became one of the principal pilgrimage sites of the whole of Christendom.

Nothing, it seemed, could rip England away from her faith, a faith that had refined and defined her.

Then came the so-called English Reformation, a Machiavellian revolution that robbed England and her people of their Christian birthright. Unlike the Protestant Reformation in Europe, the so-called "Reformation" in England had nothing to do

---

1 Hilaire Belloc to Hoffman Nickerson, 13 September 1923, Belloc Collection, Boston College; quoted in Joseph Pearce, *Old Thunder: A Life of Hilaire Belloc*, San Francisco: Ignatius Press, 2002, p.230.

with the difference between Catholicism and Protestantism and everything to do with the cynical determination of Henry VIII to have his own wicked way. And unlike the Reformation in Europe, there was little popular support for anti-Catholic "reform". The people did not want the new "church" that Henry had forced upon them and resented its oppression and its suppression of the Old Faith. In defiance of the king and his henchmen, England remained Catholic in spirit, even if not in its forbidden practice. It took 150 years of brutal and merciless persecution, including the martyrdom of hundreds of faithful Catholics, to browbeat the English into final submission.

And yet it is said that the blood of the martyrs is the seed of the Church and this is as true of England as it was of the Church of the Roman catacombs. In the resistance of the saints is the resurrection of the sinner. And this is where the present volume comes in.

Documenting those who have taken the "roads to Rome" in the years since the Reformation, the present volume encompasses converts from Scotland, Wales and Ireland, as well as those from England. This is as it must be, and should be, because England's destiny became entangled with those of her British neighbors in the wake of the Reformation (for better or worse). The Crown of Ireland Act of 1542 made the Kings of England (Henry VIII and his successors) Kings of Ireland also. In 1603, the accession of James I of England (James VI of Scotland) united the thrones of England and Scotland, thereby forming the United Kingdom of England, Scotland and Ireland, symbolized in the adoption of the crosses of St. George, St. Andrew and St. Patrick as the composite parts of the Union Flag (or Union Jack as it is now more commonly known). Wales is not represented on the nation's flag, indicative of the contemptuous way in which England annexed her diminutive western neighbor, an injustice that the Welsh nationalist convert, Saunders Lewis, lamented with acerbic eloquence.

For almost five hundred years countless Englishmen and their fellow Britons have rediscovered the Faith of their Fathers, converting to Catholicism and thereby entering into communion with their nation's past and its true being. Here we should stress that "true being" is about being true to England's God-given inheritance. The present volume is a priceless testament to those many converts who have kept the flame of faith burning through the centuries. There are the most famous of the Victorians, such as Newman, Patmore, Hopkins, Johnson, Dowson and Wilde, and the most celebrated of the last century's converts, such as Chesterton, Baring, Knox, Noyes, Waugh, Greene, Guinness, Sitwell and Sassoon. And yet the most famous are only the tip of an illustrious iceberg that has been hidden beneath the surface of the ocean of literature on Britain's recent Catholic history. This diving and delving beneath and beyond the surface is the chief strength and value of this particular volume. Here we see, meticulously assembled, a far more comprehensive list of British converts to Rome than has ever been published before. For this reason alone, *Roads to Rome* deserves a place on the shelves of every British Catholic, and indeed on the shelves of every Catholic in the English-speaking world. It serves as an inspiration and an *aide mémoire*, reminding us of who we truly are, as Catholics and as Englishmen, Scotsmen, Irishmen or Welshmen. And lest we forget, these roads to Rome do not leave the British Isles to follow a foreign path to a foreign religion. On the contrary, these roads to Rome go straight through the heart of every man to the Home that every man's heart desires.

Let's end as we began with the words of Hilaire Belloc, a cradle Catholic whose mother, *née* Parkes, is one of the converts featured herein:

> The Faith, the Catholic Church, is discovered, is recognized, triumphantly enters reality like a landfall at sea which at first was thought a cloud. The nearer it is seen, the more is it real, the less imaginary: the more direct and external its voice, the more indubitable its representative character, its 'persona', its voice. The metaphor is not that men fall in love with it: the metaphor is that they discover home. 'This was what I sought. This was my need.' It is the very mould of the mind, the matrix to which corresponds in every outline the outcast and unprotected contours of the soul. It is Verlaine's 'Oh! Rome – oh! Mere!" And that not only to those who had it in childhood and have returned, but much more – and what a proof! – to those who come upon it from over the hills of life and say to themselves 'Here is the town.'[2]

Joseph Pearce
Writer in Residence and Associate Professor of Literature
Ave Maria University, Florida
Author of *Literary Converts* and biographies of Chesterton, Tolkien, Wilde and C. S. Lewis

2 Hilaire Belloc to E. S. P. Haynes, November 8, 1923; quoted in Robert Speaight, *The Life of Hilaire Belloc*, Freeport, New York: Books for Libraries Press, 1970, p. 377. This particular letter was also quoted by Siegfried Sassoon in a letter to a friend on 29 March 1960, in which he ascribed it erroneously as being written by Belloc to Katherine Asquith. Sassoon, one of the converts documented in the present volume, selected this self-same letter by Belloc as the epigraph to *The Path to Peace: Selected Poems by Siegfried Sassoon*, Worcester: Stanbrook Abbey Press, 1960, and it was also subsequently reproduced in D. Felicitas Corrigan (ed.), *Siegfried Sassoon: Poet's Pilgrimage*, London: Victor Gollancz, 1973, pp. 181–2.

Abbreviations

References in the text of this book to "*DNB*" are to the *Oxford Dictionary of National Biography*, in particular the 2004 edition and later updates. References to "*Gillow*" are to Joseph Gillow's *A Biographical and Bibliographical Dictionary of English Catholics*, 5 Volumes (1885–1902). References to "Catholic Encyclopedia" are to what is referred to today as the *Old Catholic Encyclopedia* or *Original Catholic Encyclopedia* published between 1907 and 1914. In relation to individual entries, "b" refers to date of birth, "c" to date of conversion in the sense of reception into the Church, and "d" to date of death.

Roads to Rome

Abbot, Blessed Henry – martyr and yeoman; b. Holden, East Yorkshire; d. 4 July 1597, York; was approached by a Protestant minister who, when detained in York Castle for a misdemeanor, pretended to three Catholic prisoners to have a deep desire to become a Catholic; tried unsuccessfully to find a priest to reconcile the minister to the Church; the traitor informed the magistrate; condemned for "persuading to popery," together with the three Catholic prisoners, Bl. George Errington, Bl. William Knight and Bl. William Gibson (who were executed 29 November 1596); reprieved for six months, then hanged, drawn and quartered at York; see *Gillow*, Vol. I, p.1; *Catholic Encyclopedia*.

Abbot, John (aliases Ashton and John and Augustine Rivers) – poet and priest; b. 1587/8; c. 1623; d. c.1650, Newgate prison; parents unknown; reputed to be nephew of George Abbot, Archbishop of Canterbury in 1611; after studying logic and philosophy at Oxford, traveled on the Continent; visited the English Jesuits at St. Omer and was converted to Catholicism; admitted to St. Alban's College, Valladolid in 1609; then at English College, Douai; ordained priest in 1609 at Louvain and joined the Society of Jesus; joined the English mission in 1615; in 1621 became a secular priest; imprisoned from 1637 until his death; condemned to death in 1641, with six other priests, for being a priest, but execution not carried out because of the political struggles between king and parliament; see *Jesus Praefigured* (1623) (a poem on the holy name of Jesus); *Devout Rhapsodies* (1647) (an anticipation of Milton's *Paradise Lost*); *Gillow*, Vol. I, p.21; *DNB*.

À'Beckett, Arthur William – journalist, novelist, playwright, man of letters; b. 25 October 1844, Fulham; c. 1874 (his brother, Gilbert (see below) received earlier); d. 14 January 1907; son of Gilbert Abbott À'Beckett (1811–1856), comic writer; edited several satirical and humorous magazines; correspondent for *The Standard* and *The Globe* in Franco-German war; private secretary to 15th Duke of Norfolk 1871–1874; on staff of *Punch* 1874–1902; editor of *Sunday Times* 1891–1895 and *Naval and Military Review*; President of Newspaper Society and Institute of Journalists; genial, charming and kindly; close friend of Francis Burnand (see below); collaborated with John Palgrave Simpson (see below); wife, Susannah, a leading woman journalist; buried in Mortlake Catholic cemetery; see *DNB*.

À'Beckett, Gilbert Arthur ("Gil") – playwright, satirist and journalist; b. 7 April 1837, Fulham; c. 1869 (received with his wife, Emily); d. 15 October 1891, London; brother of Arthur William À'Beckett (see above); wrote mainly light comedies; collaborated with W. S. Gilbert on *The Happy Land*, a satirical play, which caricatured Gladstone and provoked a question in parliament; accomplished musician and librettist; on the permanent staff of *Punch* 1879–1891; friend of Francis Burnand (see below); his only son's death by drowning in 1879 greatly affected him; buried in Mortlake Catholic cemetery; see *DNB*.

Abrahams, Harold Maurice – athlete, civil servant, and sports administrator; b. 15 December 1899, Bedford; c. 1934; d. 14 January 1978, London; brought up in Jewish family; fine athlete from young age and at Cambridge; won gold medal in 100 meters at 1924 Olympic Games in Paris; silver medal in the 4 x 100 meters relay; practiced at the bar 1924–1940; engaged in athletics administrtion; journalist with *Sunday Times* 1925–1967; radio broadcaster with BBC 1924–1974; chairman of British Amateur Athletics Board 1948–1975; major force in compilation of athletics statistics; secretary of National Parks Commission 1950–1963; his story featured in the film *Chariots of Fire* (1981); buried at St. John the Baptist churchyard, Great Arnwell, Hertfordshire; see *DNB*.

Acton, Lady Daphne (*née* Strutt) – socialite; b. 5 November 1911, London; c. April 1938 (received by Mgr. Ronald Knox (see below)) in the chapel at Aldenham; d. 18 February 2003; father, 4th Baron Rayleigh, Nobel physicist and agnostic; family part agnostic, part Protestant; educated by governesses; wife of John, 3rd Lord Acton, grandson of the liberal Catholic historian; mother of eleven children; friend of Evelyn Waugh (see below), who referred to her as "a tall, elegant beauty of strong and original intellect" and "the most remarkable woman I know"; formed close platonic friendship with Mgr. Ronald Knox (see below), employing him (1939–1947) as private chaplain at Aldenham Park, creating "an atmosphere which allowed Knox the peace, confidence and purpose to produce his version of the Bible" (obituary, *The Times*, 2 April 2003); emigrated to Southern Rhodesia

after the war, where "with missionary zeal she built a school and a church to enlighten the local people and evangelize among them" (*ibid*); opponent of UDI; finally returned to England.

Adams, Blessed John – priest and martyr; b. about 1543, Winterbourne St. Martin, Dorset; d. 8 October 1586; formerly Calvinist minister; ordained priest at Rheims 17 December 1580; returned to England on the missions in 1581, working chiefly in Hampshire; helped especially the poor; good controversialist; apprehended and imprisoned in the Marshalsea in 1584; banished in 1585; returned to England, but apprehended and imprisoned in the Clink; condemned for priesthood; hanged, drawn and quartered at Tyburn; see *Gillow*, Vol. I, p.7; *Catholic Encyclopedia*.

Adelham (or Adland), John Placid, OSB – priest; b. in Wiltshire; d. between 1681 and 1685; formerly Protestant minister; joined Order of St. Benedict in France; sent to England and was at Somerset House 1661–1675; banished but returned to England; victim of Popish Plot; condemned to death as a priest in 1678/9, but reprieved and detained in Newgate prison where he died; great admirer of St. Augustine; see *Gillow*, Vol. I, p.8.

Aikenhead, Mary Frances (name in religion Sister Mary Augustine, though always known as Mrs. Aikenhead) – nun; b. 19 January 1787, Cork, Ireland; c. 6 June 1802 (some time after death of her father, David Aikenhead, a doctor, who had been received into the Church on his death-bed); d. 22 July 1858, Dublin; father a member of Church of Ireland, mother came from Catholic recusant family; baptized in father's religion; fostered out to a Catholic couple; after returning to her home at six years of age, she accompanied her father to his church on Sundays, but Catholic influences persisted as other relatives introduced her to Ursuline and Presentation nuns; came to Dublin, served the poor, and felt called to the religious life; looked in vain for an order devoted to outside charitable work, when chosen by Archbishop Murray, Coadjutor of Dublin, to found a congregation of the Sisters of Charity in Ireland; in preparation made a novitiate of three years (1812–1815) in Convent of the Institute of the Blessed Virgin in York; in September 1815 first members of new Order took their vows and she was appointed Superior-General; organized community and extended its sphere of work to every phase of charity, chiefly hospital and rescue work; health ruined by over-exertion and disease, but she worked on; buried in cemetery of St Mary Magdalen's Convent in Donnybrook, Dublin; see Cecily Hallack, *Mother Mary Aikenhead: A Sketch of Her Life* (1937); Fr. Hilary, OFM Cap, "Mother Mary Aikenhead," *Irish Ecclesiastical Record*, July 1958, p.28; M. Donovan, *Apostolate of Love: Mary Aikenhead, 1787–1858, Foundress of the Irish Sisters of Charity* (1979); Mairead Mahon, "Mary Aikenhead: Foundress of the Religious Order, the Sisters of Charity," *Catholic Life*, August 2008, p.52; *Catholic Encyclopedia*; *DNB*.

Ainsworth, Sophia Magdalene (*née* Hanmer) (in religion Sister Mary Anne Liguori of Jesus Crucified, OSSR) – nun; b. 22 July 1819; c. 14 June 1850 (received by Newman; her husband, John (d. 1871) converted in 1870; her brother, Anthony Hanmer (see below), received in 1849); d. 1 April 1882; brought up as an Anglican; greatly influenced by the treatise *On Conformity to the Holy Will of God* by St. Alphonsus; instructed by Newman; founded several Catholic missions; after husband's death became a nun of the Redemptorist Order; see *Gillow*, Vol. I, p.10.

Alabaster (or Arblastier), William – writer and scholar; b. 27 February 1568, Hadleigh, Suffolk; c. 1597; d. April 1640, London; nephew by marriage of Dr. John Still, later Anglican Bishop of Bath and Wells, who assisted with his education; Fellow of Trinity College, Cambridge, where Still was master; showed flair for literature; in 1596 joined the Earl of Essex as a chaplain on the Cadiz expedition; in that captured city he had his first contacts with Catholics and Catholic worship; in 1597 in London met Fr. Thomas Wright, a Catholic priest under house arrest ("It was hoped that the brilliant Alabaster would convert Wright, but the reverse appears to have happened" (*DNB*)); letters from Fr. Wright indicating the conversion were intercepted; wrote many of his celebrated religious sonnets at this time; sent to the Clink prison in Southwark, where unsuccessful attempts were made by Anglican theologians to sway him; escaped from prison; sheltered by Fr. Francis Gerard, who introduced him to the spiritual exercises of St. Ignatius Loyola and arranged for him to travel to Rome via Douai; in 1598 entered English College, Rome; wrote there a lengthy manuscript narrating his conversion; in 1599 went to Spain and set out for England; captured by English agents in La Rochelle and taken to the Tower of London, then on to Framlingham Castle in 1601; pardoned at accession of James I in 1603; back in Rome he wrote in 1607 a book on cabbalistic divinity, which was condemned by the Inquisition in 1610; fled to Amsterdam and returned to England; in custody, but made peace with Church of England; granted various livings, was made a royal chaplain, and married; later publications on occult, cabbalism, alchemy, and medicine (follower of John Dee's works); praised by Spenser and Samuel Johnson for his poetry and by Robert Herrick for his theological writings; buried in the churchyard of St. Dunstan-in-the–West; see *Alabaster's Conversion*, Mss, English College, Rome; Robert V. Caro, OP, "William Alabaster: Rhetor, Meditator, Devotional Poet, Parts I and II," *Recusant History*, May 1988, p.62 and October 1988, p.155; Fr. Jerome Bertram, "The Conversion of William Alabaster," *The Venerabile*, 2002, p.14; *DNB*.

Albemarle, seventh Earl of, and Viscount Bury (William Coutts Keppel) – soldier and politician; b. 15 April 1832, London; c. 13 April 1879, Easter Sunday (earlier conversion of his father-in-law, Sir Alan Napier MacNab, speaker of the Canadian parliament, had led to uproar in Canada); d. 28 August 1894, Prospect House, Barnes, Surrey; used title of Viscount Bury from 1851 until 1891; army officer and private secretary to Lord John Russell; Liberal MP for Norwich (later became Conservative); ADC to Queen Victoria in 1881; under-secretary of State for War during administrations of Lords Beaconsfield and Salisbury; had public row with Gladstone in 1880 about First Vatican Council (1870); author, *inter alia*, of history of North America, with particular reference to Canada; buried at family seat, Quidenham, Norfolk; see *DNB*.

Alfield (Aufield; Alphilde, Hawfield, Offeldus; alias Badger), Blessed Thomas – priest and martyr; b. 1552, Gloucester; d. 6 July 1585, London; brought up as Protestant; educated at Eton and Cambridge; reconciled to Catholicism; went to English College, Douai, then at Rheims; ordained priest 4 March 1581, Chalons; returned to England same month; converted another future martyr, Bl. William Deane; witnessed execution of St. Edmund Campion 1 December 1581; worked mainly in the north; arrested in 1582 and tortured; agreed to go to Protestant services and was released; great penitence and went back to Rheims to gather his resolve; in 1583 again refused to go to Protestant services; with Thomas Webley, a dyer, imported and distributed William Allen's book, *Modest Defence of the English Catholiques*; tortured and committed to Newgate prison; condemned for publishing a book against the queen; both refused to renounce the Pope and acknowledge Elizabeth's ecclesiastical supremacy; reprieve arrived for him, but too late; hanged at Tyburn (not quartered as not convicted of treason); see *Gillow*, Vol. I, p.12; *Catholic Encyclopedia*; *DNB* ("Robert Persons commented at the time: 'It is thus that these men answer our books – by hanging us'").

Allies, Thomas William – historical writer; b. 12 February 1813, Midsomer Norton, Somerset; c. 11 September 1850 (received by Newman; his wife, Eliza (1821–1902) received on 24 May 1850; his daughter-in-law, Kathleen, received in 1881); d. 17 June 1903, 3 Lodge Place, St. John's Wood, London; son of Anglican rector and brought up in country parsonage; voracious reader with love of both classical and modern languages; first in Classics at Oxford; Fellow of Wadham College, Oxford 1833–1841, when in close contact with Newman and Pusey; had religious conversion and became Anglican clergyman; committed Tractarian and chaplain to Anglican Bishop of London; affected by Gorham decision (see entry for William Maskell); much correspondence with Newman before his conversion; one of most learned of Oxford converts; renounced his living, his occupation and his prospects ("In those days ... I was supported continually by Fr. Newman's advice. He was my polar star, which never set"); secretary of Poor School Committee 1853–1890; greatly furthered work of training colleges and system of religious inspection of primary schools; first Professor of Modern History at Catholic University of Ireland, Dublin; close friend of Aubrey de Vere (see below) and Lord Acton; specialized in religious subjects; very extensive writings on history of the Church, especially predominance in history of the See of Peter; father of Mary Helen Agnes Allies (1852–1907), historian and translator (and author of a biography of her father); a son, Henry Basil (1844–1897) became a priest; buried at St Mary Magdalene's, Mortlake, by the side of his wife; see *The See of St. Peter, the Rock of the Church, the Source of Jurisdiction and the Centre of Unity* (1850), *St. Peter, His Name and His Office* (1852), *The Formation of Christendom*, 8 Vols. (1861–1895), *Per Crucem Ad Lucem* (1879), *A Life's Decision* (1880) ("More than all ... there was in becoming a Catholic, the sense of being where Christ crucified is set forth in every doctrine and principle. Protestantism had for years seemed to me nothing but Christianity without the Cross – the substitution of *human* motives, *natural* doctrines, and *natural* virtues, for grace, truth, faith, hope, and charity: a system of naturalism had been the grand result of a revolt against the divine city wherein the Crucified One is King. Whereas, at the bottom of all religious orders, of all the teachings and ministrations of the Church, what is there but the Cross? The cutting oneself off from innocent pleasures, the detaching oneself from the world and all its bonds, for Christ's sake, and after Christ's example, and to save one's neighbor and oneself. Protestantism, and specially our form of it, Anglicanism, as it reduced truth to the holding of individual opinions, so it reduced teaching and ministering from being the simple exhibition of Christ to the world, marked with the nails, the scourging and the thorns, and therefore drawing all men unto Him, to a worldly system of rewards and prizes, of comforts and home delights, tolerable as a moral police, and admirably clever in this country as a political institution, but powerless to do Christ's work. The weakness of the individual may, in the former system, fall in numberless instances below such a divine ideal, but there it is, set up in the world. If Catholics be but true to what they are taught, Catholicism is Christ Himself in the world, teaching and converting it. This is the most sovereign of proofs, the most convincing logic. Protestants may be better than their system; they often are, for 'Spiritus Domini replevit orbem terrarum'; but of no Catholic could it ever be said that he is better than his system, for the innermost principles on which it is built are Christ crucified – give up this world and all that it contains for God, for your soul, for your neighbor. To have this world and the next too is more than Christ had and more than He promised to His followers"); Mary H. Allies, *Thomas William Allies* (1924); V. Alan McClelland, "'The Most Turbulent Priest of the Oxford Diocese': Thomas William Allies and the Quest for Authority," in V. Alan McClelland (ed), *By Whose Authority: Newman, Manning and the Magisterium* (1996), Ch. XIV; Stanley L. Jaki, *Newman to Converts: An Existential Ecclesiology* (2001), Ch. 7; *Catholic Encyclopedia* ("The Fathers, especially St. Augustine, revealed to him the Catholic Church. Moreover, they revealed him to himself.... He thought to find Anglicanism in the Fathers, and his first book is the result of this delusion. It was entitled *The Church of England Cleared from the Charge of Schism....* It gives the keynote of his lifelong labor and the whole question between Anglican and Catholic in a nutshell. As he perceived early in the day, the choice of the Royal Supremacy or Peter's Primacy was the key to the whole controversy"); *DNB*.

Anderdon, William Henry, OP – priest and writer; b. 26 December 1816, New Street, Spring Gardens, London; c. 23 November 1850, France (his cousin, Blanche Anderdon (d. 1907), novelist, who wrote under name of Whyte Avis, converted in 1880); d. 28 July 1890, Roehampton; nephew of Cardinal Manning; cousin of Marquise de Salvo (see below); brought up as Evangelical; High Church leanings at Oxford; became Anglican vicar; ordained Catholic priest in 1853; DD of Rome 1869; for three years chaplain and later Dean of Catholic University College, Dublin; private secretary to Cardinal Manning 1856–1872; member of the Society of Jesus from 1872; many contributions to Catholic journals and newspapers; much writing including apologetics and Catholic tales (e.g., *The Adventures of Owen Evans* (1862), story of conversion of a marooned Welsh sailor, often referred to as "the Catholic Crusoe"); fine controversialist; see *A Letter to the Parishioners of St. Margaret's, Leicester* (1851) (description of his conversion); *Is There a Church and What is It?* (1854); *Afternoons With the Saints* (1863); *Controversial Papers* (1878); *What do Catholics Really Believe?: Confession to a Priest* (1881); *Fasti Apostolici: a Chronology of the Years between the Ascension of Our Lord and the Martyrdom of SS. Peter and Paul* (1882); *Evenings With the Saints* (1883); *Luther at Table: A Few elegant Extracts from his Talk* (1883); *Luther's Words and the Word of God* (1883); *What Sort of Man was Luther?* (1883); *Britain's Early Faith* (1888) ("A small church in Cornwall, dated from the fifth century, built by a Saint of well-known name, and recently dug out from the sand that had long concealed it, is adduced as an example of the ancient British Church having been simple in worship, and untainted by the supposed later additions of 'Roman Catholicism.' We have seen, on the contrary, that the church was invaded by the sand before the Norman Conquest, was therefore abandoned, and its furniture transferred to a new one; but that it witnessed in its ruins, to one of the most distinctive Catholic doctrines and practice, by the massive stone altar still remaining, with the Saint's relics enshrined beneath"); *Catholic Encyclopedia*; *DNB*.

Anderson (alias Munson), Lionel Albert, OP – priest; b. c.1633, Lincolnshire; c. 1655; d. 21 October 1710, London; received into the Catholic Church in Lisbon and made his way to Rome, where joined the Dominican Order; ordained priest in 1665; returned to England to work on the missions; worked in London, known at court, and personally known to Charles II; accused by Titus Oates of being a conspirator; tried and condemned to death at Old Bailey, but granted a pardon by the king and exiled for life; made pilgrimage to Holy Land; returned to England and given free pardon by James II in 1686; at Revolution in 1688, he fled with king to the Continent; returned to England, living in London until his death; buried in churchyard of St. Giles-in-the-Fields; see *Gillow*, Vol. I, p.29; *Catholic Encyclopedia*; *DNB*.

Anderson, Robin – writer; b. 1913, London; c. 17 April 1946; educated at Marlborough College and London Royal Academy of Dramatic Art; worked as a stage manager to Sir John Gielgud; conversion influenced by the writings of Gerard Manley Hopkins (see below) and

Cardinal Newman; from 1953 lived in Rome, working as a speaker for Vatican Radio and teacher of languages; writer of several papal biographies and guides to Rome; promoted the cause for beatification of the Servant of God Raphael Cardinal Merry del Val; see letter in 1974 to Fr. Winterton of the Birmingham Oratory ("I, the undersigned, who received, in 1945 in London, the great and decisive grace of approaching the Catholic Church, through reading the article in *The Times Literary Supplement*, 'Newman Decides' … and seeing Newman's portrait"); *The Quiet Grave: Intimate Journals – Part I* (1966) ("Found myself, while critically examining Newman's portrait, reverencing his face. It is the calm, sweet, bright and simple truth. What clearer testimony that this is the way? If there is nothing in it, and personal sanctity is all that counts, apart from attachment to the holy Church, why does my whole being stir, with a strange, warm, longing joy, to think of attachment to the holy Church. Saw the picture of Ven. Dominic Barberi's face next to that of Newman – and recognized truth and goodness whole and entire…

Seek God, and God only, Then all the rest will fall into place. Ultimately, all questions are between God and the person – not between persons and persons – because 'I' *am* only that particle of THOU ART which I AM. Though I cannot perfect imperfection, in imperfection, I can perfect myself. Rain must fall on the just and unjust alike. Goodness must often go unrewarded, as wickedness seemingly rewarded, since, if there were fixed rewards for being good, men might turn to goodness for the sake of the reward. One must distinguish between seeing the finger of God in accidents, and believing accidents to be the finger of God. 'To depart from evil *is* understanding; and wisdom is the fear of the Lord'"); *St. Pius V: A Brief Account of his Life, Times, Virtues and Miracles* (1973); *Between Two Wars: The Story of Pope Pius XI (Achille Ratti 1922–1939)* (1977); *Rome Churches of Special Interest for English-Speaking People* (1982); *Pope Pius VII (1800–1823): His Life, Times and Struggle with Napoleon in the Aftermath of the French Revolution* (2001).

Anderton (alias Scroop or Scroope or Scrope), Laurence, SJ (also known as Laurence Rigby) – priest; b. 1575, Chorley, Lancashire; c. 1598; d. 17 April 1643, Lancashire; conversion influenced by his historical reading, through which he developed doubts about validity of the Reformation; left for the English College, Seville, between 1597 and 1599; ordained and left for the English mission 1602/3; in 1604, in England, entered the Society of Jesus; worked around the Lancashire area; won several converts, including his relative James Anderton of Lostock (before his death in 1613), and his nephew, who later became a Jesuit; became Superior of Lancashire Jesuit District in 1625; then often in London and Rome; great controversialist and moral teacher; on the English mission for nearly forty years; see *One God, One Fayth* (1625); *The Progenie of Catholicks and Protestants* (1633); *The Triple Chord* (1634) (800 pages long defense of the Catholic faith with proofs out of Scripture); J. F. Giblin, *The Anderton Family of Birchley* (1993); *Gillow*, Vol. V, p.421; *DNB* ("Developed the doubts he had discovered before his conversion about the historical validity of Protestantism into a full-scale attack on the Reformation as an innovation").

Andrews, William Eusebius – writer and publisher; b. 1773; d. 7 April 1837; in 1813 published first number of the *Orthodox Journal*, a monthly periodical devoted to English Catholic affairs;

stimulated the debate on Catholic emancipation in its pages; buried at Holy Trinity Church, Dockhead, Bermondsey,
Southwark, South London; see *DNB*.

Angus, George – priest; b. 1842; c.
1873; d. 1909; at one time Ensign and
Lieutenant in the Indian Army; then
High Anglican curate; owed his conversion to Fr. Richard Clarke, SJ (see
below); ordained Catholic priest; chaplain of Catholic University College,
Kensington, London; contributor to *The
Tablet*; see essay in J. G. F. Raupert (ed),
Roads to Rome (1901), p.1 ("I addressed
myself to one point: What and Where is
the Church of God? What? Now, the way
was so far easy, as both High Anglicans
and Catholics were, and are, quite agreed
that the Church is a visible body. 'A city
set on a hill that cannot be hid.' Three
things, then, might be asserted concerning this Visible Body. (1) [It] has a Visible Head – the Pope. (2) [It] has no
Visible Head. (3) [It] has several Visible
Heads – the Bishops; the Universal Episcopate. Now take (2) and (3). The Visible
Body has no Visible Head. Then it is an
abortion or a corpse. Or the Visible Body
has several heads. Then it is hydra-
headed, and is – a monster. I really could
not have anything to do with (2) or (3),
so had to fall back upon (1), a Visible
Body with a Visible Head. This brought
me to where? Was there any society
claiming to be the Visible Body with a
Visible Head? If so – where? The Church
of England? No. She claims to be *a*
Church, but not *the* Church. The Greek
Church? No, again. For if she claims to
be *the* Church, she neglects her obvious
duty of trying to persuade all men to belong to her. In a word, she does not 'go
and make disciples of all nations,' nor
does she even attempt to preach the
gospel to all men. There remained, then,
the Roman Church – using popular language. About *her* position there could be

no doubt. She is a Visible Body with a
Visible Head. She claims to be the One
Universal Church. She tries to make disciples from all nations. She endeavors to
preach the gospel to all mankind. She
knows no limits of nationality or geography. Judgment, I think, goes by default. There is no other claimant. After
this, there was no course open but to submit to her claims as those of the One Divine Teacher, commissioned to guide
men into all truth. So I submitted and
was received…

Do I like everything in the Catholic religion now? By no means. As the Church
has her human element, as she is composed of men and women, of course I do
not like everything – or, for that matter,
everybody – with which, or with whom,
I come into contact. But these things are
matters of taste. In the Catholic religion
there is an amount of freedom found
nowhere else. We believe whatever the
Church teaches, simply because she is
the Church, and in all else she allows her
children a wide liberty. I do not say that
she authorizes, or even approves, every
popular devotion, practice, habit, or custom to be found here and there. But, as a
loving mother, she tolerates what she
may not approve and would not authorize. To be tolerant is one thing; to approve, or authorize, is another").

Anlaby (or Andleby), Blessed William
– priest and martyr; b. Etton, Beverley;
East Yorkshire; d. 4 July 1597, York;
brought up in Protestant religion with
strong disliking for the Catholic Church;
after Cambridge went abroad to the
Netherlands wars; paid visit to Douai out
of curiosity where he met William Allen,
which resulted in his conversion and his
joining the college; ordained priest at
Cateau Cambrésis, France, 23 March
1577; returned to England that year and
worked on the missions for twenty years,
mainly in Yorkshire and chiefly among

the poor; caught and condemned to death for being a priest; hanged, drawn and quartered at York, together with Thomas Warcop, charged with harboring him, and Edward Fulthrop, another layman; see Challoner, *Memoirs of Missionary Priests*; *Gillow*, Vol. I, p.52; *DNB*.

Anne, Duchess of York (*née* Anne Hyde) – b. 12 March 1637, Cranborne Lodge, Windsor Park; c. August 1670 (received by Fr. Christopher Davenport, alias Hunt, OSF (see below); husband converted earlier; her only sister, Frances, also became a Catholic); d. 31 March 1671; daughter of Edward Hyde, Earl of Clarendon, Lord Chancellor of England; maid of honor to Princess of Orange; she attracted attention of princess's brother, the Duke of York, afterwards James II (see below); in 1660 contracted clandestine marriage with him according to rites of Church of England; educated according to High Church wing of Church of England, but ultimately reconciled to the Catholic Church despite great opposition by her brother and the clergy; converted by study of motives and methods of Reformation, she was unable to reconcile these things with the interests of truth; became convinced that Church of England lacked that essential mark of the Church: holiness; John Dryden (see below) wrote defending the reasons given for her conversion; also partly her experience of Catholic life on the Continent brought her to Catholicism; her eldest daughter, Mary (1662–1694) married her cousin, William of Orange; her other daughter, later Queen Anne (1664–1714), succeeded to throne in 1702; buried in vault of Mary, Queen of Scots, in Henry VII's chapel at Westminster Abbey; see *A Copie of a paper written by the late Duchess of York, reprinted – Reasons of her leaving the communion of the Church of England, and making herself a member of the Roman Catholick Church* (1686); *Gillow*, Vol. III, p.522; *DNB* ("When James became a Catholic, he showed her a number of works on the Reformation, notably those of Peter Heylin, who suggested that the destruction of the old religion in England was motivated primarily by greed for church property").

Anscombe, (Gertrude) Elizabeth Mary – philosopher; b. 18 March 1919, Limerick, Ireland; c. 27 April 1938; d. 5 January 2001, Cambridge; wife of Peter Geach (see below); awarded a research fellowship for postgraduate study at Newnham College, Cambridge 1942–1945; taught philosophy at Oxford University 1946–1970; Professor of Philosophy at Cambridge University 1970–1986; an outstanding figure among twentieth century philosophers, her work ranging across logic, philosophy of mind and action, philosophy of religion, and ethics; close friend of Ludwig Wittgenstein; later translator and literary executor of Wittgenstein; original thinker with wide-ranging knowledge of history of philosophy; also wrote about moral, political, and religious issues; protested against Oxford University's decision to grant an honorary degree to Harry S. Truman, whom she denounced as a mass murderer for his use of atomic bombs at Hiroshima and Nagasaki; devout Catholic who argued in favor of traditional Catholic teachings; active role in pro-life movement; arrested twice while protesting outside an abortion clinic in Britain; see *Three Philosophers: Aristotle, Aquinas, Frege* (1963) (with P. T. Geach); *On Transubstantiation* (1967); *Contraception and Chastity* (1975) ("From '64 onwards there was an immense amount of propaganda for the reversal of previous teaching [on artificial contraception]. You will remember it. Then, with the whole world baying at him to change, the Pope acted as Peter. 'Simon, Simon,' Our Lord said to Peter, 'Satan has wanted to have you to sift like wheat, but I have prayed for thee that thy faith should not fail: and thou, being once converted, strengthen thy brethren.' Thus Paul confirmed the only doctrine which has ever appeared as the teaching of the Church on these things; and in doing so incurred the execration of the world.

But Athenagoras, the Ecumenical Patriarch, who has the primacy of the Orthodox Church, immediately spoke up and confirmed that this was Christian teaching, the only possible Christian teaching...

The teaching which I have rehearsed is indeed against the grain of the world, against the current of our time. But that, after all, is what the Church as teacher is for. The truths that are acceptable to a time – as, that we owe it as a debt of justice to provide out of our superfluity for the destitute and the starving – these will be proclaimed not only by the Church: the Church teaches *also* those truths that are hateful to the spirit of an age"); *Collected Philosophical Papers*, 3 Vols. (1981); "Faith," in *Collected Philosophical Papers, Vol. III* (1981), p.113 ("In general, 'faith comes by hearing', that is, those who have faith learn what they believe by faith, learn it from other people. So someone who so believes believes what is told him by another human, who may be very ignorant of everything except that this is what he has to tell as the content of faith.... If so, then according to faith a simple man – a man with no knowledge of evidence – may have faith when he is taught by a man ignorant of everything except that these are the things that faith believes. More than that, according to faith this simple man and his teacher have a belief in no way inferior to that of a very learned and clever person who has faith"); "Philosophy,

Belief, and Faith," *Priests and People*, October 1995, p.387 ("I remember the thrill I felt when I read God described as 'the First Cause'. (I had not been brought up as a Christian, apart from being taught the Lord's Prayer.) If I had expressed my joy, I would have said 'Of course, there must be a First Cause, and that's what God is.' The other day I heard a not irreligious natural scientist on the radio saying he could not understand the concept of 'God.' I thought about this and wondered what he would say if one told him, 'God is the intelligence that made the universe'"); Luke Gormally (ed), *Moral Truth and Moral Tradition: Essays in Honour of Peter Geach and Elizabeth Anscombe* (1994); Michael Dummett, "Obituary," *The Tablet*, 13 January 2001, p.62 ("How did she combine Catholicism with Wittgensteinian philosophy? It never occurred to her that there was any difficulty. She did not do it by interpreting Catholic doctrines in Wittgenstein's manner, as expressive of various attitudes; her understanding of them was not only undeviatingly orthodox but literal, even literalistic. An Italian priest once said of her, 'Her philosophy is subtle and sophisticated, but her religion is that of a peasant.' I have been told that she was very pleased when this remark was reported to her. She understood the divine inspiration of scripture in a highly rigorous way"); John M. Dolan, "G. E. M. Anscombe: Living the Truth," *First Things*, May 2001, p.11; Mary Geach and Luke Gormally (ed), *Human Life, Action and Ethics: Essays by G. E. M. Anscombe* (2005); David Jones, "Portrait of a Catholic Philosopher," *Pastoral Review*, May/June 2006, p.51; Mary Geach and Luke Gormally (ed), *Faith in a Hard Ground: Essays on Religion, Philosophy and Ethics by G. E. M. Anscombe* (2008).

Anson, Peter Frederick Charles – writer and painter; b. 22 August 1889, Southsea; c. 1913; d. 10 July 1975, Edinburgh; son of Admiral Charles Anson (1858–1940), often known as the father of the British Navy; brought up in Anglican family; great love of sea, but trained as architect; became member of Caldey Anglican Benedictine community from 1910; one of twenty-two monks there received into the Church and wrote biography of Abbot, Aelred Carlyle (see below); remained at Caldey until returning to outside world in 1924; writer on history and the Church; painted mainly shipping and the sea; co-founder in 1921 of the Apostleship of the Sea for the spiritual welfare of Catholic seafarers; spent much time on coast of north-east Scotland; founder of Society of Marine Artists; Franciscan tertiary from 1924; choir oblate of Cistercian Order; much illness; much traveling and restlessness of spirit; it amused him to witness the "spiritual nudity" of contemporary Catholicism that was making their churches look like Presbyterian chapels he had known in Scotland; buried at Sancta Maria Abbey, Nunraw, East Lothian, Scotland; see *The Quest of Solitude* (1932); *The Benedictines of Caldey* (1944); *A Roving Recluse: More Memoirs* (1946); *Christ and the Sailor: A Study of Maritime Incidents in the New Testament* (1954); *Fashions in Church Furnishings, 1840–1940* (1965); *These Made Peace: Studies in the Lives of the Beatified and Canonized Members of the Third Order of St. Francis of Assisi* (1963) (co-written with Cecily Hallack (see below)); *Bishops at Large* (1964) (study of episcopi vagantes); *The Art of the Church* (1964) (with Iris Conlay); *The Building of Churches* (1965); *The Call of the Desert* (1973); "An Octogenarian's Memories of the Liturgical Movement," *Clergy Review*, December 1974, p.809 ("Friends have often asked how as an octogenarian who in most ways tends to have a conservative outlook, and is a member of the Victorian Society, I can stand the wholesale innovations which have resulted from the constitution *Sacrosanctum Concilium*. The simplest answer is to quote the Profession of Faith recited in 1913 when I 'went over to Rome', 'I sincerely and solemnly declare that, having been brought up in the Protestant Religion, but now, by the grace of God, having been brought to the knowledge of the Truth, I firmly believe and profess all that the Holy, Catholic, Apostolic Roman Church believes and teaches, and I reject and condemn whatever she rejects and condemns"); Dom Bede Camm, *The Call of Caldey: The Story of the Conversion of Two Communities* (1940); Walter Romig (ed), *The Book of Catholic Authors*, Second Series (1943); Michael Yelton, *Peter Anson: Monk, Writer and Artist* (2005); *DNB*.

Anstey, Hon. Thomas Chisholm – barrister and politician; b. 1816, Kentish Town, London; c. 1836; d. 12 August 1873, Bombay, India; educated in Tasmania where his parents were among the earliest settlers; greatly influenced by Oxford Movement and was one of its earliest converts to the Catholic Church; close friend of Frederick Lucas (see below); fought for Catholic political interests in England and Ireland; for a time Professor of Law at the Catholic Priory Park College, Bath; MP for Youghal, Ireland; at first ardent supporter of Daniel O'Connell; later Attorney-General of Hong Kong; then law practice in India and judge of High Court of Bombay; his tackling of abuses in both countries led to his suspension and resignation; advocated universal suffrage; see *Catholic Encyclopedia*; *DNB*.

Antcliffe, Herbert – writer and composer; b. 1875; c. 1914; d. 1964; former Anglican layman; writer on music; composer of orchestral and chamber music, part-songs and church music; much of his working life spent as music and literary critic in London and Holland; from 1925 correspondent in Holland of the *Daily Mail*, and also contributed articles on Dutch art, music and politics to *The Times*, as well as acting as correspondent of *New York Herald Tribune*; treasurer, vice-president and president of the Foreign Press Association in Holland, resuming this last post after the war; caught in Holland by the Nazi invasion and unable to do journalistic work during Occupation (during which both he and his Dutch wife suffered from near-starvation); returned to Britain in 1949; author of several books on music; Fellow of Royal Society of Arts; see *Grove's Dictionary of Music and Musicians*.

Armstrong, (Arthur) Hilary – classical scholar; b. 13 August 1909, Hove, Sussex; c. 1942; d. 16 October 1997, Hereford; father a High Church Anglican clergyman and Tory; given a devout Anglican education and a traditional classical education; expert on Plotinus; Professor of Classics at University of Malta 1939–1943; Gladstone Professor of Greek at Liverpool University 1950–1972; visiting Professor of Classics at University of Dalhousie, Canada, 1972–1982; favored "negative theology"; growing disagreements with the Catholic Church led to his going back to Anglicanism; came to doubt the notion of personal survival; see "The Nature of Paganism," *Blackfriars*, February 1936, p.120; *The Architecture of the Intelligible Universe in the Philosophy of Plotinus* (1940); *Christian Faith and Greek Philosophy* (1960) (with R. A. Markus); *Plotinian and Christian Studies* (1979); *Hellenic and Christian Studies* (1990);

DNB ("When Malta was besieged, a friend who was an Orthodox priest chanted Greek prayers during bombing raids, an experience that Armstrong still described in his late correspondence").

Arnold, Thomas – literary scholar, teacher and barrister; b. 30 November 1823, Laleham, Middlesex; c. 18 January 1856, Hobart, Tasmania (to horror of his first wife, Julia (1825–1888), a Protestant, who wrote to Cardinal Newman, accusing him of persuading her husband "to ignore every social duty and become a pervert" and adding "From the bottom of my heart I curse you for it"; she also smashed the windows of the chapel during his confirmation!; received by Bishop Robert Willson of Tasmania); d. 12 November 1900, 16 Adelaide Road, Dublin; one of nine children of Dr. Thomas Arnold (1795–1842), headmaster of Rugby School and Anglican clergyman; brother of Matthew Arnold (1822–1888), the poet and critic; at Oxford lapsed from Anglican orthodoxy; first in Classics at Balliol; taught and farmed in New Zealand; influenced in particular by Frederic Weld of the old Catholic recusant family; after conversion Professor of English Literature at Catholic University of Dublin; classics master at Birmingham Oratory School; contributor to Catholic journals; reverted to Anglicanism when he learned of Pope Pius IX's *Syllabus of Errors*; in 1878, on the eve of being appointed Professor of Anglo-Saxon at Oxford, he reconverted to Catholicism, again to horror of his wife and leading to a "semi-detached" marriage; returned to same post in Dublin; father of Mary, Mrs. Humphry Ward (1851–1920), novelist; buried in Glasnevin cemetery, Dublin; see *A Catholic Dictionary* (editions from 1884 until 1957) (jointly with William Edward Addis); *Passages in a Wandering Life* (1900); Katherine Chorley, "Thomas

Arnold I and II," *The Month*, September 1954, p.146 and October 1954, p.209 ("Tom remembered that the early *Tracts for the Times* had dealt with the beginnings of Christianity, the first documents.... 'The unity of the Christian system from the start, and the care with which that unity was preserved seemed to me undeniable.' Other incidents contributed to fix and deepen the new direction of his thought. At a country inn, he came across the volumes of Butler's *Lives of the Saints* and took out one at random. It contained the life of St. Brigit of Sweden. Tom's attention was riveted. He began to realize the Catholic conception of sanctity and saw St. Brigit as the direct heir in an unbroken succession, contained within the firm boundary of the Roman Church, of the early saints and martyrs"); Meriol Trevor, *The Arnolds: Thomas Arnold and His Family* (1973); Bernard Bergonzi, *A Victorian Wanderer: A Life of Thomas Arnold the Younger* (2003); *DNB*.

Asquith, Lady Katharine (*née* Horner) – b. 1885; c. 1923 (followed in 1927 by her eldest daughter, Lady Helen (1908–1999), classics scholar and teacher, and in 1930 by her youngest daughter, Perdita (b. 1910), wife of the fourth Baron Hylton); d. 1976; wife of Raymond Asquith (1878–1916), scholar and army officer, killed on the Western Front; daughter-in-law of Prime Minister, Herbert Asquith; great friend of Lady Diana Cooper; inherited manor house at Mells, Somerset; Fr. Ronald Knox came to live there in 1949; social contacts with Hilaire Belloc, Christopher Hollis (see below), Evelyn Waugh (see below), Maurice Baring (see below) (latter a great influence on her conversion, as was Fr. Vincent McNabb); see A. N. Wilson, *Hilaire Belloc* (1984), *passim* ("She found, for a long period, that she was unable to believe in life after death, still less in the resurrection of the dead. But, the more she grieved and fretted, the more intolerable, and unreasonable, her unbelief appeared to her"); Emily Keyte, "Helen Asquith," in Joanna Bogle (ed), *English Catholic Heroines* (2009), p.295.

Atkinson, Thomas – architect and mason; b. 1729, York; c. 1756; d. 4 May 1798, 20 Andrewgate, York; father also a mason, with whom he worked on York Minster; conversion influenced by the family of his first wife, Anne Russell (*c*.1731–1774); first main commission Bishopthorpe Palace for the Anglican Archbishop of York; worked for many years on the convent of the Institution of St. Mary (the Bar Convent), York, where he was responsible for both the design and building of the main front and chapel; as a result his main patrons were the Catholic gentry of Yorkshire ("They included the Langdales, for whom he designed Houghton Hall, near Sancton (*c*.1765–8), the Stapletons of Carlton Hall (later Towers), the Lawsons of Brough, the Gascoignes of Parlington, the Cholmleys of Brandsby, and the Constables of Burton Constable" (*DNB*)); his works include town houses, country houses, churches, and public buildings (almost all in Yorkshire); one of the finest architects in the north of England; died penniless; buried in St. Saviour's Church, York; see *DNB*.

Attwater, Donald – lecturer and writer; b. 24 December 1892, Essex; c. 1911; d. 1977; brought up by parents who were first Methodists, then Anglican; for a time in his youth an Anglo-Catholic; worked in a publisher's office learning the art of editing; played role in Palestinian campaign in World War I and later became expert on Eastern Christianity; founder member of PAX and Vernacular Society of Great Britain; frequent contributor to *Catholic Herald*; during World War II member of Army Bureau of Current Affairs, talking to members of armed services; writer (encyclopedias, dictionaries, the Church, biography), e.g., *Butler's Lives of the Saints* (joint editor with Fr. Herbert Thurston, SJ), *Catholic Encyclopedic Dictionary*, *Dictionary of Mary*, *Dictionary of the Popes*, *Penguin Dictionary of the Saints*, *Names and Name Days*; translator; visiting lecturer at several American Universities; see Walter Romig (ed), *The Book of Catholic Authors*, Second Series (1943); Catherine Rachel John, "Donald Attwater 1892–1977: A Man for His Time and Ours," *Chesterton Review*, 2004, p.519 ("Once when Donald Attwater was dining at high table at King's College the famous Provost Dr. John Sheppard turned to him and said politely: 'I believe, Mr. Attwater, you are a Roman Catholic,' to which my father replied: 'Yes, Provost'; still politely Dr. Sheppard observed: 'And yet, you know, I should judge that you are a very sensible person.' My father's observation when relating this anecdote was that it was fair comment – two edged, after all!").

Austin, John (*pseud.* William Birchley) – religious writer and lawyer; b. 1613, Walpole, Norfolk; c. probably 1632, though some say about 1640; d. 1669, Bow Street, Covent Garden, London; student at St. John's College, Cambridge; never received a degree, undoubtedly because he converted to Catholicism; entered Lincoln's Inn in 1640; later a tutor to the Catholic Fowler family at St. Thomas's Priory, Stafford; traveled extensively on the Continent; spent his life on books and literary pursuits; wrote on Catholic controversy and devotional issues; part of a literary group (including Christopher Davenport (see below) and John Sergeant (see below)) that offered allegiance to the Cromwellian government in return for toleration for Catholics; books included *Christian Moderator* (1651–1653), published under pseudonym of William Birchley; wrote *Devotions in the Ancient Way of Offices* (1668), reprinted many times, a prayer book for laymen that takes over the structure and some of the material of the most popular Roman Catholic book of private devotion, *The Primer, or, Office of the Blessed Virgin Mary* (it was used by many non-Catholics); composed many popular original hymn texts; interred in parish church of St. Paul. Covent Garden, London; see *The Catholiques Plea, or, An Explanation of the Roman Catholick Belief* (1659); *Gillow*, Vol. I, p.87; *Catholic Encyclopedia*; *DNB*.

Ayscough, John (real name Rt. Rev. Mgr. Count Francis Browning Bickerstaffe-Drew) – priest and writer; b. 11 February 1858, Headingley, Leeds; c. 26 October 1878 ("The Pope is barely Catholic enough for some converts"); d. 3 July 1928, Salisbury; educated at Pembroke College, Oxford and whilst there converted to Catholicism; ordained priest 1884; appointed private chamberlain to Pope Leo XIII in 1891; private chamberlain to Pope Pius X in 1903 and domestic prelate in 1904; Knight of the Holy Sepulchre and Count in 1909; military chaplain at Plymouth 1892–1899, Malta 1899–1905, Salisbury Plain 1905–1909; served with distinction in World War I (decorated four times); became assistant principal chaplain royal in 1918; well known writer of the day; under the name of John Ayscough published many works, including essays, reviews, short stories, and several novels; see *Marotz* (1908), *Dromina* (1909), *San Celestino* (1909), *Mezzogiorno* (1910); *Saints and Places* (1912); *Levia Pondera: An Essay Book* (1913) ("For over three centuries and a half the pulpits of all the old Catholic cathedrals in England have been listening to an alien teaching, but the cathedrals have never turned Protestant. They express what they were built to express, and ignore the Reformation. Their air is as bland as ever, as devout; they make no descent from their serene aloofness into the lists of controversy; but their aloofness is as strong a protest as though it were not silent. No Reformer in England or elsewhere has ever converted them; the ancient cathedrals may be freeholds of new religious corporations, but the mark of ownership has never obliterated the birth-mark of origin and purpose. Perhaps that is why they have borne and bear now, so little share in the actual contemporary life of 'reformation countries.' I suppose many a Catholic has dropped in at one or the other of them, in England, and, as it chanced, heard some portion of a service, heard lovely boy-voices singing the old king's immortal songs, and watched the yellow evening light fall on the great, empty, pathetic spaces, tipping with gold, perhaps the niddle-noddling autumnal bonnets of the literal two or three gathered together for worship. Whatever else may have struck him, one thought could not fail: that it all had nothing on earth to do with the people. England was outside. Here, within, was an archaism: an attempt to pretend that something gone was present. Out in the street, beyond the green close, was the life, the interest, the business of the people; inside, nothing but a monument and a decorum"); *Fernando* (1918) (fictional autobiography); *The Compleat Protestant* (1920); *Discourses and Essays* (1922); *Dobachi* (1922); *Pages From the Past* (1922); Patrick Braybrooke, *Some Catholic Novelists: Their Art and Outlook* (1931), p.75.

Badeley, Edward Louth Q.C. – ecclesiastical lawyer; b. 1803/4, Leigh's Hall, near Chelmsford, Essex; c. 1852; d. 29 March 1868, at his chambers 3 Paper Buildings, Inner Temple; assisted Tractarian cause in courts; like his friends and fellow lawyers, James Hope-Scott (see below) and Edward Bellasis (see below), he was devoted follower of Newman, whom he first met in 1837; represented objectors to appointment of R. D. Hampden as Bishop of Hereford; one of counsel for Bishop of Exeter in Gorham case (see entry for William Maskell) after which he converted in reaction to failure of Church of England to stand up for sacrament of baptism; much correspondence with Newman before his conversion; influenced by Newman's *Difficulties of Anglicans*; after conversion devoted himself to Catholic causes; acted as assistant counsel to Newman at Achilli trial in 1852 and thereafter advised him on legal matters (it was on his advice that Newman rejected as inadequate the partial retraction of the charges leveled against him by Charles Kingsley and consequently embarked upon composition of his *Apologia*); Newman dedicated his volume of poems, *Verses on Various Occasions*, to him; author of legal texts; unmarried; see Stanley L. Jaki, *Newman to Converts: An Existential Ecclesiology* (2001), Ch. 3 ("The [Tractarian] Movement's inner logic forcefully pointed to the living word's power, in that fullest sense which only a visibly living higher authority could secure, insofar as it has been constituted by a Power from on High, who became flesh and blood, and wanted His authoritative Word to be continued through the power of a visibly living word, spoken authoritatively. So Newman said it to converts whom he preferred to instruct more by his own living word than by his letters. One who was privileged mostly to his words, instead to his letters, in this respect, was Edward Lowth Badeley"); *Gillow*, Vol. I, p.97; *DNB*.

Baggs, Bishop Charles Michael – vicar apostolic of the Western district; b. 21 May 1806, Bellville, County Meath, Ireland; c. 1820; d. 16 October 1845, Prior Park, near Bath; father was a barrister and member of the established church of Ireland; educated at a Protestant school in England; when his father died in 1820 he was removed to a Catholic school and became a Catholic himself; fine student at the English College in Rome (there for nearly twenty years); ordained priest in December 1830; vice-rector, then rector, of English College; great skill in languages and controversy; many liturgical and antiquarian writings; consecrated bishop in 1844 and appointed vicar apostolic of the western district (the only secular priest to occupy that office and ignorant of the requirements of the mission); buried in Holy Souls cemetery, Arnos Vale, Bristol; see *On the Supremacy of the Roman Pontiffs* (1836); *The Ceremonies of the Holy-Week at Rome* (1839); *DNB*; *Gillow*.

Bailey, Thomas – religious controversialist; d. 1659; son of Anglican Bishop of Bangor; made Sub-Dean of Wells; educated at Magdalene College, Cambridge; created Doctor in Divinity at Oxford; supporter of king's cause in the Civil War; wrote against Cromwell and was imprisoned in Newgate; on release went to Italy, dying shortly before restoration of Charles II; writer on theological issues, notably the *Herba Parietis; or the Wall-flower* in allusion to the walls of his prison; see *Gillow*, Vol. I, p.102 ("He was enabled to make a tour through Flanders and France, and see in practice the principles of the Catholic religion which he had for some time thoroughly considered, and the consequence was his conversion").

Bainbridge, Dame Beryl Margaret – writer; b. 21 November 1934, Liverpool; c. 1950s; relatively non-dogmatic Protestant upbringing; famous for stories of working-class families and later for historical novels; expelled from school at fourteen; began acting on stage at sixteen; conversion influenced by Graham Greene's novel *The End of the Affair*; shortlisted for Booker prize five times; friend of Alice Thomas Ellis (see below); see *An Awfully Big Adventure* (1989); *The Birthday Boys* (1991); *Every Man For Himself* (1996); *Master Georgie* (1998); *According to Queenie* (2001); "Laurie Taylor interviews Beryl Bainbridge," *New Humanist*, January/February 2004 ("She became converted to Rome as a result of visiting a church in central Liverpool.... After the relatively austere Protestantism of her youth, she was romantically overwhelmed by the sacramental ritual of Catholicism: the Latin, the incense, the confession and communion. 'All gone now,' she laments. 'All the things I liked about Catholicism have all gone. No more Latin or sin or confession or penance. There's no longer any point to it.'

So what was there for her now? Had anything taken the place of Catholicism? Did she have any sort of belief in a superior being, in some prime mover, in any sort of God or divine being? She paused for a moment as though opening and shutting drawers in her head. 'No, I don't have any of that. I now mostly feel empty'").

Baker, Augustine, OSB (original name David) – priest and mystical writer; b. 9 December 1575, Abergavenny, Monmouthshire, Wales; c. May 1603 (father converted on his deathbed in June 1606); d. 9 August 1641; youngest of thirteen children; family had a benevolent attitude towards Catholicism, but conformed to the Established Church; in dissolute company at Oxford, but changed on studying law; read many books on religion, which led to his conversion; joined the Benedictine novitiate in Padua in 1605; professed in England as a Benedictine in 1607; in 1608 started on a life of retirement and prayer at Sir Nicholas Fortescue's house at Cook Hill in Worcestershire (here he claimed to have been granted for a short time the grace of passive contemplation); ordained priest at Rheims in 1613; returned to the Continent in 1624; translated and copied out whole treatises of the contemplative masters, e.g., Walter Hilton, Richard Rolle, Julian of Norwich, etc; wrote many treatises of his own; in 1638 went on the English mission; buried in St. Holborn's churchyard; see *Sancta Sophia* (1657) (a systematic digest of his teaching); Evelyn Underhill, *Mysticism* (1960) ("He was one of the most lucid and orderly of guides to the contemplative life"); *Gillow*, Vol. I, p.112 *Catholic Encyclopedia*; *DNB*; ("The distinctive notes of his doctrine were interior freedom and responsiveness to the promptings of the spirit. He discouraged dependence on spiritual directors and stood loosely to external observances").

Baker, Pacificus, OSF – priest; b. 1695; d. 16 March 1774, London; brought up as Protestant; after conversion went over to Douai and joined Franciscan Order; ordained priest and sent to the English mission; attached to Sardinian Chapel, London; attended Simon, Lord Lovat, at his execution on 9 April 1747; twice provincial of English Province; eminent in spirituality and good preacher; author of many books of devotion; see *The Devout Christian's Companion for Holy Days* (1757); *Lenten Guide for Holy Week* (1769); *The Christian Advent* (1782); *Gillow*, Vol. I, p.117; *DNB*.

Balfour, Charlotte – writer; c. 1903 or 1904; (daughter, Hester, converted under influence of Hilaire Belloc and became a nun); d. 1937; one of eight children; daughter of Francis Warre Cornish (1839–1916), vice-provost of Eton and author of history, biography and novels; her mother, Blanche Ritchie (1848–1922), also a convert, was a novelist, brilliant conversationalist and hostess, who contributed with Shane Leslie (see below) to *Memorials of Robert Hugh Benson* (1915); wife of Reginald Balfour (see below); niece of Prime Minister, Arthur Balfour; grand-niece of Thackeray; author or translator of a number of religious works published between 1910 and 1946; contributor to Catholic periodicals; see *Saint Clare* (1912).

Balfour, Reginald – author; b. 1875, c. 1901; d. 1907; Fellow of King's College, Cambridge; sub-editor of *The Month* and the *Dublin Review*; husband of Charlotte Balfour (see above); friend of Maurice Baring (see below) on whose conversion he had an influence; co-author (with Fr. Charles Ritchie, his cousin, and Mgr. Robert Hugh Benson (see below)) of *An Alphabet of Saints* (1905); see Joseph Pearce, *Literary Converts* (1999), pp.13–14.

Bannister, Godfrey – physician and Catholic layman, "the idol of the Irish refugees" (*Gillow*); formerly a Protestant preacher, whom Lord Burleigh sent on a religious mission to the prisoners of the Tower; he subsequently became a Catholic himself; imprisoned in the Tower; racked three times; escaped to Flanders, where he lived for many years and practiced as a physician; see Angelo Bannister, *Memoirs of Godfrey Bannister, Once a Protestant Preacher, Then a Papist of the Right Class* (1596); *Gillow*, Vol. I, p.125.

Barclay, Vera Charlesworth – novelist; b. 10 November 1893, Hertford Heath,

Hertfordshire; c. 1916; d. 19 September 1989, Sheringham, Norfolk; daughter of Florence Louisa Charlesworth, noted author of romances, whose work was foreshadowed by that of her great-great-aunt, Maria Charlesworth, author of early Victorian classic for the young, *Ministering Children*; her father was Charles W. Barclay, an Anglican vicar; she was one of the founding members of the cub section of the scouting movement; first female leader of a scout troop; one of the first wolf cub Akelas; national wolf cub secretary in 1916; wartime Red Cross nurse; in Spring 1920 she became an aspirant of the Order of the Sisters of Charity, but probably did not enter the novitiate; wrote *The Wolf Cub Handbook* at direct request of the founder of scouting, Lord Baden-Powell, with whom she worked; supported by Cardinal Bourne to introduce scouting into Catholic parish life; later books on Catholic education; finally her main area of children's books, some of which were broadcast by the BBC; contributions to several periodicals; great devotee of the Turin Shroud; lived in France and Switzerland for a time; see *Stories of the Saints by Candle-Light* (1922); *Good Scouting: Notes From a Catholic Parish* (1927); *The Scout Way* (1929); *Saints of These Islands* (1931); *Darwin is Not for Children* (1950); *Challenge to the Darwinians* (1951); Matthew Hoehn, OSB (ed), *Catholic Authors* (1952) ("She became a Catholic in 1916 through reading a book on education lent her by a nurse in the Red Cross hospital, Netley. Knowing nothing previously of Catholic people, worship, or doctrine, she learned during the first four years of her life in her newly adopted religion 'to know the *Faith lived* as no grown-ups could have taught it,' as she says, from the little Catholic ragamuffins in the vicinity of Westminster Cathedral in which London quarter she was then living, occupied entirely with scout work").

Baring, Hon. Maurice – writer and journalist; b. 27 April 1874, 37 Church Street, Mayfair, London; c. 1 February 1909 (received at the Brompton Oratory by Fr. Sebastian Bowden; "the only action in my life which I am quite certain I have never regretted"; his sister, Elizabeth, Countess of Kenmare, was received earlier; his niece, Daphne, an artist, converted in 1923); d. 14 December 1945, Beaufort Castle, Beauly, Inverness-shire; member of the banking family (eighth child and fifth son of Lord Revelstoke); Protestant background, though lacking serious denominational ties; freethinker in his teens, but thoughts began to move towards the Catholic Church; educated at Eton and Trinity College, Cambridge; left the university without taking a degree; great linguist; entered diplomatic service in 1908; attaché in Paris, Copenhagen and Rome; in foreign Office in London before resigning service in 1904; correspondent for *Morning Post* in Manchuria, then in St. Petersburg and Constantinople; also represented *The Times* in the Balkans; deferred his conversion until 1909, partly due to family objections; in RAF in World War I; wrote novels, verse plays, memoirs, and studies on Russia; novels were fine character studies and depictions of society; great friend of G. K. Chesterton (see below) and Hilaire Belloc (of the latter he wrote, "But for you I should never have come into the Church ... you were the lighthouse that showed me the way"); also influenced by the French novelist, Joris-Karl Huysmans' autobiographical novel, *En Route* (1895); in his final fifteen years suffered from Parkinson's Disease; unmarried; see letters to Dame Ethel Smyth ((1) from France in 1914: "I went to Mass this morning, and it was nice to think I was listening to the same words, said in the same way with the same gestures, that Henry V and his 'contemptible little army' heard before and after Agincourt; and I stood between a man in khaki and a French Tommy, and history flashed past like a jeweled dream"; (2) 1919: "To me the difference between being a Catholic and being anything else is simply that if you are a Catholic you assume responsibility for all your acts, words and thoughts.... You assume responsibility. The priest is merely the ticket office of the journey or the *bureau d'information*. In fact this fact is the explanation of why I ever became a Catholic. At one moment I came to the conclusion that human life is either casual or divine. If divine it meant a revealed representative. Where was this? The Catholic Church. And then everything follows down to the holy water. But if it is not divine, then the only alternative would be for me complete agnosticism"); *The Puppet Show of Memory* (1922) ("[Reggie Balfour] took me one morning to Low Mass at Notre Dame des Victoires. I had never attended a Low Mass before in my life. It impressed me greatly. I had imagined Catholic services were always long, complicated, and overlaid with ritual. A Low Mass, I found, was short, extremely simple, and somehow or other made me think of the catacombs and the meetings of the Early Christians. One felt one was looking on at something extremely ancient. The behavior of the congregation, and the expression on their faces impressed me too. To them it was evidently real"); *'C'* (1924) ("But do you believe it all?" asked C. 'You are in a muddle about the meaning of the word *belief*,' Bede answered, 'You use the word *belief* in the sense of thinking something is probable or improbable in itself. When we say we believe in a dogma, we mean we are giving credit to something which is guaranteed to us by the authority of the Church. Religious belief is a mystery and an adventure. But if, like Pascal, you wish to

bet on it, you have nothing to lose if it turns out not to be true, whereas the other way round –

'I should hate to do it from fear. I have the greatest contempt for death-bed repentances; for men who have blasphemed and rioted all their lives, and then at the last moment have sent for a priest –

'That means you are not a Christian, that is to say not a Catholic. (Catholicism is Christianity. It's the same thing – and nothing else is.) Well, Christianity is the religion of repentance: it stands against fatalism and pessimism of every kind in saying that a man can go back, even at the eleventh hour...'"); *Cat's Cradle* (1925) ("If the Roman Dogmas are false, what about the Protestant ones – for these derive from those? And if the smell of Rome were but trustworthy, what a difference that would make!"); *Passing By* (1928) ("Riley said there were only two points of view in the world: the Catholic point of view or the non-Catholic point of view. All so-called religions which I could mention, including my layman's common sense view, were either lopped-off branches of Catholicism or shadows of it, or a blind aspiration towards it, or a misguided parallel of it, as of a train that had gone off the rails, or a travesty of it, sometimes serious, and sometimes grotesque: a distortion. The other point of view was the materialist point of view, which he could perfectly well understand anyone holding. It depends, he said, whether you think human life is casual or divine.

I said I could quite well conceive a philosophy which would be neither materialist nor Catholic. He quoted Dr. Johnson about everyone having a right to his opinion, and martyrdom being the test. Catholicism, he said, had survived the test; would my philosophy?"); *Robert Peckham* (1930); *In My End Is My Beginning* (1931); *Have You Anything to*

Declare? (1936) ("It would have surprised [Ernest] Renan to hear that his histories of the origin and vicissitudes of the early Church, and his touching account of the laceration he suffered when he abandoned the thought of the priesthood and left the Church, should have been instrumental in bringing more than one agnostic into the Catholic Church. Such, however, is the truth. The reasons are briefly these. First of all, his histories of the early Church reveal to the agnostic who has had for sole religious education at school a certain amount of translating and construing of the New Testament, and some 'talks' prior to confirmation, the astonishing fact that there was an early Church, of which the Apostles were the pillars; secondly, Renan informs them that his reasons for leaving the Church are not the so-called abuses of the Catholic Church, that is, the so-called 'errors of Rome.' For him, the Reformed Churches have not a leg to stand on.... 'I realized that it was only the Catholics who were logical.' Nor was it because he found it impossible to swallow Catholic dogmas.

What drove him out of the Church was neither dogmatic difficulties nor the misdeeds of the Papacy, but his belief in the infallibility of the German higher criticism of the biblical texts.... Renan probably never read the German higher criticism of Shakespeare, with a Shakespeare beside it in the original; but others did, and that shattered their faith once and for all in the German higher criticism.... And after a course of the higher criticism of Shakespeare, we become aware that it is possible, as Father Knox has so brilliantly shown, to prove that *In Memoriam* was written by Queen Victoria; and when we see the German higher criticism at work upon the Gospels, and they tell us that certain of Our Lord's answers to Pontius Pilate are authentic, but that others are not, we merely reply, 'Sez you!'

[Renan's] arguments lead to one conclusion, and to one conclusion only: namely, that if Christianity is true and has not been proved false by the German higher criticism of biblical texts, then the Catholic Church is its only possible and logical manifestation on earth"); Laura Lovat, *Maurice Baring: A Postscript* (1947); Gordon Albion, "Catholicism in Maurice Baring's 'C'," *The Month*, May 1948, p.303 ("C. who had never in his life discussed religion is suddenly asked by a new poet acquaintance: 'Are you a Catholic?' 'No,' said C., 'I'm nothing' – 'Of course not, if you're not a Catholic,' said Bede, 'There is either that or nothing. There is no third course.' 'And one can't very well become a Catholic,' said C. 'Why not?' asked Bede. C. stammered and did not answer.... It was not, however, necessary, for Bede poured our a stream of argument and exposition to the effect that Catholicism was the great reality; the only thing that mattered; the only thing that counted; the only creed a thinking man could adopt; the only solace that satisfied the needs of the human heart; the only curb to the human passions; the only system that fulfilled the demands of human nature and into which factors such as love and death fitted naturally; the unique and sole representative of the Divine upon earth. The English had gone wrong because they had fallen into a rut from the straight road of the true inheritance: Catholic England, Chaucer's England, to which the whole of Shakespeare was the dirge"); Paul Horgan (ed), *Maurice Baring Restored* (1970) (discussing Baring's novel *C*: "'C says impatiently to Beatrice, the lovely Catholic whose faith holds an irritating spiritual attraction for him: 'What can it matter what church one goes to? – If one thinks it necessary to go to church.' 'Catholics think it does matter,' said Beatrice. 'Yes, but Protestants don't,' said C. 'That's the beauty of being a Protestant.' 'Yes, but although they don't mind anything else, they do mind Catholics,' said Beatrice.

Much later C agrees with this, for he has noticed that 'what's so odd is that those who mind most that anybody is converted to the Roman Catholic Church are just those who care least about religion – those who haven't got any religion at all'"); Ian Boyd, "Maurice Baring's Early Writing," *Downside Review*, July 1974, p.160; Julian Jeffs, "The Conversion of Maurice Baring," *Chesterton Review*, February 1988, p.83 (special issue devoted to Baring) (Letter to H. G. Wells: "The difference which separates [Protestants and Catholics] is not in any special dogma but in the authority in which all dogmas root, Protestants basing their authority on the Bible which Catholics do also.... But the Roman Catholic Church's first doctrine is her own perpetual infallibility. She is inspired, She says, by the same Spirit that inspired the Bible – this voice is equally the voice of God.... Catholicism is the only real living religion at this moment that is influencing humanity. That it is a gigantic fact, that no discoveries of science which shake Bible-founded Protestantism or any Bible-founded Sect to its foundations has the slightest effect on it"); E. Letley, *Maurice Baring: A Citizen of Europe* (1991); Walter Romig (ed), *The Book of Catholic Authors*, Fourth Series (1948); Joseph Pearce, *Literary Converts* (1999) *passim*; Fr. Charles P. Connor, *Classic Catholic Converts* (2001), pp.131–133; Joseph Pearce, "In the Shadow of the Chesterbelloc," *Crisis*, December 2001; Ralph McInerny, *Some Catholic Writers* (2007); Jocelyn Hillgarth and Julian Jeffs, *Maurice Baring: Letters* (2007) ("It doesn't solve the mystery, if Christ was only a man, of how and why such an astounding thing could happen.... Given the fact that the existence of this person changed the whole face of the world, all

this is very difficult to explain. If, that is to say, the man was only a man. Some explanation is necessary. You have either to say 'Yes, but he was a very good man.' Or that he was mad, went mad. Neither explanation [is] adequate. Because no other very good man has [had] quite the same effect. Nobody, for instance, has believed that Socrates or even Buddha or Mahomet was God and madmen have not inspired people to die for them rather than deny them. On the other hand you have the Church which claims to have been founded by that Person and claims the gospels as the title deeds of her estate and an uninterrupted tradition from the days of Christ and his contemporaries. To be in fact the representative of the Divine on earth. If you admit that this claim is substantial, the whole matter is simple...

But this, you will point out, entails believing that Christ was God. And you will say this is difficult. I admit the difficulty. But I maintain it is not more difficult than it is difficult for you ... or anyone else to believe that He was not God. Because once your faith in Him as a man and ordinary like Shakespeare or Mahomet is sure and certain, once you really believe that He was not God, a host of difficulties arise. You are forced to find some explanation in order to account for the rise and growth and existence of the Church"); *DNB*.

Barkworth (alias Lambert) OSB, Blessed Mark – priest and martyr; b. 1572, Lincolnshire; c. 1594; d. 27 February 1601, London; brought up as Protestant; converted at Douai when twenty-two by a Jesuit; joined Benedictine Order; returned to England after ordination at Valladolid in 1599; arrested and sent to Bridewell; charged with being a priest; tried and condemned at Old Bailey; hanged, drawn and quartered at Tyburn; buried near Tyburn, though body later retrieved; see Dom Bede Camm, *Nine Martyr Monks* (1931); *Gillow*, Vol. I, p.129; *DNB*.

Barnard, James – priest; b. 1733, London; c. 1756; d. 12 September 1803; parents Protestants; after conversion entered English College in Lisbon or Seville; ordained priest; sent on the English mission in 1761; worked in London district until nominated for presidency of Lisbon College in 1776; in 1782 resigned that position and returned to London where appointed vicar-general of London District; wrote biography of Challoner (a friend of his) and a demonstration of divinity of Christ; see *The Divinity of Our Lord Jesus Christ Demonstrated from the Holy Scriptures and from the Doctrine of the Primitive Church* (1789); *Gillow*, Vol. I, p.136.

Barnes, Very Rev. Mgr. Arthur Stapylton (known as "Mugger") – priest and author; b. 31 May 1861, India; c. 1895 (received by Cardinal Merry del Val); d. 1936, Painswick, Gloucestershire; educated at Eton, Woolwich and University College, Oxford; lieutenant in the Royal Artillery from 1877 to 1879; took Anglican orders; after conversion studied in Rome and became an expert on the burial place of St. Peter; ordained Catholic priest in 1896; assisted Wilfrid Ward in editing the *Dublin Review*; a privy chamberlain to the Pope from 1904; chaplain to the Catholic undergraduates at the University of Cambridge 1902–1916; same role at Oxford 1919–1926; domestic prelate to Benedict XV from 1919; author of many books on Catholic topics; buried in monks' cemetery at Prinknash; see *The Popes and the Ordinal* (1898); *St. Peter in Rome and His Tomb on the Vatican Hill* (1900); *Blessed Joan the Maid* (1909); *The Man of the Mask* (1912); *The Early Church in the Light of the Monuments* (1913); *Bishop Barlow and Anglican Orders* (1922); *Catholic Schools of England* (1926); *Catholic Oxford* (1933); *The Martyrdom of St. Peter and St. Paul* (1933); *No Sacrifice – No Priest; or, Why Anglican Orders Were Condemned* (1933); *The Holy Shroud of Turin* (1934); *Christianity at Rome in the Apostolic Age* (1938).

Barrow, John, SJ (later changed name to William Bernard) – priest; b. 1810; c. 1864; d. 1 January 1880, Bordeaux; took Anglican orders in 1834; tutor and librarian at Queen's College, Oxford 1835–1846; DD in 1855; wrote the *Life of St. Herbert* for the *Lives of the English Saints*; Principal of St. Edmund Hall 1854–1861; moderate Tractarian before his conversion; joined the Society of Jesus in 1867 and changed his name to "William Bernard"; worked as a priest in India for some time.

Bartlett, Joan – b. 1 August 1911, Lancashire; c. 1941; d. 9 September 2002; brought up as Anglican; in World War II she worked by day for the European service of the BBC and by night ran a Red Cross first-aid post in Chelsea; conversion influenced by meeting a Servite friar; became a tertiary of the Servite Order; in 1945 set up Hearth and Home, an organization to provide shelter for elderly Londoners who had lost their homes in the Blitz; she was particularly inspired by the image of Mary standing at the foot of the cross; she sensed that God was calling her to a consecrated life and in 1947 founded the Servite Secular Institute, a spiritual organization for lay people who have taken vows of poverty, chastity and obedience, but who wish to work in the community; the Institute was formally recognized by the Holy See in 1964 and spread to many countries; Hearth and Home developed into Servite Houses, a housing association, of which she was first director and president in

1998; great fund raiser; served on committees and working parties for Age Concern, Help the Aged and Shelter; for many years chairman of L'Arche (organization working for people with learning disabilities); founder chairman of the Housing Associations Charitable Trust; long-standing council member of the National Housing Federation; Dame of the Order of St. Gregory 1995; see *Brushing Eternity* (2000).

Basset, Joshua – college head and controversialist b. about 1641, Lynn Regis; c. 1687 (declared himself a Catholic then, but may have converted as early as 1685); d. c.1720, London; took Anglican orders in 1666; appointed as fifth Master of Sydney Sussex College, Cambridge, by a mandamus of James II in 1687; second royal mandate issued dispensing him from taking the oaths of allegiance and supremacy; caused Mass to be said publicly within the college and procured alteration of statutes for accommodation of himself and fellow Catholics; left college suddenly upon the revocation of the king's mandamuses in 1688; man of extensive reading and able controversialist; very poor at time of death; see *Reason and Authority, or, The Motives of a Late Protestants Reconciliation to the Catholic Church* (1687) (his account of his motives for converting); *Gillow*, Vol. I, p.153; *Catholic Encyclopedia*; *DNB* ("In *Reason and Authority*..., which appeared anonymously in 1687, Basset gave a lively account of his own theological development. He had attempted to construct a scheme of divinity on rational grounds, which he found resulted in a 'confused Babel of Religion'. The Church of England did not constitute a lawful authority sufficient to oblige his reason and conscience. Only the Church of Rome provided 'fundamental doctrines, authoritatively imposed, and universally received throughout the whole

Christian world.' To the Protestant allegation that the Catholic church was corrupt in faith and morals Basset replied that, if that were the case, then 'Christ failed of his promise, and so good night to Christianity.'"

Bathurst, Catherine Anne (name in religion Rev. Mother Mary Catherine Philip) – b. 14 July 1825, Summerleaze, Wookey, Somerset; c. September 1850 (received by Fr. Brownbill at Farm Street, London; her brother, Stuart Eyre Bathurst (see below) also received in 1850; another brother, Henry Allen, became a Catholic in 1853); d. 14 December 1907, Harrow-on-the-Hill; her father, General Sir James Bathurst, son of the Anglican Bishop of Norwich, served as aide-de-camp to the Duke of Wellington (her godfather) during the Peninsular War; she was introduced to Newman, who was to remain her guide and friend until his death; after a number of false starts as a religious she joined Mother Margaret Hallahan's community of Dominican sisters; foundress and first Mother-General of the Congregation of the Rosary at St. Dominic's Convent, Harrow-on-the-Hill, Middlesex; she founded St. Philip's Orphanage for Boys at Birmingham and the Couvent Anglais at Meirelbeke, Belgium; buried at the Harrow convent; see *DNB* ("More than eighty of Newman's letters to Bathurst are extant and reveal her gradual development from scrupulous young convert to confident religious superior").

Bathurst, Stuart Eyre (name in religion Philip) – priest; b. 10 December 1815, Baker Street, London; c. 28 August 1850, Birmingham Oratory (received by Newman); d. 1900; brother of Catherine Bathurst (see above); eldest of nine children of General Sir James Bathurst; educated at Christ Church, Oxford; Fellow of Merton College 1839–1845; took

Anglican orders in 1842 and a rich living at Kibworth-Beauchamp, Leicestershire; became interested in the Oxford Movement; conversion influenced by the Gorham case (see entry for William Maskell); after becoming a Catholic he joined the Birmingham Oratory in 1851; left in 1852 believing he had no vocation, but was ordained to the priesthood by Bishop Ullathorne at Easter 1854; became a mission priest at Stone, Staffordshire, and later a canon of Birmingham; many charitable works and embraced poverty himself; great promoter of devotion to the Sacred Heart of Jesus; see Rev. Bertrand Wilberforce, O.P, *Canon Bathurst* (1901) ("Things have happened lately which have forced me to a very different conclusion. I can no longer believe that we belong to the same body with Catholics. I believe the Church of England did, at the time of what is called the Reformation, what it has since found fault with Wesley and others for doing with regard to itself, viz., separated from the One, Holy, Catholic and Apostolic Church, and so has ceased to belong to it. Such being my conviction, and firmly believing … that all the baptized are bound, in obedience to our Blessed Lord's will, to live and die in strict union with His Church, I am about to make my submission to it").

Bayly, Thomas – Catholic controversialist; c. c.1647; d. c.1657, probably in Italy; fourth son of Dr. Lewis Bayly, c.1575–1631, Bishop of Bangor; Anglican clergyman; became an officer in the royal army in 1645; after the king's execution he went abroad, touring in Flanders and France; later went to Italy where he probably lived until his death in the household of Cardinal Ottoboni, then papal nuncio at Ferrara; see *An End to Controversy between the Roman Catholique and the Protestant Religions Justified*; *DNB* ("It may be that closer ac-

quaintance with the churches [abroad] may have been influential in [his conversion], but as a long prefatory account shows he had been much affected by the collapse of the Established Church in England, a punishment, as he thought, for its schism. He was especially outraged that the execution of Charles I, the head of state and of church, had not inspired more protest from the dispossessed higher clergy").

Beardsley, Aubrey Vincent – artist (illustrator and caricaturist) and author; b. 21 August 1872, 12 Buckingham Road, Brighton, Sussex; c. 31 March 1897 ("Now Beardsley needed its certainties" (*DNB*); mother, Ellen (1846–1932) received in 1898; sister, Mabel Wright, the actress and journalist, received in 1895); d. 16 March 1898, Menton, France; father lost his inherited fortune; always frail; brought up as High Anglican; worked as a clerk in London; created a public persona for himself ("carefully posed, hollow-eyed, and literate" (*DNB*)); part of decadent movement (Roger Fry referred to him as the "Fra Angelico of Satanism"); his drawings for an illustrated edition of Oscar Wilde's (see below) *Salome* created a *succès de scandale*; editor of the *Yellow Book*; career suffered as a result of being mistakenly linked by press with prosecution against Wilde; Andre Raffalovich (see below) was a friend and mentor; helped in production of *Savoy Magazine*; wandering life style with his mother; dying of consumption when persuaded to convert by John Gray (see below); buried in public cemetery at Menton; see Alexander Michaelson, "Aubrey Beardsley," *Blackfriars*, October 1928, p.609; Alexander Michaelson, "Aubrey Beardsley's sister," *Blackfriars*, November 1928, p.669; Matthew Sturgis, *Aubrey Beardsley: A Biography* (1998); Robert Whelan, "Why did so many Victorian decadents become Catholics?" *Catholic Herald*, 5 January 2001; *DNB* ("Early in March [1898] he wrote a short letter to Smithers [his publisher]: Jesus is our Lord and Judge. Dear Friend, I implore you to destroy *all* copies of Lysistrata and bad drawings.... By all that is holy, *all* obscene drawings. [Signed] Aubrey Beardsley In my death agony".... Smithers paid no attention to it, knowing what the drawings would soon be worth").

Beckett, John William – political activist and journalist; b. 11 October 1894, Hammersmith, London; c. 1952; d. 28 December 1964; fought in World War I and wounded; early on a socialist; then Independent Labour Party MP 1929–1931 (twice suspended for calling Prime Minister a liar); impatience and passionate nature involved him in several lawsuits; joined British Union of Fascists; then formed National Socialist League with William Joyce; then British People's Party; imprisoned in World War II under emergency legislation; see Francis Beckett, *The Rebel Who Lost His Cause: The Tragedy of John Beckett MP* (1999); *DNB*.

Bedford, Henry – teacher; b. 1816, London; c. 1851; d. 1905; to Trinity College, Cambridge, then transferred to Peterhouse College; became a Tractarian; took Anglican orders; in 1852 on staff of All Hallows Missionary College, Dublin; never became priest because of a natural defect in his right hand; professor of Natural Science, then treasurer, then director of the college, working there over fifty years; popular public lecturer; articles in Catholic periodicals; see *The Life of St. Vincent de Paul* (1856).

Belaney, Robert – priest; b. 1804; c. 1852; d. 1899; at Cambridge University; former Anglican vicar; corresponded with Newman prior to Newman's conversion; stated to Fr. William Neville (see below) of Birmingham Oratory that Newman's *Lectures on the Doctrine of Justification* "proved fatal" to his Protestantism; ordained priest in 1857; introduced Jesuits to Glasgow and Servite Fathers to London; was oldest Catholic priest in Britain when he died; see *A Letter to the Lord Bishop of Chichester, assigning his reasons for leaving the Church of England* (1852); *The Bible and the Papacy* (1889); *The Kingdom of God on Earth* (1896).

Bell, Edward Ingress – architect; b. 7 February 1837, Greenhithe, Kent; d. 30 August 1914, East Preston, Sussex; joined War Office in 1859 as a draughtsman and worked there until retirement as first-class surveyor in 1898; from 1890 responsible for barrack design; appointment about 1882 as a consulting architect to the crown agents for colonies led to collaboration with Sir Aston Webb which lasted until 1909; designer (with Webb) of the University of Birmingham; his wife, Elizabeth, and children also received into the Catholic Church; buried at Broadwater cemetery, Worthing; see *DNB*.

Bellasis, Edward ("The Serjeant") – lawyer; b. 14 October 1800, the vicarage, Basilden, Berkshire; c. 27 December 1850 ("I felt thoroughly convinced that if I were to die in my then position, I could not be saved; knowing what I did I was acting against my conscience"; his three older children, Margaret (13), Katherine (11) and Mary (9), were received 17 April 1851; his second wife, Eliza Jane (1815–1898) on 22 April 1851 (all above received by Fr. Brownbill); his sister, her husband, Dr. W. E. Masfen, and their four sons also became Catholics); d. 24 January 1873, Hyères, France ("He was one of the best men I ever knew" (Newman)); son of an Anglican rector; of rather evangelical upbringing and conservative inclinations; highly successful legal career in chancery and in county palatine of Lancaster; became serjeant-at-law; associated with Tractarian movement; friend of Edward Badeley (see above) and James Hope-Scott (see below); directly influenced in his conversion by Gorham judgment in 1850 (see entry for William Maskell) and by Anglican reaction against the restoration of the Catholic hierarchy same year; noted conversations with his wife, later published as *Philotheus and Eugenia: Dialogues between Two Anglicans on Anglican Difficulties* (1874) and two pamphlets on the "papal aggression" of 1850: one as Anglican (1850), the other as Catholic (1851); left manuscript verse and autobiography; took part in famous libel action Achilli v Newman; as magistrate he secured Catholic chaplains for Catholic prisoners; he and Hope-Scott handled affairs of last Catholic Earl of Shrewsbury; active in many Catholic philanthropic and educational societies; Newman's *Grammar of Assent* bears dedication to him; father of five sons including Fr. Richard Garnett Bellasis (1849–1939), formerly barrister and then priest and Superior of Birmingham Oratory; of Edward Bellasis (1852–1922), barrister, genealogist and author; of William Dalglish Bellasis (1853–c1942), co-founder of Westminster Cathedral; and of Fr. Henry Lewis Bellasis (1859–1938), priest of the Birmingham and the Roman Oratory; three of his five daughters, Mary (1852–1927), Cecilia, and Monica (1855–1918), became nuns in Society of the Holy Child Jesus; buried St. Mary Magdalen's, Mortlake; see Edward Bellasis, *Memorials of Mr. Serjeant Bellasis, 1800–1873* (1923) ("Is it probable that the Church of England – that is to say, the independent Anglican system – will ever again obtain a hold upon my

confidence and affection? The origin of the Church of England, the characters and motives of its founders, its history, its general policy, its sympathy with Protestant and heretical bodies, the double aspect of its formularies, the untenableness of its theory as regards unity, and, as it now appears, the entire absence in it of any authority on matters of faith, have impressed me so strongly, and so unfavorably, that I cannot think it possible I can ever again admire it, or love, or even respect it, as I ought to do that Church to which I entrust myself and all that are dear to me.

Assuming that there is no probability that the Church of England will regain my confidence, what course do I propose to myself? It is plain I shall either fall into indifference, or sooner or later I shall detach myself from the Church of England for some other Church – that other, of course, the Catholic Church"); Stanley L. Jaki, *Newman to Converts: An Existential Ecclesiology* (2001), pp.94–96; *Gillow*, Vol. I, p.177; *Catholic Encyclopedia*; *DNB*.

Bellew, Harold Kyrle Money – actor; b. 28 March 1855, Prescot, Lancashire; c. 1868 (father, John Bellew (see below), mother, and brother, Evelyn Bellew, received in the same year); d. 2 November 1911, Salt Lake City, Utah; father was an Anglican clergyman who later converted; spent some years in the navy, both royal and merchant, then lived in Australia; worked as journalist; returned to England in 1875 and formed a touring company, playing mainly romantic comedy roles; successful career in England, United States, Australia, and Far East; writer of several plays and adapted others for stage; see *DNB*.

Bellew, (formerly Higgin), John Chippendale Montesquieu – preacher; b. 3 August 1823, Lancaster; c. 1868 (his son, the actor Harold Bellew (see above), also converted; his wife and another son, Evelyn, also received); d. 19 June 1874, 16 Circus Road, St. John's Wood, London; mother a Catholic; assumed his mother's family name on attaining his majority; good speaker at the Oxford Union; took Anglican orders in 1848; several posts both in India and in England; became one of the most popular preachers in London; wrote on Shakespeare and on poetry, plus a novel; on his conversion he relinquished Anglican orders; later concentrated on public readings, including in the United States; his readings raised money for Catholic charities; buried at Kensal Green cemetery, London; see *DNB*.

Bellingham, Sir (Alan) Henry, fourth Baronet, second creation – barrister and author; b. 1846; c. 1873; brought up as Low Church in Ireland; under influence of High Church party at Oxford University; conversion largely owing to conversion and example of Fr. Richard Clarke, SJ (see below); 5th Battalion, Royal Irish Rifles; called to the bar in 1876; Commissioner of National Education, Ireland; Senator of the Royal Irish University; MP for County Louth 1880–1885; married first to Lady Constance Noel Bellingham, daughter of the second Earl of Gainsborough, then to Hon. Lelgarde Clifton; Private Chamberlain to Popes Pius IX, Leo XIII and Pius X; see essay in J. G. F. Raupert (ed), *Roads to Rome* (1901), p.7 ("The chief thing that attracted me to the Church was its universality, as opposed to the insularity of Episcopalianism, in which form of Christianity I was brought up. And I felt this very strongly during my first visit to the Continent. Detail had never much difficulty for me, for when once I had grasped the notion of a Teaching Church, all followed as a matter of course.

My first impressions of Catholicism were amongst the poor in Ireland, where I was born. Brought up myself in a school of extreme Low Churchism of a deeply religious character, but surrounded by masses of practical good living Catholics, I was struck by the little impression the educated Protestant classes made on their poorer brethren, and was very favorably impressed with the simple devotion and faith of these latter"); *Reminiscences of an Irish Convert* (1919) ("The idea that if there was such a thing as a true Church, it could have fallen into error, and stood in need of reformation from such men as Henry VIII, Cranmer, Luther, and Calvin, always seemed to me to savor of the ridiculous; so that, if I had not had the grace eventually to become a Catholic, I should probably have been an unbeliever, or drifted into some vague form of agnosticism").

Benenson, Peter (born Peter James Henry Solomon) – barrister and human rights campaigner; b. 31 July 1921, 6 Albert Court, Knightsbridge. London; c. 1958; d. 25 February 2005, Oxford; born to a Jewish family; educated at home (tutors including W. H. Auden); then at Eton and briefly at Balliol College Oxford before World War II broke out; worked at Bletchley Park during the war; adopted his mother's maiden name in 1949 as a tribute to his grandfather, Grigori Benenson, a Russian banking and oil tycoon; founded *Justice* organization in 1957; at conversion disillusioned with politics; new faith led to his ceasing to look to politics for a solution to world's problems and conclusion that the answers lay in individual regeneration; co-founded *Amnesty International* in 1961 (President 1961–1966) to fight for prisoners of conscience and other victims of political ideology around the world; see *DNB*.

Benett, Harriet – nun; b. 1830; c. October 1853 (followed by the conversion of two sisters and a brother); d. 1903; just before her conversion Newman wrote to her about the oneness of the Catholic Church; after her conversion worked as governess at Liège of daughters of Baroness d'Hooghvorst, later Mother Mary of Jesus, foundress of the Society of Marie Reparatrice; became one of the first novices of the Order in Paris in 1864; later mistress of novices; Superior of the convent of the Order in London in 1864 and again in 1871; see Stanley L. Jaki, *Newman to Converts: An Existential Ecclesiology* (2001), pp.347–349 ("Newman the fearsome logician took over: 'Sanctity admits of *degrees*, unity does not admit of degrees. The Church may be more or less holy – she cannot be more or less *one* – She may be one in different senses – but in the same sense of one, there are no degrees of one'…

Newman then made his strongest point. He said he could understand the Protestant 'notion of one and *no one* body, but I have never been able to get hold of what is *meant* by saying one body, yet calling Rome, England and Greece all *parts* of that one body – I have in times past tried hard to do so, and have turned the matter in all possible ways, but none would do, and so says the common sense of the world.' He then explained that respect for common sense imposed on the mind the duty to use words with clear meaning: 'The common sense of the world says, Do not use words without meaning, if so, *call* them mysteries – We need not always have *clear* ideas of things, but if we have *not*, do not let us say we *have* – The unity of the Church is one of its notes – one of its four notes – therefore it ought to be a *clear* idea – not a mystery – not to be taken on faith but to be seen and understood – Now the Anglican idea of the Church's unity is a single [simple] mystery for no human being ever put it into intelligible words'").

Benson, Mgr. (Robert) Hugh – priest and writer; b. 18 November 1871, Wellington College; c. 11 September 1903 (received by Fr. Reginald Buckler, OP at Woodchester, Gloucestershire); d. 19 October 1914, Bishop's House, Salford, Lancashire; brought up as Anglican (son of the Archbishop of Canterbury); brother of A. C. Benson (1862–1925), poet, schoolmaster and Master of Magdalene College, Cambridge, and E. F. Benson (1867–1940), writer; at Eton and Trinity College, Cambridge; former High Anglican clergyman and member of Community of the Resurrection at Mirfield; reading Newman's *Development of Doctrine* removed last doubts; one of the most high profile converts of his day; ordained priest 12 June 1914, interior chapel of San Silvestro in Capite, Rome; purchased old house at Hare Street, Hertfordshire as a haven and base from which to set out on missions; rest of his life devoted to preaching and writing; great controversialist; very popular preacher despite stammer and shrill voice; many novels, especially historical romances (e.g., *By What Authority* (1904); *The King's Achievement* (1905); *The Queen's Tragedy* (1906); *Come Rack! Come Rope!* (1912)), and apocalyptic stories about Church history (*Lord of the World* (1908); *The Dawn of All* (1911)); wrote classic collection of supernatural stories (*The Light Invisible* (1903)); in 1911 was made a private chamberlain to Pope Pius X; buried at Hare Street House, Hertfordshire; see *By What Authority?* (1904) (novel set in Elizabethan time, which includes description of a Mass: "Then [the priest] began the preparation with the servant who knelt beside him in his ordinary livery, as server; and Isabel heard the murmur of the Latin words for the first time.

Then he stepped up to the altar, bent slowly and kissed it and the mass began. Isabel had a missal, lent to her by Mistress Margaret; but she hardly looked at it; so intent was she on that crimson figure and his strange movements and his low broken voice. It was unlike anything that she had ever imagined worship to be. Public worship to her had meant hitherto one of two things – either sitting under a minister and having the word applied to her soul in the sacrament of the pulpit; or else the saying of prayers by the minister aloud and distinctly and with expression, so that the intellect could follow the words, and assent with a hearty Amen. The minister was a minister to man of the Word of God, an interpreter of His gospel to man.

But here was a worship unlike all this in almost every detail. The priest was addressing God, not man; therefore he did so in a low voice, and in a tongue as Campion had said on the scaffold 'that they both understood.' It was comparatively unimportant whether man followed it word for word, for (and here the second radical difference lay) the point of the worship for the people lay, not in an intellectual apprehension of the words, but in a voluntary assent to and participation in the supreme act to which the words were indeed necessary but subordinate. It was the thing that was done; not the words that were said, that was mighty with God. Here, as these Catholics round Isabel at any rate understood it, and as she too began to perceive it too, though dimly and obscurely, was the sublime mystery of the Cross presented to God"); *A City Set on a Hill* (1905) ("I had come to see the need for a teaching Church to preserve and interpret the truths of Christianity to each succeeding generation. It is only a dead religion to which the written records are sufficient; a living religion must be able to adapt itself to changing environment *without losing its own identity*. One thing, therefore, is certain – that if Christianity is, as I believe it, a real Revelation, the Teaching Church must, at any rate, know her own mind with regard to the treasure committed to her care, and, supremely, on those points on which the salvation of her children depends…. She must not only know her own mind, but must be constantly declaring it, and no less constantly silencing those who would obscure and misrepresent it. I was an official in a church that did not seem to know her own mind, even in matters directly connected with the salvation of the soul…. More and more I was beginning to see the absolute need of a living authority…. Might I, or might I not, tell my penitents that they are bound to confess their mortal sins before Communion. Then on the other side was the Church of Rome. I had heard, at various times, all the theoretical and historical arguments that could possibly be brought against her; but, practically, there was no question. Her system worked…. The smallest Roman Catholic child knew precisely how to be reconciled to God, and to receive His grace…. The Roman theory worked, the Anglican did not"); *The Religion of a Plain Man* (1906); *Christ in His Church* (1910); *Confessions of a Convert* (1913) ("For years past I had claimed to be saying Mass, and that the Sacrifice of the Mass was held as a doctrine by the Church of England; and here in Elizabethan days were priests hunted to death for the crime of doing that which I had claimed to do. I had supposed that our wooden Communion tables were altars, and here in Tudor times were the old stones of the altars defiled and insulted deliberately by the officials of the Church to which I still nominally belonged, and wooden tables installed instead. Things which were dear to me … – vestments, crucifixes, rosaries – in Elizabethan days were denounced as 'trinkets' and 'muniments of superstition.' I began to wonder at myself, and a little while later gave up celebrating the Communion service"); *Paradoxes of Catholicism* (1913); *Lourdes* (1914); *Spiritual Letters to One of His Converts* (1915) ("The Inquisition. Everybody is agreed now, I suppose, that the old methods of the Inquisition are wholly indefensible, and alien to the mind of Christ. But it makes one more lenient to the persons who practiced this indefensible system, to remember: (1) That the murder of souls is a far greater crime than the murder of bodies; and that from this premise the medieval authorities (faultily) argued that, if it was lawful to punish 'body-murder' with death, and to keep civil detectives etc., it was, *a fortiori*, lawful to punish heresy with death etc. (2) That, strictly speaking, the secular arm alone punished and inflicted secular chastisement; in heresy cases as in others. And that therefore the civil power was technically to blame. (Of course this does not excuse the ecclesiastics' connivance and encouragement). (3) That in the days when Catholicism was the only guardian of morality, and other religious systems did not exist, heresy meant an influx of every kind of crime, in the long run; and the temptation therefore was great, to holy people, to use unlawful means for a good end. (4) That compulsion of a kind must always be used in teaching and maintaining religion; (e.g., education of children; legal penalties still due to blasphemy). (5) That barbarities were the general order of the day. (6) That in those days even heretics did not object to the fact of the death penalty for heresy, but only to the application of it in their own cases (e.g., Calvin's connivance at the burning of Servetus). Nothing can excuse the Inquisition therefore, but it is easy to explain it"); *A Book of Essays by Mgr. Benson* (1916); A.C. Benson, *Hugh: Memoirs of a*

Brother (1915); Blanche Warre Cornish, *Memorials of Robert Hugh Benson* (1915); C. C. Martindale, *The Life of Robert Hugh Benson*, 2 Vols. (1916); Reginald J. J. Watt, *Robert Hugh Benson: Captain in God's Army* (1920); Robert Keable, *Peradventure* (1922) (a novel featuring a Catholic priest (Fr. Vassall) modeled on Mgr. Benson); Patrick Braybrooke, *Some Catholic Novelists: Their Art and Outlook* (1931), p.113; Michael O'Halloran, "The Memory of Monsignor Benson," *Irish Ecclesiastical Record*, November 1954, p.322; Sr. M. St. Rita Monaghan, *Monsignor Robert Hugh Benson: His Apostolate and its Message for our Time* (1985); Aidan Nichols, "Imaginative Eschatology: Benson's 'The Lord of the World'," *New Blackfriars*, January 1991, p.4; Madeleine Beard, *Faith and Fortune* (1997), pp.180–188; Janet Grayson, *Robert Hugh Benson: Life and Works* (1998); George Marshall, "Two Autobiographical Narratives of Conversion: Robert Hugh Benson and Ronald Knox," *Recusant History*, October 1998, p.237; Paschal Scotti, OSB, "Necromancy and Monsignor Benson," *Downside Review*, April 2003, p.135; Patrick Allitt, *Catholic Converts: British and American Intellectuals Turn to Rome* (1997) *passim*; Joseph Pearce, *Literary Converts* (1999) *passim*; Fr. Charles P. Connor, *Classic Catholic Converts* (2001), pp.73–80; Ralph McInerny, *Some Catholic Writers* (2007); *DNB* ("He began to see no alternative but authority or skepticism")..

Bentley, John Francis – architect; b. 30 January 1839, Doncaster, Yorkshire; c. 1862 (wife, Margaret Annie, received in 1874); d. 2 March 1902, 3 The Sweep, Old Town, Clapham Common; trained in office of Henry Clutton (1819–1893) (see below), an architect in extensive domestic and ecclesiastical practice, who had become a Catholic; many designs for work in stone, metal, wood, stained glass and embroidery; firm believer in architectural principles and methods of the Middle Ages; many commissions for churches (including St. Mary of the Angels, Bayswater, London, and Holy Rood, Watford), seminary of St. Thomas, Hammersmith, London, and houses, including internal decoration and furniture of Carlton Towers, Selby, Yorkshire, for Lord Beaumont; architect of Westminster Cathedral, done in Byzantine style with tall campanile; father of four sons and seven daughters, including Bede John F. Bentley, traveler, big game hunter, prospector and photographer; and of Osmund Bentley, architect; see Winefride de l'Hôpital, *Westminster Cathedral and its Architect* (1919); *Catholic Encyclopedia*; *DNB*.

Berdoe, Edward – physician and author; b. 7 March 1836, London; c. 28 May 1866 (received by Fr. Gallwey); d. 2 March 1916; brought up as Nonconformist; worked as general practitioner in Hackney for forty years; opposed the germ theory of disease and the experimental method in research; medical advisor to Anti-Vivisection Society; editor of *The Zoophilist*; drawn to Catholicism through reading Newman's *Apologia*; great authority on Robert Browning and founder of the Browning Society; see *Browning and the Christian Faith* (1896); essay in J. G. F. Raupert (ed), *Roads to Rome* (1901), p.9 ("It has often been said that there is no logical standpoint between Agnosticism and the Catholic Faith.... I cannot be an Agnostic, because I consider Jesus Christ the greatest Fact in human history. He was either what he claimed to be, or the greatest of impostors. But He was more than man, and the Catholic Church knew Him, spoke with Him, and she speaks now with an authority no other Church claims or dares to usurp. This compels my obedience. All else is shifting sand").

Berisford, Humphrey – Catholic layman; b. in Derbyshire; d. about 1588, Derby; son of a Protestant squire; studied at Douai for about two years; on return he was fighting a legal action for his father when his opponent accused him of being a recusant; questioned by the judge he bravely professed his Catholic faith and was committed to prison; judge offered him both favor to his cause and freedom if he would say he would go to the Protestant church, but he refused; remained in prison seven years and died prisoner in Derby gaol; see *Gillow*, Vol. I, p.200; *Catholic Encyclopedia*.

Berkeley, Sir Lennox Randal (Francis) – composer; b. 12 May 1903, Melford Cottage, Boars Hill, near Oxford; c. 1928; d. 26 December 1989, London; from aristocratic family; composed music from childhood; studied French at Merton College, Oxford; met Maurice Ravel who was very impressed with his musical work; studied with Nadia Boulanger in Paris 1927–1932, where he was friends with Stravinsky, Poulenc and Fauré; musical collaboration with Benjamin Britten (1913–1976); Professor of composition at Royal Academy of Music 1946–1968; particularly at home with the voice; notable works were *Serenade for Strings*, flute sonata; four operas, a *Stabat Mater*, two masses, and Latin motets; song cycle for contralto and orchestra, *Four Poems of St. Teresa of Avila*; religious influences in much of his music; later experimented with serial techniques, e.g., in third symphony; composed in almost all genres; respectful of tradition; his pupil Peter Dickinson referred to him as dedicated to "passing on the love of music as a spiritual imperative in a foreign, material age"; knighted in 1974; papal knighthood of

St. Gregory; President of the Composers' Guild of Great Britain from 1975; ashes scattered at Cap Ferrat, France; son, Michael, a composer; see Michael Dawney, "Centenary of Sir Lennox Berkeley, Composer," *Catholic Life*, June 2003, p.27; Susan Treacy, "Lennox Berkeley: A Twentieth-Century Convert Composer," *Saint Austin Review*, July/August 2009, p.29; *DNB* ("In the wake of the Second Vatican Council, he wrote in the press urging the retention of the Tridentine Mass, since he believed the authorities were ignoring a legitimate desire expressed by a large body of the Roman Catholic laity. In private he wrote of those 'for whom the overthrow of the old tradition appears to be an end in itself,' an end which, in religion as in music, he was unable to approve").

Berry, Dame Mary – b. 1917, Cambridge; c. 1938 (received by the Bishop of Liège); d. 1 May 2008 (Ascension Day), Cambridge; daughter of the Vice-Master of Downing College, Cambridge; mother was daughter of an Anglican clergyman; brought up as an Anglican; degree in music at Cambridge; studied with Nadia Boulanger in Paris; became a novice with the Canonesses of St. Augustine at Jupille, Belgium; before war evacuated to Paris and then to Lisbon; after Vatican II exclaustrated with Margaret Aitken and Rosemary McCabe and founded the Schola Gregoriana in order to foster the Chant; played important role in preserving Gregorian Chant and reintroducing it into the Church's liturgical life; thereby helped in the resurgence of Tradition; produced many recordings to illustrate development and interpretation of Chant down the centuries; did much teaching at home and abroad; awarded *Pro Ecclesia et Pontifice* medal by Pope John Paul II in 2000; buried in cemetery of St. Birinus Catholic Church, Dorchester on Thames; see obituary in *The Gramophone*, July 2008; Bernard Marriott, "To Teach and to Celebrate," *Mass of Ages*, August 2008, p.23 ("After the war she was sent to Rome, Jupille, Dijon and Paris, but by this time the winds of change fanned by Vatican II were blowing strongly to the extent that, deeply unhappy that two promises made at her final profession – to teach and to celebrate the solemn Roman office – were being downplayed, she volunteered to be exclaustrated, and to live her vocation closer to the secular world").

Best (Beste), Henry Digby – novelist and miscellaneous writer; b. 21 October 1768, Lincoln; c. 26 May 1798; d. 28 May 1836, Brighton; son of prebendary of Lincoln Cathedral; mother a member of Catholic Digby family; Fellow of Magdalen College, Oxford; Anglican deacon and active preacher; his writings anticipated Tractarian doctrines; a Douai translation of the New Testament confirmed his early leanings towards Catholicism; inherited considerable estates from his mother and retired to Lincoln; had doubts about character of Established Church resulting in his conversion; much work for Catholic causes; traveled abroad, spending four years in France and Italy; father of John Richard Digby Beste the author; see *Four Years in France* (1826) (especially pp.71–75, which give account of conversion); *Personal and Literary Memoirs* (1829); *Poverty and the Baronet's Family, a Catholic Story* (published posthumously, 1846); *Gillow*, Vol. I, p.203; *Catholic Encyclopedia*; *DNB* ("He met Abbé Beaumont, a French émigré priest. As he was led to consider the doctrine of transubstantiation and other Catholic tenets, his doubts about Anglicanism increased.... His conversion can be attributed not only to the influence of Beaumont and to his own theological studies but also to the influence of the

Digbys, particularly his mother, who in his own words still had the 'rags of popery' about her").

Betjeman, Lady Penelope Valentine Hester (*née* Chetwode) – writer, lecturer and adventurer; b. 14 February 1910; c. 9 March 1948; d. 11 April 1986, India; daughter of Field Marshall Lord Chetwode, C-in-C in India, 1930–1935; first went to India in 1928 and often throughout her life; wife of Sir John Betjeman (1906–1984), though they separated after her conversion; Evelyn Waugh drew on her and her love of horses for *Helena*; see her unpublished "Random Thoughts" ("I know I owe my first real experience of the Reality of God to India. India made me God conscious. The two countries where the air is electric with God are India and Spain.... The Hindu idea is: I hope one day to be God. My reaction is: I don't want to be God. I don't want to be worshipped. The idea fills me with horror. My whole instinct is to WORSHIP and this is what I want to do for ever and ever because it satisfies an instinct in me and I feel I was created to do it"); Imogen Lycett Green, *Grandmother's Footsteps: A Journey in Search of Penelope Betjeman* (1994) ("My grandmother went to Assisi – the Italian home of St. Francis and the artist Giotto – when she was seventeen.... 'I just knew that I would one day come back there as a Catholic and exactly twenty years later I did. Many people have been started off on their religious pilgrimage through St. Francis of Assisi. I didn't do anything about it for a long time'.... I had always been told that Evelyn Waugh converted my grandmother to Catholicism.... Actually, it was St. Francis who had planted the seed in her young mind in 1927, and not Evelyn Waugh at all, whom she only met several years later"); Bevis Hillier, *John Betjeman: New Fame, New Love* (2002),

passim; A. N. Wilson, *Betjeman* (2006), *passim*.

Bevan, James Johnstone – priest; b. 28 May 1890; c. 1913; d. 1959; naval officer in World War I and chaplain in World War II; joined Oratorian Order; ordained priest 1922; resided at London Oratory; very influential in Catholic Evidence Guild of which he was director of studies for some time; writer of Catholic pamphlets and articles; made many converts; see *God and this War September 1939* (1939); *Why Should I Go To Mass?* (1963); Maisie Ward, *Unfinished Business* (1964), pp.358–360 ("[S]howing us supremely the road of the heart ... he was ... personally linked with the hundreds he brought into the Church and the thousands he helped to live close to God. I never knew a man to whom his friends meant more, or who had more friends and spiritual children.... [A] life utterly unselfish, totally devoted to God and man, great pain, total self-abandonment and above all unfailing love").

Bewley, Charles – barrister and diplomat; b. 12 July 1888, Dublin; c. 1911; d. 1969, Rome; brought up in wealthy Anglo-Irish family; father a Quaker, mother an Anglican; raised as a Quaker; read Law at Oxford and trained as barrister at Kings Inn, Dublin; called to bar 1914; moved to a republican position; supported Home Rule movement; defended many nationalists and republicans; during Irish civil war, took the treaty side and prosecuted many anti-treaty prisoners; Irish Minister to Holy See in 1929; Pope bestowed on him Order of Grand Cross of St. Gregory the Great; Irish ambassador to Germany 1933–1939; apologist for Nazis and anti-British; reportedly thwarted efforts to obtain visas for Jews; picked up in Italy at end of World War II; spent rest of life in Rome; in last years became great friend of Mgr. Hugh O'Flaherty, "the Vatican Pimpernel" who had rescued thousands of Jews and escaped POWs from the Nazis; see *Memoirs of a Wild Goose* (1989); Andreas Roth, *Mr. Bewley in Berlin:Aspects of the Career of an Irish Diplomat, 1933–1939* (2000).

Biggar, Joseph Gillis – politician; b. 1 August 1828, Belfast; c. 1877 ("...received into the Roman Catholic Church, which he described as the national religion" (*DNB*)); d. 19 February 1890, Clapham Common, London; son of Joseph Biggar, merchant and chairman of Ulster Bank; parents Presbyterians; adopted strong nationalistic views; MP for County Cavan, Ireland from 1874 until his death; treasurer of the Land League; one of Irish politicians whose conduct was investigated during the Parnell Commission; adopted, with considerable success, policy of parliamentary "obstruction," for example in opposing Gladstone's Irish policy; after his conversion was devout Catholic; buried in Carnmoney cemetery, Belfast; see *DNB*.

Bird (Byrd or Beard), Blessed James – martyr; b. 1572/3, Winchester; d. 25 March 1592, Winchester; educated in Protestant religion; for some time student in English College, Rheims; on return to England his zeal for the faith resulted in his apprehension; accused of being reconciled to the Catholic Church and maintaining the Pope to be, under Christ, the Head of the Church; acknowledged indictment and sentenced to death; refused offer of life and liberty if he would once go to Protestant church; hanged, drawn and quartered at Winchester; see *Gillow*, Vol. I, p.213.

Bishop, Edmund – liturgical scholar and ecclesiastical historian; b. 17 May 1846, Bridgetown, Berry Pomeroy, near Totnes, Devon; c. 16 August 1867

(received by Fr. William Lockhart (see below)); d. 19 February 1917, Caburn, Park Lane, Barnstable, Devon; brought up in Evangelical family; father a hotel-keeper; clerk in civil service; taught himself ecclesiastical history by tracking Gibbon's references; served as kind of secretary to Thomas Carlyle; worked in Education Office of Privy Council Office 1864–1885; conversion influenced by Newman, Pugin, Simpson (see all below), and Lord Acton; retired early intending to join Benedictine Order at Downside Abbey, but unable to do so, largely for health reasons; best classified as a liberal Catholic, but this "was always inclusive of loyalty to the Catholic Church" (*DNB*); unassailable knowledge of liturgiology; original scholarship on history of missal and breviary; "one of the last great English auto-didacts" (Dom David Knowles); given a gold medal in 1897 by Pope Leo XIII "in recognition of his timely and effective services and of his unflagging devotion to the Catholic cause"; unmarried; buried in the monastic cemetery at Downside Abbey; see *Notes on My Conversion* (1874), reprinted in *Downside Review*, May 1930, p.85 (letter written at the age of fourteen to his mother: "I suppose that you agree with me that the great point is the Real Presence. Now look at the Bible and tell me what are the words: 'This is my body' and 'Do this in remembrance of me.' Does the first phrase mean, This is a remembrance of my body? No. It is 'This is *my body*,' that is to say the real body whole and entire. It is no good saying *reason, our common sense* tells us differently; we must look on Christ's words with faith; we must take the words of a God implicitly, as they are, and not pervert them as our petty, nay despicable, reason may dictate. We [Protestants] say that it is impossible that Christ's natural body can be in different places at the same time. But are we to question what God does? We say that nothing is impossible for God; why therefore do we pervert the words of Christ because we do not understand them?"); *Edward VI and the Book of Common Prayer* (1891) (jointly with Abbot Gasquet); *Liturgica Historica* (1918); Nigel Abercrombie, *The Life and Work of Edmund Bishop* (1959) (quoting a letter to Everard Green: "The history of the Anglican Church always seems to me the history of an evolution, – an evolution in the Catholic sense (I mean – towards Catholicity) not from causes within but by pressure from without. Thus: in the early years of Elizabeth's reign Protestantism was supreme, and Catholicity seemed (notwithstanding the adherence of so many to the old faith, the tenderness of so many for it) doomed to extinction. Who was to step in when the old men died? Where was the promise, the hope, of continuance? In those first twenty years of Elizabeth's reign this must have been the feeling in men's hearts, and the new Church had need to trouble about little more than itself: and what an Anglicanism it was! – having little if anything in common with what we know to go by that name. Then came seminaryism, young men, a hope of life and continuance for Catholics, a hope that the blood of the martyrs might be the seed of the Church. The new establishment feels the change immediately, – it feels, as it had not felt before, the need of a basis as against the Catholic Church, and it is forthcoming in Hooker. The establishment feels the need to be a *Church*; the sectaries who had begun to be a part of the establishment ... are disavowed, must be put down. As Catholicity grows, and Catholic pressure continues to be exercised, so does the Anglican Church grow, in the whole Stuart period, more Catholicizing: do the Catholic ladies, who accompany Queen Henrietta Maria to England, read their office books devoutly? – the Protestant ladies of the court feel abashed, they must be supplied with something of the same sort, – though if it had not been for the Catholic model they would never have felt the need ..."); Shane Leslie, "The Achievement of Edmund Bishop," *The Month*, March 1960, p.172 ("It was Bishop who gave the historical stroke which settled the question of Anglican Orders *qua* Orders. He pointed out that the answer must be found in Cardinal Pole's papers, since he had been the first to deal with the confused situation which has existed to the present day"); Dom Urban Butler, "Some Memories of Edmund Bishop," *Downside Review*, Winter 1960–61, p.50; Dom Andrew Moore, "Edmund Bishop as a Commentator on Modernism," *Downside Review*, April 1983, p.90; *DNB* ("It may safely be said that he knew the western liturgies in their entire sweep as no one else in his day. He had an unrivalled knowledge of the minutest details, but liturgy interested him primarily, not as texts, nor as ceremonial, but as the expression of the religious sense of the various peoples and ages; thus he regarded liturgy as a branch of the history of religion. His outstanding single contribution was the identifying of the Roman mass book of Gregory the Great, the central point, backwards and forwards, for the history of the liturgy in the west" (taken from the *DNB* archive)); issue of *Downside Review* for October 1917 was a memorial to Bishop.

Bittleston, Henry – priest; b. 25 September 1818; c. 24 November 1849; d. 2 July 1886, St. Albans; formerly Anglican curate; because of his difference with Anglican Bishop of Worcester on auricular confession, he had to move to High Anglican parish; some correspondence with Newman arising out of his perplexity with T. W. Allies' (see above) book, *The Church of England Cleared from the*

Charge of Schism; a later conversation with Newman resulted in his reception by Newman next day; joined Birmingham Oratory in March 1850; left Oratory in July 1879 and tried to become a Carthusian at the Chartreuse in France, finally serving as a secular priest; see Stanley L. Jaki, *Newman to Converts: An Existential Ecclesiology* (2001), pp.343–345 ("[Newman] returned to Allies' book: 'To say that theory of religion is true, which is at present held by half a dozen people only on the face of the earth (for not many more hold the Pope to be so great as Allies does and no greater,) is to my feelings and judgment a simple absurdity'").

Blackfan (alias Blackman), John, SJ – priest; b. 1560, Horsham, Sussex; c. about 1587; d. 13 January 1641; after conversion escaped from England in 1587; went first to English College at Rheims, then to English College at Valladolid, where entered the Society of Jesus; confessor at English College, Rome, then at Valladolid; once the director of Dona Luisa de Carvajal, whose charitable intention he directed to suffering Catholics of England; arrested in 1612 and committed to Gatehouse prison; in 1613 banished and retired to Brussels, where appointed vice-prefect of the English mission; in 1616 became rector of Valladolid; later returned to England and worked as missioner in different districts; known as man of integrity; see *Gillow*, Vol. I, p.224.-

Blair, Anthony Charles Lynton ("Tony") – politician and lawyer; b. 6 May 1953, Edinburgh; c. 21 December 2007 (received by Cardinal Murphy-O'-Connor at Archbishop's House, Westminster); brought up as Anglican, but not really practicing one until undergraduate at St. John's College, Oxford; associated for a time with High Church Anglicanism;

Labour MP from 1983; shadow Home Secretary 1992–1994; elected leader of Labour Party in June 1994; pioneered movement known as "New Labour" to modernize Labour Party and re-claim political centre; became Prime Minister on 2 May 1997 after general election; fought and won two further terms in 2001 and 2007; announced his resignation as Prime Minister on 10 May 2007 and left office on 27 June 2007, also stepping down as MP; appointed official envoy on Middle East on behalf of United Nations, European Union, United States and Russia; after conversion there was criticism of his voting record on promoting abortion, experimentation on unborn embryos, including cloned embryos, and euthanasia by neglect; continued to criticize the Catholic Church's teaching on homosexuality and stem cells; see Gerry Burns, "Converts to Catholicism: Tony Blair," *Catholic Life*, January 2009, p.60.

Blakelock, Denys Martin – actor; b. 22 June 1901, Shelfanger, near Diss, Norfolk; c. June 1934 (his brother, Alban, converted many years before; his sister-in-law, Renee, converted in 1934); d. 7 December 1970, London; son of an Anglican clergyman; brought up in Muswell Hill, London; actor who worked with many great actors and directors; career damaged by lack of confidence and increasing claustrophobia; later joined RADA, where taught audition technique; broadcaster; close friend of Sir Laurence Olivier and later of Eleanor Farjeon, the writer (see below) and Antonia White (see below); much depression and mood swings leading to his death; possible suicide, but Antonia White casts real doubt on this in her diaries; see *Finding My Way* (1958) ("If, in spite of all this evidence [of the recorded appearances of Christ at the first Easter], I could still cast doubts upon the truth of the Resurrection, I felt I should be raising up a miracle more difficult of acceptance than the Resurrection itself. In this way: only if the Resurrection did take place; only if Our Lord did return to his disciples, after the seemingly tragic failure of that first Good Friday; only then would it have been possible for them to accomplish the amazing things they did accomplish a few weeks later.

On that Good Friday, the disciples must surely have been hoping against hope for something stupendous to happen at the eleventh hour – something that would end in the complete confusion of Christ's enemies, and the vindication of all his claims. Nothing did happen. He died; it was the end; his enemies had won. And it is extremely doubtful whether to any of Christ's disciples his, to them, rather vague words about the Son of Man rising again on the third day meant anything at all. On that first Good Friday afternoon their spirits must have been at a very low ebb indeed. Was I to believe that that small band of uneducated fishermen went out and turned their little world upside down, with the Gospel of the Christ who had failed to implement his claims and fulfill his promises? Was I to believe that these men succeeded in spreading this Gospel throughout the whole world, performing miracles, and *even influencing the Calendar*; so that, up to the present day, most of our public holidays derive their very existence from the birth, death and resurrection of Jesus Christ; the very years being divided into B.C. and A.D. – those that were before Christ, and those that are called the first, or the nineteen-thirty-fourth year of the Lord? Was I really to believe that the disciples achieved all this when they themselves were in the depths of disillusion and disappointed hopes?

This was altogether too much to demand of credulity. No, the disciples were able to achieve all this just because Christ *did* come back to them on that first Easter Day. Good Friday was *not* the end; his enemies had *not* won. He had triumphed over them; triumphed over the evil in human nature for which they stood; triumphed over Death itself; proving to his followers that there was indeed another life on the other side of the grave, and that all his other claims were more than justified...

It only remained for me, as I grew more and more puzzled, and a little dismayed, by the hundred-and-one dissentient voices within the Church of England, to ask myself to what sort of Church Our Lord was referring when he said to St. Peter: 'Upon this rock I will build *my church*'.... If his Church was meant to be one which was to speak with certainty and with an authoritative voice; and to be at unity within itself on all fundamental matters of faith and morals; if that was what Christ had intended, where was this Church today? Did it exist? And if so, which of all the Christian bodies was it? There was only one Church which could reasonably claim to 'fill the bill'; that Church which called itself the 'one, true Church' of Christ, and stated that it was *the* Catholic Church. This Church alone, in the light of history, could logically say that it was the original Church founded by Jesus Christ, from which all the others had broken away; this Church alone could say that it had never permitted its teachings to be vitiated and watered down; this Church alone could claim that it had preserved the Apostolic succession and all the sacred functions of the priesthood in an unbroken line; this Church alone had a supreme authority – the Pope, whose final decision on fundamental questions of faith and morals were unquestioned...

...When I looked around and saw the tumult of the world today; when I saw civilization, which had had its very roots in Catholic Christianity, going down and down into the abyss of disbelief and cynicism; as a direct result, it seemed, of breaking away from the one Church, which alone could, with any reason, claim to speak authoritatively and with one voice, the Church which alone could give civilization any clear positive lead in moral and spiritual matters; when I saw all this, I sometimes glimpsed, however imperfectly, something of Our Lord's purpose in safeguarding his Church in this special way, in making the Pope the lynch-pin, as it were, by which the giant wheel of that great spiritual dynamo could revolve with perfect safety to the end of time. I saw the reason for it all – I 'saw and believed.' Before many weeks had gone by the parting of the ways became inevitable, and in the June of that year I was finally received into the Church. Let me say in conclusion that from that day to this I have never ceased to be deeply thankful that I took that step: never had the briefest moment of regret"); John Beaumont, "Denys Blakelock: Actor and Convert," *Catholic Life*, September 2007, p.36.

Blamires, Cyprian – editor, writer and translator; b. 1948; c. 17 June 1979; former Church of England minister (evangelical); doctoral thesis in history at Oxford University 1985; various academic positions; district organizer for St. Barnabas Society; see "How Much Do We Leave Out?" *Priests and People*, January 1998, p.22 ("Above all I had failed to grasp that the Incarnation did not come to an end when the earthly body of Jesus ascended to heaven; for from Pentecost onwards the home of Jesus on earth was the Church, his address was the Church, the place to find him and meet him was the living body of the faithful celebrating the sacraments given to them for the nourishment of their souls…

…And then there is the problem that those who preach the Bible as sole authority in matters of faith are incorrigibly divided about what the Bible teaches, a state of affairs that raises the question: do believers not need to be subject to a binding arbiter, a person whose interpretation of the truths of revelation is received as authoritative?... To use the words of the Evangelical scholar Oliver O'Donovan, 'God was incarnate as a man, not a book'"); "The Full Gospel" in Dwight Longenecker (ed), *The Path to Rome* (1999) ("I had been struck by the wonderful examples of sacrificial love given by so many Catholic post-Reformation saints, which exploded any notion that Catholic spiritual power had been diminished by the events of the sixteenth century. Sadly, most English Protestants were told nothing about the publicly established facts of the lives of heroic post-Reformation Catholics like St. Francis Xavier, St. Teresa of Avila, St. Vincent de Paul, St. Charles Borromeo, St. Francis de Sales, St. Alphonsus Liguori, Father Damien the leper priest, St. Maximilien Kolbe and countless others. These saints combined as passionate a commitment to the love of God with love for their fellow humans as anyone could possibly ask for…. It was the wonderful saints of the post-Reformation Catholic Church which brought me little by little, step by step, kicking and screaming, to my knees in submission"); *Protestantism: From a Catholic Perspective* (2007) ("There is a difficulty inherent in the whole Protestant position which is almost never referred to, perhaps out of delicacy. While there is nothing at all objectionable in the notion of the Church needing to be reformed from within, what the Reformers ended up promoting was something entirely different: the idea that there was a better version of the Christian faith that could be practiced outside the Roman obedience.

They had discovered something better in fact than the historic Catholic Church. It is not difficult that from the Catholic perspective this position seems to be inherently self-righteous. Considering that the Catholic Church brought the bible to birth, wrote the early creeds, and spread the gospel across all of Europe, often at great costs to those involved, it seems hard to understand how there could be a better version of the faith outside the Church…

…Asked why he persisted in rejecting King Henry VIII's breach with Rome when the English bishops had accepted it, [St. Thomas More's] answer was: 'The English bishops may have done so, but not the bishops of France, Italy, Spain, Portugal, Austria, etc.' In other words the Catholic Church in any given country is always only ever a part, not the whole. She cannot act independently of the whole Body, and the spokesperson for the body is the Pope…

…The degree to which the Anglican Reformers modified Catholic doctrine is rarely acknowledged by … apologists for Anglicanism. There are places where the medieval altar stone has been found to have been placed at the entrance to the church building as a threshold, ensuring that the people trod on it when they entered: nothing could be more expressive of the general desire to turn a completely new page and make the cleanest possible break with the old religion.

Moreover the 39 Articles of the Church of England – still its official doctrinal foundation – contain decidedly anti-Catholic statements. John Henry Newman's experience of a vain struggle to reconcile these Articles with traditional Catholic belief was one of the major factors that impelled him towards being received into the Church"); *The French Revolution and the Creation of Benthamism* (2008).

Bland, Hubert – journalist and politician; b. 3 January 1851, 22 Wood Street, Woolwich, London; c. 1900; d. 14 April 1914, Well Hall, Eltham; brought up as a non-conformist; attended various local schools; early interest in political ideas; worked as a bank clerk; husband of Edith Nesbit (1858–1924) (see below), the famous children's writer; admirer of Robert Browning and William Morris; honorary treasurer of the Fabian Society from its founding until 1911 (recruited George Bernard Shaw); wrote and lectured on socialism, but also had conservative opinions; critical of democracy, opposed women's suffrage, defended the empire, and rejected republicanism; had several mistresses and offspring by them; became a journalist and contributed a weekly column of social commentary to the *Sunday Chronicle* from 1892 to his death; had bohemian social circle; friend of Mgr. Robert Hugh Benson (see above), Cecil Chesterton (see below) and Frederick Rolfe ("Baron Corvo") (see below); his practical observances of the faith were not great; buried with Catholic rites in the family plot at Woolwich cemetery; see E. Nesbit Bland (ed), *Essays by Hubert Bland: 'Hubert' of the 'Sunday Chronicle'* (1914); Doris Langley Moore, *E. Nesbit: A Biography* (1967); Julia Briggs, *A Woman of Passion: The Life of E. Nesbit 1858–1824* (1987) ("Hubert's conservatism (at odds with his socialism, though he sought to reconcile them), his respect for tradition and his admiration for discipline and good order led him towards Catholicism"); *DNB*.

Bliss, William Henry – archivist and author; b. 26 April 1835, Newton St. Loe, Bath, Somerset c. 10 July 1869; d. 8 March 1911; father an Anglican clergyman; educated at Magdalen College, Oxford; came into contact with the Oxford

Movement; ordained Anglican vicar; after conversion to Catholicism became keeper of periodicals at the Bodleian Library, Oxford; from 1877 to his death official representative of British Public Records Office in Rome, researching in Vatican archives (spent most of his time searching the medieval Papal Registers in order to find all the dealings between the Papacy and Great Britain and Ireland); tutor to Victor Emmanuel, heir to the Italian crown; father of eleven children, including Fr. Geoffrey Bliss, SJ; his wife remained an Anglican; buried in Rome.

Bluet, Thomas – priest and divine; d. 1604; formerly a Church of England minister; after conversion went to Douai and entered English College in 1577; ordained priest 23 February 1578 and sent to the English mission; apprehended in London; boldly professed his faith and refuted the arguments of his examiners; imprisoned in London and then in Wisbeach Castle; supported the appellant clergy in the quarrel between the Seculars and the Jesuits over the appointment of the Archpriest Blackwell and was admitted to the presence of the Queen; involved in the discussions in Rome over this matter in 1602 in which his deputation was held to be innocent of the charges of schism and rebellion leveled against them; returned to the mission in England where he toiled for many years; see *Gillow*, Vol. I, p.243.

Blunt, Lady Anne Isabella Noel (*née* King) (*suo jure* fifteenth Baroness Wentworth) – authoress, painter, traveler and breeder of Arab horses; b. 22 September 1837, London; c. 1879 (her mother-in-law, Mary Blunt (1806–1855) received with her three children in 1851); d. 15 December 1917, Cairo, Egypt; daughter of William King, first Earl of Lovelace (1805–1893); grand-daughter of George Gordon, sixth Lord Byron (1788–1824), the poet; educated privately; wife of Wilfrid Scawen Blunt (1840–1922), traveler and poet, who lost his religious faith later; traveled extensively in East with husband; converted to Catholicism as result of vision experienced when her husband lay seriously ill in remote spot during journey in 1879; one of very few women of the time to travel into heart of desert; did fine sketches and superb watercolors; heir to considerable fortune inherited from the Milbanke family; founded one of greatest private studs devoted to Arab horses; much writing on Arabs and Arab horses; separated from husband in 1906; buried in Nun's burial-ground at the Jebel Ahmar; see R. Archer and J. Fleming (ed), *Lady Anne Blunt: Journals and Correspondence, 1878–1917* (1986); H. V. F. Winstone, *Lady Anne Blunt: A Biography* (2003); *DNB*.

Blyth, Francis, STP (alias Francis Courtney; name in religion Simon Stock of the Blessed Trinity) – priest and writer; b. c.1705; c. when a youth; d. 11 December 1772, Portuguese embassy, London; educated in the Protestant principles of his parents, but dissatisfaction at the practices of the Established Church, e.g., on manner of administering baptism on occasions; in 1723 entered the novitiate of the Discalced Carmelites in Modena, Italy; studied for the priesthood and ordained there; returned to England in 1730, working in Wiltshire and then in the London district; in 1741 appointed assistant chaplain at the Portuguese embassy (chaplain major from 1756 until his death); vicar provincial of the English Carmelites 1742–1755, a period when much disagreement between secular and religious missioners; author of many fine spiritual works, notably a paraphrase on the seven penitential psalms; worked with Bishop Challoner in publishing a new edition of the Rheims Testament; buried in cemetery of St. Pancras; see *Gillow*, Vol. I, p.252; *Catholic Encyclopedia*; *DNB*.

Bodey (Body), Blessed John – gentleman and martyr; b. Wells, Somerset; d. 2 November 1583, Andover; studied canon law and civil law at Oxford University; disliked established religion and went to Douai College in 1577; schoolmaster; after returning to England his zeal for the old religion resulted in apprehension; prosecuted under the Article of Supremacy, tried and condemned; hanged, drawn and quartered at Andover; see *Gillow*, Vol. I, p.255.

Bolt, John – musician and later priest; b. 1563, Exeter; d. 3 August 1640; musician at court, but stole away in order to become Catholic and live with Catholics; Queen heard of it and was much annoyed, but he lived secretly in gentlemen's houses; apprehended by Topcliffe who thought he was a priest; thrown into prison; contacts at court obtained eventual release; retired to the Continent; ordained priest in 1605; acted as chaplain and organist to St. Monica's Convent, Louvain from 1613 until his death; see *Gillow*, Vol. I, p.256.

Bond, Anne (*née* Bennet) – mother; b. 1784; c. 1815 (received with her husband, William Vincent Bond (1782–1873); d. 1859; mother of six sons, three of whom became secular priests: Rt. Rev. William Bond (1811–1888); Very Rev. Canon Joseph Bond (1814–1878); Fr. James Bond (1819–1887), two Jesuit priests: Fr. Stephen Bond (1826–1871); Fr. Vincent Bond (1828–1892), and one died young as a Jesuit scholastic, Fr. John Bond (1817–1844); and of four daughters, all of whom became nuns: Miss Anne Bond (1807–1876), Sr. Anne Francis (Franciscan); Miss Mary Bond (1821–1892), Sr. Winifred Joseph (Franciscan); Miss Teresa Bond (1823–1864), Sr. Anne Teresa of the Holy Family (Carmelite); and Miss Anne Frances Bond, Sr. Anne Mary Vincent of St. Joseph (Carmelite).

Boothman, Edward Duncan – author; b. 1845; c. 8 April 1903; "I had, I remember, at three years of age, clear and vivid ideas of possessing a soul, a force within the body that would live for ever, when the body died"; brought up as a Wesleyan Methodist by devout grandparents; of delicate health as child and educated at home; "reached the age of sixteen under strict puritan rules of daily life"; moved to London with parents and started to attend the Church of England; reading of Renan's *Vie de Jesus* led to doubts; found High Church movement and ordained to Anglican ministry; in February 1903, after twenty-eight years of ministry, left his rectory to "make submission to the Holy See"; after his conversion he resolved to maintain silence for three years, then published the pamphlet referred to below; see *The Truth shall make you Free: A Letter*, (1906) ("I cannot finish this letter without telling all its readers how much I rejoice in the freedom of the Catholic Church. When you 'know the truth, the truth shall make you free'; since the Holy Spirit leads Mother Church 'into all truth,' therefore her children rejoice in 'the liberty of the children of God.' If we 'stand fast in the liberty wherewith Christ has made us free,' we rejoice, and our joy 'no man has taken from us.' This is a joy, not confined to exceptionally favored individuals or nations, it is universal. Throughout the world the children of the Catholic Church realize the blessing of this glorious liberty. It is a glorious privilege to be free, spiritually free; free from doubts, anxieties, and questionings; free from wrangling, and dissension, and 'doubtful disputations'; free from State 'bonds'; free from parliamentary politics; free from Royal Commissions and Privy Councils and legal judgments; free from autocratic State-Bishops; free to worship God in His own way, One way; free whilst worshipping the Son with holy adoration – to honor her, whom the holy undivided, ever-blessed Trinity, Father, Son, and Holy Spirit, honor; her, the great Mother of God, Mary most holy; free to speak to the Blessed Company of Heaven, the Blessed Saints and Holy Angels; free to exercise the heart's deepest devotion and aspirations; free to pray always and at all times for the souls of our loved ones departed this life; free to offer soul and body to a life of poverty, chastity, and obedience, according to our Lord's counsels of perfection; free to wash at the fountain opened in the Church for sin and uncleanness; free to draw nigh in perfect confidence and boldness to adore the Lord of Life dwelling in the Blessed Sacrament of His love in the Tabernacle; freed from that fear of death which so long held man in bondage; free, at last, to depart in peace, fortified with all the Sacraments of Holy Church; free to enter the purifying, purging fires, where (helped by the prayers of the saints and the faithful friends on earth) we may be holy souls attaining that eternal freedom, 'the bliss of the purified' in the blessed vision of 'eternal loveliness'").

Boste, Saint John – priest and martyr; b. 1544, Wellyng Manor, Dufton, Westmorland; c. 1576; d. 24 July 1594 (some accounts say 19 July), Durham; Fellow of Queen's College, Oxford; received Church of England orders and subscribed to royal supremacy; after conversion expelled from his fellowship; entered English College, Rheims, in 1580; ordained priest 4 March 1581 and sent on the English mission; worked in northern counties and Scotland; after many narrow escapes apprehended near Durham and sent to the Tower; imprisoned for long time and racked; sent back to North in 1594; accused of leaving and re-entering country without permission; tried and condemned; hanged, drawn and quartered at Durham; see Rt. Rev. B. Foley, *Bl. Christopher Robinson* (1987), pp.7–12 (gives account of martyrdom of John Boste); *Gillow*, Vol. I, p.274; *DNB*.

Botting, Joseph – Catholic layman; brought up in "Low Church" Anglicanism, then in Anglo-Catholicism; gave up church-going at age of eighteen, but began a rethink five years later, by which time he was practically a Unitarian in outlook; studied for the Anglican ministry and became High Church; took Anglican orders in 1941; began to see how wide was the gulf between High and Low Church; see "More Converts Explain," *The Month*, November 1956, p.275 ("I had the good fortune ... to set hands on Fr. Philip Hughes' *Rome and the Counter-Reformation*. The opening chapters, summarizing the course of the Reformation, completely shattered the ideas I had always accepted and clung to. I saw now that it was not a question of correcting abuses in the medieval practice of the Catholic religion. In the minds of the leaders of the English Reformation and those in power at the time, it was an earnest attempt to replace Catholicism with the Protestant religion nurtured on the Continent. There was no doubt about 'intentions'. They were all too clearly expressed.... I was able to read the first two volumes of Fr. Hughes's monumental work on the Reformation in England.... [This was] sufficient to make me see that my old arguments for Anglicanism as a purged return to primitive non-papal Catholicism, and miraculously preserved from the theological aberrations of continental

Protestantism, were exploded once and for all.... [W]hat I now saw was the further truth that those who refused to accept the new religion and died as martyrs for the old were in fact 'the Church.' The rest, even though they were perhaps the majority, who submitted under pressure applied with all the relentless insistence of a modern police state, were apostates, whatever extenuating circumstances there might have been at the time. Surveying the sixteenth-century upheaval from a distance, I realized clearly that had I lived then I ought to have been on the side of More, Fisher, the Carthusian martyrs and all the other Catholics who resisted the attempt to change the religion of their forefathers...

It only remained for the Abbot of Downside [B. C. Butler (see below)] in his essay *The Church and Infallibility* to dispel for me the notion of a 'primitive non-papal Catholicism,' and so to give me all the evidence I needed to seek reconciliation with the Holy See").

Boulton, Sir Harold Edwin, second baronet – song writer, philanthropist, editor, and poet; b. 7 August 1859, Charlton, Kent; c. 1897 (wife, Adelaide Lucy (d. 26 April 1926) received in 1904); d. 1 June 1935, Grosvenor House, Park Lane, London; involved in university settlement movement; formerly associated with High Church party; writer of *Songs of the North* (2 Vols.), *Songs of the Four Nations*, *Canti d'Italia*; writer of *Twelve Lyrics*, and of many volumes of songs and detached lyrics; author of Canadian National song "Canada"; Knight of Grace of Order of St. John of Jerusalem in England; co-founder of Federation of Working Men's Social Clubs; see *DNB*.

Bovill (or Bonvill) (alias Terrill), Anthony, SJ – priest; b. 1621, Canford, Dorset; d. 11 October 1676, Liège; after converting entered the English College, Rome, in 1640; ordained priest 16 March 1647; entered the Society of Jesus in June 1647; chair of Philosophy in Florence; later to Parma where he taught philosophy and scholastic divinity for four years; then on to Liège as director of studies and teaching theology and mathematics; rector of Liège College 1671–1674; see *Gillow*, Vol. I. p.279 ("It is stated that he was consulted far and near as an oracle of learning").

Bowden, Elizabeth (*née* Swinburne) – b. 1805; c. 8 July 1846 (received with her son, Charles, and two daughters, Mary (Marianne or Maryanne) and Emily; brother-in-law, Captain Henry Bowden (1804–1869) received in 1852, as were his second wife, Marianne Catherine, *née* Burgoyne (1806–1864), his son, Fr. Henry George Sebastian Bowden (see below), his daughter, Emma Jane (1833–1908) (whose future husband, Richard Mills (1829–1901) was received in February 1855), and the rest of his family); d. 1896; youngest daughter of Sir John Swinburne, sixth Baronet; wife of John William Bowden (1798–1844), the High Anglican ecclesiastical writer, author of some of the *Tracts for the Times* and close friend of Newman from when they were both students at Trinity College, Oxford; his premature death came at the height of Newman's difficulties about the Anglican Church (at his funeral Newman "sobbed bitterly over his coffin, to think that he left me still dark as to what the way of truth was"); influenced greatly by Newman's friendship and many letters regarding process of conversion; mother of Fr. John Edward ("Johnny") Bowden (1829–1874), who converted in August 1848, became a priest of London Oratory, and wrote *Life and Letters of Frederick William Faber* (1869) (see *Gillow*, Vol. I, p.279); of Marianne Bowden (1831–1867), who became a nun of the Order of the Visitation (name in religion Sr. Mary Francis Dominica); of Emily Frances Bowden (1833–1909), translator of Countess Hahn-Hahn's *Fathers of the Desert*; and of Fr. Charles Henry Bowden (1836–1906), godson of Newman and priest of London Oratory; aunt of Algernon Swinburne (1837–1909), the poet; she lived to attend Newman's funeral; see Joyce Sugg, *Ever Yours Affly: John Henry Newman and His Female Circle* (1996); Stanley L. Jaki, *Newman to Converts: An Existential Ecclesiology* (2001), Ch. 5 ("Mrs. Bowden, Newman argued [in a letter to her], would be most mistaken in thinking that she had to read everything in order to see clearly. In Newman's eyes Mrs. Bowden was caught in an 'unreal argument'.... Were the argument valid, then 'no pagan could become a Christian; no Jew could become a Christian; except the learned. How could a Unitarianism, or a Nestorian, or a Presbyterian, ever leave his own sect…, if it were necessary to read all that was to be said on both sides. At any rate, nobody could be so learned as to claim that 'he has read *all* that may be said.' Further, ever new arguments might be coming").

Bowden, Henry George (called in religion Sebastian) – priest and soldier; b. 1836; c. 1852 (received in Gibraltar; his sister, Emma Jane (1833–1908) received in the same year); d. 1920; son of Captain Henry Bowden (1804–1869) by his first wife; in 1855 joined the Rifle Brigade; in 1856 transferred to the Fusilier Guards; left the army in 1867 and joined the Oratory; ordained priest in 1870; Superior of the Oratory 1889–1892 and 1903–1907; see *Miniature Lives of the Saints* (1877); *Miniature Life of Mary, Virgin and Mother* (1880); *Mementoes of the English Martyrs and Confessors* (1910); *Spiritual Teaching of Father Sebastian Bowden* (1921).

Bowles, Emily – writer and translator; b. 1818; c. 1843 (received by Cardinal Acton); d. c. 1904; sister of Frederick Bowles (see below); from a large well-to-do family; at age of fifteen she doubted Christianity and was given to reading Carlyle's *Sartor Resartus*; her brother, Henry, introduced her to the Tracts and she became a supporter of the Oxford Movement; overwhelmed by Newman's preaching; became a great friend of Newman with whom she corresponded freely; conversion influenced by Miss Agnew's novel *Geraldine* and friendship with Eyston family, her neighbors at East Hendred, Berkshire; encouraged in her conversion by Lady Acton, mother of the Cardinal, and by Pierce Connelly; under influence of Newman and Wiseman she joined the Order which Cornelia Connelly was founding, the Society of the Holy Child, and went with her to Derby to opening of first convent there; later sent to make a foundation in Liverpool, but quarreled with foundress; she obtained a dispensation from her vows and left the Order; spent rest of her life writing and translating religious books and doing works of charity; also wrote several novels on Catholic themes, e.g., *St. Martha's Home* (1864); *In The Camargue* (1873); unmarried; see *A Gracious Life. Being the Life of Barbara Acarie: Blessed Mary of the Incarnation* (1879); *The Life of St. Jane Frances Fremyot de Chantal* (1888); *Madame de Maintenon* (1888); Joyce Sugg, *Ever Yours Affly: John Henry Newman and His Female Circle* (1996).

Bowles, Frederick Selwood – priest; b. 1819; c. 9 October 1845, Littlemore (received on the same occasion as Newman); d. 1900; brother of Emily Bowles (see above); educated at Exeter College, Oxford; became Anglican clergyman; at Littlemore with Newman; ordained priest in Rome 1847; joined Birmingham

Oratory in 1848; depressive in temperament and gradually withdrew from community life, leaving in 1860; continued to work as a priest.

Bowyer, Sir George, seventh Baronet – jurist and politician; b. 8 October 1811, Radley Park, near Abingdon, Berkshire; c. August 1850; d. 7 June 1883, 13 King's Bench Walk, London; received much of his early education in Italy; barrister, then drawn to academic side of law and wrote works on constitutional law, comparative jurisprudence, and Roman law; drawn to Tractarian Movement; after conversion active spokesman for the Catholic Church on legal and constitutional questions; acted as constitutional adviser to Cardinal Manning at time of public agitation against Pope's decision to create Archbishopric of Westminster (argued for legal right of Pope to exercise his spiritual authority by creating a permanent episcopacy in England, saying that the Catholic Church was recognized in English law); regular contributor to *Dublin Review*; MP for Dundalk 1852–1868 and then for County Wexford 1873–1880; passion for politics (fervent Whig but always independent minded); consistent defender of Catholic causes in parliament and the press; Knight of Order of St. John of Jerusalem; Knight Grand Cross of Order of St. Gregory the Great; Knight Commander of Order of Pius IX and Chamberlain to that Pope; unmarried; buried in family vault at Abingdon; see *Gillow*, Vol. I, p.282; *DNB*.

Boyd, Charlotte Pearson – benefactress; b. 21 March 1837, Macao, China; c. 22 September 1894 (followed by many of her Anglican friends); d. 3 April 1906, Kilburn, London; brought up as Anglican in a merchant family (inherited enormous wealth from both sides of family); on a visit to Walsingham at the age of thirteen she heard an inner call to restore as many ruined monasteries as possible; founded the English Abbey Restoration Trust in 1875; restored the Slipper Chapel at Walsingham to Catholic ownership; many charitable activities; oblate of St. Benedict; buried at St. Mary's Catholic Church, Kensal Green, London; see Mgr. George Tutto, "Walsingham: Charlotte Pearson Boyd (1837–1906)," *Catholic Life*, October 2002, p.28.

Bracey, Robert – priest; b. 1870; c. 1887; d. 1933; brought up in a decidedly Low Church home with a hatred of "Popery" and "Ritualism"; after conversion became Dominican Friar and Prior of St. Dominic's, Haverstock Hill, London; later Prior of Woodchester; see essay in J. G. F. Raupert (ed), *Roads to Rome* (1901), p.10 ("That which I think seemed to attract me most in [the Catholic Church] was her claim to infallibility. I saw clearly the uselessness of revelation without a key, of the Bible without an interpreter. Every page of the Gospel bore upon it an indication of Our Lord's own provision of such a key and such an interpreter; and the fact that only one claimant for this absolutely necessary position of infallible guide existed, seemed to leave me no power of choice save that between Catholicism and an unreasoning skepticism").

Bradburne, John Randal – mystic, poet and pilgrim; b. 1921, Skirwith, Cumbria; c. 1947, Feast of Christ the King; d. 5 September 1979, Mutemwa, Zimbabwe; brought up in cultured Anglican family (father Anglican clergyman); cousin of Terence Rattigan, the playwright and of Christopher Soames, the last Governor of Rhodesia; in World War II an officer in the Gurkhas in Malaya; later in Burma with Whingate's Chindits; long friendship with fellow Gurkha, John Dove, later Jesuit priest, who is main guardian of his memory; few brief jobs (e.g., forestry, prep school master, sailor), but spent many years seeking God in England, Europe, Israel, and Africa, often walking and begging; layman and member of Third Order of St. Francis; deeply versed in Holy Scripture and loved *The Cloud of Unknowing*; great devotion to Our Lady, making private vow to her that he would remain celibate; spent some time with Benedictines, Carthusians and Congregation of Our Lady of Sion; tried life of a hermit; caretaker at Archbishop of Westminster's country house at Hare Street, near Cambridge, living in study formerly used by Mgr. Robert Hugh Benson (see above); in 1962 went to Africa and was caretaker at house of Lady Acton (see above), given by the Actons to the Jesuits; made warden of Mutemwa Leprosy Camp, Rhodesia, and restored it from a state of dereliction; cared for the lepers, had a church built there, taught them plainchant, and read to them from Gospel when they lay dying; disagreement with Rhodesia Leprosy Association, which expelled him; he lived in tin hut nearby almost as hermit and continued to care for lepers; shot and killed during Rhodesian war by soldiers of supporters of Robert Mugabe; cause for canonization has been opened; see John Dove, SJ, *Strange Vagabond of God: The Story of John Bradburne* (1997); John D. Vose, *John Bradburne: A Magnificent Eccentric* (2003).

Brampton, first Baron (Sir Henry Hawkins, PC) – lawyer and judge; b. 14 September 1817, Hitchin; c. summer 1898 (received by Cardinal Vaughan at the age of eighty; he remarked that at least the step would not be put down to the impetuosity of youth); d. 12 October 1907, 5 Tilney Street, Park Lane, London; son of solicitor; established great reputation as barrister, especially in

criminal cases; appeared in Tichborne case for the family in civil action and for the prosecution in criminal case; Judge of Queen's Bench; standing counsel to the Jockey Club; long standing friend of Cardinal Manning; relative of Anthony Hope (Hawkins), the novelist; generous contributor to building of Westminster Cathedral; his second wife, Jane Louisa (1827–1907) a Catholic; in 1903 with his wife presented the chapel of Sts. Augustine and Gregory to Westminster Cathedral; bulk of their estates went to Archbishop of Westminster and was applied, as they wished, to the hospital of St. John and St. Elizabeth; buried at Kensal Green cemetery, London; see letter in J. G. F. Raupert (ed), *Roads to Rome* (1901), p.13 ("Those ... who look for my reasons for taking the important step I took so late in life, cannot have their expectations satisfied by me. It must suffice them to know that it was the result of my deliberate conviction that the truth – which was all I sought – lay within the Catholic Church. I thought the matter out for myself, anxiously and seriously, uninfluenced by any human being, and I have unwavering satisfaction in the conclusion at which I arrived and my conscience tells me it is right"); *Catholic Encyclopedia*; *DNB*.

Bramston, Bishop James Yorke – vicar apostolic of the London district; b. 18 March 1763, Oundle, Northamptonshire; c. 1790 (received by the notable Irish Franciscan, Arthur O'Leary); d. 11 July 1836, Golden Square, London; raised as an Anglican and trained as a lawyer, studying under Charles Butler, the well-known Catholic lawyer, who introduced the faith to him and took him to Mass at the Sardinian embassy; after conversion entered English College, Lisbon, in 1792; ordained priest in 1796 and served in Portugal, mainly as chaplain to the British troops stationed in Lisbon; returned to England in 1801; served in London district mission; appointed coadjutor to Bishop Poynter and consecrated Bishop in 1823; succeeded Poynter as vicar apostolic of London district in 1827; noted for his charity towards the poor; buried at St. Mary Moorfields, London, but later moved to the Chapel Cloister at St. Edmund's College, near Ware; see Fr. Nicholas Schofield, "A Forgotten London Bishop: James Yorke Bramston (1763–1836)," *Catholic Life*, May 2008, p.30; *Gillow*, Vol. I, p.288; *DNB* ("'A Popish priest grafted on to a Protestant lawyer', he once remarked, 'should be a switch for the devil himself'").

Braye, Lord (Hon. Alfred Thomas Townshend Verney-Cave, fifth Baron Braye) – b. 1849; c. June 1868; d. 1928; brought up as an Anglican, he recalled religious atmosphere at Eton as "elusive and curiously unsatisfying"; educated at Christ Church, Oxford; Knight of Malta; succeeded as Baron in 1879; took part in South African War as Lieutenant-Colonel of Leicestershire Militia; as Catholic he suggested to Queen Victoria that she, in the papal tradition, should celebrate her Jubilee; great interest in higher education for Catholics and in the study of Holy Scripture; see *Fewness of My Days: A Life in Two Centuries* (1927) ("It was a meditation in itself before and after mass to see the quiet yet mighty stones of Oxford all in possession of Anglican uncertainty – stones blessed and reared centuries ago by Catholic hands for Catholic teaching. For this is bare fact, and the English mind appears incapable of believing it or seeing it. Were these colleges built by *Papists*, people who really held the Pope to be the Vicar of Christ? How can there be any doubt about that? Granted. Is it, then, possible to assert that the object of the institutions is being carried out by a body of

occupiers who protest against the Pope and all his doctrines? They make out that they are the legitimate successors of the *Papist* founders, although they repudiate '*papistry*.' Is there no inconsistency? To the Anglican mind, none. The real Absence in the Sacrament is equally true as the Real Presence. Believe as you please. As at Oxford, so, too, at Eton. The toast was 'Our pious founder, Henry VI, *in piam memoriam*.' Yet this Founder expressly started his school in order that the doctrine held by the Pope should be imparted to the boys for ever. Bless the Founder with one breath and denounce his whole project in the next! All Souls was founded on purpose to endow masses for the soldiers who fell at Agincourt: the emoluments were for that object only. Not a mass has been said since 1559 – on the contrary, learned men enjoy the funds, men who are bound to aver that the doctrine of Rome is wrong. I now saw clearly from what a quagmire of contradictions I had escaped. Logic, simple logic, had triumphed...

If Christ could pass through the closed doors after His Resurrection, can He not dwell sacramentally on the altar? Long before I had entered the Church I came across a sentence in Pascal which placed the solution in a question and answer; and the question could only have one answer, and that a convincing one. Admit the omnipotence of Christ and all difficulty is removed. Once as a boy at Eton I opened a copy of Pascal in the library ... and I found the words *Si Christ est Dieu, si l'Evangile est vrai, qu'elle difficulté y-a-t'il là?* – prefaced ... by his exclamation that he cannot bear those foolish people who oppose the doctrine of the Eucharist. So I had been led on to believe in the sacramental Presence, but I applied the belief to the Anglican Lord's Supper; not till I was received into the Church did I realize that the Real Presence must be in the sacrament

consecrated by real priests"); Madeleine
Beard, *Faith and Fortune* (1997),
pp.186–190 ("The Hon. Alfred Verney-
Cave asked his parents long before he
went to Eton why every Sunday they said
they believed in the Catholic Church. No
answer was forthcoming. It was not until
he was eighteen that he realized that such
a proclamation by Anglican tongues was
misleading. The observance of saints'
days at Eton he found to be a curious
relic of the college's Catholic past. Then
in conversations with a pious contemporary, Verney-Cave became interested in
Tractarianism. Slowly he moved beyond
the theory that the Church of England
was a branch of the Church founded by
Christ, 'a branch unfortunately in antag-
onism with the two other "branches" –
all Three God's appointed Teachers of
the Nations – a trinity of schism as it
were.' Next he came across a Benedictine breviary. 'There was something,
then, beyond the Book of Common
Prayer, and Elizabethanism did not embrace the entire Christian system'").

**Brent-Dyer, Elinor Mary (real name
Gladys Eleanor May Dyer)** – children's
author; b. 6 April 1894, 52 Winchester
Street, South Shields; c. 12 December
1930 (received at St. Bede's Church,
South Shields; her mother, Eleanor, received before her death in 1957); d. 20
September 1969, 56 Woodlands Road,
Redhill, Surrey; family abandoned by
her father when she was three; brought
up in the Church of England; qualified
as teacher at Leeds Training College
1915–1917; continued to be a practicing
Anglican until her conversion; inspired
by a holiday spent in the Austrian Tyrol
at Pertisau-am-Achensee in 1924 (is evidence that she was probably considering
becoming a Catholic from that point on);
conversion influenced by seeing the Passion Play at Oberammergau in 1930;
taught in several schools, then ran her

own school 1938–1948 in Hereford;
headmistress to daughters of exiled
Haile Selassie of Ethiopia; then devoted
all her time to writing; author of the popular *Chalet School* stories, about a girls'
school based in this Austrian Tyrol area;
author of 101 books, of which around 60
comprise the series about the Chalet
School; lived in Hereford 1933–1964;
her stories advocated strong moral and
religious principles; unmarried; buried
in Redstone cemetery; see Helen Mc-
Clelland, *Behind the Chalet School*
(1996) (On the affirmation of religious
and moral principles in the stories: "To
put the scene in context: [In *The Head
Girl of the Chalet School* (1928)] Joey
and Grizel, aged 15 and 17 at this point,
are staying with Joey's sister Madge
whose husband James Russell is a doctor. On this particular evening they have
just heard some bad news about a patient
of Doctor Russell's; and, as they sit with
books in front of them 'Joey's thoughts
were all on that mysterious thing that
was happening at the sanatorium'...

'Madge divined it as soon as she entered the room ... "Joey, you need not be
sorry for this poor fellow. He has nothing
to live for and he will be joining those he
loved best tonight. The priest was here
this morning, and he is prepared." The
two girls came and sat on the floor beside her. "Madame, what is death?"
asked Grizel suddenly. "Just falling
asleep with God – to wake in His presence – that's all," said Madge Russell
quietly. "Then why are we afraid of it?"
"Because it means a change, and most of
us are afraid of changes that we don't understand. But, Grizel, there is nothing to
fear, really, any more than there is anything to fear when we fall asleep at
night." Grizel sat silent, thinking this
over. "God is with us through it all?"
asked Joey. "Yes, Jo. He never leaves us
if we have faith in Him'""); Joanna
Bogle, "The Lady Behind the Chalet

School," *Catholic Life*, March 2003, p.19 ("Doubtless her love of the Tyrol and the strong Catholic culture that she found there played a part in her discovery of the Faith. She also liked its values, its clear moral message and its sense of joy and hope. Her books reflect all of this, and are full of messages which emphasize the importance of courage and faith, the value of true friendship, and the importance of placing trust in God"); Joanna Bogle, "Elinor Brent-Dyer," in Joanna Bogle (ed), *English Catholic Heroines* (2009), p.273 ("[I]n an age where childhood innocence is being widely violated, when teenage suicide is on the increase, when girls lack wholesome and positive role models, when faith in God is mocked and reading material for adolescents too often focuses on the sordid, crude, sexually explicit or violent, here is an example of someone who used her writing talents to offer something of good cheer"); *DNB*.

Bridge, Ann (real name Lady Mary Anne Dolling O'Malley) (née Sanders) – novelist; b. 11 September 1889, Porters, near Shenley, Hertfordshire; c. 1948 (received by Fr. Martindale at Farm Street, London); d. 9 March 1974, 27 Charlbury Road, Oxford; seventh of nine children of a businessman who was later financially ruined; father English and very Low-Church, mother American and Episcopalian; educated at home; husband, Owen St. Clair O'Malley (1887–1974), worked in the Foreign Office (in particular reporting with great skill on the Katyn massacre during World War II); much foreign traveling with her husband; unhappy marriage, but she decided to make the best of it; began writing articles, poems and short stories; prolific and successful romantic novelist and travel writer; very thorough in her research; also Alpine climber, archaeologist and war relief worker; her

conversion was influenced by the writings of St. Francis of Assisi, the poetry of Dante, and the friendship of Maurice Baring (see above) and Archbishop Macdonald of Edinburgh; death of her son from heart failure affected her last years; her ashes were placed in the O'Malley grave at Cuddesdon, Oxfordshire; see *Peking Picnic* (1932); *Frontier Passage* (1942); *The Dark Moment* (1952); *A Place to Stand* (1953); *The Tightening String* (1962); *Facts and Fictions* (1968) (autobiographical); *Moments of Knowing* (1970) (about her interest in the supernatural); *Permission to Resign* (1971); Matthew Hoehn, OSB (ed), *Catholic Authors: Contemporary Biographical Sketches* (1952); *DNB*.

Bridgett, Thomas Edward, CSSR – priest and historian; b. 20 January 1829, Derby; c. 12 June 1850 (after hearing Newman's lectures on *The Difficulties of Anglicans* he went to the Oratorians and wanted to be received immediately; received a day later at the London Oratory by Fr. Richard Stanton (see below)); d. 17 February 1899, St. Mary's House, Clapham; father's background Baptist, mother's Unitarian; experienced religious awakening at Tonbridge School; at Cambridge attracted in turn by High Church and Broad Church parties; left Cambridge without a degree rather than take the oath of supremacy; influenced in his conversion by Newman's sermons; having discovered writings of Kenelm Digby, experienced "the day of grace" and thenceforward "hated the isolation and insulation of the Church of England, and felt it was a mere sham"; joined Redemptorist Order; ordained priest 4 August 1856; conducted some 80 missions and over 150 retreats; wrote mainly on history of the Reformation and restored reputations of St. John Fisher and St. Thomas More; wrote on his deathbed the following words: "Before the storm I will not quail,/ From heights or depths I will not shrink,/ Yet, gentle Lord, should courage fail/ Stretch forth Thy hand before I sink"; see *The Ritual of the New Testament* (1873) (personal account of his conversion); *The Defender of the Faith: The Royal Title, Its History and Value* (1885); *The True Story of the Catholic Hierarchy Deposed by Queen Elizabeth With Fuller Memoirs of Its Last Two Survivors* (1889); *Life of Blessed John Fisher* (1890); *Blunders and Forgeries: Historical Essays* (1891); *England's Title: Our Lady's Dowry: Its History and Meaning* (1894) (showing by many illustrations from history and literature the devotion of medieval England to the Mother of God); *The English Coronation Oath* (1896); *The Art of Lying: As Practised by Some Writers of Anti-Catholic Tracts* (1898); *Life and Writings of Blessed Thomas More* (1924); Cyril Ryder, *Life of Thomas Edward Bridgett* (1906), especially pp.10–27 ("I will merely say that among the causes that led me toward the Church were some very simple words spoken by a poor Irish laborer. I was then studying at the University of Cambridge, and a fellow-student had invited me to visit the Catholic chapel.... We got the keys from a poor Catholic man, who lived near, and after we had looked at the church, my friend, who was fond of a joke, began to banter the poor Irishman. 'Why, Paddy,' he said, 'do you think you've got the truth all-to-yourselves down in this little back street, and all our learned doctors and divines in this University are in error?' The answer that Paddy gave was this: 'Well, sir, I suppose they're very learned, but they can't agree together, while we are all one.' I often thought of that answer, and the more I thought of it the more wisdom did I see in it. And now that I have been a Catholic over thirty years, and have read many books, and seen many countries and many men, I

see the force of that answer better and better. Yes; if infidels or heretics could but agree together, they would overwhelm us with their objections, their learning, their power, and their wealth. But they have the curse of Babel on them. They can't agree together. They can't understand each other's speech. Therefore they can't unite to build up anything, or even to pull down the Church that God has built. Whereas, as Paddy said, Catholics are all one. *We* can understand each other. You may travel where you like, the world over, and have but to ask for the Catholic Church to be sure to hear the same doctrine you learnt in your catechism at home, and to see the same Sacraments administered that you and your forefathers received, the same Holy Mass celebrated of which the prophet Malachias foretold more than 2000 years ago that it should be offered from the rising and the setting of the sun"); *Catholic Encyclopedia*; *DNB*.

Brindley, Brian Dominic Frederick Titus Leo – writer and *bon viveur*; b. 4 August 1931, Harrow, Middlesex; c.1994; d. 1 August 2001, London; formerly flamboyant Anglo-Catholic canon; rescuer of Pugin screen from Birmingham Catholic Cathedral; representative of Anglo-Catholic interests on Anglican general synod; opposed women's ordination and converted after the measure had been passed by parliament; later reviewer and columnist for *Catholic Herald*; larger than life character; unmarried; see Damian Thompson (ed), *Loose Canon: A Portrait of Brian Brindley* (2004) ("No church could call itself Catholic, he believed, and follow such a course when the matter of ordination was defective. It was a breach from the Apostolic Tradition, church order, and Catholic sacramental doctrine. 'For me,' Brian recalled, 'it was as if scales fell from my eyes on that Black Wednesday [the Church of England's vote for the ordination of women to the priesthood]. I saw, all at once, that Leo XIII had been right after all. The ministry of the Church of England was not, as I fully believed it to be, a continuation of the Apostolic Church, but a new creation of the sixteenth century, with which the Church of England was free to do whatever it chose.' 'Women are no more capable of being priested than donkeys,' he bitterly observed. And he told a friend: 'I felt as if I had been a commercial traveler who had been selling vacuum-cleaners for 50 years, only to discover suddenly that they didn't work.'").

Brittain, Thomas Lewis, OP – priest; b. 1744, near Chester; c. 1760 (with his brother, William); d. 3 May 1827, Hartpury Court, near Gloucester; parents were Protestants; after converting went to France, subsequently joining Dominican Order at Bornhem; regent of studies at Bornhem where he had highest reputation as a teacher; director of English Dominicanesses in Brussels from 1790 until his death; after French revolution he escorted the community to Bornhem and thence safely to Hartpury Court in England; provincial 1814–1818; much loved by his brethren; buried in Hartpury churchyard; see *Principles of the Christian Religion and the Catholic Faith Investigated* (1790); *Gillow*, Vol. I, p.303.

Britten, James – botanist and Catholic writer; b. 3 May 1846, 18 Shawfield Street, Chelsea, London; c. 26 May 1867; d. 8 October 1924, Bedford Street, London; brought up as High Church Anglican; Senior Assistant of Natural History Museum 1871–1909; wrote several specialist works on botanical subjects; editor of *The League of the Cross Magazine*; Hon. Secretary of Catholic Truth Society, which he re-established almost single-handed in 1884; he and Alfred Newdigate (see below) worked together; Knight Commander of Order of St. Gregory the Great; editor of *Nature Notes*, *Catholic Book Notes* and *The Journal of Botany*, 1879–1924; bequeathed most of his estate to Catholic charities; unmarried; buried Isleworth cemetery, Brentford; see *The Conversion of James Britten K.C.S.G.* (reprint of a lecture delivered by Britten in March 1893) (1931) ("We Catholics are so accustomed to the unity of the Church that we do not perhaps always think what a wonderful thing it is: and Protestants, I find, often do not realize it. They sometimes point to our religious orders as if they were equivalent to their own manifold divisions! It is, I believe, the literal truth that, as the sun shines day by day on each part of the world, he sees at each moment the blessed Sacrifice of the Altar uplifted to the Eternal Father. Where, save in the Catholic Church, shall we find such a fulfillment of the prophecy 'From the rising of the sun unto the going down of the same shall incense be offered to My Name and a pure offering'? Not only so, but throughout the world – from 'Greenland's icy mountains' to 'India's coral strand' – wherever two or three are gathered together in the One Name is the same belief, the same sacrifice, mainly the same ritual: so that the Irish exile leaving the Old World for the New, where Catholicism is increasing with rapid strides, is as much at home in the churches of New York as he was in his roadside country chapel in the old country...

I have said that the Church of England neither has nor claims authority; and my last words shall be devoted to making this plain. If she has authority, as our High Church friends assert, whence does she derive it? Not from the old Church of England, for, by the Reformation of Elizabeth, the old Catholic episcopate was swept away. Of the sixteen surviving

Catholic Bishops, all save one – Kitchin of Llandaff, who took no part in the Reformation, nor in the consecration of Parker – were imprisoned, and Parker and those consecrated by him were intruded into the sees of the imprisoned Bishops. But granting that Parker and the rest were validly consecrated whence did they get jurisdiction? Certainly not from the old Catholic Bishops; most certainly not from the source whence these obtained it, namely the Pope; not by the fact of consecration, for orders and jurisdiction are distinct, and received independently of each other; not from any of Parker's consecrators – Barlow, Scory, Coverdale, and Hodgkins – for not one of these was in possession of a see, and they could not give what they themselves did not possess. The only answer possible, however unpalatable it may be to High Churchmen, is that they got jurisdiction from the Crown, or not at all. Every Protestant Bishop now takes the oath of supremacy, by which he professes that the Sovereign is the 'only supreme governor' of the realm 'in spiritual and ecclesiastical things, as well as in temporal.' Whence the Sovereign obtained this supremacy, or what 'warranty of Scripture' can be adduced for it, I do not know; nor do I think it easy to ascertain"); essay in J. G. F. Raupert (ed), *Roads to Rome* (1901), p.17 ("There came upon me more and more plainly the claims of a Church which taught with authority and uniformity all that I believed; which claimed to be the One Body having a right to teach; and which, without equivocation or hesitation, pointed out to its members one only means of salvation.... I realized, as I had never done before, that the first mark of God's Church was Unity – a mark which no one can pretend to find in the Church of England; and, after a period of anxiety such as none can know who have not experienced it, I was received into that Unity"); *DNB*.

Bromby, Hon. Charles Hamilton – barrister; b. 17 June 1843, Cheltenham; d. 24 July 1904, London; father, Charles Henry Bromby (1814–1907) was Anglican Bishop of Tasmania and later assistant at Lichfield and at Bath and Wells; brought up as an Anglican; educated at St. Edmund Hall, Oxford; Attorney-General of Tasmania 1876–1878; returned to England and practiced at the English bar; Chaucer and Dante scholar; translator of Dante; see *DNB*.

Bromley, Baron and first Viscount Bellomont (Bellamont) (Henry Bard) – soldier and diplomat; b. 1615/16; d. 1656; son of an Anglican vicar; Fellow of King's College, Cambridge, but left university and spent some years traveling through Europe and in Turkey, Palestine, Arabia and Egypt; on return in 1642 appeared at court and subsequently supported royal cause in Civil War, losing use of an arm; gained support of Queen Henrietta Maria; knighted in 1643; moved with his family to exiled court of Charles II; sent by Charles II on embassy to Shah Abbas II of Persia, in hope of obtaining money owed as a debt to help in recovery of throne; embassy failed; moved on to India to seek aid from the Mughal, Shah Jahan; died, probably from heat apoplexy, at Hodal, between Agra and Delhi, where he was buried; later his body was reburied at Agra, probably in the Catholic cemetery; one of his daughters, Frances (1646?-1708), a Catholic and Jacobite supporter, was mistress of Prince Rupert, by whom she had a son, Dudley (1666?-1686), killed at siege of Buda in reign of James II; see *Gillow*, Vol. I, p.128; *Catholic Encyclopedia*; *DNB*.

Brookfield, Charles Hallam Elton – playwright and actor; b. 19 May 1857, London; c. 1900; d. 20 October 1913, London; father Anglican clergyman, mother novelist who was a close friend of Thackeray; brought up in company of his parents' literary friends; concentrated on farce, revue and burlesque; also successful actor; controversial appointment as examiner of plays in 1911, when he was firmly against the New Drama of Shaw and Ibsen and hated Wilde; found peace and enjoyment at Downside Abbey, where his son was a monk; buried in the Catholic church at Stratton on the Fosse, Somerset; see *Random Reminiscences* (1902); *DNB*.

Brown, George Alfred (later Baron George-Brown of Jevington) – politician; b. 2 September 1914, Duke Street, Lambeth; c. 1985; d. 2 June 1985, Truro, Cornwall; grew up in working class family and community (father a grocer's packer); became committed Christian at elementary school; developed as Anglo-Catholic; trade union organizer (as his father had been); Labour Party activist; minister of works in post-war government; champion of Labour right wing and fine speaker; deputy party leader from 1960; defeated by Harold Wilson in party leadership election in 1963; Secretary of State for Economic Affairs 1964–1966; Foreign Secretary 1966–1968; made life peer in 1970; moved to cross benches in 1976; family man, but alcohol and political life put strain on his marriage and he left to live with his secretary in 1982; health deteriorated and he turned away from Anglo-Catholicism to the Catholic Church; ashes buried in garden of Golders Green crematorium; see Peter Paterson, *Tired and Emotional: The Life of Lord George-Brown* (1993) ("Canon [Michael] Walsh spent five hours talking late into the night, followed by other encounters, with George frankly discussing his life and his relationships with others. 'He had a very lucid, keen insight into matters spiritual. He then told me he would like to join the

Catholic Church. He said, 'Father, I want to come home. I want to be reconciled with God.'""); *DNB*.

Brown, George Mackay – poet and short story writer; b. 17 October 1921, Victoria Street, Stromness, Orkney; c. 23 December 1961; d. 13 April 1996, Kirkwall; almost always Orkney resident; brought up by parents who were lukewarm Presbyterians; had prolonged bouts of enfeebling ill-health; influenced by reading Francis Thompson's *The Hound of Heaven*; greatly admired the poet Edwin Muir; great love for poetry of Gerard Manley Hopkins (see below); used *The Orkney-inga Saga* as a source book; lauded in his later years; unmarried; buried in Stromness kirkyard; see *An Orkney Tapestry* (1969) ("There is a new religion, Progress, in which we all devoutly believe, and it is concerned only with material things in the present and in a vague golden-handed future. It is a rootless utilitarian faith, without beauty or mystery; a kind of blind unquestioning belief that men and their material circumstances will go on improving until some kind of nirvana is reached and everyone will be rich, free, fulfilled, well-informed, masterful. The notion of progress is a cancer that makes an elemental community look better, and induces a false euphoria, while it drains the life out of it remorselessly. I feel that this religion is in great part a delusion, and will peter out in the marsh"); "The way of literature" *The Tablet*, 12 June 1982, p.584 ("When I was in my mid-teens I read Lytton Strachey's *Eminent Victorians*, which contains his famous essay on Cardinal Manning, whom, it was soon apparent, the author disliked very much. John Henry Newman was, for Strachey, the perfect counter-balance. He had more than a passing sympathy with Newman, as a true child of the Romantic movement who wrote moreover an exact and luminous prose; but Newman, too, of course, had been fatally lured and fascinated by the enormous claims of Rome, that apostolic succession that went back eighteen and a half centuries to St. Peter. And then Strachey demonstrates gleefully how the dogmas and utterances of one Pope were contradicted out of the mouth of another Pope. What could any average rational being make of such a morass of error and human frailty and pretension?

And yet the whole pageant that Strachey unfolded before me – intended to make every reader chuckle scornfully – gave me one of the great thrills I have got out of literature.

That such an institution as the Church of Rome – with all its human faults – had lasted for nearly 2,000 years, while parties and factions and kingdoms had had their day and withered, seemed to me to be utterly wonderful. Some mysterious power seemed to be preserving it against the assaults and erosions of time.

The phrase in some book that finally, for Newman, led from Anglicanism to Catholicism (implying that this or that tenet was true, because the Pope of the time had said it) made me catch my breath, and not in derision either, as Strachey had intended. It was the same kind of astonishment as Newman had felt, though much diluted.

Soon I got hold of Newman's *Apologia*, most of which (the personalities and feuds of Oxford in his day) bored me, except for those passages, all exquisite and soaring as violin music, that rise clear above his own dilemmas and difficulties"); *For The Islands I Sing* (1997), especially pp.48–57 ("In the end it was literature that broke down my last defenses. There are many ways of entering a fold; it was the beauty of words that opened the door to me.... The beauty of Christ's parables was irresistible. How could they fail to be, when so many of

them concern ploughing and seedtime and harvest, and his listeners were most of them fishermen. I live in a group of islands that have been farmed for many centuries; all round me in summer are the whispering cornfields turning from green to gold. 'Except a seed fall into the ground, and die ...' These words were a delight and a revelation, when I first understood them. And at piers and moorings in every village and island are the fishing boats, and the daily venturers into the perilous west, the horizon-eyed salt-tongued fishermen ('The kingdom is like a net ...'; 'I will make you fishers of men ...'). The elements of earth and sea, that we thought so dull and ordinary, held a bounteousness and a mystery not of this world. Now I looked with another eye at those providers of our bread and fish; and when at last I came to work as a writer, it was those heroic and primeval occupations that provided the richest imagery, the most exciting symbolism"); Alan Bold, *George Mackay Brown* (1978); Joseph Pearce, *Literary Converts* (1999), pp.427–439, 442–445 ("Against the rootless 'Progress' heralded by the Reformation, the Catholic Church stood for Tradition. It was this aspect of Catholicism which had first impressed Brown when he was still in his mid-teens. He was intrigued by the majesty and mystery of Catholicism, by the long history of the Church from that stark beginning, that incredibly endured through the changing centuries, always adapting itself; enriched by all that poetry and music, art and architecture, could give; and still apparently as strong as ever in our grey twentieth century. This respect for tradition stayed with Brown throughout his life and was one of the factors behind his conversion. Catholicism was the Old Religion, the champion and defender of tradition and its last bastion and refuge. The new religion of 'our grey twentieth century' was Progress");

Maggie Fergusson, *The Life of George Mackay Brown: Through the Eye of a Needle* (2006); Gerry Burns, "George Mackay Brown: Orkney's Melancholy Visionary," *Catholic Life*, April 2009, p.10; *DNB*.

Brown, Bishop William Francis – priest and bishop; b. 3 May 1862, Park Place House, Dundee, Scotland; c. 1880; d. 16 December 1951, Southwark; parents were Episcopalians, but in 1873 mother became a Catholic and within eight years entire family was Catholic; ordained priest in 1886; spent most of his life as parish priest in South London slum parish; worked tirelessly for his parishioners; zeal for social and educational reform; in 1917 was appointed apostolic visitor to Scotland where he oversaw development of Catholic education system; eventually became auxiliary bishop in diocese of Southwark; close friend of Pearl Craigie (see below); see *Through Windows of Memory* (1946); *DNB*.

Browne, Henry B., SJ – priest; c. 1874 (his mother, Mrs. J. Wilson Browne, received in 1890 and his brother, William Percy Wilson Browne, in 1897); formerly Anglican; ordained to the Catholic priesthood; Fellow of Royal University of Ireland; Professor of Greek at University College, Dublin; see essay in J. G. F. Raupert (ed), *Roads to Rome* (1901), p.25 ("Before having to face the question of the claims of the Roman Church, I had previously, as an Anglican, made up my mind on another momentous controversy: the question of the Real Presence of Christ in the Eucharist. As my process of thought was identical in the two cases, and, in fact, the latter decision depended on the former, I will briefly explain both and their connection.... What finally led me to a conclusion, to an acquiescence in the doctrine of the Real Presence ...

was the following train of thought ... I felt with more and more certainty that if Christ was God, and therefore foresaw the course of events, He must have known that, as a matter of fact, the enormous bulk of His followers would take (as, indeed, they have taken) His words in the most literal sense – in a sense which, if false, has led and leads them into practices which are really, though unconsciously, idolatrous. Now, I convinced myself, gradually but more and more clearly, that Christ, foreseeing this effect following from His words, and foreseeing, on the one hand, that the effect would be most widespread, and, on the other, that it came from a too simple and too literal interpretation of His own words, would have been bound, as the God of Truth, to take some effective means towards guarding His followers against such a pernicious and (at least to take a thousand years) universal error. Now, so far from this, He had used expressions which, even though we leave their hidden meaning an open question, yet certainly give a very good *prima facie* ground for the belief in question. Consequently, I felt with more and more certainty that the belief in the Real Presence is bound up with and included in belief in the Divinity of Christ. I held then, long before I had any doubt as to Anglicanism in general, to the belief that the process of reasoning I have indicated is perfectly unanswerable and perfectly sound, and I hold to it still.

At a later date, when I came to consider the validity of the Roman claims, I saw that the position which I had previously accepted as to the Real Presence could be, and ought to be, applied to the question of the Papal Supremacy as of Divine origin. For it rests on words of Christ which, however they may be discussed and tortured by controversialists, are in reality as direct and simple, as naturally understood in the Roman sense, as are the words of institution of the Eucharist: 'Thou art Peter ... to thee I give the keys of the Kingdom of Heaven'").

Brownlow, Bishop William Robert Bernard – priest, bishop, author and archaeologist; b. 4 July 1830; c. 15 November 1863 (received by Newman at the Birmingham Oratory); d. 9 November 1901; son of Anglican minister; educated at Trinity College, Cambridge; took Anglican orders; supporter of Tractarian movement; through his friend, James Marshall (see below), he approached Newman and much correspondence between them before his conversion; studied at Collegio Pio Nono, Rome; ordained priest 22 December 1866; became fourth Catholic Bishop of Clifton in 1894; wrote classic work of reference on the catacombs, *Roma Sotterranea* (1869), with Dr. James Spencer Northcote (see below) and other works on early Church antiquities; worked for prevention of cruelty towards children; see *How and Why I Became a Catholic: A Letter to Friends in the Church of England* (1864); essay in J. G. F. Raupert (ed), *Roads to Rome* (1901), p.27 ("It was history that more than anything else brought me into the Church. And among Christian writers, St. Irenaeus and St. Vincent of Lerins influenced me more than any others. Then the history of the English Reformation – the violent break of continuity under Elizabeth, etc., etc.; the utter inability of the Anglican bishops to defend any Catholic doctrine: Baptism, the Holy Eucharist, Absolution, Inspiration of Scripture, and the Eternity of Heaven and Hell; – all this traceable to the surrender to the Crown of the Keys of the Kingdom of Heaven and contrasted with the attitude and action of the Pope in every page of the history of the past eighteen hundred years. Evils, scandals, abuse of power, and all these sort of things, did not affect me in the least, but rather showed that the institution that could survive all these abuses must be Divine"); Stanley L. Jaki, *Newman to Converts: An Existential Ecclesiology* (2001), Ch. 16.

Buccleuch and Queensbury, fifth Duchess of (Charlotte Anne Montague-Douglas-Scott, *née* Thynne) – benefactress; b. 10 April 1811; c. 1860 (received by Manning); d. 28 March 1895; wife of fifth Duke of Buccleuch, who was Lord Privy Seal, President of Council and Lord Lieutenant of Midlothian and Roxburghshire; second daughter of second Marquess of Bath; sister of Lord Charles Thynne (see below); mistress of the robes to Queen Victoria 1841–1846; much charitable work with her close friend Cecil Kerr, Marchioness of Lothian (see below); another influence was Eleanor Leslie (see below); see *DNB* ("Under the influence of Henry Manning and Cecil, Lady Lothian, she converted to Roman Catholicism in 1860, after struggling with her conscience for many years over the distress it would cause her Presbyterian husband").

Buckingham, Leicester Silk – dramatist and popular lecturer; b. 29 June 1825, Regent's Park, London; c. 1845; d. 15 July 1867, Margate, Kent; youngest son of James Silk Buckingham (1786–1855), politician, author and oriental traveler; used many pseudonyms; wrote several historical works and over thirty-five burlesques, comedies and farces; made several free adaptations of French comedies; several historical works; fine speaker; married at eighteen Sarah White, later a well-known actress under stage name of Mrs. Buckingham White; see *DNB*.

Buckland, Ralph – priest; b. 1564, West Harptree, Somerset; d. 1611; from an ancient family; sent to Magdalen College, Oxford at age of fifteen where he gained much academic learning; reading books of controversy made him doubt truths of Established Church and resulted in conversion; entered English College, Rheims, foregoing his position as heir to a large estate; completed studies at English College, Rome, and ordained priest in 7 August 1588; served on the English mission; imprisoned, then banished from the realm in 1606, but returned to England and worked as missioner until his death; wrote several volumes on saints and spiritual works; wrote against those Catholics who after the Gunpowder Plot tried to prove their loyalty to king by attending Anglican services; most pious and devoted priest; see *Gillow*, Vol. I, p.332; *DNB*.

Bullough, Edward – linguist, psychologist and philosopher of art; b. 1880, Thun in the Bernese Oberland; c. 1923 (received by Fr. Cyril Martindale, SJ (see below)); d. 1934, Bath; from a wealthy Lancashire family of industrialists; educated at the prestigious Vizthum Gymnasium at Dresden; studied Medieval and Modern Languages at Trinity College, Cambridge; career of teaching and research at Cambridge in languages; main field of study was aesthetics from a psychological and physiological perspective, notably the idea of "psychical distance," which combines both personal involvement and an awareness that the object or event is a cultural artifact; also the perception and appreciation of colors, the relation of aesthetics to psychology, and the issue of mind and medium in art; married to Enrichetta Angelica Marchetti (1882–1961), daughter of the celebrated Italian actress Eleonara Duse and the actor Tebaldo Marchetti (stage-name Checchi); lay Dominican (his wife also) and led active Catholic lives; joint President of the British Federation of University Catholic Societies and President of *Pax Romana*, the body coordinating such national networks world-wide; lecturer in German, but later Professor of Italian; translated Etienne Gilson's *Le Thomisme* into English as *The Philosophy of St. Thomas Aquinas* (1929); built a fine Italianate house, dedicated to St. Michael, which his widow bequeathed to the English Dominican friars and which became the Dominican priory in Cambridge; father of Fr. Sebastian Bullough, OP (1910–1967), noted for his biblical scholarship and writings on aesthetics, and of Leonora Ilaria Bullough, later Sister Mary Mark, OP (1912–2001), a nun with the English Dominican Congregation of St. Catherine of Siena at Stone, Staffordshire; buried in the Cambridge Dominican priory.

Bulstrode, Sir Richard – diplomat and writer; b. 1617, Astley, Warwickshire; d. 3 October 1711, St. Germain; eldest son of Edward Bulstrode, a favorite of Cromwell; practiced as barrister until Civil War broke out; joined Royalist army, where his proficiency attracted notice of Charles I, who appointed him Adjutant-General of army, and later Quarter-Master-General, a post he held until disbandment of the king's forces; committed two thefts and fled to Ireland where he was imprisoned for them; while in prison converted to Catholicism by Fr. John Cross, President of Douai College; later rehabilitated and sent by Charles II as agent to reside in Brussels, a post he held until death of the king; James II raised him to degree of envoy at same court, where he remained until after the Revolution; followed king to the Court of St. Germain where he lived in retirement until death; married twice and brought up his second family as Catholics; ten children from his two marriages, forty-four years between the eldest and the youngest; wrote biographies of kings under whom he served; spent last twenty years in dire poverty; buried at St. Germain; see *Gillow*, Vol. I, p.340; *DNB*.

Bunn, Alfred (nicknamed "Poet Bunn") – librettist and theatre manager; b. 8 April 1796; c. 1845; d. 20 December 1860, Boulogne, France; manager of Drury Lane and Covent Garden theatres; husband of Margaret Agnes Bunn (*née* Somerville) (1799–1883), actress, regarded as best Scottish-born tragic heroine of her day (marriage was not a happy one and led to much scandal); supported national composers; after great success ran into financial difficulties; controversial in respect of wide range of works he produced for stage; declared bankrupt in 1860; devout as a Catholic; buried in Boulogne; see *DNB*.

Burder, George Bernard, O Cist – priest and author; b. 1814; c. 24 January 1846 (his sister-in-law, Mrs. Henry Burder, received in 1848); d. 26 September 1881; son of George Burder (1752–1832), well-known Congregationalist minister, who founded London Missionary Society, Religious Tract Society, and British and Foreign Bible Society; ordained as Anglican curate; influenced by Tractarian movement; after conversion ordained as Catholic priest; became Cistercian monk and Lord Abbot of St. Bernard's Abbey, Leicestershire; *Gillow*, Vol. I, p.343.

Burgis, Edward, OP (name in religion Ambrose) – priest; b. 1673?, Bristol; d. 27 April 1747, Brussels; son of a Church of England clergyman; became a Dominican friar at Naples in 1697; rector of Louvain 1718–1730; elected provincial of his Order in 1730; resident in London 1730–1735; installed as prior of Bornhem Abbey in 1741; vicar provincial and vicar-general for Belgium from 1746;

see *An Introduction to the Catholic Church (1709); The Annals of the Church*, 5 Vols. (1738); *Gillow*, Vol. I, p.344; *Catholic Encyclopedia*; *DNB*.

Burnand, Sir Francis Cowley ("Frank") – playwright and humorist; b. 29 November 1836, Mortimer Street, London; c. December 1858 (received by Cardinal Manning; "Never for one single second at any period of my life have I repented of or regretted the step I then took"; both first wife, Cecilia Victoria (d. 1870), with whom he had seven children, and second wife, Lady Burnand, his deceased wife's sister, with whom he had six children, also converted); d. 21 April 1917, 18 Royal Crescent, Ramsgate, Kent; father stockbroker of Protestant Savoyard descent; at Cambridge he founded Amateur Dramatic Club; High Church Anglican at university; close friend of Arthur À'Beckett (see above); was preparing for Anglican ministry; under the influence of Manning and Newman's *Development of Christian Doctrine* he converted to Catholicism, which caused his father to cut him adrift; at one time novice of the Community of Oblates of St. Charles Borromeo of which Manning was Superior; practiced as barrister briefly; playwright and humorist (for most part his dramatic output consisted of burlesques, extravaganzas and farces, with some librettos, comedies and a few serious plays); collaborated with Arthur Sullivan on comic operetta *Cox and Box*; very successful editor of *Punch* 1880–1906; editor of *The Catholic Who's Who*; knighted in 1902; buried in cemetery attached to St Augustine's Abbey Church, Ramsgate; see *Records and Reminiscences, Personal and General*, 2 Vols. (1904) ([After meeting the famous Jewish convert Fr. Alphonse Ratisbonne, who had a vision of the Blessed Virgin Mary] "'We've been very silent,' I observed to

Walter Richards, with something of an effort. 'We have,' he replied gravely, 'but you see, my dear fellow, it isn't every day one meets a man who has actually seen Our Lady'"); Madeleine Beard, *Faith and Fortune* (1997), pp.183–184 ("Burnand faced opposition on all fronts. When his father learned of his decision to become a Catholic he was disinherited. He knew there was something wrong when his suitcase was not taken up to his room but left in the hall. After an interview with his father, it was the butler who showed him out with some kindness. He immediately went to see an old Catholic friend from Cambridge. Arriving at his house he found a note to say that dinner had been prepared for two and he would be back after Mass in Farm Street. Waiting inside the warm room, so welcoming after the coldness of his father's establishment, Burnand noticed in the corner of the room a statue of the Blessed Virgin Mary in a niche under a canopy. A light flickered at her feet and flowers were placed close by. Suddenly the door opened and in came his host, beaming with delight. Hearing the news of Burnand's decision to become a Catholic he was overcome with joy and heartily shook his hand. He had had a presentiment that this would happen and that it would occur on or about the Feast of the Immaculate Conception. And so it did"); *DNB*.

Burns, James – publisher and author; b. 1808, near Montrose, Scotland; c. 1847 (received with wife, Margaret Jane (1806–1893)); d. 11 April 1871, London; son of Presbyterian minister; became High Churchman; published Anglican works; influenced by Oxford Movement; conversion caused much dissension; founded new firm, Burns and Oates, to publish good Catholic works; his firm soon became household name (Newman wrote *Loss and Gain: The Story of a Convert* partly in order to help him); also wrote constantly on church music and edited and republished many compositions of best masters; after his death his wife became an Ursuline nun in the United States with her four daughters, the other daughter becoming a Sister of Charity in England; their son, William James Burns, became a priest; see *Gillow*, Vol. I, p.346; *Catholic Encyclopedia*.

Burrows, Eric Norman Bromley, SJ – priest and archaeologist; b. 26 March 1882, Ramsgate, Kent; c. December 1904; d. 1938, Oxford; brought up as Anglican; drawn to the Catholic Church at Oxford, but persuaded to think it over; was received after traveling in Switzerland and Germany; entered the Society of Jesus in 1905; ordained priest in 1918; studied oriental languages in Syria; official expert cuneiformist on Sir Leonard Woolley's expedition to Ur of the Chaldees, Abraham's birthplace; a leading expert in Assyriology; writer also on biblical issues; charming and humorous character; sudden death in a car crash; see Matthew Hoehn, OSB (ed), *Catholic Authors: Contemporary Biographical Sketches* (1952).

Burton, Doris Eliza (*pseud.* Lucis Amator) – writer; c. 1936; received vague Church of England upbringing at home, whilst being taught at school by a Quaker and Unitarian; became atheist at Swiss (Lutheran) finishing school, where came in contact with agnostic science teacher and atheistic literature; from realization of suffering in World War I and problems of poverty and overcrowding, dabbled with socialism, theosophy, spiritualism, moral rearmament and Oxford Group, before finally becoming a Catholic; author of books on saints, stories and articles for Catholic magazines, stories with Catholic themes for children; see essay in Walter Romig (ed), *The Book of Catholic Authors*, Third Series (1945); *From Oxford Group to the Catholic Church* (1948) ("I considered next that stupendous claim of the Catholic Church: the claim to be the universal Church founded by Jesus Christ, interpreting His true spiritual and moral doctrine to all mankind through His vicar, the Pope, the successor of St. Peter, who is guided infallibly for such purpose by the Holy Spirit. I began to perceive that Christ's doctrine must be that of unchangeable Truth (for Truth cannot contradict itself), but must be ever expanding as required by time and circumstance.

Back in London, I placed myself under instruction, and – rather scornfully – settled down to study the penny catechism with an elderly nun. What a revelation that was to me! One by one, my difficulties and doubts vanished. From the outset, the contrast between Catholic and [Oxford] Group values was obvious.

1. Who made you?
   God made me.
2. Why did He make you?
   That I might know, love and serve Him on earth and be happy forever with Him in heaven.

It made me aware that my creation – and that of every human being – was an act of love; its purpose the achievement of sanctity and the attainment of eternal bliss. I learned that His plan of perfection differs for every human soul, and that there is no enforced or fixed standard for everyone as affirmed by the Group. Then the doctrine of Original Sin taught me that man's natural tendency is to sin so that there is no short cut to sanctity, which can only be attained gradually, through continuous will and effort, in cooperation with God's grace. I discovered also, that although the Catholic Church teaches the Way to Perfection with her saints as shining examples, she is not a Society of the Perfect, but a School for the Imperfect...

I began to see that as a cell in the Mystical Body of Christ, my own sacramental life would be of far greater service to Him, for I learned that this Mystical Body was composed of the Church Triumphant in Heaven, the Church Suffering in Purgatory, and the Church Militant on Earth. It became obvious to me that it was an absurdity therefore, for a mere Protestant sect like the [Oxford] Group to hope to absorb the universal Holy Catholic Apostolic Church"); *Saints and Heroes for Boys* (1950); *Through a Convert's Window* (1950); *Great Catholic Mothers of Yesterday and Today* (1951); *Heroic Missionary Adventures* (1952); *By Courage and Faith* (1955) (brief biographies of various famous Catholics); *Daring To Live: Heroic Christians of Our Day* (1955); *Brave Wings: More Heroic Christians of Our Day* (1957); *The Girls' Book of Saints* (1958); *Pioneers for Christ: Ten Great Founders* (1958); *The Loveliest Flower: Ten Foundresses of Religious Congregations* (1958); *More Saints and Heroes* (1961*); Heroic Missionary Adventures* (1962); *Heroic Brothers: Ten Great Religious* (1965); *Heroic Nuns: Ten Great Religious* (1965); Matthew Hoehn, OSB (ed), *Catholic Authors* (1952) ("Doris Burton at last reached her goal, a key to things both eternal and temporal; a religion which taught that suffering accepted as one's Christian cross has a redemptive value, which gave the solutions to poverty and social evils in its encyclicals, which expounded the Christian Moral Law, with Holy Matrimony as a sacramental life long union, its fundamental purpose the rearing of a family").

Busk, Rachel Harriette – authoress and folklorist; b. 1831, 22 Cumberland Street, London; c. 1858 (her four sisters received later); d. 1 March 1907,

Members' Mansions, Victoria Street, Westminster; daughter of Hans Busk the elder (1772–1862), scholar and poet; sister of Julia Clara Byrne (1819–1894), authoress (see below); educated by her father involving much traveling; brought up as Protestant; enthusiastic convert of Cardinal Manning; lived much in Rome from 1862; friend of Cardinal Pecci, later Pope Leo XIII; reported from Rome to the *Westminster Gazette* 1859–1879; authority on and collector of folklore; published fiction under her own name and anonymously; contributor to *Notes and Queries*; Hilaire Belloc dedicated his *The Path to Rome* to her in 1902; buried in family vault at Frant, near Tunbridge Wells; see *The Folklore of Rome* (1874); *DNB*.

Bute, third Marquess of (John Patrick Crichton-Stuart) – civic benefactor and great patron of architecture; b. 12 September 1847, Mount Stuart, Isle of Bute, Scotland; c. 8 December 1868, chapel of Sisters of Notre Dame, Southwark; d. 9 October 1900, Dumfries House, Scotland; his father died when he was six months old, mother before he was twelve; inherited vast wealth and extensive estates; brought up in Presbyterian religion (mother staunch Protestant); Harrow and Christ Church College; passion for medievalism; greatly moved during a visit to the ancient Catholic chapel of East Hendred to learn that the lamp before the tabernacle there had never been extinguished, and Mass had been celebrated all through the worst days of penal times; his conversion caused a sensation and reputedly inspired plot of Benjamin Disraeli's novel, *Lothair*; married Hon. Gwendolen Mary Anne Fitzalan-Howard, niece of fourteenth Duke of Norfolk and eldest daughter of Lord Howard of Glossop (1854–1932) from old Catholic family; Knight Grand Cross of Holy Sepulchre,

Knight of Order of St. Gregory the Great; Lord Rector of St. Andrews University; great promoter of architecture in Scotland and Wales (especially in Gothic revival style); translator of pre-Reformation *Roman Breviary* into English, published in 1879; wrote on wide variety of subjects; said to have mastered twenty-one languages; in 1890s developed interest in spiritualism and investigation of psychic phenomena; on his death his heart taken to Palestine and buried on 13 November 1900 in garden of Franciscans on the Mount of Olives on traditional spot where Christ shed tears over the approaching fate of Jerusalem; see a memorandum in Bute's writing (preserved by his close friend, Hartwell Grissell (see below)): "I came to see very clearly indeed that the Reformation was in England and Scotland – I had not studied it elsewhere – the work neither of God nor of the people, its real authors being, in the former country, a lustful and tyrannical King, and in the latter a pack of greedy, time-serving and unpatriotic nobles.... I also convinced myself (1) that while the disorders rampant in the Church during the sixteenth century clamored loudly for reform, they in no way justified apostasy and schism; and (2) that were I personally to continue, under that or any other pretext, to remain outside the Catholic and Roman Church, I should be making myself an accomplice after the fact in a great national crime and the most indefensible act in history. And I refused to accept any such responsibility"); David Hunter Blair, *John Patrick, Third Marquess of Bute, KT (1847–1900): A Memoir* (1921) ("There were undoubtedly many sides of his character to which the appeal of the ancient Church would be strong and insistent. Her august and venerable ritual, the ordered splendor of her ceremonial, the deep significance of her liturgy and worship, could not fail to attract one who had learned to see in them far more than the mere outward pomp and beauty which are but symbols of their inward meaning.... The marvelous roll of her saints, the story of their lives, the record of their miracles, would stir the imagination and kindle the enthusiasm of one who loved to remember ... that the blood of pilgrims flowed in his veins, and found one of his greatest joys in visiting the shrines, following in the footsteps, venerating the remains, and verifying the acts of the saints of God in many lands, even in the remotest corners of Christendom.... [B]ut most of all it was the historic sense which he possessed in so peculiar a degree, the craving for an exact and accurate presentment of the facts of history, which was one of his most marked characteristics – it was these which, during his many hours of painful and laborious searching into the records of the past, were the most direct and immediate factors in convincing his intellect, as his heart was already convinced, that the Catholic and Roman Church, and no other, was the Church founded by Christ on earth, and that to remain outside it was, for him, to incur the danger of spiritual shipwreck"); Madeleine Beard, *Faith and Fortune* (1997), pp.148–153; *Catholic Encyclopedia*; *DNB* ("His profound medievalism gave him a feudal outlook, while his sense of the duties of wealth and position was reinforced by his Catholicism").

Butler, Bishop (Basil Edward) Christopher, OSB – bishop and theologian; b. 7 May 1902, Reading; c. June 1928; d. 20 September 1986, London; brought up in committed Anglican family; formerly deacon in Church of England; joined the Benedictine Order in 1929; ordained Catholic priest in 1933; internationally respected scripture scholar who defended priority of St. Matthew's Gospel; headmaster of Downside School; Abbot of Downside 1946–1966 and later Abbot-President of English Benedictine Congregation 1961– 1966; consecrated bishop in 1966; full member of Second Vatican Council and its Theological Commission; member of ARCIC; auxiliary bishop in Westminster; author of many books, articles and reviews (over three hundred) on theology; man of deep spirituality; buried at Downside Abbey; see *The Originality of St. Matthew: A Critique of the Two Document Hypothesis* (1951); *The Church and Infallibility* (1954); The *Church and the Bible* (1960); *Why Christ* (1960); *Prayer: An Adventure in Living* (1961); *The Idea of the Church* (1962); *A Time to Speak* (1972) ("The two determining issues, closely interlocked, were unity and authority.... I came to think that the early Church held that visible unity was an inalienable attribute or property of the Church ... and the divisibility of the Church was, for practical purposes, a notion that sprang from the Reformation.... As regards authority, I held that Christianity was a dogmatic religion, and that there was needed some living authority to determine its dogmatic content. The Church of England did not appear to claim such authority, and ... the option must be between Roman Catholicism and Eastern Orthodoxy.... The sweep of history showed existentially that the Western Church had continued to exhibit, in its on-going life, the characteristics of a living apostolic Church, while Eastern Orthodoxy appeared to have got stuck at a stage of arrested development I do not clearly remember my final 'case' for becoming a Catholic, the case on which I acted. On reflection, I should put things now like this. Either God is real or not. And, if God is real, either he has given a revelation of himself to man or not. And, if he has given such a revelation, either it is the alleged Christian revelation or it is not. The answers to these questions were important, not just for the satisfaction of intellectual curiosity, but for the ordering of one's life"); *The Resurrection* (1972); *Searchings* (1974); *An Approach to Christianity* (1981) ("Perhaps it will be easier to understand if one constructs a case of a Christian such as the present writer, brought up in some church other than the Catholic Church, who has come to feel intelligently uneasy about the doctrines he has been taught, whether as to their truth or as to their sufficiency.... Let us bear in mind that our hypothetical enquirer is asking, basically, which Christian body he should seek to join, it being presupposed that the Christian commitment is intended to take shape in commitment to an actual historical group. The clue to follow is the principle, recognized on all hands up until the Reformation and since then still maintained by the Catholic Church and the Eastern Orthodox Church, that by divine will the 'Church' of Christ takes shape, and will always take shape, in history as a single 'communion of the faithful'. It is from centuries in which this principle was taken for granted that we all inherit Christianity today.... If this principle is accepted, then, the position of the churches that have 'taken the Protestant Reformation into their system' is undermined. It is undermined principally because hardly any of these churches maintains, in fact, that it is – in contrast to all other Christian groupings – the one and only Church of Christ. Commonsense revolts at the idea of a Church which was really unique but which failed to claim persistently and publicly to be unique.... Which of these two bodies [the Eastern Orthodox Church and the Catholic Church] should be looked to as the heir of the divine gift of 'visible unity'?... Deep in the Christian tradition is the principle that the criterion of Christian communion is communion

with bishops who are themselves in full communion with the bishop of the local church of Rome, the 'successor of Peter' as Catholics call him. This principle was recognized by the Christian East at various crucial moments of the first Christian millennium.... Two considerations, to speak of no other arguments, recommend this principle. One is that it is of easy application and does not leave the ordinary believer at the mercy of academics and their changing views. The other is that it is at least suggested by the New Testament itself. The New Testament evidence for the primacy of Peter among the apostles is extensive and massive, and can hardly be disputed.... I think that these evidences and indications, taken all together, point rather unmistakably to the Christian body in communion with the See of Rome (where, it appears, Peter himself suffered martyrdom) as that body which has inherited and by divine grace rather than by any merits of its members, preserved the priceless gift of a unity which is the long term condition of the effectiveness and integrity of the Christian message to mankind"); *The Church and Unity* (1979) ("From 431 to 787 ... the witness of the East to the Roman primacy is impressive. The events to which I have referred relate to ecumenical councils or to the crucial conditions for the termination of a lengthy schism.... The evidence, then, may go some way to recommend the view that Eastern Orthodoxy, a Church celebrated for its devotion to tradition, has in recent centuries allowed one element of the tradition to drop somewhat into the background. History allows no doubt that – to look back no further than the fourth century – the See of Rome was, from the time of the later decades of that century onwards, making no secret of its primatial claims...

Christianity is meant for everyone, and so the Church is meant for everyone; it is 'catholic', universal of right even when it is not yet universal in fact. And since it is meant for everyone, and can only be accepted by an act of personal faith, it is apprehensible by each mature human being – at least, its credibility and its claim on his acceptance must be so apprehensible.... Christianity is intended for everyone. Everyone is capable, when he has reached a certain degree of maturity, of reflecting upon religion.... Ordinary human beings, ordinary Christians, actual or potential – what are they? They are housewives and workers, doctors, lawyers, artists, politicians; tinker, tailor, soldier, sailor, as we used to say.... It is surely probable that, if God has provided for mankind a true and universal religion, it will be fairly recognizable in its universal claims and presence. As a sore thumb stands out, so surely the true religion will stand out, for the responsible and prayerful inquirer who is not a professional theologian or a professional scholar as unique and uniquely credible.... The potential Christians of whom I am thinking are likely ... to think that it is, at the very least, probable that the Christian body which has the divine mandate and guarantee to proclaim and sustain God's message to mankind will be aware of that commission and will be vocal in publishing its awareness. They are not likely to think that a body that makes no such claim, a body, for instance, that points away from itself ... is, unbeknown to itself and despite its own disclaimers, the one mouthpiece of a divine revelation intended for all mankind and in every age.... A selection has to be made. I think most inquirers, if they are sufficiently detached and have some little common sense, will conclude that in the end the option is between the Eastern Orthodox and the Roman Catholic Church. I have tried ... to suggest that, when the issue is thus narrowed down, there is a way of reaching a conclu-

sion"); "Letters to a Man of Letters: The Correspondence of B. C. Butler and Ralph Ricketts," Parts I and II, *Downside Review*, April and July 1992, pp.131 and 177; Fr. Paul McPartlan, "The Idea of the Church: Abbot Butler and Vatican II," *Downside Review*, January 2003, p.39; *DNB*.

Butler, Elizabeth Southerden, Lady Butler (*née* Thompson) (known as "Mimi") – painter; b. 3 November 1846, Villa Claremont, Lausanne, Switzerland; c. 1869 (whole family received in Florence); d. 2 October 1933, Gormanston Castle, County Meath, Ireland; elder sister of Alice Meynell (1847–1922), poet and essayist (see below); educated entirely by her father; traveled extensively in Europe; depicted mainly "manly subjects" such as military (most famous painting *The Roll Call (Calling the Roll After an Engagement in the Crimea)*); adopted bleak and untriumphalist style; John Ruskin classified her style as Pre-Raphaelite; married Sir William Francis Butler (1838–1910), up-and-coming army officer from poor Irish Catholic family background; family moved to Florence in 1869 and converted to Catholicism; later work was largely ignored; see *An Autobiography* (1923); Wilfrid Meynell, *The Life and Work of Lady Butler* (1898); P. Usherwood and J. Spencer-Smith, *Lady Butler: Battle Artist, 1846–1933* (1987); *DNB*.

Byles, (Thomas) Roussel Davids Byles – priest; b. 26 February 1870, Shelton, Hanley, Staffordshire; c. 1894 (received at St. Aloysius, Oxford, taking baptismal name of Thomas; his brother, William, converted earlier); d. 15 April 1912; eldest of seven children of Dr. Alfred Byles, first pastor of Headingley Hill Congregational Church, Leeds; became member of Church of England whilst at Balliol College, Oxford (fine scholar); studied at the Beda College, Rome; ordained priest 15 June 1902 at St. Apollinaris, Rome; involved in founding of Catholic Missionary Society; parish priest of St. Helen's, Chipping Ongar, Essex, from where he set out on intended voyage to New York to officiate at marriage of his brother William who had emigrated; one of victims of the *Titanic* disaster, refusing to leave ship, devoting his last moments to religious consolation of his fellow passengers, hearing many confessions; much ill-health; close friend of Fr. Edward Purbrick (see below); see Ann Farmer, "Priest of Courage: Father Byles of the Titanic," *Catholic Life*, September 2002, p.44; Mark Fellows, "Fr. Byles and the Ship of Dreams," *The Angelus*, May 2004 (Statement by Miss Helen Mary Mocklare, third class passenger: "When the crash came we were thrown from our berths.... Slightly dressed, we prepared to find out what had happened. We saw before us, coming down the passageway, with his hand uplifted, Fr. Byles. We knew him because he had visited us several times on board and celebrated Mass for us that very morning. 'Be calm, my good people,' he said, and then he went about the steerage giving absolutions and blessings. A few around us became very excited and the priest again raised his hand and instantly they were calm once more. The passengers were immediately impressed by the absolute self-control of the priest. He began the recitation of the Rosary. The prayers of all, regardless of creed, were mingled, and all the responses, 'Holy Mary,' were loud and strong. One sailor ... warned the priest of his danger and begged him to board a boat. Fr. Byles refused"); Fr. Scott Archer, "Father Thomas Byles (1870–1912)," www.fatherbyles.com (Statement by Miss Agnes McCoy, third class passenger: "I first saw Father Byles in the steerage. There were many Catholics there, and he eased their minds by praying for them, hearing confessions and giving them his blessing. I later saw him on the upper deck reading from his priest's book of hours. Survivors, especially a young English lad, told me later that he pocketed the book, gathered the men about him and, while they knelt, offered up prayer for their salvation").

Byrne, Julia Clara Pitt (*née* Busk) – authoress; b. 1819, London; c. 1860 (her husband, William Pitt Byrne (1811–1861), son of the founder of the *Morning Post*, converted on his death bed); d. 29 March 1894, 16 Montagu Street, Portman Square, London; sister of Rachel Harriette Busk (1831–1907), authoress (see above); conversationalist, hostess, and friend of social celebrities, including Charles Waterton and Cardinal Manning, who converted both Julia and her sister Rachel; wrote travel books, anecdotal memoirs, and works on contemporary social issues; see *A Glance behind the Grilles of the Religious Houses in France* (1855); *DNB*.

Caldecott, Stratford – writer and commentator on Catholic affairs; c. November 1981 (his wife, Leonie, writer and co-director of Centre for Faith and Culture, brought up as an Anglican, though later ceasing to practice and flirting with Eastern religion, received in 1983); studied Philosophy and Psychology at Oxford University; editorial work for several publishers; former interest in Eastern religion; founder and co-director of Centre for Faith and Culture, Oxford; director of G. K. Chesterton Institute (UK); regular writer for *Chesterton Review* and *Communio*; editor of the journal *Second Spring*; see *Eternity in Time: Christopher Dawson and the Catholic Idea of History* (1997) (with John Morrill); (ed) *Beyond the Prosaic: Renewing the Liturgical Movement* (1999); "Gnosis and Grace" in Dwight Longenecker (ed), *The Path to Rome* (1999) ("The Church I had converted to was the same Church that had existed at the Council of Trent, and before. If thumbscrews had happened still to be in use today, or if the Vatican was being turned into a brothel by a corrupt Pope, I would still have joined it. The Church would still have been the sinless Bride of Christ, simply because the all too evident sins of her members are constantly being washed away by the ever flowing blood of Christ. The Church as institution exists to preserve the sacraments, which are the actions of Christ. It is these which caused the bridal Church to be born on earth, again and again"); *Catholic Social Teaching* (2001); *The Spiritual Vision of J. R. R. Tolkien* (2003); *The Power of the Ring: The Spiritual Vision Behind The Lord of The Rings* (2005); *The Seven Sacraments: Entering the Mysteries of God* (2006).

Caldwell (alias Fenwick), Blessed John, SJ – priest and martyr; b. 1628, County Durham; d. 20 June 1679, Tyburn; of Protestant parents; converted after arriving at mature age and was disowned by his family; studied at English College, St. Omers 1654–1656; entered the Society of Jesus at Watton in 1656; ordained priest in 1664; after ordination, was procurator or agent at St. Omers College 1665–1672; sent to England in 1673; seized in 1678 with martyr Bl. William Ireland during the Oates Plot persecution and committed to Newgate; after long imprisonment arraigned for high treason with Ireland; insufficient evidence to convict him; sent back to prison and re-arraigned with Fathers Barrow, Garven, Whitbread and Turner in 1679; convicted and executed with them at Tyburn; his remains were interred in the churchyard of St. Giles-in-the-Fields; see *Gillow*, Vol. I, p.373; *DNB*.

Calvert, George, first Baron Baltimore – courtier and colonist; b. 1579/80, Kiplin, Catterick, Yorkshire; c. October or November 1624; d. 15 April 1632, London; descended from a longstanding Yorkshire Catholic family; he and his father conformed to the Established Church; studied at Oxford with a Protestant tutor; worked as one of Sir Robert Cecil's secretaries; appointed a clerk of the Privy Council in 1610; advancement at court continued; knighted in 1617 and became secretary of state in 1619; lost influence at court through his support of the king's Spanish policy; in 1624 king created him Baron Baltimore in Ireland as reward for his loyal service; after his conversion he moved his family to Ireland; later established several colonies in America; buried at St Dunstan-in-the-West, London; see *Gillow*, Vol. I, p.374; *Catholic Encyclopedia*; *DNB*.

Cameron, James Munro – philosopher; b. 14 November 1910; c. 1944; d. 1996; a Marxist prior to his conversion; Professor of Philosophy, Leeds University (first Catholic to hold a chair in the subject in Britain since the Reformation); later Professor at University of St. Michael's College, Toronto; primarily an essayist; emphasis on philosophy of religion, especially on Newman; see "Theological Fragments," *Downside Review*, Spring 1949, p.134 (notes made at the time of his conversion) ("There is so much dialectic in the world that the words of the apologist are lost in the hubbub. But amid all the clamor man is aware of an absence, of a void which awaits a Presence. The more desperately he packs into the void the current political religions, the aestheticisms, the intellectual sophistries of the day, the more manifestly is the void a void. Wretched man that he is, who is to deliver him? He who cast out the demons, healed the sick, raised the dead, preached the

Gospel to the poor. The Church is his, in a sense the Church is he, and everything within the Church, including text-books of apologetics, is a means whereby men are joined to him. What is not such a means is nothing"); *Night Battle* (1962); Timothy Potts and Michael Higgins, "Obituary," *The Tablet*, 20 January 1996, p.93.

Camm, Dom Bede, OSB (born Reginald Percy John Camm) – priest and author; b. 1864; c. 19 June 1890 (his father was received in 1891 and other members of his family converted later); d. 1942; brought up as High Anglican; educated at Keble College, Oxford; member of Ritualist movement at Oxford; later Anglican minister; entered Benedictine novitiate at Maredsous, Belgium in 1890; ordained priest 9 March 1895 in Rome; at Erdington Priory, Birmingham; helped the Caldey Community into the Catholic Church; moved to Downside Abbey; major promoter of cause of English and Welsh martyrs; see essay in J. G. F. Raupert (ed), *Roads to Rome* (1901), p.29 ("I began to see that communion with the See of Peter was of old the essential test of orthodoxy, the *signum stantis vel cadentis ecclesiae*; and if so, why should it not be so still? St. Augustine's words haunted me: '*Extra Ecclesiam Catholicam totum potest praetor salutem ...*' And when I turned to Rome, and saw her so firm, so invincible, so serene, so unfaltering in her teaching, so uncompromising with heretics, so sure of her own rights, so immovable through the ages, I fancied that to her, and to her alone, could apply those other words of the Saint: '*Ipsa est Ecclesia sancta, Ecclesia una, Ecclesia catholica, contra omnes haereses, pugnans; pugnare potest, expugnari tamen non potest ...*'" But still I was tormented with fears and anxieties, still I did not see clearly. At last I went abroad for a holiday, and there kneeling one day in a monastic church, I heard the brethren chant those words of the *Credo*: '*Et unam sanctam Catholicam et Apostolicam Ecclesiam.*' And as they sang them the clouds rolled away from off my soul and the light of faith shone on it once for all. I saw them, in a way which I cannot describe, but, like the blind man of old, '*One thing I know, that whereas I was blind, now I see.*' I saw that all this time I had *not* been believing in *One* Church. I saw what the unity of the Church really was, and seeing, I rejoiced and thanked God"); *Forgotten Shrines* (1910); *Pilgrim Paths in Latin Lands* (1923); *Tyburn and the English Martyrs* (1924); *The Martyrs of Tyburn* (1928); *The English Martyrs and Anglican Orders* (1929); *Nine Martyr Monks* (1931); *Anglican Memories* (1935) ("[Herbert Mackay] informed me one day that there were only two positions logically possible. Either Rome's claims were true and all were bound to submit to them, or they were false and were therefore anti-Christian. In a word, Rome was either the one Church of Christ, or she was anti-Christ. I rebelled against being thrust into this dilemma, but I was none the less impaled upon its horns...

...Still the want of heroic sanctity among us [the Church of England] since the Reformation was an even greater difficulty. Why were there no Anglican *saints?*"); *The Call of Caldey: The Story of the Conversion of Two Communities* (1940).

Campbell, Archibald, seventh Earl of Argyll – magnate and politician; b. 1575/6; c. 1618; d. 1638, Drury Lane London; took part in the clan wars on behalf of James VI of Scotland against the Catholic earls; on death of his first wife, he married a Catholic, Anne Cornwallis (d. 1635), which brought him increasingly into contact with members of the

Jesuit Order and greatly altered his religious views; in 1618 he and his wife went to take waters at Spa under pretext of his poor health, but once there he announced his formal conversion to Catholicism; took service with the Spanish army in Flanders; reached an accommodation with Charles I and returned home in 1627; abandoned his Scottish estates and lived in London; see *DNB*.

Campbell Mary Margaret (*née* Garman) – b. 1898; c. 1935; d. 27 February 1979; eldest of seven sisters; had a privileged childhood; rebelled against her parents from an early age; at age twenty-one ran away to London with her sister Kitty and they worked as artists' models; adopted bohemian lifestyle; member of Bloomsbury group; in 1924 married Roy Campbell (1901–1957), the poet; they shared an unconventional lifestyle (she had a relationship with Vita Sackville-West, his response being to attack the Bloomsbury group in *The Georgiad* (1931)); later they moved to the south of France, then to Spain, finally small village of Linho in Portugal, living very simply; after her conversion she was resolute in her faith; on her reception into the Church she chose Mary Magdalene as her saint; many charitable activities; buried with Roy Campbell in the cemetery of São Pedro, near Sintra; see Teresa Campbell [daughter], unpublished memoirs ("[My mother's] great discovery ... after her conversion to Catholicism, was the tabernacle in Catholic churches where the Body of Christ remains permanently present. It was there, near the tabernacle, that my mother could spend hours absorbed and it was there that she found satisfaction and consolation"); Roy Campbell, *Light on a Dark Horse* (1935) ("Protestants go to these countries for spiritual fresh air, yet with the trained opportunism which is their chief raison d'être, they ascribe the attraction,

which is really that of the Church and the people who have not been amputated from the Church by force of tyrants like Henry VIII, or crooks like Calvin and Luther – to the climate or the landscape, or to anything else save in the culture and civilization which hold them so spellbound. They always consort with the malcontents also. They have not the courage to disown what is wrong in themselves. They would sooner join with atheists and diabolists, as they did in the Spanish War, than with anything straightforwardly European or Roman, though they will hang around a place like Spain for whatever by-products of the Catholic faith they can pick up buckshee, without any responsibilities – the courtesy, hospitality, and nobility of the people.

From the beginning my wife and I understood the real issues in Spain. There could be no compromise in this war between the East and the West, between Credulity and Faith, between irresponsible innovation (which catches all 'intellectuals' once they have been hereditarily derailed) and tradition, between the emotions (disguised as Reason) and the intelligence...

Up to then we had been vacillatingly Anglo-Catholic; but now was the time to decide whether by staying in the territorials, to remain half-apathetic to the great fight which was obviously approaching – or whether we should step into the front ranks of the Regular Army of Christ"); P. F. Alexander, *Roy Campbell: A Critical Biography* (1982); Joseph Pearce, *Bloomsbury and Beyond: The Friends and Enemies of Roy Campbell* (2001); Cressida Connolly, *The Rare and the Beautiful: The Lives of the Garmans* (2004); Joseph Pearce, *Literary Converts* (1999) *passim*; *DNB* (entry for her husband, Roy Campbell).

Campbell, Robert – Scottish advocate,

hymn writer and translator; b. 1814; c. 1852; d. 1868; from early age took great interest in theology; originally Presbyterian, before becoming member of High Church branch of Episcopal Church of Scotland; wrote and translated hymns and published the *St. Andrews Hymnal* (1850); spent much time before and after conversion in educating the poor; friend of Francis Wegg-Prosser (see below) and began to correspond with Newman about claims of the Catholic Church; father of William Campbell KC; see Stanley L. Jaki, *Newman to Converts: An Existential Ecclesiology* (2001), Ch. 14 ("Newman [turned] to the question of the factuality of the Church: 'Look then at the (Roman) Catholic Church of this day as the possible representation or continuation of the Primitive Church, confront the present with the Primitive, and see if you do not recognize an identity.' Newman hesitated not a whit to state: 'The Catholic Church of today is a polity, self-dependent, extending over the world, unattached to place, professing divine authority &c. &c, just as the Primitive was. Compare it with other bodies, Protestantism, Mahometanism, the Greek religion &c and I conceive the likeness comes out stronger from the contrast. None of these can be called a polity, self-dependent &c, &c'").

Campion, Saint Edmund, SJ – priest and proto-martyr of English Jesuits; b. 25 January 1540, London; c. 1571 (a revert); d. 1 December 1581, Tyburn; parents were Catholics; brilliant student from childhood (made the Latin address to Queen Mary on her solemn entry into London 3 August 1553); student and Fellow of St. John's College, Oxford; great public orator gaining several triumphs, in particular during Queen Elizabeth I's visit to the university in 1566; gained patronage of Robert Dudley, Earl of Leicester and Sir William Cecil, Secretary of State; Catholic opinions, but allowed himself to be ordained deacon in Anglican Church in order to obtain preferment (later had "remorse of conscience and a devastation of mind"); witnessed trial and execution of Blessed John Storey in June 1571; went to Douai where he was reconciled to the Catholic Church; in 1573 went to Rome by foot as a penniless pilgrim and was admitted into the Society of Jesus; sent as novice to Brünn, Moravia where said to have had vision in garden, in which Our Lady foretold to him his martyrdom; ordained priest in Prague in 1578 by Archbishop of Prague; sent to the English mission with Fr. Robert Persons (see below) in 1580 as first two Jesuit missionaries; great success in preaching in London and through country up to Yorkshire and Lancashire; wrote his famous controversial works there (e.g., the 'Challenge' or 'Brag' and the *Rationes Decem*); "The expense is reckoned, the enterprise is begun, it is of God, it cannot be withstood. So the faith was planted, so it must be restored"; betrayed by apostate, George Eliot, at Lyford Grange, Berkshire, moated house of the Catholic family of Edward Yates; taken to London and committed to the Tower; offered his life by the queen if he would conform; racked and tortured; took part in public disputation in chapel of St. Peter ad Vincula in the Tower; tried with several other priests at Westminster on indictment for conspiracy to compass overthrow and death of the queen; found guilty and condemned to death (sang the Te Deum laudamus on the passing of the sentence; dragged with St. Ralph Sherwin and St. Alexander Briant from the Tower by Cheapside and Holborn to Tyburn where they were hanged, drawn and quartered (when urged to confess his treason he replied, "If it be a crime to be a Catholic, I am a traitor"); see *Rationes Decem* (1581); Richard Simpson,

Edmund Campion (1867); Evelyn Waugh, *Edmund Campion* (1935) ("The thesis [of the *Rationes Decem*] may be analyzed as follows: (1) All heretics have been obliged to mutilate Holy Scripture in their own interest. The Lutherans and Calvinists have done this in several instances. (2) In other cases they retain the text, but pervert the clear message of the passage. (3) The Protestants by denying the existence of a visible Church, deny for all practical purpose, the existence of any Church. (4) The Protestants pretend to revere the first four General Councils, but deny many of their doctrines. (5) and (6) The Protestants are obliged to disregard the Fathers. (7) The history of the Church is continuous. The Protestants are without living tradition. (8) The works of Zwingli, Luther, and Calvin contain many grossly offensive statements. (9) The Protestants are obliged to employ many empty tricks of argument. (10) The variety and extent of Catholic witness are impressive"); E. E. Reynolds, *Campion and Parsons: The Jesuit Mission of 1580–1* (1980); T. M. McCoog (ed), *The Reckoned Expense: Edmund Campion and the Early English Jesuits* (1996); Alexander Haydon, *Edmund Campion* (2003); Alice Hogge, *God's Secret Agents: Queen Elizabeth's Forbidden Priests and the Hatching of the Gunpowder Plot* (2005) ("Campion had always believed he was coming home to England to die. The night before his departure from Prague a colleague had inscribed on the door above his cell *P. Edmundus Campianus, Martyr*. Earlier, another priest had painted a garland of roses and lilies on the wall above his bed – the symbol of martyrdom"); Anthony Symondson, SJ, "St. Edmund Campion, SJ," in John Joliffe *(ed), English Catholic Heroes* (2008), p.88 ("When Christopher Wray, the presiding judge, asked the accused if they had anything to say, Campion replied: 'The only

thing that we have now to say is that if our religion makes us traitors we are worthy to be condemned, but otherwise we are and have been as true subjects as ever the Queen had. In condemning us, you condemn all your own ancestors, all that was once the glory of England, the Island of Saints, and the most devoted child of the See of St. Peter. For what have we taught, however you may qualify it with the odious name of treason, that they did not uniformly teach? To be condemned with these old lights – not of England only but of the whole world – by their degenerate descendants is both glory and gladness to us. God lives; posterity will live, and their judgment is not so liable to corruption as that of those who are now going to condemn us to death'"); *Gillow*, Vol. 1, p.377; *Catholic Encyclopedia*; *DNB*.

Canes, Vincent, OSF (alias Thomas Bodwill; name in religion John Baptist) – priest and writer; b. 1608, on borders of Nottinghamshire and Leicestershire; c. 1628; d. 21 June 1672, Somerset House, The Strand, London; brought up Protestant; converted at Cambridge University; went to Douai and entered English Franciscan Convent; after ordination became Professor of Divinity; returned to England and lived for the most part in London; twenty-four years on the English mission; able controversialist and wrote many works defending the faith; association with Fr. Hugh Cressy, OSB (see below); no animosity or bitterness towards opponents; buried in vault under chapel attached to Somerset House; see *Gillow*, Vol. I, p.392; *Catholic Encyclopedia*; *DNB*.

Capes, John Moore – author; b. 1812; c. 24 June 1845 (received at Oscott by Cardinal Wiseman; his younger brother, Frederick Capes (1816–1888), solicitor, also received in 1845); d. 14 June 1889; was opposed to Tractarians and wrote against Newman; took Anglican orders; came to regard the Church of England as being in schism and wrote to Newman for advice, converting three weeks later; founder and editor of *The Rambler* (leading liberal Catholic journal of mid-nineteenth century) 1848–1858; reverted to Anglicanism in 1860; in 1870 he attacked Newman for accepting the definition of infallibility; in 1882 became Catholic once more and received last sacraments before his death; see "The Story of My Life," *The Month*, October 1884, p.182 ("When I resumed work as an English clergyman, my belief in the claims of the Church of England to my allegiance was slowly giving way. Mr. Newman's Essay on *The Difficulties in the Scripture Proof of the Doctrines of the Church* had effected a radical change in the feelings with which I regarded the claims of Rome. His aim in the bold and subtle argument which he then put forward, had not been to apologize for the doctrines supposed to be especially Roman, but to show that the characteristic High Church Anglican theories rested on as firm a Scriptural basis as do the doctrines of the Holy Trinity, the Incarnation, and the Atonement, accepted by all orthodox Protestants. In neither case, he argued, are the doctrines taught with that distinctness of definition which Protestants call for when they are asked to accept Patristic theology. Either, then, he went on to say, with a daring at which he himself trembled, accept the sacramental teaching of the early Church, or confess that all orthodox Christianity is deficient in Scriptural proof"); Newman, letter to Frederick Capes, 24 May 1865 ("He is too religious to do without religion and too clever to be satisfied with any but the Catholic").

Caradoc (formerly Craddock), Sir John Hobart, second Baron Howden – diplomat; b. 16 October 1799, St. Stephen's Green, Dublin; c. 1848; d. 8 October 1873, Bayonne, France; grandson of Dr. John Caradock (1708–1788), Protestant Archbishop of Dublin; ensign in Grenadier Guards; appointed aide-de-camp to Duke of Wellington; military career followed by entry into diplomatic service; attaché at Berlin; in 1825 he joined embassy at Paris; famous for his amorous exploits, living up to his nickname, "Beauty Caradoc"; one-time MP for Dundalk; successively British Minister at Brazil and Madrid; buried in mausoleum, Caradoc Castle, Bayonne; see *DNB*.

Carier (Carrier), Benjamin – divine; b. 1566, Boughton Monchelsea, Kent; c. c.1613; d. 1614; son of learned Protestant preacher; brought up in pious and devout manner; made Anglican minister; chaplain and preacher to James I; always denounced Calvinism; perceived the king planned coalition between the two Churches; seeing this to be impracticable he resolved to become a Catholic, which he did on visit to Cologne, Germany, where he consulted the rector of the Jesuit college; influenced in his conversion by Henry Constable (see below); king's resentment great; accepted invitation of Cardinal du Perron to Paris to assist the cardinal in writing against James I, but died shortly after arrival; see *A Treatise etc.* (account of his conversion) (1613); *Gillow*, Vol. I, p.405; *DNB* ("He ... claimed that from about 1590 he had studied church history and the fathers, finding them in opposition to current teaching and practice in the Church of England, particularly on grace, predestination, and the sacraments, which he contrasted with that of the Book of Common Prayer").

Carlyle, Aelred (formerly Benjamin Fearnley Carlyle) – priest; b. 7 February 1874, Sheffield; c. 22 February 1913;

d. 14 October 1955, Prinknash Abbey; brought up in Argentina; as young man founded Anglican Benedictine community (in 1896), which eventually moved to island of Caldey off South Wales; abbot of this community which adopted Anglo-Catholic liturgical practices; one of twenty-two monks of the community received into the Church in 1913; ordained Catholic priest in 1914; left community (which eventually moved to Prinknash in 1928) in 1920; went to Vancouver, British Columbia where he worked as secular priest until 1951; returned to England and received back into his old community, by then at Prinknash; re-made his solemn vows in 1953 and lived as an ordinary monk in community; buried under high altar of the New Abbey, Prinknash; see Dom Bede Camm, *The Call of Caldey: The Story of the Conversion of Two Communities* (1940); Peter Anson, *Abbot Extraordinary* (1958); René M. Kollar, OSB, "The Caldey Monks and the Catholic Press, 1905–1913," *Recusant History*, May 1985, p.287; Fr. Aelred Baker OSB, "Abbot Aelred Carlyle: A Spiritual Journey," *Catholic Life*, August 2005, p.52.

Carmichael, Montgomery – writer; b. 17 May 1857, Birkenhead, Lancashire; c. 1881 (his sister, Mary, composer and accompanist, also converted); d. 6 August 1936, Italy; educated at Breward, Bonn and Munich; began life in commerce but then entered consular service, becoming British vice-consul in 1892 at Leghorn, the sea port city of Tuscany, Italy, where he lived for much of time (consul from 1908 to 1922); consul general to San Marino and for Tuscany 1912–1922; love of Italian art and history led to his conversion; books on Italy, novels, many showing Italian influence, and articles in Catholic periodicals, including several on Catholic interests of poet William Cowper (1731–1800);

great authority on Franciscan lore; see *Sketches and Stories, Grave and Gay* (1896); *The Major-General. A Story of Modern Florence* (1901); *The Life of John William Walshe, F.S.A.* (1902) (a fictitious conversion story, his most representative novel) ("One of my dearest friends was an Anglican who had been in the thick of that Oxford movement.... I then sat down and copied out a page [from *Du Pape* by Count Joseph De Maistre]. It contains an argument against Anglicanism, but not the argument of a controversialist; simply the common sense conclusions of a wise man clothed in winged words. My friend read this page through thrice, knelt down in prayer for ten minutes, put on his hat, went out in search of the nearest Catholic priest, and tumultuously demanded to be received into the Church. The winged words of De Maistre had brought the card castle of the Via Media toppling about his ears beyond all earthly hope of reconstruction. These were the words which I had copied: 'The Anglican Church is, besides, the only association in the world which has declared itself null ... by the very act which constitutes it. In this act it has solemnly proclaimed thirty-nine articles, neither more nor less, absolutely necessary to salvation and which must be sworn to in order to belong to this church. But one of these articles (the XIXth) formally declares that God, in constituting his Church, has not left infallibility upon earth; that all the churches, beginning with that of Rome, have fallen into error; that they have grossly erred, even as regards dogma, even as regards morality; so that none of them possesses the right to lay down a creed, and that the Scriptures are the only rule of faith. The Anglican Church declares, therefore, to her children, that she is, indeed, entitled to command them, but that they are equally entitled to refuse her their obedience. At the same moment, with the same pen and ink, on the same paper, she enunciates dogma, and declares she has no right to do so. I think I may be allowed to entertain the conviction, that of the interminable catalogue of human follies, this is one which will always hold a distinguished rank.'

How simple the view: yet it had never occurred to my friend that his Church, while prescribing to her children the articles touching *true* religion, admitted at the same moment that she might be in error about those articles…

…But one other tribute to my Master. One, Holy, Catholic, Apostolic: those are the four great notes of the Church. But they need much proof and exposition. Joseph de Maistre has divined a fifth note, which is now-a-days every bit as conclusive: 'Tous les ennemis de Rome sont amis!' That is the great glory of the modern Church: she is one within herself, and is yet so powerful as to make all other bodies outside her one against herself'"); *In Tuscany* (1906); *Francia's Masterpiece: An Essay on the Beginnings of the Immaculate Conception in Art* (1909); Anon., "Montgomery Carmichael (1857–1936)," *Catholic Life*, March 2002, p.23.

Carson, William Robert – priest and author; b. 1874; c. 1893; d. 1903; son of Anglican clergyman and grandson of Anglican bishop; see essay in J. G. F. Raupert (ed), *Roads to Rome* (1901), p.34 ("Either God had revealed Himself to us in a way so plain that he who runs may read; or his revelation was useless – nay, no revelation at all, for each man would take his own different subjective meaning out of it. A message implies a messenger; a revelation, an interpreter and a guide. Unless God intended men to make havoc of His Truth – to render it piecemeal, to mistake the tares for the wheat – He must have instituted on earth a means by which they could know infallibly and surely, without danger of mistake, what He actually taught, and what they must believe if they would inherit eternal life.… That need for a Divine Teacher, telling me in the name of God His authentic doctrine, I saw to be satisfied by the Catholic and Roman Church, and by her alone. She claims to be the one Oracle of Truth, the sole Depository and Unfolder of the Christian revelation *as a whole*. He who rejects one part of her message because it is unpalatable to him personally, has no logical reason for not rejecting the rest. If he once ignores her authority, he has none other to substitute for it but his own. Ultimately, the issue lies between a Teacher sent from God, and the clouded guidance of the natural unaided reason").

Cary-Elwes, Valentine Dudley Henry – gentleman; b. 1832, Great Billing Hall, Northamptonshire; c. Trinity Sunday 1874 (received with his wife, Alice Geraldine (*née* Ward) (1844–1907), Nice, France; a cousin, Captain Windsor Cary-Elwes of Scots Guards (b. 1839), later father of two priests, converted in 1857, making his decision partly on basis of empty Lutheran churches and full Catholic ones in Germany; several other relatives also converted); d. 1909; brought up as a Protestant (as was his wife, daughter of a rector of the Established Church in Ireland); a sermon preached on one Fold and one Shepherd caused him and his wife to be assailed by doubts for first time; one time Cornet in 12th Lancers, serving in Kaffir War; JP and High Sheriff for Lincolnshire; JP for Leicester and Northampton; built Catholic churches on his estates; eldest son, Gervase Henry Cary-Elwes (1866–1921), celebrated tenor, who was received into the Church in 1876 and later married Lady Winefride Feilding, a daughter of Rudolph Feilding, eighth

Earl of Denbigh (see below); youngest son, Dudley (d. 1932), Catholic Bishop of Northampton; see Madeleine Beard, *Faith and Fortune* (1997), pp.75–79.

Casement, Roger David – political activist; b. 1 September 1864, Doyle's Cottage, Lawson Terrace, Sandymount, near Dublin; c. 2 August 1916, day before his execution; d. 3 August 1916, Pentonville prison, London; brought up as strict evangelical Ulster Protestant, though his mother had him secretly baptized a Catholic in August 1868 (something Casement did not recall in later life); worked in Africa for nearly twenty years as colonial administrator; pro-British then; reported on abuses in Congo and investigated atrocities in Peru, all related to the rubber trade; became Irish nationalist during World War I; joined group of Irish separatists planning with Germany a rising against British Crown; tried, convicted and executed for high treason 1916; was controversy regarding genuineness of his diaries in which homosexual relationships were recorded (tests later proved these to be genuine); his remains were returned to Ireland in 1965 and reinterred in Glasnevin cemetery, Dublin; see Alan Wharam, *Treason: Famous English Treason Trials* (1995), pp.156–165; Michael Carson, "Casement: Traitor or Hero," *The Tablet*, 14 December 1996, p.1645; Sean Ua Cearneigh, "Rebel's Faith: The Last Days of Roger Casement," *Catholic Life*, July 2005, p.19; Seamas O Siochain, *Roger Casement: Imperialist, Rebel, Revolutionary* (2008); *DNB*.

Cassel, Sir Ernest Joseph – merchant banker and financier; b. 3 March 1852, Cologne, Germany; c. about 1882 (at the wish of his wife Annette, who had already converted, expressed before her death in 1881; baptized by Fr. Cyril Forster); d. 21 September 1921, Brook House, Park Lane, London; Jewish upbringing but he was never devout; father a banker; in 1869 emigrated to England where he became extremely successful financier; naturalized British subject; gained entry into high society, being friend and companion of Edward VII; great collector of artwork; appointed to Privy Council in 1902 and received GCVO in 1906; grieved by death of his only daughter, Maud, from tuberculosis in 1911; very private man; never remarried; buried at Kensal Green cemetery, London; see *DNB*.

Casson, Christopher Thorndike – actor; b. 20 January 1912, Prestwich, Manchester, Lancashire; c. 1941; d. 9 July 1996, Dublin; son of the celebrated theatrical couple, Sir Lewis Casson (1875–1969) and Dame Sybil Thorndike (1882–1976); brought up in High Anglicanism; child and adult actor in London; since 1930s acted mostly in the Gate Theatre, Dublin, but also on radio and television; taught elocution for many years at All Hallows College, Drumcondra, Ireland; became Third Order Dominican; committed pacifist; lifelong interest in mysticism; became an Irish citizen; devout Catholic attending Mass every day; see "Conversion: The Invisible Witness," *Position Paper* (1992), p.265 ("The great medieval book *The Cloud of Unknowing* drew its inspiration, to a large extent, from the writings of Richard of St. Victor. The extraordinary interlocking of the unknowable with exactitude of dogmatic revelation is one of the wonders of the Catholic tradition, which this great book brings out, and which the history of the fourteenth century mysticism demonstrates").

Caswall, Edward (*pseud.* Scriblerus Redivivus) – priest and author; b. 15 July 1814, Yateley, Hampshire; c. 18 January 1847 (received by Cardinal Acton in Newman's presence; his wife, Louisa (1818–1849) became a Catholic on 25 January 1847; his younger brother, Thomas (1816–1862), received in 1846); d. 2 January 1878, Birmingham Oratory; son of Anglican vicar; younger brother of Dr. Henry Caswall, Prebendary of Salisbury; educated at Brasenose College, Oxford; took Anglican orders; toured the Continent with his wife in 1845 and returned with deep love of the Catholic Church; attributed his conversion in part to Newman and the *Tracts for the Times*; also influenced by Milner's *The End of Religious Controversy* and Manning's *The Unity of the Church*; wife died of Asiatic cholera 14 September 1849 and after her death he joined the Oratorian Order; ordained priest 18 September 1852; lived at Birmingham Oratory until his death; writer of devotional poetry and many hymns; wrote *Lyra Catholica*, a translation of all the Breviary and Missal hymns with some others; buried at Rednal; see *Journals* (unpublished – housed in the archives of the Birmingham Oratory) ("I must say I think it is childish and absurd to argue for the Independence of [the Church of England] from the fact of their having been a British Church here before Augustine came. Anyhow … present [Anglican] orders if derived in succession at all come from Augustine and not from the Old British Church. We are Saxons and have not connections with the older inhabitants of this country. Or at least if there is a connection it is so slight as to amount to nothing. To go back to the British Church is a mere theory and amounts to real dissimulation and false argument…

…If there is one Holy Catholic Church, then to pass from one portion of that Church into another cannot entail a real change of religion. But to pass from the English to the Roman Church is a real change of religion. Therefore either

there is not one Holy Catholic Church and the Creed is false, or else the Roman and English Churches are not two portions of the Holy Catholic Church. But if they are not two portions of it, then one of them does not belong to it. Is it then the Roman or the English that does not belong to it? Not the Roman for at best the English comes from the Roman. Therefore the English Church is not a portion of the Holy Catholic Church"); Jean Stone, *Eleanor Leslie: A Memoir* (1898) ("At last [Mr. and Mrs. Caswall] made up their minds that they had had enough theory and would like to see the Catholic religion in practice.… [S]o they went [to Ireland] and took lodgings in Dublin. As they meant to be very impartial in collecting evidence they provided themselves with two note-books, in one of which they intended to put down all they saw in favor of Protestantism, in the other all they saw favorable to Catholicism. The landlady asked Mrs. Caswall if she would like to witness the ceremony of a nun's clothing. At the convent they were put into a room overlooking the chapel with the father of the young novice who was to be clothed that day. Mr. Caswall asked him if he were not sorry to lose his daughter in such a manner. But the man replied earnestly, 'Sir, I am not worthy of it'; and Caswall said afterwards, 'I put that down.' One Sunday they passed a thatched hovel. It was a Catholic chapel; mass was going on, and it was pouring with rain. The chapel was full to over-flowing, and outside men were kneeling among the puddles. Caswall said, 'I put that down'"); Nancy Marie de Flon, *Edward Caswall: Newman's Brother and Friend* (2005) ("'Catholic' wrote Caswall, means existing everywhere. 'One' means one. Thus, to believe in one Catholic Church is to believe in a church that is everywhere one. But, he reasoned, the Church of England is not everywhere one but only in England, the colonies, Ireland, Scotland, and the United States. The Roman Catholic Church, on the other hand, really is everywhere one. It exists throughout the globe and everywhere is 'one body teaching one doctrine on fundamentals.' The Anglican Church, in contrast, is 'simply a national church, not a Catholic one'"); *Catholic Encyclopedia*; *DNB*.

Cellier, Elizabeth (*née* Dormer) – midwife; *fl.* 1668–1688; brought up Protestant in a family that remained loyal to Charles I; wife of a Frenchman; said that she converted to Catholicism out of loyalty to the crown, after her father and brother died on same day during the Civil War; also impressed by those Catholics who saved Charles II after battle of Worcester; she visited and helped imprisoned Catholics; after her conversion she was accused during Oates' plot in 1678 of conspiring to assassinate the king and of alleged treasonable practices against leading Protestants (the so-called "Meal-Tub Plot"; tried for high treason in 1680 and acquitted; later accused of libel against the king and Protestant religion in a book about the trial (in which she alleged torture of Catholic prisoners in Newgate); condemned to the pillory and to pay fine of one thousand pounds; nothing known of her after January 1688 and assumed she left country following Revolution of 1688; colorful, forthright character; her enemies called her the "Popish Midwife"; much work in developing midwifery; a tradition claims she is buried in Great Missenden Church, Buckinghamshire; see Anne Barbeau Gardiner, "Elizabeth Cellier, the Popish Midwife: A Woman for all Seasons," *Catholic Dossier*, March/ April 2002; Fiorella Nash, "Elizabeth Cellier," in Joanna Bogle (ed), *English Catholic Heroines* (2009), p.140; *Gillow*, Vol. I, p.441; *Catholic Encyclopedia*; *DNB*.

Challoner, Bishop Richard – bishop and religious writer; b. 29 September 1691, Lewes, Sussex; c. about 1704; d. 12 January 1781, Gloucester Street, London; both parents Protestants, father being rigid Presbyterian, who had his son baptized by a Presbyterian minister; father died early and mother, having become a Catholic, served as housekeeper to two ancient Catholic families, Gage at Firle Park, near Lewes, and then Holman at Warkworth Manor, Northamptonshire (Lady Anastasia Holman (d. 1719) was daughter of William Howard, Viscount Stafford, executed during the so-called Popish Plot); chaplain, John Gother (see below), received him into the Church and recommended him for education for the priesthood at Douai; entered English College in 1705; ordained priest 28 March 1716; Professor of Theology and Vice-President there; went on the mission in London in 1730; untiring worker, especially for the poor and imprisoned; elected "controversial writer" for the district in 1736, which continued until 1757; administered London district as vicar-general from 1737; co-adjutor bishop from 1741 (became Bishop of See of Debra, *in partibus*, and vicar apostolic for London district in 1758); followed the *devot* tradition of St. Francis de Sales; published in 1740 *The Garden of the Soul*, which continued to be the main devotional text for the vast majority of Catholics living in England until the late nineteenth century; re-established Catholic martyrology with *Memoirs of Missionary Priests*, 2 Vols. (1741–1742); updated the Rheims–Douai Catholic Bible (1750); published very popular *Meditations for Every Day of the Year* in 1753; many controversial and spiritual works and translations; built several schools; embassy chapels made it easier for Catholics, but later he narrowly escaped, and was greatly shaken by, the Gordon riots of 1780;

leading figure in English Catholicism for most of eighteenth century; very devout private life; buried by his friend Briant Barrett in his family vault at Milton, Berkshire; see *The Unerring Authority of the Catholic Church* (1732); *The Touchstone of the New Religion* (1734); *The Catholick Christian Instructed* (1737); *The Grounds of the Old Religion* (1742); *Britannica Sancta* (1745); Edwin H. Burton, *The Life and Times of Bishop Challoner, 1691–1781*, 2 Vols. (1909); E. E. Reynolds, *Richard Challoner* (1974); Eamon Duffy (ed), *Challoner and His Church: A Catholic Bishop in Georgian England* (1981); William Sheils, "Richard Challoner," in John Joliffe (ed), *English Catholic Heroes* (2008), p.103; *Gillow*, Vol. II, p.447; *Catholic Encyclopedia*; *DNB* ("He had, in Cardinal Wiseman's words, 'supplied, in fact, almost the entire range of necessary or useful religious literature for his Catholic fellow-countrymen': the Bible, catechetical and apologetic works, prayer books, meditations, martyrologies, and controversy. All were written in plain, sound, instructive Augustan prose, often affective in tone, yet as sober as their century, and they ensured that Challoner's church did better than survive").

Chambers, Frederick Walter – Catholic layman; b. 1881; c. 25 November 1919 (received by Fr. John Ratcliffe, SJ); d. 1967; former Anglican minister; secretary of Converts Aid Society from 1922 until his death (forty-five years); genius in personal relationships, able to enthuse others with his own personal commitment to the Society's work; buried Teddington cemetery, Richmond, Surrey.

Chambers (alias Mann), Sabine, SJ – priest; b. about 1559, Leicestershire; d. 16 March 1633, probably at College of St. Francis Xavier, Wales; dissatisfied with Protestantism when at Oxford; went to Paris and was received into the Church; appointed by Fr. Persons (see below) as Superior of Jesuit College in Eu, Normandy; entered the Society of Jesus in 1588; taught theology for several years on the Continent; then his request to work on the English mission was granted and he arrived in 1609; worked in Lincolnshire and later in London district, 1623–1628; see *The Garden of Our B. Lady* (1619); *Gillow*, Vol. I, p.460; *DNB*.

Chapman, Horace Edward – Catholic layman; b. 1842; c. 1894 (his wife, Adelaide, sister of Fr. Philip Fletcher, founder and Master of Guild of Ransom (see below), received in 1895; his daughter, later a Benedictine nun, also received in 1895; d. 6 March 1907; formerly Anglican clergyman; see *Why I Became a Catholic* (1897) ("By what law of God, written or unwritten, was the determination of religious causes transferred to the King from the Pope, who had exercised in this country supreme authority in things spiritual ever since the mission of St. Augustine?...

What led me to perceive that the Anglican Church could not be the Church of God in this land and so led me to look elsewhere for the true Church of Christ was because being convinced of the Absolute Supremacy of the Crown in things spiritual, and in consequence the complete overt-throw of all positive truth, I could no longer without grievous sin against God, remain in the Established Church, without imperiling my soul. Neither to Kings or Queens, to Parliaments, or Republics, or to any earthly form of Government whatsoever did our Divine Lord entrust the Supreme Power in the ruling of His kingdom").

Chapman, Dom John, OSB (born Henry Chapman) – priest and author; b. 25 April 1865, Ashfield, Suffolk; c. 8

December 1890 (received at the London Oratory by Fr. Kenelm Digby Beste); d. 7 November 1933; only son of Frank Robert Chapman (d. 1924), Anglican Archdeacon of Sudbury and Canon of Ely Cathedral; delicate health and so taught at home by tutors; at Christ Church, Oxford, where gained a first in Greats; influenced at Oxford by High Church Anglicanism; became Anglican curate; entered Benedictine novitiate at Maredsous, Belgium (a byword for strict observance and rigorous scholarship); ordained Catholic priest 8 June 1895; prior of St. Thomas' Priory, Erdington, Birmingham; Superior of Caldey Community on their reception into the Catholic Church; army chaplain to the British forces 1914–1919; worked on revision of the Vulgate in Rome 1919–1922; prior, then fourth Abbot of Downside from 1929 until his death; founder of Worth Abbey in 1933; greatest Patristic scholar of his time; much sought-after spiritual director and authority on prayer, spiritual life and mystical theology; see essay in J. G. F. Raupert (ed), *Roads to Rome* (1901), p.51 ("I had to study [as an Anglican student] doctrine and Church history, and soon came to see in the Reformation the uprooting of all that I was just beginning to love and venerate.... Now began my troubles in earnest. I had to teach. I asked myself on what authority. Not the bishop's. Not that of the Articles, which I hated; not that of the Prayerbook, which we all laughed at. Not of the present Catholic Church; for East and West agreed only in holding me to be a heretic. As to antiquity, if I took in the fourth and fifth centuries, why not the sixteenth or nineteenth?... It seemed to me that Christianity must be continuous, and the Church infallible. But, if Rome was right, I must be wrong.... There was only one Church possible and that must be the Church of Rome. There must be

authority and a living voice to decide controversies, and there must be supernatural sanctity and religious orders, and miracles and signs and wonders"); *Bishop Gore and Roman Catholic Claims* (1905) ("Was it chance that those who fought against the Church in the sixteenth century were the immoral Luther, the cruel Calvin, the blasphemous Zwingli, the adulterous Beza, the lying and cowardly Cranmer, Henry, model of husbands, the virgin Elizabeth, and such like? Was it chance that those who defended unity were men like More, and Fisher, and Pole, and Campion, and Allen, or Ignatius, and Charles Borromeo, and Philip and Canisius? The lies of three hundred years are melting away like smoke before modern criticism, and we are beginning to know something of the men who robbed Englishmen of their faith by the use of rack and gibbet and cauldron. We know something of Foxe's martyrs now. We wish they had been kept from the stake, but we are forced to admit that most of them deserved the prison. But the white-robed army of martyrs tortured and slain by Henry and Elizabeth, and the two Charleses, is beginning to be known and respected by Protestant historians. We are learning how much we lost by the 'Reformation.' The crushing blow dealt to the universities, the loss of popular education throughout the country, scarcely at all made good by the scanty endowments of Edward VI, the wholesale destruction of libraries, the confiscation of the patrimony of the poor, the degradation of the clergy, the cessation of religious instruction, the beginning of vagrancy, the increase of immorality. If it had not been for the Puritans and John Wesley, there would have been little religion left in the country. Is all this chance?"); *John the Presbyter and the Fourth Gospel* (1911); "The Appeal to Tradition in the Patristic Age," *Downside Review*, January 1923, p.4 ("Dead bishops have no jurisdiction over us. Dead bishops and councils only speak to us through the living voice of today. Nay, even dead Apostles are our authorities only because our Church, in which we live now, vouches for them and presents them to us"); *Studies in the Early History of the Papacy* (1928); "Newman and the Fathers," in *Blackfriars*, July 1933, p.578; *Matthew, Mark and Luke* (1937) (argued for the priority of the Greek Matthew in relation to the Synoptic Problem); *The Four Gospels* (1946); Abbot Butler, "Abbot Chapman," *Downside Review*, January 1934, p.1; Dom Bede Camm, *Anglican Memories* (1935) (letter by Dom John Chapman to the author quoted at p.64: "Who is schismatical or heretical, Rome or England? If England is right, then Rome is in schism, and especially the promulgation of the Infallibility is the most violent act of schism ever perpetrated. Also, we must suppose that the usurpations of Popes held the Church in a Babylonian captivity under the Blessed Luther, and that the Church was an unwilling captive. If *willing* (and history tells us that the Church gave the Pope his powers) the whole Western Church was schismatic. Yet the Roman Church is the Church of saints and doctors, the only Church who has shown herself to be a Church by teaching, by unswerving orthodoxy, by definitions of doctors and discipline. There is no break in her history, no heresy in her system.

And while the Roman Church since her Reformation has flourished in saints, the English Church has steadily decayed. She has had 'good men' among her Bishops and clergy, she has been an obedient servant to her chosen lord the King (and Parliament), she has kept off open fidelity by saying 'you needn't believe very much; and that little had better be quite indefinite.' She is not committed to heresy, simply because one cannot be quite certain what she means by her Articles. But she has habitually taught heresy; and her Articles only avoid heresy by a miracle.

I can't conceive how it is possible to hold the view, (which began in Laud's time, and which was never held in the Church till then) that the visible Church may consist of several bodies which hate each other and call each other heretics and schismatics. The Greeks don't hold the view, and never did. No one supposes that the early Church did"); Dom Roger Hudleston, OSB (ed), *The Spiritual Letters of Dom John Chapman OSB* (1946) ("The only way to pray is to pray; and the way to pray well is to pray much. If one has no time for this, then one must at least pray regularly. But the less one prays the worse it goes. And if circumstances do not permit even regularity, then one must put up with the fact that when one does try to pray, one can't pray – and our prayer will probably consist of telling this to God"); Bishop B. C. Butler, "English Spiritual Writers: John Chapman," in *The Clergy Review*, November 1959 (reprinted in Bishop B. C. Butler, *Searchings* (1974, p.143, under the title, "The Absurd and John Chapman"); *DNB* ("Evelyn Underhill, after encountering him, reported that he knew more about prayer than anyone she had met").

Charles II, King of England, Scotland and Ireland – b. 29 May 1630, St. James's Palace, London; c. 5 February 1685 (on his deathbed); d. 6 February 1685, Whitehall Palace, London; second (but first surviving son) of Charles I (1600–1649) and Henrietta Maria (1609–1669), daughter of Henri IV of France and Marie de Medici; mother a Catholic; spent most of Civil War with his father; then nominal leader of royalist forces in west country; when his father surrendered to Scots, he went to Isles of

Scilly, then Jersey, and finally to the French court at St. Germain where his mother was; after death of father tried unsuccessfully to organize risings in Scotland and Ireland; eventually his coronation took place 1 January 1651; led a Scottish army south to Worcester where they were defeated by Cromwell 3 September 1651; legendary escape from Worcester, remaining at large for six weeks (including finding refuge with Catholics, notably Fr. John Hudleston, in Shropshire and Staffordshire and hiding in, among other places, the famous oak tree at Boscobel (see also entry below for Fr. Richard Hudleston, OSB, uncle of Fr. John Hudleston); escaped to France and lived with his mother in the palace of the Louvre, Paris; moved to Germany and then to Bruges within the Spanish Netherlands; after many negotiations returned to England in May 1660 on the basis of a regime committed to law and the Protestant religion; restoration took place also in Scotland and Ireland; took many mistresses and had many illegitimate children; in politics moved closer to France and against Spain and the Dutch republic; married Catherine of Braganza (1638–1705) in 1662; after the time of the conversion around 1668 of his brother, James, Duke of York, he said that he also intended to convert, but did not do so (e.g., undertaking at time of secret treaty of Dover that if given financial assistance by French he would declare himself a Catholic and attempt to lead his subjects back to the Church of Rome); much expense in various military operations and many problems of debt; many crises relating to political and religious issues (e.g., the Popish Plot and the question of religious toleration); sudden illness 2 February 1685; received into the Catholic Church in the presence of James by Fr. John Huddleston, the priest he had met during his escape from Worcester; strongly attracted to the

Church for much of his life; buried in the King Henry VII Chapel, Westminster Abbey; see J. G. Muddiman, "The Death of Charles II," *The Month*, December 1932, p.520; Hilaire Belloc, *The Last Rally: A Story of Charles II* (1940); Antonia Fraser, *Charles II* (1979); Ronald Hutton, *Charles II: King of England, Scotland, and Ireland* (1989); John Miller, *Charles II* (1991); Richard Ollard, *The Escape of Charles II after the Battle of Worcester* (2002); *Gillow*, Vol. III, p.463 (entry for Fr. John Hudleston); *DNB*.

Charnock (Chernock), Robert – Jacobite conspirator; b. 2 February 1663, Warwickshire; c. early 1687; d. 18 March 1695, Tyburn; Fellow of Magdalen College, Oxford, of which he was made Vice-President in reign of James II, having then converted to the Catholic faith; on 1688 Revolution had to flee to France; fought for the Jacobite army at the Battle of the Boyne in 1690; returned to England some years later and engaged in a conspiracy against William III, for which he was tried and condemned in 1695; he repeatedly denied the charge that James II had commissioned him to assassinate William III; hanged, drawn and quartered at Tyburn with Edward King and Thomas Keys, who suffered on the same account; see *Gillow*, Vol. I, p.473; *DNB*.

Chase, Charles Rose – soldier and priest; b. 1 June 1844, London; c. 2 June 1900 (received by Fr. Vassall-Phillips (see below) at St. Joseph's, Bishop Stortford); d. 27 November 1908, Lisbon; youngest of eight children of Colonel Morgan Chase, First Madras Calvary; brought up in a military family as an Anglican; went to Sandhurst, then to 21st Hussars in India for seven years; resigned commission in 1868 and returned to England; always religious minded (had a love for the Roman missal); took Anglican orders; was an extreme Ritualist; resigned from his ministry because of ill-health; for a time the question of the papacy was a stumbling block, but influenced by Fr. Vassall-Phillips and by Tanqueray's *Dogmatic Theology*; friend of Henry Patrick Russell (see below); after his conversion went to complete his studies for the priesthood to the Beda in Rome; ordained priest by Cardinal Merry del Val in Rome 2 June 1901; preached missions in England and United States to Protestants, especially High Anglicans; given mission by Cardinal Vaughan to found the Diocesan Missionaries of Our Lady of Compassion to work for the conversion of England, which was his consuming passion; much ill-health; gave generously for charitable purposes from his private funds; buried in Lisbon; see Henry Patrick Russell, *From Hussar to Priest: A Memoir of Charles Rose Chase* (1913) ("First, there are the three great texts – 'Thou art Peter'; 'I have prayed for thee, that thy faith fail not: when thou art converted strengthen thy brethren'; 'Lovest thou Me ... feed My sheep ... feed My lambs.' These understood in the literal meaning, as we understand texts about the Real Presence, teach – the Church built on Peter as distinct from the other Apostles. Whatsoever *thou* shalt bind on earth, etc., – universal jurisdiction to St. Peter, Christ's prayer for St. Peter has been heard in that the Roman Church has never fallen into heresy as each of the other Churches founded on other Apostles. Then, again, the universal rule given to St. Peter over sheep and lambs – clergy and people, as St. Ambrose in the fifth century interpreted it. But I used to say, How can it be proved that the Pope is the successor of St. Peter? The only answer is universal tradition – East as well as West, and the assertion of two of the Ecumenical Councils accepted by all.

Ephesus, which decreed the Divine Maternity of Mary, speaks of the Pope as the successor of Peter and teacher of the whole Church. The Fathers of Chalcedon, when Pope St. Leo's letter was read to them, shouted, 'Peter has spoken by Leo,' and accepted what he had defined without further discussion, though they were nearly all Eastern Bishops. The Corinthian Church, founded by St. Paul in the lifetime of St. John, appealed in a matter of difficulty, not to him, though an Apostle, but to St. Clement, the successor of St. Peter, and afterwards read St. Clement's letter as if it were Scripture in the service of their Church. St. Polycarp, the disciple of St. John, appealed to the Pope. St. Irenaeus appealed to the Roman See as that with which all other Churches must be in agreement. Tertullian in the second century calls the Pope Universal Bishop. St. Eleutherius, a Pope and martyr, settled troubles in the Diocese of Lyons in the second century. St. Augustine, after the Pope had given his judgment, wrote: 'Rome has spoken, the cause is ended.' St. Ambrose, speaking of the Roman Church, writes, 'Where Peter is there is the Church.' St. Jerome writes to the Pope, 'Whosoever eateth the Lamb outside thy house is profane.' Tradition alone teaches us Infant Baptism, the observance of Sunday, what is the Canon of Scripture, Fasting Communion, and that the Pope is Peter's successor as Head of the Church under Christ – Vicar of Christ – and therefore able to insure jurisdiction in every diocese and to shepherd every sheep and every lamb of the flock of Christ...

Papal infallibility follows from Papal supremacy. For if the Pope, as successor of St. Peter, exerts his power of teaching the whole Church and of strengthening his brethren, then what he decides must end any question, and that is just what infallibility means – i.e., when the Pope speaks as universal teacher to the whole

Church and defines or explains a matter, then that decision of his is irreformable").

Chatterton, (Henrietta) Georgiana Marcia Lascelles, Lady Chatterton (*née* **Iremonger; other married name Dering**) – writer and traveler; b. 11 November 1806, 24 Arlington Street, Piccadilly, London; c. 20 September 1865 (received by Newman together with her second husband and her niece and ward, Miss Rebecca Dulcibella Orpen (d. 1923), shortly to marry (Marmion) Edward Ferrers (d. 1884) of the old Catholic family at Baddesley Clinton); d. 6 February 1876, Baddesley Clinton, Warwickshire; published extensively in fiction, biography, travel and devotional works; only child of Lascelles Iremonger (d. 1830), Anglican Prebendary of Winchester; married (1824) Sir William Abraham Chatterton, baronet (1794–1855) of Castle Mahon, County Cork; married (1859) Edward Heneage Dering (1827–1892) (see below); around 1870, because of the contention that arose over definition of papal infallibility, she developed doubts (also relating to Our Lady, the real presence and purgatory) and by 1873 again attended Anglican services; in 1875 she returned to the Catholic Church; counseled by Newman on many matters; see Edward Heneage Dering, *Memoirs of Georgiana, Lady Chatterton* (1878); obituary of Rebecca Ferrers, *The Times*, 13 September 1923 ("At the time of [Lady Chatterton's] second marriage [she] was 53 and Dering was twenty-two years her junior. Indeed there is good authority for the statement that it was for the hand of the young Miss Orpen, the ward, that Dering had really asked of Georgiana Lady Chatterton, and when the latter, in the mistaken belief that it was she who was being wooed, extended her own, Dering was too well-bred to explain. Soon after her reception into the Roman Catholic Church, Miss Orpen married Marmion Edward Ferrers, of Baddesley Clinton.... Ferrers and Dering had been old friends.... On the invitation of Ferrers, Dering and Georgiana Lady Chatterton went to live at Baddesley Clinton, and there the two married couples lived together for the remainder of their lives" (NB: in *Cat's Cradle* by Maurice Baring (see above) there is an important scene based on the above)); Joyce Sugg, *Ever Yours Affly: John Henry Newman and His Female Circle* (1996); Stanley L. Jaki, *Newman to Converts: An Existential Ecclesiology* (2001), Ch. 17 ("[Newman's] next lines to Lady Chatterton should make clear what he would think today of some 'leading' Catholic exponents of 'Catholicism' who claim that Paul's words about the Church as the 'pillar and ground of truth' are no proofs of the Church's infallibility: 'St. Paul says that the Church is the pillar and ground of the Truth. He says that there is *One* Body as there is *One* Faith. Our Lord has built His Church on Peter. These are great facts – they keep their ground against small objections, however many the latter may be'"); *Gillow;* Vol. I, p.478; *DNB*.

Cherois Crommelin, Andrew Claude de la – astronomer; b. 6 February 1865, Cushendun, County Antrim, Northern Ireland (but moved to England as a child); c. 1891 (wife, Letitia, received in 1898); d. 20 September 1939; brought up in Northern Ireland Protestant family; was reading for Anglican holy orders when he became unsettled in his religious views and became a Catholic; one of world's leading authorities on comets; comet 27/P Crommelin named after him posthumously; took part in several expeditions to observe total solar eclipses, including the one in Brazil in 1919, which aimed to determine amount of deflection of light caused by gravitational field of Sun (results from these observations crucial in providing confirmation of Einstein's General Theory of Relativity); also named after him are Crommelin crater on Moon, Crommelin crater on Mars, and Asteroid 1899, Crommelin; Fellow of Royal British Astronomical Society; President of the Royal British Astronomical Association, 1904–1906; one of his sons became a priest; see *Comets* (1937) (with Mary Proctor); *Diamonds in the Sky. The Story of the Stars* (1940).

Cheshire, Lord (Geoffrey) Leonard, VC, OM – air force officer and charity founder; b. 7 September 1917, Hoole, Chester; c. 24 December 1948; d. 31 July 1992, Sue Ryder home at Cavendish, Sudbury, Suffolk; father was Vinerian Professor of English Law at Oxford University; husband of Sue Ryder, later Baroness Ryder (see below); formerly Anglican; youngest group captain in RAF in 1943; flew more than 100 missions; attached to 617 Squadron ("The Dam Busters"); his VC was unique because rather than an individual act of courage on a particular day, it cited four years (1940–1944) of sustained courage, and bombing sorties in face of heavy ground reaction; one of two official British observers of dropping of atomic bomb at Nagasaki; after nursing an ex-serviceman dying of cancer, he founded Cheshire Homes for relief of suffering; great philanthropist; conversion greatly influenced by writings of Mgr. Vernon Johnson (see below) and those of C. S. Lewis; buried in Cavendish village cemetery; see *The Holy Face* (1954) (on the Shroud of Turin); "My Quest for Certainty" in John A. O'Brien (ed), *Where Dwellest Thou?* (1956) ("When Christ stood before his accusers, He had claimed, in answer to their question, that He was no less than God

Himself, and since He refused to retract He was put to death. In making this claim and maintaining it even unto repudiation and death, He was clearly either one thing or the other; either wholly mad or exactly what He claimed to be. By no possible stretch of the imagination could He be a good man slightly confused on this one point, for to make oneself out to be God is either deliberate deception, which is incompatible with goodness, or else mania, which is irreconcilable with Christ's life and teaching.

What held good for Christ now also held good for the Catholic Church, because here before my eyes she was making the selfsame and identical claim: to be nothing less than the direct continuation of His work on earth, entrusted with all His authority, able like Him to forgive sins, authorized to teach without possibility of error, and empowered to administer the helps and safeguards that man required in order to achieve his final end. In claiming to be the one and only true Church of Christ, like Him in every respect except in the sins and shortcomings of its individual members, she was making herself out to be nothing less than of divine origin"); *Pilgrimage to the Shroud* (1956); *Where is God in All This?* (1991) ("Very soon I told myself that the Church should have two characteristics. The first was, it must speak with authority. I came across this early on when reading the New Testament. Remember the crowd's remark that Jesus was a man who spoke with authority, not like the Scribes. Now that is such a forceful statement, that I said to myself, 'Well in that case, if he founded a Church, then that Church must speak with the same authority as he did, and with the same complete certainty about what it's saying'.... Also, unless the Church was teaching us about reality, it had no appeal for me.... Therefore, when you look at the different religions.... I think the important thing is to ask, 'Is there one which God founded and God guarantees?' If that wasn't the case, you could choose which you liked. But if it is true, then clearly we have a duty to look for it and, once we find it, to submit to it...

...I went to a talk that Hans Küng gave. I must say much of it was inspiring but much didn't appeal to me at all. I don't mean Hans Küng as a person, but because everything he presented was done in a way which boosted himself at the expense of somebody else. He made fun of the Pope, he made fun of the Vatican, but he did it in such a way that, very subtly, he seemed to me to be lifting himself up. And there's a very basic principle that the prophet must not profit, so that put me off. Then somebody mentioned Satan and in a very angry way, he lifted his finger and said, 'No!' But Jesus constantly talks about Satan in many different contexts. And I argue that it's another of the devil's triumphs that he's made the mention of sin something to be rather shied away from, not quite proper to talk about it in ordinary conversation. But the more you lose your sense of sin, the more you lose your sense of God and conversely, the more you approach God, the more you're aware of the reality and horror of sin...

...I think hell is something many of us wish wasn't part of the Christian Faith, but it only requires a little objective thought to realize that if it weren't, something would be wrong with the Church's teaching about heaven. What the Church is telling us is that hell is a real possibility, a possibility that you cannot deny unless you deny that God has created us free to make up our own minds about him. Therefore the Church is absolutely right in preaching about hell and doing what it can to make us take it seriously. After all if, despite everything that God has done for me and

despite his last approaches to me at the hour of my death, I remain completely and finally obdurate in refusing him, well then, he has to respect my free and deliberate choice. It will then be I, not he, who excludes myself from his presence"); *Crossing the Finishing Line* (1998); Russell Braddon, *Cheshire V.C.: A Study of War and Peace* (1954); Andrew Boyle, *No Passing Glory* (1955); Richard Morris, *Cheshire: the Biography of Leonard Cheshire VC OM* (2000) ("After three years as a Catholic I acknowledge humbly that so far as the Reformation aimed at purifying and dephariseeing the Roman Church it was right.... You on your side must try and realize that if Christ did not in fact establish an infallible, apostolic Catholic Church which really holds the keys of Heaven and wields power over sin and death, then the Apostles, the early Fathers and 1,900 years of Saints have all been deceived and are proved wrong"); Tricia O'Donnell, "Leonard Cheshire: A Modern Saint," *Catholic Life*, September 2002, p.9; John Joliffe, "Leonard Cheshire," in John Joliffe (ed), *English Catholic Heroes* (2008), p.210 ("Leonard's conversion to the Catholic Church seems to have begun in a victory celebration in a London nightclub.... One of the girls in his party – he described her as 'not the sort who would fall for religion' – asked him 'What do you know about God?' He replied that 'God is an inward conscience, personal to us all, that tells us what we ought to do, and what we ought not.' To which she answered 'Absolute nonsense. God is a *Person* – the Creator of the world. And you know it as well as I do'"); Gerry Burns, "Converts to Catholicism: Leonard Cheshire," *Catholic Life*, November 2009, p.30; *DNB*.

Chesterton, Ada Elizabeth (*née* Jones) – journalist and philanthropist; b. 30

June 1869, Oxford House, Thurlow Park Road, Dulwich, London; c. 1942; d. 20 January 1962, Croydon; born into family of journalists; worked as a freelance Fleet Street reporter from the age of sixteen; met the Chesterton brothers (see both below) in 1900 and finally married Cecil in 1917 after a long courtship; present at the military hospital in France when her husband died in 1918; much investigative journalism, especially highlighting the problems of the poor; set up Cecil houses as refuges for homeless women; also worked as journalist abroad; wrote many biographies, several popular novels, and two plays, one an adaptation of G. K. Chesterton's *The Man Who Was Thursday*; was an agnostic before her conversion to the Catholic faith; see *The Chestertons* (1941); S. J. Avens, Mrs. Cecil Chesterton, OBE," *Chesterton Review*, November 1981, p.313; *DNB*.

Chesterton, Cecil Edward – journalist and writer; b. 12 November 1879, 11 Warwick Gardens, Kensington, London; c. 7 June 1912 (brother, Gilbert (see below) received in 1922; wife, Ada (see above) received in 1942); d. 6 December 1918, Wimereux, near Boulogne, France; brought up in family with Unitarian leanings; later Anglican; Fabian socialist by 1902, then distributist from 1911; co-wrote *The Party System* (1911) with Hilaire Belloc, an attack on parliamentary system; editor of *New Witness*, seeking, sometimes recklessly, to expose corruption at all levels of government; conversion influenced by talks with Elodie Belloc, wife of Hilaire Belloc; defendant in Marconi libel trial in 1913 when *New Witness* alleged prominent members of the Liberal government, e.g., Sir Rufus Isaacs and Lloyd George, had engaged in corrupt financial dealings; convicted but fined only £100; pugnacious and polemical character;

joined army in 1916, but died from illness on active service; buried in military cemetery near Wimereux; see Brocard Sewell, *Cecil Chesterton* (1975) ("[Hilaire and Elodie Belloc's] daughter Eleanor (Mrs. Jebb) says that after one of these talks with Cecil her mother told him that if he did not become a Catholic he would 'lose his soul'. Evidently Cecil felt that she had good grounds for making this assertion"); Joseph Pearce, *Literary Converts* (1999) *passim*; *DNB*.

Chesterton, Frances Alice (*née* Blogg) – b. 1870/1; c. 1 November 1926; d. 12 December 1938; wife of G. K. Chesterton (see below); formerly devout Anglo-Catholic; her husband's general untidiness and lack of organization meant that he depended heavily upon her in all remotely practical matters (in a now famous telegram to his wife, Chesterton once wrote, "Am in Market Harborough. Where ought I to be?"); see Joseph Pearce, *Literary Converts* (1999) *passim*.

Chesterton, Gilbert Keith – writer; b. 29 May 1874, 32 Sheffield Terrace, Campden Hill, London; c. 30 July 1922 (received in the makeshift Catholic chapel at the Station Hotel, Beaconsfield; "I cannot explain why I am a Catholic, because now that I am a Catholic I cannot imagine myself as anything else"; his wife, Frances (see above), d. 1938, was received in 1926; brother, Cecil (see above), received in 1912); d. 14 June 1936, Top Meadow, Beaconsfield; dreamy and unorganized child; brought up in a nominally Anglican family, but a humanist one; studied at Slade School of Fine Art; made his name as reviewer and essayist; great friend of Hilaire Belloc (1870–1953); many books (both fiction and nonfiction), essays, short stories (especially the Father Brown stories), poems, and journalism (editor *G.K.'s Weekly*); great Catholic apologist; a constant contributor to leading periodicals of the day; famous for use of paradox; became great public figure, a modern Dr. Johnson; always generous and charitable; buried at Beaconsfield cemetery; see *Orthodoxy* (1908) ("Tradition means giving the vote to the most obscure of all classes, our ancestors. It is the democracy of the dead"); *Where All Roads Lead* (1922–3) ("As for the fundamental reasons for a man joining the Catholic Church, there are only two that are really fundamental. One is that he believes it to be the solid objective truth, which is true whether he likes it or not; and the other that he seeks liberation from his sins. If there be any man for whom these are not the main motives it is idle to enquire what were his philosophical or historical or emotional reasons for joining the old religion; for he has not joined it at all"); article from the *New Witness* (1922) ("The Church cannot move with the times; simply because the times are not moving. The Church can only stick in the mud with the times.... We do not want, as the newspapers say, a Church that will move with the world. We want one that will move it away from many of the things towards which it is now moving; for instance the Servile State. It is by that test that history will really judge, of any Church, whether it is the real Church or no"); *The Everlasting Man* (1925) ("Christendom has had a series of revolutions and in each one of them Christianity has died. Christianity has died many times and risen again; for it had a God who knew the way out of the grave.... Europe has been turned upside down over and over again; and at the end of these revolutions the same religion has again been found on top. The Faith is always converting the age, not as an old religion but as a new religion.... At least five times ... with the Arian and the Albigensian, with the humanist skeptic, after Voltaire and after Darwin, the Faith has to all appearances gone to the dogs. But in each of the five cases it was the dog that died..."); *The Catholic Church and Conversion* (1926) ("The Catholic Church is the only thing which saves a man from the degrading slavery of being a child of his age.... The New Religions are in many ways suited to the new conditions. When those conditions shall have changed in only a century or so, the points upon which alone they insist at present will have become almost pointless. If the Faith has all the freshness of a new religion, it has all the richness of an old religion; it has especially all the reserves of an old religion.... We do not really want a religion that is right where we are right. What we want is a religion that is right where we are wrong"); "The Reason Why" in John A. O'Brien (ed), *Where Dwellest Thou?* (1956) ("The difficulty of explaining 'why I became a Catholic' is that there are ten thousand reasons all amounting to one reason: that Catholicism is true. I could fill all my space with separate sentences each beginning with the words, 'It is the only thing that...' As, for instance, (1) It is the only thing that really prevents a sin from being a secret; (2) It is the only thing in which the superior cannot be superior; in the sense of supercilious; (3) It is the only thing that frees a man from the degrading slavery of being a child of his age; (4) It is the only thing that talks as if it were the truth; as if it were a real messenger refusing to tamper with a real message; (5) It is the only type of Christianity that really contains every type of man; even the respectable man; (6) It is the only large attempt to change the world from the inside; working through wills and not laws; and so on...

...Nine out of ten of what we call new ideas are simply old mistakes. The Catholic Church has for one of her chief duties that of preventing people from making those old mistakes; from making them over and over again for ever, as people always do if they are left to themselves.... There is no other case of one continuous intelligent institution that has been thinking about thinking for two thousand years"); *Upon This Rock* (1926) ("To a Catholic the Catholic Church is simply the Christian religion; the gift of Christ to St. Peter and his successors of a right to answer at all times all questions about what it really is; a thing surrounded at the edge of its own wide domain by various severed fragments of its own substance; consisting of people who for different reasons deny that right to affirm what it really is. It may be added that they differ not only about the nature of the ideal Christianity that ought to be substituted, but even about the nature of the Catholicism that is to be defied. To some it is Antichrist; to some it is one branch of the Church of Christ, having authority in certain provinces but not in England or Russia; to some it is a corrupt perversion of Truth from which religion was rescued; to others a necessary historic phase through which religion had to pass; and so on"); *The Thing* (1929); Patrick Braybrooke, *Some Catholic Novelists: Their Art and Outlook* (1931), p.3; W. R. Titterton, *Chesterton: A Portrait* (1936); Maisie Ward, *Gilbert Keith Chesterton* (1944); Maisie Ward, *Return to Chesterton* (1952); Christopher Hollis, *G. K. Chesterton* (1954); Robert Hamilton, "Chesterton and the Faith," *Irish Ecclesiastical Record*, August 1954, p.83; John A. O'Brien, *Giants of the Faith: Conversions Which Changed the World* (1957), p.187; Christopher Hollis, *The Mind of Chesterton* (1970); Jay P. Corrin, *G. K. Chesterton and Hilaire Belloc: The Battle Against Modernity* (1981); Michael Ffinch, *G. K. Chesterton: A Biography* (1986); Stanley L. Jaki,

Chesterton: A Seer of Science (1986); Quentin Lauer, SJ, *G. K. Chesterton: Philosopher Without Portfolio* (1988); Michael Coren, *Gilbert: The Man Who Was G. K. Chesterton* (1989); Kent R. Hill, "The Sweet Grace of Reason: The Apologetics of G. K. Chesterton" in Michael MacDonald and Andrew A. Tadie (ed), *In The Riddle Of Joy* (1989); Terry Teachout, "Coming to Terms with Chesterton," *The American Scholar*, 1989, p.105; Ian Crowther, *Chesterton* (1991); Kevin L. Morris, "Chesterton's Conversion: Hesitation and the Recovery of Infancy," *Chesterton Review*, August 1992, p.371; Sheridan Gilley, "Chesterton and Conversion," *Priests and People*, October 1995, p.381; Joseph Pearce, *Wisdom and Innocence: A Life of G. K. Chesterton* (1996); Sheridan Gilley, "Chesterton, Mission and Catholic Apologetics," *Chesterton Review*, August 1997, p.271; Anthony Cooney, *G. K. Chesterton: One Sword at Least* (1998); David W. Fagerberg, *The Size of Chesterton's Catholicism* (1998); Bernard Bergonzi, *War Poets and Other Subjects* (1999), Ch. 16, "Chesterton's First Novel"; David W. Fagerberg, "Would Chesterton be a Convert in 2000?" *Priests and People*, January 2000, p.18; Mark Knight, "Chesterton and the Problem of Evil," *Literature and Theology*, 2000, p.373; Dale Ahlquist, *G. K. Chesterton: The Apostle of Common Sense* (2003); Ian Ker, *The Catholic Revival in English Literature, 1845–1961* (2003), Ch. 4, "The Dickensian Catholicism of G.K. Chesterton" ("There were two ideas or facts about the world that were crucial for Chesterton's conversion first to Christianity and then to Catholicism as the form of Christianity that best realized them. They correspond to the two attitudes to life that Chesterton called optimism and pessimism, each of which is a recognition of one of the undeniable aspects of reality but each of which without the other is a serious distortion of reality. On the one hand there is the sheer goodness of human life and the world, which calls for gratitude and wonder, and on the other hand the no less striking evil that vitiates them and creates despair. These two contradictory truths, Chesterton came to believe, could be explained only by the two basic, complementary doctrines of Christianity, namely, that creation is good because created by God but also bad because spoilt by fallen human beings.... These two truths were for Chesterton most fully embodied in Catholicism, which on the one hand emphasized the goodness of creation through the sacramental principle and refused (unlike Calvinism) to reject human nature as wholly corrupt, and on the other hand, unlike liberal Protestantism, was unflinching in its acknowledgment of the awful reality of sin, for which it provided an antidote in the form of confession"); Sheridan Gilley, "Chesterton and the English Anti-Catholic Tradition," *Chesterton Review*, Fall and Winter 2004, p.293; Mark Knight, *Chesterton and Evil* (2004); Susan Hannsen, "Chesterton's Reputation as a Roman Catholic Convert in the Twentieth Century," *Chesterton Review*, Spring and Summer 2005, p.63; Dale Ahlquist, *Common Sense 101: Lessons from G. K. Chesterton* (2006); Ralph McInerny, *Some Catholic Writers* (2007); Kevin L. Morris, *The Truest Fairy Tale: An Anthology of the Religious Writings of G. K. Chesterton* (2007); Karl Schmude, *G. K. Chesterton* (2008); William Oddie, *Chesterton and the Romance of Orthodoxy: The Making of G.K.C., 1874–1908* (2008); Aidan Nichols, *G. K. Chesterton: Theologian* (2009); Gerry Burns, "Converts to Catholicism: G. K. Chesterton," *Catholic Life*, September 2009, p.38; Patrick Allitt, *Catholic Converts: British and American Intellectuals Turn to Rome*

(1997) *passim*; Joseph Pearce, *Literary Converts* (1999) *passim*; Fr. Charles P. Connor, *Classic Catholic Converts* (2001), pp.97–107; Lorene Hanley Duquin, *A Century of Catholic Converts* (2003), p.55; *DNB* ("As a very young man he had become agnostic for a time, but the sense he had found in Browning that life is splendid but somehow incomplete led him to work out a religion for himself which, he was astonished to discover, already existed in the form of orthodox Christianity...

...At its simplest, Chestertonian paradox involved seeing familiar things from an unfamiliar angle, so that a glass of water which is half empty is also, remarkably, half full; the one description might be called pessimistic, the other optimistic. In a more directly philosophical fashion, the difference between things implies a measure of similarity, in order for the comparison to be possible. And central to Christian belief is the traditional paradox, to which Chesterton often returned, of an incarnate God who is born as a helpless infant and dies an ignominious death"); on Chesterton generally, see the *Chesterton Review*, published 1982 to date.

Childe, Wilfred Rowland Mary – poet and prose writer; b. 1890; c. 1914; d. 1952; educated at Magdalen College, Oxford; lecturer in English at University of Leeds 1922–1952; chiefly remembered for *Dream English. A Fantastical Romance* (1917) see essay in Maurice Leahy (ed), *Conversions to the Catholic Church: A Symposium* (1933) ("My belief in Our Lord absolutely demanded my becoming a Catholic almost as a test of loyalty to Himself with a sudden blinding vision of the Unity of the Church. As a present objective fact – not merely in a golden mediaeval past or a hypothetical Utopian future – but here and now. And with that vision went a very clear sense of the function, organic, persisting, providential, of the Holy See.... It is the sense of the glorious and unifying function of the Holy See, I suppose, which sometimes makes converts rather bitter about the Established Church, whose 'unity' rests upon a political compromise, and which has no idea (as yet) of how utterly unphilosophical such a conception of the nature of the Church must be. To oppose patriotism to Catholicism is really a kind of intellectual suicide; it is to despair of the promises of Christ and to give the things of God to Caesar"); *Selected Poems* (1936).

Chisholm, Caroline (*née* Jones) – humanitarian and philanthropist, immigration administrator and authoress; b. 30 May 1808, Wooton, Northampton; c. 1830, on her marriage; d. 25 March 1877, 43A Barclay Road, Fulham; youngest of twelve children of farmer; from wealthy family; educated at home; brought up as Anglican; married Captain Archibald Chisholm (1798–1877), officer with the East India Company from Scottish Highland Catholic family; went to India where opened schools for soldiers' daughters in Madras; then to Australia where opened home for emigrants newly arrived in Sydney with nowhere to go; they returned to England in 1846 and their home became centre for Australian emigration, helping people to join their families in Australia; launched the Family Colonization Society in 1849; known as "the emigrants' friend"; motivation was promotion of marriage and family life; in Australia there are schools, a welfare society, and a suburb named in her honor; buried in Billings Road cemetery, Northampton; see Joanna Bogle, *Caroline Chisholm: The Emigrants' Friend* (1993); Carole Walker and Jane L. Littlewood, "A Second Moses in Bonnet and Shawl: Caroline Chisholm: 1808–

1877," *Recusant History*, May 1995, p.409; Joanna Bogle, "Caroline Chisholm," in Joanna Bogle (ed), *English Catholic Heroines* (2009), p.196; *DNB*.

Christie, Albany James, SJ – priest; b. 18 December 1817, London; c. 18 October 1845 (received by Dr. Doyle); d. 1891; studied medicine for a time at King's College, London; then at Oriel College, Oxford, before becoming a fellow there 1840–1845; pupil of Pusey and one of the more extreme of the Tractarians; his views were such that Newman, then an Anglican, advised him not to take orders; worked on Newman's editions of Fleury's *Church History* and *The Lives of the English Saints*; took up residence with Newman at Littlemore in July 1845; left at end of September for London where he was received shortly afterwards into the Catholic Church; went to Maryvale with Newman and his group and lived there until 1847, but decided against becoming an Oratorian with them; joined the Society of Jesus in 1847; ordained priest in 1852; opened the Jesuit house in Edinburgh in 1859; later life spent at Farm Street, London; at one time he received into the Church more converts than almost any other priest in London; see *Two Lectures on the Papacy* (1857); *Union With Rome* (1869); *The Philosophy of Christianity* (1874); *Luther's Jubilee* (1883); Richard Frederick Clarke, *In Memoriam: A Short Sketch of Fr. A. J. Christie* (1891) (reprinted from *The Month*, June 1891, p.153).

Christie, Lydia Rose Bonamy (*née* Price) – c. 1879 (mother of Fr. Henry James Christie (b. 1869) who converted on leaving Christ Church, Oxford in 1887 and later became a priest of the London Oratory); daughter of Bonamy Price (1807–1888), Drummond Professor of Political Economy at Oxford;

correspondence before her conversion with Newman on historical arguments and act of faith; attended Newman's funeral; see Stanley L. Jaki, *Newman to Converts: An Existential Ecclesiology* (2001), pp.364–367 ("Newman cautioned her against getting too much involved in dissecting historical arguments, in her case the debates about the canons of Nicaea and Chalcedon: 'I can't conceive that is the way we are to be led into the truth. Of course, *we* Catholics have "answers" to such objections, and I think sufficient answers.' But disposing of some difficulties was not the same as advancing towards the desired goal. The move had to come from taking seriously a principle which Newman found best expressed by Saint Ambrose, and this is why he had prefixed it to the *Grammar of Assent* as its motto: The motto was, of course, that God did not favor dialectics as the means of saving his people. Instead of wrangling over subtleties, about which 'each party has its own view,' one was to focus on 'broad arguments,' especially the Notes of the Church...

Then Newman summed up the effect which the contemplation of the Notes can make on the mind so that the mind may reach conclusions like these: 'I say there is nothing immoral in faith, if you are in that state of mind as to say 'I see clearly that the Catholic Church is from God, but I can't answer these <certain> objections.' 'I certainly should have no doubt at all could I get over these objections,' and 'I am far more sure that the arguments *for* are *good* than the arguments *against*'; and the one have a *strength* and a *completeness* which the others have not'; in that case I say that ... it is your duty to submit to the Church as the Voice in spite of certain objections to its authority or to its teaching, which you cannot satisfactorily solve'").

Clare, Countess of (Elizabeth Julia Georgiana Burrell) – benefactress; b. 1793; c. 7 September 1841, Rome (instructed by Fr. Thomas Grant, later first Bishop of Southwark); d. April 1879; wife of John, second and last Earl of Clare; daughter of Priscilla, Baroness Willoughby de Eresby and of Sir Peter Burrell, who became Baron Gwydyr; generous benefactor of Catholic Church, especially at St. Mary's, Ryde, Isle of Wight (where she also provided funds for a school) and Our Lady of Reparation in West Croydon; built Dominican priory at Carisbrooke, Newport, Isle of Wight in 1866; see Peter Clarke, "Life of Elizabeth, Countess of Clare," *Catholic Life*, November 2002, p.50; Peter Clarke, *Ryde to Rome* (2004); Madeleine Beard, Review of *Ryde to Rome*, *Mass of Ages*, November 2004 ("The foundation of the Catholic Church in Ryde was instigated by the holy example of one individual. The Countess of Clare would often see an old man, a gardener..., walking to Mass every Sunday, whatever the weather, to the Catholic church in Newport, some seven miles away. Moved by the Faith of Edward Meehan (1798–1882), the countess wrote to the Bishop of the London District, requesting a priest be sent to Ryde 'to procure the blessings and comforts of Holy Mother Church.' On being told by the Bishop that it was necessary for twelve Catholics to be resident in a town for a priest to be sent, the Countess dismissed four of her servants and replaced them with Catholics to make up the required number").

Clark, Colin Grant – economist; b. 2 December 1905, London; c. 1942; d. 4 September 1989, Brisbane, Australia; although chemist at Oxford, fascinated by economics (influence of G. D. H. Cole and Lionel Robbins); worked with Keynes and Pigou at Cambridge; three unsuccessful attempts to become a Labour MP, but then moved from Fabianism to free market economics; advisor to Queensland government 1937–1952; directorship of the Oxford University Institute for Research in Agricultural Economics 1953–1969; "able to demonstrate agriculture's remarkable capacity to increase food availability to support his contention that 'the earth can feed its people'…. He argued that progress would not be achieved by increased levels of nationally planned investment but by improving skills and fostering incentive. The latter … could only be damaged by attempts to secure welfare improvements by excessive redistribution of wealth" (*DNB*); of his nine children, his son, Gregory Clark, became an Australian diplomat and later Professor of Economics; *see Conditions of Economic Progress* (1957); *DNB* ("His conversion to Catholicism in 1942 provoked his interest in population growth, prompting him to attack Malthusian views. He became a key lay member of the Pope's commission on population (1964–6), from which Humanae Vitae appeared").

Clark, Jonathan Charles Douglas – historian; b. 28 February 1951; c. 2009 (received at St. Mary's Whittingham, England); developed a revisionist approach to seventeenth and eighteenth century British history, opposing Whig and Marxist interpretations; emphasis on the unity of the period between 1660 and 1832, seeing it as an Anglican-Aristocratic hegemony; later interested in the American revolution and then in the religious dimension of history; Joyce and Elizabeth Hall Distinguished Professor of British History at the University of Kansas; see *Samuel Johnson : Literature, Religion, and English Cultural Politics from the Restoration to Romanticism* (1994); *English Society 1660–1832: Religion, Ideology and Politics*

during the Ancien Régime (2000); *Our Shadowed Present: Modernism, Postmodernism and History* (2003).

Clark, Baron Kenneth MacKenzie, OM – art and cultural historian; b. 13 July 1903, 32 Grosvenor Square, London; c. 14 May 1983 (death bed conversion); d. 21 May 1983, Hythe, Kent; father a wealthy Scottish industrialist; educated at Trinity College, Oxford; worked for the art historian Bernard Berenson in Florence; catalogued the Leonardo da Vinci drawings at Windsor Castle; keeper of the department of fine art at the Ashmolean Museum, Oxford, 1931–1934; Director of National Gallery 1934–1945; surveyor of the king's pictures 1934–1944; Slade Professor of Fine Art, Oxford University 1946–1950; Professor of Art History at the Royal Academy; chairman of Art Council 1953–1960; chairman of Independent Television Authority 1954–1957; major influence on British cultural life; made the celebrated TV series *Civilization* (1969); his dictum was "I believe in God because I believe in inspiration"; father of Alan Clark (1928–1999), the politician, historian and diarist (about whom there were reports that he had converted some weeks before his death; this was denied by his wife, there was no reference to it in his diary or journal, and no official record of it); see *Civilization: A Personal View* (1969), especially pp.175–182 ("The great achievements of the Catholic Church lay in harmonizing, humanizing, civilizing the deepest impulses of ordinary, ignorant people. Take the cult of the Virgin. In the early twelfth century the Virgin had been the supreme protectress of civilization. She had taught a race of tough and ruthless barbarians the virtues of tenderness and compassion. The great cathedrals of the Middle Ages were her dwelling places upon earth. In the Renaissance, while remaining the Queen of Heaven, she became also the human mother in whom everyone could recognize qualities of warmth and love and approachability. Now imagine the feelings of a simple hearted man or woman – a Spanish peasant, an Italian artisan – on hearing that the Northern heretics were insulting the Virgin, desecrating her sanctuaries, pulling down or decapitating her images. He must have felt something deeper than shock and indignation: he must have felt that some part of his whole emotional life was threatened. And he would have been right"); *Piero della Francesca* (1951); *The Nude* (1956); *Rembrandt and the Italian Renaissance* (1966); *Looking at Pictures* (1972); *Another Part of the Wood: A Self-Portrait* (1974); *The Other Half: A Self Portrait* (1977); Meryle Secrest, *Kenneth Clark: A Biography* (1984) ("Kenneth Clark asserted that great art could only be understood in terms of a divine source of inspiration. Such paintings were acts of adoration and proof of celestial joy.... [H]e had always believed that, if one accepted that human beings could be inspired, one had to concede a divine source for that inspiration"); *DNB* ("At the close of a crowded memorial service in St James's, Piccadilly, most of the congregation were startled to hear that in the last days of his life he had been received into the Roman Catholic Church"); Charles Moore, "Can K still stand for civilization?" *The Spectator*, 16 October 1993, p.8.

Clark, Mrs. William – c. early October 1877 (received by Fr. H. J. Coleridge, SJ (see below); most of her children were received later); wife of William Robinson Clark, Anglican vicar and Prebendary of Wells; much correspondence with Newman before her conversion regarding the pain she foresaw her husband would feel on her becoming a

Catholic and on the question of conversion and its timing; Newman wrote to tell him of his wife's position as she was afraid to do so; see Stanley L. Jaki, *Newman to Converts: An Existential Ecclesiology* (2001), Ch. 21 ("'You say,' Newman quoted her very words, 'Thank God, I have no longer any doubt about the Catholic faith, I firmly believe Jesus Christ founded One Church, and that the head of the Church is the Pope.' Newman therefore felt obliged to tell her: 'Then you are bound to be received into that Church without delay.' Conscience, as Newman had just set forth in his *Letter to the Duke of Norfolk* 'has rights because it has duties'.... 'You must not become a Catholic merely because you like our doctrines and devotions, but because you believe the Catholic Church to be the Ark of Salvation.'").

Clarke, Richard Frederick, SJ – priest and author; b. 24 January 1839 London; c. 10 July 1869 (received at Farm Street, London, by Fr. H. J. Coleridge, SJ (see below)); d. 10 September 1900, York; Fellow of St. John's College, Oxford 1860–1869; rowed number two in the winning crew at the University Boat Race in 1859; took Anglican orders; joined the Society of Jesus in 1871; ordained priest 22 September 1878; first Master of Campion Hall, Oxford; editor of *The Month* 1882–1893; wrote many books on apologetics, philosophy of religion, and especially prayer and spirituality (series on short meditations on different themes); editor of the Stonyhurst Manuals of Philosophy series; many lectures in Britain and the United States; see *The Existence of God, A Dialogue in Three Chapters* (1887) ("Everywhere around us we perceive effects following from causes and causes producing effects. All the causes which fall within the range of our experience are at the same time both causes and effects.

While they themselves produce some effect, they are also in their turn effects of some cause. They are called subordinate or dependent causes. There is a long series of them; each member of the series is the effect of the preceding member and the cause of the member which follows it. Every cause of which we have any knowledge has this double character. But our reason tells us that this string of causes and effects must be limited at both ends. We see the limit at one end in the ultimate effect present to us. There is no doubt about that, and we cannot help a conviction that, there must be a limit too at the other end, and that we cannot go on from one cause to another *in infinitum...*

Outside the long series of dependent subordinate causes which falls within the range of our experience (whether such a series could be infinite does not matter to our argument) ... there must be a cause which is neither subordinate nor dependent, but in every possible aspect independent and the primary cause of all the rest – in other words, the First Cause, or God"); *Logic* (1889); *Lourdes, and its Miracles* (1889); *The False Decretals* (1892); *Medical Testimony to the Miracles of Lourdes* (1892); *A Pilgrimage to the Holy Coat of Treves* (1892); *Patience* (1893); *Prayer* (1900); Joseph Rickaby, "In Memoriam, Richard Frederick Clarke," *The Month*, October 1900, p.337.

Clayton, James – priest and confessor of the faith; b. in Sheffield; d. 22 July 1588; brought up in the new religion; apprentice to sickle and shear smith; up to this point his education minimal or nonexistent, but then devoted himself to study, resulting in his conversion; went over to English College, Rheims, in 1582; ordained priest in 1585 and sent on the English mission; apprehended just before Christmas 1588 whilst visiting Catholic prisoners in Derby gaol; arraigned and condemned to death for exercising his priestly offices; was either reprieved or his execution delayed, but was kept in prison, where his sufferings produced illness from which he died; see *Gillow*, Vol. I, p.495; *Catholic Encyclopedia*.

Clifford, Thomas, first Baron Clifford of Chudleigh – statesman; b. 1 August 1630, Ugbrook, Devon; c. only finally in 1673; d. 17 October 1673 (rumor of suicide probably a libel); entered Exeter College, Oxford, but expelled for royalist and Anglican views; studied law at Middle Temple; father of fifteen children in happy marriage with Elizabeth Lindridge; attended Charles II in exile; after Restoration represented Totnes in parliament; spoke in favor of royal prerogative, also toleration for Catholics and Protestant dissenters; rewarded with knighthood; distinguished service as volunteer in navy against Dutch; concluded new treaties and alliances with Courts of Denmark and Sweden; Comptroller and then Treasurer of Household; great patron of writers and obtained John Dryden (see below) office of poet laureate in 1670; in 1669 secretary in negotiations with the French, culminating in secret treaty of Dover in May 1670; at this time wished to reconcile Anglicanism with Rome by negotiation and compromise (under influence of Fr. Hugh Cressy, OSB (see below)); tried unsuccessfully to persuade Charles to make a declaration of allegiance to Rome; Privy Councillor and one of Lord Commissioners of Treasury; in 1672 created Baron Clifford of Chudleigh and then Lord High Treasurer of England; both he and his later patron, the Duke of York, were suspected to be privately in communion with the Catholic Church; Test Act was passed, which disabled all Peers from sitting in House of Lords, or bearing any office, who did not renounce by oath Papal ecclesiastical supremacy, transubstantiation, etc.; he consequently resigned; accused of attempting to further popery and arbitrary power, but died before any further persecution; founded one of England's most remarkable noble Catholic families; buried in chapel at Ugbrooke; see *Gillow*, Vol. I, p.512; *DNB*.

Clutton, Henry – architect; b. 19 March 1819, Surrey; c. 1858 (received by Manning at Farm Street, London); d. 27 June 1893, Brookside, Yiewsley, West Drayton, Middlesex; brought up as an Anglican; studied architecture through traveling on the continent; after his conversion he received no more commissions from the Anglican establishment and had to rely on Catholic clients (e.g., he was prevented from completing his restoration of the chapel of All Souls College, Oxford, as the fellows had come to realize that he was a Catholic); husband of Caroline Alice Ryder (1841–1934), daughter of George Dudley Ryder (see below) and Sophia Lucy Ryder (see below); brother-in-law was Cardinal Manning; Cardinal Newman was a family friend; expert in thirteenth century Gothic architecture and fifteenth-century French domestic buildings; built several country houses and Catholic churches; appointed architect for new Westminster Cathedral and spent from 1867 to 1873 on designs before project fell through (eventually built by his former pupil, J. G. Bentley (see above)); his prize-winning design for Brompton Oratory was rejected; buried in the family tomb at Mortlake, Surrey; see *Remarks, with Illustrations, on the Domestic Architecture of France* (1853); *DNB*.

Coetlogon, Colonel Henry Watts Russell de – soldier; b. 1839; c. 1865; d. 1908; served with 15th East Yorkshire and other regiments; then with Generals Hicks and Gordon in Sudan; was acting Governor of Khartoum until Gordon's arrival there; subsequently British Consul for Navigators Islands, New Caledonia, New Hebrides, and finally to States of North Carolina, South Carolina, Georgia and Tennessee.

Coffin, Bishop Robert Aston, CSSR – bishop and ecclesiastical writer; b. 19 July 1819, Brighton; c. 3 December 1845 (younger brother, Edmund, received in 1851); d. 6 April 1885, Redemptorist house of St Joseph at Teignmouth, Devon; from family of great wealth; vicar of St. Mary Magdalen, Oxford 1843–1845; attracted by the Tractarian movement and became follower of Newman; after conversion was tutor for a year to family of Ambrose Phillipps de Lisle (see below) at Grace Dieu Manor near Leicester; joined Oratorian Order; ordained priest 31 October 1847; joined Redemptorist Order in 1850 (provincial 1865–1882); conducted many missions and retreats and founded several houses of the Order; consecrated third Bishop of Southwark in 1882; ascetical writer; made excellent English translations of works of St. Alphonsus Liguori; see Michael Clifton, *A Victorian Convert Quintet* (1998); *Gillow*, Vol. I, p.373; *Catholic Encyclopedia*; *DNB*.

Coleridge, Henry James, SJ – priest, writer and preacher; b. 20 September 1822, London; c. April 1852; d. 13 April 1893, Manresa House, Roehampton; second son of Sir John Taylor Coleridge (1790–1876), Judge of the Court of Queen's Bench; great-nephew of Samuel Taylor Coleridge (1772–1834), poet and philosopher; brother of Lord Coleridge (1820–1894), Lord Chief Justice of England; brother-in-law of Dr. John Fielder Mackarness (1820–1889), Anglican Bishop of Oxford; Fellow of Oriel College, Oxford; received Anglican orders;

came under the influence of the Tractarian movement; ardent disciple of Newman; ordained priest in 1856; entered Society of Jesus; on staff of St. Beuno's College, North Wales 1859–1865; later priest at Farm Street, London; prolific writer mainly on ascetical topics, notably his great work, *The Public Life of Our Lord*; his harmony of the Gospels, *Vita Vitae Nostrae*, was a favorite book for meditation; first Jesuit editor of *The Month*; also editor of *The Messenger*; his remains interred in family vault at Ottery St Mary; see *The Life of Our Life*, 18 Vols. (1876–1892); *The Prisoners of the King: Thoughts on the Catholic Doctrine of Purgatory* (1882); *The Works and Words of our Saviour Gathered from the Four Gospels* (1882); *The Baptism of the King: Considerations on the Sacred Passion* (1884); *The Mother of the King: Mary During the Life of Our Lord* (1886); *The Mother of the Church: Mary During the First Apostolic Age* (1887); *Catholic Encyclopedia*; *DNB*.

Colleton (Collinton), John – priest; b. 1548, Milverton, Somerset; c. 1571 (later he reconciled his father to the old faith); d. 29 October 1635, Well Hall, Eltham, Kent, home of recusant Sir William Roper; grew up Protestant; influenced to convert by fellow students at Oxford, who put forward arguments against the Reformation that he was unable to answer; retired to Louvain intending to join Carthusian Order, but ill-health and melancholic disposition forced him to withdraw from novitiate; entered English College, Douai, in 1576; ordained priest 16 June 1576; sent on the English mission in July 1576; in 1581 taken prisoner, arraigned and tried, with Saint Edmund Campion (see above) and others, for conspiracy against queen and government; acquitted on account of evidence as to time and place of conspiracy being inconsistent, but detained in

Tower, then Marshalsea, and then banished; returned to England in 1587; worked in London and Kent; involved in appellant or archpriest controversy, 1598–1602, in which he took appellants' side; confined in the Clink prison, Southwark, for several years and in the New prison until finally released; his character straightforward and esteemed both by moderate party of Established Church and by James I, who relied on his sincerity in issues concerning Catholics; buried in churchyard of Eltham parish; see *Gillow*, Vol. I, p.538; *DNB*.

Collins, Dorothy Edith – secretary; b. 1894; c. 1932; d. 1989, Top Meadow, Beaconsfield; secretary to G. K. Chesterton (see above), though treated more like a daughter; through sheer lack of organization Chesterton was not infrequently late for, and sometimes completely missed, speaking engagements; not until 1926, when he employed her as his first trained secretary, that anything approaching order was brought out of chaos of Chesterton's working life; remained his secretary throughout his life, and also a great friend to Frances Chesterton; after G. K. Chesterton's death, continued to edit and publish collections of his writings and made the papers available to any scholars who wanted to study them; cremated and her ashes buried in the same grave as Chesterton and his wife; see Ian Boyd CSB., "Dorothy Edith Collins (1894–1988): Requiescat in Pace," *Chesterton Review*, November 1988, p.591.

Collinson, James – genre painter and poet; b. 9 May 1825, Mansfield, near Nottingham; c. 1848; d. 24 January 1881, 16 Paulet Road, Camberwell; shy and nervous young man who suffered from narcolepsy; one of seven founders of Pre-Raphaelite Brotherhood 1848–1850; when Millais' painting *Christ in* *the House of his Parents* was accused of blasphemy, Collinson resigned from the Brotherhood in the belief that it was bringing the Christian religion into disrepute; drawn to the Oxford Movement; proposed marriage to Christina Rossetti, the poet, who rejected offer because he had converted; she accepted him when he went back to High Anglicanism, but cancelled their wedding plans when he reverted to his Catholic faith in 1850; entered Jesuit college at Stonyhurst to prepare for priesthood, but later abandoned that training and returned to painting; in 1858 married Eliza Alvinia Henrietta Ann Wheeler, a Catholic, sister-in-law of Collinson's friend, the Catholic artist, John Rogers Herbert (see below); exhibited regularly at Royal Academy, British Institution and Society of British Artists; see Georgina Battiscombe, *Christina Rossetti: A Divided Life* (1981), pp.43–48; David Jones, "James Collinson – Catholic Pre-Raphaelite Brother," *Catholic Life*, January 2002, p.28; *DNB*.

Colman (Coleman), Blessed Edward – lay courtier and martyr; b. 17 May 1636, Brent Eleigh, Suffolk; c. early 1660s at Cambridge University; d. 3 December 1678, Tyburn; son of Anglican clergyman; very fine scholar at Cambridge; left Cambridge after his conversion and became secretary to the Duchess of York in which post he gave service to the Duke (whose Catholicity was suspected); named as one of conspirators in "Popish Plot" in 1678; tried for corresponding with foreign powers for purpose of subverting Protestant religion, and for complicity in a resolution to assassinate the king; he replied that letters only a scheme of his own to procure liberty of conscience for Catholics to be forwarded in parliament; evidence of conspiracy was given by Titus Oates himself and another rogue, William Bedloe; convicted, and hanged, drawn and quartered at Tyburn; charismatic advocate for the Catholic faith, influencing several highly publicized conversions (possibly including the Duke of York's); his body was buried on unconsecrated ground next to St Giles-in-the-Fields; his wife, who survived him, is believed to have committed suicide several years later; see *Gillow*, Vol. I, p.532; *Catholic Encyclopedia*; *DNB*.

Constable, Henry – poet and polemicist; b. 1562, Newark-on-Trent; c. 1591; d. 9 October 1613; from a distinguished family; after Cambridge University, he acted as gentleman-spokesman for the Protestant cause in Paris 1583–1585; a favorite of Elizabeth I and wrote texts in support of Protestantism; specialized in sonnets, particularly a series of twenty-three under the title of *Diana*; later lived abroad, mainly in France; declared himself a Catholic in 1591; worked for the welfare of English Catholics by trying to get Henri IV of France to get Elizabeth to be more tolerant to recusants; made attempts to convert James VI of Scotland and wrote on theology; after his return to England he was imprisoned in the Tower in 1604 and then confined to his own house and deprived of his inheritance; returned to Paris in 1610; went to Liège in 1613 to try to convert Dr. Benjamin Carier (see above), a Protestant divine, and died there; see George Wickes, "Henry Constable, Poet and Courtier, 1562–1613," *Biographical Studies* (1954); John Bossy, "A Propos of Henry Constable," *Recusant History*, April 1962, p.228; *Gillow*, Vol. I, p.532; *DNB* ("He was a notable Roman Catholic convert, who abandoned his home and inheritance to use his family's high standing and his own popularity at court to promote in tracts, disputations, and personal contact the controversial position that devout Roman Catholics could be loyal subjects of the English crown").

Cooper, Thompson – biographer and journalist; b. 8 January 1837, Cambridge; d. 5 March 1904, 38 Loughborough Road, Brixton, London; educated at a private school and articled to his father, Charles Henry Cooper (1808–1866), a solicitor and noted antiquary; inherited from his father a love of biographical and antiquarian research; elected Fellow of the Society of Antiquaries at the age of twenty-three; became a Catholic early in life; published two volumes of *Athenae Cantabrigienses* (memoirs of eminent Cambridge alumni); journalist with the *Daily Telegraph*, then *The Times*, mainly as a parliamentary reporter; associated with the *Dictionary of National Biography* from its start, writing 1423 entries, many more than anyone else; wrote a *Biographical Dictionary* (1873), then a series of profiles, *Men of Mark* (1876–1883) and *Men of the Time* (1872–1884); many contributions to *Notes and Queries* from the age of sixteen until his death; buried in Norwood cemetery, London; see *DNB*.

Copeman, Frederick – political and religious activist; b. 1 March 1907, near Beccles, Suffolk; c. Christmas Midnight Mass, 1946 (received with his wife, Kitty and three daughters); born and brought up in the workhouse and rebelled against injustices; when in navy he played a leading role in mutiny of British sailors at Invergordon in 1931; Communist activist who led hunger marches and riots in England; commanded 16th and 54th Battalions of International Brigade during Spanish Civil War when seriously injured; work in London air raids won him OBE; later in disgust at Communist techniques ("All for the Party"), renounced his membership of party and led British trades unionists against Communists; author and lecturer; see *Reason in Revolt*

(1948); Matthew Hoehn, OSB (ed), *Catholic Authors* (1952) ("The beauty of the Church is that it gives the teaching of one God, whilst enabling and in fact demanding that individuals be masters of their own soul and responsible for the actions they take.... In my political work ... my Christian experience has given me a fresh dynamic, to understand politics as morality enlarged and the Christian expression of the art of government").

Copleston, Frederick Charles SJ ("Freddie") – priest and philosopher; b. 10 April 1907, Claremont, Trull, near Taunton, Somerset; c. July 1925; d. 3 February 1994, London; brought up in family with strong Anglican roots; entered the Society of Jesus in 1930; ordained priest in 1937; Professor of Philosophy and History of Philosophy; writer and broadcaster (two famous radio debates with Bertrand Russell on the existence of God, and with A. J. Ayer on logical positivism); author of nine-volume history of philosophy; Gifford lecturer 1979–1981; buried in Kensal Green cemetery, London; see *A History of Philosophy*, 9 Vols. (1944–1975); *St. Thomas and Nietzsche* (1955); *Contemporary Philosophy: Studies of Logical Positivism and Existentialism* (1973); *Religion and Philosophy* (1974); *Aquinas* (1975); *Philosophers and Philosophies* (1976); *On the History of Philosophy and Other Essays* (1980); *Philosophies and Cultures* (1980); *Memoirs of a Philosopher* (1988) ("While zealously exploring the local variants of High Church practice, I could not help becoming aware that in the dim background there lurked a Church which was not only the real source of the ceremonies and ritual which at that time appealed to me but also represented authority.... It seemed to me that if Christ was truly the Son of God and if he founded a Church to teach all nations in his name, it must be a Church teaching with authority, as her Master did.... One could not decide between doctrines relating to the transcendent by empirical testing. Either one should adopt an agnostic attitude or one should invoke divine revelation mediated by a teaching institution which was divinely protected from error"; Christopher Howse, "A philosopher's testimony" in *The Tablet*, 8 December 1984, p.1230; Gerard J. Hughes (ed), *The Philosophical Assessment of Theology: Essays in Honour of Frederick C. Copleston* (1987); William Doino, "A Jesuit and His Faith: Frederick C. Copleston, SJ (1907–1994)," *Sursum Corda*, Fall 1996; Matthew Hoehn, OSB (ed), *Catholic Authors* (1952); *DNB*.

Corby (Corbie), Gerard – Catholic exile; b. 1558, Hett, County Durham; d. 18 September 1637, Watten; mother a Catholic recusant, but he was brought up a Protestant; converted to the Catholic faith as a result of meeting missionary priests; his wife Isabella, *née* Richardson (1552–25 November 1652), also a convert; they went to live in exile in County Kildare, Ireland; in the service of Lady Kildare; seven children, four sons and three daughters; three of their sons, Ambrose (1604–1649), Ralph (Bl. Ralph Corby (1598–1644), executed at Tyburn) and Robert, joined the Society of Jesus and were ordained priests; the fourth son died when a student at the Jesuit college at St. Omer; two of the daughters, May and Catharine, became Benedictine nuns at Brussels (the eldest daughter died in infancy); at length they went into permanent exile in the Spanish Netherlands and agreed to separate and consecrate themselves to religion; he entered the novitiate of the Society of Jesus at Watten as a lay brother in 1628; in 1633 (at the age of eighty) she became a professed Benedictine nun at Ghent, where

she died at the age of one hundred; see *Gillow*, Vol. I, p.563; *DNB*.

Coren, Michael – writer and broadcaster; b. 15 January 1959, Essex; c. 1986 (evangelical Christian in 1990s, then came back to the Catholic Church 5 July 2004); raised in secular home; family Jewish on his father's side (maternal grandfather also converted to Judaism); moved to Canada in 1987; columnist for *Toronto Sun* and successful television and radio broadcaster; staunchly pro-life (referred in an article to abortion clinics as "abortuaries"); social conservative; writer of biographies; major religious influences St. Thomas More, Ronald Knox (see below), C. S. Lewis, and his godfather, Lord Longford (see below); see *Gilbert: The Man Who Was G. K. Chesterton* (1989); *The Invisible Man: The Life and Liberties of H. G. Wells* (1993); *Conan Doyle* (1995); *The Man Who Created Narnia: The Story of C. S. Lewis* (1996); *J. R. R. Tolkien: The Man Who Created The Lord of the Rings* (2001); column, *Toronto Sun*, 11 September 2004 ("Please do not tell me about historical failings or current lapses because I've heard them all. I've met lapsed Catholics and lousy Catholics as well as good Catholics and glorious Catholics. Not relevant. It is the truth of a belief, not the failure or success of alleged followers to live up to that truth, that is of importance. I'm a miserable sinner. But at least I know it. Please pray for me. Or, if you can't, at least tolerate me"); correspondence with John Beaumont: "Reasons for conversion: G. K. Chesterton, C. S. Lewis (Anglican but I have no doubt where he'd be today), Lord Longford, who was my Godfather, and someone called Paul Goodman, who is now a Tory MP in the UK and one of my closest friends"; "Pope states obvious," *Toronto Sun*, 14 July 2007 ("The rallying cry of the liberal, modernist world. 'I'm offended. Please feel my pain. I'm offended.' Which is precisely what various critics, some of them conservative evangelical Christians, said this week when Pope Benedict XVI merely clarified and emphasized Roman Catholic teaching concerning the truth of Catholicism and the place of non-Catholics. The leader of the Roman Catholic Church had the audacity to say that, wait for it, Roman Catholicism was right. But in the 21st century it is not nice for anybody to say that truth is truth and therefore lack of truth is lack of truth. Everything has to be tolerated. Apart, of course, from intolerance. Unless the intolerant ones are homosexual activists, pro-abortion students or leftist zealots banning and silencing their critics. Just in case any of us are foolish enough to believe the headlines, all the Pope said was that the full understanding of Jesus Christ and the road to salvation is to be found within Catholicism. Anyone who is baptized is still a Christian and non-Christians are also loved by God. Neither of these groups are, contrary to what some pundits yelled, condemned to hell. But the Church, the Pope continued, offers the Eucharist, the body and blood of Jesus. This and Papal supremacy and the Sacraments make it unique. Not particularly surprising. What, one wonders, did people expect the Pope to say? 'Well, Catholicism is quite fun but then so is Islam. I also hear that Hindus have great parties and as for Zoroastrianism, it's really cool, man.' Give us a break here. He's a Catholic. He's the Catholic! Nobody is obliged to be Catholic, but if they say they are they should live as though they are. Which means they have to observe Catholic teaching. Requiring that they know what Catholic teaching is in the first place. It's precisely because so many Catholics have been confused by decades of dreadful education and poor formation that they need reminding of basic Catholicism. Who better to do that than the Pope? One of the reasons his latest statement has caused offence is because so many people, Catholic or otherwise, have all too often lost any sense of what constitutes a claim to truth. Not that it's a difficult concept. If I believe in the exclusive truth of something, I cannot believe in the exclusive truth of something that contradicts it"); *As I See It* (2009).

Corker, James, OSB (name in religion Maurus) – priest; b. 1636, Yorkshire; c. 1656; d. 22 December 1715, Paddington, London; son of vicar of Bradford and brought up Anglican; reacted against father's actions as a spy against royalty during interregnum; after conversion admitted to English Benedictine Abbey at Lambspring, Germany; taught for some years before being sent to the mission in Benedictine South Province in 1665; chaplain to a distinguished widow, Frances Cotton, until 1677; later chaplain to Queen Catherine of Braganza; when mentioned in Titus Oates' narrative as being involved in that supposed plot went into hiding for several months; apprehended and committed to Newgate; tried in 1679 for endeavoring to raise rebellion, subvert Government, introduce popery, and conspiracy to murder the king; found not guilty by jury after vigorous defense of himself; detained in custody because of his religious profession and indicted again for receiving orders under authority of See of Rome; convicted and sentenced to death, but reprieved and detained in Newgate (during which time he was installed as President-General of English Benedictines); during time in prison he received over a thousand people into the Catholic Church; released by James II in 1685; responsible for receiving poet John Dryden (see below) into the Catholic Church in 1685; worked many years in London for the poor; in Newgate he formed close friendship with martyr, St. Oliver Plunkett, Archbishop of Armagh; in 1683 responsible for exhumation of quartered remains of Plunkett and supervised their transfer to Lambspring; on release from prison received by king at court as resident ambassador of Elector of Cologne; in 1688 Revolution forced to seek refuge on the Continent; in 1690 elected Abbot of Lambspring; in 1695 resigned and returned to England where he remained until his death; interred at St. Pancras; see *Roman Catholic Principles with Reference to God and King* (1680); *A Rational Account given by a Young Gentleman to his Uncle of the Motives and Reasons why he is become a Roman Catholick* (1698); T. A. Birrell, "James Maurus Corker and Dryden's Conversion," *English Studies*, Vol. 54 (1973), p.461 ("*A Rational Account* is a short pamphlet, in the form of an imaginary letter from a recently converted Catholic to his Protestant uncle, in which the nephew sets out his motives for his recent conversion. The line of argument of the nephew is remarkably brief. His reason shows him the insufficiency of reason as the rule of faith, and his reason shows him the necessity of a Church; that Church cannot be the Church of England (and the same may be said of the Presbyterian, Anabaptist or other Dissenting Churches) because it did not exist before the Reformation"); *Gillow*, Vol. I, p.568; *Catholic Encyclopedia*; *DNB*.

Cornwell, Peter – priest and writer; b. 19 May 1934; c. 12 July 1985 (wife, Hilary, received in 1996); former Anglican minister and chaplain at Oxford University; ordained Catholic priest 1988; see *One Step Enough* (1986) ("The reasons for my decision are inevitably complex but, at the heart of it, lies a growing conviction that the Christian enterprise is

not a book or a club for religious do-it-yourself enthusiasts but a movement, a stream of life passing through different ages and cultures. In mid-stream are those Christians in communion with the Bishop of Rome. That stream has encountered log-jams of rubbish, the product of human sin and inertia. So I can understand frustrated reformers who have felt compelled to divert from the main stream. Yet I have come to see that such separation is ultimately destructive and diminishing. Christian creativity lies in unity.... I can no longer see any reason of substance and principle to hold apart from the main-stream. Life is too short, the Gospel too precious, the human issues too serious to waste time thinking up reasons for preserving division"); *On The River's Edge* (1988); John Haldane, "In Retreat from Historical Faith," *Contemporary Review*, 1989, p.316 ("In the same month that the Pope visited Holland and the Bishop of Durham again gave public voice to his version of the Creed, the Anglican vicar of the University Church of St. Mary's, Oxford announced his intention to seek membership of the Roman Catholic Church and thereby followed in the pathway trodden by one of his predecessors in the post, viz. John Henry Newman. It is no accident that among the reasons he is quoted as having given for his decision is his search for a church equipped to say: 'This is the faith of the Church whatever professor X or Y says it is'").

Cottington, Francis, first Baron Cottington of Hanworth – diplomat and politician; b. about 1579, Godminster, near Pitcombe, Somerset; c. 1651/2 (in 1607 in Spain unsuccessful attempt to convert him by Fr. Joseph Creswell, who knew of his younger brother Edward's Jesuit training; little evidence to support the claim that he converted during periods of illness in 1623 and in 1630s);

d. 19 June 1652, Valladolid, Spain; educated privately; in 1605 entered service of Sir Charles Cornwallis, English ambassador at Madrid; under James I made clerk in council; ambassador to Spain 1616–1622; on return made secretary to Prince Charles in 1623 and created a Baronet; under Charles I was Under Treasurer and Chancellor of Exchequer; ambassador to Spain 1629–1631; one of Commissioners of Treasury during king's progress through Scotland; became Lord Treasurer at start of Civil War; oversaw surrender of Oxford, leaving city with rest of court; most of his property appropriated by parliament; left England and resided in Rouen; sent on a mission to Court of Spain to solicit financial assistance for royalist cause from Philip IV, but failed; spent last few months of his life in Valladolid; able statesman and fine linguist; buried in chapel of English College, Valladolid, but in 1678 remains reburied beside those of his wife in St Paul's Chapel, Westminster Abbey; see *Gillow*, Vol. I, p.576; *DNB*.

Cowans, Sir John Steven ("Jack") – army officer; b. 11 March 1862, Woodbank, St Cuthbert Without, Carlisle; c. 11 April 1921; d. 16 April 1921, Villa Louise, Garavan, Menton, south of France; went to the Royal Military College, Sandhurst (passed out near top of list); passed Staff College course with distinction in 1890; served in India for several years; made colonel in 1903; in 1912 appointed quartermaster general (supreme administrator of the supply services of the army); pioneer in enlarging the quartermaster-general's functions in mass warfare; his reputation survived criticisms arising from the support he gave Mrs. Patrick Campbell, the actress, in her pursuit of grievances against two officers and recommendation of another for promotion, leading to accusations of

jobbery and "petticoat influence"; he was a new type of military leader, a preeminent military administrator with little experience of the battlefield; made general in 1919; converted five days before his death; lay in state in Westminster Cathedral; buried in Kensal Green cemetery, London; four years after his death his name was dragged into a lurid alimony case, Dennistoun v. Dennistoun (1925), when Mrs. Dorothy Dennistoun testified that he was her lover; see Desmond Chapman-Huston and Owen Rutter, *General Sir John Cowans GCB GCMG: the Quartermaster General of the Great War*, 2 Vols. (1924); *DNB*.

Craigie, Pearl (*née* Richards) (*pseud.* John Oliver Hobbes) – novelist and playwright; b. 3 November 1867, Boston, Massachusetts; c. 5 July 1892; d. 13 August 1906; brought up in upper middle-class American Protestant family (father a Calvinist), which settled in London immediately after her birth; voracious independent reader; disastrous marriage to Reginald Walpole Craigie (1860–1930), a man about town; she obtained a legal separation; on conversion she adopted the name Mary-Teresa and took vow of celibacy; significantly influenced by Oscar Wilde; wrote several novellas, novels and plays, which were great successes; in later works religious element was more and more prominent (e.g., *The School For Saints* (1897); *Robert Orange* (1900)); contributor to *The Times, The Fortnightly Review, The Anglo-Saxon Review* and *The North-American Review*; conversationalist and hostess; many platonic friendships with men (notably with Bishop William Brown (see above) and Lord Curzon, whose memorial address depicted how "in a time of trouble she found refuge in the Roman Catholic Faith ... and a solace in its authority"); see William Archer, *Real Conversations* (1904)

(Conversation with Mrs. Craigie: "Has it ever struck you that the Church of Rome, which alone among the Churches of Western Europe enjoins and enforces continual examinations of conscience, is the real creator of modern analytical fiction?"); M. D. Harding, *Air-Bird in the Water: The Life and Works of Pearl Craigie (John Oliver Hobbes)* (1996); *Catholic Encyclopedia; DNB* ("Certain themes resonated more and more firmly as their author matured: individual responsibility for one's fate; love as the primal force and the great educator; the importance of rational, unselfish love and the dangers of sentimentality, hypocrisy, and egotism; the inevitability of suffering; the necessity of renunciation, courage, and compassion; the strong vocational attractions of art and religion; and an unmilitant, apolitical feminism—a feminism based on a belief in women's worth, intelligence, and right to a good education and financial independence, but also on a conviction of women's essential psychological difference from men").

Crashaw, Richard – poet and divine; b. 1612/3, London; c. by 1645; d. 1648, Loreto, Italy; son of preacher of Established Church who was very anti-papal; in 1633 published volume of Latin poems, in one of which ("Sacred Epigram") occurs well-known reference to the miracle of conversion of water into wine: "Nympha pudica Deum viditet erubuit," translated by John Dryden when a schoolboy as "The conscious water saw its God and blushed" (though literally "The chaste nymph saw …"); Fellow of Peterhouse College, Cambridge; associated himself with Laudianism; entered into Anglican orders and became popular preacher; remembered for his devotional poems, many in Latin; ejected from University in 1644 for refusing to subscribe to the Covenant; after converting went to France and lived in poverty; influence of Queen Henrietta Maria procured him post of secretary to Cardinal Palotto; later canon of the Cathedral of Loreto; skilled in music and drawing, and was fine linguist; great admirer of St. Teresa of Avila who inspired some of his best poetry; in later life, became more mystical; buried in Loreto; his motto was "Live, Jesus, live, and let it be my life to die for love of Thee"; see Abraham Cowley (1618–1667), "Ode on the death of Richard Crashaw" ("Poet and Saint! To thee alone are given/ The two most sacred names of earth and heaven"); Edward Hutton, *The English Poems of Richard Crashaw* (1901) ("Crashaw's religion does not seem to have been so much a matter about which it was possible to argue, not so much a matter of difference in belief or creed between the opinions he held when 'he was among the Protestants' and after he became a Roman Catholic; it does not seem to have been an act of faith, or credulity, so much as an attitude of mind, a coloring of his spirit that he was probably born with, and that no amount of fortune, good or bad, no influence exercised by his father over him could ever have changed. He was born to appreciate and care strongly for those things which the Romanists, as distinct from any other body of Christians, express most perfectly"); E. I. Watkin, *Richard Crashaw, 1612–1649* (1933); Rev. C. J. Curtin, "Crashaw: A Great Religious Poet," *Irish Ecclesiastical Record*, September 1948, p.816; R. V. Young, *Richard Crashaw and the Spanish Golden Age* (1982); R. V. Young, *Doctrine and Devotion in Seventeenth-Century Poetry* (2000); R. V. Young, "John Donne, Richard Crashaw, and the Mystery of God's Grace," *Catholic Dossier*, March/April 2002; Alan Frost, "Richard Crashaw," *Catholic Life*, August 2007, p.60; *Gillow*, Vol. I, p.584; *Catholic Encyclopedia; DNB*.

Craven, Augustus – diplomat and writer; b. 1806; c. 1834; d. 1884; illegitimate son of Keppel Richard Craven (1779–1857) of the court of Queen Caroline, consort of George IV; private secretary to Lord Palmerston (1784–1865), then successively *attaché* of Naples, Paris and Brussels; *chargé d'affaires* at Darmstadt; translated Lord Bulwer and Evelyn Ashley's *Life of Palmerston* into French, and at the request of Queen Victoria made an abridged translation into French of the *Life of the Prince Consort*; husband of Pauline Craven (*née* de La Ferronnays) (1808–1891), authoress and from a family of Catholics who had taken refuge in England after losing their estates in the French Revolution (chief work, *Recit d'une Soeur*); see *Catholic Encyclopedia* (entry for Mrs. Augustus Craven); *DNB* (entry for Pauline Craven).

Crawford, Virginia Mary (*née* Smith) – writer and social worker; b. 20 November 1862, Gosforth House, Northumberland; c. 4 February 1889; d. 19 October 1948, 48 Holland Park, London; daughter of Newcastle shipping magnate; educated by Calvinist governess; traveled widely from early age; wife of Donald Crawford MP (1837–1919); party in divorce case relating to Sir Charles Dilke when she named Dilke as her lover; in the process she ruined Dilke's career, discredited her family and made herself a social outcast; later influenced by *The Confessions of St. Augustine*; Cardinal Manning became her firm friend and mentor before her conversion; friend of Wilfrid Meynell (see below) and of George Moore; wrote books on art, foreign literature, and social issues; contributed more than 130 articles to periodicals between 1895 and 1947; very active member of Catholic Guardian's Association and untiring worker in cause of Poor Law Reform; co-founder of the Catholic Social Guild in 1909; first woman labour councillor on Marylebone Borough Council; supporter of women's suffrage; helped to aid the plight of unmarried mothers; after conversion she led exemplary single life and followed Franciscan ideal, becoming a Franciscan tertiary; see *Ideals of Charity* (1908), *The Church and the Worker* (1916); *Catholic Social Doctrine, 1891–1931* (1933); Francis Bywater, "Cardinal Manning and the Dilke Divorce Case," *Chesterton Review*, November 1992, p.539; Robin Gard, "The Cardinal and the Penitent: Cardinal Manning and Virginia Crawford," in Sheridan Gilley (ed), *Victorian Churches and Churchmen: Essays presented to Vincent Alan McClelland* (2005), Ch. 3; *DNB*.

Crawley, George John Lloyd, OMI – priest; c. March 1851 (received by Newman); d. 8 November 1874; formerly Anglican curate at St. Saviour's, Leeds, founded by Dr. Pusey to exhibit impact of Anglican Church upon the masses of the working population in large towns; High Church practices took place there (see entry for Thomas Minster); influenced by the Tractarian movement; joined Missionary Congregation of Oblates of Mary Immaculate in 1856; ordained priest; see *Reasons for Leaving the Church of England: A Letter to a Late Parishioner* (1852); *Gillow*, Vol. I, p.588.

Cressy, Hugh Paulinus Serenus, OSB – priest; b. 1605, at Thorp Salvin, Yorkshire; c. 21 July 1646, Rome; d. 10 August 1674, East Grinstead, Sussex; father a King's Bench Judge; Fellow of Merton College, Oxford; took Anglican orders; chaplain to Thomas, Lord Wentworth; traveled through Europe, giving him opportunity to inquire into the Catholic religion, which resulted in his public renunciation in the offices of the

Inquisition in Rome of Protestantism; Queen Henrietta Maria provided him with means to go to Douai, where he entered Benedictine Order; sent to the English mission in 1656; chaplain to Charles II's wife, the Infanta of Portugal; wrote several controversial, devotional and historical works; preserved the work of the early English mystics; association with Vincent Canes (see above) and Thomas Clifford (see above); see *Exomologesis* (1647) (on motives of his conversion); *Gillow*, Vol. I, p.592; *Catholic Encyclopedia*; *DNB* ("The present Roman Catholick religion hath from the beginning, without interruption or change, been professed in this our island").

Croft (Crofts, Craftes), Sir Herbert – administrator and landowner; b. c.1565; c. 1617; d. 1 April 1629, St. Gregory's monastery, Douai; heir to Croft Castle, Herefordshire, an ancient family seat; sat in parliament in later part of Elizabeth I's reign; served with Robert Dudley, Earl of Leicester, in the Netherlands 1585–1586; knighted by James I in 1603; left England in 1617 for France and then the Spanish Netherlands where he converted to the Catholic faith; he had professed Protestantism for fifty-two years before his conversion; went to Rome, then retired to St. Omer in 1619; in 1626 admitted as lay brother at the English Benedictine Monastery of St. Gregory, Douai; spent the rest of his life in recollection and strict religious observance; wrote several works justifying his own conversion and encouraging his family to convert; one son knighted and colonel during the Civil War, the other, also Herbert, converted in 1619 and joined the Society of Jesus, but later returned to the Church of England and became Anglican Bishop of Hereford as reward for his activities against Catholics; see *Arguments to Show that the Church in Communion with the See of Rome is the True*

Church (1619); *Gillow*, Vol. I, p.597; *DNB*.

Crofton, Morgan William – mathematician; b. 26 June 1826, Dublin, Ireland; c. 15 July 1851 (received by Newman); d. 13 May 1915, 23 Montpelier Place, Brighton, Sussex; eldest of twelve children of William Crofton (1795–1851), rector of Established Church; very much influenced by Newman; successively Professor of Natural Philosophy (Physics) at the Queen's College, Galway and Professor of Mathematics at Catholic University College, Dublin; leading authority on geometric probability; author of scientific and philosophical essays; of his five children one, Fr. William John Camille Crofton, SJ (1858–1940), rector of St. Aloysius' College, Glasgow, teacher and astronomer within the Jesuit Order; another child became a nun; brother, Henry (1827–1894), made his career in the Established Church; see obituary in *The Tablet*, 22 May 1915, p.662 ("[H]e remained to the end a staunch and uncompromising Catholic, singularly pious and devout in his bearing and in his habits"); *DNB*.

Crombie, Alistair Cameron – historian and philosopher of science; b. 4 November 1915, Brisbane, Australia; c. 1944 (his wife, Nancy (1914–1993), received earlier in same year ("she first and he later 'with difficulty'" (*DNB*)); d. 9 February 1996, Orchard Lea, Boars Hill, Oxford; central interests were the methods and modes of scientific thinking and reasoning in medieval and early modern Europe, also on Galileo; cofounder of British Society for the History of Science in 1964, and of British Society for the Philosophy of Science; President of Académie Internationale d'Histoire des Sciences 1968–1971; buried beside his wife at Ramsgill church, Yorkshire; see *The Classics of*

Science (1951); *Augustine to Galileo: the History of Science, AD 400–1650* (1952); *DNB*.

Cronin, Archibald Joseph ("A. J. Cronin") – writer; b. 19 July 1896, Cardross, Dumbartonshire, Scotland; d. 6 January 1981, Glion, near Montreux, Switzerland; mother was devout Catholic; for many years he was agnostic; reverted to the faith; qualified as doctor; medical inspector of mines for Great Britain; became full time writer of novels, often containing religious themes and matters of conscience (e.g., *Hatters Castle* (1931) (made him famous overnight), *The Citadel* (1937), *Keys of the Kingdom* (1942); *The Spanish Gardner* (1950)); great narrative and descriptive skill; lived in United States during World War II, then in Switzerland; several of his books made into films; collection of short stories, *Adventures of a Black Bag* (1969), was made into very popular television and radio series *Dr. Finlay's Casebook*; eldest son, Vincent, writer; buried at La Tour de Peilzsee; see Fr. Charles P. Connor, *Classic Catholic Converts* (2001), pp.206–207; Alan Frost, "A. J. Cronin – Catholic Author," *Catholic Life*, June 2008, p.56; *DNB*.

Currie, William Bertram Wodehouse – banker and politician; b. 25 November 1827; c. late October 1896 (his wife, Caroline Louisa, *pseud.* Minima Parspartis (1837–1902), author of *Some Sidelights on the Oxford Movement* (1895), received in 1862; d. 29 December 1896; second son of Raikes Currie (1801–1881); brother of Philip Henry Wodehouse Currie (1834–1906), diplomat; contributed significantly to English political life; MP for Northampton; President of City of London Liberal Association; close friend of Gladstone; financed Manchester Ship Canal in late 1880s; lived at Coombe Warren, Surrey,

immortalized in *The Forsyte Saga*; until his last year, when he was informed that his cancer was fatal, he had moved from superficial Anglican religious observance into confirmed agnosticism, but his religious testimony which he wrote at this time has the hallmark of sincerity; see *The Conversion Testimony of Bertram Wodehouse Currie*, November 1896 (quoted in the article by John Powell, referred to below: "I had long been of opinion that the world was tending towards Agnosticism on the one hand, and Catholicism on the other, and that the other religions had a much less logical basis on which to rest than the Catholic Church, whose ubiquity, uniformity, and piety had long been the wonder of the world. She at any rate speaks with authority, and her authority is the same wherever she speaks. I admit that, to one who has contemned religion as I have done, and who has been wanting in reverence for all kinds of authority, the struggle is a hard one, but being firmly convinced that my former opinions were utterly wrong, and that most of my bad actions proceeded from irreligion and want of reverence, I thought it best to join a Church which represents the principle of authority in its highest form. I endeavor humbly to accept its dogmas, and to submit to its teaching on spiritual things"); Louisa Currie, *Bertram Wodehouse Currie: A Memorial* (1897); Caroline Louisa Currie (ed), *Bertram Wodehouse Currie, 1827–1896, Recollections, Letters and Journals* (1901); John Powell, "Testimony in High Places: The Conversion of Bertram Wodehouse Currie," *Recusant History*, October 1988, p.198; *DNB*.

Custance, Olive (*pseud.* "Opals") – poet; b. 7 February 1874; c. 1924; d. 12 February 1944, Viceroy Lodge, Hove, Sussex; daughter of Col. Frederic Hambledon Custance; on 4 March 1902 married Lord Alfred Douglas (see below) with whom she eloped in 1901; radiant beginning to their relationship, but separated ten years after their marriage (though remained respectful of each other); poet caught up in the concerns of her generation, resulting in her tackling decadent themes; three years after converting she lapsed from the faith, something about which she expressed her deep regret five weeks before her death; see Brocard Sewell, *Olive Custance: Her Life and Work* (1975); Brocard Sewell, *Like Black Swans: Some People and Themes* (1982), Ch. 5; *DNB*.

Dalbiac, Lieutenant-General Sir James Charles – army officer; b. 1776, Hungerford Park, Berkshire; c. 1843 (received with his wife, Lady Susanna Isabella Dalbiac); d. 8 December 1847, at his chambers in the Albany, London; spent his whole military life in 4th Light Dragoons rising to Major-General; took part in famous charges at Talavera in Portugal (1809) and at battle of Salamanca (1812); commanded Goojerat district of the Bombay Army 1822–1824; knighted 1831 by William IV; Conservative MP for Ripon 1835–1837; see *DNB* ("Napier commemorated not only this charge [at Salamanca], but the conduct of Mrs. Dalbiac at the battle: 'An English lady of a gentle disposition, and possessing a very delicate frame, had braved the dangers and endured the privations of two campaigns.... In this battle, forgetful of everything but the strong affection which had so long supported her, she rode deep amidst the enemy's fire, trembling, yet irresistibly impelled forwards by feelings more imperious than terror, more piercing than the fear of death'").

Dalgairns, John Dobrée (name in religion Bernard) – priest and scholar; b. 21 October 1818, Guernsey; c. 29 September 1845 (received by Bl. Dominic Barberi at Aston Hall; his sister, Elizabeth, wife of Robert Ornsby (see below), was received in 1848); d. 6 April 1876, Burgess Hill, near Brighton; brought up Anglican; friend of Newman at Oxford University, where he became a member of radical wing of the Oxford Movement; first to reside with Newman at Littlemore; studied for the priesthood at Langres, France; ordained priest 19 December 1846; one of original Oratorian community and arguably its finest scholar; followed Frederick Faber (see below) to London to found London Oratory; in 1863 succeeded Faber as second Superior; an Ultramontane; prepared George Robinson, first Marquess of Ripon (see below) for his reception into the Catholic Church in 1874; author of several mystical and metaphysical works; in later life lost contact with Newman; buried at London Oratorians' private cemetery at Sydenham; see *Life of Stephen Harding, Abbot of Citeaux* (1844); *The Devotion to the Heart of Jesus* (1854); *The Holy Communion, Its Philosophy, Theology and Practice* (1861); letter to Marquess of Ripon on the latter's worries concerning Pius IX's *Syllabus of Errors* ("You seem to think that anyone who believes the Syllabus would be bound to affirm that in the best state of society some penalties ought by law to be laid on the professors of false religions. I do not think so. The stress of the condemnation lies elsewhere. You must remember the drift of the whole document. The Pope is vehement throughout against what he calls indifferentism, that is, the notion that there is no one ascertainable true religion, and therefore that all religions have a right to be treated as equal before the law. The authors of this condemned proposition made one exception to this right: namely they allowed the justice of punishing those who broke the public peace In other words, they affirm that a religion which caused public troubles, tumults, and revolutions might be coerced by legal penalties. In other words, the condemned authors asserted that no account whatever was to be taken of the truth or falsehood of a religion, but simply of its tendencies to disturb the public peace. It is plain that if this were allowed to pass not only the Roman Emperors were right in persecuting Christianity, but the Jews would have been justified in crucifying our Lord for 'raising a tumult among the people.' What, therefore, the Pope intends to condemn is not the principle that no penalties are to be inflicted on false religions, but the principle that there is no reason for punishing them except on purely political reasons.... [The Syllabus] is a protest in favor of truth against indifferentism; it is a re-assertion of a principle which the Reformation and the French Revolution have well-nigh made to disappear from the earth"; *Gillow*, Vol. II, p.3; *Catholic Encyclopedia*; *DNB*.

Dalton, Marmaduke (alias Joseph Booth) – priest; d. 5 April 1695; member of ancient Yorkshire family; brought up Protestant; converted after his father's death and was ostracized by his mother; went over to Douai, but was eventually ordained priest in Ireland about 1670; ministered to the poor Catholics around Crathorne; died after being taken ill at Burniston, near Scarborough; fine controversialist; see *Gillow*, Vol. II, p.6.

Daniels, Augustine – c. Holy Week 1893; formerly Anglican curate; joined Benedictine Order; ordained priest; see essay in J. G. F. Raupert (ed), *Roads to Rome* (1901), p.65 ("The truth of the Resurrection was the principal question to which I turned my attention. Amongst my German friends I had a number of Rationalistic theologians, who also admitted the fact which must strike every reader of the New Testament. I mean the prominence assigned by the Apostles to the doctrine that their Lord had really risen from the dead. My friends, however, would not admit what seemed to me to be the only reasonable explanation of this fact, viz. the historical reality of Christ's resurrection. They essayed to explain away the supernatural element, and I found their attempt unsatisfactory. The causes assigned were inadequate to account for the effects which were to be explained. The existence of Christianity and the growth of the Christian Church are facts so weighty that they cannot be reasonably supposed to have their origin in the ecstatic illusions or spiritualistic fancies of the first disciples and followers of Jesus. Such an assumption would involve such an enormous number of difficulties that common sense and reason both prefer to accept the simple statement of the evangelists as historical fact. Further inquiries led to the confirmation of my belief in the genuineness of the New Testament as a whole. I found that a false assumption, express or implied, invariably underlay all the arguments of the negative critics, viz. the impossibility of miracles. This supposition, however, seemed to me to be entirely untenable, and indeed philosophically absurd. Thus I was led by the grace of God to accept the Christian revelation as contained in the New Testament.

Like many others, I soon found in this collection of books many 'things which are hard to be understood' – things capable of various, even apparently contradictory, explanations. Which of these was I to accept? Certainly the one suggested by that Spirit Whom Christ had promised to send to lead His Disciples into all truth. The question then arose in my mind, Where is this Holy Spirit now to be found? I knew that the Roman Church claimed to be the sole heir of this promise, and, as I have already hinted, I had a certain predisposition of mind towards Catholicism. The wondrous unity of its doctrine, the unsurpassed beauty of its liturgy, and the glorious traditions of its past, had often combined to impress me in the course of my studies.... I began to see that the Church of England could be no part of Christ's visible kingdom on earth, for the latter, according to the explicit statements of the Gospel, must not only possess the *potestas docendi*, but also exercise it").

Darwin, Sir Robert Vere ("Robin") – landscape and portrait painter; b. 7 May 1910, Chelsea, London; d. 30 January 1974, Chelsea; son of Bernard Darwin (1876–1961), the writer on golf; great grandson of Charles Darwin and of Erasmus Darwin, the physician; studied painting at the Slade School of Fine Art, London; art master at Eton College 1933–1939; in 1939 gave up the post to concentrate on painting; in 1946 appointed Professor of Fine Art at Durham University; Principal (and later Rector) of the Royal College of Art 1948–1973; widened the college's range of provision and made it into the leading organization of its kind; painted in a realist style with much originality, especially in his water colors; influenced by Courbet and Derain; worked to encourage excellence in art and design; knighted in 1964; childless; see *DNB* ("He was a man of outward gravity and inner gaiety; he made working for him seem of the greatest importance but also the greatest fun").

Daunt, William Joseph O'Neill (*pseud. Denis Ignatius Moriarty*) – politician and author; b. 28 April 1807, Tullamore, King's County, Ireland; c. 1827; d. 1894, Kilcascan, Ballyneen, County Cork; came from a family of English Protestants which had obtained land in County Cork in the late sixteenth century; MP for Mallow 1832–1833; ardent nationalist; one of original members of the Repeal Association in 1840; secretary to Daniel O'Connell when latter became Lord Mayor of Dublin in 1841; co-founder of the Dublin *Nation*; in 1856 helped found the Irish church disestablishment movement which led to the Disestablishment Act 1869; urged complete separation of Church and State; "viewed home rule as the best attainable goal short of full repeal of the union" (*DNB*); wrote four novels, three under his pseudonym, plus books about Ireland, politics and economics; see *A Catechism of the History of Ireland Ancient and Modern* (1845); *Ireland and Her Agitators* (1867); *Essays on Ireland* (1886); *Eighty-Five Years of Irish History 1800–1885* (1888); *A Life Spent for Ireland* (1896); *DNB*.

Davenant (D'Avenant), Sir William – poet, playwright and theatre manager; b. 1606, Oxford; c. 1645; d. 7 April 1668, Duke's Playhouse, Lincoln's Inn Fields, London; introduced by his father to William Shakespeare; his elder brother, Robert, was Doctor of Divinity at Oxford; was a page to noble families until the success of his first play; succeeded Ben Johnson as poet-laureate in 1637; fought for Royalist army in Civil War; afterwards withdrew to France and became a Catholic there; imprisoned in the Tower 1650–1651 by the government forces; his life and freedom were saved through efforts of John Milton, which favor he returned after the restoration of Charles II; wrote many works of different kinds, keeping up with changes in taste; buried in Poets' Corner, Westminster Abbey; see *Gillow*, Vol. II, p.19 ("It has been asserted that, in 1646, the Queen [Henrietta Maria] commissioned him to try and persuade Charles to give up the Church of England for his security, which so displeased the king that he forbade him ever to appear before him again"); *DNB*.

Davenport Christopher, OSF (name in religion Franciscus a Santa Clara) (sometimes used the names of Francis Hunt and Francis Coventry) – priest and theologian; b. about 1598, Coventry; c. between 1613 and 1616; d. 26 May 1680, Somerset House, London; at Oxford he conversed on religion with a Catholic priest and was convinced by his arguments; he renounced his own errors and declared himself a Catholic; as a result he left Oxford and went to Douai in 1615; entered Flemish Franciscans at Ypres in 1617, later joining his English brethren in Douai in 1618; ordained priest 14 March 1620; Professor of Divinity with many publications; friend of John Austin (see above); later came on the English mission for many years and was informal chaplain to Queen Henrietta Maria, wife of Charles I; in his book *Deus, natura, gratia* (1634) he argued that the Thirty-nine Articles were not incompatible with Catholic doctrine, which led to much controversy; three times provincial between 1637 and 1665; after Restoration he was chaplain to Catherine of Braganza; he reconciled Anne, Duchess of York, to the Church; buried in St. John's Church of the Savoy Hospital; his brother, John, became Puritan and then independent preacher, who refused to conform to the Established Church and emigrated to the United States; see Fr. John Berchmans Dockery, OFM, *Christopher Davenport: Friar and Diplomat* (1960); *Gillow*, Vol. II, p.24; *Catholic Encyclopedia*; *DNB*.

Davies, Michael Treharne – writer and schoolteacher; b. 13 March 1936, Yeovil, Somerset; c. 17 April 1957; d. 25 September 2004; father Welsh and a Baptist, mother English and an Anglican; for a time was an Anglican; on leaving school at eighteen, joined the Somerset Light Infantry as a regular soldier; took part in the Malayan Emergency, the Suez Crisis,

and in the civil war in Cyprus; teacher in Catholic primary schools for thirty years until retiring in 1992; supporter of Archbishop Marcel Lefebvre, although he criticized the Episcopal consecrations in 1988 against the will of the Pope; powerful critic of the alleged apparitions at Medjugorje; prolific writer from the traditionalist perspective on Vatican II and the liturgical changes thereafter; committee member and then Vice-President of the Latin Mass Society of England and Wales; President from 1995 to 2003 of Una Voce, an international federation of organizations attached to the Tridentine Mass; buried in the churchyard of St. Mary's, Chislehurst, Kent; see *Cranmer's Godly Order* (1976); *Pope John's Council* (1977); *The Order of Melchisedech* (1979); *Pope Paul's New Mass* (1980); *Apologia Pro Marcel Lefebvre*, 3 Vols. (1979, 1983, 1988); *Partisans of Error (St. Pius X Against the Modernists)* (1983*); The Second Vatican Council and Religious Liberty* (1992); *Medjugorje After Twenty-One Years: The Definitive History* (2002).

Davies, Rowland – priest and composer; b. 9 May 1740, London; d. 16 March 1797, probably at Bosworth Hall; pupil of George Frederic Handel; said to have played organ at coronation of George III in Westminster Abbey in 1760; after conversion went to English College, Douai, in 1765; ordained priest in 1772; taught classics and philosophy at Douai; went on the English mission and worked at Cliff in Yorkshire, Warwick Street in London, and Bosworth Hall, the residence of Francis Fortescue Turville; composed a number of Masses, a Te Deum, a Magnificat, and responses for the dead; see *Gillow*, Vol. II, p.29; *DNB*.

Davis, Francis (*pseud.* "The Belfast Man") – poet and Young Irelander; b. 7 March 1810, Ballincollig, County Cork;

c. November 1874; d. 7 October 1885, Belfast; family originally from Belfast and moved back there when he was a child; brought up as a Presbyterian; self-taught man; trained as muslin weaver; wrote nationalist and radical poetry; lived from hand to mouth and worked at several jobs to support his family; from 1865 he disappeared from public life; his conversion alienated many of his friends and patrons; during his last five or six years he lived as a recluse, devoting himself totally to religion; buried in Milltown cemetery, Belfast; see *DNB*.

Dawson, (Henry) Christopher – historian of religion and culture; b. 12 October 1889, Hay, Brecknockshire; c. 5 January 1914 (daughter, Juliana, received later and afterwards became a nun of the Assumption sisters); d. 25 May 1970, Fountain Hill House, Budleigh Salterton, Devon; brought up as Anglican in the Anglo-Catholic tradition; later loss of faith, but influenced to come back to the faith by the lives of the Catholic saints and medieval mystics (and by E. I. Watkin (see below), a lifelong friend); educated at Trinity College, Oxford; frail and very shy; unworldly and impractical scholar and thinker; showed that religion is the dynamic of all social culture, and notably that the "dark ages" were in fact the most creative period in the culture of the Western world; editor *Dublin Review*; first Professor of Roman Catholic Studies at Harvard University 1958–1962; deplored the changes in the Mass after Vatican II ("I hate the changes in the liturgy and even the translations are so bad" (letter to E. I. Watkin)); buried in the churchyard at St. Wilfrid's Church, Burnsall, near Skipton, Yorkshire; see "Why I am a Catholic" in *The Catholic Times*, 1926 (reproduced in *Christopher Dawson Special Issue*, *Chesterton Review*, May 1983) ("My first visit to Rome, at the age of nine-

teen, came as a revelation to me. It opened out a new world of religion and culture. I realized for the first time that Catholic civilization did not stop with the Middle Ages, and that contemporary with our own national Protestant development there was the wonderful flowering of the Baroque culture.... To me at least the art of the Counter Reformation was a pure joy, and I loved the churches of Bernini and Borromini no less than the ancient basilicas. And this in turn led me to the literature of the Counter Reformation, and I came to know St. Teresa and St. John of the Cross, compared to whom even the greatest of non-Catholic religious writers seem pale and unreal...

...It was by the study of St. Paul and St. John that I first came to understand the fundamental unity of Catholic theology and the Catholic life. I realized that the Incarnation, the Sacraments, the external order of the Church and the internal working of Sanctifying Grace were all parts of one organic unity, a living tree, whose roots are in the Divine Nature and whose fruit is the perfection of the Saints. Thus the life of the Saints is not, as the eclectic student of mysticism believes, the independent achievement of a few highly gifted individuals, but the perfect manifestation of the supernatural life which exists in every individual Christian, the first fruits of that new humanity which it is the work of the Church to create.

This fundamental doctrine of Sanctifying Grace, as revealed in the New Testament and explained by St. Augustine and St. Thomas in all its connotations, removed all my difficulties and uncertainties and carried complete conviction to my mind"); *The Age of the Gods* (1928); *Progress and Religion* (1929); *The Making of Europe* (1932); *The Spirit of the Oxford Movement* (1933); *Religion and Culture* (1948); *Religion and the Rise of Western Culture* (1950);

Dynamics of World History (1962); *The Dividing of Christendom* (1965); *The Formation of Christendom* (1967); *Dawson Special Issue, Chesterton Review*, May 1983; Christina Scott, *A Historian and His World: A Life of Christopher Dawson, 1889–1970* (1984) ("Ironically, in Christopher's case, it was the writings of a 19th century German theologian, Adolf Harnack, which finally convinced him that it was the Church of Rome which alone held the true faith in an unbroken tradition from the Apostles. He once said: 'Harnack, a liberal Protestant, never knew how much he contributed to the process of my conversion to the Catholic Church! He had never heard of me, of course, but I wonder if it ever occurred to him that he might have helped anyone along that particular road.' In volume vii of his *History of Dogma*, Harnack deals with Luther's criticism of dogma, and he made it clear at the outset that Luther attacked the whole Catholic (not only the medieval) idea of Christian perfection and so made the break with the Christian past which was finally sealed with the Reformation...

Christopher Dawson never changed his views on Luther's reformation.... This is not to say that he did not think that there should have been a reformation. As a historian, fully aware of the corruption of the Church in the later Middle Ages, he could not have thought otherwise. He ... showed that there were two movements in the Reformation, the first was one of religious reform represented by Erasmus and More and Pole and the other was one of religious revolution, anti-Humanist in character, represented by Luther and Calvin and Munzer, who broke with the whole Catholic tradition and did their best to destroy the Church and the sacraments. As he described the Protestant Reformation in an earlier writing: 'It was a classic example of emptying out the baby with the bath. The reformers revolted against the externalism of medieval religion, and so they abolished the Mass. They protested against the lack of personal holiness, and so they abolished the saints. They attacked the wealth and self-indulgence of the monks and they abolished monasticism and the life of voluntary poverty and asceticism. They had no intention of abandoning the ideal of Christian perfection, but they sought to release it in Puritanism instead of Monasticism and in pietism instead of mysticism'"); James Hitchcock, "Christopher Dawson," *The American Scholar*, 1993, p.111; Christina Scott, "The Vision and Legacy of Christopher Dawson," *Downside Review*, October 1996, p.283; Aidan Nichols, "Christopher Dawson's Catholic Setting," in Stratford Caldecott and John Morrill (ed), *Eternity in Time: Christopher Dawson and the Catholic Idea of History* (1997); Kevin Dean, "Christopher Dawson (1889–1970): A Great Catholic Historian," *Catholic Life*, January 2005. p.54; Bradley J. Birzer, "Christopher Dawson: The Historian of the Twentieth Century," *Saint Austin Review*, September/October 2005, p.6; Gerry Burns, "Converts to Catholicism: Christopher Dawson," *Catholic Life*, May 2009, p.52; Patrick Allitt, *Catholic Converts: British and American Intellectuals Turn to Rome* (1997), *passim*; Fr. Charles P. Connor, *Classic Catholic Converts* (2001), pp.197–200; Joseph Pearce, *Literary Converts* (1999) *passim*; Lorene Hanley Duquin, *A Century of Catholic Converts* (2003), p.36; *DNB*.

Dean, Blessed William – priest and martyr; b. c.1557, Grassington, Linton in Craven, Yorkshire; c. 1581; d. 28 August 1588, Mile End Green, Middlesex; attended school in Leeds and Clitheroe; father was a retainer of Richard Norton, one of the principals of the 1569 northern rising; conformed to the Church of

England after the rising failed; at Oxford University and then ordained to the Anglican ministry; converted to the Catholic faith by Thomas Alfield, a Rheims seminarian; entered the English College, then at Rheims, in 1581; ordained priest 21 December 1581; went on the English mission in 1582, but arrested within a month in London; imprisoned in Newgate for three years, then tried and convicted of high treason; exiled in 1585 with twenty other priests, but returned to England very soon; after less than two years arrested again in London; tried, condemned and executed by hanging (with great cruelty); see *Gillow*, Vol. II, p.37; *DNB*.

Deane, Thomas – Catholic layman; b. 1651, Malden, Kent; c. March 1686; d. 10 November 1735, Malden; Fellow of University College, Oxford from 1684; conversion influenced by Obadiah Walker (see below) and he became one of Walker's "three disciples"; at the Revolution of 1688 he privately withdrew from Oxford to avoid an attack from the mob; lived in London where he suffered imprisonment once or twice, charged with being a Jesuit or priest; in 1691 placed in pillory at Charing Cross for concealing a pamphlet against the government; lived on charity; confined for debt in the Fleet prison during most of his last days; see *Vindication; being another Argument of the Schism of the Church of England* (1688) (pamphlet); *Gillow*, Vol. II, p.36; *DNB*.

Denbigh, eighth Earl of (Lord Rudolph William Basil Feilding) – b. 9 April 1823; c. 23 August 1850 (received with his wife, Louisa Pennant (1828–1 May 1853), granddaughter of the sixth Earl of Cardigan and heiress of Downing estate, near Holywell); d. 10 March 1892; claimed descent from the imperial Habsburgs; father a member of court of

William IV; known as Viscount Feilding until 1865; brought up as Low Church Anglican by his parents; educated at Eton and Trinity College, Cambridge; doubts about Anglican orders and worries when crumbs after Anglican Holy Communion had been swept away; he and his wife impressed by the Holy Week ceremonies in Seville and by Catholic literature; conversion influenced by Bishop Gillies, vicar apostolic of the Eastern District of Scotland; their conversion opposed by his family and he was disinherited; after his first wife's death of consumption in Naples, he married Mary Berkeley from an old Catholic family and couple led devout Catholic life; of their seven children, Hon. Basil became a priest in 1898 working in a poor area of Wolverhampton (eventually drowned on a boating trip down the Rhine), and Lady Edith a Sister of Charity (religious name Sister Clare) who worked in China; Count of Holy Roman Empire; Knight Grand Cross of Order of Pius IX; Colonel of second V.B. Royal Welsh Fusiliers; took active part in many acts of Catholic charity under Cardinal Wiseman; one of founders of *Universe* newspaper; Honorary President of Peter's Pence Association; after his conversion advised by Newman in relation to objections from his family; built a beautiful chapel at his home and, as a thanksgiving for his conversion, built Catholic Church and Capuchin Monastery at Pantasaph, North Wales; at a public meeting he declared that, though he was proud of his nationality, he was "An Englishman if you please, but first of all a Catholic"; buried at Pantasaph in the habit of a Capuchin friar; see R. F. Clarke, "Rudolph, Eighth Earl of Denbigh," *The Month*, May 1892, p.1; David Hunter-Blair, *Memories and Musings* (1929), p.27 ("One of the handsomest and most aristocratic-looking men of his generation"); Madeleine Beard, *Faith and Fortune*

(1997), pp.63–75 ("[Lord Feilding] wrote [to his sister]: 'Your Faith – if Faith that can be called which is but opinion, is founded upon your own imperfect interpretation of Scripture…. You can only refer back 300 years at most for its beginning and it owed its origin solely to an incontinent monk, who in order to escape the trammels which the Catholic religion imposed on him, threw off every yoke and carved out a religion for himself. I, on the other hand, have the uninterrupted faith of eighteen centuries to support me (for it has never yet been determined by Protestants when what they call "Roman errors" began'"); Stanley L. Jaki, *Newman to Converts: An Existential Ecclesiology* (2001), pp.345–347; *Catholic Encyclopedia.*

Dering, Edward Heneage – author; b. 15 March 1827; c. 20 September 1865 (received with his wife, Lady Georgiana Chatterton (see above) and her niece and ward, Rebecca Dulcibella Orpen, shortly to be married to (Marmion) Edward Ferrers (d. 1884)); d. 1892; son of Anglican prebendary of St. Paul's who was chaplain to Queen Victoria; formerly of the Coldstream Guards (retired 1851); wrote novels on Catholic conversion themes; after his marriage to Lady Chatterton (see account under entry relating to her) he and his wife lived with Edward and Rebecca Ferrers at their home, Baddesley Clinton Hall, Warwickshire; after the deaths of Edward Ferrers and Lady Chatterton, Rebecca Ferrers became his wife and lived at Baddesley until her death in 1923; see *Lethelier* (1860); *A Great Sensation* (1862); *Florence Danby* (1868); *Sherborne; or, The House at the Four Ways* (1875); *Freville Chase* (1880); "Given a First Cause – What Then?" *The Month*, March 1889, p.388 ("We must affirm the existence of a First Cause; for otherwise we should have to suppose either an infinite succession of causes and effects, or a time when nothing was, and a First Something created by itself before it was. If the First Cause were not intelligent, we, who are caused, could not be intelligent (as in fact we are) because it is evidently impossible for the nature of any effect to exceed the nature of its cause. Therefore the First Cause must be intelligent. Where intelligence is, free will must be, in contradistinction to blind impulse: and therefore there must be free will in the intelligent First Cause, who therefore must be either good or bad, and being infinite, either infinitely good or infinitely bad. But evil is evidently privation of good, as darkness (which it morally is), is privation of light: and if we say that the First Cause is infinitely bad, we have to suppose either pre-eternal privation, which would be privation of nothing by nothing, or privation by Himself afterwards, which, by the fact of his being infinite while evil is destructive, would mean infinite destruction, which would involve the self-destruction of the First Cause Himself, and the consequent destruction of all besides Himself – the inconceivable advent of absolute and infinite nothing. His goodness therefore must be infinite, and His treatment of us in accordance with it somehow, while, on the other hand, we, who naturally long for permanent happiness, and aspire beyond the utmost that is possible here, have a short life, chequered at the best, often miserable, and generally disadvantageous to the good. The contradiction is evident, and we cannot avoid it without supposing 1. a future life, according to our deeds here, and 2. a visible Church, to teach us what we are required to do. Therefore we must conclude 1. that a visible Church exists, and 2. that it has a character of its own, by which it may be distinguished…

Where then is it? It must be one, being True, because Truth is essentially exclusive.

It must be holy, being the Church of God, whose goodness is infinite. It must be universal, not national; or it would not be one, since Truth is exclusive. It must have a visible Theocratic continuity; and any one who believes in the New Testament must, if he thinks, expect it to be the same as that which our Lord founded, when He said, 'Thou art Peter; and upon this Rock I will build my Church,' and promised that He would be with it 'all days, even to the consummation of the world.'

That these marks of the One True Church are to be found in the Catholic Church, and are conspicuously absent in the Churches and sects outside – that these are not true, not holy as such, not universal, not founded on the rock of Peter – any one can see who will fairly take the trouble of looking"); *The Lady of Raven's Combe* (1891); *The Ban of Maplethorpe* (1894).

Devas, Charles Stanton – political economist and author; b. 26 August 1848, Long Ditton, Surrey; c. 1867; d. 6 November 1906, Farningham, Kent; converted whilst at Eton College; first in Law and Modern History at Balliol College, Oxford; rest of life devoted to study, writing and lecturing on religious subjects; *The Key to the World's Progress* his main work in defending Catholicism (in the preface he wrote of his "guide and teacher the Great Master on the nineteenth century John Henry Newman … whose work … was mainly concerned with the lasting needs and chronic infirmities of our nature"); Professor of Political Economy at Catholic University in Kensington; external examiner in Political Economy at Royal University of Ireland 1889–1898; contributor to *Dublin Review, The Month*, and other journals; several texts on economics and politics from a Catholic perspective, insisting on relevance of ethics

to subject and including historical importance of the Catholic Church and Christian family; a man of singular piety, zealous member of Society of St. Vincent de Paul and active friend of the poor; his wife, Eliza Mary Katherine, *née* Ward (1853–6 June 1889) died a holy death, leaving eight young children (three of their six sons joined religious orders, all three serving as chaplains in World War I and winning awards for gallantry, and one of their daughters became a nun); see *The Groundwork of Economics* (1883); *Studies in Family Life* (1886); *The Meaning and Aims of Christian Democracy* (1899); *The Key to the World's Progress* (1906) ("The Church is ever being defeated and yet is ever victorious. Failure and defeat seem from the first the lot of the Church and the Divine operations everywhere frustrated. Instead of carrying their dominions to the bounds that had been assigned to them, the chosen people themselves were carried into captivity. There was but one temple of the true God, and this was profaned and destroyed.

And the Old Dispensation was here but the anticipation of the New; wherein the flight of Christ into Egypt appears perpetually re-enacted; and if the hardness of men's hearts extorted divorce under the Old Law, men's unbelief hindered the miracles of Christ under the New. We have to confess the apparent triumph on all sides and through all ages of man's will over God's will, the course of multitudes along the dark and miry paths of error and vice instead of walking in the luminous road which leads to the mountain of Sion, and we are confronted by an appalling mystery – appalling till we understand the necessity of free-will, the power of Divine grace, the efficacy of prayer, the meaning of omnipotence in bonds, the glory of the hidden victories of the Most High.

Moreover, if the Christian Church can

show no more than a partial fulfillment of the Kingdom of the Messiah, she knew her own prospective future from the beginning, warned her preachers of the fate before them, that they would be as sheep among wolves, would be hated for Christ's name, nay, that persecution was to be their blessing, and those their encouragement who had been racked, mocked, stoned, cut asunder – the example of men who suffered and who failed. From the beginning she knew and avowed the weakness and seeming folly of her preaching, that yet was to overcome all the strength and wisdom of the world – weakness and folly, lest God's work should perchance be taken for man's work.

Thus over and over again the Divine Pilot seemed to slumber while the ship was sinking; over and over again the Lord of all seems to keep silence, to yield, to fall back, to cast aside all carnal weapons, to leave the issue to time, waiting in a way scarce endurable to our impatience, till pride should be its own correction, broken without hands, dissolved under its own insufficiency. Indeed if the life of the Church was to be the continuation of the life of her Divine Founder, how could it be other than a life in appearance of defeat and humiliation, and in reality of victory? She must needs practice her Founder's new manner of warfare, whose triumphs are the depths of his abasement; and around her, as they stood around Him, must stand the five mystical figures, bearing on their foreheads their names of Poverty, Abandonment, Rejection, Secrecy and Mortification"); *Political Economy* (1907); Oscar Browning, *Memories of Sixty Years at Eton, Cambridge and Elsewhere* (1910) (Browning's comment as his house master at Eton: "It soon became apparent to me that he had a strong inclination to study history, and I made the suggestion that he should do this,

which was readily accepted. I advised him to read Gibbon's *Decline and Fall of the Roman Empire* completely through, making an abstract of it as he proceeded, which he did, of course, in his spare time. The effect of this study upon him was very remarkable. The aspect of his face changed, he became methodical and industrious in all his work…

…He was to leave Eton at the end of July, and a few days before he left he came and said that he … was a Roman Catholic, and wished to be admitted to that Church. I asked him how he had been converted, and he replied that he had been converted by no man and by no book, but that the serious study of history had convinced him that Roman Catholicism was the only true religion. I should imagine that this was the first time that any one was made a Roman Catholic by the study of Gibbon.… I said that I had so deep a respect for his mind and character that I could not but feel that he had done what was right. My only fear was lest he might be disappointed.… He said that he was sure that that would not be the case. The event proved that he was right"); *Catholic Encyclopedia*; *DNB* ("Devas was concerned to find an alternative to both socialism and *laissez-faire* individualism. He admitted that socialism had a number of attractive features, and there is a welcome absence from his writings of the simplistic dismissal of it frequently found in contemporary Catholic writings. He was no dreamy-eyed medievalist and welcomed modern industrialized society; the challenge was to structure it so as to benefit all its citizens. Socialism was not the answer: its view of humanity was fundamentally unhistorical, its programs would be unworkable, and, above all, there was total incompatibility between it and the family. The family was the basic unit of society, with rights and duties anterior to those of the state, to be protected at all costs. The solution lay in the establishment of a Christian democracy. This would not provide easy answers, but would protect labour by supporting trade unions and end cut-throat competition among employers: 'there must be regulated trading and collective bargaining'").

Dewar, Captain James Cumming – soldier and benefactor; b. 1857; d. 1908; of the 1st Dragoon Guards; served in the Zulu Campaign of 1879, and severely wounded at Sekukini; served in India with the Guards and then exchanged into 11th Hussars; member of Royal Company of Archers; JP for Midlothian; Private Chamberlain to Popes Leo XIII and Pius X; Knight of Sovereign Order of Malta; Knight of Sacred Military Order of Holy Sepulchre; great benefactor to several Catholic missions in Scotland.

Digby, Sir Everard – courtier; b. about 1578, Drystoke, Rutland; d. 30 January 1606, London; parents staunch Catholics from ancient family, but early death of his father left him ward of Crown and so educated in Protestant religion; attracted notice of Queen Elizabeth at court, but retired to his estates and became Catholic (his conversion, and that of his wife, Mary (1581–1653), influenced by Fr. John Gerard, SJ); knighted by James I; persuaded by Robert Catesby to join in the Gunpowder Plot (probably by false statements that it would be lawful activity and approved by Jesuit fathers); arrested and brought to the Tower; tried at Westminster and condemned to death; hanged, drawn and quartered at St. Paul's churchyard; said to have been "the handsomest man of his time"; see *Gillow*, Vol. II, p.62; *DNB*.

Digby, George, second Earl of Bristol and Baron Digby of Sherborne –

politician; b. 1612, Madrid; c. about 1657 (his eldest daughter also became a Catholic); d. 20 March 1677, Chelsea; eldest son of John Digby, first Earl of Bristol (1580–1653), ambassador to the Spanish court; lived in Spain for first eleven years; at Oxford University had reputation as good scholar, with main interests astrology and theology; in 1638–1639 in correspondence with his relative Sir Kenelm Digby (see below) he advanced claims of Church of England against that of Rome; entered parliament and joined the discontented party; acted against Strafford, but saw injustice of accusations against him and changed sides and became supporter of Charles I; after Civil War defeat fled to the exiled court in France; served bravely with the French royal army; one of inner circle of exiled court until he made a personal conversion to the Catholic faith (wholly sincere since he never reversed it when it was a political disadvantage, Charles II wishing to distant himself from Catholicism); dismissed from all his offices, though he was restored to all his lands and titles at the Restoration; feud with Clarendon finally ended his political career and he had to go into hiding for several years, only coming back into favor at Clarendon's impeachment; though a Catholic, he spoke in favor of Test Act, drawing a distinction between a "Catholic of the Church of Rome" and a "Catholic of the Court of Rome"; brilliant but irresponsible; buried in Russell family chapel at Chenies, Buckinghamshire; see *Gillow*, Vol. II, p.65 ("The Earl openly reproached [Charles II] with his amours, his indolence, and his extravagance"); *Catholic Encyclopedia*; *DNB*.

Digby, Sir Kenelm – courtier and natural philosopher; b. 11 June 1603, Gothurst, Buckinghamshire; c. (publicly) 1636; d. 11 June 1665, Covent Garden, London; eldest son of Sir Everard Digby (see above); from an ancient Catholic family; after his father's untimely death his guardians caused him to be brought up as Protestant under the supervision of Laud, later Archbishop of Canterbury; referred to at Oxford University as the Mirandula of his age, such were his great abilities and knowledge; traveled through France, Italy and Spain, where reconciled privately to the Catholic faith; knighted by King James I in 1623; married to childhood sweetheart, the beautiful Venetia Anastasia Stanley (1600–1633, dying suddenly of cerebral hemorrhage) of the Derby family; won several naval victories for Charles I; appointment resulted in his taking oaths of supremacy and allegiance; in 1636 announced publicly his reconciliation to the Church; patron of Ben Jonson; in 1640 obliged to retire into exile; recalled in 1641 and, on breaking out of Civil War, imprisoned at Winchester House; retired to France and then on to Rome as Resident on behalf of Queen Henrietta Maria, who made him her Chancellor; disagreements with Pope Innocent X over appointment of bishops in England; through him Cromwell offered some toleration for Catholic worship on conditions, but this fell through; did not lose the confidence of English court and after the Restoration returned to England; spent rest of his life studying and writing philosophy and science; buried with his wife in crypt of Christ Church, Newgate Street; one of most distinguished men of his time, but eccentric and lacking judgment, and his works have not lasted; never remarried; see W. J. Blyton, "A Versatile Jacobean: Sir Kenelm Digby: 1603–1665," *The Month*, January 1938, p.23; M. Foster, "Sir Kenelm Digby (1603–65) as Man of Religion and Thinker," Parts I and II, *Downside Review*, January and April 1988, pp.35 and 101; *Gillow*, Vol. II, p.70; *Catholic Encyclopedia*; *DNB*.

Digby, Kenelm Henry – writer and poet; b. 1795/6, Geashill, King's County, Ireland; c. 1825 (his cousin, Mother Mabel Digby, Superior General of the Society of the Sacred Heart (see below) converted partly on the strength of knowing Digby's family and his writings); d. 22 March 1880, Shaftesbury House, Hammersmith, London; born into aristocratic, clerical, Church of Ireland family; brought up as staunch anti-Catholic; early deaths of father and mother left him with ample independent means; early travels on the Continent exposed him to Catholic culture; devotee of culture of Middle Ages and concept of chivalry; in early 1820s he was Anglo-Catholic; monarchist and conservative; one of the "Cambridge converts"; long friendship with Ambrose Phillipps de Lisle (see below); husband of Jane Mary Dillon (1816/7–1860) (seven children of marriage, Marcella joining the Society of the Sacred Heart); lived for several years in France, but moved back to England in 1857; influenced by Ultramontanism; buried in Kensal Green cemetery, London; see *The Broadstone of Honour: True Sense and Practice of Chivalry* (1826–1829) ("Much, I am aware, remains to be said respecting the vices which desolated society during the Ages of Faith. Great and beyond all description were the calamities of the city of God, when those two luminaries and immortal columns of the Church, Dominic and Francis, came into the world. As the historian of the Minors observes, 'the demon having persecuted the infant Church by tyrants, and the more advanced by heretics, endeavored now to oppress with both the joyful and flourishing Church, afflicting it with horrors on all sides, perils of the sword without, heresies within, and the iniquity of corrupt manners. But then historians of all ages, like modern newspapers, are more inclined to record deeds of violence and sin than to record quiet virtues, of which yet we can know if we search the humble and not the most ostentatiously striking of popular records.

Who can estimate the multitude of the golden angelic souls, candid, puerile, and at the same time profound, to which the Middle Ages gave birth, and which passed without observation, or leaving behind in history any vestige or memorial of their transit? It was enough for the just that their death was precious in the sight of God, and that their lot was amongst the saints"); *Mores Catholici, or, Ages of Faith*, 11 Vols. (1831–1842) ("To a Catholic, not only the philosophical but also the literary history of the world, is prodigiously enlarged; objects change their relative position, and many are brought into resplendent light, which before were consigned to obscurity. While the moderns continue, age after age, to hear only of the Caesars and the philosophers, the Catholic discovers that there lies between the heathen civilization and the present, an entire world, illustrious with every kind of intellectual and moral greatness; the names which are first upon his tongue are no longer Cicero and Horace, but St. Augustine, St. Bernard, Alcuin, St. Thomas, St. Anselm; the places associated in his mind with the peace and dignity of learning, are no longer the Lycaeum and the Academy, but Citeaux, Cluny, Crowland, or the Oxford of the Middle Ages"); *Compitum, or, The Meeting of the Ways at the Catholic Church*, 7 Vols. (1848–1854); *The Lover's Seat* (1856); Bernard Holland, *Memoir of Kenelm Digby* (1919); M. Girouard, *The Return to Camelot: Chivalry and the English Gentleman* (1981); Kevin L. Morris, "Chesterton and Kenelm Henry Digby," *Chesterton Review*, August 1985, p.332; Kevin L. Morris, "Kenelm Henry Digby and English Catholicism," *Recusant History*, May 1991, p.361; Margaret Pawley,

Faith and Family: The Life and Circle of Ambrose Phillipps de Lisle (1993); Madeleine Beard, *Faith and Fortune* (1997) ("He … regarded Anglo-Catholics as the type who 'procured copies of pinnacles and crosses, and even the iron hinges of the old doors of churches; while the spiritual hinge, on which the whole system turns, they were content to suppress for ever…'"); *Gillow*, Vol. II, p.81; *Catholic Encyclopedia*; *DNB*.

Digby, Mother Mabel Mary Josephine – nun; b. 1835, Ashford House, Staines, Middlesex; c. 19 March 1853 (her mother and sister, Geraldine, converted in September 1852); d. 21 May 1911; daughter of the heiress of last Baron Haversham; in 1849 the family moved to France because of ill-health of her mother; when mother and sister converted, her father objected and family split up temporarily; she went with her father; a friend was told by the Curé d'Ars that God would soon have complete mastery over Mabel's heart; deeply affected by witnessing the Blessed Sacrament raised in Benediction and converted; joined the Society of the Sacred Heart in 1857; influenced by the Order's foundress, Mother Madeleine Sophie Barat; in France at the convent at Marmoutier until returning to England to the Order's convent at Roehampton in 1872, where she became superior; cousin of Kenelm Digby (see above) whose *Mores Catholici* was read to her by her mother and influenced her conversion; buried at Roehampton; see A. Pollen, *Mother Mabel Digby, A Biography of the Superior-General of the Society of the Sacred Heart, 1835–1911* (1914) ("[Mabel] remained impassive. The chants ended; the Bishop slowly removed the monstrance from the throne; the throng bowed low; Mabel, still seated, threw back her head haughtily as if in protest; the bell tinkled as the

Blessed Sacrament was now raised in Benediction. In an instant Mabel Digby had slipped from her seat on to her knees and flung her arms across her breast with a clutch that gripped both shoulders. Her face seemed to be illumined; her tearful eyes were fixed upon the Host until the triple blessing was complete, and It was replaced in the tabernacle. Then she sank crouching to the ground, whilst the last short psalm was intoned; she remained bent low and immovable...

Mabel rose to her feet, and followed Geraldine to the church porch. Here she placed her hand upon her sister's arm. 'Geraldine,' she said, 'I am a Catholic. Jesus Christ has looked at me. I shall change no more'"); Madeleine Beard, *Faith and Fortune* (1997), pp.97–102.

Dingle, Reginald James – scientist and author; b. 1889, Plymouth; c. 1919; educated privately; writer and translator on faith and science, political history, and the Church; see *The Faith and Modern Science* (1935); *"Democracy" in Spain* (1937); *Russia's Work in France* (1938); *Russia's Work in Spain* (1939); "St. Alphonsus Liguori," *The Month*, January 1955, p.21 ("Whenever the plea is advanced that the deposit of faith, of which the Church is the eternal custodian, must be re-expressed or re-interpreted, according to current scientific or philosophic fashions, Authority will pronounce its anathema. 'The One remains the many change and pass.' The Church until the end of this dispensation will contend for the Faith that was once delivered to the saints").

Dinnis, Enid (real name Mrs. William Cassell) – writer; b. 1873, London; c. 1897, Ursuline convent, Thildonck, Belgium; d. November 1942; daughter of Anglican clergyman; brought up as Protestant; novelist mainly on historical themes from Catholic perspective (e.g.,

Mr. Coleman, Gent. (1914) (on Popish Plot of Titus Oates), *The Three Roses* (on Edward VI) and *Bess of Cobb's Hill* (on Elizabeth Barton)); also short story writer focusing on combining supernatural with touch of realism (e.g., *Mystics All*, inspired by the writing of Mgr. Robert Hugh Benson (see above)); poet and essayist; contributor to *Punch*; spent her life writing as an apostolate, aimed at inspiring readers to live the faith or become Catholic if not already one; see Walter Romig, *Book of Catholic Authors*, First Series (1942) ("It is sometime before a convert from Protestantism realizes that religion is no longer a Sunday affair which can only intrude into weekday life without unseemliness in the form of good behavior implying a religious basis"); Joseph Kelly, "Enid Dinnis, 1873–1942," *Catholic Life*, April 2002, p.39 ("Enid ... was 'received into the City set on a hill' having made the discovery that 'the Church is a living reality, not a fancy name for a school of morality'.... She devoted her pen 'to the only thing worth writing and singing about,' the supernatural, of which she said, 'to the convert, Catholicism presents itself as the embodiment'.... A rare spiritual quality characterized all of Enid's work, which are inspired greatly by her work with the poor.... In the simple and humble she recognized souls touched by the special grace of God, seeing his hand in all things").

Dodsworth, William – theological writer; b. 19 March 1798, Kirk Ella, Yorkshire; c. 31 December 1850; d. 10 December 1861, 7 York Terrace, Regent's Park, London; began as Evangelical; became Anglican curate influential in Tractarian movement, where worked with Manning and Pusey; friend of Newman's from late 1820s; helped set up first Anglican religious sisterhood at Park Village West; resigned his ministry as result of judgment in Gorham case (see entry for William Maskell) and joined the Catholic Church; father of Fr. Cyril Dodsworth (1844–1907), Redemptorist priest in the West Indies and Canada; after conversion led quiet life as layman, publishing Catholic apologetic works; one of the original promoters of the plan for an Oratory school; had large family; buried in Kensal Green cemetery, London; see *Popular Objections to Catholic Faith and Practice Considered* (1858); *DNB*.

Dors, Diana (real name Diana Mary Fluck) – actress and film star; b. 23 October 1931, Swindon, Wiltshire; c. Spring 1973 (her third husband, Alan Lake (1940–1984) also received); d. 4 May 1984, Windsor, Berkshire; only child of a railway clerk and former army captain; enrolled at the London Academy of Music and Dramatic Art; spotted and put into films; given a ten-year contract by the Rank Organization; promoted as a celebrity and sex symbol; married three times; after her memoirs were published by the *News of the World*, the Archbishop of Canterbury denounced her as a "wayward hussy"; later in pantomimes, cabaret performer and agony aunt; courageous fight against cancer; buried at Sunningdale Catholic cemetery; Alan Lake never got over his grief and committed suicide 10 October 1984; see Joan Flory and Damien Walne, *Diana Dors: Only a Whisper Away* (1987); *DNB*.

Douglas, Lord Alfred Bruce ("Bosie") – poet and socialite; b. 22 October 1870, Ham Hill, near Worcester; c. 1911 (his wife, Olive Custance (1874–1944), poet (see below), with whom he eloped in 1901, received in 1924, though lapsed later); d. 20 March 1945, Old Monks Farm, Lancing, Sussex; son of 9th Marquess of Queensberry (see below); editor

of *The Academy* 1907–1910; was amour fatale of Oscar Wilde (see below); part of the decadent movement; one of the minor poets of "the eighteen-nineties," several of his poems rise above his own affectations and end-of-the-century decadence, *The City of the Soul* (1899) and *Sonnets* (1900) containing his most graceful writing; conversion influenced by reading the lives of the saints, and by mystics such as St. Teresa and St. John of the Cross; buried beside his mother in Franciscan friary cemetery in Crawley, Sussex; see *The Autobiography of Lord Alfred Douglas* (1929); *Without Apology* (1938); essay in Maurice Leahy (ed), *Conversions to the Catholic Church: A Symposium* (1933) ("What changed me from High Anglicanism to Catholicism was simply that reading history, and finding out all the lies that had been taught to me as truth at school and at Oxford, convinced me that the High Anglican position, however attractive it may be, does not hold water. The theory that the Church of England is a 'branch of the Catholic Church,' and that the continuity was never broken at the Reformation, seems to me to be demonstrably false…. What finally converted me to Catholicism, though I did not actually become a Catholic till more than a year after I read it, was Pope Pius X's *Encyclical Against Modernism*…. It had the effect of convincing me that the Catholic Church in communion with the See of Peter in Rome, is the only true Church"); H. Montgomery Hyde, *Lord Alfred Douglas: A Biography* (1984); Douglas Murray, *Bosie: a Biography of Lord Alfred Douglas* (2000); *DNB*.

Douglas-Irvine, Helen Florence – writer; b. 29 February 1880, Grangemuir, Pittenweem, Fife, Scotland; c. 1917; d. 1947; related to family of Marquess of Queensberry; educated in several countries; member of International Institute of Agriculture from 1916 and later of agricultural section of International Labour Office; published work on agrarian history, *The Making of Rural Europe*, and histories of London and the Royal Palaces of Scotland; made her home in Chile from 1931 onwards and wrote much for *The Times* about Chile, Peru and Argentina; turned to fiction and published four novels and one book of stories of which the scenes are mainly laid in Chile and Peru, e.g., *Magdalena* (1936); *Fray Mario* (1939); *Mirror of a Dead Lady* (1940); *Angelic Romance* (1941); and *Torchlight Procession* (1946); see Anon., "Helen Douglas-Irvine," *Catholic Life*, October 2002, p.22.

Dowland, John – musician and composer; b. 1563, Westminster, London; c. 1580, France; d. 1626; little known of his early years; in 1580 in service of ambassador to French court; by 1588 listed as one of most famous musicians of the day; specialized as lutenist; in 1594 rejected for appointment as one of Queen's lutenists; went abroad working in Germany (courts of Wulfbuttel and Hasse) and Italy; lutenist at court of Christian IV in Denmark 1598–1606; wrote many songs and instrumental music; in 1612 appointed one of King's lutenists; most famous English musician of his age; buried at St. Ann's, Blackfriars, London; neglected in eighteenth and nineteenth centuries, but revived interest in the twentieth century, mainly in his instrumental music; known also for his melancholy songs (called "The Melancholy Madrigalist"); now recognized as the greatest English composer of lute music and lute songs; father of Robert Dowland (c. 1591–1641), also lutenist and composer; see Diana Poulton, *John Dowland (1982); Grove Music Online; DNB*.

Dowson, Ernest Christopher – poet and author; b. 2 August 1867, 11 The Grove, Lee, Kent; c. September 1891; d. 23 February 1900, 26 Sandhurst Gardens, Catford, London; left Oxford University without a degree; preferred to be in London literary society (member of Rhymers' Club, which included W. B. Yeats and Lionel Johnson (see below)); frequent contributor to literary magazines, *The Yellow Book* and *The Savoy*; well read in Catholic apologetics and Walter Pater's aesthetics; in 1891 fell in love with twelve-year-old Adelaide "Missie" Foltinowicz (1878–1903), daughter of the Polish owner of a Soho restaurant, and reputed to be the subject of his best-known poem, *Non Sum Qualis Eram Bonae Sub Regno Cynarae*; pursuit was unsuccessful and he was crushed; in 1895 his parents both committed suicide and he declined rapidly, dying of alcoholism; unmarried; buried in Ladywell cemetery, Lewisham, London; see Jad Adams, *Madder Music, Stronger Wine: The Life of Ernest Dowson, Poet and Decadent* (2000) ("There may have been something of a deep childhood memory in his wish to convert: churches would have been beautifully awesome places for the young Dowson as he trekked across Catholic Europe with his parents. There is more than a little in the jib that many artists converted not because they found Catholicism more spiritually true than other forms of faith, but just more beautiful. They would answer that beauty is a form of spiritual truth, and if religion is not beautiful it cannot be true. As Frank Harris said Dowson told him, 'I am for the old faith. I've become a Catholic, as every artist must.'

The decadent life was said to be destined to lead to suicide or the foot of the Cross. Religion, but specifically Catholicism, was always part of the decadent make-up"); Robert Whelan, "Why did so many Victorian decadents become Catholics?" *Catholic Herald*, 5 January 2001; *DNB*.

Drane, Augusta Theodosia (name in religion Rev. Mother Francis Raphael) – nun and author; b. 28 December 1823, Bromley St. Leonard's, Middlesex; c. 3 July 1850 (received at Tiverton with her friend Mary Moore (1813–1855), later also a nun at Mother Margaret Hallahan's convent; sister, Louisa, received in 1852; another friend, Susan Du Boulay (1826–1906), later sister Mary Gabriel, with whom she spent a year traveling in Italy, was received 15 April 1850, and together they entered religious life); d. 29 April 1894, Stone convent, Staffordshire; brought up in Church of England; when still a girl came under influence of Tractarian teaching through a friend, William Maskell (see below); conversion influenced by several writers, but especially Burnet's *History of the Reformation*, St. Augustine's *Confessions*, and Newman; entered Mother Margaret Mary Hallahan's convent of the Third Order of St. Dominic at Clifton; moved to the Convent of St. Catherine of Siena, Stone, Staffordshire; prioress in 1872; provincial in 1881, succeeding Mary Imelda Poole (see below); many books on history and the lives of the saints, plus some fiction; voracious reader all her life; buried in choir of conventual church; see *The Life of St. Dominic* (1857); *History of England for Family Use* (1864); *Christian Schools and Scholars* (1867); *The Life of Mother Margaret Mary Hallahan* (1869); *The History of St. Catherine of Siena and Her Companions* (1880); *The Spirit of the Dominican Order* (1896); Rev. Bertrand Wilberforce, OP (ed), *The Conversion of Miss Drane* (1900); *Catholic Encyclopedia*; *DNB*.

Drummond, James, fourth Earl of Perth and Jacobite first Duke of Perth – politician; b. 7 July 1648; c. June 1685 (he persuaded his wife, Lady Jane Douglas (d. 1678), and his brother, Lord John Drummond (1649–1714) (see below), to do the same shortly after); ; d. 11 May 1716, Château-Vieux de St Germain-en-Laye; became actively involved in Scottish politics and then became Lord Chancellor; his mother a Catholic but he so far a convinced Episcopalian; his conversion to the Catholic faith was influenced by the details of the deathbed conversion of Charles II, particularly when supported by a private correspondence with Bishop Bossuet of Meaux; accusations that he and his brother converted for political reasons are untrue; in 1688 he tried to reach France by boat, but was arrested and imprisoned in Stirling Castle until 1692; went abroad permanently; appointed by James II as his ambassador extraordinary to the Pope to obtain political and financial support for the Jacobite cause; appointed governor of the education of the Prince of Wales at St. Germain; in March 1708 he accompanied James III on his unsuccessful attempt to invade Scotland; a noble character; buried in the chapel of the Scots College, Paris, at the foot of the monument to the memory of James II, which he had paid for; see A. Joly, *Un Converti de Bossuet: James Drummond, Duc de Perth, 1648–1716* (1934); *DNB*.

Drummond, (James) Eric, seventh Earl of Perth – diplomat; b. 17 August 1876, White House, Fulford, near York; c. 1903; d. 15 December 1951, Fyning House, Rogate, Midhurst, Sussex; son of tenth Viscount Strathallan; joined Foreign Office; private secretary to Asquith, Grey and Balfour; member of British delegation at Versailles Peace Conference; first Secretary General to League of Nations 1919–1933; Ramsay Macdonald, the Prime Minister, vetoed his appointment as ambassador in Washington and in Paris, allegedly because he never forgot his fellow Scot's conversion to Catholicism; British ambassador in Rome 1933–1939; deputy leader of Liberals in House of Lords; his wife, (Angela) Mary (1877–1965), was a member of the Catholic Constable-Maxwell family; see *DNB*.

Drummond, John, styled first Earl of Melfort and Jacobite first Duke of Melfort – politician; b. 1649; c. Summer 1685; d. 25 January 1714, rue de la Planche, Paris; younger brother of James Drummond (1648–1716), fourth Earl of Perth (see above); joined army, then went into Scottish politics; appointed as secretary for Scotland; James II made him Viscount, then Earl Melfort; accused of converting for political reasons, but was sincere; in 1688 made his way to St. Germain-en-Laye; then James II's principal secretary of state and the dominant voice at the Jacobite court; eventually lost his position; buried at St. Sulpice; see *DNB*.

Drummond, Hon. Lister Maurice – barrister, KC; b. 1856; c. 1875 (his mother, Hon. Adelaide Drummond (b. 1826) received in 1896, together with his sister); descendant of Lord Strathallan, Jacobite leader killed at Culloden in 1745; secretary and founder with Fr. Philip Fletcher (see below) of Guild of Our Lady of Ransom for the Conversion of England; Knight of St. Gregory the Great; speaker for Catholic Evidence Guild and brought many converts to the faith; known as the "Escaped Protestant"; see R. E. Noble, *Lister Drummond, K.S.G., Barrister-at–Law* (1922); Madeleine Beard, *Faith and Fortune* (1997), pp.207–208 ("He left Catholic Truth Society pamphlets on railings, in railway carriages and on omnibuses, and in railway station waiting rooms. He would walk down a street and with a gesture of contempt throw down a tract to watch it being picked up by someone else. He once said the rosary alone, walking along the Martyrs Way from Newgate to Tyburn, which later became a crowded annual pilgrimage").

Drury (alias Bedford and Stanley), Robert, SJ – priest; b. 1587, in Middlesex; c. 1601 (his father was reconciled to the Church on his death-bed); d. 26 October 1623; brought up Protestant; conversion mainly due to his sister, Bridget; went to St. Omers and then admitted to English College, Rome, in 1604; joined the Society of Jesus in 1608; ordained priest 1622 and then went to England; became celebrated preacher until losing his life when the floor of an overcrowded room in Hunsden House, Old Blackfriars, London (French ambassador's residence), in which he was preaching, collapsed; many people killed, including his brother, William, also a priest; see *Gillow*, Vol. II, p.108; *DNB*.

Dryden, Charles – poet; b. 27 August 1666, Charlton, Wiltshire; c. 1685 (with his father (see below) and brother Erasmus (see below)); d. 1704; eldest son of John Dryden, the poet-laureate; wrote English and Latin poetry; went to Rome in 1692 where, by the influence of Cardinal Howard, Pope Clement XI appointed him one of the chamberlains of his household; returned to England in about 1697; drowned in attempt to swim across the Thames, near Datchet ferry; buried at Windsor; see *Gillow*, Vol. II, p.110; *Catholic Encyclopedia*; *DNB*.

Dryden, Sir Erasmus-Henry Thomas, Baronet, OP – priest; b. 2 May 1669; c. 1685 (with his father (see below) and brother Charles (see above)); d. 3 December 1710, Canons Ashby, Northamptonshire; third son of John Dryden, the poet-laureate; went to Douai and studied philosophy; admitted to English College, Rome, in 1690, but left in 1691 and joined Dominican Order; ordained priest in 1694; sub-prior of Convent of Holy Cross, Bornheim 1697–1700, then returned to England where worked on the mission in Northamptonshire; succeeded to baronetcy in 1710, but as a recusant he did not inherit family estates, though he went to family residence, Canons Ashby, Northamptonshire; buried in family vault at parish church there; see *Gillow*, Vol. II, p.111; *DNB*.

Dryden, John – poet-laureate; b. 9 August 1631, at Vicarage, Aldwincle All Saints, Northamptonshire; c. 1685 (his wife, Lady Elizabeth (d. 1714), was received some time before, as was his second son, John (1667–1701) (see below); his eldest son, Charles (1666–1704) (see above) and his third son, Erasmus (1669–1710) (see above), were received with their father); d. 1 May 1700, London; his father and maternal grandfather were zealous Puritans; eldest of fourteen children; early taste for poetry and translation; after Cambridge entered the world with the patronage of Puritans, though never much sympathy with them; rejoiced in Restoration of monarchy; reputation advanced during a period when the popular taste was for melodramatic and rhyming plays; appointed poet-laureate in 1670; wrote his great satirical poem, *Absalom and Achitophel* (published 1681) against "Protestant party," which was working to exclude Duke of York from succession in favor of Duke of Monmouth; after conversion was a sincere Catholic; more at ease under James II; translated Bouhours' life of St. Francis Xavier and made beautiful translations of hymns and poetry; at 1688 Revolution dispossessed of his offices of poet-laureate and historiographer royal; major Catholic work was *The Hind and the Panther* (1687), dealing with controversy between the Hind (the Catholic Church) and the Panther (Church of England) ("Theological discussion about the nature of the true church, the authority of tradition, and the need for individual reason to subordinate itself to Pope and councils" (*DNB*)); kept the faith despite enduring in last twelve years of his life loss of office and income, separation from his three sons, and ceaseless attacks on his good name; died in poverty of gangrene; reburied in Chaucer's grave in Westminster Abbey; see *A Defence of the Papers* (1686) (defense of reasons for conversion given by Anne, Duchess of York (see above)) ("The Church of England has no authority of reforming herself, because the doctrine of Christ cannot be reformed, nor a National Synod lawfully make any definitions in matters of Faith, contrary to the judgment of the Church Universal of the present age, shown in her public liturgies; that judgment being equivalent to that of a General Council of the present age"); Sir Walter Scott, *The Life of John Dryden* (1808) ("If we are to judge of Dryden's sincerity in his new faith, by the determined firmness with which he retained it through good report and bad report, we must allow him to have been a martyr, or at least a confessor, in the Catholic cause"); Christopher Hollis, *Dryden* (1933); Edward Hutton, *Catholicism and English Literature* (1942), pp.159–171; Arnold Jordan, "The Conversion of John Dryden," *The Month*, July 1931, p.18; T. A. Birrell, "James Maurus Corker and Dryden's Conversion," (1973) *English Studies*, Vol. 54, p.461 ("Now so far as one can judge, it was the chain of events … – the Popish Plot, the Exclusion Crisis, and the Rye House Plot – which provoked Dryden to a serious reconsideration of his religious position. The hysteria of the mob and of Parliament, the unscrupulous use by the Whigs of informers like Oates, the readiness of Shaftesbury and the Whig Plot-managers to send palpably innocent men to their death in order to attain political ends, and, one regrets to say it, the pusillanimous and times-serving attitude of many of the Anglican bishops – these were all contributory factors"); Anne Barbeau Gardiner, *Ancient Faith and Modern Freedom in John Dryden's The Hind and the Panther* (1998) ("Perhaps more than anything else, the Real Presence is a key to Dryden's conversion, for he describes his conversion to Catholicism as a surrender to Christ in the sacrament.... The poet asks whether he can believe that God, by his omnipotence, *disguised* himself in the flesh of a child. And then, since he does believe this, he asks himself what prevents his believing that God could, by the same omnipotence, *disguise* himself in the sacrament...

So now Dryden asks himself this question: If Christ had the power to *veil* his divinity with his humanity to redeem us, why should he not have the power to *veil* both his divinity and humanity with the sacramental forms to nourish us?... Could he hide himself in the Incarnation and not be able to do the same in the sacrament? If he can, then there is no need to make all this effort to deny the literal meaning of his words, 'This is My Body'.... He urges the clarity and plainness of 'This is My Body' as an argument for a literal reading of the text.... He makes belief in the Real Presence a matter of taking the Divine Word at his word...

In the end the poet decides that the literal meaning of 'This is My Body' is the safest assurance of eternal life.... Unless Heaven should go bankrupt, the reward of eternal life is promised to those who eat Christ's body and drink his blood (Jn. 6). Thus he has all to gain and nothing to lose by taking literally what Christ said plainly about the bread of life.... Either the Word speaks truly, or there is nothing

true"); R. J. Stove, "Steel-White Logic: Dryden in His Time and Ours," *Annals Australasia*, January-February 2006 ("For that cultivated remnant among liberal arts students capable of serious thought, and that still smaller remnant capable of separating religious allegiance from careerism, the question which overwhelmed Dryden and drove him away from his mild Protestant upbringing is as urgent as ever: where can active, visible religious authority be found? Hence these crisp lines from Dryden's *The Medal* (1682): 'Our own worship is only true at home,/ And true but for the time; 'tis hard to know/ How long we please it shall continue so;/ This side today, and that to-morrow burns;/ So all are God Almighties in their turns./ A tempting doctrine, plausible and new;/ What fools our fathers are, if this be true!' (Chesterton phrased the point more crisply still: 'How can a man know what he wants, how can he even want what he wants, if it will not remain the same while he wants it?')"); Robert Caballo, "John Dryden and the Concept of Authority," *Saint Austin Review*, March/April 2009, p.8; *Gillow*, Vol. II, p.112; *Catholic Encyclopedia*; *DNB*.

Dryden, John Jr. – poet; b. 1667; c. about 1684; d. 28 January 1701, Rome; second son of John Dryden, the poet-laureate (see above); in 1685 elected to a scholarship to Christ Church College, Oxford, but had already become a Catholic and so could not matriculate as a member of the university; education at Oxford University committed to the care of Dr. Obadiah Walker (see below), master of University College; at the Revolution obliged to leave Oxford; followed his brother Charles to Rome, where Pope Clement XI allowed him to officiate as his brother's deputy in the Pope's household; died of pleuritic fever; see *Gillow*, Vol. II, p.131; *DNB*.

Duckett, Blessed James – bookseller and martyr; b. Gilfortrigs, Skelsmergh, Westmoreland; d. 9 April 1601, London; brought up as Protestant, though his godfather, James Leybourne, was executed at Lancaster on 22 March 1583 for denial of the queen's supremacy; apprenticed to a bookseller in London; during his apprenticeship he was persuaded of the truth of the Catholic religion by reading a book, *The Foundation of the Catholic Religion*, lent to him by a friend, Peter Mason; before he could be received into the Church he was imprisoned for not attending the Protestant services; bought out remainder of his time, set up as a bookseller, and received into the Church by Fr. Weekes (who was imprisoned in the Gatehouse prison); married a Catholic widow in 1589, but spent nine of next twelve years in prison; last arrest was when betrayed by Peter Bullock, a bookbinder; Catholic books found on his premises in 1601; imprisoned in Newgate, then tried, Bullock testifying against him; convicted, and sentenced to death (jury originally acquitted him, but judge urged them to reconsider and they convicted); hanged at Tyburn (with Bullock); son was prior of English Carthusians at Nieuwpoort, Flanders; see M. M. Merrick, *James Duckett: A Study of His Life and Times* (1947); *Gillow*, Vol. II, p.133; *Catholic Encyclopedia* ("On the way to Tyburn he was given a cup of wine; he drank, and desired his wife to drink to Peter Bullock, and freely to forgive him. At the gallows, his last thoughts were for his betrayer. He kissed him and implored him to die in the Catholic Faith"); *DNB*.

Dudley, Owen Francis – priest and writer; b. 1882; c. 1915; d. 1952; Anglican minister 1911–1915; ordained Catholic priest in Rome in 1917; chaplain to British gunners on Italian and French fronts in World War I and was wounded; superior of Catholic Missionary Society 1933–1946; lecturer and novelist (wrote trilogy: *Will Men Be Like Gods?* (1924), *The Shadow on the Earth* (1926), *The Masterful Monk* (1929)); see *Deathless Army-Advance! A Battle Cry* (1927); essay in Maurice Leahy (ed), *Conversions to the Catholic Church: A Symposium* (1933) (reprinted under the name of "What I Found" in John A. O'Brien, *The Road to Damascus* (1949)) ("Infallibility is the only guarantee we have that the Christian religion is true. Actually, if I, at this moment, did not believe in an Infallible Teacher, appointed by God, then nothing on earth would induce me to believe in the Christian religion. If, as outside the Catholic Church, Christian doctrines are a matter of private judgment, and therefore the Christian religion a mere matter of human opinion, then there is no obligation upon any living soul to believe in it. Why should I stake my immortal soul upon human opinion? For that is all you have if you refuse the Infallible Church"); *You and Thousands Like You* (1948) ("When Christ said to His Church: He that heareth you heareth Me, He laid upon Himself the obligation of making His Church recognizable, so that in hearing the voice of His Church we should know that we were hearing His own voice; and not only recognizable but *verifiable* for all time, otherwise His followers down the ages would have no means of knowing whether they were in His own Church or not. He laid such tremendous stress on being in His Church that people who did not 'hear' it were to be treated as heathens and publicans, outcasts, excommunicated. He made it *One*, *Holy*, *Catholic* and *Apostolic* so that there should be no mistake about His Church, and no difficulty in recognizing it.

It is no good telling me that those words are in the Protestant Creed, because the Protestant Creed is ours; there was no Protestant church in the year A.D. 325, the year of the Nicene Creed in which those four words occur"); Walter Romig, *Book of Catholic Authors*, Second Series (1943).

Dudley, Sir Robert – mariner and landowner; b. 7 August 1574, Sheen House, Richmond, Surrey; c. winter 1605/6; d. 6 September 1649, Villa di Castello, Florence; titular Duke of Northumberland and Earl of Warwick; son of Robert Dudley, Earl of Leicester (1532/3–1588); status of his birth still debated; provided for by Leicester in his will; came into his inheritance in 1590; became fascinated with the sea and navigation; main ambition was to circumnavigate the globe; made several lesser voyages; knighted in 1596; in 1605 took legal action (unsuccessfully) to prove himself Leicester's legitimate son and heir; went abroad with Elizabeth Southwell in September 1631, his first cousin once removed and a great beauty; they announced their conversion to the Catholic faith and applied to the Vatican for a dispensation to marry on grounds of consanguinity (Dudley claimed a contract with the maid of honor, Frances Vavasour, in 1591 to invalidate both his earlier marriages); their conversion influenced by a group of English exiles presided over by the Jesuit Robert Persons (see below); they married and lived in Florence; he built warships for patrons in Italy; famous for his nautical and navigational writings; drained the marsh between Pisa and the sea and made Leghorn one of the best ports in the world; one of his sons became a Dominican friar; buried with his Duchess in the church of St. Pancratius, Florence; see *Gillow*, Vol. II, p.137; *DNB*.

Duffus-Harris, John – stockbroker and barrister; b. 2 January 1855, Halifax, Nova Scotia; c. 7 May 1898; brought up in Church of Scotland until age of twelve; then Anglican until age of twenty-two; then long period of doubt and agnosticism before conversion; educated at Rugby School and Trinity College, Cambridge; see essay in J. G. F. Raupert (ed), *Roads to Rome* (1901), p.72 ("It ... became clear to me that, instead of trying to grapple with this or that doctrine, perhaps specially obnoxious to Protestants, the following were really the questions which would have to be answered: 'Do I believe in Our Lord's charge to Peter? Do I believe that He founded an indestructible Church on earth? Is the Roman Church that Church, or is it not?'.... Would that what I have written would go to encourage others, and show them where an inward happiness, such as they would not dream of, is to be found! The Church has widened my sympathies, it has cast down many prejudices, it has provided me with a spiritual support such as outsiders can have no possible idea of. My intellect is satisfied, and if there be trials and discouraging moments in life, the Church has innumerable remedies to cure them; they all proceed from and return to the one point – the manger of Bethlehem. Let no one say that submission is an act of servility. Submission of our individual opinions to the Vicar of Christ is no more servility than is an inferior officer's submission to his superior. He may not be able to see the situation in all its bearings, but he obeys because he believes that his superior represents his country and his Sovereign. In like manner, when the Vicar of Christ speaks to define a disputed question of faith, or to give a moral counsel, or to warn the world of certain dangers, the Catholic humbly and cheerfully obeys, because he believes that God is true to His promises, and that He is teaching truth by the mouth of His Vicar on earth").

Dummett, Sir Michael Anthony Eardley – philosopher; b. 27 June 1925; c. 1944; educated within traditions of the Anglican Church, but regarded himself as an atheist by age of thirteen ("As a schoolboy, long before any thought of becoming a Christian had crossed my mind, I was deeply impressed when one of my teachers came into class and said, 'I did not invent the Christian religion'"); Fellow of All Souls, Oxford; Wykeham Professor of Logic, Oxford 1979–1992; has written both on the history of analytic philosophy, and made original contributions to subject, particularly in areas of philosophy of mathematics, philosophy of logic, philosophy of language and metaphysics (e.g., *Frege: Philosophy of Language* (1973), *Truth and Other Enigmas* (1978), *The Logical Basis of Metaphysics* (1991)); historian of the Tarot; alleged that Catholic scholars who cast doubt on traditional Church doctrines are turning the Church into "a laughing stock in the eyes of the world" (see debate in *New Blackfriars*, 1987–1988); see "A Remarkable Consensus, " *New Blackfriars*, October 1987, p.424 ("We know that men and women have died rather than renounce, or rather than adhere to, the Catholic Church: if there is no rationale in the matter, they were pitiably deluded. There is no sense to be made of the history of Christianity unless we regard one proposition as held in common by Catholics and Orthodox, and rejected by Protestants. The proposition is that it is enjoined on us, whatever the provocation, never to take any step to disrupt the unity of the Church: let us call this the paramountcy of unity.... Suppose you reject the principle, and think it of little intrinsic importance to which institutional church one belongs: then respect for the beliefs of others ought to lead you to separate yourself from a church the rationale for whose existence is adherence to the principle; by remaining within it, you are treating unseriously the beliefs of those who do adhere to the principle, and whose acceptance of it may be their chief reason for belonging to that church, and, by implication, treating them unseriously, as people who do not matter"); "The Impact of Scriptural Studies on the Content of Catholic Belief," in Thomas Flint and Eleanore Stump (ed), *Hermes and Athena: Biblical Exegesis and Philosophical Theology* (1993), p.3 ("The Catholic Church has always required the acceptance of certain beliefs as a condition of membership; and, until recently, the universal understanding has been that the fact of requiring them is a guarantee of their truth. The centuries-old claim of the Church has been to have a commission from Christ to safeguard the truths revealed by him and to the Apostles, and a promise to be protected from misinterpreting them. That there should be such a custodian is intrinsically plausible. For it is not credible that God should have intervened in human life in so extraordinary manner, in part to reveal truths that we could not otherwise have known, and then allowed that revelation to suffer the garbling and distortion that is the normal fate of human theories and speculations.... It would be hard to accept that there had been a revelation from God if he had not also supplied such a means of keeping it intact and warding off destructive misinterpretations of it"); Gerald Priestland, *The Case Against God* (1984) (Interview with Michael Dummett: "The most important thing is that it makes sense to talk about doing things for the love of God. Now, it is presumptuous of me to mention such things, but the fact is that the few lives that exemplify something far above the average are the lives that are devoted to the love of God. For the love of God people do what, from any other standpoint, is throwing away their lives. I'm not talking only about people who risk martyrdom but who give up their whole lives to relieving the suffering of the utterly wretched, or for that matter those who give their lives to penance and contemplation. I don't know anywhere else we can find anything that counterbalances the extremes of human wickedness which very frequently occur. The one thing I feel I cannot do is to adopt a view of the world which would make nonsense of such lives. When it comes to it, that is where my loyalty lies"); John Beaumont, "Michael Dummett: Oxford Logic and Conversion to the Catholic Faith," *Catholic Life*, November 2007, p.54.

Duncan Smith, (George) Iain – politician; b. 9 April 1954, Edinburgh, Scotland; c. 1967; educated at Sandhurst military college; Scots Guards 1975–1981, including service in Rhodesia and Northern Ireland; Conservative MP; leader of Conservative party 2001–2003; from 2005 chairman of Social Justice Policy Group of Conservative Party; committed Euroskeptic; established Centre for Social Justice, centre-right thinktank.

Dunraven and Mount Earl, third Earl of (Edwin Richard Windham-Quin) – landowner and archaeologist; b. 19 May 1812, London; c. 1855; d. 6 October 1871, Imperial Hotel, Great Malvern, Worcestershire; known as Viscount Adare from 1824 until inherited earldom from his father in 1850; Conservative MP for Glamorgan 1837–1851; main political activity was to safeguard religious education in Ireland, where very popular landlord; in 1866 created a peer of the United Kingdom, with the title Baron Kenry, of Kenry, co. Limerick; Lord Lieutenant of County Limerick 1864–1871; Fellow of the Royal Archaeological Society in 1831; helped to found Irish Archaeological Society in

1840 and the Celtic Society in 1845; President of a section of the Royal Archaeological Institute in 1871; keen archaeologist with many publications, whose main interest was Irish archaeology; also interested in astronomy and investigated claims of spiritualism; devout Catholic and admirer of French liberal Catholic, Montalembert; much influenced by Newman; would have converted earlier but for opposition of his wife, Augusta, whose tactic was to threaten to have a heart attack when he seemed to be about to convert (his conversion led to serious estrangement and bitter quarrel over education of their eldest son, the fourth Earl, who finally became an agnostic); buried at Adare; see *DNB*.

Eaglesim, Thomas Arnot (name in religion Paul) – priest; b. 1840; c. 1878 (received by Newman); d. 1894; brought up a Presbyterian; became an Anglican at Oxford; took Anglican orders; joined the Birmingham Oratory in October 1878; ordained priest in 1882; in April 1879 accompanied Newman to Rome when he went to receive the Cardinal's hat; taught for a while in the Oratory school, then as a parish priest; learned man who assisted Newman with the fourth edition of the *Select Treatises of St. Athanasius*.

Edwards, Francis Oborn, SJ – priest and historian; b. 16 January 1922, Clapham; c. 15 January 1944; d. 14 September 2006; studied history at Birkbeck College, London University; fought in World War II as member of Ayrshire Yeomanry; entered the Society of Jesus in 1947; ordained priest 6 July 1957; from 1959 to 1986 archivist of the English (later British) Province of the Society of Jesus and, after 1964, its official historian; director of Roman Archives 1986–1989; fascinated with Gunpowder Plot and argued that plot was concocted by Sir Robert Cecil (at the Public Record Office he was known as "Gunpowder Edwards"); see *The Dangerous Queen: Mary Queen of Scots* (1964); *Guy Fawkes: The Real Story of the Gunpowder Plot* (1969); *The Marvellous Chance* (1969*); The Jesuits in England* (1985); *Plots and Plotters in the Reign of Elizabeth I* (2002); *The Succession, Bye and Main Plots of 1601–1603* (2006); *The Enigma of the Gunpowder Plot 1605: The Third Solution* (2008); review of Highley and King, *John Foxe and His World*, in *Recusant History*, May 2003, p.521 ("What does the New Testament really mean? The irony is that there was no such entity before 397 AD when the third Council of Carthage defined the canon of Scripture, ratified by Pope St. Siricius, which was confirmed by the Council of Trent and the First Vatican Council.... The canon, which was also that largely accepted by the 16th century Reformers, including John Foxe, was originally established as the bedrock of the Catholic Church both east and west. When the renaissance papacy forced a rethink on all believers, the Catholic reformers stood by a papacy which had erred but was an integral part of the system as founded by Christ. The Protestant reformers decided that an institution which had sunk so low was irreformable and concluded further that the only guide of conduct had to be the same New Testament which had been a pillar of the Church as accepted hitherto. Although the New Testament claimed to be a supernatural revelation, it had to be put across in the normal language of everyday. This meant that there was, as there had always been, room for misunderstanding and diverse interpretation. Hence the reluctance of the universal Church to put the book in the hands of everyone. Its true meaning was a matter for exact study by trained scholars and authoritative definition by the successors of St. Peter. So Tyndale's idea that once the Word was translated and made available even to ploughboys, everybody could know by spiritual insight what it meant, was decidedly naïve. In practice, a variety of clever and often learned men took over and reached, as one might expect, very different conclusions. One thing they all agreed on was that the former bulwark of the old Church was now transparently evident as the foundation of a new faith or faiths, which could be subsumed under the one word 'Protestant.' How the pillar of Catholicism became the main support of all that it opposed presents a question of human psychology, perhaps, as much as theology"); "The Jesuits and Devotion to Our Lady in the England of Elizabeth I and James I," *Recusant History*, May 2007, p.345; Rev. Thomas M. McCoog, SJ, "Francis Oborn Edwards, SJ (1922–2006)" (homily preached at the funeral), *Recusant History*, May 2007, p.342.

Ellis, Alice Thomas (real name Anna Margaret Haycraft (*née* Lindholm)) – novelist and Catholic columnist; b. 9 September 1932, 2 St. John's Road, Wallasey, Birkenhead; c. 1951 or 1952; d. 8 March 2005, Meadow House Hospice, Southall, London; parents were members of "Church of Humanity," which preached "ethical" atheism and human perfectibility; became Catholic because she "no longer found it possible to disbelieve in God"; was postulant nun for six months, but left and later married Colin Berry Haycraft (1929–1994), publisher; mother of seven children (deeply affected by death in 1978 of her second son, Joshua, in an accident); author of twenty-one novels, mainly black comedies about domestic issues, which drew on her own life and Catholicism (e.g., *The Sin Eater* (1977), *Birds of the Air* (1980), *The 27th Kingdom* (1982),

Unexplained Laughter (1985), *The Inn at the Edge of the World* (1990), *Pillars of Gold* (1992) and *Fairy Tale* (1994)); also non-fiction books; columnist for *Spectator*, *Oldie*, *Universe*, and *Catholic Herald* (dismissed from latter for accusing Archbishop Worlock of diluting the faith with his ecumenism); highly critical generally of liberalizing elements in the Church; strongly anti-feminist; buried in the churchyard of St. Melangell at Pennant Melangell, close to her husband, and her son Joshua; see *Cat Among the Pigeons: A Catholic Miscellany* (1994); *Serpent On The Rock: A Personal View of Christianity* (1994) ("Nowhere have I found any evidence of Vatican II having had a beneficial influence. In place of the old rigors we have sentimentality, confusion, untruth, meaningless talk of 'renewal' and 'improvement,' and 'sharing' and 'caring,' where once these were taken for granted and practiced in a specifically recognizably Catholic fashion. As Paul VI lamented, a few years later, it provided an inbuilt agency for Satan to enter and stifle the fruits of the Council. Pope John XXIII had proclaimed that Vatican II would open the windows of the Church to the world and great gusts of fresh air would flow in. All that seems to have happened is that someone of unsound architectural mind and uncertain grasp of structure opened up the floodgates letting in a tide of sewage...

Luther, who was, on the evidence, more than a little nuts, said: 'I affirm that all brothels, murders, robberies, crimes, adulteries are less wicked than this abomination of the Popish Mass.' He observed of the Canon, which is central to the Mass: 'This abominable Canon is a confluence of puddles of slimy water, which have made the Mass a sacrifice. The Mass is not a sacrifice. It is not the act of a sacrificing priest. Together with the Canon, we discard all that implies an oblation.' The most fervent ecumenicist would find it difficult to reconcile this view with that of, say, Pope Urban VIII, who said: 'If there is anything divine among the possessions of man, which the citizens of Heaven might covet (were covetousness possible for them) it would certainly be the most Holy Sacrifice of the Mass, whose blessing is such that in it man possesses a certain anticipation of Heaven while still on earth, even having before their eyes and taking into their hands the very Maker of both Heaven and earth'''); *God Has Not Changed* (2004) ("As Arthur Machen observed, '"spiritual" does not mean "respectable," it does not even mean "moral," it does not mean "good" in the ordinary acceptation of the word. It signifies the royal prerogative of man, differentiating him from the beasts.' The atheist is uneasy with this idea: it strikes him as irrational and, while he must know that man differs from the ape and the dog in certain respects, he sees it mostly as a matter of degree. One of the extraordinary things about atheists is their conviction that their point of view comes as a great surprise to the theist. 'Come on,' they scoff, 'You can't believe all that stuff about the Virgin Birth and the Resurrection.' To which the answer is – I've thought about it and no I can't but I do. This response arises, not from stubborn stupidity or a failure to listen to the arguments, but from an awareness of our lack of understanding, combined with a sense of something just beyond the borders of consciousness, just out of reach but not to be denied. Refusal to contemplate this something leads not to peace of mind but to a sort of irritable confusion. I had a friend, a noted atheist, who, after an argument, made me think of a savage dancing triumphantly round a tree treading on the supposed bones of his enemy, while the said enemy perched in the branches gazing down with a puzzled expression. There is no common ground and no point in sitting down round that table, so dear to the rationalist, to 'talk it out'"); Marian E. Crowe, "Unexplained Laughter: The Life and Work of Alice Thomas Ellis," *Crisis*, October 2005 ("She decided to become a Catholic: 'Then after due time and instruction I became a catholic because I no longer found it possible to disbelieve in God.... I felt entirely at home with the conviction, aims and rituals of the Church and secure in the certainty that it was immune from frivolous change and the pressures of fashion; primarily concerned with the numinous rather than with the political concerns of its members'...

The *New York Times* noted in its obituary that Ellis 'rebelled' against her secular humanist parents by converting to Catholicism. The version of the story she told me was somewhat different: 'I realized this makes a lot of sense. This is an ancient, ancient structure. What I think is interesting is that no one has any faith in age and experience anymore. I think authority is vital for sort of freedom. Anarchy is not freedom. One of the nuns told me, "Once you're inside the Church, you can shake a pretty loose leg." It gave you much more freedom once you knew the rules than just floundering around in this complete permissiveness and liberalism. You've got the structure, and within that you can be very free, and you can actually be very happy'"); J. C. Whitehouse, "Sin-Eating and After: First Thoughts on the Fiction of Alice Thomas Ellis," *Saint Austin Review*, September/October 2007, p.15; *DNB*.

Ellis, Bishop Philip, OSB (name in religion Michael) – bishop; b. 1652, Stratford, London; c. 1668; d. 16 November 1726, Segni, Italy; son of Anglican clergyman; eldest brother, John (d. 1733), under-secretary of state to William III;

next brother, William (d. 1734), secretary of state to exiled James II; next, Elbore, Church of Ireland bishop; converted whilst at Westminster School; went over to Benedictine monastery at Douai; ordained priest and sent to work on the English mission; preacher and chaplain to James II from 1685; consecrated bishop for western district 6 May 1688; in November when the Revolution broke out, arrested and thrown into Newgate prison; soon freed and withdrew to France to court in exile at St. Germain; went to Rome where close friend of Cardinal Howard and assistant prelate to the pontifical throne; never able to return to England; made Bishop of Segni in Papal States in 1708 where he founded a seminary and improved condition of the poor; buried in centre of seminary church; see *Gillow*, Vol. II, p.161; *Catholic Encyclopedia*; *DNB*.

Elvins, Mark Turnham OFM Cap – priest and writer; b. 1939, Whitstable, Kent; c. 24 December 1968; son of Anglican clergyman; commission in the army; studied art and joined an art dealer; life turned upside down by St. Francis; worked as volunteer with Anglican Brothers of Prayer and Action; took Anglican orders; intellectually converted by Newman's *The Development of Christian Doctrine*; ordained priest in 1973; Secretary of the Association for English Worship; joined Capuchin Order in 1999; in 2007 appointed Warden of Greyfriars Hall, Oxford; much work for the homeless; author of many articles, mainly on historical issues; see *Towards a People's Liturgy* (1994); *Catholic Trivia: Our Forgotten Heritage* (2002) ("Many Catholic customs had a liturgical inspiration associated with religious festivals. Today these festivals have mostly changed, leaving their associate customs misunderstood and disconnected. Old customs have become new superstitions.

One reason for this was the massive social and cultural dislocation wrought by the Reformation, and another was the puritanical attitudes of many liturgists of more recent (post-conciliar) times. A number of interesting reversals have occurred. The spilling of salt, today associated with bad luck, had a Catholic origin, salt being used in the preparation of holy water, the time-honored protection against the Devil. The number thirteen used to be considered lucky, representing the twelve disciples with Our Lord (hence the baker's dozen); but Puritan extremists reversed the custom to produce the modern superstition of bad luck.... Religious extremists even regarded Christmas as superstitious, and Cromwell in his day actually outlawed the consumption of Christmas puddings and mince pies. In fact the zeal to stamp out popery turned many religious customs into negative superstitions, like walking under ladders (ladders were seen as a symbol of Our Lord's Passion and were walked under to invoke divine protection). The same zeal led to the dropping of the papal tiara in the arms both of the See of York and of the Guild of White Bread Bakers. Winchester scholars used to bow to a statue of Our Lady; the bowing continues but the offending statue has long been removed. In fact, as religious customs declined real superstitions increased in a kind of inverse ration. The crucifix or St. Christopher medal, which was once invoked for divine aid, has now been replaced by a rabbit's foot for good luck. Without the anchor of religion, superstitions, and even occult practices, have become more widespread"); *Gospel Chivalry: Franciscan Romanticism* (2006); *A Eucharistic Vision and the Spirituality of St. Francis of Assisi* (2007); "The Friar" in Greg Watts, *Catholic Lives* (2001) ("[The] cross for some people is a threat. But for those who believe it is a

sign of love and triumph; the triumph of love. By submission and suffering Jesus conquered the world. God as God is beyond our comprehension. God as Man is the bridge between Heaven and earth").

Ely (alias Havard, Harvard and Howard), Humphrey – priest; b. about 1539, Herefordshire; d. 15 March 1602 or 1603, at Pont-a-Musson; declared himself a Catholic at Oxford and was obliged to leave the university; conversion influenced by Nicholas Sander's *Image of Christ* (1567); went to Douai and trained as a canon lawyer, becoming an eminent Professor at Douai University; affected by troubles at Douai in 1578; worked in Rome on revision of several controversial works; visited England in June 1580 in same ship as three priests, Thomas Cottam, John Hart and Edward Rishton, the first two being arrested in Dover; believing him to be a military man, the mayor of Dover handed Cottam over to him to be delivered up to authorities; he let Cottam go, but was later arrested himself (Cottam voluntarily gave himself up and was later executed); spent some time in Marshalsea prison; ordained priest in April 1582 in Rheims; Professor of Canon and Civil Law at University of Pont-à-Mousson from 1586 and buried there in church of Poor Clares; see *Gillow*, Vol. II, p.164; *DNB*.

Embry, Sir Basil Edward – air force officer; b. 28 February 1902, Longford, Gloucestershire; c. 1940; d. 7 December 1977, Boyup Brook, Western Australia; father an Anglican clergyman; love for flying; joined Royal Air Force in 1921; service in Iraq and work with air ambulance service; posted to India in 1934; promoted to squadron leader in 1936 and flew with courage and leadership in the 1937 and 1938 campaigns on the northwest frontier; on outbreak of war was put in directorate of operations in Whitehall; took him eight days to get out and to take command of 107 day bomber squadron, where he personally led the squadron on very dangerous missions and won great affection from his men; finally wounded and shot down over France; captured, but escaped twice and finally arrived safely in Gibraltar; in England promoted to group captain and took part in fighter operations; in 1943 given command of 2 bomber squadron with rank of Air Vice-Marshal; again flew with his crews and carried forged identity documents, for fear of execution if captured; awarded DFC and third bar to his DSO, both in 1945 (one of most highly decorated officers in the three services); after war supervised complete overhaul of RAF training; promoted Air Marshal (later Air Chief Marshal) and made commander-in-chief Fighter Command; commander of allied air forces central Europe in NATO 1953–1956; started new life with his family farming in Western Australia, becoming President of Farmers' Union there; first chairman of the worldwide RAF Escaping Society; see *Mission Completed* (1956); *DNB*.

Eppstein, John – writer and diplomat; b. 1895; c. 1919 (received by Fr. Martindale (see below)); son of Anglican clergyman; served with Friends' Ambulance Unit during World War I when he received many decorations; formed Catholic Council for International Relations in 1922; during 1930s private secretary to Viscount Cecil of Chelwood with whom he served on British delegations to League of Nations; in 1938 formed British Society for International Understanding (director until his retirement in 1966); in 1952 set up international Atlantic Treaty Association to sustain popular support for Atlantic Alliance (secretary general until 1961); writer on international law and relations

and the Catholic Church (author of *The Catholic Tradition of the Law of Nations* (1935)); critic of developments in the Church after Second Vatican Council; see *Has the Catholic Church Gone Mad?* (1971) ("The Catholic Church has *not* gone mad. In so far as Catholic minds have gone mad it is not a universal phenomenon: it is a European phenomenon, and is the consequence of attempts to adapt and accommodate a religion based upon man's entire dependence on God (a humble and contrite heart and the fear of the Lord which is the beginning of wisdom), to the conditions of a society in which pride in man's scientific achievement and his supposed social and intellectual emancipation has led to a general impatience with authority at every level and disbelief in the moral law itself. The solidity and sanity of the Church recently established in the far poorer but more naturally God-fearing society of Africa – shared, as we believe it to be, by a large but inarticulate part of the Catholic clergy and people in other continents – is proof that what is trumpeted abroad as progress, whether in the form of loosening ecclesiastical authority and discipline or in modernizing faith and morality, is in reality the peculiar product of a decadent European civilization, which, historically Christian in origin, can no longer claim the name of Christendom.... The fact remains that it is chiefly in Western Europe and North America that this disarray has been created, and it is there that the struggle to counteract it must be waged. Important as may be the debates about the distribution of powers in the Church, or regard for human freedom, or the adaptation of doctrine to the scientific or philosophical fashions of the day, or the social order, it is time to recall that these at best are only means to an end, which is a spiritual end. The first and most important mark of the Church of Christ is holiness. It is a mark which today is much beclouded. Charity and justice indeed are the adjuncts of sanctity, but so, in this boisterous world, are reverence, awe, humility, and quiet in the contemplation of divine mysteries. These, and not the reorganization of human society are what at its best the Catholic Church has offered to humanity in past centuries, and it is these intangible qualities and virtues which at all costs must be restored and preserved").

Erskine, Hon. Stuart Richard (known as Ruaraidh Erskine of Mar) – political activist and Gaelic entrepreneur; b. 15 January 1869, 1 Portland Place, Brighton; c. 1897; d. 5 January 1960, Chartham, Bridge, Kent; son of fifth Baron Erskine (1841–1913); from family with Scottish roots; learned Gaelic from a childhood nurse; inspired early by Irish nationalist movement; prominent Gaelic nationalist, who dreamed of a self-governing Celtic Scotland; editor of several Gaelic supporting periodicals, notably *Am Bard* ('The Poet'), the nationalist Gaelic newspaper, and *Guth na Bliadhna* ('The Year's Voice'); laid foundations for a resurgence in Gaelic writing; see *DNB*.

Estcourt, Edgar Edmund – priest and author; b. 7 February 1816; c. December 1845, Prior Park; d. 17 April 1884, Leamington Spa; son of Anglican rector; educated at Exeter College, Oxford; became Anglican curate; came under influence of Oxford Movement whilst student there and converted; ordained priest in 1848 by Bishop Ullathorne; canon at St. Chad's Cathedral, Birmingham (assistant to Ullathorne); excellent financial administrator; wrote fine work on Anglican orders; patiently endured much suffering; buried at Kenilworth, Warwickshire; see *The Question of Anglican Ordinations Discussed* (1873); *Gillow*, Vol. II, p.179; *DNB*.

Euan-Smith, Colonel Sir Charles Bean – army officer and diplomat; b. 21 September 1842, Georgetown, British Guiana; c. 1908 (wife, Lady Edith, musical composer and friend of Fr. Basil Maturin (see below), received in 1898); d. 30 August 1910, 51 South Street, Park Lane, London; entered Indian Army 1859; served in the Abyssinian and Afghan Wars; became colonel 1885; retired 1889; knighted 1890; Consul-General at Zanzibar 1887–1891; HM envoy to Morocco 1891–1893; offered by Lord Salisbury post of minister resident at Bogota, Colombia, but did not take up the post; pioneer in the commercial development of wireless telegraphy; see *DNB*.

Evans, Charles Smart – singer and composer; b. 1778, London; c. 1808; d. 4 January 1849, London; gentleman of Chapel Royal; for several years organist at St. Paul's, Covent Garden; as adult he had very fine alto voice; after his conversion he was member of choir of chapel of Portuguese embassy in South Street, Grosvenor Square, London, for which he wrote a Magnificat and several motets; see *Gillow*, Vol. II, p.185; *DNB*.

Evans-Pritchard, Sir Edward Evan ("E.P.") – social anthropologist; b. 21 September 1902, Sussex; c. 1944; d. 11 September 1973, Oxford; son of Welsh-speaking Church of England clergyman; worked at London School of Economics with C. G. Seligman and B. Malinowski; much research in Sudan and Egypt, especially among Nuer tribes; international academic reputation; wrote from an explicitly theistic viewpoint; served in World War II in North Africa; Professor of Social Anthropology at Oxford University 1946–1970 and Fellow of All Souls; President of Royal Anthropological Institute, 1949–1951; knighted in 1971; rejected the view that anthropology was a natural science, arguing instead that it should be grouped amongst the humanities, especially history; of his five children, his daughter, Deidre, was an expert on folklore and Middle Eastern studies and his son, Ambrose, was an investigative reporter for the *Daily Telegraph*; see *DNB* ("Though he was not, as some were led to suppose, a zealous convert, he advocated religious faith, which for him was an answer to his own inveterate skepticism. This religious stance and his dismissive attitude to claims then being made for social anthropology as 'a natural science of society' raised controversy and some polemic among professional colleagues").

Everard, Robert – religious writer and controversialist; fl. 1647–1664; d. 1664; from humble origins; of liberal education; served as captain in Cromwell's regiment in the New Model Army; was one of the representatives elected to express the regiments' grievances against parliament; spoke on the side of the Levellers and took part in the 1649 mutinies by the Levellers; adopted the General Baptist Faith after trying several Christian sects; did much preaching and published several pamphlets 1649–1655; little more known about him until 1664 when he reappeared and detailed his recent conversion to Catholicism; renounced his previous beliefs and offered an apology to Charles II for his part in the New Model Army; see *An Epistle to the Several Congregations* (1664); Gillow, Vol. II, p.189; *Catholic Encyclopedia*; *DNB*.

Faber, Frederick William – priest, poet and devotional writer; b. 28 June 1814, Calverley, West Yorkshire; c. 16 November 1845 (received with Francis Knox and ten other friends and servants; brother, Major Faber, received in 1848); d. 26 September 1863, Brompton Oratory,

London; of Huguenot descent; brought up as an Evangelical Anglican; then leaned towards Evangelical Calvinism, but later influenced by Tractarianism; Fellow of University College, Oxford; ordained into Anglican ministry, introducing Confession and devotion to the Sacred Heart in his parish; friend of William Wordsworth; developed fascination with Catholicism and devotion to St. Philip Neri; only Newman's influence kept him from the Catholic Church and Newman's reception in 1845 removed that obstacle; in 1846 established a religious community, the "Brothers of the Will of God" or "Wilfridians," as they were called from St. Wilfrid, their patron; ordained priest 3 April 1847; in 1848 presented himself and his community to Newman's new Congregation of Oratory of St. Philip Neri; for some time Superior of London Oratory; DD of Rome; wrote eight religious treatises, most notably *The Creator and the Creature* (1858), also numerous hymns, including *Faith of Our Fathers*; fine preacher; his influence in the Church was said by Fr. R. Addington, another Oratorian priest, to have been like "fireworks over water – a pyrotechnic display, whose effects linger and remain in the mind's eye"; see Rev. James Cassidy, *The Life of Father Faber, Priest of the Oratory of St. Philip Neri* (1946) ("You walk through the streets [of Rome] – there stood the centurion's house, and beneath that church St. Luke wrote the Acts of the Apostles – there St. Ignatius shed his blood – from that pulpit St. Thomas preached – in that room St. Francis slept – in that house St. Dominic first began his Order"); Ronald Chapman, *Father Faber* (1961); Madeleine Beard, *Faith and Fortune* (1997) ("At an audience with Pope Gregory XVI the Holy Father said simply: 'You must not mislead yourself in wishing for unity, yet waiting for your *church* to move. Think of the salvation of your own soul.' Faber knelt, the Pope laid his hands on his shoulders and said: 'May the grace of God correspond to your good wishes and deliver you from the nets of Anglicanism, and bring you to the true Holy Church'"); Alan Frost, "Frederick William Faber," *Catholic Life*, Parts 1, 2 and 3, June, July and August 2004; Melissa Wilkinson, *Frederick William Faber: A Great Servant of God* (2007); *Gillow*, Vol. II, p.207 ("On Sunday, Nov. 17, 1845, he officiated for the last time as rector of Elton, and announced to his people that the doctrines he had taught them, though true, were not those of the Church of England; that as far as the Church of England had a voice, she had disavowed them, and that consequently he could not remain in her communion, but must go where truth was to be found"); *Catholic Encyclopedia* ("With his zealous community [the Wilfridians], now forty in number, [Faber] converted the whole parish, except 'the parson, the pew-opener, and two drunken men'"); *DNB*.

Fairfield, (Josephine) Letitia Denny – public health physician and social campaigner; b. 10 March 1885, St. Kilda, Melbourne, Australia; c. 1922; d. 1 February 1978, London; Anglo-Irish father who traveled widely; sister of Rebecca West (1892–1983), writer, critic and journalist; family moved to Britain in 1888 and finally settled in Edinburgh; qualified as a doctor at Edinburgh University with several medals; worked in public health for London County Council 1911–1948 (became first woman senior medical officer there); in 1918 chief medical officer to new Women's Royal Air Force; called to the Bar in 1923; senior woman doctor for medical services in World War II; campaigned for social causes, e.g., women's suffrage, Irish independence; opposition to birth control, eugenics and euthanasia; co-founder in 1926, with Halliday Sutherland (see below) of the League of National Life, set up to fight against the promotion of birth control as an instrument of social control; said that if voluntary euthanasia ever introduced, the mentally handicapped would be "murdered" and homes for the aged poor would become "slaughter houses"; combated anti-semitism and gave support for Catholic converts from Judaism; co-editor of Medico-Legal and Criminological Review, and President of Medico-Legal Society in 1957 and 1958; regular contributor to Catholic press on matters such as medical evidence for miracle cures, the supernatural, and exorcism (opposed moves to canonize Teresa Higginson and accounts of case of Therese Neumann, the apparent stigmatic); writings on social and welfare responsibilities of the Church; unmarried; *see Catholics and the Public Medical Services* (1930); *The Case Against Sterilization* (1935); Ann Farmer, *Prophets and Priests: The Hidden Face of the Birth Control Movement* (2002), pp.121–123; *DNB*.

Falconer (or Falkner) (alias Dingley), John, SJ – priest; b. 25 March 1577, Litton, Dorset; c. 1598; d. 7 July 1656, London; from wealthy family; parents died early; neglected his studies; joined the expedition of the Earl of Essex to Spain in 1589; returning to London, he decided to repent and reform his life; converted under the influence of Catholics in Henry, Lord Windsor's household, where he served for two years; went to English College, Rome, in 1600; ordained priest 20 December 1603; entered the Society of Jesus in 1604 and sent to England in 1607; banished from the country in 1618, but soon returned and served in London and then in Northamptonshire and Oxfordshire; served in Jesuit houses in Belgium 1631–1648; wrote several lives of saints; see *Gillow*, Vol. II, p.223; *DNB*.

Falkland, Lady Elizabeth (Elizabeth Cary, *née* Tanfield) – b. 1585, Burford, Oxfordshire; c. 1626 (husband received later; also two sons and four daughters); d. October 1639; only child of Sir Lawrence Tanfield, later Lord Chief Baron of the Exchequer, a devout Protestant; very studious from early age and taught herself French, Spanish, Italian, Latin, Hebrew, and Transylvanian; when her father gave her a copy of Calvin's *Institutes*, she pointed out contradictions in the book; married to Sir Henry Cary, first Viscount Falkland, Comptroller of the Royal Household, a Protestant; she brought up ten of their eleven children, but not Lucius, the future second Viscount Falkland, who was removed by her father because of her Catholic leanings; her reading of the early Church Fathers unsettled her; husband appointed Lord Deputy of Ireland; she accompanied him and did much work for the poor, but returned alone to England; invited to court and got on well with Queen Henrietta Maria; in 1626 a Benedictine priest, Fr. Dunstan, received her into the Catholic Church; her conversion greatly displeased the king and by his order she was confined in her house for six weeks; her husband attempted to starve her into submission; rejected by her mother; forced to live on the charity of her friends and was almost destitute; translated Cardinal du Perron's reply to the attack on his works by James I; wrote several lives of saints and poems on them; first English female dramatist; first Englishwoman to write a tragedy (*Mariam*) and a history play (*Edward II*); Queen Henrietta Maria's mediation brought about complete reconciliation between her and her husband and he became a Catholic before his death in 1633 (she instructed her dying husband how to prepare for death); of the two sons and four daughters who converted, all of the daughters became Benedictine nuns at Cambrai, and of the two sons, Henry and Patrick, Henry (d. 1653) joined Benedictine Order and assumed the name of Placid; she was buried by Queen's permission in Her Majesty's Chapel of St. James; see Georgiana Fullerton, *The Life of Elizabeth Lady Falkland, 1585–1639* (1883); Antony Charles Ryan, "Elizabeth Cary, Lady Falkland, the First English Female Dramatist," *Catholic Life*, May 2003, p.47; Heather Wolfe (ed), *The Literary Career and Legacy of Elizabeth Cary (1613–1680)* (2007); *Gillow*, Vol. II, additions and corrections, p.ix; *DNB*.

Falkner, Thomas, SJ – priest, doctor and missionary; b. 6 October 1707, Manchester; c. 1732; d. 30 January 1784, Plowden Hall, Salop, Shropshire; brought up as Presbyterian; studied mathematics and physics under Isaac Newton; became doctor like his father; went out as surgeon on a slave-ship to Africa and then to Buenos Aires, where he became sick; cared for by Jesuits (in particular Sebastian de San Martin) and both converted and entered the Society of Jesus there in 1732; ordained priest in 1739; missionary and famed doctor to Indians in Paraguay for thirty-eight years; published treatise on Indian medicines for Royal Society; moved to college of Córdoba in 1756, where he converted to Catholicism twenty British survivors from man-of-war *Lord Clive*; expelled with the other Jesuits from South America in 1768; returned to England and joined English Province about 1771; chaplain to several houses, including the Berkeleys and the Plowdens; buried at Lydbury North, Shropshire; see R. F. Doublet, "An Englishman in Rio de la Plata," *The Month*, April 1960, p.216; *Gillow*, Vol. II, p.224; *Catholic Encyclopedia*; *DNB*.

Farjeon, Eleanor – writer; b. 13 February 1881, Buckingham Street, London; c. 22 August 1951; d. 5 June 1965, 20 Perrins Walk, Hampstead, London; father Jewish but did not practice his religion; mother taught her children their Christian prayers "to be on the safe side"; had no formal education, but member of a literary family living in a bohemian literary and dramatic world; access to her father's large library; brought up in a God fearing manner, but without any particular religion; always belief in supernatural life, but not until later – nominally – a Christian; writer of plays and verses, children's literature, and family memoirs (e.g., *Ten Saints* (1936), *The Glass Slipper* (1944), *The Silver Curlew* (1949)); wrote the hymn, "Morning Has Broken"; long platonic friendship with Denys Blakelock, the actor (see above); buried in churchyard which spans side of Hampstead Hill between Protestant church in Church Row and Catholic church in Holly Walk; see Denys Blakelock, *Eleanor: Portrait of a Farjeon* (1966) ("When friends have entered that part of each other completely, we cannot come out from it alone as we were before, for he whom we entered is now some of oneself. And that is why, I believe, we must enter Christ through His Passion; it is only after we have been with Him in Gethsemane that we can have Him in Heaven"); A. Farjeon, *Morning Has Broken: A Biography of Eleanor Farjeon* (1986) ("The romance of Christianity, with its emphasis on Mother and Child, was something she had responded to always. The Christmas festivity, birth, pity and generosity, brought out strong feelings to be expressed in poems flecked with a dry realism which kept them from becoming too sentimental…

Later … Eleanor reflected on Purgatory and 'the purgation of Self which stands between us and God,' concluding: 'Only the choosers of, and rejoicers in, mortal sin, are those who need to fear because they have pushed Him away. If this were not so, where is the hope He holds out to us millions of poor imperfect sinners? For how many can go perfect to Heaven'"); Anne Harvey, "Fresh from the Word," *The Tablet*, 22/29 December 2007, p.11; Matthew Hoehn, OSB (ed), *Catholic Authors* (1952); *DNB*.

Farren, William – actor; b. 28 September 1825, 30 Brompton Square, London; c. 1883 (received with his wife); d. 25 September 1908, Siena; from acting family, his father, also William Farren (1786–1861), being a celebrated performer; the "third Farren" (his younger brother, Henry, also being an actor) who during his father's life played under the name of "William Forrester"; extensive career playing many roles; formed the English Comedy Company, which toured the provinces; retired to Siena where he became a Franciscan Tertiary; buried in Siena, wearing habit of his Order; see *DNB*.

Fawkes, Guy – soldier and conspirator; b. April 1570, Stonegate district of York; d. 31 January 1606; parents had conformed to the new religion (some say father staunch Protestant); brought up Protestant; after his father's death (1578) his mother married Dionis Bainbridge from ancient Catholic family of Scotton, West Yorkshire and was reconciled to the Church; converted whilst at Scotton; became soldier of fortune in Spanish army in the Netherlands; conscientious and brave; one of conspirators involved in Gunpowder Plot of 1605, whose task was to set fire to the gunpowder; arrested and brought to trial at Westminster Hall in January 1606; convicted of high treason and executed; see Lingard, *History of England*, Vol. VII; *Gillow*, Vol. II, p.228; *DNB*.

Fellows, Reginald Bruce – barrister; c. 1898; assistant district auditor of Local Government Board 1897; auditor 1901–1906; ordained Catholic priest; see essay in J. G. F. Raupert (ed), *Roads to Rome* (1901), p.81 ("Some years ago I became convinced that the doctrine of the Real Presence was of the essence of Christ's teaching, that it had been taught by the Apostles and insisted on by the primitive Church and that the same doctrine had been taught as essential … down to the time of the Reformation. At that period, however, it appeared that a belief in the doctrine of the Real Presence ceased to be any longer necessary for membership of the Established Church. It seemed to me that strong and cumulative evidence of this change – this protest against the ancient faith – was found in the incidental notices which we have, e.g., in Churchwardens' Accounts, both of the payments which were made for the removal of altar stones and for the demolition of altars, and also of the sales of those sacred vessels and vestments which had for centuries formed part of a ritual which had been the expression of a belief in the doctrine of Christ's Presence on the Altar…

But if the doctrine of the Real Presence is really an essential part of Christ's teaching, it must also (I argued) form an essential part of the Christianity of this or of any other age. Now, it appeared to me that there actually existed in England a body corporate claiming to be the Church of Christ, and also to be the legitimate descendant of the pre-Reformation Church and teaching; moreover, that a belief in the Real Presence was absolutely essential for Church membership. The conclusion at which I arrived was that this body, the Catholic and Roman Church, was *prima facie* the true Church of Christ…

Further evidence in favor of submitting to the Catholic Church was found in the fact that Protestantism tended to reject, or at least to minimize, those precepts of Christ which are difficult to obey and irksome to human nature: e.g., abstinence and fasting; confession; voluntary poverty and the other counsels of perfection. A strong presumption appeared to me to be raised by this consideration alone against the claim of any Protestant Church to be the true Church of Christ").

Fenby, Eric William – composer, conductor, teacher, and author; b. 22 April 1906, 92 Candler Street, Scarborough, Yorkshire; d. 18 February 1997, 1 Raincliffe Court, Stepney Road, Scarborough; brought up as an Anglican; exceptional musical ability from very early age; after conversion considered becoming a Benedictine monk; acted as amanuensis to the blind and paralyzed composer Frederick Delius (1862–1934) from 1928 at Grez-sur-Loing in France, taking down some of his late works from dictation; also arranger of music of Delius; his own compositions (most of which he destroyed) include Overture "Rossini on Ilkla Moor"; wrote the film score for Alfred Hitchcock's *Jamaica Inn* (1939); many musical appointments and honors, including prestigious Royal Philharmonic Society award in 1984; buried in St. Laurence's Church, Scalby, Scarborough; see *Delius As I Knew Him* (1936); *Grove Music Online*; *DNB*.

Ffinch, Michael – writer; b. 7 March 1934, Rochester, Kent; c. about 1962; d. 14 September 1999, Dodding Green, Kendal, Cumbria; tutored for a time at Oxford by W. H. Auden who recognized his talents as poet; biographer, poet, librettist, broadcaster, and teacher; flamboyant figure who frequently recited his own poetry; convinced it was impossible to be wholly English without embracing the faith of his ancestors; buried in ancient graveyard of Ravenstonedale parish church; see *Voice Round a Star. And Other Poems* (1970); *G. K. Chesterton* (1986); *Newman: The Second Spring* (1991); obituary, *The Times*, 28 September 1999 ("He embraced Roman Catholicism and his faith was profound, passionate and enlightened. It gave him the interior stamina to endure adversity and misfortune and enhanced his natural generosity of spirit.... Michael felt an affinity for [Chesterton], who was also sustained by faith. Both believed that 'beer is best' although Michael would advance a good case for claret and port as lubricants of wit and imagination"); obituary, *The Independent*, 12 October 1999 ("His last awful years as the cancer went on and on have been an example to everyone who knew him. Somehow he made a joke of it until the end and his faith never faltered even after his much younger wife died so tragically, not long before he did").

Field, Henry Ibbot ("Field of Bath") – pianist, performer and teacher; b. 6 December 1797, Bath; c. 22 November 1835 (feast of St. Cecilia, patroness of music; received by Peter Baines, Bishop of Siga); d. 19 May 1848, Northumberland Buildings, Bath; eldest of seven children; father organist at Bath Abbey; in 1807, at age of ten, Field made his first appearance in public, playing duet with his father; he went on to secure successful career as performer and teacher; best pianist of the day and several distinguished composers dedicated compositions to him; whilst employed as music teacher at Prior Park College, near Bath, converted by Luigi Gentili; see *Gillow*, Vol. II, p.255; *DNB*.

Filmer, John Henry – priest; c. 1900; formerly High Anglican clergyman; ordained Catholic priest (Diocesan Missionary of Our Lady of Compassion); co-founder of the Catholic Missionary Society (dedicated to the re-conversion of the non-Catholic people of England to the Catholic Faith); Master of Guild of Our Lady of Ransom; see essay in J. G. F. Raupert (ed), *Roads to Rome* (1901), p.84 ("I regard my conversion as the result of the Holy Spirit's gradual education in the truth of God, and my submission to the Church as the logical consequence of principles which I learnt to hold while still a member of the English Church. For I had learnt, step by step, to believe the whole body (with one exception) of Catholic Doctrine, from the Church as a teaching body, through the whole list of distinctively Catholic tenets, such as the Seven Sacraments, Invocation of Saints, Purgatory, finding each in turn (to my surprise, for I had at one time held them in abhorrence) bear the tests of Scripture and of Reason. And I remained a member of the Church of England ... merely because I believed her to be a true part of God's One Church, and that therefore her formularies must be, and honestly could be, interpreted in the Catholic sense; while their mistiness, together with the difficulties encountered by any Catholic-minded person within her Communion, were simply the natural result of the sins of our forefathers who at the Reformation compromised themselves and their Church with foreign Protestantism. This was my position when it dawned upon me that I had built up this superstructure of Catholicity upon two foundations, the truth of which I had taken for granted, viz. that the Church of England was a true part of the One Catholic Church, in spite of appearances to the contrary, and that the claim of the first bishop in Christendom to be infallible was a new and a false claim.

Then, asking myself, Why do I believe Infallibility alone of all other Catholic doctrines to be false? I found I only rejected it (not knowing anything about it) because I was prejudiced against it, and because to accept it meant to give up the whole Anglican position. I had accepted all other truths which at one time in my ignorance I rejected, simply because I had learnt more about them. I now knew what they meant. I saw they were scripturally and reasonably sound; might it not be the same with this one? So I felt bound to learn more about it, and, applying the same tests of Scripture and Reason, I was convinced first of its necessity, then of its reasonableness, last of its scriptural authority").

Firbank, (Arthur Annesley) Ronald – writer and aesthete; b. 17 January 1886, 40 Clarges Street, Mayfair, London; c. 6 December 1907 (received by Mgr. Robert Hugh Benson (see above)); d. 21 May 1926, Hotel Quirinale, Rome; of wealthy upper middle class parents; from childhood enduring fascination with both royalty and Catholicism; left Cambridge University without degree (converted whilst there); lived off his inheritance traveling around Spain, Italy, Middle East and North Africa; of delicate and sensitive nature, lived life of aesthete; writer of novels written in highly personal and satirical style with no conventional plots (e.g., *Vainglory* (1915), *Valmouth* (1919), *Prancing Nigger* (1924), *The Flower Beneath the Foot* (1923), *The Eccentricities of Cardinal Pirelli* (1926)); interred in Campo Verano, Rome; see Jocelyn Brooke, *Ronald Firbank* (1951) ("Perhaps the most noteworthy event of his time at Cambridge was his reception into the Roman Catholic church, though his Catholicism might be described, perhaps, as 'pratiquant' rather than 'croyant': the appeal of the Church, in fact, was for Firbank more aesthetic than theological, and in his later novels he adopts an attitude of affectionate mockery towards the hierarchy"); M. J. Benkovitz, *Ronald Firbank:*

A Biography (1969); Ellis Hanson, *Decadence and Catholicism* (1997); *DNB*.

Fitzgerald, Geraldine Penrose – b. 27 January 1846, Corkbeg, Cork, Ireland; c. May 1869 (received by Fr. T. F. Knox at the London Oratory); from an Irish Protestant family; she became High Church; in 1867 began to write to Newman, who was impressed by her "simplicity and frankness"; faced opposition from her own family before her conversion; author of several novels, viz. *Ereighda Castle* (1870), *Only Three Weeks* (1872) (both published anonymously), *Oaks and Birches* (1885), *The Silver Whistle* (1890) (both under the pseudonym "Naseby"); see Joyce Sugg, *Ever Yours Affly: John Henry Newman and His Female Circle* (1996) ("As a very old lady she set out in a long letter [dated 9 march 1938] to a Jesuit friend [Fr. Francis Brown] the story of reading Newman's *Apologia*: 'When I was a young girl I used to read his Apologia sitting on top of a ladder in my cousin Willy Cumleton's library.... When Willy found me doing this he took it away and locked it up and said – "There's been enough of that" but it had set me off on the road to popery; I longed to read more, but it was a dear book. I had but little pocket money.... I pawned a valuable gold and ruby brooch one of my aunts had given me, and bought it.... Finally I was praying in the chapel he [Newman] built in Stephens Green, when the truth of the Catholic Church came over me like a thunderclap: but I would not join. I was afraid of being turned out of the house'").

Fitzgerald, Field-Marshall Sir John Forster – army officer; b. 1784/5, Carrigoran, County Clare, Ireland; c. short time before his death; d. 24 March 1877, Tours, France; son of an Irish MP;

fought during the Peninsular War, notably at Badajoz; held commands in India and Canada; at his death the oldest officer in the British Army; Liberal MP for County Clare 1852–1857; buried in St. Symphorien cemetery, Tours; see *DNB*.

Fletcher, Margaret – authoress; b. 5 December 1862; c. 9 September 1897, Park Town, North Oxford; d. 21 December 1943, Begbroke, Oxfordshire; daughter of Rev. Fletcher, Anglican vicar, who was acquitted in the last heresy trial carried out in Church of England; studied art at the Royal Academy, London, and in Paris, and worked as professional painter; conversion was influenced by reading St. John of the Cross and lives of the Saints; editor of *The Crucible*, aiming at better educational opportunities for women; pioneered development of women's issues in the Church; publication of her *Light for New Times* and *School of the Heart* led to inauguration of Catholic Women's League, which "aimed to unite Catholic women in bond of common fellowship for promotion of religious and intellectual interests and social work"; launched *Catholic Women's Outlook*; developed International Union of Catholic Women's Leagues; returned to Paris in 1940 at nearly eighty and organized escape of refugees; buried in churchyard of St. Michael, Begbroke; see Elizabeth Usherwood, "Call Back Yesterday: Margaret Fletcher (1862–1943)," *Catholic Life*, November 2002, p.38; David Jones, "Margaret Fletcher: In A Life of Her Own," *Catholic Life*, December 2004, p.54.

Fletcher, Philip – priest; b. 30 October 1848, Walton-on-Thames; c. 1878 (sister received in 1899); d. 13 January 1928; brought up by saintly mother in Low Church Anglican household for sixteen years; influenced by High Anglicanism as boy and then at Oxford University; became Anglican curate; ordained Catholic priest for Southwark Diocese; first master and founder with Lister Maurice Drummond (see above), barrister and fellow convert, of the Guild of Our Lady of Ransom for the Conversion of England, for which he was allowed to relinquish his parish and devote himself entirely; major role in helping Sacred Heart nuns of Montmartre to re-settle at Tyburn in central London; played central role in re-establishing Marian devotion at Walsingham; see essay in J. G. F. Raupert (ed), *Roads to Rome* (1901), p.87 ("I had become convinced that Rome was the real centre of the real Christendom. We in the Church of England were cut off – at least were outside the circle.... The storm burst midway in the reading of the *Apologia*. When the last page was reached – indeed before, I was a castaway. I could not resist the logic of the great thinker, the great convert. He held out as long as he could, but *had* to go. So must I. It was painful holding on by that one rope; but I did for more than a year. Other ropes, too, were tugging hard – 'the cords of a man'; my love for my family and my people. They pulled at my heart. My mind still clung to the hope that I was a priest. Meantime Rome was drawing, drawing still. Who was that in the October of my last year, drawing so gently, yet so strongly – in the month of his feast, too, though I knew it not? Ah! It was St. Francis of Assisi. In my last retreat at Cowley I took in with me the Life of St. Francis by St. Bonaventure and read it – a new Saint to me. He won me to himself completely. His was the influence – his, St. Francis' – which I am sure, under God, drew me at length to the shore"); Joseph Clayton, "Philip Fletcher, KCHS," *Blackfriars*, May 1928, p.270; Fr. Richard Whinder, "Father Philip

Fletcher: First Master of the Guild of Our Lady of Ransom," *Catholic Life*, February 2005, p.6 ("The catalyst for his conversion, oddly enough, was the death of Blessed Pius IX, in 1878. The furore this caused, the frenzied grief and speculation, brought home to Fletcher the rock-solid global significance of Catholicism – and the relative insignificance of Anglicanism. It was a decisive moment").

Flowers, George French – composer and musical theorist; b. 28 June 1811, Boston, Lincolnshire; c. 1860 or 1869; d. 14 June 1872, London; son of Anglican rector; founder of the Contrapuntists' Society in 1843; fine organist; music critic of the *Literary Gazette*; contributor to *Musical Examiner* and *Musical World*; set up a British school of vocalization to cultivate and bring forward English talent; may have been unsuccessful candidate for the music professorship at Oxford in 1848; composed an elaborate mass setting (1860?); see *DNB*.

Foley, Henry – Jesuit lay-brother; b. 9 August 1811, Astley, Worcestershire; c. 1846; d. 19 November 1891, Manresa House, Roehampton; son of Anglican clergyman; formerly practiced as solicitor; converted under influence of the Oxford Movement; on death in 1851 of his wife, Anne, he sought admission as lay brother into the Society of Jesus; urged to enter as scholastic and to prepare for priesthood, he said it was Our Lady's wish that he should be a lay brother; for thirty years he occupied post of lay brother *socius* to the English provincial, during which time he produced his gigantic work, *The Records of the English Province of the Society of Jesus* (8 octavo volumes); remarkable bodily austerities and great spirit of prayer; see *Catholic Encyclopedia*.

Ford, Ford Madox (formerly Ford Hermann Hueffer) – writer and editor; b. 17 December 1873, 5 Fair Lawn Villas, Merton, Surrey; c. 7 November 1892 (though rarely a practicing Catholic); d. 26 June 1939, Deauville, France; father German, music critic for *The Times*; mother English, daughter of Ford Madox Brown (1821–1893), painter associated with the Pre-Raphaelites; after his father's premature death in 1889 he went to live with his grandfather, whom he adored; moved through important bohemian, musical and intellectual circles, Dante Gabriel and Christina Rossetti being his uncle and aunt; eloped with and married his school girlfriend, Elsie Martindale (1877–1949), but they later separated; friend of Henry James and collaborated with Joseph Conrad; fought on Western Front in World War I; wrote eighty-one books, mainly fiction, but also history, reminiscence, cultural criticism and travel-writing; several very successful novels, notably *The Good Soldier* (1915) and tetralogy *Parade's End* (1924–1928); wrote over four hundred articles; editor of *English Review* and founder of *Transatlantic Review*, through both of which he helped careers of many modernist and avant-garde writers; lifelong friend of Ezra Pound; buried in Deauville, France; see Alan Judd, *Ford Madox Ford* (1990) ("As a kind of Catholic, or agnostic, or Catholic-agnostic – what he would have said would have depended upon his audience and when he was speaking – Ford would almost certainly have known Ignatius Loyola's 'Teach us to give and not to count the cost.' He never made the mistake of preaching it, but that was how he lived"); Max Saunders, *Ford Madox Ford: A Dual Life*, 2 Vols. (1996) ("On 7 November [1892] he was received into the Church. Immediately after his baptism he went to see Father Peter, whose 'eyes shone at the netting of this one more soul.' He clasped Ford's hands, kissed him on the cheek, slapped him gently on the shoulder, and exclaimed: 'Now you're a b—y Papist'"); Ralph McInerny, *Some Catholic Writers* (2007); *DNB*.

Forest, Antonia (real name Patricia Giulia Caulfield Kate Rubenstein) – children's writer; b. 26 May 1915, Hampstead, London; c. 1947; d. 28 November 2003, Bournemouth; daughter of an emigré Russian Jewish father and an Ulster Protestant mother; brought up in the tradition of Reformed Judaism; studied journalism at University College, London, but lived most of her adult life in Bournemouth; briefly a librarian and in a government clerical job, before writing full-time; a very private person; great interest in literature, especially Shakespeare, and the navy; fervent monarchist; turned from Judaism and became a Catholic; her books are superbly crafted and make intellectual as well as emotional demands on her readers; she suffered from the "political correctness" movement, which criticized her as elitist and too inaccessible; remained a devout Catholic, though increasingly critical of post-Vatican II developments in the Church; summed herself up as "middle-aged, narrow-minded, anti-progressive and proud of it"; unmarried; buried in Charminster Cemetery, Bournemouth; see *Autumn Term* (1948); *The Marlows and the Traitor* (1953); *Falconer's Lure* (1957); *End of Term* (1957) (religion and belief lie at the centre of this book); *Peter's Room* (1961); *The Ready-Made Family* (1967); *The Player's Boy* (1970); *The Players and the Rebels* (1971); *The Attic Term* (1976) (includes her criticisms of the changes in the Catholic Church following the Second Vatican Council); *Run Away Home* (1982); Sue Sims, "Antonia Forest – The Interview," *Folly*, July 1995 ("I was brought up

Reform Jewish, but it struck no roots. Later, when I opted for Christianity, I would have preferred to become an Anglican, except that it was still hung over with Red Deans and unbelieving Bishops, while the Roman Catholic Church had apparently no doubts about its teaching. This, obviously, comes into the Little-Did-I-Know category. If I *had* known what lay ahead in the shape of Vatican II, I really can't say what I might or might not have done. To be fair, Vatican II itself was not the destructive force. It was what came to be known as 'The Spirit of Vatican II', a phrase much used by clerics who wished to push through Protestantizing 'reforms', and used the phrase to distort the original mild concessions of Vatican II itself into the devastation which has followed. Yes, indeed, Patrick's views [a character in The Attic Term] are mine"); Sue Sims, "The Life and Fiction of Antonia Forest," *Children's Literature in Education*, March 2005, p.69 ("In *End of Term* (1959), all these [religious] threads are woven together using the weft of the school nativity play.... The play is taking place at Wade Abbas Minster (which Forest bases on Chichester Cathedral ...), and this serves to locate us not only in space but in time: through Patrick's reaction to the Minster ('I think I'll have this one back ... from you – from the Church of England'), we are reminded of the tragedies and conflicts which lie behind the serene beauty of the mediaeval churches and cathedrals; or perhaps, for those who read Forest as children, are led to discover this history for the first time"); Hilary Clare, "School Stories Don't Count: The Neglected Genius of Antonia Forest," in Pat Pinsent (ed), *Out of the Attic: Some Neglected Children's Authors of the Twentieth Century* (2006), Ch. 8 ("Forest is a very great writer. Her books are technically brilliant, her style witty and elegant, her dialogue a joy and her characterization superb. She deals with the universal subjects of death, loss, catastrophic life changes (whether real or potential), and religion, as well as divorce, crime and romance, all with a matter-of-fact lack of sentiment which focuses everything under the clear light of a microscope"); Sue Sims and Laura Hicks, *Celebrating Antonia Forest* (2008).

Formby, Henry – priest and author; b. 1816; c. 24 January 1846, Oscott; d. 12 March 1884; the family had been Catholic until the eighteenth century, when, with the exception of a younger branch, they lost the Faith; whilst at Brasenose College, Oxford, profoundly influenced by the Oxford Movement and in particular by Newman; took Anglican orders, but resigned his living in autumn 1845; ordained Catholic priest 18 September 1847; wrote many books on liturgical music (great enthusiast for plainchant), apologetics, and books emphasizing the use of instructive pictures as a means of spreading knowledge of the Scriptures and Catholic doctrine; see *The March of Intellect: Or the Alleged Hostility of the Catholic Church to the Diffusion of Knowledge Examined* (1852); *Our Lady of Salette* (1857); *A Guide for All to the Catholic Church* (1863); *The Book of the Holy Rosary* (1872); *Ancient Rome and its Connection with the Christian Religion* (1880); *Safeguards of Divine Faith in the Presence of Skeptics, Freethinkers and Atheists* (1882); *Gillow*, Vol. II, p.309; *Catholic Encyclopedia*.

Forster, Thomas Ignatius Maria – naturalist, astronomer and poet; b. 9 November 1789, London; c. 1824 (wife, Julia, and daughter, Selena, also became Catholics); d. 2 February 1860, Brussels; eldest son of botanist and antiquarian, Thomas Furley Forster (1761–1825); brought up by Rousseau's principles; no formal schooling; studied at home, especially natural science, then at Cambridge, London and Edinburgh; Fellow of Linnean Society; qualified doctor and master of several languages; member of Astronomical Society of London; discovered a comet in 1819; much traveling and many publications on wide range of scientific subjects, but also poetry; remarkable for his versatility and industry; friend of many of the prominent authors and scholars of the time; retired to Bruges; see *Gillow*, Vol. II, p.318; *Catholic Encyclopedia*; *DNB* ("He signalized his conversion by publishing the 'Circle of the Seasons and Perpetual Companion to the Calendar and Almanack of the Holy Catholic Church,' to which he added short Lives of the Saints under each day of the year").

Frankau, Gilbert – novelist and poet; b. 21 April 1884, Gloucester Terrace, London; c. 1952, a few months before his death; his daughter, Pamela (see above) converted in 1942; d. 4 November 1952, 4A King's Gardens, Hove, Sussex; of Jewish descent; mother, Julia Frankau (1859–1916) a successful novelist under the name of Frank Danby; went into family cigar merchant business; served on Western Front in World War I; wrote many successful novels and a number of plays; sympathized with extreme right between the wars; always "inclined towards Rome" and converted a few months before his death; one of the most widely read novelists between the wars; see *Peter Jackson, Cigar Merchant* (1920); *Seeds of Enchantment* (1921); *Gerald Cranston's Lady* (1924); *Masterson* (1926); *My Unsentimental Journey* (1926); *Self-Portrait: A Novel of his own Life* (1940); *Unborn Tomorrow* (1953); Pamela Frankau, *Pen To Paper: A Novelist's Notebook* (1961); *DNB*.

Frankau, Pamela Sydney – novelist; b. 3 January 1908, 14A Great Cumberland Place, London; c. 1942 (father, Gilbert Frankau (see below) converted in 1952); d. 8 June 1967, 55 Christchurch Hill, Hampstead, London; well known in literary circles; author of several successful novels, e.g., *The Bridge* (1967) (concerned with the imperatives of the Catholic faith); wide readership in Britain and United States; had an affair with Humbert Wolfe (1885–1940), the poet and civil servant; always troubled by her sexual identity, although did marry; close relationship in last ten years of her life with Margaret (Peggy) Webster (1905–1972), actress and theatre director; great courage in the face of cancer; see *She and I* (1930); *I Was the Man* (1932); *Tassell-Gentle* (1934); *The Willow Cabin* (1949); *Ask Me No More* (1958); *Pen To Paper: A Novelist's Notebook* (1961); *DNB.*

Franks, Richard – priest; b. 1630, Knighton, Yorkshire; d. 1696/7; brought up in family originally recusant, but which at this period had lost the faith; soon joined the faith of his ancestors; went to English College, Valladolid; ordained priest; came on the English mission about 1656 and worked in Yorkshire (residing with the Beckwiths at Marton, in Holderness); chosen as Archdeacon of Yorkshire in 1674; in 1692 elected as vicar-general of Northumberland, Lancashire, Yorkshire, and Durham; "learned and virtuous"; see *Gillow*, Vol. II, p.331.

Fraser, Hamish – writer and publisher; b. 16 August 1913, Edinburgh; c. 4 June 1948, Feast of the Sacred Heart (received by Fr. A. A. Stephenson, SJ; his wife was received in 1947); d. 17 October 1986; baptized in Church of Scotland; as a teenager turned to Revolutionary Marxism and active in Young Communist League; served with the International Brigade during Spanish Civil War 1936–1939; on return shop steward in Clydebank shipyard and organized party cells in other shipyards and factories; propaganda secretary for the Communist Party in Scotland; then dissented from Moscow's ruthless use of totalitarian power; left Communist Party in 1945; conversion influenced by the social teaching of the Catholic Church, which he continued to promote; great promoter of the message of Our Lady of Fatima; editor of *Approaches* magazine to combat what he saw as a "fifth column" of modernists in the Church; see *The Truth About Spain* (1949); *Fatal Star* (1964) ("Paradoxically, my first faint stirrings of belief arose from mere human respect: from an acknowledgment of the fact that a man, a humble peasant craftsman who had lived most of his life in an obscure village in one of the farthest outposts of the Roman empire, had nevertheless possessed such outstanding intuitive knowledge of the nature of man that the Church he had founded two thousand years ago was the only organization in existence capable of grappling effectively with the social problems deriving from modern large-scale production. The more I pondered on this 'mystery,' the more did I become intrigued. There was something about it which seemed positively uncanny. How could one find words adequate to its description? It was certainly not 'natural.' It was even more certainly not 'sub-natural.' Thus it was that the one word I had sought to eliminate from my vocabulary was the only one that could adequately express the conviction to which I was forced. It was 'supernatural.' That is how I arrived at the conclusion that Jesus Christ might well be indeed the Son of God").

Fraser, Muriel – medical doctor; b. 1911, Lisburn, County Antrim, Northern

Ireland; c. 27 May 1955 ("The only solidly good, undilutedly good, thing I ever did"); brought up in committed Anglican family in Northern Ireland; non-religious at university, but read Newman; one of United Kingdom's first female medical consultants; specialized as neonatologist; after Vatican II she was commissioned by Cardinal Conway to translate the Council documents; in 1987 awarded Pro Ecclesia et Pontifice medal; see Carmel McQuaid, "Irish Catholic Personalities," *Catholic Life*, April 2003, p.46 ("I could pass an examination on Vatican II documents. I always break my heart over some of the changes in the liturgy that came along which I hated and still do. Though I did not go along with the interpretations of a lot of young experts, I went along with Vatican II because that is the key to all my grown up life in the Church – being faithful to Rome. I am totally conservative and obedient. I am nothing but a Catholic. I am not an Irish Catholic, nor an English Catholic. I am a Roman Catholic and a papist, belonging to Rome. The only flag I would be interested in is a papal flag"); Carmel McQuaid, "An Interview with Dr. Muriel Fraser," *Catholic Life*, August 2003, p.42 ("An only child of committed Anglicans … she found fascination in the Consecration Prayer when left in the pew during Communion. Told later that the words didn't mean what they said, she was incredulous. 'They did not say it was a Catholic belief. I had always accepted transubstantiation. I decided their denial was nonsense'").

Froude, Catherine Henrietta Easterbrook (*née* Holdsworth) – b. 1809/10; c. 17 March 1857 (received with all of her five children, except her youngest daughter, Mary Catherine (died young of tuberculosis in 1864); her husband did not convert; her half sister, Eliza Holdsworth (1803–1873) was received

in 1856); d. 1878; wife of William Froude (1810–1879), railway engineer and naval architect (assistant to Brunel); sister-in-law of Richard Hurrell Froude (1803–1836), great influence on Newman, his colleague at Oriel College, Oxford, and on the Oxford Movement, and of James Anthony Froude (1818–1894), historian; she and her family much involved in the beginning of the Oxford Movement; much correspondence with Newman before her conversion; her husband remained a close friend of Newman and they corresponded on the nature of proof in science and religion, with William Froude becoming steadily more agnostic; the friendship was strained, but not broken, by rest of family's conversion; Newman's *Grammar of Assent* aimed partly at rebutting William's belief that "Our sacred duty is to doubt each and every proposition put to us including our own"; William's views became increasingly opposed to those of Newman who was to write "I try my ideas on you as one might send an iron girder to the test house"; see Joyce Sugg, *Ever Yours Affly: John Henry Newman and His Female Circle* (1996); Stanley L. Jaki, *Newman to Converts: An Existential Ecclesiology* (2001), Ch. 6 ("At least [Newman] could point out something all-important. It was not enough to know that the Church of England failed as a Church. To come to the true Church could not be done on such grounds, because this would still leave one in the world, which is full of troubles and failing: 'You must come to the Church, not to avoid it [the world], but to save your soul. If this is the motive all is right – you cannot be disappointed – but the other motive is dangerous.' One impression he did not wish to leave, namely, that he had tried 'to disguise that Catholicism is a different religion from Anglicanism – You must come to learn that religion which the Apostles ntroduced and which was in the world long before the Reformation was dreamed of'").

Froude, Eliza Margaret (always known as "Isy") – b. 1840; c. May 1859; d. 1931; eldest daughter of William and Catherine Froude (see above); in 1880 she married Baron Anatole von Hügel (1854–1928), brother of Friedrich von Hügel (1852–1925); went to live in Cambridge when her husband was appointed curator of the University Museum of Archaeology and Ethnology in 1883; their house, Croft Cottage, became a popular meeting place; always a loyal friend of Newman and gave readings from his works.

Froude, (Richard) Hurrell – b. 1842; c. 24 December 1859 (received by Newman); d. 1932; eldest son of William and Catherine Froude (see above); to be distinguished from Richard Hurrell Froude (1803–1836), Newman's colleague at Oriel College, Oxford; godson of Newman; being already a convert, he was unable to enter a good college at Oxford and studied informally, residing with William Donkin, Fellow of University College and Savilian Professor of Astronomy; married in 1847 Beatrice (known as Bice, pronounced in the Italian way), daughter of George and Sophia Ryder (see below); moved to India; after his wife's sudden death in 1877, leaving a small daughter, Mary, and a baby (William Hurrell), he married in 1881 Agnes, daughter of Henry and Mary Wilberforce (see below); after her death in 1890 he married Ruth Collis, who brought up the three children of his second marriage.

Fry, Sir (Theodore) Penrose – lay Catholic; b. 1892; c. 1929 (with his wife, Sheila Kaye-Smith (see below)); d. 6 August 1970; of Quaker antecedents and upbringing; former High Anglican minister; buried beside his wife in grounds of St. Thérèse of Lisieux church, Little Doucegrove; see *The Church Surprising* (1932), *The Making of a Layman* (1938), essay in Maurice Leahy (ed), *Conversions to the Catholic Church: A Symposium* (1933) ("Anglo-Catholicism acts in some cases as a nursery for those growing towards Catholicism, teaching them at least what they should look for and expect, till in due time they go forth on their own and 'embrace Catholicism.' This, I am sure, is what happened to me, and in this sense I can certainly say that the Church of England greatly helped me in making the decision whereas she offered no assistance to her doubting children in the past century. I suppose which of these two alternatives present Anglicans adopt is often decided by the temperament of the individual. Easy-going, static characters probably stay where they are, and those who dislike confusion, and expect to find completeness and cohesion in religion become in the end dissatisfied with Anglicanism and slowly turn towards Rome").

Fullerton, Lady Georgiana Charlotte (*née* Leveson-Gower) – novelist and philanthropist; b. 23 September 1812, Tixall Hall, Staffordshire; c. Passion Sunday, 29 March 1846 (husband, Alexander George Fullerton (1808–1907), of county Antrim, captain in the Royal House Guards and attaché in Paris, received in 1843 in Rome; and niece, Emily, received in 1884); d. 19 January 1885, Ayrfield, Bournemouth; third of four children of Lord Granville Leveson-Gower (1773–1846), diplomat and later first Earl Granville; her mother was Lady Henrietta Elizabeth (Harriet) Leveson-Gower (1785–1862), second daughter of William Cavendish, fifth Duke of Devonshire (1748–1811); educated at home, first in England, and from

1824 in Paris, where her father was appointed ambassador; much influenced by the Tractarians; wrote eight novels all of which turn on religious questions; also biographies of eminent Catholics, poetry and drama; wrote primarily to gain money for charity; after her only son died at the age of twenty-one, she dressed poorly and devoted the rest of her life to charitable works; both she and her husband joined the Third Order of St. Francis in 1857; she brought the Sisters of Charity to England; co-founded with Margaret Frances Taylor Order of "Sisters of the Poor Servants of the Mother of God Incarnate" for women who could not afford dowries for established orders; lifelong friend of Marquise de Salvo (see below); see *Ellen Middleton* (1844) (novel which turns on the necessity of for sacramental absolution and the question of whether Anglican clergy should hear confessions and absolve); *Grantley Manor* (1847); *St. Frances of Rome* (1855); *Too Strange not to be True* (1864); *Constance Sherwood* (1865); *Mrs. Gerald's Niece* (1869); *A Will and a Way* (1881); H. J. Coleridge, *Life of Lady Georgiana Fullerton, From the French of Mrs. Augustus Craven* (1888); Fanny Margaret Taylor, *The Inner Life of Lady Georgiana Fullerton* (1899); Margaret M. Maison, "Lady Georgiana Fullerton," *Irish Ecclesiastical Record*, August 1958, p.104; Joyce Sugg, *Ever Yours Affly: John Henry Newman and His Female Circle* (1996); Madeleine Beard, *Faith and Fortune* (1997), pp.165–169 ("One evening Lord Harrowby said to her: 'It is quite wrong to call the Roman Catholics idolaters, because they worship the Host. They only worship it because they believe that our Lord Jesus Christ is present in It'"); *Gillow*, Vol. II, p.336; *DNB*.

Fulthroppe, Edward – gentleman; d. 4 July 1597; executed at York for having been reconciled to the old faith; see *Gillow*, Vol. II, p.339 ("It is possible that he is the same with the Mr. Fulthroppe, mentioned by Fr. Richard Holtby, in his account of the persecution in the North, who delivered his wife to the custody of the Lord President of the North and the Ecclesiastical Commissioners on account of her recusancy. Many gentlemen who had been induced to act in a similar manner, were afterwards sorely distressed at the cruel way in which their wives were treated, and, their eyes being opened to the means by which the new religion was supported, were themselves reconciled to the Catholic Church").

Fytche, William Benedict, OSF – priest; b. about 1562, Canfield, Essex; c. 1586; d. 21 November 1611, Paris; brought up as a Puritan in ancient family; after conversion went to France and joined Order of Capuchins in the province of Paris; spent rest of his life in Paris, of which he was elected provincial in 1596 and again in 1608; one of best preachers of the time and esteemed pious and strict in morality; see *Gillow*, Vol. II, p.343.

Gainsborough, second Earl of (Charles George Noel) – b. 5 September 1818; c. 1850 (received with his wife, Ida Harriett Augusta Hay, eldest daughter of the sixteenth Earl of Erroll, and children; rest of his family remained committed Protestants); d. 13 August 1881; son of Lord Barham (1781–1866); interest in the Oxford Movement whilst at Trinity College, Cambridge; until 1866 known as Viscount Campden; founder in 1838 of Cambridge Camden Society, which subsequently became the Ecclesiological Society; at one time Liberal MP for Rutland; Lord Lieutenant and Custos Rotulorum of Rutlandshire; succeeded to Earldom in 1866; resided at Exton Park; built on his estates domestic chapels, which became new centers of Catholic life in those areas; patron of Pugin (see below); staunch conservative in later life; Knight of the Order of Christ; his wife was known as Queen Ida because of her descent from King William IV; his daughters, Lady Constance and Lady Edith (latter became a Sister of Charity), influenced when children the development towards Catholicism of Janet Erskine Stuart (see below); see David Hunter-Blair, *Memories and Musings* (1929), p.26; Madeleine Beard, *Faith and Fortune* (1997), pp.93–95; *Gillow*, Vol. V, p.182.

Gainsford, W. D. – barrister; b. 1842; d. 1926; JP for Lincolnshire and West Riding; belonged to family always Catholic; baptized and educated Catholic; but lived for many years as Protestant and professed himself Anglican; had "reverted" to Catholicism by the early 1890s; see essay in J. G. F. Raupert (ed), *Roads to Rome* (1901), p.98 ("The outcome of twenty-eight years' honest trial of Anglicanism is the conviction that its *fons et origo mali* is far more serious and far more deeply rooted than Catholics usually suppose. When remorselessly probed to the bottom, I found it to be nothing less than a positive (though unconscious) disbelief in a *present* supernatural. I mean that Anglicans do not believe in any supernatural existence *hic et nunc*.

They believe there *was* a supernatural creation and a supernatural Incarnation, and that *in days long ago* physics and miracles were very mixed up in a perplexing manner; and, moreover, they believe that a similar condition of things will arise at the Last Day. But, *hic et nunc*, all is understandable enough. Both God and the devil, no doubt, exist somewhere, but they don't interfere with the decent order of things here below nowadays. Of course, no Anglican would

admit that to be his belief; he would most strenuously deny it. But such is really his unconscious conviction – the real belief on which his life and conduct are based That such is so is apparent in many outward indications; e.g., by his contemptuous rejection of all latter-day miracles – though he readily admits the principle of miracle formerly; by his disbelief in the intercession of saints – which really means that he does not believe the saints to be now actually existing in Heaven; by his disbelief in prayer for the dead, and the general doubt of any conscious existence between death and the Last Judgment (i.e., no supernatural state *now*); and lastly, by his utter repudiation of all notion of sacerdotalism (by which I mean the administration of supernatural power through human beings and the existence of supernatural function in a material object). For a long time I held these rationalistic prejudices, without realizing that it is upon an exclusively materialistic basis alone that such can be held consistently").

Gardiner, Sir George Arthur – politician and journalist; b. 3 March 1935, Witham, Essex; c. 1994; d. 16 November 2002, Westminster; Christianity played only small role in early life; brought up in straitened circumstances, but won a state scholarship to Balliol College, Oxford; passionate anti-socialist; became Anglican at university; first class degree in PPE; worked as journalist, becoming deputy political correspondent of *The Sunday Times*; Conservative MP 1974–1997 (backbencher and loyal Thatcherite); wrote column in the *Sunday Express*; severe critic of John Major's government; much charitable work involving children's health issues; converted after Church of England ordained women; see "The Political Journalist" in Greg Watts, *Catholic Lives* (2001) ("Now, I've nothing against women playing a very full role in the Church. I'm sure that many of the women who have been ordained in the Anglican Church are much better Christians than I am. But the idea that a middle-class body like the General Synod should just bow to political correctness rather than the collective wisdom of the apostolic Church went totally against the grain with me"); *DNB*.

Garner, Thomas – architect and designer; b. 12 August 1839, Wasperton Hill, Wasperton, Warwickshire; c. 1896 (received with his wife, Rose Emily); d. 30 April 1906, Fritwell Manor, Fritwell, Oxfordshire; arts and crafts style; pupil of George Gilbert Scott; partnership with George Frederick Bodley (1827–1907) from 1869 until 1897 (resulted in a series of beautiful works in ecclesiastical, domestic, and collegiate architecture); designer of reredos of St. Paul's Cathedral, London; in 1899 appointed architect to Downside Abbey, Bath, where he designed choir in which his own interment was to take place; buried at Downside Abbey; see E. Green, "In Memoriam Thomas Garner: Artist, Architect and Archaeologist," *Downside Review*, 1906, p.116; *DNB*.

Garnett, Henry, SJ – priest and martyr; b. second half of 1555, Heanor, Derbyshire; d. 3 May 1606; family conformed to religious changes introduced by Elizabeth I; after converting went to Rome and entered the Society of Jesus in 1575; studied at Roman College under Fathers Bellarmine, Clavius and Suarez; ordained about 1582; Professor of Hebrew and Mathematics at Roman College; went on the English mission with Fr. Robert Southwell in 1586, where supported by Vaux family throughout; became Superior of Jesuits in England in 1587; survived much danger and suffering until arrested in 1605; the planned Gunpowder Plot was revealed to him under the seal of the confessional (he learned of plot from Fr. Oswald Tesimond, SJ, who with permission of his penitent, Robert Catesby, had discussed it with him); horrified by this and worked to prevent its execution; after discovery of plot, he was arrested and taken to the Tower, where ill-treated; found guilty of misprision of treason; hanged, drawn and quartered at St. Paul's churchyard next to bishop's house and his remains dispersed; his death greeted with no applause by crowd; regarded as martyr to sacredness of seal of Sacrament of Confession; great holiness of life and very learned with many publications on devotion and controversy; wrote treatise on subject of equivocation; venerated as a martyr by English Catholics; name originally included in list of martyrs submitted to Rome in 1874 by archdiocese of Westminster, but later his cause put off (dilatus) for further inquiry because of fears of possible political involvement; see Foley *Records SJ*, Vol. IV; Philip Caraman, *Henry Garnett, 1555–1606, and the Gunpowder Plot* (1964); *Gillow*, Vol. II, p.390; *Catholic Encyclopedia*; *DNB*.

Garrod, Dorothy Annie Elizabeth – archaeologist and prehistorian; b. 5 May 1892, 9 Chandos Street, London; c. 1913; d. 18 December 1968, Hope House (Catholic) Nursing Home, Cambridge; daughter of Sir Archibald Garrod (1857–1936), Regius Professor of Medicine at Oxford; studied History at Cambridge and Anthropology at Oxford; war service with the Catholic Women's League in France and Germany; expert in the Paleolithic, the Old Stone Age; pupil of the Abbé Henri Breuil; much pioneering work in prehistoric archaeology; in 1939 elected Cambridge University's Disney Professor of Archaeology, becoming the first woman to hold a chair at Oxford or Cambridge; over one hundred academic papers and articles; unmarried (unofficial fiancé killed in World War I, as were two of her brothers); her ashes were buried in her parents' grave at Melton, Suffolk; her reputation has increased since her death; see *The Upper Palaeolithic Age in Britain* (1926); *Environment, Tools and Man* (inaugural lecture) (1946); *DNB* ("Described as calm, self-assured, perfectly confident, and authoritative, Garrod is remembered by an expedition member, Bruce Howe, as 'unique, rather like a glass of pale fine stony French white wine'").

Garside, Charles Brierley – priest and author; b. 6 April 1818, Manchester; c. 21 June 1850 (sister received in 1854); d. 21 May 1876, Posolippo, near Naples area; at Brasenose College, Oxford; took Anglican orders; lost faith in Church of England as a result of Gorham case (see entry for William Maskell); ordained Catholic priest 23 December 1854; domestic chaplain to Bertram, last Catholic Earl of Shrewsbury; see *The Preaching of the Cross* (1869); *The Sacrifice of the Eucharist* (1875); *Gillow*, Vol. II, p.397; *DNB*.

Garson, Mother Mary Sunniva – nun and educational psychologist; b. 3 October 1921, Udney Green, Aberdeenshire, Scotland; c. 1947; d. 8 March 2007, Bognor Regis, West Sussex; daughter of a merchant navy captain; Presbyterian background; gained master's in psychology at Aberdeen University; early career involved wartime service in the Women's Auxiliary Air Force, industrial work and educational psychology in child guidance clinics; conversion influenced by the faith of a Catholic family with whom she stayed on the Continent; enlisted by Fr. Bernard Bassett, SJ into the Cell movement; discovered her vocation

through work with elderly needy people; professed a nun in 1962; founded Sisters of Our Lady of Grace and Compassion; built a network of homes and sheltered housing in several countries; ran the Order for over fifty years (Prioress-General 1985–2005) by which time there were over two hundred sisters; community adopted Rule of St. Benedict as a way of life in 1978; awarded Papal Cross, Pro Ecclesia et Pontifice, in 2002 for services to the Church.

Gawen, Thomas – religious writer and traveler; b. 1612, Marshfield, Gloucestershire; c. unclear date: some say 1658, but probably after the Restoration in 1660, but before 1669); d. 6 March 1684, Pall Mall, London; son of Church of England minister; made perpetual Fellow of New College, Oxford in 1632; took Anglican orders in 1639 and traveled in France and Italy; returned to England in 1642 and became chaplain to Dr. Curl, Anglican Bishop of Winchester; "foreseeing the ruin of the Church of England" (*DNB*) he traveled again to Italy and France, meeting notable Catholics; after becoming a Catholic returned to France and was introduced into the household of Henrietta Maria, wife of Charles I; moved to Rome in 1669 and married an Italian woman (had one child); returned to England alone and lived in London until his death; was in some trouble in 1679 over the Popish Plot; writer of doctrinal, liturgical and spiritual works; buried in church of St. Martin-in-the-Fields; see *Gillow*, Vol. II, p.408; *DNB*.

Gay, Richard John Neville – priest; b. 7 April 1889, Ealing Dene, Hanwell, Middlesex; c. 1913 (also eventually received his parents into the Church); d. 31 October 1969; brought up formally as Anglican; in youth drawn to extreme form of socialism which carried with it

militant atheism and secularism; then
Fabian socialist; traveled and worked in
United States; influenced by Ruskin; ordained priest 1919; enormous work as
member of Catholic Evidence Guild;
buried in St. Patrick's cemetery, Leytonstone; see J. B. O'Keefe, "Prison Camp
Seminary," *Catholic Life*, April 2004,
p.46; Fr. Stewart Foster, "Fr. Richard
Gay: A Remarkable Priest," *Catholic
Life*, June 2004, p.14).

Geach, Peter Thomas – philosopher; b.
29 March 1916, Lower Chelsea, London;
c. 31 May 1938 ("Increasingly, as time
went on, I found myself arguing with
Catholics. I was certainly cleverer than
they, but they had the immeasurable advantage that they were right – an advantage that they did not throw away by
resorting to the bad philosophy and
apologetics then sometimes taught in
Catholic schools. One day my defenses
quite suddenly collapsed: I knew that if
I were to remain an honest man I must
seek instruction in the Catholic Religion"); husband of Elizabeth Anscombe
(see above); until eight years old brought
up by a ward who was a pious non-conformist Protestant; taught philosophy by
his father, a brilliant student at Cambridge; studied at Balliol College, Oxford; lecturer at Birmingham University
1951–1966; Professor of Logic, University of Leeds 1966–1981; influenced
particularly by McTaggart, Aquinas,
Frege, and Wittgenstein; see *Three
Philosophers: Aristotle, Aquinas, Frege*
(1963) (with G. E. M. Anscombe)
("Aquinas would not be embarrassed by
the question: If it is reasonable to ask
who made the world, then why is it not
reasonable to ask who made God? For
the world shares with its parts certain attributes that give rise to causal questions:
it is a complex whole of parts and is in
process of change. But, Aquinas would
say, God is not a whole of parts and is

unchangeable; so the same causal questions need not arise about him. Moreover, precisely because we should soon
find ourselves in difficulties if we raised
questions about the whole consisting of
the world *plus* God – e.g., whether it is
caused or uncaused, changeable or unchangeable – Aquinas would deny the le-
gitimacy of speaking of such a whole");
God and the Soul (1969), *Providence
and Evil* (1977) ("Truth … does not perish and does not change. If it was true
1900 years ago to say that man was made
upright in will, and immune, if he remained in that uprightness, from misery
and death, but that by his own misdeed
man fell from that blessed state, then this
cannot have ceased to be true by lapse of
time.… It is a matter of history that for
1800 years, despite the division of Christendom, this doctrine counted as what C.
S. Lewis called 'mere Christianity.' If
Christian tradition could be in error
about this, then either it has been irre-
trievably corrupted in transmission or it
was gravely wrong from the first. In the
latter case we certainly cannot be Christians: if what was taught in the first century as Divine revelation was in large
measure false. Things are not much better in the other case: if there was once a
Divine revelation, but it was early corrupted in a substantial way. For how
could we then reconstruct the content of
the original revelation? And without
such reconstruction we should be almost
as ill-informed of the truth about God
and man as if no revelation had been
given at all. That is my first thesis: that
if the doctrines of the Fall and Original
Sin are rejected then this involves such a
skeptical attitude towards Christianity
that we can have no possible reason to be
Christians"); *The Virtues* (1977) ("In history, testimony to a happening is worthless unless we can believe it derives by a
chain of tradition from contemporaries
who knew the facts. So here; we have no

warrant for belief unless the chain terminates in someone who did not believe but knew; in Moses who saw God's face, or in Christ who had all the treasures of wisdom and knowledge. People nowadays readily speak of Christ's *faith* in his Father and his mission, even, God help us all! his faith in humanity; but if he only had faith, he walked in the dark as we do, step by step, and why should we now believe because he only believed? He was a very impressive man by any standards, but very impressive men have believed all sorts of things and cannot all have been right. Can the blind lead the blind? A long line of blind men can all perhaps keep to the road, each clinging trustfully to the one in front, if the leader of them all is sighted; if he is blind too, they will all end up in the ditch.

Again, if an authority admits to being fallible, it is fallible; one that claims to be infallible *may* be so. But a claim to infallibility carries commitments.... An authority claiming infallibility cannot also claim the right to change its mind. 'This we teach and have always taught because it is God's truth': such a claim can perhaps be heard. 'You must interiorly assent to the assertion that *p*, because we make it now, although with the same authority we demanded interior belief that not-*p* some years ago': such a demand, if ever made, would be a staggering effrontery"); *Truth, Love, and Immortality* (1979) ("A further condition *sine qua non* is that a revelation must be consistent if it is to be credible. I do not say that a revelation must be provably consistent; by now, the information really ought to have got around from formal logicians to the learned world in general that the credibility of a system does not depend on our having a proof of its consistency.... What can be required for a revelation's credibility is that it should not be provably inconsistent; and it will certainly be that if the story

authoritatively told changes from one generation to another. The truth about God cannot itself change; and if a professed witness of the truth changes his story, then one time or the other he must have been demanding assent when such a demand was mere impudence"); *Truth and Hope* (2001) ("It was for me a single act to accept the reality of time and the unchanging eternity of God; I never for a moment thought of accepting a changeable God.... A changeable God, who can be affected causally by change and activities of his creatures, is no God at all, and there can be no reason to believe in the existence of such a being.... It would be quite arbitrary to allow the question 'How come?' for changeable things in the world, but disallow it for a changeable God. If on the contrary God is supposed eternal and changeless, then to ask 'Who then made God?' is manifestly silly"); Harry A. Lewis (ed), *Peter Geach, Philosophical Encounters* (1991) ("I began thinking about the philosophy of religion under the influence of McTaggart's *Some Dogmas of Religion*. I have ever since believed that the holding of some dogmas as true is essential to any religion's being worth serious consideration: dogma is essential to religion as a shell to an egg or a skeleton to a human body, without it we have only a shapeless jelly. Undogmatic Christianity is a plain absurdity; as McTaggart pointed out, the recorded teaching of Christ includes dogmas; and as Hobbes pointed out, the earliest Christian writings contain a credal formula just as dogmatic and propositional as any later creeds: 'Jesus is the Christ, the Son of God.'.... I add only this: Truth is what matters. A religion that makes no claim to offer truth and to oppose the contrary errors deserves no serious consideration.... Nothing in the end matters except Truth; for God himself is Truth; God is that which all true speaking and thinking points towards and from which all false speaking and thinking points away.... To God all falsehood is hateful, especially if it is supposed to help religion; God has no need of our lies...

...The prospect for a rethought or revised Christianity seem to me dim. I remember somebody once asked me whether some complex form of words did not express what we must 'now' mean by affirming that Jesus Christ was born of a Virgin. Naturally I dissented: what it means to us now to say a young woman is a virgin is not all that different, despite advances in physiology, from what the corresponding statement meant in the first century; whatever that man meant, it was certainly not this. I can see no point in a man's wanting to use the old words when he does not take them in the old sense: except indeed that he is trying to deceive himself and others.... If people no longer believe the old dogmas, they should plainly say so, and not go on uttering the old affirmations...

The attitude of revisionary Christians to their Master is indeed hard to understand. On the one hand they view with considerable skepticism the reports of his teaching in the Gospels; on the other hand they are prepared, when occasion offers, to reject some of his views as mistaken, e.g., concerning the Old Testament or the reality of devils and hell. If the Gospels are historically as unreliable as they hold them to be, clearly they are on shaky ground in ascribing these 'mistaken' teachings to the alleged source. Whether the Gospels are unreliable or not, it is absurd of such thinkers to claim to follow a teacher whose mind was either so gravely in error, or so gravely misrepresented, as they suppose; although through the mists there might dimly shine a noble figure, the case would be like that of Socrates. Julian the Apostate indeed, if my memory serves, spoke of 'being saved by Socrates

through philosophy'; but the salvation Christians have looked for is different; if someone thinks that is not to be had, his profession of Christianity is merely farcical"); Luke Gormally (ed), *Moral Truth and Moral Tradition: Essays in Honour of Peter Geach and Elizabeth Anscombe* (1994); John Beaumont, "Resisting the Revisionists: The Catholic Writings of Peter Geach," *Downside Review*, October 2000, p.271; John Beaumont, "Peter Geach: Catholic Convert and Philosopher," *Catholic Life*, October 2007, p.58.

Geldard, Peter – priest; b. 1945, Bexhill-on-Sea; c. 1995; brought up in a non-practicing Anglican family; introduced to the Oxford Movement by reading Canon Ollard's *The Short History of the Oxford Movement* at seventeen; ordained as High Church Anglican; acted as secretary of the English Church Union; leading speaker against women's ordination at the Anglican Synod debate in 1992; ordained Catholic priest 1996; chaplain at University of Kent at Canterbury; see "Women's Ordination Was Non-Negotiable," *This Rock*, July-August 2005, p.36 (with Joanna Bogle) ("It seemed to me that the issue was whether or not the Church of England Synod, as one group of Christians, meeting on its own, could make a definitive decision on this crucial matter without reference to the wider Church.... From that moment, [the decision by the Church of England to ordain women], everything changed. It was, as John Henry Cardinal Newman had written a century or more earlier, like seeing a ghost. It is impossible to behave as though one has not seen it. Until then I had believed that I belonged to a Catholic Church that had many Protestants in it. Now I saw that I belonged to a Protestant Church that had people claiming to be Catholic in it. Scales fell from my eyes. Everything had to be seen in a new light"); *EWTN Audio Library* (12 May 2008) ("If the Church of England Synod could change the apostolic ministry, it could change whatever it wanted.... If we claimed to have the apostolic ministry of bishops, priests and deacons, which we shared with Orthodoxy and we shared with the Catholic Church ...; if we claimed to have a common currency, we can't mint our own coinage. And yet we did.... And so that night, on reflection, I felt that was the end of the Oxford Movement.... If you haven't got the apostolic ministry, how can you have the apostolic sacraments?"); *EWTN Audio Library* (26 May 2008).

Gennings (alias Ironmonger), Saint Edmund – priest and martyr; b. 1566, Lichfield, Staffordshire; c. 1583 (his brother, John (see below) received shortly after his death); d. 10 December 1591, London; brought up Protestant; after his conversion received into Douai College in 1583; ordained priest 18 March 1590, by papal dispensation because still under canonical age; sent to the English mission; landed near Whitby, Yorkshire and remained six months in the north; then in Lichfield and London where he made extraordinary recognition of his one living relation, his brother John, who remained then very anti-Catholic; arrested in November 1591, together with another priest, Polydore Plasden, and several lay Catholics, by Topcliffe, the priest-catcher, after saying Mass in Swithin Wells' house in Holborn; taken to Newgate prison; condemned for priesthood; hanged, drawn and quartered at Gray's Inn Fields, uttering "Sancte Gregori, ora pro me"; see *Gillow*, Vol. II, p.415; *Catholic Encyclopedia*; *DNB* ("Gennings and Wells were dragged on a sledge to a scaffold set up outside the latter's house. Once again Gennings refused to conform or admit treason. This infuriated Topcliffe, who ordered him to be immediately hung, drawn, and quartered, giving him leave to say no more, and scarce to recite the Pater Noster. With Gennings crying upon St. Gregory his patron to assist him, the hangman astonished said with a loud voice, 'God's wounds! His heart is in my hand and yet Gregory is in his mouth'").

Gennings (alias Perkins), John, OSF – priest; b. about 1570, Lichfield, Staffordshire; c. 1591 or 1592; d. 2 November 1660, St. Bonaventure's monastery, Douai; brought up Protestant and had inclination to Puritanism; moved to London where accidentally met his brother, Edmund, the martyr (see above) after eight years' separation; made no contact with his brother and rejoiced in his death, but shortly afterwards had conversion experience; went to English College, Douai, then entered English College, Rome, in 1598; ordained priest in 1600; sent to the English mission in May 1601; imprisoned in Newgate in 1611; joined Franciscan Order 1614/5 and restored English Franciscan Province (first provincial); wrote biography of his brother; buried in church of St. Bonaventure, Douai; see *Gillow*, Vol. II, p.419 ("His conversion bears some resemblance to that of St. Paul. About ten days after the execution [of his brother], he retired to rest after a day's pleasure. He was no sooner alone than his heart grew heavy, and he began to consider how idly he had spent the day. A mysterious feeling came over him as he thought of his brother's death; how he had forsaken all worldly pleasures, and for religion only had suffered such a cruel death. Entering into himself, he compared his own life with that of his brother and, struck with horror and remorse, he burst into tears and implored God to enlighten his understanding that he might see the truth. At that moment he was filled with consolation and joy; strong emotions took possession of his soul, and he vowed on the spot to forsake kindred and country to find out the true knowledge of that faith which his brother had sealed with his blood"); *Catholic Encyclopedia*; *DNB*.

Giberne, Maria Rosina – authoress and artist; b. 13 August 1802, Clapton, London; c. 19 December 1845 (received by Fr. Brownbill, SJ; her great friend, Selina Copeland, née Bacchus (d. 1850) was received in 1848); d. 2 December 1885, Autun, France; seventh child of a family from French Huguenot stock; an elder sister married Anglican clergyman, Walter Mayers, the schoolmaster who had converted Newman to a living faith in 1816; at first an Evangelical Low Church Anglican; met Newman about 1827 and became High Church and later a Tractarian; corresponded with Newman (who became her spiritual director); disturbed by Newman's doubts and hesitations, then by his conversion to Rome, but followed him into the Catholic Church (disregarding Pusey's advice); moved to Rome in 1846 and made a living as a painter; wild and passionate nature; did much work for Newman at the time of the Achilli case, going to Italy to escort witnesses; after some setbacks (rejected by several religious houses) she became a nun (Sister Maria Pia) of the Visitation Order at Paray-le-Monial, then at Autun, France; friendship and correspondence with Newman continued throughout; related to Gerard Manley Hopkins (see below); see Lance Sieveking, *The Eye of the Beholder* (1957); Joyce Sugg, *Ever Yours Affly: John Henry Newman and His Female Circle* (1996); Stanley L. Jaki, *Newman to Converts: An Existential Ecclesiology* (2001) ("[Newman pointed out] to Miss Giberne that a convert's chief duty was

to work and, above all, to pray for the conversion of others. 'And now, my dear Miss Giberne,' so Newman wrote to her … 'that you have the power, pray begin your intercessions very earnestly … for those dear friends of mine, or ours, who are still held back, or rather imprisoned in their old error, and that by their own good feelings and amiable affections. You have all the saints of heaven to aid you now, especially that first and most glorious of Saints whose name you bear'"); *DNB*.

Gibbes, William – physician; b. late 16th century, Bristol; educated at Brasenose College, Oxford; married Mary Stonor, of Stonor Park, near Henley, Oxfordshire, a recusant house; his wife, a Catholic, instrumental in his conversion; settled in London where he practiced for some time; greatly persecuted on account of his religion and as a result he went to the Continent in about 1615 and lived for some years in Rouen, France; returned to England in about 1625; appointed physician-in-ordinary to Queen Henrietta Maria, wife of Charles I; father of celebrated Latin poet and physician, James Alban Gibbes (1611–1677), who practiced at Santo Spirito and was appointed by Pope Alexander VII Professor of Rhetoric at the Sapienza University, Rome, and is buried in the Pantheon; see *Gillow*, Vol. II, p.437.

Gibbs, Sir Philip Armand Hamilton – writer; b. 1 May 1877, 33 Redcliffe Road, Kensington, London; c. 1898 (his wife, Agnes Mary (d. 1939), authoress, plus his father and mother also converted); d. 10 March 1962, Godalming, Surrey; mainly privately educated; literary editor; journalist with several London newspapers, being appointed one of the five journalists selected by the government to become official war correspondents with the British army in World

War I; first journalist ever to obtain an interview with the Pope (1919); resigned from *Daily Chronicle* in 1921 in protest at newspaper's support of Lloyd George's policy of reprisals in Ireland; author of many books on history, war and European politics; wrote several novels (e.g., *The Street of Adventure* (1909), *Intellectual Mansions* (1910)); worked for Ministry of Information in United States in World War II; four volumes of autobiography (*Across the Frontiers* (1938); *The Pageant of the Years* (1946); *Crowded Company* (1949); *Life's Adventure* (1957)); had one son, Anthony, who also became a novelist; see Patrick Braybrooke, *Some Catholic Novelists: Their Art and Outlook* (1931), p.147; Joseph Kelly, "Sir Philip Hamilton Gibbs," *Catholic Life*, March 2003, p.23; *DNB*.

Gifford (married name Plunkett), Grace Evelyn Mary Vandeleur – artist and Irish nationalist; b. 4 March 1888, 8 Temple Villas, Palmerston Road, Rathmines, Dublin, Ireland; c. 7 April 1916; d. 13 December 1955, 52 South Richmond Street, Dublin; one of twelve children; boys raised as Catholics, religion of their father, while girls raised as Protestants, religion of their mother; grew up to become supporter of Nationalist cause; attended meetings of Gaelic League, Irish Women's Franchise League, and Inghinidhe na Eireann (Daughters of Ireland); became engaged to Joseph Mary Plunkett (1887–1916), poet, editor of the *Irish Review*, devout Catholic (ancestor of St. Oliver Plunkett), and member of Irish Republican Brotherhood; at the time she was questioning her Protestant faith and shortly afterwards converted; at the Easter Monday rising in 1916 Joseph Plunkett helped to occupy the General Post Office and was present at Patrick Pearse's reading of proclamation of a republic; he was

court-martialled and sentenced to death; she married him in the chapel at Kilmainham gaol at 11.30pm 3 May 1916 and was allowed ten minutes to speak to him before his execution at 3.30am; withdrew her support for Sinn Fein when treaty granting Ireland dominion status within British Empire was signed; in civil war was a prominent republican spokeswoman; in 1923 interned in Kilmainham gaol as political prisoner and painted there the Kilmainham Madonna; much work as a caricaturist; sister, Muriel, married the poet, Thomas MacDonagh, who was also executed for his part in the rising; another sister, Sidney Czira (1889–1974), journalist and Irish republican activist; buried at Glasnevin cemetery with full military honors; see Marie O'Neill, *Grace Gifford Plunkett and Irish Freedom: Tragic Bride of 1916* (2000); Dominic Dowling, "The Kilmainham Madonna," *Catholic Life*, April 2005, p.24.; *DNB*.

Gilbert, George, scholastic, SJ – gentleman; b. about 1559, Suffolk; c. 1579; d. 6 October 1583, Rome; brought up in London in new religion, but inclined to Puritanism; succeeded to extensive estates; great favorite at English and French court, where he was introduced to Fr. Thomas Darbyshire who opened his eyes to the Catholic religion; went to Rome where instructed by Fr. Robert Persons (see below), who received him into the Church in 1579; returned to London and in 1580 formed association of twenty-six Catholic young men of birth and property without wives or offices to work for the Catholic cause; gave up his intended marriage and made vow of perpetual chastity "till the Catholic religion should be publicly professed in England"; placed himself at complete disposal of Persons (see below), Campion (see above) and their companions; pursued closely by Council, but evaded pursuivants and escaped from the country; went to Rouen, Rheims and Rome, where entered the English College as a pensioner and devoted himself to promoting Catholic cause in England; Cardinal Allen described him as the greatest patron of the Catholic clergy; covered walls of English College, Rome, with frescoes of the English martyrs; admitted into the Society of Jesus on his deathbed; buried in church of Sant Andrea; the Pope declared his death a serious blow to Catholicism in England; see *A way to deal with persons of all sorts so as to convert them and bring them back to a better way of life* (essay in Latin); *Gillow*, Vol. II, p.461; *DNB*.

Gill, (Arthur) Eric Rowtin – sculptor, engraver, writer, and typographer; b. 22 February 1882, 32 Hamilton Road, Brighton, Sussex; c. 22 February 1913 ("I found a thing in my mind and I opened my eyes and found it in front of me. You don't become a Catholic by joining the Church; you join the Church because you are a Catholic"; received with his wife; his younger brother, Cecil, former Anglican clergyman and missionary in New Guinea, was received 29 September 1934 with his wife); d. 17 November 1940, Uxbridge, Middlesex; father Congregational minister; brought up in atmosphere of religious controversy and holy poverty; formerly interested in Fabianism and Nietzsche; social critic (dealing with his various crafts, thoughts, and religious beliefs); greatest artist-craftsman of twentieth century; founded community at Ditchling 1907 to reinvent a holy tradition of workmanship; his many adulteries and incest became public knowledge in late 1980s; buried in churchyard of Baptist church at Speen, near High Wycombe; see *The Way of the Cross* (1926); *Christianity and Art* (1927); *Autobiography* (1940) ("Religion was the first necessity, and that meant the rule of God. If then there be a God, the whole world must be ruled in his name. If there be a religion it must be a world religion, a Catholicism. In so far as my religion were true it must be catholic. In so far as the Catholic religion were catholic it must be true! The Catholic Church professed to rule the whole world in the name of God – so far as I could see or imagine, it was the only institution that professed to do so.... Of course if the Catholic Church were simply an arrogant upstart institution, with no roots and no history and, more important to the innocent person, no fruits by which you might know her – no good fruits nourishing and delectable – then there would obviously be no point in considering her. But this was clearly not so; there was fruit in plenty, and, in my mind, very good fruit, even though they seemed to be fruits of the past"); *Christianity and the Machine Age* (1940); *Essays* (1947); Donald Attwater, *Eric Gill: Workman* (1945); Walter Shewring (ed), *Letters of Eric Gill* (1947); Robert Speaight, *The Life of Eric Gill* (1966); Donald Attwater, *A Cell of Good Living* (1969); M. Yorke, *Eric Gill: Man of Flesh and Spirit* (1981); Fiona MacCarthy, *Eric Gill: A Lover's Quest for Art and God* (1989) ("Gill, although painstaking in mapping out his faith, was at least in theory a Catholic already, knowing he believed and welcoming the nature of belief which was bestowed on him. It was homecoming, a return to the familiar, but it also had its sense of the supra-ordinary, the outlandish, like erotic experience of the highest order: 'I would not have anyone think that I became a Catholic because I was *convinced* of the truth, though I *was* convinced of the truth. I became a Catholic because I fell in love with the truth. And love is an experience. I saw. I heard. I felt. I tasted. I touched. And that is what lovers do'"); Brocard Sewell, "Aspects of Eric Gill,

1882–1940," *Chesterton Review, Eric Gill Special Issue*, November 1982, p.295; Sir John Rothenstein, "Eric Gill: Some Recollections," *Chesterton Review, Eric Gill Special Issue*, November 1982, p.321; Walter Romig (ed), *The Book of Catholic Authors*, Fifth Series (1952); Patrick Allitt, *Catholic Converts: British and American Intellectuals Turn to Rome* (1997) *passim*; Joseph Pearce, *Literary Converts* (1999) *passim*; *DNB* ("In 1911 he visited the abbey of Mont César in Louvain, where his first experience of hearing monastic plainchant brought him to an overwhelming moment of religious certitude: 'I knew, infallibly, that God existed and was a living God—just as I knew him in the answering smile of a child or in the living words of Christ'").

Gillett, (Henry) Martin Francis – writer; b. 11 November 1902, Andover, Hampshire; c. 1933 (received at the Brompton Oratory, London); d. 23 April 1980; from family with Tractarian associations; educated at Durham University; former Anglican minister; English and History teacher; lecturer and writer on Catholic history, relics, churches, and shrines (especially those to Our Lady); organizer of national pilgrimages to Walsingham; founder of Ecumenical Society of the Blessed Virgin Mary (his "supreme hope that Mary, Mother of the Church, will unite her dispersed children"); was given privilege of having his ashes placed in the Slipper Chapel at Walsingham for a lifetime of service to Our Lady; see *St. Bede the Venerable* (1935); *The Story of the Relics of the Passion* (1935); *Walsingham* (1946), *Famous Shrines of Our Lady*, 2 Vols. (1949 and 1952); Matthew Hoehn, OSB (ed), *Catholic Authors* (1952) ("A serious illness obliged him to convalesce in Italy, where he made many important Catholic contacts. More and more he found his interest in Marian devotion to be utterly

incompatible with the doctrine and discipline of the Church of England. Studying the facts of the various apparitions of Our Lady, including those at Fatima and La Salette, he became conscious, he says, that the urgent messages addressed by Our Lady to 'her people' contained singularly little reference to the Church of England, wherein appeals to say the Rosary could hardly be obeyed without fundamental dishonesty").

Gilley, Sheridan – historian and biographer; b. in Australia; c. 10 April 1993; Reader in Theology in University of Durham; became an Anglican in his late twenties; saw the Church of England as very middle-class and her separation from Western Christendom as a "terrible crime"; attracted by Irish Catholicism; influenced intellectually in his conversion by Newman, especially his objection to Victorian liberalism, and by Edward Norman; converted after the Church of England ordained women; much writing in favor of traditional liturgy and Church architecture; see "The Foolishness of Espousing a Fashion," *Church Times*, 16 April 1993 ("The first shock to my 'mere Christianity' came in Durham in the 1980s when the then Bishop opposed attempts to reform the 1967 Abortion Act. The views of the present Bishop [David Jenkins], whose books seemed perfectly orthodox, were a still greater surprise. I knew the history of Anglican modernism and thought it *passé*. But there it was: the Anglican hierarchy was willing to consecrate a theologian who rationalized the central mysteries of the virgin birth and resurrection, by denying the miraculous conception of Our Lord and that he rose bodily from the dead.... What was at issue here was common Christianity, as all Christians had received it, from the Ecumenical Patriarchs to the humblest captain of the Salvation Army...

I will still always honor the uncounted Anglicans, living and dead, who have kept the Catholic faith in their generation.... But in the end, Keble's congregationalism is not enough. There is something beyond it, Catholic Christendom in its fullness, as it exists in the Roman and Orthodox Churches. It is a humbling thing to enter the great communion of Christendom, which invokes the prayers of Augustine and Aquinas, and which is of all the Churches the mother and mistress, if sometimes a harsh and human one. For that it is worth being Campion on the hurdle, or Crashaw at Loreto, or Newman at Littlemore, or Ronald Knox pondering his dons' delight, or even an exile from our great cathedral, which ever haunts my dreams. But there are other and greater shrines. Long may the holy bells of Durham ring. They move me to tears. But they do not ring for me"); *Newman and His Age* (1990); "A place of worship where he comes first," *Catholic Herald*, 3 December 1993; "The End of the Oxford Movement," *The Tablet*, 18 March 1995, 352 ("The ordination of women has, moreover, revealed further difficulties in [the Anglo-Catholic] theory of the episcopate. The Anglo-Catholic bishops have allowed the ordination of women to the priesthood in their dioceses while opposing such ordinations in principle. Never, I think, in 20 centuries of Christianity, has a bishop sanctioned the ordination of a body of clergy whom he is unable in conscience to ordain himself. This conception of the episcopal office is unknown in the history of the Christian Church"); "Chesterton and Conversion," *Priests and People*, October 1995, p.381 ("I sometimes feel myself that I have a clearer view of Christianity than many who have only half left it, and who have never been wholly outside it themselves. It is from a journey which begins in the rejection of Christianity that one

can see most clearly how both like and unlike other religions it is, and that, while there are many mansions in the Father's house but only one house, so they all find their home under Peter's dome. Modern Western man may have to make a lengthy pilgrimage to find his true native land where it has always been, still awaiting him"); "Newman and the Convert Mind" in Ian Ker (ed), *Newman and Conversion* (1997); foreword to John Saward, *The Beauty of Holiness* (1997) ("There are three gateways to God, of goodness, truth, and beauty, yet in the Christian West, they have been sundered by the emergence of first a Protestant and then a secular culture. Neither truth nor goodness now need seem beautiful, and beauty in creation and creature has become, at best, a mere projection of subjective experience, at worst, a worldly temptation and a snare to turn the heart and mind from the eternal"); "The Abolition of God: Relativism and the Center of the Faith," in David Mills (ed), *The Pilgrim's Guide: C. S. Lewis and the Art of Witness* (1998); "Loss and Gain: Conversions to Catholicism in Modern Britain" in Dwight Longenecker (ed), *The Path to Rome* (1999); "Holy Words, Sacred Silence," *Catholic Herald*, 7 July 2000; letter to The Times, 6 September 2001 ("David Hume's argument against miracles..., when the impossible is claimed we must always conclude that somebody's senses must have deceived them, was answered by John Henry Newman. The balance of probabilities for miracles is altered if on other grounds (reason, faith, tradition, conscience) one already believes in a God with the power and goodness to perform them. There may be some people who believe in God on the evidence of miracles, but generally Christians (and not just Catholics) believe in miracles because they believe in God, not in God because they believe in miracles").

Gladstone, Helen Jane – b. 28 June 1814, 62 Rodney Street, Liverpool; c. June 1842; d. 16 January 1880, Hotel Disch, Bruckenstrasse, Cologne; daughter of Sir John Gladstone, first Baronet (1764–1851); sister of Right Hon. William Ewart Gladstone (1809–1898), statesman and four times Prime Minister (with whom she formed a close and confidential bond); reared mainly by her elder sister, Anne, an intense evangelical; suffered from a compulsive eating disorder and was invalided; nearly became a Greek Orthodox, but finally converted to the Catholic faith (William was furious at this; a cousin and sometime assistant of William Gladstone, Mrs. Anne Ramsden Bennett, also converted and was then shunned by him); reclusive for a time and later an opium addict; became tertiary of Order of St Dominic, and eventually settled in Cologne; buried in the Gladstone family vault in St. Andrew's Chapel, Fasque, Scotland, but without the commendatory prayer; see *DNB* ("Her brother William, at least, [was] convinced that she rejected the Pope's infallibility and died an Old Catholic").

Glasgow, George – writer; b. 1891, Bolton; c. 1939 (received (by Fr. Martindale) with his wife, Una Geraldine, daughter of Dr. C. J. Ridgeway, Anglican Bishop of Chichester); educated at Manchester University; authority on diplomacy and finance; journalist of international fame who on his conversion found much of the higher journalism irreconcilable with Catholic truth and concentrated on writing for Catholic papers; assistant editor of *The New Europe* 1916–1920; special correspondent in foreign affairs to *Manchester Guardian* 1920–1928; diplomatic correspondent of *The Observer* 1940–1942; correspondent to several European and American newspapers; advisor and contributor to

Encyclopedia Britannica; see *Diplomacy and God* (1941); Matthew Hoehn, OSB (ed), *Catholic Authors* (1952).

Goad, John – headmaster and meteorologist; b. 15 February 1616, Bishopsgate Street, London; c. 1686 (openly declared himself Catholic then, having been so in mind for many years); d. 28 October 1689; educated at St. John's College, Oxford, then took Anglican orders; headmaster of Merchant Taylors' School 1661–1681; much writing on many subjects, but main interests religion and meteorology; kept weather diary 1652–1685 and compared observations (most non-quantitative) to planetary aspects; at time of Popish Plot, charged with writing and teaching "certain passages savoring of popery" and dismissed from his post as headmaster; opened a private school in Piccadilly, which continued until shortly before his death; unmarried; buried in church of St Helen, Bishopsgate, London; see *Gillow*, Vol. II, p.500; *DNB*.

Godden, (Margaret) Rumer (Peggie) – writer; b. 10 December 1907, Meads, 30 Milnthorpe Road, Eastbourne; c. 1957 (daughter, Jane, received in 1956; both received by Archbishop Roberts); d. 8 November 1998, Kirkmichael, Dumfriesshire; daughter of a shipping company manager; spent first half of her life living in India; originally a dance teacher with a dance school in India; she made her name with her novel *Black Narcissus*; returned to England in 1945; wrote novels for adults and children, and poetry; author of over sixty books; several novels dealing with the subject of women in religious communities; when a friend asked her why she had chosen to write a novel about the religious life, she said, "My writing self, which is the more truthful, answered: Because nuns are dramatic. Theirs is the greatest love story in the world"; friendship with the Benedictine nun, Dame Felicitas Corrigan, led to *In This House of Brede*; see *Black Narcissus* (1938), *In This House of Brede* (1969); *Five for Sorrow, Ten for Joy* (1979); Ann Chisholm, *Rumer Godden: A Storyteller's Life* (1998) ("In the light of her conversion she came deeply to regret the mistakes of her past, especially her divorce; but the Catholic Church's strictness on such matters also appealed to her. Forty years later, she said, 'Catholicism suits me because I like the way everything is clear and concise. You'll always be forgiven, but you must know the rules.'"); *DNB*.

Godolphin, Sir William – diplomat; b. 1635, Spargor, Cornwall; c. 1671; d. 11 July 1696, Madrid; at school a friend of John Locke, later philosopher; after Christ Church, Oxford and the Inner Temple, assistant to Henry Bennet, Earl of Arlington, secretary of state; awarded Oxford DCL in 1663; in 1665 entered parliament for Camelford, Cornwall; in 1666 assisted the Earl of Sandwich in negotiations in Spain and Portugal; friend of Samuel Pepys; knighted in 1668; in 1671 appointed ambassador to Spain (his secretary was Edward Meredith (see below)); on arrival joined the Catholic Church; in 1678 named by Titus Oates as a "popish" agent; he was recalled but chose to remain in Spain; unmarried; buried in Madrid; see *DNB*.

Goffe (Goff, Gough), Stephen – priest; b. 1605, at Stanmer, Sussex; c. about 1649; d. 5 January 1682, in house of fathers of French Oratory in rue St Honoré, Paris; son of Puritan rector; took orders in Church of England; made a royal chaplain by Charles I and employed by court party in private negotiations on the Continent; after king's cause was lost he retired to France; heard lectures on early Church and as result

received into the Catholic Church; entered French Oratorians in 1651 and ordained priest in 1654 (reordained on orders of Rome); chaplain to Queen Henrietta Maria; assisted many distressed gentlemen; had two brothers, one, John (d. 1661), a Protestant clergyman, the other, William (d. 1679?), a colonel in the parliamentary army and one of the regicides who sat on the bench at the trial of Charles I; see Lingard, *History of England*, Vol. III; *Gillow*, Vol. II, p.506; *Catholic Encyclopedia*; *DNB*.

Gonne, (Edith) Maud – Irish nationalist; b. 21 December 1866, Tongham Manor, near Farnham, Surrey; c. 1903; d. 27 April 1953, Roebuck House, Clonskeagh, Dublin; mother died early; brought up by governesses in England, then France; had become a nationalist by 1886; inherited a fortune on her majority; close friend of the poet W. B. Yeats (1865–1939) for twenty-five years, but refused to marry him (she was the subject of more than eighty poems by Yeats); her politics were confused, but based on the formula: "to look on which side England ranges herself and go on the opposite"; mother, by Lucien Millevoye (1850–1918), of Iseult Gonne, wife of Francis Stuart (see below); converted and married Major John MacBride (1868–1916), member of the Irish Republican Brotherhood and later executed for his part in the Easter rising; their divorce in 1906 damaged her position in nationalist circles; went to France, where active in social causes and nursing during World War I; returned to Dublin in 1918; continued her activism by way of speeches, writings and demonstrations; mother of Sean MacBride (1904–1988), IRA chief-of-staff and cabinet minister; buried in Glasnevin cemetery; see *A Servant of the Queen* (1974) ("I never doubted the existence of spiritual forces surrounding us, some friendly, some hostile, more completely blind to human needs, pursuing their own existence with the same disregard of us as the birds or the insects. I knew it was possible to break the dividing barrier which separates us from this world and once had been eager to do so in the hope of gaining power to further the cause to which I had devoted my life. Then I had realized the danger of playing with forces without sufficient knowledge, – danger to one's own sanity and still more danger to those one loves and may be unable to protect. I looked on the Catholic Church as the repository of spiritual knowledge and sometimes I longed for its protection and guidance.

I believe every political movement on earth has its counterpart in the spirit world and the battles we fight here have perhaps been already fought out on another plane and great leaders draw their often unexplained power from this. I cannot conceive a material movement which has not a spiritual basis. It was this that drew me so powerfully towards the Catholic Church…"); *DNB*.

Goodall, Sir Reginald ("Reggie") – orchestra conductor; b. 13 July 1901, Lincoln; d. 5 May 1990, Bridge, near Canterbury; father, a solicitor's clerk, was imprisoned for forgery and he and his brother taken by his mother to United States for education; left school at fifteen; in 1925 returned to England to study at Royal College of Music, London, and then in Munich, Salzburg and Vienna; fine organist; flirted with Fascism, supporting Sir Oswald Mosley; joined Sadlers Wells Company 1944; conductor Royal Opera House from 1947; turned his career around and became Wagner conductor without equal (also earlier a champion of Britten's music); great understanding of the architecture of Wagner's music; modest and much loved by musicians and singers with whom he worked; wife, Eleanor Katherine Edith, devout Catholic; according to opera singer, Victor Godfrey, a close associate, "he was totally out of his time. He did not really comprehend the 20th century. He converted to the Catholic Church because 'it is timeless, dear' (and felt betrayed when the Latin text was dropped). He yearned for an earlier age when gifted artists were supported and encouraged by, as he saw it, enlightened rulers"; see J. Lucas, *Reggie: The Life of Reginald Goodall* (1993); *DNB*

Goodfellow, Lieutenant General Charles Augustus, VC – soldier; b. 27 November 1836; c. 1867; d. 1 September 1915; formerly of Royal Bombay Engineers; won his Victoria Cross for valor during Indian Mutiny in which he took part with Central India Field force (on 6 October 1859 during an attack on Fort of Beyt, India, a soldier was shot under the walls in a sharp fire of matchlock; he, a lieutenant at the time, carried away the body of the man who was then dead, but whom he had at first thought was only wounded); he also served in Abyssinian campaign; JP for Kent.

Goodhart-Rendel, Harry Stuart – architect; b. 29 May 1887, Plas Dinam, Newnham, Cambridge; c. 1924 ("His faith thereafter became the core and mainstay of his life") (*DNB*)); d. 21 June 1959, 114 Eaton Square, Westminster; from wealthy family; showed very early talent for music and construction; he added in 1902 the name Rendel taken from his maternal grandfather, Baron Rendel (1834–1913); devout Anglican in early life; unlimited leisure to develop his interests in music and architecture; graduated from Cambridge University in music in 1909; began an architectural practice; commissioned in the special reserve, Grenadier Guards, in 1915 and found soldiering was his true vocation; prominent architect between the wars; influenced by nineteenth century architects; President of Architectural Association 1924–1925 and of Royal Institute of British Architects 1937–1939; Slade Professor of Fine Art in Oxford 1933–1936; criticized "official" architecture; built in a variety of styles; wrote many essays on nineteenth century architecture, especially on Victorian Gothic Revival; unmarried; buried at Prinknash Abbey; see *Vitruvian Nights: Papers Upon Architectural Subjects* (1932); *Fine Art* (1934); *English Architecture Since the Regency: An Interpretation* (1953); *DNB*.

Goodman, Godfrey – b. 1583, Ruthin, Denbighshire; c. some say 1642, others 1650, others say on his deathbed; and some deny conversion); d. 19 January 1655, Westminster, London; Anglican rector; then Dean of Rochester; made Anglican Bishop of Gloucester in 1624; refused to sign the seventeen new canons drawn up at 1640 Convocation and was suspended by Archbishop Laud and committed to the Gatehouse prison; impeached and committed to the Tower twice; retired into private life in Westminster and concentrated on literary and historical research; gentle character and great charity to the poor; unmarried; buried in St. Margaret's Church, Westminster; see Geoffrey Ingle Soden, *Godfrey Goodman, Bishop of Gloucester, 1583–1656* (1953); Edward Ingram Watkin, *Roman Catholicism in England From the Reformation to 1950* (1957) ("[Bishop Goodman] asked for a priest to reside in his palace with a view presumably to a deathbed reconciliation, refused to subscribe to the Canons passed in 1640 because, though anti-Puritan, they denied the Real Presence in the Eucharist as it is understood by Catholic theology, and appears to have been in fact reconciled on his deathbed"); *Gillow*, Vol. II, p.528; *Catholic Encyclopedia*; *DNB*.

Goodman, Venerable John – priest and confessor of the faith; b. 1590, Bangor, North Wales; c. about 1621; d. Good Friday 1642, Newgate, London; brought up Protestant; received orders in Church of England; grew dissatisfied with Protestantism; went to Paris and was converted by Richard Ireland; entered seminary at Douai in 1621; ordained priest about 1631; on return to England, zealous in missionary work; in 1635 apprehended by pursuivant and imprisoned in Newgate; discharged, but in 1639 again was apprehended and committed to Gatehouse for a time; later in Newgate again; in January 1641 condemned to death for being a priest, but Queen Henrietta Maria interceded for him with the king who reprieved him; both houses of parliament demanded his execution; Goodman intervened personally, petitioning Charles that he, Goodman, might be executed rather than be source of division between the parties; compromise effected and he was committed to prison indefinitely, dying there; see Fr. John Berchmans Dockery, OFM, *Christopher Davenport: Friar and Diplomat* (1960), pp.55–59; *Gillow*, Vol. II, p.530; *Catholic Encyclopedia*; *DNB*.

Gordon, John (known as John Clement Gordon) – b. 1644, Ellon, Aberdeenshire, Scotland; c. 1704 (the only convert bishop from the British Isles since the reconciliation of England by Cardinal Pole in 1554); d. 1726, Rome; chaplain of Episcopalian Church ministering to navy, then a royal chaplain in New York; became Scottish Episcopal bishop of Galloway in 1688; remained loyal to James II during the Revolution and followed him to royal court at St. Germain; in about 1702 converted by

Bossuet and privately received into the Catholic Church; then went to Rome, where he made a public abjuration of Protestantism before Cardinal Sacripanti, the Cardinal Protector of Scotland; at his conditional baptism he took the additional name of the reigning pontiff, and always afterwards signed himself John Clement Gordon; the Pope caused Holy Office to enquire into validity of Gordon's Protestant orders; in 1714 the Pope confirmed decision of Holy Office that all his orders were null from beginning (in *Apostolicae Curae* in 1898 Pope Leo XIII referred to this case as standard judgment); he received sacrament of confirmation, and Clement XI conferred on him the tonsure, giving him benefice of abbey of St. Clement (after which he commonly went by name of the Abate Clemente); he never received other than minor orders in the Catholic church; see James Quinn, "The Case of the Convert Bishop: John Clement Gordon, 1644–1726," *The Month*, February 1958, p.102; *DNB*.

Gordon, Joseph (born John) – priest; b. 1811; c. 24 February 1847 (received at Taunton by Bishop Hendren; his brother, Fr. William Gordon (see below), also received); d. 1853; after Rugby School he became a cadet in the Indian Army, where he was moved towards religion by an Evangelical officer; invalided home in 1831 and went to Trinity College, Cambridge; took Anglican orders in 1837; influenced by Tractarianism and by Newman's *Sermons*; joined the Birmingham Oratory in 1848; ordained priest; went to Italy to collect witnesses for the Achilli trial in 1852; died of pleurisy; in 1865 Newman dedicated *The Dream of Gerontius* to Joseph Gordon; see *Reasons for my Conversion* (1847); Henry Tristram, *Newman and his Friends* (1933), pp.111–116 (a memoir by Newman).

Gordon, William Philip – priest; b. 1827; c. 15 September 1847 (received at Downside Abbey); d. 1900; brother of Fr. Joseph Gordon (see above); educated at Christ Church, Oxford; joined the Oratory in 1848; sent to the London Oratory in 1849; ordained 1850; Superior of the London Oratory 1868–1871, 1880–1889, 1892–1895, 1898–1900.

Gorman, William Timothy – c. 1900; formerly Anglican curate in Cambridge, then novice with Cowley fathers, Oxford; see essay in J. G. F. Raupert (ed), *Roads to Rome* (1901), p.102 ("The Holy Spirit brought to my recollection Isaiah's prophecy of the Church (Ch. xxxv), with its promise that 'the wayfaring man, though a fool, shall not err therein.' Well as I had known the words before, it was then for the first time that I saw their force, and that they contained the answer to my perplexity. The finding of the true Church of God (and the consequent certainty about revealed truth) was not really a matter for learned investigation at all, otherwise there could be no responsibility to find it resting on almost any one, and the only alternative was the ultra-Protestant dogma, 'One Church is as good as another.' God had promised by His prophet that the "fool" – the ordinary unlearned person – should be able (at the very least) to find the Catholic Church, and so with certainty to avoid error.... I therefore had to look, in a candid and simple way, for the body which obviously and clearly presented those characteristics which God had appointed to be the signs or marks of His Church – Unity, Sanctity, Catholicity, and Apostolicity. Any body which failed in any one of these points might be dismissed at once, and, unless Christ's promises had failed utterly, there must be a Church which showed them unmistakably...

Of course the matter was then ended; for the positive side, the recognition of all the notes of the Church, clearly, evidently, and indisputably in the Holy Roman Church had proceeded *pari passu* with the perception of their absence in the Anglican body. No one who accepted Catholic principles made any serious attempt to deny her possession of them; that she was One, Holy, Catholic, Apostolic, was obvious to the man in the street, once the terms were explained to him and the fact pointed out. Plain hard fact as to the actual belief even of those who rejected the Catholic idea of the Church abundantly proved this...

With what relief and gratitude one kept listening to the words of the good priest who later on received me into the Church: 'Remember, our Lord really did say, 'Tu es Petrus'...

The two chief things that the process of my conversion has impressed on me are – that faith is the gift of God, given according to the inscrutable mysteries of the Divine Vocation; and that the means to obtain it are in the hands of every one who perseveringly prays, and has recourse to the unfailing patronage of our Blessed Lady, *Sedes Sapientiae*. 'Thou hast hid these things from the wise and prudent, and hast revealed them unto babes.' Fundamental truths, indeed, and simple; but, alas! Put quite out of sight, from the necessities of their position by Anglican controversialists").

Gosselin, Sir Martin Le Marchant Hadsley – diplomat; b. 2 November 1847, Walfield, near Hertford; c. 1878; d. 26 February 1905, Busaco, Portugal (car accident); educated at Eton and Christ Church College, Oxford; entered diplomatic service in 1868; attaché at Lisbon and Berlin; second secretary to British embassy at St. Petersburg 1874–1879; attached to the special mission of Lord Beaconsfield and Lord Salisbury at the Congress of Berlin 1878; posts in Rome, St. Petersburg and Berlin; pro-

moted secretary of legation and appointed to Brussels 1885–1892; secretary to the Duke of Norfolk's special mission to Pope Leo XIII on the latter's jubilee in 1887; one of secretaries to the international conference for the suppression of the African slave trade held in Brussels in 1889 and 1890; promoted to be secretary of embassy at Madrid in 1892; transferred to Berlin in 1893; minister-plenipotentiary in Paris embassy 1896–1898; home appointment of assistant under-secretary of state for foreign affairs 1898–1902; British envoy at Lisbon; see *DNB*.

Gother (or Goter), John – priest and religious writer; b. in Southampton; c. about 1667; d. 2 October 1704; parents strict Presbyterians, who taught him anti-Catholic prejudice; reacted against this and converted; Catholic relative, Thomas Tylden (see below), arranged voyage to Lisbon; entered English College in 1668; ordained priest and taught there; sent to the English mission in 1681; located in London when James II came to throne; principal Catholic controversialist during James II's reign and wrote long series of apologetic and spiritual works; later chaplain to George Holman (see below) at Warkworth Castle in Northamptonshire, where he instructed and received into the Church the future Bishop Challoner (see above), then a boy (Challoner's mother having come as housekeeper to the Castle); he directed the boy be sent to Douai College; famous for series of devotional books; wrote guides for laity on sacraments and hearing Mass; died on a voyage to English College at Lisbon; buried in College church; see *A Papist Misrepresented and Represented* (1665); Sister Marion Norman, IBVM, "John Gother and the English Way of Spirituality," *Recusant History*, November 1972, p.306; *Gillow*, Vol. II, p.540; *Catholic Encyclopedia*; *DNB*.

Goulder, Mgr. Laurance – priest; b. 10 May 1903; c. 1937; d. 29 June 1969; freelance journalist before his ordination into the Anglican ministry in 1927; ordained Catholic priest in 1942; Master of the Guild of Our Lady of Ransom 1951–1968; organized more than six hundred pilgrimages to ancient shrines; for fifteen years he led the annual Walsingham pilgrimage; see *Pilgrimage Pamphlets*, a series on the following: Canterbury; Westminster; The Universities; London; York; Winchester; Church Life in Medieval England; Norwich.

Goulding, Lady Valerie Hamilton (*née* Monckton) – campaigner for disabled people; b. 12 September 1918, Ightham Mote, a manor house near Sevenoaks, Kent; d. 28 July 2003; daughter of Sir Walter Monckton (1891–1965), first Viscount Monckton of Brenchley; brother, Major-General Gilbert Monckton (1911–2006) (see below) also converted; acted as her father's secretary when he was advisor to Edward VIII during the abdication crisis (carried letters between the king and the Prime Minister, Stanley Baldwin); trained nurse; wife of Sir Basil Goulding (1909–1982), Irish Baronet; in 1951 founded in Dublin Central Remedial Clinic, now the largest organization in Ireland looking after people with physical disabilities (chairman and managing director until 1984); member of the Irish Senate 1977–1981.

Graef, Hilda Charlotte – writer; b. 1907, Berlin; c. March 1941 (at Farm Street, London); brought up as Protestant in name, though both parents unbelievers; some Jewish grandparents; really pious as a child; teacher in Germany; settled in England in 1936; for many years lived without any religion; did theology degree and joined the Church of England; conversion to the Catholic Church influenced by St. Thomas Aquinas, St. John of the Cross, G. K. Chesterton (see above) and Robert Hugh Benson (see above); in 1941 worked on the *Lexicon of Patristic Greek* at Oxford; articles for Catholic journals; several books mainly on spiritual topics; see *The Way of the Mystics* (1948), *The Case of Therese Neumann* (1950) (was controversy over her conclusion that a supernatural explanation was no more probable than a natural one); *God in Our Daily Life* (1951); *The Scholar and the Cross : The Life and Work of Edith Stein* (1955); *From Fashions to the Fathers: The Story of My Life* (1957); *The Light and the Rainbow* (1959) (study in Christian spirituality); *Mystics of Our Times* (1962); *Devotion to the Blessed Virgin* (1963); *Mary: A History of Doctrine and Devotion* (1963); *Adult Christianity* (1965); *The Story of Mysticism* (1966); *God and Myself* (1967); CatholicAuthors.com website ("When I was seventeen I had a strange experience. By way of broadening my horizon, I went into a Catholic church one evening, where they were having May devotions. Then something extraordinary happened. I, who had hardly ever gone into a Protestant church because I found the services intolerably boring, was completely carried off my feet. I could not imagine why. So strong was the inexplicable attraction I felt that I went again two days later, and after that to Mass on Sunday. That finished me. I felt sure that if I went once more into a Catholic church I should want to become a Catholic – without even believing in God. This was absurd, and I decided then and there never again to enter one"); Matthew Hoehn, OSB (ed), *Catholic Authors* (1952) ("When she studied doctrine, she discovered that Christianity, which her Protestant teachers had always presented as some emotional experience divorced from reason, was a perfectly reasonable and consistent whole").

Graham, Bishop Charles Morice – bishop; b. 5 April 1834, Mhow, India; c. 1844; d. 2 September 1912; eldest son of Lieutenant-Colonel William Henry Graham of the Royal Engineers (d. 1888); child convert on conversion of his father; educated at Prior Park and the English College, Rome; ordained priest 1857; became canon and vicar-general of Plymouth Diocese; consecrated coadjutor to Bishop Clifford of Clifton in 1891; succeeded Bishop William Vaughan at Plymouth in 1902; retired as bishop 1911.

Graham, Bishop Henry Grey (usually known as Grey Graham) – bishop and writer; b. 8 March 1874, the manse, Maxton, Roxburghshire, Scotland; c. 15 August 1903 (received at Fort Augustus Abbey); d. 5 December 1959, Bon Secours Nursing Home, Glasgow; son of Scottish Presbyterian Minister; his grandfather and great-grandfather were ministers of Established Church of Scotland; Assistant Professor of Hebrew and Oriental Languages; became Scottish Presbyterian minister; became attracted to the Catholic Church and its liturgy; conversion influenced by an older Presbyterian minister, John Charleson, who converted in 1901, and by the issue of authority in the Church; ordained Catholic priest 12 December 1906 in Rome; in 1917 consecrated auxiliary bishop to the Archbishop of St. Andrews and Edinburgh; reverted to being a parish priest; buried in St. Peter's cemetery, Dalbeth, Glasgow; see *From the Kirk to the Catholic Church* (1910) ("To me it seemed that the Incarnation of the Son of God, and His sojourn among men, and His teaching His apostles and declaring God's truth to them, and His founding a Church, would have been superfluous and absurd and useless if He had not intended that man should be taught with unerring certainty what to believe…. An authority, therefore, teaching with divinely-protected inerrancy, which could assure me this was false and that was true, with the same certainty as Our Lord assured his companions – for I felt we had as much right to certainty in matters of religion as the first disciples – this was what I wanted. And precisely this was what no Protestant authority could give me: what in fact they expressly declared they could not give…. The Catholic Church was the only Christian body on earth that claimed to have the light and the truth, and to give it with infallible certainty. That was so much in her favor to begin with…. She was the only Church that could reasonably and plausibly pretend to speak with authority, because she was the only one that could trace her ascent back to the Apostles… Besides, I saw plainly that Unity, which was to be a mark of the true Church, and which Our Lord had absolutely willed and required among His disciples, never had been and never could be secured in any other way than by the supreme authority of the Roman Pontiff…. Presuming that unity was demanded by Jesus Christ…. I saw that as a matter of historical fact, it never existed out of the Roman communion"); *Where We Got the Bible: Our Debt to the Catholic Church* (1911) ("People who could read at all in the Middle Ages could read Latin: hence there was little need for the Church to issue the Scriptures in any other language. But as a matter of fact she did in many countries put the Scriptures in the hand of her children in their own tongue. (1) We know from history that there were proper translations of the Bible and Gospels in Spanish, Italian, Danish, French, Norwegian, Polish, Bohemian and Hungarian for the Catholics of those lands before the days of printing, but we shall confine ourselves to England, so as to refute once more the common fallacy that John Wycliffe was the first to place an English translation of the Scriptures in the hands of the English people in 1382"); *Prosperity, Catholic and Protestant: The Relation Between the True Religion and Prosperity Examined* (1912); *Hindrances to Conversion to the Catholic Church and Their Removal* (1913), *What Faith Really Means* (1914); Hugh G. McEwan, *Bishop Grey Graham, 1874–1959: An Essay on His Life and Times* (1973) ("The original error, as Henry Graham came to see it, had been to give the Bible a false place in the divine economy. It was never meant to be the sole and self-sufficient guide to God's revelation. To set it up as the sole court of appeal was to tear it from the context of living authority and tradition and to throw it open to private and contradictory interpretation. In two of the three parishes where Henry Graham had labored, he had known of houses divided against themselves – the father going to one meeting and the mother to another – and in one instance of the congregation of the Lord's people consisting of one family only, who took consolation from the fact that Our Lord had spoken of His little flock.

On historical grounds he could not persuade himself that the Kirk was the church founded by Christ; and if it could not make that claim, it was nothing. It was simply a sectarian device adopted by one small nation in an out-of-the-way corner of the earth. In spite of its scriptural claims, the Church of Scotland had no continuity. The true church of Christ must have preserved its identity from the beginning, must have taught the same truths in every age, must have kept an unbroken succession. She must have a continuous historic memory, a constant ability to explain and restate her doctrine, to attest, as from personal experience, the faith once delivered to the saints. The church must be a living organism, with an enduring personality, growing like a human being from childhood to maturity

but maintaining all through her change and growth and development the same individuality. This continuous succession and history of preservation the Presbyterian Church made no attempt to claim. The Protestant thesis was that the church had at one stage become incurably corrupt in doctrine and morals, and that only through the reformers had the true Gospel been recovered. But if the promise of Christ meant anything, it surely meant that the church cannot be corrupted beyond redemption. It meant that you cannot leap-frog over all the centuries, over the heads of Saints and Doctors and Fathers, right into the Acts of the Apostles. You cannot repudiate the past. You cannot write off the Fathers and the mediaeval church. 'Take care, young man,' Dr. MacLeod had admonished him once at Park church, 'Once you get to the Fathers, you are like Newman – on an inclined plane that leads straight to Rome.' To Henry Graham it looked very much as if there had been a religious somersault in the sixteenth century and that the only honest course was to somersault back again"); *DNB*.

Granard, seventh Earl of (George Arthur Hastings Forbes) – Irish peer and soldier; b. 5 August 1833; c. 1869 (received with his wife, Jane, the Countess of Granard (1840–1872)); d. 25 August 1889; son of Major-General George Forbes, Viscount Forbes; educated at Eton; styled Viscount Forbes 1836–1837; succeeded his grandfather as Earl Granard in 1837; Lieutenant-Colonel Commandant of the 9th Battalion of the Rifle Brigade; Knight of St. Patrick in 1857; Knight and President in Great Britain and Ireland of the Sovereign Military Order of Malta from 1875 until his death; Knight Grand Cross of Order of St. Gregory the Great; member of the Senate of the Royal University of Ireland; President of the Catholic Union of

Ireland; Lord Lieutenant of County Leitrim; had eight children by two wives.

Grant, James – novelist and writer on history; b. 1 August 1822, Edinburgh; c. 1875 (one of his sons, Roderick (1860–1934), converted previously and became a priest; his father-in-law, James Browne (1793–1841), formerly a minister of the Church of Scotland, converted in his later years); d. 5 May 1887, Westbourne Park, London; son of an army captain; related to Sir Walter Scott through his mother; a younger brother was John Grant, the distinguished heraldic scholar; raised in Newfoundland; returned to Scotland in 1839; period of military service, then entered an architect's office before devoting himself to a literary career; novels very often on military themes, some based on Scottish history; wrote fifty-six novels and several histories; contributor to *The Dublin University Magazine*, *The United Service Magazine*, etc.; most of his works were printed in the United States; all were translated into German and Danish, and several into French; founder and secretary of the National Association for the Vindication of Scottish Rights 1852–1853; by 1880s his popularity had declined and he died in relative poverty; his political views were of a broadly Jacobite nature; see *Romance of War* (1845); *The Highlanders in Belgium: The Adventures of an Aide-de-Camp* (1848); *Jane Seton* (1853); *The Yellow Frigate* (1855); Stewart Foster, "Two Nineteenth-Century Literary Converts," *The Innes Review*, Autumn 1984, p.96; *DNB*.

Grant, John – statistician; b. 24 April 1620, Birchin Lane, Cornhill, London; d. 18 April 1674; brought up a rigid Puritan; later inclined towards Socinianism; held many offices of trust in the City of London; one of the original members of the Royal Society; at length became a Catholic; his conversion necessitated the resignation of his public offices; falsely accused of aggravating the effect of the Fire of London by turning off many cocks, thereby emptying many water pipes; buried in St. Dunstan's church, Fleet Street, under the pews in the nave; see *Gillow*, Vol. III, p.4 ("He was esteemed not only for his great candor and rectitude, but also for his singular penetration and judgment. Combining study with natural ingenuity, his observations were always valuable. He was a faithful friend and a great peacemaker, being frequently called upon as an arbitrator").

Grant, William Augustine Ignatius – artist (landscape painter) and theological controversialist; b. 1838; c. 1857 (left in 1868, but reverted in 1880 (wife also received in 1880)); d. 21 May 1883; brought up amongst Scottish Presbyterians; later became Anglican; brought into the Catholic Church by growing appreciation of the position of Our Lady in the Christian economy and of the Communion of Saints; in 1868 he left the Catholic communion for the sect of Irvingites; then returned to Anglicanism, championing the Ritualists; reconciled to the Church finally; see *Gillow*, Vol. III, p.11.

Gray, John Henry – priest, poet and author; b. 10 March 1866, 2 Vivian Road, Bethnal Green, London; c. 14 February 1890 (St. Anselm's and Cecilia's church, Lincoln's Inn Fields, London; his mother, Hannah Mary (1845–1903), converted in 1893); d. 14 June 1934, Edinburgh; son (eldest of nine) of carpenter; brought up in family originally non-conformist; passed civil service examinations and worked as librarian in Foreign Office; part of the decadent movement; Oscar Wilde's principal protégée before Lord Alfred Douglas; some would say he was the original for Dorian Gray, though he successfully sued *Star* newspaper for libel for saying so; *Pall Mall Gazette* called him "Le Plus Decadent des Decadents" in 1893 when his book of verse, *Silverpoints* published; in 1892 he suddenly suffered mental collapse, apparently precipitated by a spiritual crisis, recovery resulting in translations of devotional verse, later published in *Spiritual Poems* (1896); the wealthy Russian-Jewish émigré and poet André Raffalovich (see below) rescued him with financial and emotional support; also influenced by J-K Huysmans, the French novelist, and his view that "the Church was the only body to have preserved the art of past centuries, the lost beauty of the ages" (*Against Nature* (1884)); persuaded Aubrey Beardsley (see above) to convert to the Catholic faith; ordained Catholic priest in 1901 (later a canon); spent last years as parish priest in Edinburgh; continued literary career, writing *Park* (1932), experimental novel; buried in Mount Vernon cemetery outside Edinburgh; see Brocard Sewell (ed), *Two Friends: John Gray and Andre Raffalovich: Essays Biographical and Critical* (1963) (essay by Fr. Edwin Essex: "He had been walking abroad, I think he said in Brittany, when the faith finally came to him. Early one morning he found himself at Mass in a small, wayside chapel, with half-a-dozen peasant women. It was an untidy, neglected place, and the priest an unshaven figure at the altar, slovenly, and in a hurry. Vividly and slowly, as if savoring afresh each tiny detail, Canon Gray reconstructed the scene, without a hint of criticism, leaning forward in his chair, hands on knees, and, in his grave eyes, a look of brooding wonder even after so many years. 'Yes, Father,' he said, with a slow turn of his head in my direction, 'it was then that it came to me. I said to myself, 'John Gray, here is the real thing'"); Brocard Sewell, *Footnote to the Nineties: A Memoir of John Gray and Andre*

Raffalovich (1968); Gary H. Paterson, "Spiritual Decadence? Some Religious Poetry of John Gray," *Antigonish Review*, Autumn 1979, p.89; Brocard Sewell, *In the Dorian Mode: A Life of John Gray, 1866–1934* (1983); Jerusha Hull McCormack, *John Gray: Poet, Dandy, and Priest* (1991); Jerusha Hull McCormack, *The Man Who Was Dorian Gray* (2000); Robert Whelan, "Why did so many Victorian decadents become Catholics?" *Catholic Herald*, 5 January 2001; *DNB*.

Green, Blessed Hugh (known on the mission as Ferdinand Brooks) – priest and martyr; b. about 1584, London; c. about 1608; d. 19 August 1642, Dorchester; both parents Protestants; traveled on the Continent where the zealous religious practice made such an impact on him that he became a Catholic; entered English College, Douai, in 1609; ordained priest 14 June 1612; went to the English mission and worked there for nearly thirty years, mainly in Staffordshire, finally as chaplain at Chideock Castle, Dorset, seat of Lady Arundell; when Charles I issued the proclamation ordering all priests to depart the realm within a stated time, he admitted to custom-house officer at the port of Lyme that he was a priest, not realizing that leaving date had passed; committed to Dorchester gaol and five months later tried and sentenced to death for being a priest; converted two condemned women criminals whilst in prison; went to his death with holy joy; hanged, drawn, and quartered at Dorchester (a hotbed of Puritans who played football with his head); buried that day, near to the gallows; *Gillow*, Vol. III, p.18; *Catholic Encyclopedia*; *DNB*.

Greene, (Henry) Graham, OM – writer and journalist; b. 2 October 1904, St. John's, Berkhamsted, Hertfordshire; c. 1926 (received by Fr. George Trollope of

Nottingham Cathedral; wife, Vivienne (see below) converted earlier in 1926); d. 3 April 1991, Corseaux, Switzerland; educated at Balliol College, Oxford; served in Foreign Office; outstanding writer (great many novels, stories, plays; biography; film criticism); also worked as an intelligence officer; his Catholic novels have theme of human justice as inadequate and irrelevant to real struggle against evil; friendship with Evelyn Waugh survived religious arguments and opposed political opinions; relationship with Church never easy; later referred to himself as a "Catholic atheist," subsequently modified to "Catholic agnostic"; long affairs with Catherine Walston (1916–1978) and Yvonne Cloetta, (1923–2001); later support for international socialism and criticism of American capitalism and military expansion; to his dying day he kept a photograph in his wallet of the Italian stigmatic Padre Pio; brother, Hugh (1910–1987), became Director-General of BBC; see *Brighton Rock* (1938); *The Power and the Glory* (1940), *The Heart of the Matter* (1948)); *The End of the Affair* (1951); *A Sort of Life* (1971); W. Gore Allen, "The World of Graham Greene," *Irish Ecclesiastical Record*, January 1949, p.42; A. A. DeVitis, *Graham Greene* (1986); Patrick Sherry, *The Life of Graham Greene*, 3 Vols., especially Volume I (1989), pp.254–265 and Volume III (2004), pp.682–706; Michael Shelden, *Graham Greene: The Man Within* (1994); Anthony Mockler, *Graham Greene: Three Lives* (1994); W. J. West, *The Quest for Graham Greene* (1997); Fr. Leopoldo Duran, *Graham Greene: Friend and Brother* (1994); Bernard Bergonzi, *War Poets and Other Subjects* (1999), Ch. 18, "Graham Greene at Eighty"; William Thomas Hill (ed), *Perceptions of Religious Faith in the Work of Graham Greene* (2002); David Jones, "A Writer Who Happened to be a Catholic,"

Catholic Life, February 2003, p.62; Ian Ker, *The Catholic Revival in English Literature, 1845–1961*, (2003), Ch. 5, "The Catholicism of Greeneland"; Bernard Bergonzi, *A Study in Greene: Graham Greene and the Art of the Novel* (2006); Michael G. Brennan, "Graham Greene's Catholic Conversion: the early writings (1923–29) and *The Man Within*," *Logos* (2006), p.134; Ralph McInerny, *Some Catholic Writers* (2007); Patrick Allitt, *Catholic Converts: British and American Intellectuals Turn to Rome* (1997) *passim*; Joseph Pearce, *Literary Converts* (1999) *passim*; Lorene Hanley Duquin, *A Century of Catholic Converts* (2003), p.74; *Graham Greene: The Spoken Word* (British Library CD); *DNB*.

Greene, John Raymund, OP – priest; b. 1655, Oxfordshire; c. 1674; d. 28 July 1741, Louvain; brought up in royal household; sent to Oxford to be educated for Established Church, but was reconciled to the faith by Fr. Philip Howard, OP, then chaplain to Catharine of Braganza, consort of Charles II; anger of authorities forced both to retire to the Continent; entered English Dominican convent at Bornhem, near Antwerp, in 1674; ordained priest in 1679; chair of Philosophy and Theology at Bornhem; in 1694 elected prior; in 1700 twice attempted to reach England, but captured and re-landed in Netherlands; various other posts on the Continent; instituted provincial of English Congregation; came on the English mission intermittently; retired to the college at Louvain; see *Gillow*, Vol. III, p.32.

Greene, Vivienne (later shortened her name to Vivien) (*née* Dayrell-Browning) – poet and essayist; b. 1 August 1905, Bristol; c. 1926; d. 19 August 2003, Oxford; first wife of Graham Greene; converted to Catholicism before her marriage (to her mother's horror);

they separated in 1948, though they never divorced; expert on dolls' houses about which she wrote extensively; see Graham Greene, *A Sort of Life* (1971) ("I met the girl I was to marry after finding a note from her at the porter's lodge in Balliol protesting against my inaccuracy in writing, during the course of a film review, of the 'worship' Roman Catholics gave to the Virgin Mary, when I should have used the term 'hyperdulia.' I was interested that anyone took these subtle distinctions of an unbelievable theology seriously, and we became acquainted").

Gregory, Theophilos Stephen MC – author and journalist; b. 23 November 1897; c. 1935; d. 1975; Methodist minister (reputedly a fiery circuit preacher) 1921–1935; secretary of Aquinas Society; editor *Dublin Review*; an accepted authority on the Eucharist; advocate of a Catholic University for England; see *The Unfinished Universe* (1935) ("Papal authority rests on the word of Jesus and on nothing else. That is its strength. To discuss its title deeds, and to reach an independent decision either for or against the authenticity of His words to St. Peter, or St. Peter's occupancy of the Holy See, is *ipso facto* to deny the presence of divine authority here and now…. Such a question is finally settled before it can be discussed. An event like the speaking of certain words to Peter either happened or not: it must be straightly affirmed or denied. The sovereign authority of such an event rests absolutely upon the deity of Him who spoke the words. The statement: 'Upon this rock will I found my Church,' appeals to no criteria that man can assess and cannot rest upon any human approval. Before we can believe in the Papacy we must settle one question, not whether Jesus answers the demands of moral judgment or religious intuition, but whether in fact He was the Christ, the son of the living God. The mind that accepts the fact, independently of self-constituted approval, cannot raise the Protestant doubt. A Pope is the effectual symbol of man's submission to the Christ, which must be beyond scientific criticism and prior to any moral judgment. If the unappealing and savorless absolutism of the Papal claims repels us, it does so precisely as the original claim that this Jesus is the Son of God repelled the Jewish and Gentile foes of the primitive Church"); *According to Your Faith* (1966) ("The Cross is Love without remorse or reprieve, sovereign and everlasting, the sole image of omnipotence known to me"); letter to *The Tablet*, 6 January 1968 ("What matters [at Mass] is the central mystery, so vast, so searching, so overwhelming that you might find it almost impossible to speak of it whether in Latin or in English. One virtue of Latin, perhaps the least, is that it makes no attempt to get everybody talking: it is the language of Holy Church, of God's priest, not 'my' language. And it is a language imposed by the Mystery itself, the language of Pontius Pilate and of those who being his contemporaries crucified the Incarnate Lord as our agents, the language of penitent Gentiles. It lifts us out of our complacent English suburb and our self-sufficient century into that universal moment in which man first acknowledged the divine Savior, the Son of the Living God.

The vernacular reverses the procedure. The whole change has been made in concession to ourselves. The vernacular is the language of our private prayers, the grammar of our private life. It accompanies an extensive and potentially disastrous change of mind which I have heard expressed by a number of priests saying that 'We are the Church.' With a like logic we might substitute collar-and-tie and two-piece for chasuble and alb, a tumbler for the chalice, ordinary bread for the hosts, a dining table for the altar and sit round it instead of kneeling or standing. Many Catholics might respond to such a stimulus for a time and find the new liturgy nearer to the Last Supper. For a time. But our hearts know better. We do not go to church to please or stimulate or express ourselves; we do not need the Church for such purposes. We go to Church to be present in and at God's Act, which God does for and in and by His holy Church").

Griffiths, Dom Bede, OSB (born Alan Richard Griffiths) – priest; b. 17 December 1906, Fritton, Rydens Road, Walton-on-Thames, Surrey; c. 24 December 1932; d. 13 May 1993, Shantivanam, Tamil Nadu, India; brought up in difficult circumstances financially, his father having lost all his money; "aged seventeen, he had a mystical experience in which he glimpsed the unfathomable mystery behind creation. This changed his life" (*DNB*); pupil of C. S. Lewis at Oxford; former Anglican; influenced in his conversion by Newman's *Development of Christian Doctrine*; entered Benedictine Order 1933; ordained priest 9 March 1940; at Prinknash, until sent as Superior to Farnborough in 1947; then in 1951 to Pluscarden; reading Yeats' translation of the Upanishads led to an interest in eastern spirituality; went to India in 1955 and founded a monastery there; from 1968 until his death ran the Shantivanam ashram in Tamil Nadu; tried to bridge Hinduism and Christianity; see *The Golden String* (1954) ("The discovery that the Church of England had been founded by a Roman Pope and that the first Archbishops of Canterbury and York had been sent from Rome came as a new light to me. It was as though there had been a blank space in my map on history; which was now filled in, so that the whole was seen in a new perspective. Instead of looking back from the Renais-

sance to the Middle Ages, I now began to see the Middle Ages emerging from the Roman Empire, and the history of England took its place in the history of Europe. I saw that just as England had been part of the Roman Empire, so the Church of England had been part of Roman Church.... It may seem strange but it had never occurred to me before that our old English village churches had once known the rite of the Latin Mass...

...It was clear ... that the infallible guidance in the teaching of the Church came through the bishops, and this I knew was the universal belief of the early Church. Among these bishops the Bishop of Rome was held to have a unique position because he was the successor of St. Peter.... Newman was able to show me that this doctrine was no less universal in the early Church.... What Newman showed of the Papal authority he showed also of all other doctrines which were in dispute, of Purgatory and Indulgences, of the cultus of the Saints and their relics; all alike could be seen to be organic developments of the original doctrine of the Gospel, evolving by the same law as an oak tree develops from an acorn, or an embryo into a complete animal.... The effect of this argument on my mind was immense"); Shirley du Boulay, *Beyond the Darkness: A Biography of Bede Griffiths* (1988); K. Spink, *A Sense of the Sacred: A Biography of Bede Griffiths* (1988); *DNB*.

Griffiths, Bishop Thomas – vicar apostolic of the London district; b. 2 June 1791, London; c. 1805; d. 12 August 1847, 35 Golden Square, London, his residence; his father was Protestant; brought up in Established Church; influenced to convert by prayers and good example of his fervently Catholic mother; admitted into St. Edmunds College, Ware; ordained priest in July 1814; President of the college 1818–1833; in July

1833 appointed coadjutor bishop for London District, to which he succeeded in July 1836; improved priestly education and discipline, and instituted wearing of clerical dress; lukewarm towards the Oxford movement; brought about steady pastoral expansion; buried in St. Thomas's chantry in the college chapel at St. Edmund's College; see *Gillow*, Vol. III, p.61; *Catholic Encyclopedia*; *DNB*.

Griggs, Frederick Landseer Maur – artist, architectural draftsman, and conservationist; b. 30 October 1876, Hitchin, Hertfordshire; c. 19 February 1912 (his sister, Gladys, was received in 1911); d. 7 June 1938, Campden, Gloucestershire; brought up in a Baptist family; youthful interest in Catholicism followed by a period of agnosticism; real interest in Catholicism from 1909; influenced in his conversion by meeting the priest and polymath, Dr. Adrian Fortescue (1874–1923); friend of Graham Sutherland (see below) and of Wilfred Childe (see above); doughty champion of rural preservation; fine pen-and-ink and pencil drawings enriching the thirteen volumes of the *Highways and Byways* series; on conversion he took the baptismal name of Maur; see introduction by Malcolm C. Salaman to *Modern Masters of Etching: F. L. Griggs, ARA, RE* (1926) ("The soul and significance of the etchings … draw their inspiration entirely from the artist's own imaginative contemplation of medieval England. That is the England of his dreams, his ideals and his love, England as, with the eyes of his soul, he pictures her to have been before the Reformation and Henry VIII did their devastating work among the religious houses and, as Mr. Griggs believes, robbed the land and the people of so much beauty, grace, and goodness; long, of course, before men even dreamt of the Renaissance or the Industrial Revolution, the effects of which the artist equally deplores. And that is the England, single-hearted and faithful, expressing herself in beautiful buildings and loving craftsmanship, that he aspires, with an extraordinary unity of idea pervading his work, to reconstruct on his copper-plates"); Francis Adams Comstock, *A Gothic Vision: F. L. Griggs and His Work* (1966); interview with Graham Sutherland in Roger Berthoud, *Graham Sutherland: A Biography* (1982) ("His [Griggs] medievalism was part of his Catholicism: he dreamed of old cities and towns furnished with pure and perfect Gothic churches, and of the monastic life. He thought real England had been damned, as one of his titles, *Ex Anglia Perdita*, suggests"); Jerrold Northrop Moore, *F. L. Griggs: The Architecture of Dreams* (1999) ("The institution which had stood out against change longer than any other in the western world was the Catholic Church. That meant a very great deal to such as Griggs in such a time. 'It's the history of the Church … that is the greatest argument for its divinity.… The Canon of the Mass is from Apostolic times, *without a change*'"); Grove Art Online.

Grimshaw, (John) Atkinson – landscape painter; b. 6 September 1836, 9 Back Park Street, Leeds; c. 1856 (received with his wife, Frances Theodosia (1835–1917), a cousin); d. 31 October 1893, Old Hall, Knostrop, Leeds; parents Baptists of stern Protestant variety, who opposed his painting; no formal training as an artist; clerk with the Great Northern Railway Company, but later gave up his job in order to paint full-time; early paintings influenced by the pre-Raphaelites; later influence was John Ruskin; majestic Roman ceremonial suited his Romanticism; famous for depiction of moonlight; settled at Old Hall, Knostrop, a seventeenth century manor house, which suited his Romanticism;

father of fifteen children (only six survived to adulthood); rented a second home in Scarborough, Castle-by-the-Sea, Mulgrave Place, overlooking the North Bay, and the town became his favorite subject; fine views of London and the Thames; friend of Whistler; lapsed from the faith eventually; son, Arthur, organist and choirmaster at St. Anne's Catholic Cathedral Leeds for thirty years, then ceased to practice, as did Frances, a daughter; Lancelot, another son a devout Catholic who trained for the priesthood, but was never ordained; Enid, a daughter, popular vocalist, who kept the Faith; buried at Woodhouse cemetery, Leeds; see Sandra K. Payne, *Atkinson Grimshaw: Knight's Errand* (1987); Alexander Robertson, *Atkinson Grimshaw* (1988); *DNB*.

Grissell, Hartwell de la Garde – author; b. 14 December 1839; c. 2 March 1868; d. 10 June 1907; educated at Brasenose College, Oxford; formerly High Anglican and secretary of Association for Promotion of Unity of Christendom; Oxford convert; lived in Rome from his conversion until November 1870; he amassed superb collection of relics and ecclesiastical art, which he placed in his private chapel in Oxford; discovered and excavated the site of Eleusis; Fellow of Society of Antiquaries; of the Royal Academy of Raphaello in Urbino; of the Roman Arcadia; Chamberlain to Popes Leo XIII and Pius X; Commander of Order of Pope Pius IX; personal friend of Pius IX who granted him indulgences for a painting of Our Lady as "Mother of Mercy," currently in St. Aloysius' Church, Oxford; close friend of third Marquess of Bute (see above); see essay in J. G. F. Raupert (ed), *Roads to Rome* (1901), p.110 ("I came, after careful study of the question, to the conclusion that the Church of England, being a purely national church, could

hardly be considered Catholic and universal, in the sense of its being the Divine teacher of all nations, and that it was in schism.... The Catholic Church I knew from our Lord's promise was *one*, and could not be divided, although it could be diminished in size. I began to see that at the Reformation it was not divided but only diminished, and that there were still many old Catholic families in England who had never ceased to belong to the pre-Reformation Church and had kept the faith, though the majority of the English people had fallen away from it. I saw that its unity still remained, after this loss, the same as before...

I should like to say, in reference to one's attitude towards those outside the Church, that I have always felt that argument and controversy more often provokes than does good. We should endeavor, it seems to me, to show our separated brethren that we Catholics love truth for the truth's sake, and that we sympathize with the struggles of those who are groping their way towards the light. I feel persuaded that mere controversial victories and smart sayings in many cases repel rather than attract. Men are convinced not so much by reasoning as by a clear conception of positive truth. As Cardinal Newman so justly remarks, false ideas may be *refuted* by argument, but only by true ideas can we hope to *expel* them").

Guinness, Sir Alec – actor; b. 2 April 1914, 155 Lauderdale Mansions, Paddington, London; c. 24 March 1956 (son, Matthew, received 1955; wife, Merula (1914–2000) (see below) received December 1956); d. 5 August 2000, Eastbourne, Sussex; name of his father never been established; start of his acting career helped by John Gielgud; established himself in a series of classic stage plays in London; served in the Royal Navy in world War II; former

Anglican; later atheist/agnostic, then interest in Buddhism; outstanding stage actor and film star; made his name in films directed by David Lean and in Ealing comedies; many major roles; international star after the *Star Wars* trilogy; later a fine writer of memoirs and diarist; knighted 1959; Companion of Honour 1994; distressed at the liturgical changes after Vatican II, but remained a convinced Catholic; see *Blessings in Disguise* (1985), especially pp.36–50 ("The longevity of the Holy Roman Catholic and Apostolic Church, her wisdom and kindness, can well embrace the naïve strugglings of an adolescent English schoolboy kicking, so to speak, against the pricks. She has books to read aloud, pictures to show, consolations to offer, strength to give and some marvelous people, from all ages, to hold up for the world's admiration, not many in high places perhaps, but thousands in the market square, hospital ward, back pew, desert and jungle"); *My Name Escapes Me* (1997); *A Positively Final Appearance* (1999); *A Commonplace Book* (2001); Piers Paul Read, *Alec Guinness: The Authorised Biography* (2003), especially pp.265–282 ("The most evident change following Vatican II was to the liturgy, and one of the greatest trials for those like Alec and Merula who had joined a Church with a Latin Mass was suddenly to find it said in an English of great triteness and banality. The officiating priest, who had mysteriously re-enacted the sacrifice of Christ upon the Cross with his back to the congregation, now faced his parishioners from the other side of a table like a jovial scoutmaster serving orangeade and cupcakes in a village hall. The age-old plainchant, or the melodious hymns of the pre-Conciliar Church, were replaced by commonplace ditties or African dirges"); Joseph Pearce, *Literary Converts* (1999) *passim*; Lorene Hanley Duquin, *A*

Century of Catholic Converts (2003), p.161; *DNB*.

Guinness, Merula (*nee* Salaman) – actress and painter; b. 1914; c. December 1956 (son, Matthew, received 1955; husband, Sir Alec Guinness (1914–2000) (see above) received 24 March 1956); d. 18 October 2000; father, who had much property and financial investments, came from a family of Ashkenazi Jews; both parents atheists; the children were raised as atheists; educated by a governess and then at a boarding school; went to the Old Vic School, then to the London Theatre School; ended her acting career at request of her husband; made paintings and embroidered pictures and wrote children's books; in 1941 baptized into the Church of England and confirmed in 1944; was member of High Church wing before finally converting to the Catholic Church; see Piers Paul Read, *Alec Guinness: The Authorised Biography* (2003) ("She had read the New Testament for the first time and 'had been bowled over, knocked sideways, turned upside down. I read St. Luke straight through at a sitting and it seemed to me that no one could have invented such an extraordinary story, it just had to be true'"); Gerry Burns, "Converts to Catholicism: Sir Alec Guinness," *Catholic Life*, December 2009, p.52.

Gummer, John Selwyn – business publisher and Conservative politician; b. 26 November 1939, Brompton, London; c. 1993; son of Anglican minister; read History at Cambridge and President of the Union; formerly prominent Anglican layman (member of General Synod 1978–1992); chairman of the Conservative party 1983–1985; Secretary of State for Agriculture 1989–1993; Secretary of State for Environment 1993–1997; converted after Church of England ordained women; see "Betraying history," *The*

Times, 23 April 1993 ("The Church of England has always claimed that it has no doctrines or orders of its own but only those of the universal church. It was on that basis that it demanded the allegiance of the people of England. It sought both to insist upon the Catholic essentials and to uphold the necessity of reform. Now the Church of England has changed all that. By asserting that it can alter doctrine and order unilaterally it has relinquished its apostolic claim to the allegiance of the people of England").

Gunston (alias Blunt), John Chrysostom Gregory, (commonly known as "Dr. Sharp") – priest; b. 12 October 1693, London; c. 1715; d. 24 June 1736, London; brought up a Protestant; probably educated at Cambridge University; went to English College, Rome; ordained priest 8 April 1719; Doctor of Divinity; went to the English mission in 1720; worked for part of time in London; popular preacher; pronotary apostolic; see *Gillow*, Vol. III, p.67.

Haigh, Daniel Henry – priest, antiquary and author; b. 7 August 1819, Brinscall Hall, Wheelton, Lancaster; c. 1 January 1847; d. 10 May 1879, Oscott College; orphaned early and came into large fortune; resolved to join Anglican ministry and went into residence at St. Saviour's Church, Leeds; converted together with the four clergymen there, all of whom became Catholic priests (see entry for Thomas Minster); ascribed his conversion to the writings of Bede; went to St. Mary's College, Oscott; ordained 8 April 1847; paid for the Gothic revival church at Erdington, near Birmingham and worked on the mission there until 1876; contributed financially to other Catholic projects; devoted himself to looking after orphans; retired to Oscott; expert in Anglo-Saxon studies, numismatics, and biblical archaeology; chief authority in England on Runic literature; buried in the Blessed Sacrament chapel, Erdington Abbey; see *Gillow*, Vol. III, p.84; *DNB*.

Hales, Sir Edward, third Baronet and first Earl of Tenterden – statesman; b. 28 September 1645, Tunstall Place, Kent; c. 11 November 1685 (publicly, followed by several or perhaps all of his children, three of his daughter becoming nuns); d. 1694, St. Germain; brought up as Protestant; his father, also Sir Edward Hales, had attempted to rescue Charles I from his confinement on the Isle of Wight; at University of Padua been convinced of truth of Catholicity, but was not publicly received into the Catholic Church until more tolerant times of James II; given commission in the army without having taken oaths of supremacy and allegiance necessary for Catholics under Test Act, in order for king to test whether sovereign's prerogative allowed him to give a dispensation from such penal laws (court held it did); when Revolution of 1688 broke out he was committed as prisoner to the Tower; released in 1690 on bail and left England for James II's court at St. Germain; buried in church of St. Sulpice, Paris; the eldest of his twelve children was killed at battle of the Boyne; see *Gillow*, Vol. III, p.88; *DNB*.

Hall, Herbert Edward – writer; d. 1932; former Anglican layman; see *The Shadow of Peter* (1914) ("The true Church of Jesus Christ ... can always be distinguished and known from all rival bodies by its possession of its original form: the Petrine Primacy, the Apostolic Episcopate, the body of the faithful Laity, or the baptized believers abiding in communion through the Episcopate, with the Primate. The only society, or religious body, in the world, which bears the test is the Holy Roman Catholic Church. She alone has the Primacy. She alone is founded on 'this Cephas.' In her we have the certain faith, the forgiveness of sin, the fullness of the covenant of grace, peace with God, the hope of Eternal Life. 'Ubi Petrus est ibi Ecclesia; ubi Ecclesia nulla mors, sed vita aeterna' (St. Ambrose)"); *Authority or Private Judgment* (1917); *The Petrine Office* (1917); *Catholic and Roman: A Reply to Anglican Criticisms* (1918) ("The real difference between Catholics and all Protestants is quite as much in the 'why' and 'how' they hold their religion, as in the substance or content of the religion. The Catholic believes in the authority of the Church. The Protestant does not, in the true sense, *believe* at all, but agrees with a selection of doctrines which he, or the party to which he belongs, makes: (a) If High-Church, of doctrines taught in different parts of what he terms 'Catholic Christendom'; (b) If Low-Church, of doctrines which he thinks are taught by the Bible; (c) If Broad-Church, of doctrines which he thinks are in accordance with right reason"); *For It Was Founded on a Rock* (1918).

Hall, Herbert F. – priest; brought up as Anglican (with occasional sight of High Church services) by parents with a real loving affection for Christ and the characters of Bible history; ordained Catholic priest; priest at the Cathedral Choir School, Westminster, London; see essay in J. G. F. Raupert (ed), *Roads to Rome* (1901), p.114 ("I do not think I ever sincerely accepted the High Church branch theory. I passed through that phase in the space of two years or thereabouts, but my nineteenth year found me a Catholic, and I was only kept back so long by the influence of a friend, whom I hope I am not wrong in believing to be sincerely good, but who could never give me a satisfactory answer to the radical difficulty – the absence of definite, living teaching authority...

The greatest factor, however, of my preparation for the Church was a visitation made by Cardinal Manning to the church of the neighboring Roman Catholic Mission. I attended the High Mass, and with the man's history and his ever-present personality in my mind, his ascetic and emaciated form and features; the princely and yet tender pastoral bearing – the glory of his pontifical dress making him look like one of the old stained-glass figures which I loved so much; – the beautiful simplicity of his homily on the Gospel of the day: all these things drew me like a magnet ever nearer and nearer. Inclination was all towards the Church. The will moved by grace – as I firmly believe and know – was not long behind. I spoke to the priest: it was the first time to my knowledge that I had ever spoken to a *real* Catholic. I thought in my simplicity he would receive me into the Church the next morning. Instead of that he said, 'This is a grave step, my boy, and requires prayer and preparation. I will lend you a book to read.' Though it mortified and humbled me, there could not have been an attitude more calculated to confirm me in my resolution if confirmation were wanted. It was my first experience of the thorough genuineness and reality of Catholicism, and was fraught with influence for good. After a time of careful instruction I had the happiness of becoming a Catholic").

Hallack, Cecily Rosemary – writer; b. 11 October 1898, Littlehampton, Sussex; c. 5 October 1918 (received at Farm Street, London, by Fr. Daniel Considine, SJ, who decided not to wait any longer after her parents had refused their consent for more than two years); d. 23 October 1938, Mount Alvenia Nursing Home, Guildford; daughter of a Congregationalist minister and her ancestors had been Protestants; wrote novels, poetry, journalism, and biographies, especially of saints; great devotion to St. Francis of Assisi and became a Franciscan tertiary; in turn secretary to H. G. Wells and assistant secretary to Lord Baden-Powell; held positions with the publishers Cassells and Burns, Oates and Washbourne (editor of the children's book department); many financial difficulties, increased by her great generosity; long illness caused by a tumor on the brain; unmarried; buried in the cemetery adjoining the Franciscan friary at Crawley, Sussex; see *Beardless Counsellors* (1923); *Candlelight Attic and Odd Job's* (1924); *The Sword Blade of Michael* (1929); *Mirror for Toby* (1931); *All About Selina* (1932); *As Common as Daisies* (1932); *Miss Becky O'Toole* (1932); *The Bliss of the Way: A Bedside Book for the Tramp* (1932); *The Saints' Animals' Annual* (1932); *Having a Guardian Angel* (1933); *To Miranda* (Essays) (1934) ("My elders labeled me 'a child of fears' in very early days. That label is a useful witness that a fearful nature is not incurable. The Faith gives to the convert so tremendous a knowledge of touching and being held by Reality – by an Eternal and Invincible Personality – that all the dreads which breed in abstract ideas of space and time are brought to nought … no, not like shadows before the sun, but like nervous cogitations when one is surrounded by strong friends.

Patiently Christ used that greeting: 'Fear not.'

'Cowards do not count in battle,' said stern Euripides. 'They are there, but not in it.' The fearful do not count in Christendom because they are there but not in it: they are in a horrid world of their own imagining. On the other hand, each time we despise a terror, poking fun at our own trembling as we get through it, the force of fear is lessened, the soul gains in power over itself, and some great good is obtained.

'I couldn't read that book,' said a woman to me the other day. 'It made me feel what a dreadful place the world is.' So it is, but it is already defeated by a God-Man, who said, *before* Gethsemane: 'Fear not, I *have overcome* the world'…

The most inexplicable mystery of all is Providence. The only fool is the human being who is afraid of Him. For the Christian who takes care to live in Christendom and not in a world of his own, there is a security independent of walls and candles and means of defense. He may walk the world and lose his fears one by one as he finds himself 'everywhere at home' in a real world where, as the old mystic says, 'there is only God and nothing strange'"); *Lady Georgy's House* (1935); *Saint Philomena, Virgin Martyr and Wonder Worker* (1936); *The Adventure of the Amethyst* (1937) (novel about the instruction in the Catholic faith of the children of a family); *St. John Bosco, Franciscan Tertiary* (1937); *The Happiness of Father Happé* (1938); *Out of the Blue* (1939) (account of a pilgrimage to Rome); *The Legion of Mary* (1950); *These Made Peace: Studies in the Lives of the Beatified and Canonized Members of the Third Order of St. Francis of Assisi* (1963) (co-written with Peter Anson, (see above)); Peter Anson, "Cecily Hallack and Her Writings," *Franciscan Annals*, May 1939, p.146; June 1939, p.169; July 1939, p.198 ("At the age of eighteen, so she wrote … the Faith came to her: 'It came at a first going into Westminster Cathedral – after a walking round, wondering at everything, which ended with: "Well, goodness knows what it is all about, but it is the True Faith." Impression made neither on intellect nor heart, but only on the spirit. The Gift of Faith.'"); Mary Sheila Williams, *A Biobibliography of Cecily Rosemary Hallack, 1898–1938* (1962); Joseph Kelly, "A Perfectly English Lady: Cecily Hallack, 1898–1938," *Catholic*

Life, January 2002, p.38; Pat Pinsent, "Two Catholic Writers for Children: Cecily Hallack and Meriol Trevor," in Pat Pinsent (ed), *Out of the Attic: Some Neglected Children's Authors of the Twentieth Century* (2006), Ch. 7.

Hamilton, Elizabeth – writer; b. 3 April 1908, County Wicklow, Ireland; c. late 1920s; d. 1999; classics teacher (inspired by A. E. Housman) and author of books about the natural world and lives of Catholic mystics; her mother was Protestant descendant of John Knox; unmarried; see *A River Full of Stars* (1954) (describes her religious development); *The Great Teresa* (1960); *I Stay in the Church* (1975) ("You know my difficulties in the Church. Some are of an intellectual nature. Others, though seeming to be of this kind, are ... emotional in origin, emanating from a sense of disillusion at not finding in the Church a perfection I am not, in fact, entitled to expect: in brief a failure to distinguish between the Church as an institution, with the human failings of such, and the Church as the mystical body of Christ: between the earthly Jerusalem and the Jerusalem that is above. And yet, however deep my disillusion; however violent, however justifiable, my bouts of indignation provoked by certain facets of the Church, I know, as George Bernanos knew, that, ultimately, all I have has come to me through the Church, in that the Church, despite its shortcomings, has given down the centuries, and still gives, unique witness to the truth revealed in Christ – namely, that Love is the heart of reality. I know that, were I to cut myself off from the Church, I would be as a branch broken from the tree from whose sap it derives life"); *The Priest of the Moors: Reflections on Nicholas Postgate* (1980) ("'It is the Mass that matters.' The words are those of Augustine Birrell, the Non-conformist scholar. 'It is the Mass,'

he goes on, 'that makes the difference, so hard to define, so subtle is it yet so perceptible, between a Catholic country and a Protestant one, between Dublin and Edinburgh, between Havre and Cromer'...

It is the Mass that gives to the life of Nicholas Postgate its distinctive quality. It is the significance of the oratory hidden under the thatch at Egton. It is the significance of his death – his death as a priest...

...Nicholas Postgate died for the Mass; not for ritual and ceremony in general, but for sacrifice – the sacrifice made once and for all, for us men and for our salvation, on Calvary, and at the same time the closest bond possible on earth between God and man, man and his fellowmen. The Mass, this *mysterium fidei*, gave to Nicholas Postgate, when he was an old man, the impetus to tramp the moors to feed God's people and his own, the strength, too, to die with dignity and lightness of heart").

Hanmer, Anthony John – Catholic layman; b. 1817; c. 15 December 1849 (received at Spanish Place, London; "The die is consequently cast – I have resigned my curacy – and am now preparing to go out, like Abraham.... What I am doing seems scarcely to be real but I know and feel that thus it must be, or my damnation is forever sealed"; sister, Sophia Ainsworth (1819–1882) (see above), converted in 1850 and her husband, John Lees Ainsworth, in 1870); d. 1907; son of Anglican clergyman; at St. John's College, Cambridge; took Anglican orders; much correspondence with Newman before his conversion, especially about papal infallibility; after conversion tried his vocation at London Oratory without success; lived rest of his life as a layman; always most supportive of Newman; unmarried; see Stanley L. Jaki, *Newman to Converts: An Existential Ecclesiology*

(2001), Ch. 9 ("As a Catholic Hanmer naturally became concerned about the spiritual fate of Protestants. The reply he received from Newman should be compulsory reading in all seminaries and clergy meetings now that it has become so natural to assume that hardly anyone can fail to be saved.... Those who died in Protestantism, Newman began, could be saved if they were in invincible ignorance and, 'if they make an act of contrition on their deathbeds or rather their dying moments so as never to fall into mortal sin after it.' This too had been an old truth among Catholics, although here too Newman was able to express old truths with the force that would strike one as novel. Newman then drew the existential conclusion: 'Now considering the anxious thought these two conditions give rise to, it seems to me you have ground enough to urge any, the most holy (to human eyes) of Protestants, to be converted.' Surely, it would make a great novelty within latter-day ecclesiological literature to introduce there a modicum of that anxiety which filled Newman's soul *vis-a-vis* Protestants, including such saintly souls ...").

Hannah, Walton – priest and writer on social issues; b. 1910, Sussex; c. 7 September 1955; d. February 1966; father teacher of theology, writer, and MP; took Anglican orders; converted at time of South India question; worked to expose Freemasonry as anti-Christian; studied at the Beda College in Rome; ordained priest in 1958; worked in Canada for the rest of his life; see *Darkness Visible: A Revelation and Interpretation of Freemasonry* (1952); *Christian By Degrees: Masonic Religion Revealed in the Light of Faith* (1954); "Recent convert clergy tell how and why," *The Month*, September 1956, p.149 ("The Church, the Body of Christ, which [Christ] promised should be guided into all truth by the Holy Ghost, carries the authority of Christ and should speak and teach with that authority. In the early centuries of her history it is plain that she taught with certainty against the various heresies that assailed her, in marked contrast to the vague and uncertain teaching and diversity of beliefs on vital questions to be found in the Church of England today. Was this teaching authority lost, whether at the Great Schism or at the Reformation?"); *The Anglican Crisis* (1957).

Hanse, Blessed Everard – priest and martyr; b. in Northamptonshire; d. 31 July 1581; took orders in Established Church; serious illness made him weigh up his position; converted by his brother, William, a priest of Douai College; resigned his living and went to English College, Rheims in 1850; ordained priest 25 March 1581 and left for the English mission; apprehended in July 1581 whilst visiting Catholic prisoners in the Marshalsea; confessed to being Catholic and priest and imprisoned in Newgate; tried and condemned; hanged, drawn and quartered at Tyburn; see *Gillow*, Vol. III, p.114 ("It is said in the Douai Diary that when the executioner had his hand upon his heart, the martyr was heard distinctly to pronounce the words, *O diem felicem*").

Hanson, Eric D., SJ – priest; b. 1860, London; c. 6 August 1886 (wrote as follows to Newman the next day: "I owe simply everything, under God, to your Eminence's published works, which were my continual study and delight at Oxford"); brought up in Protestant Clapham until fourteen years of age, when he was brought under High Church influences; formerly member of English Church Union and of the Ritualist party of Church of England; ordained Catholic priest; entered the Society of Jesus; also influenced in his conversion by Henry

Wilberforce (see below); see essay in J. G. F. Raupert (ed), *Roads to Rome* (1901), p.126 ("I found that at no time since the breach with Rome was the final Court of Appeal one whit less secular in its source and authority than at present; in short I saw for the first time that the Reformation Settlement was in this and many other respects a rendering to Caesar of the things of God.... [T]he Reformation in England was mere State-craft, that at every stage it was marked by the surrender of inalienable spiritual prerogatives to Caesar, that it was heretical and schismatical in the most exact sense of those words as used by the Fathers; in short, that it was an apostasy...

I always came back to my first principle. If the Christ has come, He must have provided us, here and now, with ready and certain means of access to His revealed truth. Moreover, what my reason demanded, His own word had promised and guaranteed for all time. No 'Appeal to Antiquity' could survive that test. For you can make no adequate use of the early Christian records for this purpose without immense labor. Do what you will, you must distinguish between essentials and accidentals, the permanent and the temporary elements, the explicit and the implicit; you have to estimate how much is due to exaggeration, to reactionary influences within, to local and secular influences without; you have to deal with schools of thought, differences of practice, novelties and individual mistakes. You cannot aim simply at a blind reproduction of all that was currently accepted and practiced during a certain more or less arbitrarily selected century or age. You must largely exercise your critical faculties. And then, what principles are to guide you in this work of discrimination? And where are you going to stop? You will have embarked on an enterprise of a lifetime, with no prospect of attaining any certain result at the end of it...

There is but one society in the world answering to the *ecclesia* which Christ founded. Only one possesses, and has continually possessed, the distinguishing features of that mystical Kingdom of which He spoke so often and so profoundly. If Anglicanism, in any of its many varieties, is true, that Kingdom has come to nought, Christ's word has failed, and the Incarnation, on intrinsic grounds, is incredible; for on that hypothesis (i.e., of the Establishment being the visible Church of Christ or any part of it) it would follow that the essential notes of Christ's Kingdom, its most elementary and indispensable functions, have become not only inoperative but impossible. Christ is the Truth, the essential Truth of God. And the fullness of that living Truth was committed to His Church that thereby He might be with us always. Whom God has joined together let not man think to put asunder. You cannot part Christ and His Bride. If the Church has spoken falsely, whether early or late, then Christ is false. If the Church is divided, then is Christ divided. If Christ 'taught as one having authority, and not as the scribes,' so also must the Church teach her disciples. If Christ is risen from the dead, if Death has no more dominion over Him, neither shall the gates of Death prevail against His Church built upon Peter").

Harari, Manya (*née* Benenson) – publisher and translator; b. 8 April 1905, Baku, Russia; c. 1932; d. 24 September 1969, London; daughter of very wealthy Jewish financier; family migrated to London in 1914; husband of Ralph Andrew Harari (1893–1969), merchant banker and art scholar and collector; saw her conversion as not detracting from her Jewish identification; associated with inauguration of Sword of the Spirit movement by Cardinal Hinsley in 1940; worked on *Dublin Review*; translator at political warfare department; co-founder of Harvill Press, small publishing house specializing in books on religion, metaphysics, arts, and psychology; translated and published much modern Russian literature, e.g., Solzhenitsyn; see *DNB*.

Hardie, Colin Graham – classical scholar; b. 16 February 1906, Edinburgh; c. 1945; d. 17 October 1998, Chichester; son of William Ross Hardie (1862–1916), the most brilliant classicist of his generation; educated at Balliol College, Oxford, where he gained a first and all the major prizes (as had his brother, William Francis Ross [Frank] Hardie (1902–1990), classical scholar and philosopher); Fellow of Balliol 1930–1933; Director of British School at Rome 1933–1936; Fellow of Magdalene College, Oxford 1936–1973 (except for war service); member of the Inklings, and a friend of C. S. Lewis and J. R. R. Tolkien; specialist on Virgil and Dante; gave Waynflete lectures on the 700th anniversary of Dante's birth; public orator in Oxford 1967–1973; see *DNB*.

Harding, Gilbert Charles – broadcaster; b. 5 June 1907, Hereford; c. 29 June 1929; d. 16 November 1960, London; became strong Anglo-Catholic at Cambridge University and trained for Anglican priesthood at Mirfield (leaving on his conversion to the Catholic Church); schoolmaster and Professor of English at St. Francis Xavier University, Antigonish, in Nova Scotia; became radio and television broadcaster, where he was probably the best known performer in the country at that time in the 1950s; on radio he appeared in *The Brains Trust*, *Twenty Questions* and *Round Britain Quiz*; main role on television was the panel game, *What's My Line?*; many emotional pressures; a lonely man who donated much money to charity and helped many people in need;

politically on the left; much ill health; unmarried; see *Along My Line* (1953); *Master of None* (1958) (both books autobiographical); *Face to Face with John Freeman*, BBC Television interview, September 1960; *DNB* ("A man of very deep religious feeling … he became a convert to, and a devoted member of, the Roman Catholic church, but he remained sympathetic to Anglicanism from the emotional point of view and never spoke of Mirfield with anything but the warmest affection and admiration").

Hardy, Thomas J. – c. 1940; formerly Anglican vicar and examining chaplain to Anglican Bishop of Southwell; see *How I Came to Acknowledge the Pope* (1940) ("Our investigations arose out of your wondering how I could possibly acknowledge the Pope as the visible Head of the Church on earth. I set out to show you as simply and frankly as I could the steps by which I was led to make this acknowledgement. First, my search for grounds of belief in *institutional* Christianity; and then arising inevitably out of this a further search for the provision Christ had made for the unity, perpetuity and recognizability of the Church He founded. We noticed in what the *formal* visibility of a Society must consist, and how natural – and, speaking humanly, inevitable – it was that a Society to be recognizable should have a visible Head. We paid the closest attention to the singular Commission our Lord conferred on St. Peter at Caesarea Philippi, carefully weighing every word He used both then and on other occasions when He ratified that Commission. We then turned to the Church and inquired whether from the first our Lord's words were understood in the sense which the Church requires today; and we found it was so.

Am I not in order in asking you to tell me how it is possible not to acknowledge the Pope in the sense in which the Church justly requires that acknowledgement, viz., as the Vicar of Jesus Christ and visible Head of the Church on earth?").

Harper, Thomas Morton, SJ – priest; b. 1821; c. 1851; d. 1893; educated at Queen's College, Oxford; became High Church curate and ritualist and came into conflict with the Anglican authorities; joined the Society of Jesus in 1852; ordained priest 1859; Professor of Theology at St. Beuno's College; later taught at Stonyhurst College, then a parish priest; criticized Newman's *Grammar of Assent*, taking a scholastic approach; see *Peace Through the Truth, or Essays on Subjects Connected with Dr. Pusey's Eirenicon*, two series (1866–1874); *The Metaphysics of the Schools*, 3 Vols. (1879–1884).

Harris, James, SJ – priest; b. 25 August 1824, London; d. 4 December 1883, Kentish Town, London; came from poor family; brought up in Established Church; in anti-corn law agitation a talented public speaker, but persuaded by his mother to abandon any political ambitions; converted by poor Irish youth who attended him in his lodgings and lent him Bishop Milner's *The End of Religious Controversy*; entered the Society of Jesus in Belgium in 1850; then at Namur, Louvain and St. Beuno's College, North Wales, where ordained priest 22 September 1861; Professor of Ecclesiastical History and then of Moral Theology; in 1865 went to St. Francis Xavier's College, Liverpool, where he spent rest of his life (superior from 1879); great sense of humor; severe illness late in life; see *Gillow*, Vol. III, p.139.

Harris, William – priest; b. about 1546, Lincolnshire; c. about 1573; d. 1602,

England; Fellow of Lincoln College, Oxford, and college Bursar; forsook the Established Church ("Left the College, his friends, religion and the little all he had") and went to Louvain to study; there he was ordained priest; then entered English College, Douai, in 1574; sent to the English mission in 1575; in 1591 he returned to Douai where he became acting principal of the college; later went back to England; see *Theatrum, seu, Speculum verissimae et antiquissimae ecclesiae magnae Britanniae* (a work of ecclesiastical history in ten parts); *Gillow*, Vol. III, p.145; *DNB* ("Like similar contemporary studies, in his ecclesiastical history Harris set out to defend the historically close relationship of the English church with the see of Rome").

Harrison, Alice (known as "Dame Alice") – schoolmistress; b. about 1680, Fulwood Row, near Preston, Lancashire; c. while still a minor; d. about 1765, Garswood Hall, near Ashton in Makerfield; brought up in Church of England; influenced by reading Catholic books to convert, to annoyance of parents; treated very severely by them when she became a Catholic; protected by Edward Melling, a Catholic priest serving the hamlet of Fernyhalgh, near to her home, together with other Catholics in the area; opened a school at start of 18th century at a house and barn (both still standing) at Haighton Top, Durton Lane, Fernyhalgh, close to ancient Catholic chapel, holy well and shrine to the Blessed Virgin Mary at Ladywell; escaped prosecution because children of all religious backgrounds were admitted; children went daily to the shrine, but Protestant children allowed to absent themselves if they wished; school acted as nursery for English colleges abroad; retired from her work in about 1760; provided for in her last days by the Gerard family; buried in unmarked grave at old Catholic cemetery at Windleshaw, near St. Helens, Lancashire; see Rt. Rev. B. C. Foley, *Some People of the Penal Times* (1991), p.51; *Gillow*, Vol. III. p.145; *DNB* ("Such was the solid grounding in religious education provided by Dame Alice that a steady stream of boys began to proceed from Fernyhalgh to the English College at Douai, many of them subsequently continuing to holy orders. Her many students included the future priests Alban Butler (1709–1773), author of *Lives of the Saints*; Thomas Southworth (1749–1816), President of Sedgley Park; John Daniel (1745–1823), last President of the English College, Douai; John Gillow (1753–1828), President of Ushaw College; and the layman Peter Newby (1745–1827), poet and schoolmaster, who carried on the dame's educational work at Haighton after her death").

Harrison, George Bagshaw – scholar and literary critic; b. 14 July 1894, 6 Brunswick Place, Hove, Sussex; c. 14 June 1947 (received with his wife, Dorothy (1894–1986)); d. 1 November 1991, Palmerston North, New Zealand; brought up as an Anglican; educated at Queen's College, Cambridge; served in India and Middle East in World War I; taught at King's College, London; specialized in Shakespeare and Elizabethan period (author of twenty-five books); editor of Elizabethan and Jacobean Journals series; co-editor (with Harley Granville-Barker) of *A Companion to Shakespeare Studies* (1934); editor of the *Penguin Shakespeare*; in intelligence corps 1940–1943, but then Professor at Queen's University, Kingston, Ontario; finally at University of Michigan 1949–1964; after Vatican II worked for International Commission on English in the Liturgy (ICEL) on translation of liturgy; Knight of the Order of St. Gregory the Great 1981; conversion influenced by sudden death of two of his four children

(a third dying of cancer later); see "Finding a Way of Life" in John A. O'Brien (ed), *The Road to Damascus (1949); Introducing Shakespeare* (1968); *The Bible in the Mass* (1982); *Background to the New Testament: An Introduction to the World of Jesus and the Apostles* (1985); *One Man in His Time: the Memoirs of G. B. Harrison, 1894–1984* (1985) ("My work on John Bunyan had given me a fair insight into the nature and grim tenets of Puritanism – far from being the champions of true liberty, the Puritans were the most oppressive of all, clamoring for freedom only to force their own doctrines on others. There was more hope, I felt for Catholic Everyman, whose Good Deeds helped his entry into heaven than for Puritan ignorance, predestined to hell no matter what his efforts. It was possible to admire the depth of conviction and astute analyses of John Bunyan, but not his beliefs. And how could a literal interpretation of the Bible explain away the text 'Thou art Peter and upon this Rock I will build my Church' when that church was the Church of Rome?

On the other hand, research into sixteenth century England also provided historical examples of admirable Catholics, from the brilliant Thomas More to those cheerful martyrs, Edmund Campion and Robert Southwell. Thomas More was the kind of saint that everyone can understand – a successful man of the world, an adored father, a scholar, a lawyer, perfectly honest, unostentatiously devout, an entrancing wit, very good company for all occasions, and yet on a matter of ultimate principle utterly rigid. After studying the life of More I felt that the English Reformation, viewed solely as a political event, was an incomparable blunder.

The ultimate choice of a philosophy or religion thus lay between the Catholic faith, which demanded acceptance of dogmas that seemed, at first, as quite irrational, and an agnosticism which recognized that the knowable was very limited but the scientist was likely to be better informed than the theologian, in the twentieth century. At the same time, I was convinced that while I might not understand the visions and ecstasies of the saints and mystics they were obviously very real to those experiencing them, even if they could not be recorded by physical means. Because I had no experience of such personal commitment, I lapsed into Epicureanism, a passive, fatalistic acceptance of life – what would be, would be. Such rational but vague philosophy was useless in the event of the death of both our sons. There must be an answer and a consolation in religion. The serenity and strength of the Roman Catholic Church, the air of supreme and certain authority, remained rock-hard in the face of the malice and abuse of her enemies...

From the moment we decided to explore the Catholic faith the urge became more insistent every day. It was a force external, uncontrollable and quite different from anything that either of us had ever experienced. Psychiatrists doubtless have a name for it; Catholics call it an act of grace. We thought our way carefully through the various problems: the fact that Church authority is based on supernatural as well as historical origins; confession and absolution; the faith to believe the unprovable; the doctrine of papal infallibility; transubstantiation. Once we could accept the central position – that the Church as a corporate body, divinely and supernaturally founded, fortified by centuries of wisdom and experience, was more capable of interpreting the supernatural and defining a dogma than any one individual – then all difficulties would disappear. Could we accept all that the Church claimed? We believed so"); *DNB*.

Harrison, Herbert – priest; b. 1843; c. 3 March 1861, London Oratory; d. 1867; father was Protestant rector of Bugbrooke, Northamptonshire; captain of the Queen's Scholars of Westminster School; was first choice for entry to Christ Church College, Oxford, but his conversion meant he had to leave school and forfeit his place at Oxford; two years after his conversion his father wrote to *The Times* newspaper complaining of the behavior of Fr. Henry Bowden and Fr. Frederick Faber (see above) of the London Oratory in baptizing and receiving his son into the Church; in reality he had been considering religious questions for some months, reading such books as Newman's *Difficulties of Anglicanism*, had often attended the Oratory, and asked the fathers to receive him into the Church; ensuing controversy in the press; entered novitiate at the Oratory in 1861; ordained deacon in 1866; taken ill with advanced pulmonary tuberculosis from which he died; his illness precluded his ordination to the priesthood; in 1870 his father blamed the Oratory for his early death; see Gilbert Thompson, "Fr. Herbert Harrison: A Victorian Schoolboy Convert," *Catholic Life*, February 2009, p.48 ("In reply [to the father's criticisms in 1870] Fr. Gordon [then the Superior] quoted a letter which Herbert had written to his brother Henry in India soon after his conversion in which he describes the circumstances of his conversion, how his Protestant doubts and prejudices gradually dissipated after he attended Sunday services at the Oratory and how he could no longer blind himself to the truth and beauty of the Catholic religion. It concludes 'I became a Catholic of my own perfect free will and conviction'").

Harrison, Mary St. Leger (*née* Kingsley) (*pseud.* Lucas Malet) – novelist; b. 4 June 1852; the rectory, Eversley,

Hampshire; c. 1902; d. 27 October 1931, 18 The Norton, Tenby, Wales; daughter of the novelist Charles Kingsley (1819–1875); educated at home and traveled widely; studied at the Slade School of Fine Art; married in 1876 to William Harrison (d. 1897), a curate of her father's, but they separated amicably shortly afterwards; enjoyed great literary success; moral themes in her novels attracted criticism; her writing was admired by Henry James the novelist, who became a close friend; after her conversion she revised her earlier work to bring it in line with her new faith and published a religious novel, *The Far Horizon* (1906), but her other books continued to shock; spent much time abroad, especially in France; see *Da Silva's Widow and Other Stories* (1922); *The Survivors* (1923); *The Dogs of Want* (1924); William Archer, *Real Conversations* (1904) (Conversation with Lucas Malet: "Puritanism is so stupidly afraid of the lessons of life as a whole, and so resolute never to learn from them, that it insists on our wearing, or pretending to wear, blinkers, so as to see nothing that is inconsistent with its preconceived moral scheme. Think of the weakness, the unphilosophic quality of Puritanism, compared with Catholicism, as a basis or background for art! And then the eventual outcome of Puritanism is of necessity rationalism; and there we have the real enemy!"); *DNB*.

Hart, John, SJ – priest; b. in Oxford; c. about 1570; d. 19 July 1586, Jarislau, Poland; whilst at Oxford University showed dissatisfaction with new religion; went to Douai and was reconciled to the Church; admitted into English College in 1570; ordained priest 29 March 1578; sent to the English mission in 1580, but arrested on landing at Dover and imprisoned; released by Sir Francis Walsingham on condition that he conferred with a Protestant divine; just as resolute in faith afterwards; sent to the Tower; tried and condemned day after condemnation of Edmund Campion (see above); was to have been executed on 1 December 1581 with Campion, Sherwin and Bryant, but when placed on the sledge his fears overcame him and, returned to prison, he wrote to Walsingham an act of apostasy; recovered and would not yield later and put in irons and in the pit; admitted into the Society of Jesus in 1583 while in prison; in 1585 removed from the Tower and banished; see *Gillow*, Vol. III, p.153 ("The interpretation of the change is probably to be found in the fact told by Cardinal Allen to Fr. Agazzari, in a letter ... that Hart's mother had been to visit him in the Tower, and that she, 'a gentlewoman of a noble spirit,' spoke to him in such lofty tones of martyrdom, that if she found him hot with the desire of it, she left him on fire; and the report of this great deed on her part, and its merited promise, was widespread among the Catholics"); *DNB*.

Hart, Blessed William – priest and martyr; b. 1558, Wells, Somerset; d. 15 March 1583, York; became Catholic at Oxford University; went to Douai, Rheims and Rome, entering English College there in 1579; ordained priest and left for the English mission in 1581; worked chiefly in York area; eloquent preacher; visited many prisoners for recusancy; present at Mass at which Bl. William Lacy was captured, and only escaped by standing up to his chin in muddy moat of York Castle; betrayed by an apostate on Christmas Day, 1582, put in dungeon in castle; at trial for exercising his priesthood, foreman of jury petitioned for a discharge, but judges directed jury to convict; hanged, drawn and quartered at York; see *Gillow*, Vol. III, p.155; *Catholic Encyclopedia*.

Hartley (alias Garton), Blessed William – priest and martyr; b. about 1557, Wyn, Derbyshire; d. 5 October 1588, Shoreditch; formerly Anglican minister; Fellow of St. John's College, Oxford, at the time when Edmund Campion (see above) was there; went to Rheims and entered English College 1579; ordained priest February 1580 at Chalons; set out on foot on 16 June to proceed to the English mission; printed and distributed books of Persons (see below) and Campion (see above); apprehended at Stonor Park, near Henley, on 13 August 1581 and sent to Marshalsea prison; detected saying Mass in a cell before Lord Vaux, and indicted for high treason; not tried, but sent into exile in 1585; returned to England; eventually rearrested and condemned to death for being a priest; executed at Shoreditch; see *Gillow*, Vol. III, p.160; *Catholic Encyclopedia*.

Hartwell, Louisa Teresa (name in religion Sr. Teresa Gonzaga) – nun; b. 20 June 1813; c. 1832 (received with her mother, Lady Louisa Hartwell (*née* Aldridge) (1778–1843); d. 1 March 1854; her father Sir Francis Hartwell (d. 1831) Deputy Controller of Royal Navy; brought up in Protestant family which was very suspicious of the Catholic Church; Anglicanism failed to satisfy her and she was always attracted to Catholicism (partly by living in Ireland for some of her childhood where she saw Catholic chapels, convents and schools); affected by fact that father refused to have clergyman attend him at his death-bed, showing his attachment to Anglicanism had been more from political than religious motives; shortly afterwards she became gravely ill and decided to become a Catholic; she and her mother went to live in Italy; in 1835 became nun at convent of Reformed Carmelites at Ronciglione (her mother, after much work in

the service of the poor, became Third Order Carmelite and spent rest of her days in convent at Ronciglione); both women helped to restore the monastery and were noted for their piety; see *An Account of the Conversion of Louisa Teresa Hartwell, Written by Herself* (1832) ("From the moment that they began to teach me the Apostles' Creed, certainly I was no longer a Protestant. The words 'I believe in the Holy Catholic Church' were enough for me; that a person could be and could not be the same thing at the same time was to my youthful mind an absurdity too patent to be believed in. I said, 'But we are not Catholics. Why are we not Catholics? It is a lie to say we believe in her, because we do not believe in her.' 'But we are Catholics, though not Roman Catholics,' they answered me. 'No,' I said, 'I will never believe that; it is not true. Why are we never called Catholics or our churches called Catholic ones?' No one could make me understand the Creed in the Protestant and negative sense. Everyone told me I ought to say it because everyone else said it, even though I was too young to understand it. And so I believed in the Holy Catholic Church, but not in the English Church, because I knew well that she was not Catholic, and I also quickly convinced myself, in thinking things over, that she was not Holy"); Dom Bede Camm, *Pilgrim Paths in Latin Lands* (1908), pp.165–218 (includes the account referred to above and other documentation); Richard Whinder, "The Conversion of Louisa Hartwell," *Catholic Life*, February 2007, p.12.

Harvey, Frederick William – poet and solicitor; b. 26 March 1888, Hartpury, Gloucestershire; c. 1915; d. 13 February 1957; educated at King's School, Gloucester and Rossall School; private soldier in France in World War I with the Gloucestershire Regiment; awarded

Distinguished Conduct Medal in 1915 and returned to England for officer training; captured behind the German lines in 1916; best known for poems composed in prisoner–of–war camps; returned home in 1919; friend of Ivor Gurney, poet and composer, and Herbert Howell, composer, both of whom set some of his poems to music; career faltered later; see *Comrades in Captivity: A Record of Life in Seven German Prison Camps* (1920) (war memoirs); essay in Maurice Leahy (ed), *Conversions to the Catholic Church: A Symposium* (1933) ("It pleased me to see laborers in rough clothes and soldiers in common khaki coming to kneel simply by an altar and going into the confessional to receive pardon for their sins instead of driving up in 'Sunday-best' to listen to some popular preacher.... I became a Catholic because I was a sinner. And for the same reason remain under those healing wings"); Anthony Boden, *F. W. Harvey: Soldier, Poet* (1988); Frances Townsend, *The Laureate of Gloucestershire: The Life and Work of F. W. Harvey, 1888 – 1957* (1988).

Haskell, Arnold Lionel David – ballet critic; b. 19 October 1903, London; d. 15 November 1980, 6A Cavendish Crescent, Bath; son of banker; childhood friendship with Alicia Markova enabled her to be involved with Diaghilev ballet; trained as lawyer, but worked unsuccessfully in business for short period; in 1934 wrote very successful book, *Balletomania*; dilettante, especially in painting and sculpture; worked with various ballet companies; ballet critic for *Daily Telegraph* 1935–1938; director of new Royal Ballet School, 1946–1965; wrote about ballet in popular style; urbane and civilized; son, Francis (1928–2000), Professor of History of Art at Oxford; see *In His True Centre* (1951 (autobiography) ("I had yet to realize that one could reconcile a certain anti-clericalism with

Catholicism, believe in the Church yet have doubts about the men who compose it at certain periods in its long history. I should have realized that the Church has survived the leadership of mediaeval banditti and inspired great saints, great scholars and great artists. That while some bishop may have been worldly, a Sainte Thérèse in the calm of her convent gave evidence that God still speaks to the humble, that religion was not something that had happened in ancient times, but was no longer a living force. Later a visit to Lourdes moved me deeply. There I found what I had missed in Rome. For all its flamboyance and vulgarity, the crudely painted stucco saints and madonnas, the commerce in the healing waters, the shops with their religious tourist souvenirs, Lourdes had an atmosphere both of mystery and holiness. One could not doubt that Bernadette had been touched by God, that millions had flocked to the spot believing it, that some had been healed and that many had been comforted.

Not only did I gain a special affection … for this simple village girl, but I have since then come more and more to regard her as one of the most significant figures of modern times. Bernadette suddenly appears at a period that prides itself on its rationalism, that believes there is a concrete answer to every problem, that science is the only truth. With great courage and simplicity she stands up to exhaustive cross-examination as did another village girl and succeeds in shaking many of the complacent rationalists…

Bernadette, incapable herself of philosophical argument, has forced many of us to think and to become more humble; her very strength lies in her complete simplicity. Aquinas and Bernadette; what wealth and variety they represent under the same wide roof!...

If there are sinners there must be

saints, whose aid we can invoke, if there is evil there must be good for which we can pray. If there is nothing but a blind madman trampling his creations at the dictate of a whim, then the sooner we end it all the better. There would at any rate be logic in suicide").

Hawes, John Cyril (Fra. Jerome) – priest and architect; b. 7 September 1876, Richmond, Surrey; c. 1911 (received in New York); d. 1956; showed early talent for drawing and was articled to a firm of architects; influenced by Arts and Craft movement, the work of Ninian Comper and Charles Voysey, and the writing of John Ruskin; started in practice in 1897; had a religious conversion in 1899 and in 1903 took Anglican orders; High Anglican in outlook; joined the Anglican Benedictine community on Caldey Island, but left in 1907; in 1909 joined a Church of England mission in the Bahamas where many churches had been damaged by a hurricane; ministered and repaired and built churches there; after becoming a Catholic he went to the Beda College in Rome; ordained priest in 1915; recruited for the dioceses of Western Australia, where he worked on outback missions and designed and built several churches, notably the Cathedral of St. Xavier; in 1937 became a monsignor; in 1939 he returned, via England, to the Bahamas where he built a hermitage on Cat Island and attempted to live as a hermit under the name of Fra Jerome, also designed and built churches; buried in the cave he had prepared below the hermitage; see Peter Anson, *The Hermit of Cat Island* (1958).

Hawker, Robert Stephen (*pseud.* Reuben) – poet (also wrote hymns and ballads) and antiquary; b. 3 December 1803, Charles church vicarage, Plymouth; c. 14 August 1875 (death bed conversion); d. 15 August 1875,

Plymouth; son of Anglican vicar; grandson of Dr. Robert Hawker (1753–1827), celebrated Calvinist Divine and author who brought him up; Anglican vicar himself with mission for many years to those shipwrecked off Cornish coast; student of history and legends of Cornish people; became well known not only as romantic poet ("the Bard of the Tamarside") but as eccentric vicar ("He dressed flamboyantly, wearing a brown cassock, scarlet gauntlets, and a hat like a fez, or a claret-colored coat, fisherman's jersey, and sea boots. He talked to birds, and his congregation often included his nine cats and many dogs, which he preferred to the uncharitable farmers, over whom he once read the Exorcistic Service" (*DNB*)); assimilated some ideas of the Oxford Movement; his mind had long been tending towards the Catholic Church; when he was dying his wife, a daughter of a Polish exile, sent for a priest who received him into the Catholic Church; buried in Plymouth cemetery; see Frederick George Lee, *Memorials of R. S. Hawker* (1876) ("Hawker's clear mind ... went straight to the heart of the question of validity. Again he wrote: 'A National Church (acting) apart from foreign Catholics, has never been able to retain its own flock, let alone the folding of others'"); C. E. Byles, *Life and Letters of R. S. Hawker of Morwenstowe* (1905); Michael Sewell, "Hawker of Morwenstowe," *Blackfriars*, October 1933, p.854; H. E. G. Rope, "The Catholicism of R. S. Hawker," *The Month*, August 1934, p.451; J. Lewis May, "Hawker of Morwenstow," *Dublin Review*, October-December 1939, p.375; Piers Brendon, *Hawker of Morwenstow* (1975); Brocard Sewell, *Like Black Swans: Some People and Themes* (1982), Ch. 3; *Gillow*, Vol. III, p.183; *Catholic Encyclopedia*; *DNB* ("Latterly Hawker found himself increasingly at odds with the secular and religious temper of his day. His letters suggest that he was turning from Protestantism, which amounted to nothing more than 'a gigantic sneer of religious negation' towards the positive dogmas of the Roman Catholic Church. Nevertheless it was a shock to almost everyone except his wife when the vicar of Morwenstowe was baptized a Roman Catholic on his deathbed. Pauline wrote afterwards that her husband had been 'at heart a Catholic' ever since she had known him").

Hay, Bishop George – bishop and writer; b. 24 August 1729, Edinburgh; c. 21 December 1748; d. 15 October 1811, Aquhorties, Aberdeenshire; parents Scottish Episcopalian (father, a Jacobite, imprisoned after the 1715 rising); after school in Edinburgh apprenticed to a surgeon; gave medical service to Prince Charles' army and was imprisoned; after conversion unable to qualify as doctor because of his religion; introduced to Bishop Challoner (see above) who persuaded him to study for the priesthood; entered Scots College, Rome, in 1751; ordained priest in Rome 2 April 1758; returned to Scotland in 1759 and served on the mission; on 21 May 1769 at Scalan he was consecrated titular bishop of Daulis and coadjutor to Bishop Grant; printed 10,000 copies of a catechism; became vicar apostolic of the lowland district in 1778; Catholic Relief Bill led to his new chapel and priests' house being destroyed by Edinburgh mob; his writings on the faith had great influence; many churches built and new missions; buried in the old chapel of St. Ninian, Fetternear; see *The Sincere Christian* (1781) (an apologetic for the Catholic faith); *The Devout Christian* (1783); *The Pious Christian* (1786); *Catholic Encyclopedia*; *DNB*.

Headlam-Morley, Agnes – historian; b. 10 December 1902, 1 Benet Place, Cambridge; c. 1948; d. 21 February 1986, Cheam, Surrey; daughter of Sir James Wycliffe Headlam (1863–1929), diplomatic historian; her uncle was Arthur Cayley Headlam (1862–1947), Anglican Bishop of Gloucester; studied History at Oxford and was a Fellow at St. Hugh's College 1932–1970; Professor of International Relations 1954–1970 (the first woman to be elected to a full professorship at Oxford); specialist in interwar European diplomatic history; Conservative in politics; member of the Longford committee investigating pornography, which reported in 1972; unmarried; her ashes were buried in her parents' grave at St. Mary's Church, Whorlton, Barnard Castle; see *DNB* ("Her essay [in her introduction to her uncle's posthumous book *The Fourth Gospel as History* (1948)] does ... reveal her sadness at the division of European Christendom into different states, churches, and sects, and it identifies strikingly with the bishop's role in the ecumenical movement and his belief in a 'higher loyalty to the Universal Church'. It helps to explain her decision to be received into the Roman Catholic Church").

Heard, Cardinal William Theodore – Cardinal priest; b. 24 February 1884, The Lodge, Fettes College, Edinburgh; c. 1910 (received by Fr. Stanislas St. John at Farm Street, London); d. 16 September 1973, San Stefano Rotondo, Rome; father headmaster of Fettes College; brought up in Scotland in a house of stern discipline; educated at Balliol College, Oxford; won a rowing blue in the boat race of 1907; became a solicitor; ordained Catholic priest in 1918; obtained doctorates in theology and canon law; judge and later Dean of the Sacred Roman Rota; worked on the canonizations of the English martyrs; member of curial party and of central preparatory commission at the Second Vatican Council; his motto was *Recte et sapienter*; buried in the Campo Verano, Rome; see C. burns, "His Eminence Cardinal William Theodore Heard," *Venerabile*, 1973, p.7; Hugh McLoughlin, "From the Blue of Oxford to the Purple of Rome," *Catholic Times*, 8 April 2007, p.11; *DNB* ("He liked to work on marriage annulments in the morning and canonizations in the afternoon, because they were less depressing and even the failed candidates had tried hard").

Heath, Blessed Henry, OSF (name in religion Paul of St. Magdalen) – priest and martyr; b. about 1599, Peterborough, Northamptonshire; d. 17 April 1643; parents Protestants and sent him to Cambridge to study for ministry; studied writings of the fathers and works of controversy; influenced by the writings of Cardinal Bellarmine; openly exposed errors of the Reformation, fled to London and reconciled to the Church by Fr. George Fisher (alias Musket or Muscote); admitted to English college, Douai; became Franciscan in 1623; ordained priest at Douai; almost nineteen years in convent of St. Bonaventure at Douai, becoming Guardian of convent three times, and leading saintly life; went on the English mission; apprehended at once and on confessing himself to be a priest, committed to Newgate; found guilty of being a priest and entering the realm; hanged, drawn and quartered at Tyburn; reconciled in the very cart one of the criminals that were executed with him; very learnèd man who wrote on spirituality; his father, John Heath (d. 29 December 1652), when nearly eighty and a widower, went over to Douai, was reconciled to the Church in convent of St. Bonaventure, and became lay-brother in the community; see *Gillow*, Vol. III, p.239; *Catholic Encyclopedia*; p.239; *DNB*.

Heigham, John (alias Roger Heigham) – bookseller and Catholic apologist; b. 1568; d. 1632; convert from extreme Protestantism; two of his sons became priests; he was exiled from England c.1603 on account of his Catholic religion; lived in Douai and then in St. Omer; devoted all his time, working with his wife Mary, furthering the Catholic cause in England by preparing English texts (many being translations) and smuggling them across the Channel; very productive publisher; also fine controversialist; he accused the Protestant Reformers of heresy and innovation, and provoked the Calvinist/Arminian division in Church of England, a religious controversy one of the causes of the English Civil War; see *The Gagge of the Reformed Gospell* (1623); *Via Vere Tuta, Or the Truly Safe Way* (1631); A. F. Allison, "John Heigham of St. Omer (c.1568–c.1632)," *Recusant History*, October 1958, p.226; Thomas Scheck, "The Polemics of John Heigham and Richard Montagu and the Rise of English Arminianism," *Recusant History*, May 2008, p.12 ("Heigham's apologetic principles are clarified in his works. In *Via Vere Tuta*, Heigham repeats the question to the Protestants: 'Where was your Church before Luther?' Heigham's thesis is that the Roman Catholic Church, and not any of the new Protestant Churches, can be demonstrably proven to be the same visible and publicly worshiping Church of all previous ages reaching back to antiquity, both in its doctrine and practice.... Heigham was well aware of the scorn to which the leading Protestants, especially Luther, had subjected the ancient Fathers and he makes capital use of such statements in his works.... For Heigham such statements proved that the Protestant Reformers themselves, for all their claims to be 'primitive', recognized that their new churches had innovated doctrinally and did not teach and practice the same as the Ancient Church. For by accusing the Church Fathers of fundamental doctrinal error, the Protestant Reformers proved that they themselves were discontinuous with the Catholic Church of the past.

In his earlier work, *The Gagge*, the leading idea of Heigham's Catholic apologetics is his rejection of the *sola scriptura* doctrine of the Protestants. As Heigham sees it, the affirmation of this doctrine is the principal error of Protestantism, since it entails the repudiation of the Church's infallible magisterium and the substitution of the Rule of Faith with private interpretation.... [F]or Heigham oral tradition, delivered by word of mouth, is of equal or greater authority with what was written. For before the New Testament was even completely written, the Apostles had delivered everything by Tradition and word of mouth.... [W]e see here one of the perennial questions Catholic apologists posed to the Protestants: 'Why do you accept the canon of Scripture, when it was a formal decision of the Church to include those books in its canon?' Does not the acceptance of the canon imply the admission of an external ecclesiastical authority? In short, for Heigham the crucial issue dividing Catholics and Protestants is that of authority. The Protestant assertion that the Bible is the sole authority begs the question of ecclesiastical authority, since the Church has decided the canon"); *DNB*.

Helbert, Magdalena – married lady; b. 1838; c. March 1874 (shortly before her death); d. 8 March 1874; had four children; associate of the High Anglican House of Mary at Clewer; very devout; strongly drawn towards the Catholic Church, but had particular difficulties about papal infallibility and the Marian doctrines; consulted Manning, who recommended her to write to Newman; much correspondence with Newman in 1869, but was persuaded to remain an Anglican; became a Catholic before her death; her husband wrote to Newman six days after her death: "I am very grateful that she was permitted to join the Roman Communion before her death. I am sure that her mind was more at ease and her last moments more peaceful in consequence of the step she took"; see Stanley L. Jaki, *Newman to Converts: An Existential Ecclesiology* (2001), Ch. 18 ("Newman ... [stated] that the kind of ancient Church he had just described was no different from the present Catholic Church and that the similarity of the two was his reason for having become a Roman Catholic. He ... added the graphic point ... about the resemblance of the primitive Church to the present Roman Church as being as unmistakable as the resemblance of the photograph taken of a man when he was twenty, with that of a man taken twenty years later: *'You know it is the same man.'*

...[Mrs. Helbert] must have gasped on seeing Newman turn around the thrust of a long worn objection: 'My dear Madam, as to the scandalous lives of some Popes ... we not only allow but glory in, as showing the Divine Care of the Church, that, even in the case of those very men, the See of Peter spoke truth, not falsehood.... God was 'glorified in that respect in which the Pope is His appointed teacher in Alexander VI and Leo Tenth. They have never spoken false doctrine.'

...The best part of Newman's answer concerning papal infallibility was his insistence on an outstanding series of undeniable facts showing Rome's stubborn, incorrigible readiness to interfere with other sees: 'There were continual collisions between Rome and nearly every Church and that Rome was always in the right.... *Why* did the Pope always nterfere and (if you will) dictate, except that he had a tradition of his infallibility? And why was he always right, except that he *was* infallible?'

[Newman] called Mrs. Helbert's attention to the fact that 'the Assumption of Our Lady is more pointedly and in express words held by all Catholics, and has been for a thousand years, than the proposition "The Holy Ghost is God" was held by the Catholic world in St. Basil's time...'

Then he gave the priceless rule of thumb relating to the use of private judgment: 'Private judgment *must* be your guide, till you are in the Church. You do not begin with faith, but with reason, and you *end* with faith. How are you to get into the way of faith, but by history or some other equivalent method of inquiry? You *must* have some *ground* of becoming a Catholic, or you will not make a good one'").

assumption that the Catholic Church can be and is in fact divided. They postulate separated bodies, owning different authorities, differing to some extent in faith, yet all parts of the Catholic Church. But both Rome and the East deny this, and each claims to be, alone, the whole of the true Church of Christ on earth. If the Anglican theories are true, then both Rome and the East are formally teaching falsehood in a very grave matter.... For a Papalist, as I was, [this] was a *reductio ad absurdum*. Scripture and the Fathers alike set forth the Church as One, unique and indivisible. I accepted Rome's claim to be that Church. I must accept her teaching on her own nature and her own frontiers. By that teaching, the Church of England cannot be both separate and Catholic. It is separate and autonomous, as a matter of principle. Therefore it cannot be part of the one Catholic Church").

Henderson, Sir George Francis Robert – army officer, historian and military writer; b. 2 June 1854, St. Helier, Jersey; d. 5 March 1903, Aswan, Egypt; son of Anglican Dean (eldest of fourteen children); for many years director of Military Art and History at Army Staff College; served in Egypt; director of military intelligence during Boer War; been described as most scientific British strategist of his time; most famous for his work regarding American civil war and Stonewall Jackson, the Confederate general; buried in Catholic cemetery, Cairo; see *DNB*.

Hepburne-Scott, Hon. Patrick J. – c. 15 August 1955; former Church of England minister and "Papalist"; converted at time of South India question; see "Recent convert clergy tell how and why," *The Month*, September 1956, p.143 ("All Anglican theories of the Church, even the most extremely 'Papalist,' involve the

Herbert, John Rogers – portrait and historical painter; b. 23 January 1810, Maldon, Essex; c. most sources indicate 1836 (sister, Elizabeth received in 1845 and became nun; brother, William, received in 1846); d. 17 March 1890, London; noted especially for Italianate scenes; when drawn to Catholicism developed close friendship with Augustus Welby Pugin (see below); thereafter concentrated on religious subjects with Catholic theme; Officer of Legion of Honour; father of, *inter alia*, Arthur John Herbert (1834–1856), Cyril Wiseman Herbert (1848–1882), and Wilfrid Vincent Herbert (d. 1891), all also artists; his wife's sister married James Collinson, the painter and Catholic (see above); buried in upper catacombs of Kensal Green cemetery, London; see *DNB* ("Herbert's obsession with religion is evident in his art from 1840 onwards when he exhibited *The monastery in the fourteenth century: boar-hunters* *refreshed at St. Augustine's monastery, Canterbury.* The painting evoked pre-Reformation England, still wholly Catholic, with the church as benevolent provider for all").

Herbert, (Mary) Elizabeth, Lady Herbert of Lea (*née* Acourt Repington) – philanthropist and authoress; b. 21 July 1822; c. 5 January 1865 (at Palermo, Sicily; her seven children being made wards of court by family trustees so they could not follow her into the Catholic Church (only Mary, wife of Baron Friedrich von Hügel (1852–1925), author, philosopher and mystic, able to do so, in 1873)); d. 30 October 1911, Herbert House, 38 Chesham Place, Belgrave Square, London; brought up as devout Anglican; moved in "the best circles"; wife of Sidney Herbert (1810–1861), first Baron Herbert of Lea, Secretary of State for War, friend and supporter of Florence Nightingale, and great army reformer (also devout Anglican); mother of thirteenth and fourteenth Earls of Pembroke, of Mary Catherine Herbert and of Elizabeth Maude, wife of Sir Hubert Parry, the composer; influenced by the Oxford Movement; close friend of Florence Nightingale, Gladstone and Manning; devoted herself to charitable work and, together with Fr. Herbert Vaughan, with whom she had an extraordinary spiritual friendship, developed St. Joseph's Missionary College, Mill Hill; member of Third Order of St. Francis; wrote and translated several books on variety of subjects, mainly from Catholic perspective; see *The Mission of St. Francis of Sales* (1868); *The Passion Play at Ammergau* (1890); *How I Came Home* (1893) ("I do not think I was ever attracted to the Catholic Church by the gorgeousness or beauty of its services. I always prefer a Low to a High Mass; it is to me more devotional.... But the Adoration of the Blessed Sacrament; the

little light telling of the perpetual Presence in the Tabernacle; the inexpressible relief of Confession; and the intimate union with and nearness to the Sacred Humanity of Our Divine Lord which breathes in every form of Catholic worship, these had from the first the strongest possible hold upon me. People were always talking to me about the 'Church of my baptism.' What Church is that but the Church of our Baptismal creed – the One Holy Catholic Church? Our baptism binds us to *this*, not to the Church of England, except so far as the Church of England is one with the Church Catholic; and if you feel convinced that the Anglican Church is at variance with the Catholic Church throughout the world, your very baptism, as it appears to me, binds you to leave it'…

The gist of the whole matter is this: 'Whatsoever is not of faith is sin.' If people are content with Anglicanism, and have no doubts or fears of its truth, they are comparatively safe. But to remain in it, when you are convinced that she is in error, or when you have grave doubts of the validity of her orders, and consequently of her Sacraments and authority, is imperiling your own salvation; to stifle such doubts is immoral; and this was my case at that time. Certainly on coming to a decision on so vital a matter we must use all the faculties God has given us, and in that way incur the reproach of acting on our private judgment. But if people remain in the Church of England, they must live and die in a perpetual exercise of private judgment upon every doctrine in the Thirty-nine Articles. There are no two Bishops and scarcely two clergymen who think alike or teach alike on the most vital and important doctrines. Anglicanism professes to include within her pale all extremes, from the Calvinist to the highest Ritualist; and the latter utterly contemn all ecclesiastical authority, have made to themselves a sect and a

Church of their own within the Establishment, and then call themselves Catholics! On the other hand, by submitting, once for all, to the Church of God, we rest our faith for ever on a rock, and form one of a body which through the continual presence of Our Divine Lord and the teaching of His Holy Spirit, is infallible and unchangeable to the end of the world"); *Anglican Prejudices against the Catholic Church* (1899); Madeleine Beard, *Faith and Fortune* (1997), pp.171–173; Raleigh St. Lawrence, "Lady Elizabeth Herbert of Lea, 1822–1911," *Catholic Life*, December 2003, p.50; *DNB*.

Hewins, William Albert Samuel – economist and politician; b. 11 May 1865, near Wolverhampton; c. September 1914; d. 17 November 1931, 25 Chester Square, London; fourth of ten children; father lapsed Catholic; specialized in economic history; first director of London School of Economics 1895–1903; supporter of tariff reform and imperial preference and advisor to Joseph Chamberlain; Unionist MP 1912–1918; never returned to parliament, believing it to be as result of anti-Catholic prejudice; conversion influenced by Fr. Pollen, SJ; advisor to Cardinal Bourne; isolated and marginal figure in 1920s; buried at Kensal Green cemetery, London; see *DNB*.

Heydt, Baroness Vera von der (*née* von Schurabach) – Jungian analyst; b. 11 December 1899, Berlin; c. 1937 (received by Fr. Martin D'Arcy); d. 14 November 1996, London; member of aristocratic family with Jewish banker father, who converted at sixteen to Protestantism, and mother of German Lutheran and Irish Ulster Catholic parentage, who gave up her religion on her marriage; fled from Berlin in 1933 with rise of Nazis and lived in London; became a leading influence on Jungian circles in Britain; after conversion her religion became the focal point in her life; studied connections between Christian faith and psychology; see *Prospects for the Soul* (1976), p.xii ("I was attacked by quite a number of people who could not understand why I wished to join a church at all, particularly one as rigid as the Roman. I was told of crimes committed through the centuries by the Church, the Popes, priests, monks and nuns. Such arguments seemed strange and irrelevant to me; I could not see the point of arguing such matters at all but only knew that I had stumbled upon my truth"); "A Journey," in Shirley du Boulay (ed), *The Light of Experience* (1977) ("One night I dreamed, yet I was half awake, and I saw a statue of the Sacred Heart come alive and I heard Christ calling me three times. This happened three nights running. I followed the call as I understood it and I joined the Roman Catholic Church").

Higgins, Matthew James (*pseud.* Jacob Omnium) – journalist and author; b. 4 December 1810, Benown Castle, County Meath, Ireland; c. 1852; d. 14 August 1868, Abingdon, Berkshire; from wealthy family; close friend of W. M. Thackeray; contributor to *The Times* (many of his letters instrumental in exposing abuses), *The Morning Chronicle*, *Pall Mall Gazette*, *Edinburgh Review*, and *Cornhill Magazine*; assisted famine relief committee in Ireland; wrote especially on administrative and army reform; son-in-law of Sir Henry Tichborne, eighth Baronet; had many additional pseudonyms, e.g., Civilian, Paterfamilias, West Londoner, Belgravian Mother, Mother of Six, and John Barleycorn; see *DNB*.

Hill (alias Buckland), Edmund Thomas, OSB (name in religion Thomas of St. Gregory) – priest; b. 24

June 1564, Somerset; d. 7 August 1644; formerly minister in Church of England; after conversion went to English College, Rheims, in 1590; ordained priest 12 March 1594; sent to the English mission in 1597; apprehended in 1602 and sent to Newgate; in 1612 condemned to death for being a priest, but reprieved and banished in 1613; received the Benedictine habit whilst in prison; retired to St. Gregory's monastery at Douai; see *Gillow*, Vol. III, p.305.

Hoare, Frederick Russell – writer; b. 1888, China; c. January 1923; d. 1951, St. Bonaventure's, Cambridge; son of Bishop of Victoria, Hong Kong; devoted many years of his life to social work; contributor to Catholic periodicals; lecturer in sociology; see *The Papacy and the Modern World* (1940); *Catholicism and the State* (1944): *The Original Order of St. John's Gospel* (1944); *The Gospel According to St. John* (1950); *St. Paul, the Galatians and the Church* (1951); "The Testimony of a Convert," *The Tablet*, 2 June 1951, p.435 and 9 June 1951, p.456 ("The late Abbot Vonier, of Buckfast, was instructing me; and the actions of Pius X against Modernism must have come up in our talks, for I remember being suddenly struck with something incongruous in the situation. Not only was I asking to be received into the Church whose disappearance, except for a few fools and knaves, I had so confidently predicted; but I was conscious of a particular impulse of gratitude towards the very man who had once played a leading part in making Catholicism seem intellectually impossible. But how could I not feel grateful to the Pope who had braved the ridicule of the whole world of 'intellectuals' to preserve an Ark of intellectual sanity above the flood of skepticism that had submerged me for so many years? For, now that by faith I was already

within the citadel, the picture of the obscurantist peasant trying laughably to turn back the tide had been replaced in my mind by an image of the mighty defender of the historical basis of Christianity...

At the root of [Modernism] was subjectivism, that is to say, the rejection of objective or absolute standards of ultimate truth in favor of such tests as whether a belief 'works' (pragmatism) or whether it has 'spiritual value.' And the purpose of it all was alleged to be the defense of Catholic dogma by showing that it rests on spiritual values that are not endangered by the results of the Higher Criticism. In practice this meant, and could only mean, that dogma was detached from historical fact. Dogmas, it was affirmed, were the fruit of the Church's reflections upon truths in the spiritual order. If they were sometimes cast in the form of historical statements (as in the case of the Virgin Birth and the Resurrection), these statements must be regarded simply as symbols of the inward experience of the Christian Church, gradually elaborated as that experience matured. For dogma, it was said, has its own laws of evolution, and 'the Christ of faith' is independent of 'the Jesus of history.'

The result could be foreseen and was, indeed, intended. The Catholic Higher Critics who adopted this philosophy were soon exercising, not more, but less restraint than their non-Catholic opposite numbers (if we exclude those who were the avowed enemies of Christianity in any form)...

Such being the situation, the essential task of the new Pope, as he himself saw it, was not so much to condemn this or that particular error in Biblical criticism as to strike at the root of the danger, the false philosophy of these self-appointed apologists for the Church. That was the task that he accomplished in the great encyclical *Pascendi.…* Certainly I know that, when, in that January of 1923, I set foot spiritually upon dry land at last, my mind went back to those Cambridge days when I foretold that Pius X had doomed the Church, and I thank God with all my heart that Giuseppe Sarto had lived, for without his courage there would have been, humanly speaking, little prospect that the Church would still have been standing intellectually upon the rock"); *Eight Decisive Books of Antiquity* (1952); *The Western Fathers* (1954).

Hodgson, Blessed Sydney – layman and martyr; d. 10 December 1591, Tyburn; apprehended by Topcliffe, the priest hunter, while attending Mass in house of Mr. Swithin Wells in London; the celebrant, Fr. Edmund Gennings (see above), was just at the consecration; some of men present resisted the entrance of the intruders until Mass was finished, and then gave themselves up; tried for receiving and relieving priests, and for being reconciled to the Church of Rome; he chose to die for his religion rather than save his life by occasional conformity to the Established Church; executed at Tyburn; see *Gillow*, Vol. III, p.320; *Catholic Encyclopedia*.

Hoey, Frances Sarah Cashel (*née* Johnston) – authoress and journalist; b. 15 February 1830, Bushy Park, near Dublin; c. 1858 (on her marriage); d. 9 July 1908, Beccles, Suffolk; one of eight children; wife of John Baptist Cashel Hoey (1828–1892), barrister and journalist, who was for a time sub-editor of the *Dublin Review* and contributor to, e.g., *The Spectator*; after meeting Daniel O'Connell she became and remained fervent Irish nationalist for rest of her life; published eleven novels between 1868 and 1886 (*A Golden Sorrow* (1872) and *Griffith's Double* (1876) perhaps the best); regular contributor to *The Specta-*tor, *Chamber's World*, *The World* and *The Australasian*; translated thirty-five or more books from French, including biographies of Marie Antoinette and the Empress Josephine; buried in the grounds of the Benedictine church at Little Malvern; see *DNB* ("Her faith is often evident in her novels, notably *Out of Court* (1874), which exposes the evils of divorce and applauds Ireland for rejecting it, and *The Question of Cain* (1882) and *The Lover's Creed* (1884), both of which feature providential conversions on the brink of death").

Holden, Angus William Eden, 3rd Baron Holden of Alston in the county of Cumberland – politician; b. 1 August 1898; c. 1916; d. 6 July 1951, London; educated Eton and Magdalen College, Oxford; for a time in diplomatic service; honorary attaché to Holy See 1918, then to British embassy, Madrid 1922, then to British embassy in Berlin 1925; succeeded in the barony on his father's death in 1937; at first member of the Liberal party, then in 1937 joined National Labour party; in May 1945 joined Labour party; speaker and deputy chairman of committees in the House of Lords 1947–1950; served in the Labour government of Clement Atlee as Under-Secretary of State for Commonwealth Relations March 1950–July 1950; author of several books; unmarried; on his death barony became extinct.

Holford, Peter (alias Lostock) – priest; b. about 1690; c. about 1707 (later his nephew, also Peter Holford (d. 1803), was sent to Cambridge to take Anglican orders, but becoming dissatisfied with the reasons given for the Reformation, went to London with his sister, Elizabeth (d. 1814), and both were instructed and received into the Church by Bishop Challoner (see above); his sister became a nun); d. 31 August 1722; brought up as

Protestant; left home unknown to his parents and received into the Church by John Jones, alias Vane, London agent of the English College at Lisbon, to where he was sent by Bishop Giffard in 1708; ordained priest 30 October 1712 and made prefect of studies; further studies at the Sorbonne and received into English seminary at Paris; died of sudden illness at age of thirty-two; humble and gentle personality; see *Gillow*, Vol. III, p.342.

Holford (alias Acton and Bude), Blessed Thomas – priest and martyr; b. at Acton, Cheshire; d. 28 August 1588, London; father Protestant minister; schoolmaster in Herefordshire; converted by priest, Richard Davies, who was visiting his parents; arrived at English College, Rheims, in 1582; ordained priest 7 April 1583 and went on the English mission; several close escapes in south of England; then went to Cheshire, where apprehended and imprisoned in Chester Castle; taken to London, but escaped on the way; in Gloucester, but in 1588 returned to London, where apprehended; tried and condemned for receiving orders abroad and coming into the realm; brutally executed at Clerkenwell; see *Gillow*, Vol. III, p.343.

Holland, Bernard Henry – civil servant and barrister; b. 23 December 1850, Kent; d. 25 May 1926, Kent; son of canon of Canterbury Cathedral; spent much of his life as insider in public affairs; private secretary to Duke of Devonshire 1892–1894 and subsequently wrote his biography; private secretary to Secretary of State for Colonies; author of book on imperialism; member of many Royal Commissions; see *Memoir of Kenelm Digby* (1919); William C. Lubenow, *The Cambridge Apostles: 1820–1914* (1998) ("On reading *Eminent Victorians*, 'with much pleasure and

admiration,' Holland wrote to Strachey: 'I became a Catholic myself some years ago, and oddly enough it is about the only step in life which I have never at any time regretted.... Don't you think that there is something Apostolic both in the doctrine of transubstantiation and the doctrine of infallibility?'").

Holland, Catherine, OSA – nun; b. 1635; d. 6 January 1720, Bruges; daughter of Sir John Holland and Lady Sands; father rigid Protestant and bad tempered, mother Catholic and amiable; father educated her narrowly ("The religion I follow seems to be but an empty shadow; there must be one true and only faith. Where can I find it?"); after Civil War, father moved her to Holland and then she settled in 1651 in Bruges, where she was attracted by the Catholic religion and the Mass ("Here is God truly served"); tried unsuccessfully to persuade her father to let her convert; family returned to England at the Restoration; fled her father's house and went to the Augustinian convent at Bruges; before her profession wrote to her father for his pardon and consent, which she received; spent rest of her life in the convent at Bruges; wrote her apologia and translated French and Dutch works of piety; see *Gillow*, Vol. III, p.347.

Holland (alias Holt), Guy, SJ – priest; b. c. 1585/6, Gainsborough, Lincolnshire; c. about 1607; d. 16 November 1660, Oxfordshire; at St. John's College, Cambridge, but being converted, went to English College, Valladolid, in 1608; ordained priest in 1613 and sent to England same year; joined the Society of Jesus in 1615; at House of Probation of St. Ignatius in Clerkenwell, London as a missioner 1621–1636; at length seized with other fathers by pursuivants in 1628 at the house, but released; worked mainly in London and

Oxford; virtuous, prudent and learned; see *Gillow*, Vol. III, p.349; *DNB*.

Holland, Hugh – poet; b. 1563, Denbigh; d. about 18 July 1633, London; son of the Welsh poet, Robert Holland; pupil of William Camden; at Balliol College, Oxford and Trinity College, Cambridge; after his conversion traveled to Rome, then to Jerusalem, and then to Constantinople, where Sir Thomas Glover, the English ambassador, imprisoned him for abusing Queen Elizabeth; one of several poets and parliamentarians (e.g., John Donne, Inigo Jones, and John Hoskyns) who met at the Mitre tavern in about 1610; friend of, and worked with, William Alabaster (see above) and Ben Jonson (see below), who called him the "black swan" due to his dark hair and skin; all three men were converted by Fr. Thomas Wright; he was patronized by Buckingham and contributed a sonnet to the First Folio of Shakespeare; submitted to the Established Church in 1626 after having been indicted for recusancy; wrote many poems, in English, Latin, Greek, and Welsh; buried in Westminster Abbey, near the door of St. Benet's Chapel, without any monument; see *DNB*.

Hollis, (Maurice) Christopher – writer, publisher and politician; b. 29 March 1902, Axbridge, Somerset; c. late summer 1924 (received by Mgr. Barnes); d. 5 May 1977, Claveys, Mells, Somerset; son of Anglican Bishop of Taunton; brother of Sir Roger Hollis (1905–1973), the intelligence officer; great-nephew to celebrated Tractarian, R. W. Church; skeptic for a short time; President of Oxford Union 1923; teacher at Stonyhurst; Conservative MP 1945–1955; visiting Professor, University of Notre Dame, Indiana; chairman of *Hollis and Carter*, publishers; conversion strongly influenced by Newman and Chesterton (see

above); see *Glastonbury and England* (1927); *Saint Ignatius* (1931) ("Take the early history of the Church, the history of her rise within the Roman Empire. The broad historical facts are there, necessarily admitted by believer and skeptic alike. How are these facts to be explained? The believer's explanation is that the Church triumphed through the direct, supernatural action of God. For the life of me I cannot see any other explanation which at all adequately accounts for that triumph. This which is true of the history of the Church at large, is equally true of the history of some of her saints"); *European History 1713–1914* (1929); *The Monstrous Regiment* (1932), *Dryden* (1933); *Erasmus* (1933); essay in Arnold Lunn (ed), *Public School Religion* (1933) ("If the skeptic denies the resurrection, he is under obligation to explain what happened to the body of Our Lord after death. In the same way, if the skeptic rejects the Gospel story, he is under obligation to tell us who made that story up.... Who made up the Gospel story? Is it a story which we can imagine anyone inventing? If Jesus Christ was not God, what was He? An enlightened economist upon whom unscrupulous or misguided disciples forced baseless claims to Divinity? The thesis can only be sustained by a distortion of the evidence so pitiably contemptible that one hardly has the patience to refute it – yet it must be refuted. A deliberate deceiver? A madman? Does it seem probable that the figure which has dominated the history of two thousand years, the figure to whom men and women of every age and of every nation have turned for comfort and for confirmation is the figure either of a deceiver or of a madman?"); essay in Maurice Leahy (ed), *Conversions to the Catholic Church: A Symposium* (1933) (reprinted in John A. O'Brien (ed), *The Road to Damascus: Vol. II: Where I Found Christ* (1950), p.143) ("If

Christ was the Son of God I did not doubt that the Roman Church was the Church of Christ. The 'churches' were all agreed that Christ had founded a church; none venture to assert that He had founded the present variety of 'churches.' All were agreed, too, that His Church was imperishable, that 'the gates of hell' were not to prevail against it. That being so, the 'one, holy, Catholic and Apostolic Church' of which the Creed speaks, must be in existence somewhere today, and must have been in existence continuously ever since the times of the Apostles. There seemed, as there still seems, to me to be nowhere that that Church could be found save in the obedience of Rome. The very definitions of the Church, as given by those outside this obedience, are a denial of her unity. She alone is Catholic. And, if she be not Apostolic, certainly nobody else is, for all others can only trace their ancestry back to the Apostles through her. If Christ was God, the Church must exist, and, if the Church exists, the Church of Rome cannot but be the Church"); *Religious Persecution in the Sixteenth Century* (1936); *Noble Castle* (1941) ("It is common in certain circles to ascribe the growth of the Christian Church entirely to the genius of St. Paul.... Naturally enough I have no wish at all to quarrel with those who exalt either the genius or the common-sense of St. Paul. But, if the critic tells us that the Roman world accepted Christianity because of St. Paul, we have the right to push the question a stage further back, and ask, 'What can possibly have induced St. Paul to accept it?' The higher the abilities of St. Paul are rated, the less likely it clearly is that his reason for acceptance would be a trivial one. Now we know about St. Paul that he had no preliminary bias in favor of Christianity. His preliminary bias was all the other way. As a pious Jew, he was shocked by the

appalling blasphemy of the Christian claims, as he thought them at the time when he believed them false. We know also that he had every opportunity of investigating the Christian claims, and every motive for exposing their falsity, were it possible to do so. He was in Jerusalem. A short walk would take him to see for himself the site of the Empty Tomb. He had facilities for cross-questioning any who put forward the Christian claims, and we are told that he used those facilities to the full.

In later days, when he was meditating the acceptance of the Christian faith, it is not to be believed that he did not return to the attack and question and cross-question all the Christian witnesses, determined not to make his submission until utterly convinced that their story was irrefutable. Both in the last stages of skepticism, and on the first flush of penitent love, he must necessarily have demanded of those who were now to be his colleagues that they recount to him every detail of their relations with the Master. What could have convinced him of the truth of the claims save only their truth?"); *Quality or Inequality* (1944); *Fossett's Memory* (1944); *Death of a Gentleman* (1945); *Letters to a Sister* (1947) (the last three texts form the Fossett trilogy, a series of novels reflecting on religious issues); *History of Britain in Modern Times, 1688–1939* (1946); *Evelyn Waugh* (1954); *G. K. Chesterton* (1954); *Along the Road to Frome* (1958) ("The attraction to me [of the Church] was predominantly that of a society which had been, as it seemed to me, the sustainer of civilization throughout the nations and throughout the ages.... If Christ was God and founded a Church, it was of the very essence of that Church that it should be One. *Scindi non potest.* The weakness of a branch-theory of the Church is that it says that the one, true, holy, and apostolic Catholic Church, the seat of all truth and the channel of all revelation, consists of three branches, each of which gives an account of itself radically different from what, on the branch-theory, must be the true account"); *St. Thomas More* (1961); *The Papacy* (1964); *A History of the Jesuits* (1968); *Holy Places* (1969); *Newman and the Modern World* (1970); *The Seven Ages* (1974); Patrick Allitt, *Catholic Converts: British and American Intellectuals Turn to Rome* (1997) *passim*; Joseph Pearce, *Literary Converts* (1999) *passim*; *DNB*.

Holman, George – gentleman; b. 1630, Warkworth Castle, Northamptonshire; d. 19 May 1698; from the time of his conversion, his home became a refuge for persecuted priests and neighboring Catholics; inherited several large estates; remarkable for his charities; his wife, Lady Anastasia (d. 1719), daughter of William Howard, Viscount Stafford, one of most well-known victims of Oates Plot in 1680, continued the good works for many years; three eminent Catholics had links with Warkworth, John Gother (see above), chaplain there, Bishop Challoner (see above), son of the housekeeper at Warkworth, and Alban Butler, who was indebted to Warkworth for most of his education; see *Gillow*, Vol. III, p.358.

Holmès, Augusta Mary Anne (*née* Holmes) – musical composer; b. 16 December 1847, rue de Berri, Paris; c. 1902 (Dominican friary church in Faubourg St Honoré, Paris); d. 28 January 1903, Versailles, France; of Irish parentage; brought up in Versailles; attracted attention as a piano prodigy and singer of French songs of her own composition; pupil of César Franck; in 1879 she became a French citizen, and thenceforth wrote her name as Holmès; wrote several symphonies, symphonic poems (notably *Irlande* (1882)), operas, and a large number of songs; was for many years the mistress of the novelist Catulle Mendès (1841–1909), husband of Judith Gautier, French supporter of Wagner; with him she had three daughters; was a theosophist for a time and later a spiritualist before finally becoming a Catholic; buried in St. Louis cemetery, Versailles; see *Grove Music Online*; *DNB*.

Holtby, Richard, SJ (alias Andrew Ducket, Robert North, and Richard Fetherston) – priest; b. 1552, Fryton, Yorkshire; c. August 1577, Douai; d. between 15 and 25 May 1640, Durham district; studied at Cambridge, then Oxford; in 1577 went to the English College, Douai, where he was received into the Catholic Church; ordained priest at Cambrai 29 March 1578; in 1579 went on the English mission where he worked successfully in Yorkshire; in 1581 visited by St. Edmund Campion (see above) and found Campion a suitable place where he could write the *Rationes Decem*); felt he needed more expertise on theological controversy and entered the Society of Jesus in Paris in 1582; Superior of Scots College at Pont-à-Mousson, when he was one of few survivors of the plague; sent to England in 1588/9 and worked in the north again from 1590 until his death; great apostolate to secular clergy and lay people; wrote no controversy, but admired the controversial writings of Robert Persons (see below); made many hiding places and used many aliases; on the martyrdom of Henry Garnet (see above) in 1606, he became Superior of the Jesuits on the English mission; very clever in evading capture and was never apprehended or imprisoned despite ceaseless activity; see *Gillow*, Vol. III, p.366; *DNB*.

Hone, Eva Sydney ("Evie") – artist and craftswoman; b. 22 April 1894, Roebuck Grove, County Dublin; c. 1937; d. 13

March 1955 (during Mass); severely disabled as result of fall in 1905 whilst decorating local church for Easter; grew up to be devout Anglican; studied art in London, Italy, France and Spain; joined Anglican Community of the Epiphany in Truro, Cornwall, but resumed her art studies a year later; her lifelong friend and fellow painter was Mainie Jellett (although not a Catholic, the latter considered this an absolutely essential step, since Evie Hone's warm and passionate nature demanded the mysticism which Catholicism provided); disregarded perspective in favor of strictly two-dimensional surface; developed from abstract art to religious art, influenced by Rouault; became one of greatest stained glass artists, doing windows in many churches, especially Jesuit ones; formed link between early medieval glass painters and modernism; buried at St. Maelruan's church, Tallaght, Rathfarnham, near Dublin; see Derek Hill, "Evie Hone," *The Month*, March 1950; Paul Hurley, SVD, "Evie Hone (1894–1955)," *Catholic Life*, March 2005, p.52; *Grove Art Online*; *DNB* ("They found direct parallels between the forms and construction of early Christian art and cubism in what Hone described as 'a direction to the spirit to contemplate the Divine Author of the rhythm and form of all created life by a composition of form and color, by a circular movement symbolic of eternity, by a sublimity of form, by simplicity and severity of color'").

Hooke, Nathaniel, Jacobite first Baron Hooke – Jacobite politician; b. 1664, Corballis, County Meath; c. 1688; d. 25 October 1738, France; brought up a Puritan; left Glasgow University and Cambridge University without taking a degree; in 1685 landed with Duke of Monmouth at Lyme Regis, acting as his independent private chaplain; later became loyal servant of James II and

converted to the Catholic faith; after James II's abdication, committed to the Tower of London, but released in 1690; served in the Jacobite army at the battle of the Boyne; entered the French service and served with the army; took no active part in the Jacobite rising of 1715; James III appointed him envoy to Prussia in 1718; see *Gillow*, Vol. III, p.372; *DNB*.

Hope, Anne (*née* Fulton) – historian and authoress; b. 7 September 1809, Calcutta, India; c. 1846; d. 12 February 1887, The Hermitage, St. Marychurch, near Torquay; daughter of prosperous merchant; brought up in County Antrim, Ireland, and London; much ill health; wife of James Hope (1801–1841), famous physician and cardiologist; her interest in ecclesiastical history led to conversion; developed close links with the Oratorians, in particular Fr. Dalgairns (see above) who was her guide and main literary counselor; author of *The Conversion of the Teutonic Races*, 2 Vols. (1872), and several books on the lives of the saints; simple, direct style of writing; high ability to sift evidence and assess conflicting narratives; her son, Sir Theodore Hope, financial secretary to Indian government; see *The Early Martyrs* (1858); *The Life of St. Thomas à Becket* (1868); *Franciscan Martyrs in England* (1878); *The First Divorce of Henry VIII* (1894); *Gillow*, Vol. III, p.375; *DNB*.

Hope-Scott (originally Hope), James Robert – parliamentary barrister and author; b. 15 July 1812, Marlow, Buckinghamshire; c. Passion Sunday, 6 April 1851 (received on same occasion as Henry Manning; Charlotte Lockhart-Scott (1828–1858), his first wife and grand-daughter of Sir Walter Scott (1771–1832), was received six weeks later; in 1852 his sister, Louisa Dorothea (1811–1884), and her husband, Lord

Henry Kerr (1800–1882), became Catholics); d. 29 April 1873, 7 Hyde Park Place, London; third son of General Sir Alexander Hope (1769–1837), founder and first governor of Royal Military College, Sandhurst; educated at Eton and Christ Church, Oxford; Fellow and first Bursar of Merton College, Oxford; close and long friendships with Gladstone, Manning, Newman and Bishop Grant of Southwark; Chancellor of Diocese of Salisbury; called to the bar where specialized in railway legislation, making great fortune; closely involved in the Tractarian movement and became Newman's confidant (when still Protestant he told Newman, then still sure that he would never become a Catholic: "Ah Newman, there may be abuses and scandals in Rome, but there is a higher region and wider views in the governing part"); Gorham trial and judgment of 1849–1850 (see the entry for William Maskell) and Newman's lectures on *Difficulties of Anglicans* in 1850 brought his religious crisis to a head leading to conversion; much correspondence with Newman before conversion; assumed name of Hope-Scott on inheriting Sir Walter Scott's home, Abbotsford, in 1853; in 1855 he conducted negotiations which ended in Newman's accepting the rectorship of the Catholic University of Ireland; Newman constantly turned to him for advice and "ask Hope" was a proverb; great benefactor to several Scottish Catholic missions, convents, schools and church buildings (from 1860 onwards he spent £40,000 in hidden charity) and in Ireland; second wife Lady Victoria Fitzalan Howard (d. December 1870), daughter of Henry Granville, fourteenth Duke of Norfolk; father, by his second wife, of Josephine Mary Ward (1864–1932), Catholic novelist and mother of Maisie Ward (1889–1975), Catholic writer and publisher; both of his wives died in childbirth (in case of first wife, Charlotte

(d. 20 October 1858), daughter born to her died two weeks after and a year old son a week later); strikingly handsome but reserved; practiced much private piety; Newman preached at requiem at Farm Street, London; buried at St. Margaret's convent, Edinburgh; see R. Ornsby, *The Memoirs of James Robert Hope-Scott of Abbotsford, D.C.L., Q.C.*, 2 Vols. (1884); Madeleine Beard, *Faith and Fortune* (1997), pp.155–159 ("It was not the state of the Church of England which had prompted him to leave, but a review of the chain of events which led up to the Reformation. 'I can safely say that I left her because I was convinced that she never from the Reformation downwards, had been a true Church'"); Stanley L. Jaki, *Newman to Converts: An Existential Ecclesiology* (2001), Ch. 4 ("Newman explained: 'Surely, enough has been written – all the writing in the world would not destroy the necessity of faith – if all were made clear to reason, where would be the exercise of faith? The simple question is whether *enough* has been done to *reduce* the difficulties so far as to hinder them absolutely blocking up the way, or excluding those direct and large arguments on which the reasonableness of faith is built.' Hope could not ignore the point. In Newman's most considered view it was useless for him to engage in further studies. Rather he should pray and then act. Newman said it sweetly, but peremptorily, because the duty to act was fundamental and all had to comply with it"); *Gillow*, Vol. IV, p.377; *Catholic Encyclopedia*; *DNB*.

Hopes, Bishop Alan Stephen – bishop; b. 14 March 1944, Oxford; c. December 1994; brought up as a High Anglican; formerly Anglo-Catholic minister for 27 years; ordained Catholic priest in 1995; consecrated Auxiliary Bishop of Westminster in 2003; see "I think your heart has already become Catholic," *Catholic Herald*,

22 July 2005 ("There were voices in the Church of England which, while desiring unity as a goal, held other desires to be equally important…. This caused me some real misgivings. How did the Church of England make its decisions, some of which seemed to go against the teaching that I knew I shared with the Catholic Church? How could it be right that decisions about doctrine, for instance, were made by a vote in the General Synod? I recognized a lack of Magisterium, which for me, at least, was vital. Often scripture and tradition were dismissed, by some, as outmoded. Decisions of the Lambeth Conference which had bound us together as an Anglican family were rejected by some parts of the Anglican Communion. Although it was called a 'Communion,' it was in fact a co-existence…

When the vote for the ordination of women came in 1992, I realized that I must now be where I had always longed to be. At the heart of my decision was the desire to continue to be faithful in the ministry of the priesthood. I believe that God used my Anglican ministry for his good purposes – but it had been based on my understanding of what a priest is and does, rather than that of what the Church believes about priesthood.

My reception into the Catholic Church was a real coming home – and that has brought great peace and consolation. I now know and experience communion – a real unity with the bishop and through him, with all the bishops and the successor of St. Peter, the Holy Father. I now know and experience the authority of the teaching voice of the Catholic Church – a voice which continues to teach both in matters of faith and morals what it has always taught and believed, a prophetic voice in a world caught up in relativism and unbelief ").

Hopkins, Gerard Manley, SJ – priest and poet; b. 28 July 1844, 87 The Grove, Stratford, London; c. 21 October 1866 (received by Newman at the Birmingham Oratory); d. 8 June 1889, 85 St. Stephen's Green, Dublin, Ireland; son of Manley Hopkins, average adjuster in marine insurance; eldest of nine children; brought up in moderately High Church, mainstream Anglicanism; always small and delicate; High Church influences at Oxford, especially Canon H. P. Liddon and Dr. Pusey (reacted against liberalism and Darwinism); close friendship with Robert Bridges and Bridges' schoolboy relative, Digby Dolben (drowned at the age of eighteen); obtained double first in Greats and proclaimed "the star of Balliol"; conversion to the Catholic faith primarily influenced by Newman; joined the Society of Jesus; ordained priest in September 1877; had eleven postings, in four countries, in eight years; Fellow of the Royal University of Ireland; Professor of Classics at the Catholic University College, Dublin; friendship with Coventry Patmore (see below), the poet; on joining the Jesuits he burned his poems, but had previously sent copies of them all to Bridges who later published them after his death; experimented with poetic form, especially with "sprung rhythms"; suffered from regular depression; buried in Jesuit burial plot in Prospect cemetery, Glasnevin, Dublin; see *The Collected Works of Gerard Manley Hopkins* (2006); Rev. Joseph Keating, "Impressions of Father Gerard Hopkins, SJ," *The Month*, July 1909, p.59, August 1909, p.151, September 1909, p.246; Lance Sieveking, *The Eye of the Beholder* (1957); Peter Milward, *Landscape and Inscape* (1975); Bernard Bergonzi, *Gerard Manley Hopkins* (1977) ("[I]n a letter to Ernest Coleridge, Hopkins made an eloquent statement of his beliefs about the Incarnation, culminating in a quasi-Metaphysical paradox or conceit: 'I think that the trivialness of life is, and personally to each one, ought to be seen to be, done away with by the Incarnation – or, I should say the difficulty which the trivialness of life presents ought to be. It is one adorable point of the incredible condescension of the Incarnation (the greatest of which no saint can ever have hoped to realize) that our Lord submitted not only to the pains of life, the fasting, scourging, crucifixion etc. or the insults, as the mocking, blindfolding, spitting etc., but also to the mean and trivial accidents of humanity. It leads one naturally to rhetorical antithesis to think for instance that after making the world He should consent to be taught carpenteering, and, being the eternal reason, to be catechized in the theology of the Rabbis"); Walter J. Ong, SJ, *Hopkins, the Self, and God* (1986); Catherine Phillips (ed), *Gerard Manley Hopkins: Selected Letters* (1990) (Letter to his father, 16 October 1866: "If the question which is the Church of Christ? could only be settled by laborious search, a year and ten years and a lifetime are too little, when the vastness of the subject of theology is taken into account. But God must have made his Church such as to attract and convince the poor and unlearned as well as the learned. And surely it is true, though it will sound pride to say it, that the judgment of one who has seen both sides for a week is better than his who has seen only one for a lifetime. I'm surprised you should say fancy and aesthetic tastes have led me to my present state of mind: these would be satisfied in the Church of England, for bad taste is always meeting one in the accessories of Catholicism. My conversion is due to the following reasons mainly (I have put them down without order) – (i) simple and strict drawn arguments partly my own, partly others, (ii) common sense, (iii) reading the Bible, especially the Holy Gospels, where texts like 'Thou art Peter' (the evasions proposed for this

alone are enough to make one a Catholic) and the manifest position of St. Peter among the Apostles so pursued me that at one time I thought it best to stop thinking of them, (iv) an increasing knowledge of the Catholic system (at first under the form of Tractarianism, later in its genuine place), which only wants to be known in order to be loved – its consolations, its marvelous ideal of holiness, the faith and devotion of its children, its multiplicity, its array of saints and martyrs, its consistency and unity, its glowing prayers, the daring majesty of its claims, etc etc. You speak of the claims of the Church of England, but it is to me the strange thing that the Church of England makes no claims: it is true that Tractarians make them for her and find them faintly or only in a few instances borne out for them by her liturgy, and are strongly assailed for their extravagances while they do it"); Robert Bernard Martin, *Gerard Manley Hopkins: A Very Private Life* (1991); Norman White, *Hopkins: A Literary Biography* (1992) ("There is a tradition among the Jesuits ... that before the final blessing and absolution he was heard two or three times to say 'I am so happy. I am so happy'"); Bernard Bergonzi, *War Poets and Other Subjects* (1999), Ch. 13:, "Hopkins the Englishman" and Ch. 14, "Hopkins, Tradition and the Individual Talent"; Ian Ker, *The Catholic Revival in English Literature, 1845–1961* (2003), Ch. 2, "From Oxford to Liverpool: The Conversion and Poetry of Gerard Manley Hopkins"; Jill Muller, *Gerard Manley Hopkins and Victorian Catholicism: A Heart in Hiding* (2003); Aidan Nichols, OP, *Hopkins: Theologian's Poet* (2006); "Newman, Manning and Their Age," *Saint Austin Review*, September/ October 2008 (special issue devoted to Newman, Manning and Hopkins); Gerry Burns, "Converts to Catholicism: Gerard Manley Hopkins," *Catholic Life*, October

2009, p.68; Joseph Pearce, *Literary Converts* (1999) *passim*; *DNB*.

Horne, (Percy) Ethelbert, OSB – priest and writer; b. 1858; c. 1874; d. 1952; ordained to the priesthood in 1889; Benedictine monk at Downside Abbey, Somerset; also archaeologist; see *Reasons for Being a Catholic* (1945) ("Remember that Christ was *God*. As such He could look into the future, and He could see what men would say about His religion after He had gone back to Heaven. He knew that they could not teach by themselves *with certainty*, and that as time went on they would be at a loss to know *exactly* what were the doctrines of the religion which He founded. Also, being God, He had infinite power, and so could design any sort of religion He liked, and could make any kind of safeguards to prevent it from falling into error or decaying.

Christ having infinite knowledge and infinite power, what sort of a religion would you expect Him to found? Is it not more probable that He left 'a Church' – that is, a teaching body that cannot teach wrong – to instruct you, than that He left a book out of which you were to help yourself?"); *Relics of Popery* (1946); *Catholic Customs in the Church* (1935); *Catholic Customs in the Home* (1935).

Hough, Stephen – classical pianist, composer and writer; b. 22 November 1961, Heswall, Wirral Peninsular; c. 1980; brought up as a Methodist, but Evangelical in his teens; began piano lessons at the age of five; finalist in BBC "Young Musician of the Year" competition in 1978, winning the piano section; master's degree from the Juilliard School; many recordings; composer of, for example, masses (*Missa Mirabilis*, and *Mass of Innocence and Experience*); and a cello concerto; visiting Professor of piano at the Royal College of Music,

London; became Australian citizen in 2005; has written about his homosexuality and its relationship with his music and religion; see "An Equal Music," *The Tablet*, 29 April 2006; *The Bible as Prayer: A Handbook for Lectio Divina* (2007); "Heavens Above," *The Tablet*, 21 April 2007; "Grace Notes for Advent," *The Tablet*, November-December 2008.

Houghton, Bryan Richard Staples – priest and writer; b. 2 April 1911, Dublin; c. 1934; d. 19 November 1992, Montelimar, France; father professional soldier, mother wealthy; from an Anglican family; brought up in Europe, mainly in France and Germany until going to Stowe school at thirteen; took first-class degree in Modern History at Christ Church College, Oxford; came under the influence at Oxford of Fr. Martin D'Arcy, SJ, who subsequently became a firm friend; worked as a banker in Paris until his mother's death in 1936; converted after a visit to the Soviet Union where he was appalled by the Communists' cruelty to minorities; studied for the priesthood at the English College, Rome; ordained priest 30 March 1940; of independent means; served in the diocese of Northampton for twenty-eight years, notably at Bury St. Edmunds; opposed theological modernism; declined to acknowledge the orthodoxy of Teilhard de Chardin when so asked by the Secretary of the Higher Studies Conference of the English hierarchy; put much of his own money into Catholic education; believed that the liturgical changes after the Second Vatican Council were ill-advised and resigned his parish on the introduction of the *Novus Ordo Missae*; retired to Viviers on the edge of Provence, France, where he took advantage of papal indult to say the old rite of Mass; opposed to the Lefebvrist schism ("You do not save the Faith by destroying the Church"); close friend from schooldays of E. J. Oliver (see below); consummate English gentleman; wrote many articles defending the traditional faith; see *Saint Edmund: King and Martyr* (1970); *Mitre and Crook* (1979) (analysis, set out in the form of a novel, of problems in the Church since the Second Vatican Council); "Irreligion, Part I and II" *Christian Order* (1983), pp.267 and 375 ("The trouble with truth is that inevitably it is both exclusive and universal. It is truth which is 'catholic' and the term is applied to Christianity merely because it claims to be true. If, however, religion is not thought of as being true, it automatically becomes tolerant and oecumenical. This, indeed, was the primary characteristic of pre-Christian religions: they were oecumenical to the point of building the Pantheon and sufficiently tolerant to erect altars to the Unknown God. The one exception was Judaism, which claimed precisely to worship the 'true' God. But even it was persecuted primarily because of the exclusiveness of the race rather than because of the exclusiveness of truth – an idea incomprehensible to the pre-Christian in matters of religion. Hence the extraordinary fact that purely religious persecutions and wars of religion are post-Christian phenomena. As Jesus said: 'Do not imagine that I have come to bring peace to the earth; I have come to bring a sword, not peace' (Mt. 10:34). No prophecy has ever been more clearly or more constantly fulfilled"); *Judith's Marriage* (1987) (fictional study of the modern Church) ("You told me, girl, that you had bought a very beautiful crucifix and you wanted to know what it was about. Very well, it is proof of the truth of Christianity. In all other religions man is more noble than God. God eternally enjoys the beatitude of His own infinite perfection, yet he expects miserable creatures to love him disinterestedly and to suffer nobly. Alone in Christianity is this not so.

God becomes incarnate precisely to do as man what He cannot do as God: suffer. The personality of the man who is dying on the cross is the personality of God. He does not ask you to do what He is unwilling to do Himself. Indeed your suffering nobly borne, your disinterested love are justified by His. Nothing is more terrible than unrequited love; and no love goes more unrequited than that of God"); *Pretre Rejeté* (1999); R. Michael McGrade, "Father Houghton, Rejected Priest," http://unavoce.org/uva-archive.

Houldsworth, Mrs. Henry – Catholic laywoman; c. 1 July 1872 (received by Newman); of Craigforth, Stirling, Scotland; mother of several children and an ailing husband hostile to the Catholic Church; friend of Catherine Froude (see above); much correspondence with Newman before her conversion, in particular on question of the need for evidence in relation to religious belief; see Stanley L. Jaki, *Newman to Converts: An Existential Ecclesiology* (2001), Ch. 19 ("[Newman wrote regarding Mrs. Houldsworth]: 'She *must* take *something* on faith. The question is whether she has enough evidence in order to make it her duty to put away questions she cannot answer to her satisfaction, as mere difficulties. If she inquired in the New Testament in the same minute way, she would not believe in the Bible, if into the proofs of God, the bare existence of evil would hinder her from believing in Him'.... Newman took up the matter that in this life man, through God's will, had to be satisfied with probabilities, in much of his reasoning.... [H]e referred to ... Bishop Thompson, who wrote: 'One property of highly probable judgments is that the favorable evidence for them, not preponderates, but utterly expels the unfavorable. Adverse arguments must, when we have once made up our minds, be ignored entirely. If a jury find a man guilty, because ten credible witnesses have sworn against him, and one or two for him, they consider that the testimony of the ten annihilates that of the two.' Newman's comment was weighty: 'This is a law of the human mind -, that is, the will of God'").

Houselander, (Frances) Caryll – writer; b. 29 October 1901; c. 1907 (received with her sister, though practice of the faith did not begin until later; lapsed, but reverted in 1925; mother, Gertrude, received subsequently); d. 12 October 1954; parents separated permanently when she was nine; plagued by ill-health from childhood; schooling never completed; in mid-teens abandoned practice of Catholicism for several years and explored many different religions; returned to the Church in 1925; conversion greatly influenced by George Spencer Bower, KC, an agnostic; writing career began in late 1920s; contributor to *The Children's Messenger* and *The Messenger of the Sacred Heart*; poet and mystic, who wrote several books on spiritual issues; also painter and woodcarver; friend of Eric Strauss (see below); see *This War is the Passion* (1941), *The Reed of God* (1944), *The Passion of the Infant Christ* (1949); *Guilt* (1952); *A Rocking-Horse Catholic* (1955) ("It was to Smokey [George Spencer Bower KC] that my mother turned for advice, and he who convinced her that if Jesus Christ was really God, and if he founded a Church, it was absolutely certain that this Church was none other than the Roman Catholic Church. He examined the evidence for this with the searching methods of an experienced lawyer, convincing my mother of the integrity of the witnesses, the four evangelists. Only absolutely honest witnesses determined to give the facts, he said, would have recorded the words of Christ on the Cross, 'My God, my God,

why hast thou forsaken me?' – words which, Smoky used to say, could easily have 'lost the cause' for the divinity of Christ. He stressed the importance of the fact that the same honest witnesses told the story of the Resurrection, and of the forty days on earth of the Risen Christ.

There were two other points which Smoky was fond of repeating (and all the arguments he put forward to my mother, he put to me years later in my adolescence). The first of these points was that unless the visible Church was divine, and was really protected by the Holy Ghost, it could not have survived all the corruption that had assailed it in the course of history, through its own members. He gave it as his opinion that the Church's survival, with the absolute purity of its doctrine, was the strongest argument that existed for the divinity of Christ.

His second favorite point was the beauty and the all-inclusiveness of Catholicism. He used to say that it was the only religion in the world that includes all that is beautiful and good in every other, and all the poetry that is innate in the human race"); Maisie Ward, *Caryll Houselander: That Divine Eccentric* (1962); Maisie Ward (ed), *The Letters of Caryll Houselander* (1965) (letter to Archie Campbell-Murdoch, 13 September 1943: "The way I look upon the abuses and so on which inevitably crop up in the visible Church is that they are necessary, because they are the Passion. You see, the Church *is Christ*, and therefore Christ's Passion must go on in the Church. Tragic, even frightening though it is, we know Christ better with the kiss of Judas on His face. But how to stand, what could be the bleak misery of that, and to know the glory in it as well as the tragedy? There is a problem, and if you don't solve it, it breaks you.

I am sure the solution is to abandon yourself to the contemplation of the love and beauty of God, to the mystery of the

Trinity, to the unutterable bliss of the indwelling of the Holy Spirit; because if you do allow your soul to be swept along on this great storm-wind of love, like the bird with spread wings, you will find that one day you can look upon the face of the Passion, on what is ugly and confusing in the world, without faltering and with an increase of compassion for God and man"); Joyce Kemp, *The Spiritual Path of Caryll Houselander* (2001); Leonie Caldecott, "Caryll Houselander," in Joanna Bogle (ed), *English Catholic Heroines* (2009), p.282 ("Another paradox of Caryll's is that whilst she was able to write sublime prose on Our Lord, his mother and the saints, she herself was far from being in some plaster-cast mode of holiness. For most of her life Caryll smoked like a chimney; she was apt to swear and she liked a drink").

Howard, Anne, Countess of Arundel (*née* Dacre) – noblewoman and priest-harborer; b. 1 March 1557, Carlisle; c. 1583 (received by a Marian priest; her half sister, Margaret, also received at this time; her husband converted in 1584); d. 13 April 1630, Sifnel, Shropshire; daughter of Thomas Dacre, fourth Lord Dacre (1526?-1566); mother and grandmother (Lady Mounteagle) Catholics, and she was influenced by the latter and by her tutor, Gregory Martin, who was wholly Catholic in his judgment; wife of St. Philip Howard, Earl of Arundel (1557–1595) (see below); conversion resulted from reading a book on the dangers of schism (probably *Treatise of Schism* by Gregory Martin, then teaching Scripture at the English College, Douai); after husband's death in the Tower in 1595 dedicated herself to her religious duties, education of children, and acts of charity; founded English College of the Society of Jesus in Ghent in 1622; housed many priests, including St. Robert Southwell, later martyred; close

friend of Mary Queen of Scots; her son, Thomas, apostatized, but later returned to the Catholic faith, and his son, Viscount Stafford, died for the profession of his Catholic faith at the time of the Oates Plot; buried in Fitzalan Chapel, Arundel Castle; see *Gillow*, Vol. I, p.65; *DNB*.

Howard, Esme William, first Baron Howard of Penrith – diplomat; b. 15 September 1863, Greystoke Castle, Cumberland; c. 1898 (received in St. Dominic's Chapel, Port of Spain Cathedral, Trinidad; "from that day I can say that, although the first exaltation passed away in the hurly-burly of terrestrial occupations such as rubber-planting or diplomatic work, I have never looked back. Indeed, the security in the protection of mother Church has grown from year to year"); d. 1 August 1939, Ridgecoombe, Hindhead, Surrey; youngest son of Henry Howard (1802–1875); of Greystoke Castle and Thornbury Castle, Gloucestershire; brought up as an Anglican, assistant private secretary to his brother-in-law, Earl of Carnarvon, Lord Lieutenant of Ireland; third secretary at embassy in Rome; then private secretary to ambassador in Berlin; left diplomatic service in 1892; explorer; rubber planter in Trinidad and Tobago; conversion influenced by Mgr. Merry del Val; fought in the Boer War (was captured and escaped); married an Italian Catholic noblewoman, Donna (Maria) Isabella Giovanna Teresa Gioacchina Giustiniani-Bandini (1867–1963) of a noble Scottish family that went into exile with the Stuart kings; returned to diplomacy, becoming honorary second secretary at embassy in Rome 1903; then consul-general for Crete 1903–1906; counselor in Washington embassy 1906–1908; consul-general in Hungary 1908–1911; minister to Switzerland 1911–1913; minister in Sweden 1913–1918; member of British delegation to the Paris peace conference 1919; ambassador in Madrid 1919–1924; ambassador in Washington 1924–1930; one of Britain's greatest diplomats of twentieth century; see *Theatre of Life: Life Seen from the Pit, 1863–1905* (1935) ("As soon as ... I had gone over all the well known texts in support of the doctrine of the real Body and Blood of Our Lord actually being in the bread and wine of the Eucharist in accordance with His promise to remain with His Church on earth for ever; after I had studied the sacrifice of the Mass and seen how this differed from the purely human services of other churches, I felt that this was the loadstone that would draw me irresistibly into the arms of the Church. Surely nothing so spiritual and at the same time so genuinely tangible could have been 'invented' by any mere man. Our Lord's words in regard to this seemed to me perfectly clear, and their meaning not open to doubt. Those who would not accept them in their obvious significance He allowed to leave Him without any word of explanation in a Protestant sense. In fact, those disciples who left Him at Capharnaum over this question and 'walked no more with Him' became for me the first Protestants

It might be a hard saying indeed but what a marvelous help and support when once accepted with mind and heart and soul. It is quite incredible that any mere man should have conceived so amazing a thing as this, so utterly simple and yet so utterly divine. For this reason, if for no other, it appeared to me to bear the stamp of divine truth which to deny was to deprive oneself of the greatest assistance which the Savior left behind him on earth for men"); *Theatre of Life: Life Seen from the Stalls, 1905–1936* (1936) ("It would seem ... that the central question at issue between the Catholic and the 'Reformed' faith resolves itself into the one simple query: Are we to believe

what Christ said or not, and, if we believe Him to be what He declared Himself to be, namely the Son of God, how can we suppose it possible for Him to speak anything contrary to the truth or to deceive those whom He was teaching the Way of Life"); "No Other Way," in John A. O'Brien, *Where Dwellest Thou?* (1956), p.175 ("Had I remembered Newman's *Apologia pro vita sua* I should have quoted perhaps one sentence of his when a controversialist declared that Dr. Arnold vouched for his interpretation: 'Dr. Arnold vouches for his interpretation, but who vouches for Dr. Arnold?' There is the crux of Protestantism. Who vouches for Luther, for Zwingli, for Calvin, for John Knox, for Cranmer, for Parker, or for any of the other leaders of Protestant thought?...

One day I asked how I was to know that the Church differed from other self-styled teachers of revealed as opposed to natural Law. [Mgr. Merry del Val] asked me if I believed Christ to be the Son of God, and I declared I did because He spoke as no man had ever spoken and because He clearly taught that He was the Son of God. 'Then,' he said, 'you must believe Him to be infallible and no word of His can have been spoken in error.' I replied that of course I believed that. And then we proceeded to go through the various texts of the New Testament on which the Papal claims for the infallibility of the Church, not only at that time but for the future, are based"); B. J. C. McKercher, *Esme Howard: A Diplomatic Biography* (1989); Anon, "Esme William, Baron Howard of Penrith," *Catholic Life*, December 2002, p.27; *DNB*.

Howard, Mary of the Holy Cross – abbess; b. 28 December 1653, Berkshire; d. 21 March 1735, Rouen, France; brought up Protestant in wealthy family; to escape the admiration of Charles II she went away to Paris; placed in Benedictine convent of Val de Grace to learn French; holy life of nuns made strong impression upon her and very soon she was received into the Church; admitted into the English convent of Poor Clares at Rouen; elected Abbess in 1702; governed with great judgment and wisdom; wrote spiritual and devotional books; great suffering in her last ten years; see *Gillow*, Vol. III, p.435; *Catholic Encyclopedia*.

Howard, Saint Philip, thirteenth Earl of Arundel – magnate and martyr; b. 28 June 1557, Arundel House, The Strand, London; c. 30 September 1584 (received at Arundel Castle by Fr. William Weston, SJ); d. 15 October 1595, Tower of London; only child of Thomas Howard, fourth Duke of Norfolk (1538–1572) and Mary Howard, (*née* Fitzalan) (1539/40–1557) (died from complications arising from the labor), daughter of Henry Fitzalan, twelfth Earl of Arundel (1512–1580); from a family of great wealth and property; his father richest man in England; named after Philip II of Spain, his godfather; brought up in Howard House, which used to be the London Charterhouse, home of the Carthusian martyrs; father conformed to the new religion, but Lady Mounteagle, mother of father's third wife, who came to care for the children, was loyal to the old religion; as a boy he showed little concern for religion; father executed for treason 2 June 1572; married to Anne Howard (*née* Dacre) (see above); after Cambridge University, took up residence at court and led a life of dissipation, neglecting his wife; became deeply in debt and forced to leave court in disgrace, but then succeeded to Earldom of Arundel in 1580, becoming premier Earl in England; grew closer to his wife and when she converted, he drew attention to himself by not criticizing her; had begun favoring the Catholic faith himself after attending disputations of Edmund Campion (see above) with Protestant divines in August 1581 and his trial in November; did not tell the queen of his later conversion; very devout after his conversion; fearing arrest he set out from Lymington, Hampshire for the Continent in April 1585, but ship boarded in Channel; taken to the Tower; charged with reconciliation with the Catholic Church, attempting to flee from kingdom without the queen's permission, and correspondence with Cardinal Allen; fined and imprisoned at queen's pleasure; spent his time (eleven years) in the Tower in pious exercises and writing and translating spiritual works (never saw his wife and son again); St. Robert Southwell, SJ, the martyr, sent him spiritual letters, later published as *An Epistle of Comfort* (the two men never met); later able to hear Mass said by an imprisoned priest, Fr. William Bennett; charged with asking for prayers and Fr. Bennett for a Mass for the success of the Spanish fleet (in reality prayers were to ward off the rumored massacre of Catholics); tried in Westminster Hall in 1589 (Fr. Bennett testified against him); condemned to death, but sentence never carried out; continued his prayer life and fasting, and died peacefully; buried in his father's grave in chapel of St. Peter ad Vincula in the Tower (later his remains were taken in 1624 by his wife to West Horsley, Surrey, then on to Arundel Castle, finally, in 1971, to the Catholic Cathedral in Arundel); see A. C. Kerr, *The Life of the Venerable Philip Howard, Earl of Arundel and Surrey* (1926); Margaret Waugh, *Blessed Philip Howard, Courtier and Martyr* (1961); John Martin Robinson, *The Dukes of Norfolk; A Quincentennial History* (1982); Philip Caraman, SJ, *St. Philip Howard* (1985) ("Campion proclaimed himself 'a man dead to the world who traveled only for souls.' In that moment Philip saw himself for what he himself was, a man devoted to worthless pleasure-seeking"); *DNB* ("Catholics generally celebrate Arundel for his behavior while a prisoner and the ultimate sacrifice he made for his religious beliefs. Much is made by his admirers of the Latin inscription carved into the wall of his octagonal room in the Tower, 'quanto plus afflictionis pro Christo in hoc saeculo, tanto plus gloriae cum Christo in futuro' ('the more affliction we endure for Christ in this world, the more glory we shall obtain with Christ in the next')").

Howitt, Mary (*née* Botham) – writer and translator; b. 12 March 1799, Coleford, Gloucestershire; c. 26 May 1882 (daughter, Margaret, received in 1880); d. 30 January 1888, via Gregoriana, Rome; brought up according to strict Quaker principles; wife of William Howitt (1792–1879), Quaker poet and author; wrote many poems; published translations of Fredrika Bremer and Hans Andersen, and successful children's books; she and her husband resigned from Quakers in 1847; phases of Unitarianism and spiritualism, followed by attendance at Church of England services; always interested in Catholics, seeing them as faithful guardians of medieval Christianity and showed much affection for the old religion in her poetry; moved around England and Europe, settling in Rome; the Penny Catechism her constant companion; buried by special permission beside husband in Monte Testaccio Protestant cemetery, Rome; see Margaret Howitt (ed.), *Mary Howitt: An Autobiography*, 2 Vols. (1889); James Britten, *Mary Howitt* (1895) ("In the winter of 1879–80 [she] read *All For Jesus* by Father Faber.... She met with the following passage...: 'One of the most divine and striking characteristics of the Catholic religion is the Commun-

ion of Saints, the way in which everything belongs to everybody, and nobody has any spiritual property of his own. The merits and satisfactions of our dear Lord, the joys and woes of Mary, the patience of the martyrs, the perseverance of confessors, and the purity of virgins, they all belong to all of us. Just as the blood circulates from and to the heart all over the body, so in the Church there is no division or separation. Heaven, purgatory and earth, it is all one body.... We talk of the other world, as if it was a city we were familiar with from long residence; just as we might talk of Paris, Brussels or Berlin. We are not stopped by death. Sight is nothing to us; we go beyond it as calmly as possible. We are not separated from our dead. We know the Saints a great deal better than if we had lived with them upon earth. We talk to the Angels in their different choirs as if they were, as they are, our brothers in Christ. We use beads, medals, crucifixes, holy water, indulgences, sacraments, sacrifices, for all this, as naturally as pen, ink and paper, or axe and saw, or spade and rake, for our earthly work. We have no sort of distrust about the matter. We are all one household and there is an end of it ...' Human words are powerless to describe the love and thanksgiving which filled Mary Howitt's soul by this revelation of the Catholic Church"); *DNB*.

Huddleston (alias Dormer and Shirley), John, SJ – priest; b. 27 December 1636, Clavering, Essex; d. 16 January 1700, London; uncertain parentage; sent to St. Omer's College in 1649, where received into the Church; admitted into English College, Rome, in 1655; then to Jesuit novitiate in Bonn in 1656; ordained in 1669; served on the English mission in Lincolnshire from 1673; James II made him one of royal preachers at the court of St. James; at the outbreak of the Revolution in 1688 he fled to the Continent and in 1689 was appointed rector of college at Liège, though replaced in 1691; returned to the English mission, covering London district; see *Gillow*, Vol. III, p.460; *DNB*.

Huddleston (alias Parkinson), Richard, OSB – priest; b. 1583, at Farington Hall, Leyland, Lancashire; d. 26 November 1655, Stockeld Park, Ilkley, Yorkshire, seat of the Middletons; attended the Established Church with his father, who had outwardly conformed under coercion; from 1594 studied for several years at Grange-over-Sands under a Catholic teacher, Bl. Thomas Sommers (later a priest on the English mission, who was hanged, drawn and quartered at Tyburn, 10 December 1610); whilst there he often visited a relative, Francis Duckett, a staunch Catholic and there was reconciled to the Church by Fr. William Smith, a devout priest, who had often been imprisoned and exiled; set off for St. Omer's College, but after many adventures arrived at Douai; sent to English College, Rome, in 1601; later returned to Douai College where ordained priest in 1607; sent to the English mission in 1608; later returned to Italy and joined the Benedictine Order at the monastery of Monte Cassino; in 1619 returned to the English mission; resided at Farington Hall, where he had particular success in reconciling aristocratic families to the Church; later worked in Yorkshire; fine controversialist and preacher; see *Short and Plain Way to the Faith and Church* (published in 1688 by his nephew, John Huddleston, OSB, 1608–1698); this book was influential in the conversion of King Charles II (see above) who was received into the Church on his deathbed by the nephew); *Gillow*, Vol. III, p.466 ("Speaking of his uncle's treatise in his address to the reader, Fr. John Huddleston says – 'that (God so ordaining) it became an occasional instrument

towards the conversion of our late Sovereign Lord King Charles II to the faith and unity of the Catholic Church.' When Charles was hiding in Mr. Whitgreave's house at Moseley he entertained himself with perusing the MS of Fr. Richard's treatise, which lay on the table of his nephew, who was then chaplain at Moseley Court. Charles seriously considered it, and, after mature deliberation, said, 'I have not seen anything more plain and clear upon this subject. The arguments here drawn from succession are so conclusive, I do not conceive how they can be denied'"); *DNB*.

Hudleston, Dom Roger, OSB (born Gilbert) – priest; b. 27 December 1874, Hutton John, Penrith, Cumberland; c. 8 January 1896 (received by Fr. Luke Rivington; his first communion was made in Rome from the hands of Pope Leo XIII); d. 5 August 1936, Downside Abbey, Somerset; went to Keble College, Oxford, but left after a year, was received into the Church and joined the Benedictine community at Downside; spent time at Fort Augustus, Belmont, and the College of St. Anselm in Rome; returned to Downside and was ordained priest 24 September 1904; secretary to Abbot Chapman (see above) and editor of the *Downside Review*; chaplain to the Forces in Salonika in 1918; wrote and edited works, in particular on ascetic theology, the spiritual life, and prayer; related to Fr. Richard Huddleston (see above) and to his famous nephew, Fr. John Huddleston, who reconciled Charles II (see above) to the Church on his deathbed; see *The Duty of Prayer* (1915); *God's Will in Death* (1917); *God's Will in Happiness* (1917); *God's Will in Suffering* (1917); *Why Must I Pray?* (1922); *Mystic Voices* (1923); *My Cousin Philip* (1924) (the last two are novels written under the name of Roger Pater); Dom Hugh Connolly, "Obituary," *Downside Review*, October 1936, p.566.

Hull, Ernest Reginald, SJ – priest; b. 1863; c. 1882; d. 1952; worked for the Society of Jesus in India; author and editor of *The Bombay Catholic Examiner*; see *What the Catholic Church Is and What She Teaches* (1902) ("In the course of the answer [to the question: *What is the Catholic Church?*] five important facts ... come to light:

First fact. The Protestant churches came into existence some 400 years ago by separating themselves from a much older Church, and by adopting the Bible as their only Rule of Faith.

Second fact. They have never been able to form one corporate body such as the Church of Christ *ought* to be, since they cannot find one creed and code of worship to which they can all subscribe – though even if they could, this would not ensure that they were the Church of Christ, since they repudiate any Christ-founded authority.

Third fact. The older Church from which they broke away is the Roman Catholic Church (which can be traced back right to the time of the Apostles) with its bishops appointed by the Apostles to carry on their work – which they have been doing ever since.

Fourth fact. Their powers of ruling and teaching are those conferred by Christ on the Apostles, and passed on by them to their successors; and the validity of their acts rests entirely on the promises of Christ – promises which are to hold good until the end of the world.

Fifth fact. The identity of the Church of Christ in the time of the Apostles with the Roman Catholic Church of today cannot honestly be denied; it is written plainly across the pages of history"); *Devotion to the Sacred Heart* (1909); *The Early Life of Our Lady* (1910); *Why Should I Be Moral? A Discussion of the Basis of Ethics* (1911); *Essay on Love* (1912); *Galileo and his Condemnation* (1913); *Civilization and Culture* (1916);

A Practical Philosophy of Life (1921); *Our Modern Chaos and the Way Out* (1925).

Hulme, Mgr. Benjamin – priest; b. Lane-End with Longton, Staffordshire; d. 9 August 1852, Aston Hall, near Stone, Staffordshire; brought up in the Protestant religion of his parents; when grown up was introduced to Fr. Robert Richmond, chaplain to the Benedictine convent at Caverswall Castle, who received him into the Church (mother received later); in 1824 went to Oscott College to study for the priesthood; ordained priest in 1831; worked on the mission in Leicestershire and Staffordshire; at Aston Hall he found under the altar the relics of St. Chad, lost for many years; chaplain at Mawley Hall, Shropshire 1843–1847, then at Haversage in Derbyshire; retired to Longton; friend of Cardinal Wiseman; left much money for foundation of a convent for tertiaries of the Third Order of St. Dominic; buried at Aston Hall; see *Gillow*, Vol. III, p.470.

Humphery-Smith, Cecil Raymond Julian (known as "Humph") – genealogist and heraldist; b. 1928; c. 1953 (received at St. James's, Spanish Place, London); brought up in Sussex as a "middle churchman"; went to High Anglican school; graduated in science from London University, then worked in antibiotics under Alexander Fleming's pupil, Harold Raistrick (converted whilst there); influenced in his conversion by a fellow researcher, Juan Galarraga, later a priest of Opus Dei; also influenced by his Catholic wife-to-be, Alice; worked in the Po Valley, Italy, for the Heinz Company on quality control in the tomato fields; in 1955 had a very serious car crash in Italy and was visited in hospital by Padre Pio, whom he did not know, and who heard his confession; in 1962 he met again Padre Pio who cured his severe headaches at a touch; they became close friends; in 1968 he had a vision of Padre Pio on the night of the latter's death; brought the concept of family history to the subject of genealogy with his lecture in 1957 on "Introducing Family History"; in 1961 founded the Institute of Heraldic and Genealogical Studies in Canterbury (editor of its journal from 1962); lecturer at many universities; became the only non-British member of the Council of L'Académie Internationale d'Heraldique; in 2004 made OBE for "services to education in heraldry and genealogy"; many publications; see *A Saint On My Back: Personal Experiences of Padre Pio by a Spiritual Son* (1983).

Hunter, Sylvester Joseph, SJ – priest and educator; b. 13 September 1829, Bath; c. 1857 (two of his sisters, one later a Benedictine nun, received in 1860); d. 20 June 1896, Stonyhurst; his father, Joseph Hunter, himself descended from a long line of English Roundheads, was a Presbyterian minister, but better known as antiquarian writer and Shakespeare critic; early on very able in classical literature; fine student at Trinity College, Cambridge in Mathematics and Physics; barrister who wrote two legal texts and practiced at the Chancery bar; entered the Society of Jesus in 1861; ordained priest in 1870; taught physics and mathematics at Stonyhurst; later rector of St. Beuno's college, St. Asaph, North Wales; finally at Stonyhurst, began *A Short History of England*, unfinished at his death; see *Outlines of Dogmatic Theology* (1894); *Catholic Encyclopedia*.

Hunter-Blair, Rt. Rev. Sir David Oswald, fifth Baronet, OSB – priest and author; b. 1853; c. 25 March 1875, both Maundy Thursday and Lady Day (received at St. Alphonsus church, Rome; d. 1939; educated at Eton and Magdalen College, Oxford; friend of Oscar Wilde (see below) whom he tried to convert; became Benedictine monk (Dom Oswald); for five years rector of Fort Augustus Abbey School; later Master of Hunter-Blair's Hall, Oxford; Private Chamberlain of Sword and Cloak to Popes Pius IX and Leo XIII; see *A Medley of Memories: Fifty Years' Recollections of a Benedictine Monk* (1919); *A New Medley of Memories* (1922); *Memories and Musings* (1929); *More Memories and Musings* (1931); *A Last Medley of Memories* (1936); Madeleine Beard, *Faith and Fortune* (1997), pp.153–155 ("For Hunter-Blair, it was reading Sir Walter Scott's novels with their gallant knights and gracious ladies which suddenly made him realize that it was Catholicism that had made them what they were. Scott's writings 'first helped me throw off the incubus of acquired and inherited prejudice which had weighed upon me from childhood.' Newman's novel *Loss and Gain* and the conversion of the Marquess of Bute (which was featured in Newman's novel) both played their part").

Hutchison, William Antony – priest; b. 27 September 1822, London; c. 21 December 1845; d. 12 July 1863; educated at Trinity College, Cambridge, where a member of Cambridge Camden Society; went to Birmingham to be received and met Fr. Faber (see above) (not yet ordained), with whom he remained close friends until his death, and acting on his advice, he was received without delay; went on tour of France and Italy with Faber in 1846; joined Faber's community of Brothers of the Will of God; ordained priest 15 August 1847; in February 1848 community joined the Oratory of St. Philip Neri; man of independent financial means who supported the Oratory, e.g., started large schools for boys and girls; expert on holy house of Loreto on which he wrote a book; long illness before his death; buried in cemetery of the Fathers of the Oratory at St. Mary's, Sydenham; see *Loreto and Nazareth* (1863); *Gillow*, Vol. III, p.511.

Hutchison, William Corston – Catholic layman; b. 1820; c. 1851; d. 9 September 1883, Holly Place, Hampstead, London; formerly Anglican curate; follower of Puseyite party in Established Church; converted at the sacrifice of every worldly interest; after converting spent most of his life on the Continent; close friend of Mgr. Dupanloup, Bishop of Orleans; tutor to Prince Imperial of France; member of Third Order of St. Francis; chevalier of Holy Cross of Jerusalem and private chamberlain to Pius IX and Leo XIII; had a great share in the successful production of Dr. Faà di Bruno's *Catholic Belief*; eldest son became Benedictine monk; seriously ill in final years; see *Gillow*, Vol. III, p.514 ("It was whilst translating the words, *In manus tuas commendo spiritum meum*, that he fell back and calmly expired").

Hutton, Edward – writer on travel and art history; b. 12 April 1875, Cambridge Villa, Ealing, Middlesex; c. 1928 (received at the same time as Mason Perkins, collector and Italian art connoisseur, in the Porziuncola, built above the spot in Assisi where St. Francis died); d. 20 August 1969; one of a family of five, including his brother Robert Salmon Hutton (1876–1970), Professor of Metallurgy, Cambridge University; learned the writing trade at Bodley Head publishers; came into contact with a number of writers and aesthetes linked with the "decadent movement," e.g., Aubrey Beardsley (see above), Ernest Dowson (see above), Frederick Rolfe (see below), Lionel Johnson (see below), George Moore, Arthur Symons, and Oscar Wilde (see below); first went to Italy in 1896,

where he wrote several articles and reviews on Italian art history; married Charlotte Miles (1875/6–1960) in 1898 and they lived in Casa di Boccaccio (once owned by Boccaccio's father) at Ponte a Monsola, east of Florence; friend of Bernard Berenson; also friend of Hilaire Belloc and Richard Terry (see below); wrote great number of books on travel and art history, and many other topics (e.g., art criticism, topography, mosaic, polyphonic church music in 16th and 17th centuries), and collaborated with Norman Douglas (1868–1952), the travel writer; great devotion to St. Francis; helped to found British Institute in Florence; helped to improve the decoration of Westminster Cathedral; in World War II he used his unrivalled knowledge of topography of Italy to help the allied forces; greatly saddened by what he saw as the downgrading of Latin, which was to him the sign of the Church's universality; see *Studies in the Lives of the Saints* (1907); *The Life of Christ in the Old Italian Masters* (1939) ("The subject of Jesus Christ, directly or indirectly, was necessarily the main inspiration of Christian, that is modern, art. Indeed, that Figure, at first mysteriously and with the greatest reserve, but soon with ever-increasing freedom and enthusiasm, has been its chief concern and subject matter from the earliest times; so that presently the Life of Christ, beginning with the great central fact of Christianity, the Incarnation, with all that radiated from it, fills the art of more than a thousand years, from the Catacombs to the Reformation – and thenceforward appears with ever-decreasing interest, till today it would be hard to find a single artist of the first rank, whose art is in any way concerned with it...

That story able to be expressed at first in art, in its enormous significance, only in symbol and pictured dogma, little by little becomes, in the hands of these Italian painters, the most wonderful, the most beautiful, the most enthralling and touching story in the world, beside which, even as a story, the Odyssey itself is a shadow of a shadow, the loveliness of Greek mythology an inhuman fairy tale without consolation. For, as Giotto and Daddi and Angelico and Benozzo Gozzoli and Botticelli, and Duccio and all the Sienese perceived, there is no other story to compare with this story, no other that like this touches the heart; that begins with an idyll far lovelier than ever Theocritus conceived, passes into a discourse more sublime than any Plato knew, proceeds to a tragedy more awful than Aeschylus could imagine, and ends in an apotheosis beyond the power of Sophocles"); *Catholicism and English Literature* (1948); "Catholic English Literature," in George Andrew Beck *(ed), The English Catholics 1850–1950* (1950); *Rome* (1950); Anon, "Profile: Edward Hutton," *Apollo: The International Magazine of the Arts*, October 1963, p.317 ("Throughout his books, whatever their subject, one detects the author's interest in classical culture, a certain Latinity which is summed up by his reply to the prelate who asked him why he had become a Catholic: 'Because it is the next best thing to Paganism'"); *DNB* ("He became interested in both Italy and Catholicism, largely through the study of Virgil and the reading of the Italian novels of Marion Crawford and J. H. Shorthouse's Anglo-Catholic novel *John Inglesant* (1881)").

Hyde, Douglas Arnold – journalist and political campaigner; b. 8 April 1911, Worthing, Sussex; c. 1948 (received with his wife, Carol); d. 19 September 1996, Kingston upon Thames, Surrey; brought up as Methodist; twenty years a Communist, including news editor of *Daily Worker* (resigned 1948); member of Communist Party of Great Britain from 1928; supporter of Popular Front government during Spanish Civil War; converted many of his local Labour party to Communism; in 1950 published his book, *I Believed*, in which he explained his disagreements with the Communist Party; wrote for the *Catholic Herald*; later came to believe Pope John Paul II was too conservative; in sympathy with liberation theology; worked for release of political detainees in developing world; ended his life no longer practicing Catholic but once more a socialist (described himself as an "agnostic Christian"); lifelong passion for the work of William Morris; love of plainsong and Gothic architecture; see *From Communism Towards Catholicism* (1948) ("The new element was, in fact, simply that I had once again started differentiating between right and wrong, accepting once again the old discarded values. Right and wrong, I knew, were in their final analysis, spiritual values – utterly un-Marxist. In concerning myself about the fate of bourgeois democratic leaders who were being hunted for their lives I was admitting the intrinsic value of the individual when as a Marxist I should regard the individual as being of no consequence and the mass as being all that mattered...

...Suddenly we awoke to the fact that the period we loved most in history was a Catholic period, that its music and art and learning were part of a Catholic culture which existed in Britain for centuries and was still the culture, often in somewhat degraded form, of large parts of the Continent...

...I saw Fr. Francis Devas SJ and told him my position. One cannot spend years in the Communist Party playing with dirt without being soiled. I wanted to know if despite my years as an atheist and their irrevocable consequences I could yet become a Catholic. He cleared my doubts with the Jesuitical but profoundly understanding observation that it is better to be even a bad Catholic than a Communist.

Then I discovered St. Etheldreda's… Here was a [Gothic church] that had been restored to the ancient Faith, its walls hallowed by hundreds of years of Catholic prayer; the stoupes, the images of saints, everything once again serving their true purpose, not just quaint survivals in an Anglican setting…

…The bitterest epithets the [Communist] party could find were not too bad for me, for Communists regard the Catholic Church as the spearhead of the opposition to everything at which they are aiming. In this they are quite logical, for ultimately either Communist materialism or the Catholic Church must prevail. Against the cynicism, the hate, the blind bigotry, the destruction of ethics and morality by the Communists the Church can pose the dignity, sanctity and responsibility of man as an individual, the conception of an extended Christendom which must ultimately include all nations of the earth, the return to spiritual values and a belief in God who, as Father, unites the human race in a way which no materialist creed can hope to do"); *I Believed* (1950) ("Instead I found myself saying: 'The Catholic Church against the twentieth century? So what? So am I, if the twentieth century means the crazy world I see about me which had endured two world wars and goodness knows how many revolutions already, and with the war-clouds gathering so soon after the last war'…. And in any case was it really so certain as we had imagined it to be that the world must inevitably 'progress', that the past was necessarily less good and civilized than the *present and still less so than the future?"); The Answer to Communism* (1951); "From Marx to Christ" in John A. O'Brien (ed), *The Road to Damascus* (1949) ("My cultural interests had

always been with the Middle Ages: in poetry, Chaucer and Langland; in architecture, Norman and Gothic; in music, plainsong and Gregorian chants. The *Weekly Review* brought home to me the fact that the Middle Ages were those when men still loved God and that was the reason for the great outpouring of the human soul of that period; that their culture was a Catholic culture and that the Catholic Church today was the sole custodian of that grand and ancient culture"); Francis Dufay and Douglas Hyde, *Red Star Versus the Cross: The Pattern of Persecution* (1954); Matthew Hoehn, OSB (ed), *Catholic Authors* (1952).

Hyde (formerly Bayeart), William – priest and divine; b. 27 March 1597, London; c. 1622; d. 22 December 1651, English College, Douai; avid reader from childhood; unable "to get over that great point of the judge of controversies," became a Catholic; entered English College, Douai in 1623; ordained priest 24 September 1625 at Cambrai; Professor of Philosophy at college until went on the mission in 1631; acted as chaplain to Catholic families before returning to Douai in 1633; returned to England to avoid the plague; back to Douai as Vice-President, then President (1646) of college; many honors; restored Douai College to sound condition; profound theologian; buried in lady chapel of church of St. Jacques close by the college; see *Gillow*, Vol. III, p.527; *DNB*.

Ingram, Blessed John – priest and martyr; b. about 1565, Stoke Edith, Herefordshire; d. 26 July 1594, Gateshead; parents Protestants or lapsed Catholics; was reconciled to the Church and so ejected for recusancy; went to Douai and then Rheims in 1582; on to Rome, where admitted into English College in 1584; ordained priest 3 December 1589; left for the English mission in 1591, but plan changed to mission to Scotland; landed in Scotland where pursued and arrested before had performed any priestly function in England; argued he did not come within the statute under which he was arraigned; sent to London where racked, then returned to Newcastle; tried at Durham Assizes for being ordained priest abroad and for having returned to England to exercise his function; condemned and hanged, drawn and quartered at Gateshead; see M. J. Cashman, "The Gateshead Martyr," *Recusant History*, October 1971, p.121; *Gillow*, Vol. III, p.543 ("[In the Tower], in the expectation of martyrdom, Mr. Ingram cut on the walls of his cell some Latin verses, of one of which the following translation is a specimen: 'Men to the living rock resort/ for their sepulchral stones:/A living tomb is mine, unsought -/The crow that picks my bones'"); *Catholic Encyclopedia*.

Ireland, Richard – headmaster; c. 1610; d. about 1636; elected student of Christ Church, Oxford, in 1587; headmaster of Westminster School in 1599; withdrew to France on his conversion; when the College of Arras, in the University of Paris, was set up as a house for Catholic writers under the commendation of the Pope, he resided there for rest of his life; he gave literary and monetary assistance to the controversialists there; worked to reconcile regulars and seculars; left ecclesiastical education funds to Douai College, to Benedictine College at Douai and to Franciscan College at Douai; see *Gillow*, Vol. III, p.550.

Isaacs, Godfrey Charles – industrialist; b. 1866; c. about 1913; d. 17 April 1925, Lyne Grove, Virginia Water, Surrey; one of nine children from well-known Jewish family; brother of Rufus Isaacs (1860–1935), Lord Reading (Attorney-General in Asquith's Liberal Government and later Lord Chief Justice); built up assets of Marconi company of which he was managing director; plaintiff in "Marconi scandal" case 1913, involving allegations of impropriety by Rufus Isaacs as Attorney-General and speculation in Marconi stock by Rufus Isaacs and the Chancellor of the Exchequer, Lloyd George; after attacks on his role in the Marconi case he brought a successful libel action against Cecil Chesterton (see above); director of the newly formed British Broadcasting Company in 1923; see *DNB*.

Jackson, Captain Sir Henry Moore – diplomat; b. 1849, Grenada; c. 1880 (from the day of his reception into the Church he never willingly missed daily Mass); d. 29 August 1908, London; son of Anglican bishop of Leeward Islands; trained at Royal Military Academy; member of Royal Artillery 1870–1885; commissioner for Turks and Caicos Islands 1885–1890; Colonial Secretary of Bahama Islands 1890–1893; Colonial Secretary of Gibraltar 1894–1901; Governor of Leeward Islands, then Governor of Fiji Islands and High Commissioner of Western Pacific; Governor of Trinidad and Tobago; Order of St. Gregory the Great; Grand Cross of St. Michael and St. George; see *Catholic Encyclopedia*.

Jacob, Naomi Eleanor Clare (*pseud.* Ellington Gray) (known as Naomi Ellington Jacob) – writer; b. 1 July 1884, 20 High Street, Agnes Gate, Ripon, Yorkshire; c. 1907; d. 27 August 1964, Sirmione, Lake Garda, Italy; father a German Jew, but she was brought up in Church of England; became socialist and involved in suffrage movement; prolific writer of popular fiction and some acting on stage and in films; her own lesbianism is never put forward in her books; flamboyant appearances for Entertainments National Service Association in World War II; lecturer and contributor to BBC's *Woman's Hour* program, plus several autobiographical works; friend of Radcliffe Hall and appeared for the defense of her novel, *Well of Loneliness*; see *Jacob Ussher* (1925); *Four Generations* (1934); *Me: Yesterday and Today* (1957); *DNB*.

James II and VII, King of England, Scotland and Ireland – b. 14 October 1633, St. James's Palace, London; c. exact date uncertain, but after 1676 completely committed to the Catholic faith; d. 5 September 1701, St. Germain; third (but second surviving son) of Charles I (1600–1649), and Henrietta Maria (1609–1669), daughter of Henri IV of France and Marie de Medici; mother a Catholic; relatively stable childhood; was made Duke of York and Albany shortly after his baptism; spent some time with his father during the Civil War; then in Oxford, where taught by several fellows of colleges; after surrender of Oxford to parliamentarians in 1646, went to London; escaped from England in 1648 and went to the Hague; in 1649 went to St. Germain to his mother, spending a month on the way at Benedictine monastery at St. Armand greatly enjoying his first experience of a Catholic community; failure of royal cause at home left him very short of money and he joined French army; fought with bravery; later joined Spanish army; after Restoration of 1660, married Anne Hyde (1637–1671) (see above, under "Anne, Duchess of York"), but had several mistresses; he and his wife both extravagant; appointed Lord High Admiral (obliged to resign after the passing in 1673 of first Test Act, disqualifying Catholics from holding office under the crown); took part in second Dutch war; outwardly conformed to Church of England in 1660s, but by 1669 convinced only Catholic faith could procure salvation; on coming to the throne he wished to put Catholicism on same footing as Anglicanism; risings by Earl of Argyll and by Duke of Monmouth crushed; ignored Test Act and appointed many Catholics to crown posts, both political and religious; enacted religious toleration to protect both Catholics and dissenters; on the invasion by William of Orange in 1688 he eventually fled to France and chateau of St. Germain-en-Laye, provided by Louis XIV; led uprising in Ireland, but defeated at Battle of the Boyne on 1 July 1689 and returned to France; body dissected (corpse buried in English Benedictine church in Faubourg St. Jacques, Paris, but destroyed during French Revolution; brain in Scots College, Paris; heart in convent at Chaillot; other relics taken to England); see Hilaire Belloc, *James the Second* (1928); John Miller, *James II* (2000); W. A. Speck, *James II* (2002); *Gillow*, Vol. III, p.559; *DNB* ("According to his own testimony, what had converted him had been: 'the divisions among Protestants and the necessity of an infallible judge to decide controversies, together with some promises which Christ made to his church in general that the gates of hell should not prevail against it and some others made to St Peter, and there being no person that pretends to infallibility but the Bishop of Rome.'
'He concluded the Catholic church to be the sole authoritative voice on earth,' observed his Catholic biographer Hilaire Belloc, 'and thenceforward ... he not only stood firm against surrender but on no single occasion contemplated the least compromise or by a word would modify the impression made. It is like a rod of steel running through thirty years'").

James, Bruno Scott – priest and writer; b. 1906; c. 1935; d. 16 March 1984; educated mainly at home owing to ill-health; entered Anglican Benedictine monastery; never comfortable in Church of England; instructed by Carthusians at Parkminster; tested his vocation until health broke down again, then studied for secular priesthood at the Beda in Rome; ordained priest in 1935; in Spanish Civil War traveled to front line to say Mass; first administrator of Walsingham shrine; began apostolate there and inspired many seminarians to join him on pilgrimages around the country; after further ill-health, began apostolate in Naples; appointed Monsignor by Pope Paul VI; traveled widely in Europe, United States and North Africa; see *Asking For Trouble* (1962) ("I could not find the slightest justification for the Church of England in the writings of the Fathers, in fact I think it was Origen, who said that schism was the sin against the Holy Ghost. In short I could not find the slightest justification for being in schism from the Church of Rome. That dear institution we call the Church of England is altogether too well-bred, too good if you will, to be true. Quite certainly, she had not been founded by the Divine Son of a Galilean carpenter, with a fisherman as his representative on earth. She speaks with a well-bred voice, but she does not speak with authority. But this is not to say that I did not and do not still admire and love the Church of England. I respect the learning and the devoted lives of her clergy.... Only I cannot think of them as priests in the sense that the Catholic Church uses and has always used the word, nor do I for one moment believe that the founders of their Church meant them to be.... In a world torn by conflicting counsels and warring creeds only the Catholic Church speaks with authority. In spite of all that I find distressing in her superficial appearance – and there is very much – I have never for one moment had the slightest doubt that the Roman Catholic Church is the Church that Christ founded on the rock

of Peter, the Church of the Catacombs, the Church of the Fathers"); review of *A Time to Speak* by B. C. Butler, *Downside Review*, April 1973, p.154 ("We are treated to all the old emotive phrases and words, the obscurantism of the Roman Curia, the forward-looking liberals – the lot. (I confess I find it hard to endure the arrogance of the self-styled progressives and also their lack of humor.) To be forward-looking is no doubt a fine thing, but it is as well to glance back now and then when you are slipping down a precipice.... No one in their senses would wish to belittle the aims and achievement of the Second Vatican Council. Pope John hoped that it would lead to a spiritual renewal in the Church, and this may still happen, but the immediate results have been quite other: numerous priests have abandoned their vocation and monks as well, there has been a notable and grave fall-off in vocations to the priesthood as well as to the monastic life, and there has been a serious fall-off in attendance at Mass"); *Bruno Scott James Papers*, Georgetown University (description by Rt. Rev. William Gordon Wheeler, former Bishop of Leeds (see below): "The vision of this.... priest enveloped in a black cloak, his head shorn, and with a Siamese cat perched on his shoulder, sitting on the steps of the Slipper Chapel [at Walsingham] and pouring out patristic pearls is a memorable one. He undoubtedly had a great gift of prayer himself and was able to communicate this to others...").

James, David Pelham (later known as David Guthrie-James) – author, traveler and politician; b. 25 December 1919; c. 1943; d. 15 December 1986; son of Wing Commander Archibald William Henry James; born into a Church of England family; married in 1950 Jaquetta Mary Theresa Digby (b. 28 October 1928), daughter of Edward Kenelm

Digby, eleventh Baron Digby of Dorset and sister of Pamela Churchill Harriman; left Oxford University before completing his studies to sail around the world; in the RNVR 1939–1946; prisoner of war from 1943 after his motor gun boat was sunk, escaping twice, the second time successfully; embarked on several polar expeditions; Conservative MP 1955–1964 and 1970–1979; cofounder of Loch Ness Phenomena Investigation Bureau in 1962 (firm believer in the existence of the "Loch Ness monster"); in 1979 took the name David Guthrie-James (Guthrie his mother's maiden name); see *Prisoner's Progress* (1947); John Robson, *One Man In His Time* (1998).

James, Stanley Bloomfield – writer; b. 9 December 1869; c. 1923 (wife and two children received 1927); d. 1 December 1951; successively tramp, newspaper manager, cowboy, soldier in Spanish-American war, Nonconformist minister, and labor agitator; then curate to W. E. Orchard (see below) and member of his "Free Catholic" movement; on staff of *Catholic Herald*; see *The Adventures of a Spiritual Tramp* (1925) "During my visits to the tenements to awaken interest in our Special Services I had invaded the room of an old Irishman. 'Who are yez?' he asked. 'I come from the little church in Darby Street,' I said. 'There's only wan Church,' he hissed. 'It's the Howly Catholic Church.' There was much more to the same effect, but I scarcely stopped to listen. There was a fierceness in his manner, a violent dogmatism with which I could as well have argued as I could argue with a mad bull. Before this storm I bowed.... This tempestuous assault expressed my own secret thought. I knew he was right. From that moment, I think, my mind was made up. There was only 'wan Church.'

I did not balance the advantages of making my submission against the 'advantages' of not doing so. I did not put the values of Catholicism against any alleged values of Protestantism. I saw clearly that in choosing Catholicism I chose the whole against the part. Nothing would be lost. If that had seemed even possible, I could never have taken the step I did. I wanted everything the universe had to give and would not be satisfied until I secured a pledge of it. No star must be missing from my firmament. A joy for ever forbidden, however small, would make my heaven a hell. The Church could be rigorously exclusive, I seemed to see, because it was so magnificently inclusive. It could brand as schismatic every sect that rose above the horizon, with whatever splendor the new body shone, only because that splendor already glittered in its crown"); *The Evangelical Approach to Rome* (1933).

Jameson (Jamieson), John Paul – priest and antiquary; b. 1659, Aberdeen; d. 25 March 1700; brought up as Protestant; after being converted to the Catholic faith he went on to Rome and entered the Scots College in 1677; graduated doctor of theology and ordained priest in 1685; Professor of Theology at the seminary in Padua; entered Cardinal Carlo Barberini's household; worked as a priest in Scotland from 1687 until his death; best known for his work on Scottish history; praised for his character and spirituality; at the Revolution he was imprisoned for some time and in poor health; see *DNB*.

Jarrett, Keith – Catholic layman; b. 1937; c. 1982 (received with his wife); d. 20 November 2000; brought up in Open Brethren Assembly; took Anglican orders in 1970; became an organizer for the Converts' Aid Society in 1988 and acting secretary in 1992; secretary of the St. Barnabas Society; see *One Step*

Enough: A Short History of the St. Barnabas Society (1996); "Doing it by the Book" in Dwight Longenecker (ed), *The Path to Rome* (1999) ("For many converts to Catholicism there is a final straw. For me it was something very small, an almost throwaway line which St. Paul had written. I had started to read St. Paul's great letter to the Roman Church and there in the first few verses of his greetings to that church I read 'your faith is proclaimed throughout the world' (Romans 1:8). At its most basic level St. Paul was saying something about the faith of the Roman church of the first century. The Roman church even then proclaimed the faith which was to spread throughout the world. In a much wider and deeper sense what was true then is more true today. For the Roman Catholic Church has gone into all the world and preached the Gospel and is still doing so today").

Jenner, Henry Lascelles – librarian and promoter of Cornish language; b. 8 August 1848 Union Hill, St. Columb Major, Cornwall; c. late in 1933; d. 8 May 1934, Bospowes, Cornwall; brought up in extreme Anglo-Catholic family; in 1866 father consecrated first Anglican Bishop of Dunedin, New Zealand, but diocese rejected him because of his High Church views; husband of Katherine Jenner, authoress (see below); assistant in British Museum's department of manuscripts and later department of printed books, where he studied Cornish material and became foremost authority on Cornish affairs, writing extensively on the subject; friend of Ruskin, Dickens and Gladstone; only child, Cecily Katharine Ysolt (b. 1878), later Sister Mary Beatrix Jenner of Order of the Visitation; Tory and committed Jacobite; buried in cemetery of church of St. Uny, Lelant; see D. R. Williams (ed), *Henry and Katharine Jenner: A Celebration of Cornwall's*

Culture, Language and Identity (2004); *DNB* ("Much of the ethos of the movement's early period constituted a middle-class, apolitical harking back to a semi-mystical, pre-industrial, Catholic Cornwall").

Jenner, Katherine Lee (*née* Rawlings) ("Kitty") (*pseud.* Katherine Lee) – author and artist; b. 12 September 1853, Hayle Foundry, Cornwall; c. about 1873; d. 21 October 1936, Bospowes; brought up as an Anglican; home education and from 1873 Slade School of Fine Art; wife of Henry Jenner (see above); European sketches and domestic watercolors, but greater recognition came as a writer (six novels, three books on Christian art and symbolism, and poetry); made a bard of the Welsh gorsedd; buried with her husband at Lelant; see *A Western Wildflower* (1882); *In the Alsatian Mountains* (1883); *In London Town* (1884); *Katharine Blythe* (1886); D. R. Williams (ed), *Henry and Katharine Jenner: A Celebration of Cornwall's Culture, Language and Identity* (2004); *DNB*.

John, Gwendolen Mary ("Gwen") – painter; b. 22 June 1876, 7 Victoria Place, Haverfordwest, Pembrokeshire, Wales; c. 1913; d. 18 September 1939, Dieppe, France; elder sister of the artist Augustus John (1878–1961); brought up in somber household; studied at Slade School of Art 1895–1898; worked briefly in Paris with Whistler; returned to London and exhibited her work; set out to walk to Rome in 1903, but settled in Paris and continued to paint; began modeling for Rodin and became his mistress; in later life concentrated on small-scale portraits, female figures and still-life; came into contact with the convent in Meudon and painted portraits of founder of Order, the nuns, and girls at their school; became reclusive; unmarried; see Susan Chitty, *Gwen John 1876–1939*

(1981); James Sullivan, "Gwen John: Art and Faith in the Shadows," *Crisis*, September 1995; Alicia Foster, *Gwen John* (1999); Sue Roe, *Gwen John: A Life* (2001); David Jones, "Gwen John: God's Little Painter," *Catholic Life*, July 2004, p.12 ("Friends around her ... began to worry that she was increasingly bent on detachment from the world. And their fears were not allayed when Gwen, who described herself as 'God's Little Painter,' began proclaiming: 'Aloneness is nearer God, nearer reality'"); *DNB*.

Johnson, Lionel Pigot – poet and literary scholar; b. 15 March 1867, Broadstairs, Kent; c. 22 June 1891 ("It is a great piece of courage: his [Johnson's] 'first general confession' must have been extremely disagreeable" (Ernest Dowson to Arthur Moore, 25 June 1891)); d. 4 October 1902, London; brought up in High Church tradition; very small in stature and frail; educated at Winchester and New College, Oxford; strongly influenced by Walter Pater at Oxford; well read in Catholic apologetics; for a time in great demand as Catholic lecturer; part of 1890s poetic movement (friend of Ernest Dowson (see above) and W. B. Yeats); love of Celtic things; supporter of Irish nationalism; contributor of essays and reviews to *The Academy*, the *Anti-Jacobin*, the *Daily Chronicle*, *The Pageant*, *The Savoy*, *The Speaker* and *The Spectator*; his poems explore Catholicism, classicism and Celticism; became more and more solitary, then paranoia and alcoholism; fell off a bar stool in the Green Dragon, Fleet Street, cracked his skull and died; unmarried; buried in Kensal Green cemetery, London; see *The Art of Thomas Hardy* (1894); Fr. John Gerard, "Of Lionel Johnson (1867–1902)," *The Month*, November 1902; Robert Shafer (ed), *Reviews and Critical Papers of Lionel Johnson* (1921); Ian Fletcher (ed), *The*

Complete Poems of Lionel Johnson (1982); *Catholic Encyclopedia* ("He greatly loved his friends in a markedly spiritual way, always praying for them, absent or present. His sound Catholic principles, his profound scholarship, his artistic sensitiveness, his play of wisdom and humor, his absolute literary honor, with its 'passion for perfection' from the first, show nobly in his prose work. His lyrics are full of beauty and poignancy, but perhaps have in them something taxing"); Derek Stanford, "Lionel Johnson as Critic," *The Month*, August 1954, p.82; Gary H. Paterson, "The Religious Thought of Lionel Johnson," *Antigonish Review*, Spring 1973, p.95; Robert Whelan, "Why did so many Victorian decadents become Catholics?" *Catholic Herald*, 5 January 2001; *DNB*.

Johnson, Rt. Rev. Mgr. Vernon Cecil – priest and writer; b. 1886; c. 1929 (received by Fr. Vincent McNabb, OP); d. 21 October 1969; educated at Charterhouse and Trinity College, Oxford; took Anglican orders and was high churchman; converted after spiritual experience at Lisieux; studied for the priesthood at the Beda College, Rome; ordained Catholic priest in 1933; chaplain to Catholic undergraduates at Oxford 1941–1947; became known for his devotion to St Thérèse; served in Westminster Diocese at St. James' Spanish Place; famous for his preaching; gentle, spiritual and accessible; domestic prelate to Pius XII from 1951; see *One Lord – One Faith* (1929) ("It will be seen that the supreme reason [for my action in becoming a Catholic], behind all others, was that I could not resist the claim of the Catholic Church to be the one true Church founded by Our Lord Jesus Christ to guard and teach the truth to all men till the end of time. She alone claims to be infallibly guided by the Holy Spirit in her teaching: she alone possesses the authority and unity necessary for such a Divine Vocation; and she alone, in the Papacy, gives any effective and working meaning to the position of St. Peter in Scripture. It was the positive fact of the Catholic Church from which I could not escape.

Thus the state of the Church of England was a very secondary difficulty and only served to confirm my growing belief in the Catholic Church. The Prayer Book controversy was, to me, more a symptom than anything else; though serious, it was never so serious, to me, as modernism. Modernism, I saw, as I came to understand it better, was clearly destroying the true conception of, and belief in, the Personality of Christ and His Godhead – the Foundation Truth of the Christian Religion"); *The Message of St. Thérèse of Lisieux* (1936); *The Mission of a Saint: Essays on the Significance of St. Thérèse of Lisieux* (1947); *Our Guiding Star: A Short Life of St. Thérèse of Lisieux* (1951); *Spiritual Childhood: A Study of St. Thérèse's Teaching* (1953); *In Lisieux With St. Thérèse: A Simple Guide (1954); Suffering and Lourdes* (1956); "My Journey to Rome" in J. A. O'Brien (ed), *Roads to Rome* (1955) ("Can the Anglican Church in any way claim to represent the Church which we have seen was founded by our blessed Lord in the Gospels? She cannot do so for two great reasons: she has no authority; and she has no unity. She does not even claim to be an infallible teacher, and consequently she can exert no authority – can call forth no obedience. Those other members who desire some authority, the Anglo-Catholics, have either to look to the past and in so doing have to admit that the Church of Christ has ceased to speak with authority; or else they have to look to the future, to a day when Christendom may again be reunited: but one thing they cannot do, and that is point to a divine authority speaking in clear and certain tones today. And because there is no authority in the Anglican Church therefore there is no unity. Contradictory doctrines are taught within her fold both as to the meaning of Apostolical succession and as to the meaning of the sacraments themselves. How can a Church which allows contradictory doctrines to be taught be in any way a guardian of the one truth?"); G. J. MacGillivray, *Father Vernon and His Critics* (1930).

Jones, Blessed Edward – priest and martyr; b. Lyndon, St. Asaph; d. 6 May 1590; formerly member of the Established Church; admitted into English College, Rheims, in 1587; ordained priest 11 June 1588 and went to England four months later; worked in and about London where esteemed as preacher; arrested by priest-catcher in shop in Fleet Street and committed to the Tower; racked by Topcliffe and under torture acknowledged he was a priest; at trial argued that forced confession not legally enough to convict him, and put up learned and detailed defense; condemned to death for being a priest and hanged, drawn and quartered on the same day, with another priest, Bl. Anthony Middleton, in Fleet Street, near Conduit, facing the shop in which he was taken; see *Gillow*, Vol. III, p.647; *Catholic Encyclopedia*.

Jones, John, OSB (in religion Leander a Sancto Martino) – priest and theologian; b. 1575, Llanfrynach, near Brecon, Wales; d. 27 December 1635, Somerset House, London; family had conformed to the Established Church; shared rooms at St. John's College, Oxford, with future Archbishop of Canterbury, William Laud; knowledgeable and eloquent student of law; brilliant in debates on the new religion, charged with being secretly a Catholic, and expelled from university for his Catholic principles; converted in Oxford by a Jesuit disguised as a layman; went to Valladolid and received into English College, then directed by the Jesuits, in 1596; outstanding student; in 1599 allowed to join Benedictine Order and studied at University of Salamanca; ordained priest; intended to go on the English mission, but superiors asked him to teach theology and train their novices, which he did at Rheims and Douai for twenty-four years; held many offices in the Order, notably President-General of English Congregation; frequent visits to England, notably in 1634 on behalf of Pope Urban VIII to examine real state of things in England at time when the marriage of Charles I and Henrietta Maria of France resulted in courtesies being exchanged between the king and the Pope; several literary works and great linguist; buried in cemetery of Capuchin friars attached to Queen Henrietta Maria's chapel in Somerset House; see *Gillow*, Vol. III, p.660; *DNB*.

Jones, (Walter) David Michael, MC (*pseud.* Dai Greatcoat) – poet and prose writer, painter, calligrapher, and sculptor; b. 1 November 1895, Brockley, Kent; c. 7 September 1921 (received by Fr. John O'Connor ("Fr. Brown")); d. 29 October 1974, Harrow; father of Welsh chapel upbringing, mother English and Anglican; great artistic potential at early age; served World War I on Western Front where injured; member of Arts and Crafts movement; worked with Eric Gill (see above) at Ditchling and at Capel-y-ffin; admirer of Christopher Dawson (see above), T. S. Eliot, Baron Friedrich Von Hügel, James Joyce, and Père de la Taille; won many prizes and awards, e.g., his poem, *In Parenthesis* won the Hawthornden Prize in 1938; lamented the passing of the old Latin Mass; unmarried; buried in Ladywell cemetery, South East London; see *In Parenthesis*

(1937); *The Anathemata* (1951); "Art and Sacrament: An Enquiry," in Elizabeth Pakenham (ed), *Catholic Approaches* (1955), p.143; *The Sleeping Lord* (1974); Rene Hague (ed), *Dai Greatcoat: A Self-Portrait of David Jones in His Letters* (1980) ("I don't know whether I ever told you of my first sight of a Mass. It was after the Somme, I think, so when I had returned to France from being wounded.... Just a little way back that is between our support trench and the reserve line I noticed what had been a farm building now a wreckage in the main, owing to shell fire. No individual of any sort was about and I noticed that one bit of this wreckage, a byre or outhouse of some sort still stood.... I found a crack against which I put my eye.... [W]hat I saw through the small gap in the wall was not the dim emptiness I had expected but the back of a sacerdos in a gilt-hued *planeta*, two points of flickering candlelight no doubt lent an extra sense of goldness to the vestment and a golden warmth seemed, by the same agency, to lend the white altar cloths and the white linen of the celebrant's alb and amice and maniple (the latter, I notice, has been abandoned, without a word of explanation, by these blasted reformers). You can imagine what a great marvel it was for me to see through that chink in the wall, and kneeling in the hay beneath the improvised mensa were a few huddled figures in khaki.... I can't recall at what part of the Mass it was as I looked through that squint-hole and I didn't think I ought to stay long as it seemed rather like an uninitiated bloke prying on the Mysteries of a Cult. But it made a big impression on me. For one thing I was astonished how close to the Front Line the priest had decided to make the Oblation and I was also impressed to see Old Sweat Mulligan, a somewhat fearsome figure, a real pugilistic, hard-drinking

Goidelic Celt, kneeling there in the smoky candlelight. And one strong impression I had (and this I have often thought about over this last ten years of change when clerics of all sorts declare that the turning-round of the mensa and the use of the vernacular and much besides made the faithful more at one with the sacred minister and so get back nearer to the Coena Domini) for at that spying unintentionally on the Mass in Flanders in the Forward Zone I felt immediately that oneness between the Offerant and those toughs that clustered round him in the dim-lit byre – a thing I had never felt remotely as a Protestant at the office of Holy Communion in spite of the insistence of Protestant theology on the 'priesthood of the laity'"); Jonathan Miles and Derek Shiel, *The Maker Unmade* (1995); Hilary Davis, "An Artist For Our Age" *The Tablet*, 28 October 1995, p.1385; *David Jones Special Issue*, *Chesterton Review*, February and May 1997; Bernard Bergonzi, *War Poets and Other Subjects* (1999), Ch. 17, "David Jones and the Idea of Art"; Bishop Daniel J. Mullins, "David Jones: Artist and Writer," *Saint Austin Review*, November 2001, p.8 (transcript of a broadcast talk, 25 July 1954); Keith Aldritt, *David Jones: Writer and Artist* (2003); David Jones, "An Odd, Unassignable, Modern Genius," *Catholic Life*, August 2002, p.38; Christopher C. Knight, "Some Liturgical Implications of the Thought of David Jones," *New Blackfriars*, July 2004, p.444; Thomas Dilworth, *Reading David Jones* (2008); Joseph Pearce, *Literary Converts* (1999) *passim*; *DNB*.

Jonson, Benjamin (Ben) – poet and playwright; b. 11 June 1572, in or near London; c. 1598; d. mid-August 1637; of Scottish descent; father an Anglican clergyman; close friend of Hugh Holland (see above); several court masques; worked as bricklayer for some time, but gave this up and in early 1590s joined the English expeditionary forces to the Low Countries; then actor and director and writer of plays; in September 1598 imprisoned for manslaughter, having killed in a duel the actor Gabriel Spencer; converted to the Catholic faith whilst in prison (perhaps by Fr. Thomas Wright, a loyalist, anti-Spanish Jesuit, who living in semi-detention in London's gaols); started to write poetry, some having references to Catholicism; made no attempt to mourn death of Elizabeth I and wrote entertainments and masques for James I, collaborating with Inigo Jones; imprisoned for offensive and "popish" references in his plays; attended supper party with the Gunpowder Plot conspirators shortly before the incident took place (his role unclear); he and his wife charged several times with recusancy; returned to Church of England about 1610 when there was further tightening of anti-Catholic laws, but retained Catholic sympathies and mixed in Catholic circles (e.g., close friend of Sir Kenelm Digby (see above)); fine epigrammist; buried in north aisle of Westminster Abbey, the slab being later inscribed with the words, "O rare Ben Jonson"; see T. A. Stroud, "Ben Jonson and Father Thomas Wright," *ELH: A Journal of English Literary History*, Vol. 14 (1947), p.274; Robert S. Miola, "Ben Jonson, Catholic Poet," *Renaissance and Reformation*, Vol. 25, 2001, p.101; *DNB*.

Joyce, George Hayward, SJ – priest and author; b. 1864; c. 1893; d. 1943; son of Anglican vicar; formerly Anglican curate himself; priest of the Society of Jesus; some time Professor of Dogmatic Theology at St. Beuno's College, St. Asaph, North Wales; see *The Question of Miracles* (1914) ("The Christian religion has ever professed itself to be a religion of miracles.... The miraculous element in Christianity is in accordance with its internal character as a religion. For the Christian revelation is no mere ethical system. It claims to be nothing short of a vast inrush of supernatural forces upon the human race, elevating man to a new plain of being, and conferring upon him an altogether new destiny. According to Christian belief, by the Incarnation and the Atonement, man is raised to sonship to God: his soul becomes the seat of a divine indwelling: and through membership in Christ's body he receives the pledge of an eternal beatitude to which his nature gives him no claim. Thus Christianity as a religion supposes that God has superseded the natural order on man's behalf. And considered in the light of these truths, external miracle appears but the congruous expression of the tremendous spiritual transformation"); *The Catholic Doctrine of Grace* (1920); *Principles of Logic* (1949); *Principles of Natural Theology* (1924); *Christian Marriage: An Historical and Doctrinal Study* (1948).

Joyner (alias Lyde), William – writer and playwright; b. 24 April 1622, Oxford; c. 1644; d. 1706, Holywell, Oxford; Fellow of Magdalen College, Oxford, but concerned about religious practices and resigned; after converting to the Catholic faith he became secretary to Earl of Glamorgan, a royalist, and went with him to Ireland, France and Germany; then resided with Hon. Walter Montague (see below), abbot of St. Martin, near Pontoise, and with him in Paris as domestic steward for several years; returned to England and devoted himself to study; persecution caused by Oates Plot in 1678 forced him to leave London for his family's estate at Oxford; arrested as Jesuit or priest and retired to sister's house in Ickford, Buckinghamshire, where he converted his nephew, the father of Fr. Thomas Phillips, SJ; in

household of Queen Henrietta Maria; James II restored him to his fellowship at Oxford in 1687, but he was expelled at the Revolution in 1688; lived rest of life in some poverty; devout and religious; unmarried; buried in Holywell churchyard; see *Gillow*, Vol. IV, p.355 ("The vagaries of the Puritans opened his eyes to the fallacy of the doctrines of the Anglican Establishment, so he resigned his fellowship and became a Catholic"); *DNB*.

Katharine, Duchess of Kent (née Katharine Lucy Mary Worsley) – member of British Royal Family; b. 22 February 1933, Hovingham Hall, Yorkshire; c. 14 January 1994 (her son, Lord Nicholas Windsor (see below) (b. 1970), received in 2001; her grandson, Edward Windsor, Lord Downpatrick (see below) (b. 1988), converted in 2003); wife of Edward, Duke of Kent; cousin of Queen Elizabeth II; former Anglican with Anglo-Catholic leanings (in 1980 she became the first member of the Royal Family since the Reformation to visit the Shrine of Our Lady of Walsingham in Norfolk); patron of many charities; first member of Royal Family to convert to Catholicism for more than three hundred years (but see Appendix Four); long history of ill-health and later stood down from royal duties and dropped "Her Royal Highness" title; see reported statement of Bishop Gordon Wheeler, former Bishop of Leeds: "She was very interested in the Church of Rome because, like Our Lord, it speaks with authority on questions of faith and morals"; interview on BBC Television: "I do love guidelines and the Catholic Church offers you guidelines. I have always wanted that in my life. I like to know what's expected of me. I like being told: You shall go to church on Sunday and if you don't you're in for it!"

Kaye-Smith, Sheila – writer; b. 4 February 1887, Battle Lodge, 9 Dane Road, St. Leonards, Sussex; c. 1929 (received with her husband, Sir Penrose Fry (see above)); d. 14 January 1956, Little Doucegrove, near Northiam, Sussex; privately educated; brought up as an Evangelical; then Anglo-Catholic; best known for novels about Sussex; writings reflect interest in questions of religious faith and include novels, ballads, plays, stories and criticism, e.g., *Willow's Forge* (1914), *Sussex Gorse* (1916), *Joanna Godden* (1921), *The Village Doctor* (1929), *Selina* (1935), *The Secret Son* (1942), *Mrs. Gailey* (1951); friend of G. B. Stern (see below), both being influenced by St. Thérèse; her house, Little Doucegrove, was later owned by Rumer Godden, another convert novelist (see below); buried beside her husband in grounds of St. Thérèse of Lisieux church, Little Doucegrove; see *Why I Am a Catholic* (1931); *Three Ways Home* (1937) ("The change I made in 1929 when I joined the Church of Rome was mainly a change of allegiance, due to my conviction that Catholicism cannot exist apart from the Church which Christ himself established on the rock of Peter...

I was disturbed by the holiness of Rome – or rather, I should say, by the fact that I was cut off from it. This surely was the heart and blackness of schism. I was cut off from the Altar of the Saints – of St. Thérèse of Lisieux, of St. Teresa of Avila, of St. John of the Cross, of St. John Vianney, and all the rest of that great cloud of witnesses – just as I was cut off from the altar of the people – the people of Palermo, Preston, Peking, every part of the world where the Catholic Church draws together all classes, colors and races. I was cut off, not by any personal conviction but because I belonged to a Church which had deliberately cut itself off four hundred years ago"); *Dropping the Hyphen: A*

Story of a Conversion (1938) (reprinted from the *Dublin Review*, January 1930) ("It is difficult to describe the impression this young saint [Thérèse of Lisieux] made upon me. It was not only the beauty of her life, the charm, wit, and sweetness of her recorded words, of the lovely simplicities of her Little Way. It was rather the realization of that sanctity, that heroic virtue, that sublime love, being offered to the modern world. Here was a saint who, if she had been alive today, would scarcely have been old ... a saint of our times, whose features and expression have been given us not only by the painter and ecclesiastical image-maker, but by the photographer. In Lisieux are still living men and women who knew her and spoke to her, including her own sisters; her canonization miracles were not found in documents or in tradition, but on the lips of living witnesses. And when I looked at her I saw not merely myself, but the living, unfailing fountain of sanctity which is the Church that made her what she was...

...In the Church of England one is given the impression that sanctity as well as miracles came to an end with the early Church. The Anglican Calendar is astonishingly poor and bare; it was drastically cleared after the Reformation, and no name has since been added to it (with the doubtful and disputed exception of King Charles I), till the Revised Prayer Book cautiously inserted a few commemorations, the latest of which is some five hundred years old"); essay in Maurice Leahy (ed), *Conversions to the Catholic Church: A Symposium* (1933) (reprinted as "Only One Thing to Do" in John A. O'Brien (ed), *The Road to Damascus* (1949) ("Once one conceives the Church as a living personality, it is impossible to see it divided and yet remaining alive. The hand cannot say to the foot: 'I have no need of thee.' My branch theory would not work once I saw the Church no longer as a mere organization but as the living Body of Christ"); Patrick Braybrooke, *Some Catholic Novelists: Their Art and Outlook* (1931), p.179; W. Gore Allen, "Sheila Kaye-Smith: A Convert Novelist of Britain," *Irish Ecclesiastical Record*, June 1947, p.518; Walter Romig (ed), *The Book of Catholic Authors*, Fourth Series (1948);

Keepe, Henry – antiquary; b. 1652, Fetter Lane, London; c. in the reign of James II; d. early June 1688, Carter Lane, near St. Paul's Cathedral, London; studied at Oxford and then law at the Inner Temple, but abandoned both; member of Westminster Abbey choir for eighteen years; wrote detailed historical account of Westminster Abbey and its contents, "accurately recording the church's many monuments, complete with their heraldry, several of which have subsequently been destroyed or displaced" (*DNB*); also accounts of genealogies and antiquarian objects; began about 1684 a manuscript survey of York, with details of coats of arms in the city's churches; buried in St. Gregory by Paul, adjoining St. Paul's Cathedral; see *Monumenta Westmonasteriensia* (1682); *Gillow*, Vol. III, p.677; *DNB*.

Kennard, Right Rev. Mgr. Charles Henry – priest; b. 11 October 1840; c. 9 July 1868 (received by Newman); d. 6 August 1920, Burnham-on-Sea, Somerset; brother of Coleridge John Kennard, MP for Salisbury; educated at Harrow and University College, Oxford; formerly High Anglican curate; ordained Catholic priest in 1872; served on the mission; chaplain to the Catholic undergraduates of Oxford 1896–1911; Canon of Diocese of Clifton; Domestic Prelate of Pope Pius X; one time captain of the Royal and Ancient Golf Club, St. Andrews; see essay in J. G. F. Raupert (ed), *Roads to Rome* (1901), p.144 ("I could

not but see … that the primary cause of the final destruction of … heresies was the direct action of Church Authority, which was both organized and effective. Furthermore, I noticed that the rulers of the Church knew that they possessed this authority, and were moreover certain in their own minds of what really was 'the Faith once delivered to the Saints,' I could not but contrast this '*certainty*' and this '*authority*' with the uncertain teaching prevalent in the Church of England, as, e.g., on such important dogmata as the Eternity of Punishment, the Inspiration of Scripture, the Eucharistic Sacrifice, and the Communion of Saints, to say nothing of the equally tenable but vastly different views held by Churchmen on Justification and the Sacramental System…

It seemed to me that, as long as one remained apart from that Church which had undoubtedly come down in its chief See in an unbroken line from the Apostles, and which had even claimed the allegiance of mankind on the basis of Divine Authority, it was impossible to escape from making '*self*' and '*private judgment*' the sole arbiter in matters of faith…

If Christ had really revealed a supernatural religion and intended it for *me*, it could only be brought home to me (if I was to have certitude, or, in other words, *faith*) by some living organized teaching Body preserved from error, and so infallible. To find this I had to go back to the Church which had sent Augustine to England, and which, up to the time of the so-called Reformation, had taught with Divine authority throughout the length and breadth of the land; and so, by the mercy and goodness of God, I was led to look for the Rock out of which all dissentient Churches at one time or another had been hewn – to the Rock of Peter, which alone now and at all times was able to withstand the destructive forces of the ever-active mind of man. It was, of course, intensely painful to leave all that was most dear, and oppose the will of those one loved best and admired most in the world; but '*fiat Voluntas Tua*' was all one could say and pray; and so I made my way to Edgbaston to be further enlightened and consoled by the saintly Newman, to be by him in due time reconciled to 'the Church of the Living God, the pillar and ground of the Truth'"); Stanley L. Jaki, *Newman to Converts: An Existential Ecclesiology* (2001), pp.357–359.

Ker, Ian Turnbull – priest and writer; b. 1942; brought up in a conventional Church of England home and school; his mother's family was related to Ronald Knox (see below); stopped going to church on entering Oxford University; influenced at Oxford by C. S. Lewis' books, *Surprised by Joy* and *Mere Christianity*; had conversion experience in Italy (removing doubts stemming from the problem of evil), which brought him back to Anglicanism; attended Anglo-Papalist church; conversion to the Catholic Church also influenced by C. S. Lewis; taught theology in universities in both Britain and United States; Catholic chaplain to University of Oxford 1989–1990; member of Theology Faculty at Oxford University; author of many books on Newman; see *John Henry Newman: A Biography* (1988); *Newman on Being a Christian* (1990); *The Achievement of John Henry Newman* (1991); *Newman and the Fullness of Christianity* (1993); *Newman and Conversion* (1997); "The Hall and the Side Rooms" in Dwight Longenecker (ed), *The Path to Rome* (1999) ("[Newman] so clearly saw that if development was a necessary part of any living organism, such as the Church claimed to be, then ipso facto a legitimate authority was needed to distinguish genuine developments from inauthentic corruptions. But only one Christian communion claimed to possess such an authority and that was the Roman Catholic Church. In consequence any other Christian body must either become fossilized, as Newman thought that the Orthodox had, or else risk heresy and liberalization of doctrine, like the Church of England"); *The Catholic Revival in English Literature* (2003); *EWTN Audio Library* (19 May 2003) ("I'd been impressed by C. S. Lewis's argument he got from Origen, that Jesus Christ is either God or he's a bad man. The Jesus of the Gospels seemed to me obviously not somebody who just went around preaching a kind of morality or being meek and gentle. This was clearly a very formidable figure. And it seemed to me quite obvious, and he made claims. That was obvious to me. And his followers have made claims for him. So it seemed to me that either you take the line that he is indeed, as Lewis argues I think in *Mere Christianity*, that he's God, or a bad man. And it seemed to me the same was true of the papacy. I couldn't see how Anglo-Catholics could avoid the papacy. It seemed to me that either the Pope is the Vicar of Christ or he is the Anti-Christ.... You couldn't take a kind of halfway position. That seemed to me to be totally unreal because the Pope made certain claims and his Church makes claims for him and these had to be taken seriously. One could take the ultra-Protestant line certainly and dismiss them, but it seemed to me that either one did that or one had to take them on board"); *Mere Catholicism* (2006) ("The most fundamental difference between Catholics and Protestants is not always understood. Many people suppose that Catholicism is simply Bible Christianity, that is, Protestantism, plus a whole lot of accretions, some bad, some indifferent, some perhaps acceptable but not necessary. The truth is that the two religions are essentially different in kind, because they have diametrically opposed views of the relation of the Church to the Christian faith, as well as to the Bible. The crucial and fundamental difference between Catholic and Protestant understanding of the nature of the Church is that Protestants think of the Christian faith as existing somehow independently of the Church, whereas, for Catholics, you cannot separate the two from each other. For many Protestants, the Christian faith is something you find in the Bible, and you then look around for the church which seems most in conformity with this. But for Catholics, the Bible is the possession of the Church, which is entrusted with interpreting it. They point to the fact that it was the Church, which called itself Catholic, that decided in the early centuries what books of the Old Testament and which writings relating to Jesus Christ were to be included as authentic parts of Scripture…

But quite apart from that, Catholics also point out that the first preaching of the Gospel was done before any of the New Testament writings were even available – for they were written by that Church of the New Testament. In other words, it was the Church which began at Pentecost to announce the news about the risen Jesus and that there was now a new People of God which one had to join by baptism in order to be a follower of Jesus. This same Church also took upon itself, as Jesus Himself had done, to interpret the Old Testament in the light of God's self-revelation in Jesus. Obviously, the Church at the beginning could not even appeal to the New Testament because it had not yet been written").

Kerr, Lady Amabel (*née* Cowper) – authoress and benefactress; b. 1846; c. 1872; d. 1906; wife of Admiral of the Fleet, Lord Walter Talbot Kerr (see below), son of the seventh Marquess of Lothian; cousin of Marquess of Ripon, George Robinson (see below); mother of Fr. Ralph Francis Kerr, priest of the London Oratory; of Lieutenant Andrew William Kerr, RN; of Catherine Cecil Kerr, a nun; and of Lieutenant John David Kerr, Gold Staff Officer at Coronation of King Edward VII; foundress of several Catholic churches; authoress on Catholic topics (both adult and children's books) and editor of *The Catholic Magazine*; see *Joan of Arc* (1895); *Unravelled Convictions* (1897) ("What I wish now to consider is the Established Church, which does not reject the name of Protestant, and which was set up (never mind when) and is set up in protest against the Church of Rome, and as a bulwark against any approaches to or from her. I begin by applying the test which, I maintain, must be applied to every Rule of Faith. Could it have lasted through all ages? Could it be universal? There is a difficulty to be met at the very outset; for anything to last, it must have a beginning, and I do not see that the Established Church of England, or any other of the same stamp, could have had a beginning without the pre-existence of the Catholic Church. I do not think its foundation could have had that misty outline, which once formed its strength and is now beginning to prove its weakness, if there had not been a powerful and distinct system in semi-contradiction to which, and in semi-protestation against which, it drew up its codes. How, for instance, could the nature of the Sacraments be left as vague as it is, had they not somehow or somewhere been defined, rightly or wrongly, so that a half acceptance, half rejection of such definitions was enough to satisfy men's minds? It seems to me that the effect of the Church of England's foundations is very similar to that of the tracing of a drawing, in which the tracer has tried to correct the original by leaving out some portions, inserting others, and rendering some indistinct and obscure. So long as the tracing is laid on the drawing we can perceive the draughtsman's object, for the perfect outline and the distinct lights and shadows of the drawing underneath are still visible, and give their own meaning to the imperfect 'modified' outline over it. Once, however, remove the tracing, and by itself it looks so flat, so angular, so unfinished, that you are obliged to refer to the drawing in order to connect its various parts...

And secondly, as to whether such a system ... could be universal.... No! Christianity was never meant to be a national institution. One thing that, more than many, makes me look on the Catholic Church as the true representative of Christianity, is that she alone has always had in view the making of the world into one vast brotherhood. She hates nationalities, and she alone had tried to efface them instead of fostering them. What other Christian creed is there that is not in some measure national? She alone may dare say, as said St. Pacianus of old: 'Christian is my name, Catholic is my surname'"); *A Life of Our Lord* (1900); *St. Antony of Padua* (1901); *Saint Cecilia* (1902); *The Whole Difference* (1902); *Saint Thomas Aquinas* (1905); *Common Sense Talks* (1907).

Kerr, Fergus Gordon Thomson, OP – priest, theologian and philosopher of religion; b. 16 July 1931, Scotland; c. 1954; entered Dominican Order in 1956; ordained priest in 1962; director: Aquinas Institute, Blackfriars, Oxford; taught Philosophy and Theology at Oxford 1966–1986; prior at Blackfriars, Oxford, 1969–1978; prior at Blackfriars, Edinburgh 1992–1998; regent at Blackfriars, Oxford 1998–2004; editor of *New Blackfriars* from 1995; see *Theology After Wittgenstein* (1986); *Immortal Longings: Versions of Transcending*

Humanity (1997); *After Aquinas: Versions of Thomism* (2002); *Twentieth Century Catholic Theologians: From Neoscholasticism to Nuptial Mysticism* (2006); numerous articles and reviews.

Kerr, Rev. Mother Henrietta Mary Emma – nun; b. 1842; c. 20 October 1852; d. 1884; daughter of Lord Henry Kerr (see below) and Lady Louisa Kerr; sister of Fr. Henry Schomberg Kerr (see below); brought up in strongly Catholic atmosphere; inspired by lives of Japanese martyrs; became sister of Society of the Sacred Heart; later Superior of Roehampton convent; see Richard F. Clarke, SJ, "Henrietta Kerr," *The Month*, September 1886, p.8 and October 1886, p.163; John Morris, SJ, *The Life of Mother Henrietta Kerr, Religious of the Sacred Heart, Roehampton* (1887); Madeleine Beard, *Faith and Fortune* (1997), pp.86–89 ("Her mother, Lady Louisa Kerr, had saintly qualities; on first meeting her one Jesuit regretted that the times of persecution were over; 'I know of no one who would have walked up to the scaffold so gallantly as she'").

Kerr, Lord Henry Francis Charles – b. 1800; c. 24 August 1852 (received at Clifton; his wife, Louisa Dorothea (1811–1884), sister of James Hope-Scott (see above), and five of his six children received a month later, the sixth, Henry Schomberg Kerr (see below) being received in 1855); d. 1882; second son of the sixth Marquis of Lothian; took Anglican orders; influenced by the Oxford Movement; visited Newman at Littlemore in 1843 and heard him preach at St. Mary's; confidence in the Church of England shaken by the Gorham case (see entry for William Maskell) and he resigned his living and became a Catholic; eldest son, William (1836–1913) also became a Jesuit priest; also father of Rev. Mother Henrietta Kerr (see above).

Kerr, Henry Schomberg, SJ – priest and sailor; b. 15 August 1838; c. May 1855 (in Scotland while on leave; parents became Catholics three years before whilst he was away at Winchester School); d. 1895, son of Lord Henry Kerr (see above); brother of Rev. Mother Henrietta Kerr (see above); joined Royal Navy in 1852 and became a commander with a brilliant future ahead of him; served in the Crimea; in 1867 left the navy to join the Society of Jesus (recalling that he and Henrietta had made promise as children to serve God in the religious life); ordained priest in 1873; army chaplain in Cyprus, then, 1880–1884, chaplain to Viceroy of India, George Robinson, Marquess of Ripon (see below); later at Jesuit Zambesi mission where he died; see Hon. Mrs. Maxwell-Scott, *Henry Schomberg Kerr, Sailor and Jesuit* (1901); Madeleine Beard, *Faith and Fortune* (1997), pp.89–91 ("He died on the mission. The priest who was with him in his last moments said that half an hour before he died he raised his arm to his forehead to make the Sign of the Cross and Father Ryan finished it for him. He ceased to breathe so gently that the priest was praying with him for some minutes after his death. Another priest recalled taking his leave from the dying Father Kerr: 'I still remember the cheerful, encouraging farewell he gave me as I parted with him'").

Kerr, Admiral of the Fleet Lord Walter Talbot – naval officer; b. 28 September 1839, Newbattle Abbey, Midlothian, Scotland; c. January 1854 (received with his brother, Lord Ralph Kerr (1837–1916)); d. 12 May 1927, Melbourne Hall, Derby; fourth son of John William Robert Kerr, seventh Marquess of Lothian (1794–1841); husband of Lady Amabel Kerr (see above); soon after entered the navy; widowed mother, Marchioness

of Lothian (see below) became, with her younger children, Catholic, and he thenceforth was a devoted Catholic; served in Baltic during Crimean War; during Indian Mutiny he took part in the Relief of Lucknow; Commander of Channel Squadron and First Sea Lord of Admiralty; Grand Cross of Charles III of Spain; Royal Humane Society's silver medal for saving life; was ADC to Queen Victoria; member of Catholic Education Council; President of Catholic Union of Great Britain; see *DNB*.

King, Archdale Arthur – liturgical scholar; b. 10 April 1890; c. 1937; d. 10 July 1972; son of an Anglican minister; read History at Oxford; took Anglican orders and was vicar of Holy Trinity church, Reading, very High Anglican; writer on Catholic matters; many books and monographs on the oriental and western liturgies; after conversion devoted his life to his studies and his books are standard and authoritative; in addition to consulting all the relevant documents, he traveled widely to research his subject; a man of deep faith; great friend of Bishop William Wheeler (see below); see *The Rites of Eastern Christendom*, 2 Vols. (1947–1948); Liturgies *of the Religious Orders* (1955); *Rites of Western Christendom* (1955*); Liturgies of the Primatial Sees* (1957); *Liturgy of the Roman Church* (1957); *Liturgies of the Past* (1959); *Eucharistic Reservation in the Western Church* (1965); *Concelebration in the Christian Church* (1966).

Kingsford, Anna (*née* Bonus) – physician, writer and spiritualist; b. 16 September 1846, Maryland Point, Stratford, Essex; c. 1870; d. 22 February 1888, Kensington, London; wrote on religious themes and short stories; youngest daughter of twelve children; functioned within theosophy and spiritualism (also radical views on vegetarianism and anti-vivisection); experienced a religious reawakening after receiving three nocturnal visits from Mary Magdalen (by this time her husband was an Anglican curate); subsequently made a life outside her marriage, training as a doctor; supported English women's movement, but became dissatisfied with what she saw as denigration of women as wives and mothers; never seems to have acquired a secure sense of who she was; buried at Atcham; see E. Maitland, *Anna Kingsford: Her Life, Letters, Diary and Work*, 2 Vols. (1913); *DNB*.

Knowles, Richard Brinsley – barrister, author and journalist; b. 17 January 1820, Glasgow; c. 1849; d. 28 January 1882, Regent's Park, London; son of James Sheridan Knowles (1784–1862), dramatist and Baptist preacher; editor of *The Weekly Register* (a Catholic journal), *The Illustrated London Magazine*; on the staff of *The Standard* (anti-Catholic prejudice of proprietors led to his dismissal); father of Richard Brinsley Sheridan Knowles (1848–c.1930), author; catalogued many valuable collections of historical manuscripts, mainly belonging to Catholic families; see *Gillow*, Vol. IV, p.78; *DNB*.

Knox, Rt. Rev. Mgr. Ronald Arbuthnot – priest and writer; b. 17 February 1888, Kibworth rectory, Leicestershire; c. 22 September 1917 (received at Farnborough Abbey by the abbot, Dom Fernand Cabrol); d. 24 August 1957, Manor House, Mells, Somerset; son of Evangelical bishop; brilliant student; Anglo-Catholic at Eton; made private vow of celibacy at seventeen; at Balliol College, Oxford; President of the Oxford Union; Fellow of Trinity College, Oxford; took Anglican orders; after his conversion studied for the priesthood at St. Edmund's, Old Hall, Hertfordshire; ordained Catholic priest by Cardinal Bourne 5 October 1919 "on his own patrimony"; Catholic chaplain to University of Oxford 1926–1939; wrote five detective stories to finance the chaplaincy to the disapproval of Cardinal Bourne; close platonic friendship with Daphne Lady Acton (see above); translated the Vulgate Bible; last years (1947–1957) spent at Mells, Somerset, with the Asquiths; great preacher; many books on religious themes; Harold MacMillan, a student of his at Oxford, said he was "the only man I have ever known who really was a saint ... and if you live with a saint, it's quite an experience, especially a humorous saint"; buried at Mells; see *A Spiritual Aeneid* (1918) (account of his conversion); *The Belief of Catholics* (1927); *The Church on Earth* (1929) ("It matters little whether we define the attitude of Protestants by saying that they believe in a Church that is divided, or by saying that they believe in a plurality of churches. The whole issue depends upon your answer to the question, 'What happens when there is a schism in the Christian body? What is left?' If you answer, 'Two churches' or 'Two divided parts of the Church,' you are not a Catholic. If you say, 'One Church and one sect,' you are in agreement with Catholic Christendom"); *Difficulties* (1932) (with Arnold Lunn); *In Soft Garments* (1942), *I Believe* (1944); *The Mass in Slow Motion* (1948); *The Creed in Slow Motion* (1949) ("[W]hen we call the Church holy we don't simply mean that it is a collection of holy people.... And I think it is a really startling difference between the Catholic Church and any other Christian denomination, that other Christians think it is up to *them* to be holy in order to bring up the average of holiness, so to speak, in their particular denomination; but we Catholics have a quite different instinct – we think of the Church as a holy thing, whether we are holy or not. We expect it to make us holy; we don't imagine it to be our job to make it holy"); *Enthusiasm* (1950); *The Hidden Stream* (1952) ("For St. Paul, the Church is at once something wholly united, and something wholly unique. The Bride of Christ, how could there be more than one Bride of Christ? The building of which Christ is the corner-stone; what more compact idea could you get of Christian fellowship? The Body of which Christ is the Head; how could there be more than one such Body, or how, outside the unity of that Body, can a man have a right to think of himself as united to Christ?...

The Church, as Christ himself envisaged it, is a visible Church, rogues and honest men mixed; not all members of the Church are bound for heaven by any means.

And if you look around, today, for a visible Church which is visibly one, there is hardly any competition, is there? I mean, Christians who belong to other denominations don't even claim, as a rule, that their denomination is *the* Church.... Anybody who has reached the point of looking round to find a single, visible fellowship of human beings which claims to be the one Church of Christ, has got to become a Catholic or give up his search in despair"); "The Pull of Truth" in J. A. O'Brien (ed), *Roads to Rome* (1955) ("Now, it is evident that both the Scriptural writers and the early Fathers treated the Church as axiomatically one. It is evident that in the mind of the early centuries the effect of schism was not to produce two Catholic churches (which would be a contradiction in terms), nor two parts of the Catholic Church, for this would be the formal abandonment of the unity which all their thought postulates. How, then, can I imagine that when the eastern dioceses fell out of communion with the west, or when England abandoned its former connection with Rome and threw in its lot with the continental Protestants,

schism had any other effect than it had in the days of Nestorius or of Eutyches? Which, in either case, was the true Church, and which the schismatical? I only know of two tests which have ever been proposed for finding the true church in such an emergency. One rule is to take your stand with the majority of the Catholic episcopate; the other is to take your stand with that part in the dispute which includes the Bishop of Rome"); *Proving God: A New Apologetic* (1959); Evelyn Waugh, *The Life of Ronald Knox* (1959); Philip Caraman, SJ (ed), *The Occasional Sermons of Ronald A. Knox* (1960); Philip Caraman, SJ (ed), *The Pastoral Sermons of Ronald A. Knox* (1960); Thomas Corbishley, SJ, *Ronald Knox the Priest* (1964); Denis Gwynn, "Monsignor Ronald Knox," *Irish Ecclesiastical Record*, October 1957, p.240; Denis Gwynn, "Evelyn Waugh and Ronald Knox," *The Irish Ecclesiastical Record*, May 1966, p.288; Milton T. Walsh, "Ronald Knox the Apologist," *Priests and People*, October 1988, p.401 ("In trying to explain to his father the object of his search, he compared the Church of Rome to a shop window where there was no need to examine the goods because over the door was a sign: 'THIS IS THE TRUE DEPOT ORDAINED BY CHRIST HIMSELF'"); Paul Dean, "The Consecration of the Heart: Ronald Knox Reconsidered," *The New Criterion*, September 1997; George Marshall, "Two Autobiographical Narratives of Conversion: Robert Hugh Benson and Ronald Knox," *Recusant History*, October 1998, p.237; Milton Walsh, *Ronald Knox As Apologist: Wit, Laughter and the Popish Creed* (2007); James Chappel, "Ronald Knox: A Bibliographic Essay," *Theological Librarianship*, an online journal, December 2008; David Rooney, *The Wine of Certitude: A Literary Biography of Ronald Knox* (2009); Milton Walsh, *Second Friends:*

C. S. Lewis and Ronald Knox in Conversation (2009); Terry Tastard, *Ronald Knox and English Catholicism* (2009); Patrick Allitt, *Catholic Converts: British and American Intellectuals Turn to Rome* (1997) *passim*; Joseph Pearce, *Literary Converts* (1999) *passim*; Fr. Charles P. Connor, *Classic Catholic Converts* (2001), pp.143–155; Lorene Hanley Duquin, *A Century of Catholic Converts* (2003), p.43; *DNB*.

Knox, Thomas Francis (name in religion Francis) – priest and scholar b. 24 December 1822, Brussels, Belgium; c. 17 November 1845 (received with Faber (see below) and his followers); d. 20 March 1882, Brompton Oratory, London; brought up in Protestant family; educated at Trinity College, Cambridge, where he gained first in Classical Tripos; eventually told Oxford Movement's leader, Dr. Pusey, that Church of England was "a delusion of Satan"; joined the Oratorian Order in 1848; ordained priest 2 June 1849; one of founders of the London Oratory (third Superior there); DD of Rome; Westminster diocesan archivist; much work on causes of English martyrs; became known as a historian of the English Catholics; a high Ultramontane; buried at Oratorian private cemetery, Sydenham, South London; see *When Does the Church Speak Infallibly? or, the Nature and Scope of the Church's Teaching Office* (1870); *Gillow*, Vol. IV, p.79; *DNB*.

Kolnai, Aurel Thomas – philosopher; b. 5 December 1900, Budapest, Hungary; c. 10 July 1926 (wife, Elisabeth, *née* Gemes (d. 1982) received in August 1940); d. 28 June 1973, Hampstead, London; parents both liberal Jews (father's name was Stein); prosperous family; paternal grandfather was a rigorous Orthodox Jew; changed his name to Kolnai while a teenager; distinguished

education at the Lutheran Obergymnasium, Budapest and later at Universities of Vienna, Freiburg and Berne with such as Moritz Schlick, Ludwig von Mises, and Edmund Husserl; influenced in his conversion by Max Scheler and especially by G. K. Chesterton (see above), whose writings he discovered in 1919 (said in 1936: "Chesterton's death is like a permanent eclipse of the sun"); said that only in Catholicism was the true presupposition of religion, 'response' comes before 'fiat', to be found; main interests were ethics and political philosophy; worked as a writer and journalist 1926–1936; wrote *The War Against the West* (1938), a critique of Nazi ideology ("In Kolnai's view, Nazism was not an inexplicable efflorescence of unfathomable evil, but the result of a pathological overemphasis on some human values at the expense of others" (*DNB*)); wrote against pacifism, arguing that absolute non-violence precluded moral responsibility; escaped to the United States in 1940, moving later to Canada and settling in London in 1955; British citizen from 1962; adopted a philosophy of imperfectionism or anti-utopianism; buried in Hampstead cemetery; see *Twentieth Century Memoirs* (1952–1955), pp. c.700 (unpublished) (excerpts from the memoirs under the title of "Chesterton and Catholicism," are published in the *Chesterton Review*, May 1982, p.127) ("The mental aura of my conversion, which to some extent has permanently tinged my faith, reminds me more or less of Mark the Roman in the *Ballad of the White Horse*: 'And belief that stood on unbelief/ Stood up iron and alone.' Few things, indeed, have done so much to convince me of the authenticity of Jesus's miracles and the claims of the Church as the episode of Thomas, the Apostle, who would doubt and test the improbable thing ere he surrendered to belief, and some of whose sober rationalism recurs in that other great Thomas in the Church's history, Aquinas. Long after my conversion, I discovered a phrase of St. Paul's which impressed me with a similar note of dry authenticity: *Scio enim cui credidi...*

I did have a most vivid experience of the alternative: either *no* religion or an *embodied* religion – with its symbols, traditions, historic figures (beyond more abstract concepts or allegoric personifications) and with its arbitrary accents and its corporate authority. Having chosen religion in place of irreligion, which meant entrusting myself to God and not inventing a concept of Divinity that might best suit my fancy, I chose, *uno ictu*, submission to the Church...

Like so many other converts of my time, I was won for Catholicism largely, if not chiefly, by the wisdom and wit of Gilbert Keith Chesterton. One of my prevailing moods in those years could be phrased thus, 'Not to share Chesterton's faith is, after all, a thing of rank absurdity.'

Sound reason aware of its limitations but trustful of its application to objects outside the mind, reverence for the manifoldness of reality, open-minded acceptance of the order of the universe and the realm of values as 'given' in our world-experience – to maintain or safeguard any of these, it was by no means necessary to embrace Catholicism; but the historical linkage between these principles and the Catholic intellectual tradition, the dominant general propensity of mankind to turn against the former in proportion as it deserted the latter, seemed to bear witness, if not to the truth of Catholicism, at least to a deep enduring concordance of Catholicism with the spirit of Truth. Sanity, morality, and the full experience of a world undeprived of its wealth of meaning, dimension, color, savor and weight were undoubtedly possible without the Faith; but they were all

of greater intrinsic perfection and endowed with greater security under the Faith. Above all, the Faith alone would guarantee their status and effective presence on the vast scale of our common civilization. Entering the Church not only placed me in the supernatural presence of God and offered me access to the Communion of Saints; it also made me feel as if I were firmly lodged in the one valid, universal and imperishable medium of communication with my fellow man"); *Ethics, Value and Reality* (1977); Andrew C. Vorga, "Aurel Kolnai, Philosopher in Troubled Times," *Chesterton Review*, February 1983, p.31; Francesca Murphy (ed) *Political Memoirs* (1999); Pierre Manent, "Aurel Thomas Kolnai (1900–1973)," *Chesterton Review*, 1982, p.162 ("A. Kolnai, like Chesterton, understood admirably that when man conceives of himself as God's guest on earth, innumerable paths are open to him, whereas when he believes himself – and wishes himself – to be the master and creator of his own destiny, he petrifies both the world and himself"); Francis Dunlop, "Aurel Kolnai," *Salisbury Review*, Autumn 1997, p.8; Francis Dunlop, *The Life and Thought of Aurel Kolnai* (2002); John Haldane, "Ethics, Politics and Imperfection," *New Blackfriars*, July 2008, p.389 ("Kolnai's adopted theology gave him reason to believe in the Fall, but experience taught him about human fallen-ness – indeed recognition of this as a recurrent feature of mankind was part of the reason for his conversion. It is rhetorical to say, with G. K. Chesterton, that 'the only Christian doctrine for which there is empirical evidence is that of original sin'; but it is not at all an exaggeration to observe that every thoughtful person knows that human beings have recurrent liabilities to injustice, cruelty, malice and other forms of maltreatment of others, and destruction of self'"); *DNB*.

Laing, Francis Henry, SJ – priest and author; b. 9 April 1816; c. 1846 (his brother, an Anglican clergyman, converted in October 1889); d. 17 December 1889; formerly Anglican curate; joined the Society of Jesus in 1849; ordained priest in 1855; DD of Rome; taught at St. Beuno's College, St. Asaph; left Jesuits in 1862; see *Gillow*, Vol. IV, p.93 (referring to a letter from a "Scottish Recusant" in *The Tablet*, 11 January 1890: "With no uncertain sound he denounced the adoption by Catholics of the political heresies of the age. He declared that they should be distinct and different from the Protestant world around them; that their politics should be Catholic, their social life Catholic, their journalism Catholic. To those who, faithful to the memory of the great Pontiff, Pius IX, strive to make the 'Syllabus' their rule of conduct and opinion, his loss will hardly be replaced by any living English Catholic writer").

Lamb, Lady Margaret Pansy Felicia (*née* Pakenham) (known as "Pansy") – writer and translator; b. 18 May 1904; c. 1981; d. 19 February 1999, Rome; eldest daughter of fifth Earl of Longford (killed at Gallipoli); sister of Lord Longford (see below); wife of the Bloomsbury artist, Henry Lamb (1883–1960), who painted her almost continuously; sister-in-law of Anthony Powell (1905–2000); celebrated by John Betjeman and Evelyn Waugh (see below); wrote two novels and a biography of Charles I; translated Charles Peguy's poetry; influenced in her conversion by the early Fathers and by Newman (it was merely a case, she said, of "When in Rome ...", though she always suspected that Catholics held the stronger position); moved to Rome in 1981 so as to be near Pope John Paul II whom she greatly admired; in her last years she acted as a voluntary guide for pilgrims to St. Peter's.

Langdale, Marmaduke, first Baron of Holme – gentleman soldier; b. 1598, Pighill, near Beverley, Yorkshire; d. 5 August 1661, Holme-on-Spalding-Moor, Yorkshire; most of relations were Catholic (uncle, Christopher Wharton, martyred at York in 1600 for being a priest), but father was temporizer and brought him up in the Established Church; knighted by Charles I in 1627; one of Charles I's most distinguished supporters and generals in the Civil War; taken prisoner after battle of Preston in 1648 and sent to Nottingham Castle; escaped and withdrew to Flanders, where reconciled to the Church; served as soldier for several continental sovereigns; Charles II created him peer; his estates sequestered after the Civil War; returned to England in 1660; very austere man; buried in sanctuary on right side of altar at All Saints' parish church, Sancton; see *Gillow*, Vol. IV, p.123.

Langrishe, Helen Amelrosa – Catholic laywoman; c. 1894; d. 14 December 1955; of County Kilkenny, Ireland; daughter of Right Hon. Fitzwilliam Hume-Dick; wife of Hercules Robert Langrishe, JP, only son of Sir James Langrishe, fourth Baronet; see essay in J. G. F. Raupert (ed), *Roads to Rome* (1901), p.150 ("Believing as I did in the necessity of valid orders for valid Sacraments, I could not, once I had begun to ponder on these matters, remain in the Church of England, whose orders are repudiated not only by the *whole* of Christendom, but also by half her members and many of her clergy. The risk to my mind was too great. Rome might err, but she could give me true Sacraments; no one could dispute that. And what doubts or difficulties I might have to encounter could come up to those I faced in the Anglican Church, as to whether her Sacraments were genuine or not? What greater evil could befall me than the risk I might run if they were not? And so unhesitatingly I went over to the old faith; and I can safely say, once in the true fold, all doubts and difficulties vanished").

La Primaudaye, Charles John – b. 1807; c. December 1850 (in Marseilles; followed by his wife, Anne Hubbard (1812–1854), received in 1851, and his children); d. 1859; member of a Huguenot family exiled at the time of Louis XIV; educated at St. John's College, Oxford; took Anglican orders and became Manning's curate and confessor; with his wife brought up nine children religiously; father of Maria Margaret Pollen (1838–1919) (see below); another daughter, Catherine (1839–1864), became at the age of seventeen a Holy Child nun (soon became an invalid and died a holy death); after his wife's death he joined Manning's Oblates of St. Charles and went to Rome to study for the priesthood; nursed a student there who had smallpox on the basis that an older person was less likely to catch the disease; he became infected and died.

Law, Augustus Henry, SJ – priest and sailor; b. 21 October 1833, Trumpington, near Cambridge; c. 16 May 1852 (father converted earlier); d. 25 November 1880, South Africa; son of Anglican vicar; naval cadet for eight years; conversion influenced by the Gorham judgment (see entry for William Maskell); joined the Society of Jesus in 1854; very able student; ordained priest on 24 September 1865; served on many missions, finally in South Africa; died on missionary expedition to valley of Zambesi, worn out by yellow fever, privation and fatigue; see Ellis Schreiber, *The Life of Augustus Henry Law, Priest of the Society of Jesus* (1893); R. F. Clarke, *Augustus Henry Law, Sailor and Jesuit* (1894); James Wallace, "Augustus Henry Law 1833–1880," *The Month*, February 1962, p.90; *Gillow*, Vol. IV, p.152.

Law, Hon. William Towry – army officer and author; b. 16 June 1809; c. 19 September 1851 (received at Oscott; his eldest son, Augustus Henry (see above), was received in 1852; another son, Thomas, joined the London Oratory, but in 1878 left the Catholic Church); d. 31 October 1886, Hampton Court Palace, Middlesex; youngest son of the Chief Justice, Edward, first Lord Ellenborough; grandson of Anglican Bishop of Carlisle; commission in the Grenadier Guards; took Anglican orders and held several curacies and benefices; at first Evangelical, then attracted to Tractarianism; President of the Church Union (protested against "papal aggression" at time of restoration of the Catholic hierarchy); influenced greatly in his conversion by secession of Henry Manning; eight children by his first marriage and six by his second; see *Unity and Faithful Adherence to the Word of God are only to be Found in the Catholic Church: A Letter to His Late Parishioners* (1852); *Gillow*, Vol. IV, p.154 ("[Having a numerous family] this change involved many bitter sacrifices, which he cheerfully endured during the thirty-five years that he spent as a devout and fervent Catholic"); *DNB* (entry relating to his father) ("[I]n.... *A Letter to his Late Parishioners*, [he] explained that he never had any authority as a priest in the Church of England, as there was only one indivisible church").

Lawton, Sir Frederick Horace, PC, QC – judge; b. 21 December 1911, 1 Fenwick Road, Camberwell, London; c. 1936; d. 3 February 2001, York; educated at Corpus Christi College, Cambridge; long and very successful career as barrister, primarily in criminal law work; temporary flirtation with fascism when member of British Union of Fascists 1936–1940; invalided out of the war and went back to practice at the bar; Judge of Queen's Bench Division 1961–1972; presided over Richardson and Kray gang trials; also presided over the famous libel trial, Dering v. Uris (1964), over allegations of the plaintiff's conduct in a Nazi concentration camp; Lord Justice of Appeal 1972–1986; member of Criminal Law Revision Committee 1959–1986 and other bodies considering reform of the criminal law; *DNB*.

Lechmere (alias Stratford), Edmund – priest; b. c.1586, Fownhope, Herefordshire; d. September 1640, English College, Douai; educated at Brasenose College, Oxford; became a Catholic and went to the English College, Douai; later taught philosophy there; studied at the Sorbonne and graduated BD; returned to Douai where he became Vice-President; ordained priest 18 December 1622; created DD at Rheims in 1633; wrote several works defending the Catholic faith; see *A Disputation of the Church wherein the Old Religion is Maintained* (1629); *DNB*.

Leckonby, John – schoolmaster; b. at Shadforth, Durham; student at Oxford during the Civil War; made examination of authenticity of Protestant religion, which resulted in his becoming a Catholic; admitted at Douai College in 1649; returned to London and worked at school opened in Whitefriars by dramatist and poet, James Shirley (see below), who had also become a Catholic; indicted for hearing Mass and for being recusant-schoolmaster and thrown into prison; ultimately gained release, but died shortly afterwards in great distress; high reputation as classical scholar and for knowledge of ecclesiastical history; see *Gillow*, Vol. IV, p.176.

Lee, Christopher Robin James – historian, writer and broadcaster; b. 13 October 1941, Kent; c. 11 May 2008; form- erly Anglican; freelance writer 1962–1967; journalist for the *Daily Express* 1967–1976; defense and foreign affairs correspondent BBC Radio 1976–1986; Fellow in History, Emmanuel College, Cambridge 1986–1991; also author and scriptwriter for various BBC radio drama and comedy series; see *1603: A Turning Point in British History* (2003); *This Sceptred Isle: Empire* (2005); "Becoming a Catholic without illusions," *Catholic Herald*, 30 May 2008 ("So what does bring me to Rome? First, I feel at home in its structure, its ritual, its devotion to Our Lady and the sacrament of Confession. But above all, I am brought to Rome by one simple celebration of Faith: the Mass. I am welcomed by the unswerving devotion in the Liturgy of the Eucharist. It is a devout and profoundly personal moment when that wafer is indeed the Body. It is a moment that has no need for the debate between a philosophical and anthropological approach to the Eucharist. The Dominican Edward Schillebeeckx wrote that 'the basis of the entire Eucharist event is Christ's personal gift of himself to his fellow-men and, within this, to the Father.' For me, it is a moment of almost medieval simplicity.... It is a personal experience that is both frightening and a blessed excitement.

Did I not find it elsewhere? No, no I did not. Yet, I have no evangelic message, certainly no sense of ecumenism. To my mind, one is one and the other is the other. There is no reason for wishy-washy diplomatic compromise and certainly not reconciliation. Moreover, the Church of Rome is not a refuge of downtrodden worshippers. It is the true home of the expression of the Trinity and the Liturgy of the Mass. That is an awesome responsibility and one that it must with much louder voice more publicly celebrate").

Lee, Frederick George – writer on theology; b. 6 January 1832, School House, Thame, Oxfordshire; c. 11 December 1901; (wife, Elvira (1838–1890), hymnologist and authoress, second cousin once removed of Newman, received in 1881; second son, Gordon, writer, received in 1879; sister-in-law, also converted, later becoming a nun); d. 1902, 22 Earl's Court Gardens, London; father a High Church vicar; he himself vicar of All Saints, Lambeth 1867–1899; at St. Edmund Hall, Oxford, but failed to graduate; promoter of corporate reunion between Church of England and the Catholic Church; set up Association for Promotion of Unity of Christendom; Anglican disciple of Pugin (see below) and friend of Ambrose Phillipps de Lisle (see below); founded Order of Corporate Reunion in 1857; took part in clandestine episcopal consecration near Venice; reconciled to the Catholic Church six weeks before his death; buried in Brookwood cemetery, Surrey; see H. R. T. Brandreth, *Dr. Lee of Lambeth* (1951) (statement by Dr. G. C. Williamson: "Dr. Lee was a lovable man and all who knew him were ready and willing to follow his guidance, caring little whither it led, as long as he was its leader. He gathered round him a faithful band of followers and not one of them, I believe, has ever broken the confidence Lee reposed in him. Very many of them, probably most of their number, eventually joined the Catholic Church: many preceded him, and others followed him. We all loved him. May he rest in peace"); J. H. Crehan, "Black Market in Episcopal Orders," *The Month*, June 1953, p.352; *DNB*.

Leech, Humphrey, SJ (alias Henry Eccles) – priest; b. in 1571, Drayton in Hales, Shropshire; c. 1608 (received by John Floyd); d. 18 July 1629, Puddington Hall, Cheshire; formerly Anglican vicar and then chaplain or minor canon of Christ Church College, Oxford; reputed as a preacher; after studying writings of St. Vincent de Lerins began to doubt authenticity of the Established Church; after giving two sermons, charged with having introduced new doctrine and favoring Catholic doctrine, and suspended; suspecting arrest, went over to St. Omer and was received into the Catholic Church; entered English College, Rome, in 1609; ordained priest 21 April 1612 and stayed at college; entered the Society of Jesus in 1618; sent to the English mission, resided at Puddington Hall, Cheshire, attending Catholics in that area; see *A Triumph of Truth* (1609); Barbara Coulton, "'Casting Anchor in the Harbour of Religion': The Peregrination of Humphrey Leech (1571–1629)," *Recusant History*, May 2006, p.55; *Gillow*, Vol. IV, p.184; *DNB*.

Lees-Milne, (George) James Henry – diarist, biographer, architectural historian and conservationist; b. 6 August 1908, Wickhamford Manor, Worcestershire; c. 26 March 1934; d. 28 December 1997, Tetbury; read Modern History at Magdalen College, Oxford; vowed to preserve the country houses of England; pioneer of National Trust from 1936 to 1966; his diaries (running from 1942 to 1997) are seen as some of the finest of their kind in twentieth century; wrote several biographies and histories; reverted to High Anglicanism in the wake of the Second Vatican Council; disliked the new liturgy; his wife, Alvilde (1909–1994), a celebrated gardener; their ashes scattered together in the garden at Essex House, Badminton, his last home; see *Roman Mornings* (1956); *St. Peter's: The Story of St. Peter's Basilica in Rome* (1967) ("It is remarkable how the four great Eastern Churches never had the will or the wish to dispute Rome's superior claims. The see of Antioch, reputedly founded by St. Peter, had consistently been contested by rival claimants and its line vitiated by heretical bishops. Alexandria, which by the time of Julius I ranked immediately after Rome as the second patriarchal see, was then a seat of Arianism. Constantinople, because only newly founded on the site of the Greek Byzantium where certainly there had been a Christian community since the second century, could advance no pretensions. Lastly Jerusalem, which of the four cities boasted the greatest antiquity in that it was the scene of Christ's ministry, crucifixion and resurrection, the disciples' first teaching, and so was the virtual nursery of Christianity, yet put forward no right to pre-eminence. That the heresies which flourished like weeds in the fourth century were eradicated one by one or rendered innocuous, was without question owing to Rome's firmness in denouncing them. By the fifth century the Pope in Rome was invariably consulted by overseas bishops for rulings in matters of faith and policy. He responded in what are known as decretal letters having the force of law within his supreme jurisdiction. The first was issued in 385. All bishops throughout Christendom were ostensibly nominated by the Pope. Leo the Great (440–61) became the first true Pope in the modern sense because he was the unquestioned supreme head of Christendom. He raised himself to this dignity through staunchly upholding not only the primacy of Peter over the other apostles, but that of his successors in Rome over other bishops. By a process of gradual evolution, the primacy of Rome had become firmly established. For a thousand years it did not occur to anyone in Christendom to question it"); *Another Self* (1970), especially pp.136–138 ("In the spring of 1934 I became a Catholic. I was twenty-five. Why at an age past sentimental adolescence, and one of full-blown earthy youth, did I do it? Not for pietistic, but for temperamental reasons. I was a Christian. I did not feel that I belonged exclusively to the Church of England nor, as my father did, that God was an Englishman. So why not? I did not like to be called a convert. I saw myself as a re-vert to the ancient faith of my forebears. The Church of Rome was the original Christian church which for nearly two thousand years had survived countless heresies and schisms. I revered its endurance and its historic continuity which seemed to me divine. I admired the unbroken apostolic succession from St. Peter down to Pope Pius XI. I dearly loved the heraldry and symbolism of its ministry. I loved the Gothic sanctity, the Renaissance paganism, the Baroque opulence of the Catholic ritual and ceremonial. The smell of vellum missals, candle wax, chrism and incense was the breath of life to me. Genuflexions and signs of the Cross seemed the natural pledges of devotion, just as Gregorian chants and the *missa cantata* were the fitting stimulants and accompaniments to worship. I bitterly deplore the policy of the hierarchy today in depreciating and doing away with these time-honored usages and practices.

I also think ... that I had need of a discipline from outside, a discipline with which unaided I was incapable of providing myself. Conscience was certainly not enough. Since no man's conscience agreed with another's why should mine be infallible? Of course I found much Catholic doctrine unpalatable. Several tenets seemed to me then, and still do seem, nonsensical. Very well, I ignore or flout them at my peril. But because they seem nonsensical I am not so arrogant as to presume they must be wrong. They may for all I know be useful yardsticks of ethical conduct. Besides, I believe in having pricks to kick against so long as one cannot kick them quite away. In the same sense I believe in outward proprieties. I don't care a fig what people do in private. In any case they all do it. I just don't want to see them do it, because 'it' is usually unaesthetic. There is much to be said for dissimulation as opposed to cant. For whereas the last clogs the wheels of daily intercourse the first often oils them.

On the whole then I found little hardship in accepting the Catholic dogmas. I have never, for instance, worried over the literal meaning of obscure passages in the Missal. Again it is the symbolism of the phraseology, tried and proved by countless assaults, and the poetry of the Latin words, weathered with the lichen and patina of the centuries, which are the ultimate beauties worth dying for. The reformers are mad – or wicked – to tamper with a foundation sanctified and beautified by the devout past, and to substitute makeshift structures of gimcrack materials merely in order to placate the ephemeral tastes of the vulgar and ignorant. By chucking overboard the Latin Mass these philistines are threatening the basic fabric of the Church's universality – an alarming and terrible thing to do.

My reversion to Catholicism had also a political connotation. I saw the Church as the last and impregnable bulwark against Communism in western Europe. The sequence of events in Spain throughout the Thirties confirmed my faith"); "The Sale of Treasures from Catholic Churches" in Marcus Binney and Peter Burman (ed), *Change and Decay: The Future of Our Churches* (1977) ("Throughout the Dark Ages and during the medieval and Renaissance periods the Catholic Church was the greatest inspiration of western art, the greatest patron of artists. Churches were built and adorned, firstly, for the glory of God and, secondly, for the worship and delight of the people. These purposes, in this order, persisted throughout Europe and the Christian world until the present century.

Holiness and beauty walked hand in hand.

But with decreasing spiritual fervor, artists tended to derive less spiritual inspiration from religion. Fewer works of art were dedicated to it.... On the whole church artifacts from 1900 to 1960 were in extremely poor taste.... Then came the Second Vatican Council of 1962–6, and to everyone's surprise, things suddenly went from bad to worse.... Like Cromwell's soldiers, the bishops and clergy turned upon the Church treasures.... Statues, candelabras, chalices, vestments, jeweled reliquaries, votive offerings are being thrown out, given away, sold. God knows what happens to them in England. In Italy they can be bought in every antique shop and junk market. The parishioners ... are not consulted, nor are they told to what purpose the accruing funds are devoted. The whole business is conducted *sub rosa*, and those people who have the temerity to enquire are either snubbed or ignored"); *The Last Stuarts* (1983); *Fourteen Friends* (1996); Michael Bloch, *James Lees-Milne: The Life* (2009); *DNB*.

Leigh, William – benefactor; b. 4 November 1802; c. 10 March 1844; d. 4 January 1873; son of wealthy Liverpool merchant; of very serious nature and deeply religious; interested in the Tractarian movement before his conversion; Lord of Manor of Woodchester and Nympsfield; founder of Passionist Church and Monastery at Woodchester, Gloucestershire (both built by Charles Hansom in Gothic style), but with death of Dominic Barberi shortly before, Passionists moved on and Dominicans moved in; great generosity to the Church, both in England and Australia, and to the poor; Knight of St. Gregory the Great; corresponded with Newman about the teaching that man is a fallen being needing redemption, in a supernatural form, and whether one can learn from pagan writers; three of his four children pre-deceased him, one dying in infancy; buried in the Church of the Annunciation, Woodchester; see *Gillow*, Vol. IV, p.196; Stanley L. Jaki, *Newman to Converts: An Existential Ecclesiology* (2001), pp.411–412 ("Although Newman was fully aware of the difficulty of giving a balanced answer about the relation between a fallen nature and a nature rescued by the supernatural, he was not hesitant to tell Mr. Leigh that it was not right to say that what one could learn from Horace could be learned only better from Thomas à Kempis, as if they represented two stations on a continuous line: 'I think not – because a heathen's experience of life is not the same as a Christian's.' The latter's experience was derived from no less source than Christ himself: 'Our Lord has a full knowledge and love of fallen man. He came to save that which was lost. And St. Paul had that love according to his measure after Him – and so the great missionaries, as St. Francis Xavier.

Newman went on to explain what may be gained from studying the classics. A good deal, he said. But what was really that 'good deal'? It was the misery which sin dealt to man.... 'It is most piercingly sad to observe how the heathen writers yearn for some unknown good and higher truth and cannot find it – how Horace, in particular, tries to solace himself with the pleasures of sense, and how stern a monitor [the conscience] he has within him, telling him that Death is coming'...

Newman then draws a conclusion that demolishes by one stroke the opinion of those Newmanists who present him as a 'humanist' enchanted by man's natural powers and virtues. On the contrary, he bemoaned man's fallen misery in a Pascalian vein: 'Who can but pity such a race – so great and so little! Who does not recognize the abyss of misery which lies in that wound which sin has made in us! Who does not begin to see from such a spectacle, the Love of the Eternal Father, who felt it in fullness, and came to die for His dear rebellious children!'").

Leonard, Rt. Rev. Mgr. Graham Douglas – priest; b. 8 May 1921; c. 1994 (received by Cardinal Basil Hume; his wife, Priscilla, *née* Swann, also converted); d. 6 January 2010; father an Evangelical clergyman; educated at Balliol College, Oxford where he became Anglo-Catholic; took Anglican orders; Anglican bishop of Willesden (1964–1973), then Truro (1973–1981), then London (1981–1991); opponent of liberal developments there, especially ordination of women; ordained Catholic priest 23 April 1994 (ordained conditionally, having persuaded the Vatican that he might already possess valid orders by virtue of an Old Catholic apostolic succession); created papal chaplain with title of Monsignor; appointed Prelate of Honour by Pope John Paul II in 2001; brother-in-law to Michael Swann, Lord Swann of Colne St. Denys, and Hugh Swann, cabinet maker to Queen Elizabeth II; see essay in Rowanne Pasco (ed), *Why I Am a Catholic* (1995) ("One of the major differences between the Catholic Church and other Christian denominations is that there is a continuity between the early Church and the present Catholic Church, which doesn't exist with the others. Whether you take the Protestant Church on the Continent, or the Church of England here, they have sort of bypassed the Middle Ages and tried to go back to the primitive Church. So where is the continuity of the faith? Newman wrote, 'Did Saint Athanasius or Saint Ambrose come suddenly to life, it cannot be doubted what communion he would take to be his own.' The Catholic Church certainly does have this continuity right back to the earliest days and, indeed, to the Lord himself"); "By Whose Authority" in Dwight Longenecker (ed), *The Path to Rome* (1999) ("I came to recognize the need for an authority which declares what interpretations and expositions of doctrine are consonant with the Catholic Faith. Only so is the Church capable of living under the authority of revealed truth.... I came to see that the Petrine and Papal ministry gives to the Church a central authority which is both universal and personal. It is difficult to overestimate the significance of the fact that in the Catholic Church, obedience is given not to a book nor to the resolutions of a committee nor to formularies nor to a trust deed but to a person who exercises his ministry as *servus servorum Dei* – Servant of the Servants of God"); "Searching for obedience down the path that leads to Rome," *Catholic Herald*, 1 October 1999; "Former Anglican bishop of London explains why he became a Catholic," *AD 2000*, March 2002 ("As a member of the Anglican Church I was very concerned that increasingly greater importance was given to private, individual interpretations of the faith – interpretations that depended on the situation, the environment, on what the Church felt should be decided or commented on at any given moment"); *EWTN Audio Library* (2002); Michael Jackson, "The Case of Dr. Leonard," *The Tablet*, 30 April 1994.

Leslie, Mrs. Cuthbert – of Hassop Hall, Derbyshire; formerly member of Church of England; see essay in J. G. F. Raupert (ed), *Roads to Rome* (1901), p.151 ("When before my conversion, I had to define for myself, and for others, the reasons which forced me to enter the Catholic Church, I wrote down several statements, the substance of which I now give; as they bring out very clearly the motives which urged me to leave the Church of England and to join the Church of Rome.

First of all, I could not understand any Church being the true one in which the professing members are allowed to hold such contradictory opinions on the most important subjects.

Secondly, I had a very strong feeling that a Church cannot be called *Catholic* in which there is no pretence even of one central authority which all the world is bound to obey, and in which every one is allowed what is called liberty to accept one fundamental doctrine and reject another, and in which such different and contradictory practices are tolerated in dealing with the most sacred subjects – as, for example, Holy Communion and Devotion to Our Lady.

Thirdly, I never could understand the possibility of a Church teaching a consistent body of doctrine without the presence in the Church of a teaching authority which should not only be *Universal* but *Infallible*. The Church of England was to me the best example of the chaos and confusion of thought which result, and must of necessity result, from the absence in a Church of an infallible teaching authority which all are bound to obey.

Fourthly, I hoped and expected to get greater comfort from the Catholic Church than I had ever got from the cold formalism of the Establishment; but I did not argue that because the Catholic Church would be more consoling, it must therefore be the right Church; but I argued thus: 'If it be the Church of God, it will as a matter of fact satisfy all the longings of the human heart better than the Church established by law in this land'").

Leslie, Eleanor (*née* Falconer-Atlee) – b. 3 December 1800, Wandsworth; c. 3 December 1846 (received by Bishop Gillis; two daughters, Charlotte Cumming and Mary Margaret, both later nuns, received in 1847; son, Eric

William, later Jesuit priest, received 8 September 1848; eldest daughter, Eleanor, received 19 March 1850; finally her husband, Archibald Leslie (1789–26 February 1851), son of a Scottish Presbyterian minister, received in 1850); d. 8 April 1892; eldest daughter of John Falconer-Atlee; brought up and lived in Edinburgh; influenced in her conversion by Bossuet's *Exposition de la Doctrine de L'Eglise Catholique*, by some letters of Fénelon to a Protestant gentleman, and by Milner's *End of Controversy*; instrumental in conversion of many well-to-do English women, including Duchess of Buccleuch (see above); closely connected with St. Margaret's convent in Edinburgh; see Jean Stone, *Eleanor Leslie: A Memoir* (1898) (On the conversion of her son: "The young man then reflected as to what he would say if an unlearned pagan came to him for instruction. First he would ask him whether he believed that our Lord Jesus Christ was God. If he got an answer in the affirmative, he would then ask, 'Did not Jesus Christ give us a religion and promise that this religion should not go wrong?' The conclusion was evident, and reasoning thus he overcame the difficulties raised by his learned friends"); W. Gordon Gorman, *Converts to Rome* (1910) ("Of this lady, Charlotte [Montague-Douglas-Scott], fifth Duchess of Buccleuch, 1811–1895 (see above), wrote: 'I look upon her as our mother who helped to bring us into the true Church. We are all her children – good Father Robertson [Thomas Charles Robertson, chaplain to the Duke of Buccleuch, who converted in 1847], his aunt and her children, dear Lady Lothian and her children, myself, and I do not know how many others'").

Leslie, George (name in religion Archangel) – priest and missionary; b. in Scotland; d. 1637?, Aboyne, on Dee-side, Scotland; brought up as Protestant; after converting entered the Scots College, Rome, but left to become a Capuchin friar; acted as confessor in Bologna to the many Scottish, English, and Irish banished for their religion and living there; missioner for many years in Scotland, where he made many converts, including his own family; wrote a polemical tract, *Where was your Church before Luther?* (no copy extant); buried in Glen Tanar churchyard; see Giovanni Battista Rinuccini, *Il Cappuccino Scozzese* (1644) (account of Leslie's conversion, but containing also many marvelous incidents, which are apocryphal); *DNB*.

Leslie, Sir John Randolph ("Shane"), third Baronet – historian, biographer, and poet; b. 24 September 1885, Stratford House, 11 Granville Place, London; c. about 1907; d. 14 August 1971, 14 New Church Road, Hove; descended from adoptive daughter of Mrs. Fitzherbert; first cousin of Winston Churchill (his mother, Leonie Jerome, was American heiress whose sister, Jennie, was married to Lord Randolph Churchill); born into Anglo-Irish Protestant ascendancy; left school in 1901 to study in Paris; educated at King's College, Cambridge; became Catholic and Irish nationalist at Cambridge; influenced in conversion by Mgr. Robert Hugh Benson (see above) and Fr. Basil Maturin (see below); editor of *Dublin Review* 1916–1926; worked for a united Ireland; fine lecturer; see *The End of a Chapter* (1916) (description of a civilization he saw coming to an end); *Henry Edward Manning: His Life and Labours* (1921); *Mark Sykes: His Life and Letters* (1923); *The Poems of Shane Leslie* (1928); *The Oxford Movement 1833–1933* (1933); *The Film of Memory* (1938), *Mrs. Fitzherbert: A Life* (1939); *An Anthology of Catholic Poets* (1952); *Cardinal*

Gasquet: A Memoir (1953); *Long Shadows* (1966) ("On the whole the Latin and Catholic countries treat the Magdalen more charitably than the English-speaking world, though never up to the white heights from which Our Lord surveyed the problem. He pardoned the Magdalen *quia multum amavit* and for no other reason! As Monsignor Hemmick said: 'Only a God could have said that!'"); Patrick Allitt, *Catholic Converts: British and American Intellectuals Turn to Rome* (1997) *passim* ("All the Anglican factions, high and low, Leslie believed, had been weakened by the rise of modernism.... Leslie openly defended Pius X's excommunication of Tyrrell. Catholics, he insisted, had benefited from having a clear line of authority and a clear papal prohibition on modernism, while the Anglicans' lack of an effective authority principle condemned them to theological confusion"); *DNB*.

Leslie, Walter (Count Leslie in the nobility of the Holy Roman Empire) – army officer and diplomat; b. 1606, Aberdeenshire; c. 1634; d. 3 March 1667, Vienna; Calvinist background; gained prestige fighting in the imperial army; involved in the plot that led to the murder of the imperialist general Albrecht von Wallenstein in 1634; subsequent unsuccessful military career; constantly in diplomatic service of the Habsburgs; buried in the Scottish Benedictine abbey in Vienna; see *DNB*.

Leslie, Bishop William – bishop; b. 1657, Aberdeenshire; c. 1675; d. 4 April 1727, Laibach; son of a Scottish laird; schoolmaster for a while, then traveled to Padua, Italy; entered the Scots College, Rome; ordained priest 5 April 1681; returned to Padua, then settled in Graz, before studying philosophy, theology, and church law in Vienna and Rome; later held several ecclesiastical

positions in Austria and Hungary; appointed Professor of Theology at Padua University in 1698; membership of the Privy Council of Emperor Joseph I led to several successful diplomatic missions; appointed Bishop of Waitzen in 1716; made Prince-Bishop of Laibach in 1718; buried in Laibach Cathedral on the bank of the Ljubljanica River; see *DNB*.

Lester, Edmund, SJ (originally Edward) – priest; b. 1866; c. 1883; d. 24 October 1934, Osterley; christened Edward, but took name Edmund on reception into the Church; of delicate health; joined the Society of Jesus in 1885; ordained priest 30 July 1899; Superior of Campion House, Osterley, devoted to late vocations to priesthood and religious life; editor of *Stella Maris*; founder of new sodality, Knights of the Blessed Sacrament; see essay in Maurice Leahy (ed), *Conversions to the Catholic Church: A Symposium* (1933) (reprinted under the title of "Mailing a Letter," in John A. O'Brien (ed), *The Road to Damascus: Vol. III; The Way to Emmaus* (1953) ("The Catechism ... tells [us] that 'Faith is a supernatural gift of God, which enables us to believe without doubting whatever God has revealed.' There can be no conversion without this gift and God may not give it to all. We can have conviction without conversion but we cannot have conversion without conviction. The conviction may be the result of study, clear thinking and absence of prejudice, without which there can be no clear thinking, or it may be included in the Gift of Faith. An illiterate Catholic has the Faith and the conviction. He might be defeated in argument but that will not shake his Faith...

[A man] would find it as easy to determine where each color of the rainbow begins and ends as to tell you why and when he became a Catholic. He might say: I became a Catholic because God in

His infinite mercy gave me the grace to believe without doubting all that He has revealed. Can any convert say more?"); Daniel Kearney, "Fr. Edmund Lester, SJ and Campion House, Osterley," *Catholic Life*, September 2003, p.62.

Lewgar, John – colonial administrator and writer; b. about 1601, Sussex; c. 1634; d. 1665, London, parish of St Giles-in-the-Fields; descended from ancient family; received Anglican orders at Cambridge; rector in Somerset; conversion brought about by friend William Chillngworth, recent convert who later fell; after conversion became secretary to Cecil Calvert, second Lord Baltimore, and his representative in government of Maryland; several posts in Maryland assembly; much opposition from the Jesuits who complained of his harsh government; after his wife's death he became a priest (1647); returned to England just before the Restoration in 1660 and retired; worked to assist the poor when plague broke out in London, regardless of danger and finally died of the disease; see *Gillow*, Vol. IV, p.202; *DNB*.

Lewis, David – author and translator; b. 1814; c. 30 May 1846; d. 1895; Fellow and then Vice-Principal of Jesus College, Oxford; Anglican curate of Newman at St. Mary the Virgin, Oxford; assisted Frederick Lucas (see below) with the editing of *The Tablet* in 1848; translator of Nicholas Sander's *The Rise and Growth of the Anglican Schism* (1581) from original Latin into English and of works of St. Teresa of Avila and St. John of the Cross; a patron of the London Oratory; *DNB*.

Lewis (alias Charles Baker), Saint David Henry, SJ – priest and martyr; b. 1617, Abergavenny, Monmouthshire, Wales; c. 1633; d. 27 August 1679, Usk, Monmouthshire; both parents Catholic, though father Protestant for some time before being reconciled to the Church; brought up in conformity with the established religion by his father, whilst eight siblings educated by mother in the Catholic faith; visited France when sixteen and by means of Fr. William Talbot, SJ, became Catholic; after studying law in England, went to Rome in 1638 and received into English College; ordained priest 20 July 1642; entered the Society of Jesus in 1645; sent to the English mission twice and spent thirty years there; much bravery and suffering and commonly called Father of the Poor; at time of Oates Plot betrayed and seized in house in Llantarnam, Monmouthshire, whilst preparing to say Mass, 17 November 1678; confined in Monmouth prison; tried for high treason by coming into or remaining in the kingdom; condemned and executed at Usk, Monmouthshire; much sympathy with his innocence, so that body not cut down until life extinct and not quartered; buried in churchyard of priory church of St. Mary at Usk; very devout and respected greatly both by Protestants and Catholics; see *Gillow*, Vol. IV, p.205; *Catholic Encyclopedia* (under the name of Charles Baker); *DNB*.

Lewis, (John) Saunders – Welsh dramatist, poet and nationalist; b. 15 October 1893, 61 Falkland Road, Poulton-cum-Seacombe, Wallasey, Cheshire; c. 16 February 1932 (his wife, Margaret, *née* Gilcriest (1891–1984), daughter of Irish Wesleyan parents, teacher and Irish nationalist, also a convert); d. 1 September 1985, Cardiff; family on mother's side long line of Welsh Presbyterian (Calvinistic Methodist) preachers and ministers; served and severely wounded in World War I; conservative minded and acknowledged a debt to Charles Maurras as a literary figure; friend of David Jones, the poet (see above); co-founder of Welsh Nationalist Party and President in 1926; teacher and lecturer in English and Welsh literature; wrote fine Christian poetry and drama dealing with public and private morality; examined Welsh writers in wider context of European literature; defended the Welsh language; loyal and devout Catholic, but critical about the downplaying of the old rite of Mass, which he felt was "the perfect way for a human being to worship God"; buried with his wife in Penarth public cemetery; see David Jones, "John Saunders Lewis: A Man of Great Contradictions," *Catholic Life*, July 2002; David Jones, "Y Cylch Catholig – The Welsh Catholic Circle," *Catholic Times*, February 2009, p.14 ("[He] decided to convert to Catholicism because he strongly believed that only in the Catholic Mass could God be fittingly worshipped"); *DNB* ("As a nationalist politician, as in his literary work, Lewis not only looked back to the medieval period when Wales had a degree of autonomy but also outward to continental Europe of his day. He eschewed the old romantic nationalism of most nation states and … asserted it was the rise of nationalism in Tudor times which had destroyed European nations such as Wales and Ireland…

…He attempted to reveal the glories of the literature of what he saw as the golden age: the period when Wales was Catholic and had a degree of political autonomy, before she was annexed by England in 1535–6 and her religion and language proscribed. He tried to elucidate the medieval mind for a mainly nonconformist audience, drawing on authors from Catholic and classical Europe … to illustrate the background of scholastic philosophy and theology which was the patrimony of the poets and scholars of the period, and the basis of their poetic aesthetics").

Lewis, (Dominic) Bevan Wyndham (born Llewelyn Bevan Wyndham Lewis) – journalist and author; b. 9 March 1891, Seaforth, Litherland, Lancashire; c. 1921; d. 21 November 1969, Altea, Spain; family originally from Wales; brought up in Cardiff; fought in World War I; much humorous and satirical writing, plus several biographies; wrote "Beachcomber" column in *Daily Express* 1919–1924; close friend of J. B. Morton (see below), his successor as Beachcomber; conversion influenced by Hilaire Belloc; see *DNB* ("Lewis was a leading member of an influential group of Catholic writers who flourished between the wars, including Hilaire Belloc, G. K. Chesterton, J. B. Morton, Compton Mackenzie, and Evelyn Waugh. Many of them used to meet regularly at Shirreff's wine bar under Ludgate Circus where, despite a lifelong stammer, Lewis more than held his own; he was indeed described by Belloc as the wittiest man he had ever known").

Liddell, (John) Robert – novelist and literary critic; b. 13 October 1908, Tunbridge Wells; d. 23 July 1992, Athens; son of a retired army office who was later in service of Egyptian government; spent early childhood in Cairo; sent to Haileybury College, then Corpus Christi College, Oxford on a classical scholarship; formerly Anglo-Catholic; met Barbara Pym at Oxford in 1933 and they remained life-long friends (she admired his novels; he was known to her as "Jock"); many literary friends and admirers, e.g., Walter Allen, John Bayley, Ivy Compton-Burnett, Fr. Martin D'Arcy, Francis King; Peter Levi, Olivia Manning, Iris Murdoch, Elizabeth Taylor (the novelist), Honor Tracy); taught for some time in Middle East (in Alexandria, then lecturer at University of Cairo 1941–1951 and University of Alexandria 1953–1972); later Head of English Department, Athens University; did not revisit England after 1947; his work was re-discovered in mid-1980s; great moral rectitude; "One of those novelists who sit quietly writing classics over a lifetime" (Patrick White); unmarried; see *The Last Enchantments* (1948); *Unreal City* (1952, *The Rivers of Babylon* (1959), *An Object for A Walk* (1966); J. V. Guerinot, "The Exiled Sons of Eve: Robert Liddell's Egyptian Novels" *New Blackfriars*, April 1994, p.200 ("[In *Unreal City*] Charles's friendship with the old and disreputable Eugenides, whose companionship he comes to value in his loneliness and grief, is a remarkable study of homosexuality.... It is remarkable for its compassion and for its unspoken conviction that sex outside marriage is sinful. It is this Christian awareness of sin that makes the novel so different from the more celebrated novels of Gide, Proust, and Forster. 'L'amour, hors du marriage, ne desiras,' so Flora in *An Object for a Walk* reads in a French prayer book while bored during the sermon, and it is entirely characteristic of Robert Liddell's habitual indirection that the moral absolute is given us not by the narrator but by a banal text which is made flatly and ironically to rhyme with 'Vendredi chair ne mangeras.'

When Charles grieves over his inability to comfort Eugenides who has just learned of [a close friend's] death, he remembers 'the three terrible words of Pascal, 'Je mourrai seul.' 'There was only one death in all history in which we could share'").

Lilly, William Samuel – barrister, writer and controversialist; b. 10 July 1840, Fifehead, Dorset; c. about 1869; d. 29 August 1919, 36 Fitzgeorge Avenue, West Kensington, London; after Cambridge was in Indian civil service 1862–1872; under-secretary to the government of Madras 1869; called to the bar 1873; secretary to the Catholic Union of Great Britain 1874–1912; wrote many articles on history, religion and politics, plus an anthology of the writings of Newman; see *Characteristics from the Writings of John Henry Newman* (1879); *Ancient Religion and Modern Thought* (1884); *The Great Enigma (An Enquiry into the Tenableness of the Christian Religion)* (1893); *The Claims of Christianity* (1894); *Essays and Speeches* (1897); *Christianity and Modern Civilization* (1903); *Studies in Religion and Literature* (1904); *The Christian Revolution* (1905);

Lindsay, Hon. Colin – theological writer; b. 6 December 1819, Muncaster Castle, Cumberland; c. 28 November 1868 (received by Newman; Lindsay's wife, Lady Frances (1821–1897), received 13 September 1866; the four younger of his eight children also became Catholics; of the two girls, Alexina and Harriett Maria (b. 1850), the latter, received in 1868, was later a nun; of the two boys, one, Claude, was later a priest); d. 28 January 1892, London; fourth son of twenty-fourth Earl of Crawford; before conversion adhered to Tractarian views and founded English Church Union (first President 1860–1867); led into the Church by studying the Roman question and Catholic position; buried with his wife at St. Thomas's Church, Fulham; see *Evidence for the Papacy* (1870) (includes account of his conversion) ("One [Anglican theologian] suggested that there was a variety of interpretations put by the Fathers upon the words, 'Thou art Peter,' and 'Feed my sheep'; that the Popes were fallible men, and that they had erred in faith, as for instance Honorius; and another informed me that the opinions of the Fathers were not binding upon us; and that no dogma whatever was of faith unless formally decreed by a Free Oecumenical Council. After ruminating upon this, I concluded that there was something fundamentally wrong in the arguments of my friends. In the first place, I could not conceive how the Fathers could *really* vary in their teaching on any essential or fundamental point of Faith.... Then with respect to Pope Honorius, it is evident, after reading his extant letters, that he was no heretic, though he was blameworthy in not detecting the deceit of Sergius, Patriarch of Constantinople. And as regards the opinion that no dogma or doctrine is binding unless formally decreed by an Oecumenical Council, if this was true, much of the Catholic Faith would even now be reduced to a nullity. If this opinion be sound, then it was permissible, without censure, for one of the Faithful, before the Council of Nicaea, to deny the Divinity of our Lord, simply because, though believed as *de fide*, it had not been formally and dogmatically affirmed by a General Council"); *De Ecclesia et Cathedra: or The Empire Church of Jesus Christ*, 2 Vols. (1877); *Gillow*, Vol. IV, p.243; *DNB* ("Lindsay's researches on the Reformation in England convinced him of the impossibility of maintaining a Catholic position within the Church of England").

Line, Saint Anne (*née* Heigham) – laywoman and martyr; b. c.1567, Dunmow, Essex; d. 27 February 1601, Tyburn; father rigid Calvinist who disinherited her when she became Catholic (and her brother, William, who also converted); married Roger Line (1568–1594), staunch convert who was disinherited by his own father; husband exiled after hearing Mass and settled in Flanders where he died suddenly; she was left destitute, but helped financially by Fr. John Gerard and his friends; put in charge of house of refuge for priests in London established by Fr. Gerard; took a vow of chastity and poverty; had much illness; her residences in London became centers for priests and for lay Catholics; she desired martyrdom above all things;

on Candlemas day 1601 pursuivants broke into her house when Mass just finished, the celebrant being able to use a secret hiding place; tried at the Old Bailey for harboring and supporting priests (when accused of sheltering priests she replied: "My Lords, nothing grieves me more but that I could not receive a thousand more"); sentenced to death (which she received with joy); hanged at Tyburn together with martyrs, Ven. Roger Filcock, SJ, her confessor and friend, and Bl. Mark Barkworth, OSB (see above)); brother joined the Society of Jesus in Spain; see Mac McLernon, "St. Anne Line," in Joanna Bogle (ed), *English Catholic Heroines* (2009), p.120; *Gillow*, Vol. IV, p.247 ("Addressing the assembled people in a loud voice she declared, 'I am sentenced to die for harboring a Catholic priest; and so far I am from repenting for having so done that I wish with all my soul that where I have entertained one I could have entertained a thousand.' Then kissing the gallows with great joy, she knelt down, and continued praying till the hangman had done his work"); *DNB*.

Lisle, Ambrose Lisle March Phillipps de (born Ambrose Lisle March Phillipps) – theological writer and philanthropist; b. 17 March 1809, Garendon Park, Leicestershire; c. 21 December 1825 (received at the church of St. Peter, Birmingham by Canon Macdonnell); d. 5 March 1878; of Grace-Dieu Manor, Leicestershire; in youth delicate and solitary; small and slight in appearance; influenced by Abbé Giraud, elderly émigré priest, whose simplicity and holiness made him want to know more about the Catholic faith, and removed prejudices of his upbringing; insisted on becoming a Catholic, to the dismay of family, at the age of sixteen, claiming to have had a heavenly intimation that Mohammed and not the Pope was Antichrist; educated at

Trinity College, Cambridge; associated with the "Cambridge converts"; religious affiliation as Catholic reinforced by friendship with Kenelm Digby (see above); changed name to de Lisle in 1862 on death of father and inheritance of Garendon estates; friend of John, sixteenth Earl of Shrewsbury, Pugin's patron; married Laura Maria Clifford (1811–1896) ward of Hugh Clifford, seventh Baron Clifford from recusant family (sixteen children of marriage); in 1838 joined his friend George Spencer (see below) in establishing and propagating Association of Universal Prayer for Conversion of England; gave land in Charnwood Forest to found Trappist Monastery of Mount St. Bernard, first mitred abbey in England since Reformation; great benefactor to several Catholic missions; his friendship with Rosmini led to Rosminians coming to Leicestershire to run new school, Ratcliffe College; in January 1843 first public Calvary erected in England since Reformation blessed on one of Gracedieu rocks; advocate of corporate reunion; principal founder in 1857 of Association for Promotion of Unity of Christendom (later banned by Rome, forcing him to withdraw); influential in persuading Newman to write *Letter to the Duke of Norfolk*; translated many Catholic devotional works; portrayed as Eustace Lyle, a Catholic philanthropist, in Disraeli's novel *Coningsby*; buried in Abbey Church of Mount St. Bernard; father of, among others, Ensign Everard Aloysius Lisle Phillipps (1835–1857), of 11th Bengal Native Infantry, who was gazetted for Victoria Cross for several deeds of heroism, but did not live to receive it as killed at siege of Delhi; and of Lieutenant Rudolph Edward March Phillipps de Lisle (1853–1885), of the Royal Navy who, after involvement in attempted relief of Gordon in Khartoum, killed at battle of Abu Klea; see *Notes of*

My Conversion to the Holy Catholick and Apostolick Faith (n.d.) ("I was hardly seven years of age when the thought struck me that it was extraordinary that as Protestants, we should say, we believed in the Catholick Church (in the Apostles' Creed), when, so far from believing in it, we considered it to be full of error..[T]he impression always remained on my mind that by these words in the Creed, 'I believe in the holy *Catholick* Church,' must originally have been designated some *particular* Church, to which it was necessary that all should belong; for that in the time of the Apostles, who composed this Creed, there could have been but *one* Church, and that as those solemn words of belief were applied to itself alone, so they would continue to be applicable to *that same* Church, wherever it might be, to the end of the world. Equally was it imprinted on my mind, as it were by intuition, that the Protestant Church could not be this Church; and the more so as it did not even pretend to have any claim to this title of 'Catholick' in virtue of its calling itself the 'Protestant Church'"); Alexander P. J. Cruikshank, Laura de Lisle (1897); Jean Stone, *Eleanor Leslie: A Memoir* (1898) ("From Mr. Caswall Mrs. Leslie heard a great deal about the conversion of his friend Ambrose Lisle Phillipps, and the kind of persistent annexing of every fragment of Catholic truth remaining in the Church of England which led him up to it. When a boy he read something in Edward VI's first Prayer Book about a cope. He went to the old parson and said to him, 'Sir, I find you might wear a cope.' 'Oh, yes, my dear boy, but it's never done.' 'But, sir,' he persisted, 'I should like to see you in a cope. I'll get you one.' Another time he went to him and said, 'Sir, I find I might go to confession.' 'Yes, my boy,' answered the parson, 'but no one does now.' 'But, sir, I'll come tomorrow and make my confession.' He was as good as his word, went to the old man's study and knelt down. In terror the parson urged him not to say a word, but the boy got his way, and, having made his confession, asked for absolution. The parson asked him which he preferred, as there were two in the Prayer Book – the general absolution and the one in articulo mortis. The boy answered, 'Please, sir, I would like the best.' The next thing young Ambrose suggested was a cross on the Communion Table in the church. He got one made, and a procession of the school children followed him, carrying it through the park to the church, the poor old parson, a maiden sister on each arm, bringing up the rear. The boy put the cross on the Communion Table, and heard the parson say to his sisters with a sigh, 'Ain't it awful!'"); E. S. Purcell, *Life and Letters of Ambrose Phillipps de Lisle*, 2 Vols. (1900); Bernard Elliott, "Laura Phillipps de Lisle: A Nineteenth-Century Catholic Lady," *Recusant History*, May 1991, p.371; Margaret Pawley, *Faith and Family: The Life and Circle of Ambrose Phillipps de Lisle* (1993); Madeleine Beard, *Faith and Fortune* (1997), pp.109–111; 135–137 ("In 1857 Newman wrote to Ambrose Phillipps De Lisle: 'If England is converted to Christ, it will be as much due under God, to you as anyone'"); *Gillow*, Vol. II, p.38; *Catholic Encyclopedia*; *DNB*.

Livius, Thomas Stiverd – priest and author; b. 1828; c. 1857 (received by the Redemptorists at Clapham); d. 1902; brought up as Evangelical Anglican; later moderate High Church holding "branch theory"; later Anglican curate; ordained as priest of Redemptorist Order in 1862; gave missions for many years, then Professor of Scripture for the English Redemptorists; see *St. Peter: Bishop of Rome* (1888); *The Blessed Virgin in the Fathers of the First Six Centuries*

(1893); essay in J. G. F. Raupert (ed), *Roads to Rome* (1901), p.153 ("I became more and more convinced that, save the Sacrament of Baptism, Anglicanism was not a religion of Sacraments at all; and that when it is attempted to make it so, it is only a hollow outward imitation and sham. Since I became a Catholic, received the gift of faith, and read something for myself on the whole question, I have seen that the notion of the Church of England having anything to do with the Holy Catholic Church in its origin or principles, is the most absurd that can be conceived. A very superficial glance over its history from its first start in the sixteenth century abundantly shows this; and that its founders were actuated by the very same Protestant anti-Catholic spirit as the continental reformers, whom they even exceeded by their persecutions, and in their destroying and plundering everything that Catholics most cherished...

When one began to learn something of what true Christian faith was, it became very clear that Anglicans had it not, and indeed, could not have it in any proper sense; for it is quite evident that a Divine supernatural revelation absolutely demands, for man to believe it, that there be a Divine, external, infallible authority to set forth to him the divine supernatural truths and obligations which it contains. This infallible authority, once given, must ever exist in the world, to preserve this divine revelation, one and the selfsame in its integrity and purity, free from error, and to teach and explain it to men of all generations in every land and age.

I saw that there is such an infallible authority, and that there can be but one only – and that this is the Roman Catholic Church, which has ever made itself known to be such throughout the world from the beginning of Christianity; whereas it is held as a first principle in every other so-called Christian Church, and in the Anglican amongst the rest, that there is no such Divine infallible authority existing on earth at all, and consequently no means for man to know for certain what was divinely revealed, and what he is properly to believe. For it appeared to me utterly unreasonable and absurd to think of believing with Divine infallible faith supernatural mysteries, that are above the reach of reason, on merely human and fallible teaching").

Lloyd, Venerable William – priest and confessor; b. about 1610, Carmarthenshire; d. 1679, Brecon, Wales; went to Lisbon in 1635 and admitted into English College; ordained priest 26 April 1639; in 1642 came on the mission to Wales; early in Oates Plot apprehended and committed to Brecon gaol; tried for high treason, for being ordained priest abroad and coming into realm; found guilty and sentenced to death, but died in Brecon gaol six days before the date fixed for his execution; see *Gillow*, Vol. IV, p.291.

Lobb, Emmanuel, SJ (alias Joseph Simeon or Simons) – priest; b. 1593, Bournemouth, Hampshire; d. 24 July 1671; parents were not Catholics; as youth went to Portugal with view to mercantile life; soon converted by Fr. Henry Lloyd (or Floyd), SJ, of Lisbon, and sent by him to St. Omer's College, thence to Rome and English College 1616; entered the Society of Jesus in 1619; Professor of Theology, Philosophy, and Sacred Scripture for several years at different colleges; rector at Rome, Liège and London; sent to the English mission; in 1669 he received the Duke of York, later King James II, into the Church; see *Gillow*, Vol. IV, p.292.

Locke, Matthew – organist and composer; b. about 1622, Devon; c. probably 1649; d. August 1677, The Strand, London; chorister and pupil of organists at Exeter cathedral; activities during the Civil War unknown; probably joined exiled court at The Hague in 1648; then in Antwerp in early 1649, where probably converted; married into the recusant Garnons family of Herefordshire; much instrumental chamber music and music dramas under the Commonwealth; highly regarded by Charles II and after the Restoration appointed composer in the private music and composer for the violins; wrote much of the music for Charles II's ceremonial progress through London on the eve of his coronation; organist of Queen Catherine's Catholic chapel 1662–1671; composed several operas and anthems, and many Latin hymns; a major composer in the generation before Purcell (who recognized his abilities); probably buried in Anglican churchyard at St. Mary Savoy; see *Gillow*, Vol. IV, p.293; *Grove and Oxford Music Online*; *DNB*.

Lockhart, Elizabeth (in religion Mary Elizabeth, OSF) – nun and authoress; b. 1812; c. 1848; d. 23 July 1870; daughter of Alexander Lockhart, High Church Anglican curate and his wife, Martha (see below); sister of William Lockhart (see below); foundress of one of earliest Anglican sisterhoods at Wantage; later Catholic nun of Order of St. Francis; founder and later Abbess of Franciscan convent at Notting Hill, London; writer and translator of lives of various saints; see *Gillow*, Vol. IV, p.297.

Lockhart, Martha – authoress, printer and publisher; b. about 1798; c. 9 July 1845; d. 15 January 1872; second wife of Alexander Lockhart, High Church Anglican curate; mother of William Lockhart (see below) and Elizabeth Lockhart (see above); after husband's death, she entered religion, but obliged to leave because of failing health; bought *Catholic Opinion* and *The Lamp*, and established St. Joseph's Press, in order to promote cheap, sound and interesting Catholic literature; see *Gillow*, Vol. IV, p.298.

Lockhart, William, OC – priest; b. 22 August 1819; c. 26 August 1843 (first of the Tractarians to convert; received by Fr. Gentili); d. 15 May 1892, St Etheldreda;s, Ely Place, Holborn, London; only son of Alexander Lockhart, High Church Anglican curate, and his wife, Martha (see above); brother of Elizabeth Lockhart (see above); educated at Exeter College, Oxford; at Oxford attracted by the Catholic Church, his friends there including Edward Douglas (later Superior of the Redemptorists in Rome), John Ruskin, Wilfrid Scawen Blunt, James Hope-Scott (see above) and J. B. Dalgairns (see above); on advice of Manning, lived 1841–1842 at Littlemore with Newman in order to prepare for Anglican ordination; his conversion led Newman to resign from his living at St. Mary's; immortalized in *The Parting of Friends*, Newman's last sermon preached as an Anglican; greatly influenced by Milner's *End of Religious Controversy* and later by Fr. Gentili; joined the Rosminians three days after conversion; ordained priest 19 December 1845; much work giving missions and retreats in England, Scotland and especially Ireland; did much writing, especially on apologetics and on Antonio Rosmini; editor of *The Lamp: An Illustrated Catholic Journal of General Literature*; buried at Ratcliffe College, Leicestershire; see *The Communion of Saints* (1869); *The Old Religion* (1870); Joseph Hirst, *Biography of Father Lockhart* (1893); *Gillow*, Vol. IV, p.301 ("It was the reading of Froude's *Remains* and Faber's *Foreign Churches and Peoples* that opened to Lockhart a new view of Christianity.

Hitherto he had without reflection, really thought that Catholics were not, properly speaking, Christians, and supposed that Protestantism was the same as the primitive Christianity"); Fr. Nicholas Schofield, "Fr. William Lockhart," *Catholic Life*, November 2007, p.28; *DNB*.

Lockwood, Harriet – nun; b. 1823; c. 8 March 1849; d. 1912; friend of Henry Wilberforce (see below) and his family, and of Elizabeth Bowden (see above); as a result of seeing the Good Shepherd nuns working during the summer of 1849 among the cholera-stricken Irish hop-pickers in Kent, she entered the Hammersmith convent on 8 December 1849; worked as a nun in Bristol and Glasgow; appointed prioress at Limerick in 1860; in 1862 became the first mother provincial of the newly established Irish Province; returned to Hammersmith in 1872.

Lodge, Thomas – poet, physician and traveler; b. about 1558; c. 1597 (some say he was a Catholic earlier); d. September 1625, Old Fish Street, London; son of Sir Thomas Lodge (1509/10–1585), grocer and Lord Mayor of London, who later went bankrupt; already attracted favorable notices by his verses written at Oxford; several voyages to distant parts, during which he was kindly received by the Jesuits in Brazil; contributed many verses and other writings, plus translations; turned to studying medicine and took his MD degree at Avignon in 1598; received another MD degree from Oxford in 1602 and thereafter practiced medicine in London and in Brussels, where he took refuge as a recusant following exposure of the Gunpowder Plot (1605); back in England by 1612; one of chief physicians of the day, but had financial difficulties and was imprisoned as a debtor; died of the plague;

his poetry was more popular after his death; best remembered for *Rosalynde*, a prose romance, the source of Shakespeare's *As You Like It*; see *Gillow*, Vol. IV, p.314; *DNB*.

Logan, Henry Francis Charles – priest; b. 1800; c. 1818; d. 1 December 1884, Clifton Wood Convent, Clifton; went to Corpus Christi College, Cambridge, but at age eighteen left without graduating; and was received into the Catholic Church in France; studied at the English College, Rome, and then taught mathematics at Prior Park College, near Bath; ordained priest Advent 1830; Vice-President of Oscott College 1840–1846; succeeded Wiseman as President 1847–1848; Vice-President again in 1850, then on various missions, followed by period at Ushaw College 1862–1871; see *Gillow*, Vol. IV, p.741.

Londonderry, Marchioness of (Elizabeth Frances Charlotte Jocelyn) – b. 1813; d. 1884; eldest daughter of the third earl of Roden; famous as a beauty; married the sixth Viscount Powerscourt (d. 1844) in 1836; married the fourth Marquis of Londonderry (d. 1872); after becoming a Catholic she concentrated on works of charity with Lady Georgiana Fullerton (see above), Lady Lothian (see below) and others.

Longford, Elizabeth Pakenham, Countess of (*née* Harman) – writer; b. 30 August 1906, 108 Harley Street, London; c. 21 April 1946 (Easter Sunday); d. 23 October 2002, Bernhurst, Hurst Green, Sussex; marriage of nearly seventy years to Lord Longford (see below); niece of Joseph Chamberlain; her family was Unitarian, but mother died young and her religious education entrusted to a strongly Baptist nurse; Anglican at school; felt first strong pull of Catholicism while reading Evelyn Waugh's *Ed-*

mund Campion; wrote biography; mother of eight children, including several notable writers; staunch Labour party supporter; see "Marriage and the Family," in Elizabeth Pakenham (ed), *Catholic Approaches* (1955), p.97; *Wellington*, 2 Vols. (1972 and 1975); *Piety in Queen Victoria's Reign* (1973); *Byron* (1976); *Winston Churchill* (1978); *Eminent Victorian Women* (1981); *Elizabeth R* (1983); *The Royal House of Windsor* (1984); *The Pebbled Shore* (1986), especially pp.238–239 ("Another source of trouble was the Roman Priesthood and, of course, the 'Black Popes', whom all potential converts feel bound to trot out. Gervase [Fr. Matthews who instructed her] saw the priesthood as a system of pipes, some lead, some copper, some silver, along which the priestly power flows. The value or otherwise of the pipes makes no difference to the purity of the water." I found all Gervase's images vivid and relevant. The Catholic faith, he told me, had been regarded by Catholics in two different ways, one right and one wrong. The wrong way (that of 'poor girls brought up in convents') is to think of it as a small white room in which you come and switch on the light, whereupon everything is immediately dazzlingly clear. The right way is to think of Catholicism as a huge dim room lit only by firelight.... As the firelight flickers certain things in the room become visible and then fade away again, brightening the next moment. But there are many, many things in the recesses and corners of the room which we never see at all. Catholic faith is still a 'Mystery' even after reception into the Church"); *Queen Victoria* (1999); *DNB*.

Longford, seventh Earl of (Francis Aungier Packenham, first Baron Pakenham) ("Frank") – politician, writer and philanthropist; b. 5 December 1905, 7 Great Cumberland Place, London;

c. November 1940 (wife, Elizabeth (see above) received in 1946; sister, Lady Pansy Lamb (1904–1999) (see above) received in 1981); d. 3 August 2001, London; father fifth Earl of Longford (killed at Gallipoli); from Anglo-Irish family; educated Eton and New College, Oxford; first class degree in PPE; lecturer at Oxford; moved from Conservative to Labour party in thirties; influenced in conversion by Evelyn Waugh (see below); invalided out of army; in charge of British zone in occupied Germany 1947–1948; Labour MP; Minister of Civil Aviation 1948–1951; First Lord of the Admiralty 1951; Secretary of State for Colonies 1965–1966; social reformer, especially in respect of welfare state and penal reform; nicknamed "Lord Porn" by media following his anti-pornography campaigns of the 1970s; see *Born to Believe* (1953) ("The three great questions for me were these. Does God exist? Was Our Lord divine? Is the Catholic Church His Church? I soon had little doubt that if I could satisfy myself on the first two counts I should have no hesitation about the third…

After a few months I knew in outline the main arguments for and against the existence of God. But I soon saw that some of the deepest philosophical problems centering around God's existence – I mention only the problem of suffering – were not going to decide the issue one way or the other for me. If I could believe in the Son of the Gospels I could believe in the Father described there…

So back I came to what was for me the crucial question. Was Jesus God?... The Gospels say that Our Lord was God. Can we accept the broad account in the Gospels as true?...

How many religious books I read during that period I have no idea. St. Augustine's *Confessions* was the first one recommended to me by Father D'Arcy. Arnold Lunn's controversy with Haldane

removed my sneaking suspicion that in a real showdown there would be materialist questions the man of religion could not face. Grandmaison's great three volumes on Our Lord did more than any other single work to give ultimate assurance that the Gospel Life occurred.

In the end the conclusions I reached can be summarized in this way. I. The gospels were written in the first century by writers some of whom had known Our Lord. 2. He therefore lived and made the general impression described. 3. The Gospels themselves represent the highest ethical teaching known to us. (Even the bitterest critics seemed hardly to dispute them). 4. Our Lord must therefore be regarded at the very least as a sublime and wonderful Man. 5. But He claimed to be God, and setting aside in the case of such a Man the only possible alternative of insanity, the claim must be accepted. 6. In that case, so must the rest of His theological teaching and the authority of the Church He established"); "The Catholic in Politics," in Elizabeth Pakenham (ed), *Catholic Approaches* (1955), p.201; "My Search for Faith" in John A. O'Brien (ed*), The Road to Damascus: Vol. IV: Roads to Rome* (1955); *Humility* (1969); *A Grain of Wheat* (1974); *The Life of Jesus Christ* (1974) ("Past attempts to separate the moral teaching from the claims of Jesus to divinity have never succeeded, even when undertaken by a man of genius like Renan in the last century. The dilemma before a rationalist who pursues this line is surely beyond solution. It can be stated in simple terms. No other founder or leader of a great religion claimed to be divine; Jesus did so. We must assume *ex hypothesi* his good faith. We are left then to conclude that he was, or became, totally demented, presenting a claim which would render him a suitable candidate for a mental home. The rationalist is left muttering that whatever one may say things like that – like the life, death, and resurrection of Jesus Christ – just don't happen. And yet if we once accept the possibility that God exists, we can readily accept the further possibility that he became incarnate, and, in that case, one would expect the events of his life to be unlike those of any other, before or since"); *Francis of Assisi* (1978); *Pope John Paul II* (1982); *One Man's Faith* (1984) ("Today hundreds of millions throughout the world are followers of Christ.... He rose from the dead, so Christians believe, on the third day after his crucifixion.... No human being has ever influenced world history so profoundly. But Christians believe he was not just a human being. They insist that he was at once man and God. The duality in Jesus Christ's nature sets him apart from any other religious leader. Many millions follow the teachings of Buddha, Mahomet and others. None of these leaders ever claimed divinity.... My conviction that the Resurrection did indeed occur was crucial to my renewed Christianity. No one has summed up the whole issue better than Sir Norman Anderson ...: 'There is reliable testimony that the Tomb was empty. A large number of witnesses attested that Jesus appeared to them after His death. The lives of the original disciples changed dramatically from that point (and led them into heroic courses). The Christian Church has borne witness to the same faith all down the centuries.' Anderson goes on to point out that St. Paul must have received an outline of it some two to five years after the Crucifixion itself. Those who insist dogmatically that the Resurrection *could not* have occurred are flying in the face of historical evidence. Once the Resurrection is accepted, the other miraculous features of Christ's life need cause us no special trouble...

I conclude ... that no one could make the claims that Jesus made unless either he were insane or, alternatively, they were true. Yet it is conceded that the ethics of Jesus were the noblest product of the human mind. His healing and caring for the sick illustrated the beauty of his character. The idea that he was insane is itself insane. There is no escaping the conclusion that what he said about himself was true and, accepting that testimony, we must acknowledge that he was divine"); *Saints* (1987); *Suffering and Hope* (1990); *Avowed Intent: An Autobiography of Lord Longford* (1994); Dr. Vincent McKee, "Lord Longford (1905–2001): Social Conscience of Catholic Britain," *Catholic Life,* December 2002, p.42; Peter Stanford, *The Outcast's Outcast: A Biography of Lord Longford* (2003); *DNB.*

Longley, Clifford Edmund – writer, journalist and broadcaster; b. 6 January 1940; c. 1961; worked for *The Times* 1967–1992, *Daily Telegraph* 1992–2000, editorial consultant and columnist *The Tablet* from 1996; much independent journalism; freelance broadcaster and author; see "A Conservative Case for Christ," *The Times,* 4 June 1984, p.18 ("If ... nothing miraculous occurred at the event of Jesus's conception, the implications are enormous.... It means that Jesus had a natural father. This was either Joseph or someone else. If it was Joseph, those New Testament references to his thinking his betrothed wife was made pregnant by another man are not just 'religious myth' – they are deliberate lies, either by Joseph himself, or someone else who made them up. If it was not Joseph but indeed another man, then Mary's story was a lie, Joseph was deceived (or an accomplice in the lie), and the Gospel writers were 'taken in'.... The Resurrection is a similar case. If there was no empty tomb, no early morning sightings, then Jesus lies buried still in Palestine. The implications are again enormous. Many people lied"); essay in Rowanne Pasco (ed), *Why I Am a Catholic* (1995) ("I am a Catholic because I couldn't be anything else. None of the alternatives is better, because Catholicism is true.... I am quite ready to accept the Church's self-definition as the community Christ founded on the Apostles and that its history can be traced straight back to the original. That seems to me to authenticate it. I am quite happy therefore to journey on in this ancient and rather rusty old ship"); "Imagine a World Without Evil," *The Tablet*, 30 March 1996, p.453 ("Try this. Faced with a daunting or even insuperable 'problem of evil,' attempt the mental exercise of constructing an imaginary world without evil. It leads to interesting conclusions. The challenge to faith presented by some sudden catastrophe is usually in the form of 'How can there be a God who loves us if he allows *this* to happen?...

So what does the hypothetical 'world without suffering' look like? Much suffering results from mechanical failure, for instance from metal fatigue in an aircraft part which might cause a catastrophic breakage leading to tragedy. So does our all-powerful, all-loving God ensure that no metal parts ever fail from metal fatigue, and by the same token, that no engines ever fall off because somebody forgot to tighten a bolt? But what then is the point of maintenance, or research into aircraft safety? We are postulating a world where, every time some unforeseen misfortune overtakes an aircraft in flight, a miracle is performed automatically to put it right. And we have to say the same about every other form of human activity.

It is, in short, a world where the law of cause and effect has been abolished.... Actually it is worse than that. The principle of cause and effect is the fundamental reason why we find the world rational: do this, and that follows; do it over and over again, and we have a scientific law by which means we can begin to make sense of the world. Furthermore there is an extraordinary (and surely divinely arranged) association between the rationality of the world, and the rationality of our minds. If the world was irrational ... our minds would surely be irrational too. Would we even exist?"); "Me and My Faith" *The Tablet*, 24 April 1999, p.572; *The Worlock Archive* (1999)

Lorimer, Hew – sculptor; b. May 1907, Edinburgh; c. 1941; d. 1993, Kellie Castle, Fife, Scotland; second son of Robert Lorimer, Scotland's greatest artist of the Arts and Crafts movement; nephew of John Henry Lorimer (1856–1936), painter; left Oxford University early to study design and sculpture at Edinburgh College of Art; stayed a few months with Eric Gill 1934–1935, where he learnt letter cutting and the correct use of tools (influence of Gill seen in his work); influenced by Aquinas and Eckhart, and Ananda Coomaraswamy's idea that the purpose of beauty is to be the attractive power, in kind, of truth; links to the medieval artist-craftsman; greatest work probably his twenty-eight foot tall sculpture, "Our Lady of the Isles," in South Uist on the Outer Hebrides; great majority of his eighty commissions are to be found in Scotland; influenced the conversion of Russell Kirk, the American conservative writer; see J. R. H. McEwan, "A sculptor who shuffles us Godwards," *Catholic Herald*, 15 June 2007, p.8 ("He looked back not merely to a time before industrialization – as the Arts and Crafts movement had looked – but to a time before the Renaissance, when art was dominated by the Eternal Idea, the source of which is what Augustine of Hippo called, 'Wisdom Incarnate, the same now as it ever was and the same to be forevermore'").

Lothian, Cecil, Marchioness of (Lady Cecil Chetwynd Kerr) (née Chetwynd Talbot) – b. 17 April 1808, Ingestre Hall, Staffordshire; c. 11 June 1851 (received by Fr. Brownbill at Farm Street, London); her children, Lord Walter Kerr (see above), Cecil (1835–1866), subsequently a nun of Society of the Sacred Heart in France, Alice and John, all later converted, plus other relatives; her brother-in-law, Lord Henry Kerr (1800–1882) (see above) and his wife, Lady Louisa Dorothea (1811–1884), sister of James Hope-Scott (see above), received in 1852 and their children); d. May 1877, Rome; daughter of second Earl Talbot of Hensol; from family of twelve children; brought up in father's moderate High-Churchmanship; married seventh Marquess of Lothian; after husband's death in 1841, she moved from services in the Kirk to the Episcopal Church; one of earliest financial supporters of Tractarianism in Scotland; her conversion to the Catholic Church influenced by Gorham judgment (see entry for William Maskell) and by conversion of Manning (see below); sponsor of Catholic Church in Scotland; close friend of Charlotte Montague-Douglas-Scott, Duchess of Buccleuch (see above) with whom she did much charitable work; influenced in her conversion by Mrs. Eleanor Leslie (see above); buried at the foot of the altar in the church at Dalkeith; see C. Kerr (ed), *Cecil, Marchioness of Lothian: A Memoir* (1922); *Madeleine Beard, Faith and Fortune* (1997), pp.81–86; 164–165; *DNB* ("Her conversion imperiled her guardianship of her sons, as the other guardians appointed by her husband's will sought to have them removed from her custody lest she attempt to convert them to Rome. (They were not concerned about the religion of her daughters.) In a midnight adventure, she escaped from Newbattle Abbey with her younger children, taking them to Edinburgh where they were received into the Catholic Church. Her eldest son, William, the eighth Marquess, was away at Oxford at the time, and remained a staunch Episcopalian").

Loveday, Emily Mary – nun; b. 28 December 1799; c. 1821; father a barrister and a Protestant, who moved to Auteuil, France; he returned to England in 1819, but placed her, together with her sister, Matilda Susan, then eighteen, and his niece, Mary Loveday, in a boarding school in Paris; he returned to Paris in 1821 to find all three had converted to the Catholic faith; they were removed; Matilda renounced her new faith, but Emily fled twice to convents, latterly to the convent of the Sisters of Notre Dame in the rue de Sèvres in Paris; the matter became a cause célèbre in both France and England; father accused the headmistress of kidnapping by seduction, but Emily had reached the age of majority (twenty-one) in France; father's claims dismissed, and his request for custody, and Emily allowed to stay in the convent; she insisted that her conversion was inspired by "the piety of her school companions and her own reading of the theologian Bossuet"; no further public references to her after 1822; see Caroline Ford, "Private Lives and Public Order in Restoration France: the Seduction of Emily Loveday," *American Historical Review*, February 1994, p. 21; *DNB*.

Lowe, Blessed John – priest and martyr; b. 1553, London; d. 8 October 1586, Tyburn; formerly Protestant minister for a short time; after conversion went to Douai College and then to English College, Rome, in 1581; ordained priest in September 1582; went to the English mission in 1583; worked chiefly in or about London; his exorcisms produced a great effect and caused many conversions to the Catholic Church;

apprehended and sent to the Clink prison; at trial falsely impeached by apostate priest, Anthony Tyrrell; condemned to death for his exorcisms, and with him two other priests, Ven. John Adams and Ven. Richard Dibdale, who were condemned for being ordained by authority of the Holy See; all drawn to Tyburn and hanged, drawn and quartered; see *Gillow*, Vol. IV, p.334.

Lucas, Frederick – journalist, barrister and politician; b. 30 March 1812, Westminster, London; c. February 1839 (he and his wife, Elizabeth, received by Fr. Lythgoe, SJ, before their marriage in 1840; brothers, Edward (1822–1899), journalist and writer (secretary of the Academia of the Catholic Religion), Henry, of the Australian civil service, both received in 1853, and another brother later); d. 22 October 1855, Staines; son of Samuel Hayhurst Lucas, prominent Quaker; brought up as Quaker (as was his wife); later became very sympathetic to feudal and Catholic spirit of medieval Christendom; influenced by the Oxford Movement and by close friend, Thomas Chisholm Anstey (see above); reading Milner's *End of Religious Controversy* convinced him of the truth of the Catholic claims; wrote for *Dublin Review*; founder and first editor of *The Tablet* in 1840 (advocated Ultramontane and pro-Irish policies); in 1849 transferred publishing offices of *The Tablet* from London to Dublin and from then on became "more Irish than the Irish themselves"; MP for County Meath; identified himself with Irish Nationalist party, but questioned sincerity of some of the Irish politicians; friend of Mill and Carlyle, and later Newman; buried in Brompton cemetery; see *Reasons for Becoming a Roman Catholic, Addressed to the Society of Friends* (1839); Edward Lucas, *The Life of Frederick Lucas, MP*, 2 Vols. (1886); *Gillow*,

Vol. IV, p.336; *Catholic Encyclopedia*; *DNB*.

Lunn, Sir Arnold Henry Moore – writer and controversialist; b. 18 April 1888, Madras, India; c. 13 July 1933 (received at the university chaplaincy, Oxford, by Mgr. Ronald Knox (see above); son, Peter Northcote Lunn (b. 1914), diplomat, captain of British ski team at 1936 Olympics, received in 1934); d. 2 June 1974, London; son of a Methodist lay preacher, author and entrepreneur; as child taken to Anglican service in the morning and Methodist service in the evening; later agnostic and outspoken opponent of Christianity; influenced strongly in his conversion by Mgr. Ronald Knox; supporter of Franco in Spanish Civil War; saw Communism as the ultimate enemy of the Catholic faith; intense opposition to Hitler; pioneer of development of skiing and winter sports; knighted in 1952; religious controversialist who wrote sixteen books on apologetics ("the most tireless Catholic apologist of his generation" (Evelyn Waugh)); wrote over 60 books in total; President of the Latin Mass Society on its founding; see *Difficulties* (with Ronald Knox) (1932), *Is Christianity True?* (1933) (with C. E. M. Joad), *Now I See* (1933) ("Those who maintain that Christians do not need a teaching Church, since Christ promised that the spirit of truth would guide them, never face the awkward fact that the Holy Ghost, if this assumption be correct, provides no clear guidance on many of the questions which perplex divided Christianity. Is hell a reality? Is there a visible Church? Is confession to a priest essential? May the innocent party remarry after divorce? Is birth control sinful? Christians differ on all these points, from which one of two conclusions must follow. Either Christ was mistaken in believing that God would implement his promises, in which case what becomes of the deity of Christ? Or one Church alone of many rival Churches has a monopoly of guidance. If we adopt the former hypothesis, we must reject Christianity, if the latter, we should submit to Rome, for no Church but the Roman Catholic Church can make any intelligible claim to infallibility. Once again we are driven by the logic of fact to choosing between two alternatives. Either Christ was not God, or the Catholic Church is infallible"); "The Road to Rome," *Dublin Review*, October-December 1933, p.181 ("If one has come to the conclusion that Christ was true God and true man, it is natural to prefer the Church which has taught this doctrine from the first, and which still teaches it, to the Churches which permit their priests to proclaim doctrines which are indistinguishable from Unitarianism.... Against the confused and shifting background of the modern world Catholic order alone can resist the erosion of modern chaos. Where others are content to express opinions, this impenitent old Church still thunders, with all her own confidence, ex cathedra denunciations of sin and error"); "Orthodoxy and the New Religions," in Sidney Dark (ed), *Orthodoxy Sees It Through* (1934); *Science and the Supernatural* (1935) (with J. B. S. Haldane); *Within This City* (1936); *Spanish Rehearsal* (1937); *Communism and Socialism: A Study in the Technique of Revolution* (1938); *Come What May: An Autobiography* (1940) ("I discovered, of course, that most of the beliefs with which Catholics were credited were not, in fact, held by Catholics.... Why is it that so few people pause, as I paused, after asking themselves how Catholics can hold such and such a belief? Why is it that so few people are interested to discover whether in point of fact Catholics do hold the belief in question?"); *The Good Gorilla* (1943); *The Third Day*

(1945); *Is The Catholic Church Anti-Social?* (1946) (with G. G. Coulton); *The Revolt Against Reason* (1950); *Memory to Memory* (1956); *And Yet So New* (1958); *Unkilled For So Long* (1968); Walter Romig (ed), *The Book of Catholic Authors*, Fourth Series (1948); William F. Buckley Jr., *Nearer My God: An Autobiography of Faith* (1997), pp.49–90; John Fry, "Up and Down the Holy Mountains," *The Tablet*, 19 December 2009; Patrick Allitt, *Catholic Converts: British and American Intellectuals Turn to Rome* (1997) *passim*; Joseph Pearce, *Literary Converts* (1999), *passim*; Fr. Charles P. Connor, *Classic Catholic Converts* (2001), pp.134–136; *DNB*.

Lyons, Richard Bickerton Pemell (first Earl Lyons) – diplomat; b. 26 April 1817, Lymington, Hampshire; c. November 1887 (death bed conversion); d. 5 December 1887, London; elder son of Admiral Lord Lyons (1790–1858), first Baron; brother of fourteenth Duchess of Norfolk (see below); educated at Christ Church, Oxford; entered diplomatic service; attaché at Athens, Dresden and Florence; very tactful British envoy in Washington, U.S.A. during American Civil War; ambassador at Constantinople, and then very effectively for twenty years (1867–1887) at Paris at very difficult period; Privy Councillor; offered Foreign Office by Salisbury in 1886, but declined on grounds of ill-health and age; reliable and conciliatory figure; some authorities deny he converted despite receiving permission from Lord Salisbury to begin to study Catholicism and to attend Mass, on the grounds that whilst he on path to conversion, serious stroke, in November 1887, rendered him both paralyzed and incapacitated; buried at Arundel; see *DNB*.

McCewan, Sir John Helias Finnie, first Baronet of Marchmont – writer, poet and conservative politician; b. 21 June 1894; c. 1945; d. 19 April 1962; MP for Berwick and Haddington 1931–1945; served under Neville Chamberlain as Under Secretary of State for Scotland 1939–1940; served under Winston Churchill as a Lord of the Treasury 1942–1944; created a Baronet, of Marchmont in the County of Berwick and Bardrochat in the County of Ayr.

McClellan, David – political philosopher; b. 1940, Hertfordshire; c. 1958 or 1959; brought up in Congregational church; converted whilst at Oxford University; was leading figure in Marxist thought; Professor of Political Theory at University of Kent at Canterbury; influenced profoundly by Simone Weil; see "The Marxist Historian" in Greg Watts, *Catholic Lives* (2001) ("He had investigated various Christian traditions before arriving at the conclusion that it was only the Catholic Church that could trace its roots back through the centuries to the New Testament. 'I thought to myself that all these Christian churches have got a bit of the truth, while the Catholic Church had a more rounded truth'").

MacDonald, Minna – c. 1898 (received with her family); wife of Lochlin Macdonald, JP of Skeabost, Isle of Skye; see *Why I Became a Catholic* (1903) "I had not realized that 'Unity,' in the Catholic meaning of the word, was entirely lost at the 'Reformation.' And later, it came with a shock when I made the discovery that were all the discordant factions to agree; that were the bishops that are 'High' and the bishops that are 'Low' to square their differences, and be of one mind; that were the clergy and the congregation to conform to every rite and rule, and abide by every decision – that, in short, were Anglicans to sink their differences in every particular, and become one, even then they would still be outside

the pale of the Church, cut away from the main body, and so forfeit the promises and blessings!...

It has passed into a truism, and forms a powerful argument for Catholic Christianity, that when Agnostics change they find a ready refuge in the Catholic arguments, but in no others; the obvious conclusion being that where materialism is set aside as an intellectual failure, no logical reasoning can withstand the arguments involved in Catholic theology.... We want religion and not theology, but we want it secured to us after the manner our Lord Himself has ordained He should be worshipped, and not a Christianity after 'the inventions of men.' Ordination either meant something or it meant nothing; and if our Lord ordained the apostles, who, in their turn, were commanded to ordain others, and so on down to the present century, all I could say was – let us not lightly cast away a heritage descended to us through the 'Laying on of Hands!' If in our Church, we had not valid orders, it was unsafe to remain in it...

I knew [the Reformation] was the turning point on which all had hinged – a crisis of tremendous importance.... Dr. Pusey had said: 'The sale of indulgences very chiefly caused the Reformation'; but I had never given it a thought.... If a certain number of rogues, disguised as friars, or who were renegade friars, imposed on a certain number of ignorant and credulous persons in the fifteenth or sixteenth century, and turned a dishonest penny by professing to be licensed vendors of 'indulgences,' there is no good reason why it should be looked at in the light of a life and death question for the Church. Luther called the attention of the world to these abuses; but he need not have done so, for a remedy was possible without the resort of cunningly working them up into an excuse for a religious revolution to the detriment of the Church...

The 'Reformation' was a grave evil. The very gravity of it is like dust in the eyes; and there are many who labor under the delusion that the period preceding it cannot be painted in colors black enough! 'Enslaved minds,' 'blunted consciences,' a 'Catholicism that paid little heed to social righteousness,' it is often said, had prepared the way for 'the blessed movement' known as the 'Reformation'! What? Such trivialities as Luther falling in love with a nun in Germany, and the later circumstances of Henry VIII wishing to divorce one wife and marry another in England, occasioned the catastrophe of bloodshed and burning, first for a doctrine professed and then for a doctrine recanted! Impossible that such slight causes should lead up to, and account for, the extraordinary confusion which led solemn divines to compile a prayer book with a set of doctrines in one reign, and withdraw them in the next!

Arguments could not be evaded. The Catholic Church and the Anglican Church had formerly been one; but, with a curious inconsistency, it was pleaded that 'errors' had crept in, and had permeated the whole, so that it had become steeped in 'error,' which was finally resolved into an excuse for a portion to break away and constitute themselves a new Church, while the Church they had deserted followed on in the groove of its ancient traditions. According to the apostles and the early saints, this breaking away would be deemed heresy. Heresies were from the beginning. The bible and writings of the early saints confirmed it, and it was significantly alluded to in the saying of St. Augustine, to the effect that in pagan times the devil was busy multiplying gods, but, after the advent of Christianity, he transferred his mischievous propensity to multiplying sects!...

My reasoning was very simple. The Church, guided by the Holy Ghost, could not fall into 'error,' however much it might suffer from the evil deeds of evil men. To admit defection of any other kind would, in my humble opinion, close the argument for the Christian Church: 'Lo, I am with you to the consummation of the world'! Wickedness might abound – history was not silent; and it was no secret that wolves clad in the soft fleeces of sheep are a scandal in every age. St. Catherine of Siena, urging reforms in the fourteenth century, could say: 'The depth of calamity overwhelmed the Church!' but added: 'All men may indeed, in their wickedness, wound her, but they cannot destroy her, for she bears a divine principle of life'.... And no history of the Christian Church is complete that records the blemishes, and leaves unrecorded the triumphs of faith …").

MacGillivray, George John – priest and writer; b. 1876; c. 1919; former Church of England minister; ordained Catholic priest in 1922; Cambridge University Catholic chaplain; writer of books, articles and pamphlets on Catholic themes; see *The Way of Life: An Introduction to the Catholic Religion* (1931); *Through the East to Rome* (1932) ("If Jesus Christ was God, and founded a divine body to be the teacher and source of grace to the world until he comes again, that body must exist today. It is inconceivable that he should allow his purpose to be frustrated. The question, therefore, arises: Where is that body? And to this there is only one possible answer, because there is only one reasonable claimant. There is practically only one body which claims to be, to the exclusion of every other, the Body of Christ, and that is the Holy Catholic Roman Church. Anglican writers have expended a vast amount of energy in trying to establish their claim to be part of the Catholic Church. But … when all is said, it remains according to any Anglican theory (and Anglican theories are legion) the Church of Christ today is not one body but several. And it is certain that such an idea is wholly repugnant to the New Testament conception, and was never dreamt of for 1,500 years after Christ. It is absurd to speak of a number of antagonistic and mutually exclusive communions as one body in the New Testament sense"); *The Christian Virtues* (1934); *Can I Change my Religion?* (1941); *An Introduction to the Mass* (1950);

MacIntyre, Alasdair Chambers – philosopher; b. 12 January 1929 Glasgow, Scotland; c. early 1980s; Protestant upbringing; educated at London University; lectured at several English universities; professorial chairs at several American universities until Professor at University of Notre Dame 2000–2007; critic of Marxism and at first Christianity; broad range of subject areas, but emphasis lately on ethics; defender of Thomism, who does his work against background of what he calls an Augustinian Thomist approach to moral philosophy; see *After Virtue* (1981; 3rd edition, 2007); *Whose Justice? Which Rationality?* (1988); *Three Rival Versions of Moral Enquiry* (1990); *Dependent Rational Animals: Why Human Beings Need the Virtues* (1999); *God, Philosophy, Universities* (2009); Maurice Cowling, "Alasdair MacIntyre, Religion and the University," *New Criterion*, February 1994, p.32; Edward T. Oakes, "The Achievement of Alasdair MacIntyre," *First Things*, August/September 1996, p.22; Maurice Cowling, *Religion and Public Doctrine in England, Volume III: Accommodations* (2001), pp.374–384; Lucy Beckett, *In the Light of Christ* (2006) ("That there would one day be agreement on, for example, the rational basis for morality or the rational basis for aesthetic judgment – truth upon which the judgment of the good or the

beautiful might be founded – was the hope of the Enlightenment. It rested on the assumption that reason is universal and that its proofs are bound to be accepted by everyone sufficiently educated to follow its arguments. It was assumed, in other words, that there is a common, neutral ground from which all traditions, all claims to truth, including the Christian, can be rationally assessed. As time went by, the ground shrank, eventually leaving only facts, only what is empirically verifiable, as that upon which we may properly stand, while 'all those large dreams by which men long live well' evaporated into mere personal opinion. The hope of the Enlightenment turned out to be forlorn, its assumptions baseless. In an acute analysis of the resulting disappointment, and the resulting consensus that there is no consensus, Alasdair MacIntyre in *Whose Justice? Which Rationality?* wrote: 'The most cogent reasons that we have for believing that the hope of a tradition-independent rational universality is an illusion derive from the history of that project. For in the course of that history liberalism, which began as an appeal to alleged principles of shared rationality against what was felt to be the tyranny of tradition, has itself been transformed into a tradition whose continuities are partly defined by the interminability of the debate over such principles.' He goes on to concede that the failure of liberalism to 'provide a neutral tradition-independent ground' does not prove that there is no such ground. However: 'Liberalism is by far the strongest claimant to provide such a ground which has so far appeared in human history or which is likely to appear in the foreseeable future. That liberalism fails in this respect, therefore provides the strongest reason that we can actually have for asserting that there is no such neutral ground.'

If there is no such ground, we are left

with two possible ways in which to think of ourselves and our lives. One is to trust nothing but empirically verifiable facts.... But there is an alternative choice, as MacIntyre convincingly argues. The alternative is to choose to trust a tradition in which to think, to judge, to live, because we discover that a tradition does exist, a collaborative achievement of coherent intellectual effort with a long history still accessible, that confirms our own experience of what we have found – using, quietly, words we cannot do without – to be good, beautiful and true. What we may then discover is that the tradition we have come upon makes more and more sense to us, makes more and more sense of our own lives, which begin to take on ... a unity that turns out to be real and full of infinitely explorable meaning. If we choose a Christian tradition – MacIntyre distinguishes the Augustinian from the Thomist – we will discover that this unity is in God").

Mackenzie, Sir (Edward Montague Anthony) Compton – writer; b. 17 January 1883, West Hartlepool, County Durham; c. April 1914, Capri; d. 30 November 1972, 31 Drummond Place, Edinburgh; went through Anglo-Catholic phase and pondered ordination; military service in World War I; prolific output of novels, essays, criticism, history, biography, autobiography, and travel writing – in all a total of 113 published titles; worked in intelligence service; Jacobite tendencies and co-founder of Nationalist Party of Scotland; rector of Glasgow University; lived for many years in Capri; broadcaster, raconteur and mimic; knighted in 1952; buried on the island of Barra, Scotland; see *Altar Steps* (1922), *The Parson's Progress* (1923), *The Heavenly Ladder* (1924); *My Life and Times* (1963–71), especially Octave 4 (1965), pp.214–215 ("I made it clear to him [the priest instructing him] that my

reception into the Church was not to be regarded as a conversion but as a submission, a logical surrender to an inevitable recognition of the fact that Jesus Christ had founded his Church on the rock of Peter"); Andro Linklater, *Compton Mackenzie: A Life* (1992); Patrick Allitt, *Catholic Converts: British and American Intellectuals Turn to Rome* (1997) *passim*; Joseph Pearce, *Literary Converts* (1999), *passim*; *DNB*.

McKerlie, (Emmeline) Marianne Helena – writer and traveler; b. in Kensington, London; parents were Presbyterians (her mother having been an Evangelical Episcopalian before her marriage); occasionally visited Catholic churches as a child and was attracted by Benediction; influenced by the Catholic aspects of Sir Walter Scott's novels; read *The Imitation of Christ* every day; became an Anglo-Catholic; conversion to Rome influenced by traveling in Catholic countries and seeing the practice of Catholics there; see *Mary of Guise-Lorraine: Queen of Scotland* (1931); *Rome Via Whithorn: Autobiographical Notes of a Protracted Journey* (1934) ("What a struggle it was with one's conscience to believe that the Anglican establishment was indeed a branch of the Catholic Church. In Italy this belief had received a rude shaking.... Questions I had wanted to ask remained unput. Strangely enough, they were answered by [an Anglican] Canon in one of his addresses ... viz. about the Holy Sacrifice of the Mass, Devotion to St. Joseph, to the Sacred Heart, each of which he pointed out as being incompatible with the teaching of the Church of England. With the feeling that I wished to believe in them came, that in this case I had no business to be where I was...

...Receiving the sacramental bread in the palm of one's hand always left me with anxiety about crumbs, and even that anything else should touch that palm. It was always the left one, and I kept a tiny handkerchief to cover it before pulling on my glove. On reaching home I put the handkerchief in water and wrung it out into the roots of some growing plant, or, failing that, on to the window sill. How many people must share these anxieties who believe in the Real Presence. John Ayscough, in one of his books, relates how as a boy he used to go and gather up the crumbs of the sacramental bread on the altar steps and consume them").

McLaren, Agnes – physician; b. 4 July 1837; c. 20 November 1898; d. 18 April 1913; daughter of Duncan McLaren (1800–1886), Scottish Presbyterian minister, at one time MP for Edinburgh; mother a Quaker; worked for the Women's Suffrage Movement; later first woman graduate in medicine at Montpellier in 1878; worked as a doctor in France for twenty years; attracted by Catholic liturgy and made a yearly retreat with the Dominicans, but remained a Presbyterian until she was sixty; in 1900 became a Dominican tertiary; great efforts to abolish the white slave trade; Fellow of Academy of Dublin; member of Arcadia of Rome; in 1910 founded first Catholic Medical Mission to Women and Children of India; member of the International Federation for the Abolition of State Regulation of Vice; see Katherine Burton, *According to the Pattern: The Story of Dr. Agnes McLaren and the Society of Catholic Medical Missionaries* (1946); Anna Dengel, "Doctor Agnes McLaren: Lay Apostle and Dominican Tertiary," *Blackfriars*, March 1950, p.125; Rev. Bernard J. Canning, "A Great Scot – Dr. Agnes Mclaren," *Catholic Life*, September 2008, p.26.

Maitland, Sara – writer; b. 27 February 1950; c. 1993; brought up as Presbyterian; educated at Oxford University; left-wing libertarian in 1960s and 1970s; then Anglo-Catholic before being received into the Catholic Church; novelist (feminist fiction) and writing on religion; see "A feminist's path to Rome," *The Tablet*, 3 April 1993 ("As I wrestle (and I will continue to wrestle) with the theological issues that have concerned me for the last twenty years – gender, sexuality, creativity, power – I desire to do so in a community which will hold me accountable, which insists that I am one member of a universal body and cannot just make it up to suit myself. I want to be held answerable to both Scripture and history, just as any sane trapeze artist wants a safety net: not to stop her flying but to catch her when she falls… I love Mary. My spirituality is increasingly Marian: grounded in the *Magnificat* and in the idea that 'what we believe of Mary, we hope for ourselves.' How can I not then love a Church which holds Mary as the model of normative humanity? Which proclaims, so openly, that salvation comes into the world, in the most basic genital way, through a woman?"); *A Big Enough God* (1994); *Awesome God* (2002); *A Book of Silence* (2008); *Stations of the Cross* (2009) (with Chris Gollon).

Malleson, Colonel George Bruce – army officer and military historian; b. 8 May 1825, London; c. 1891; d. 1 March 1898, Kensington, London; given direct commission to Bengal Staff Corps; served through Second Burmese War; was in Indian Military Finance Department; Sanitary Commissioner for Bengal; for seven years guardian of the Maharajah of Mysore; author of several works, e.g., *History of the French in India, Historical Sketch of the Nation States of India, History of the Indian Mutiny, Histories of Afghanistan and Herat, Life of Lord Clive*, etc.; *Times* correspondent; see *DNB*.

Mallock, William Hurrell – writer; b. 2 February 1849, Cheriton Bishop, Devon; c. 2 April 1923, in extremis ("It was only on his deathbed that semi-conscious movement was charitably interpreted as a conscious sign of acquiescence by the waiting priest" (Arnold Lunn, *Now I See* (1933). p.121); sister, Mary Margaret Mallock (1846/7–1938), authoress, converted in 1874); d. 2 April 1923, the infirmary, Wincanton, Somerset; son of Anglican clergyman; nephew of James Anthony Froude (1818–1894), historian, and of Richard Hurrell Froude (1803–1836), one of authors of *Tracts for the Times*, etc; grew up in traditional world of local gentry, whose Tory and High Church sympathies he shared; educated privately then at Balliol College, Oxford; writer of satirical fiction; conservative political and religious polemicist; forceful defender of dogmatic Christianity; main object in his political and economic writing to expose fallacies of radicalism and socialism; his philosophical writings aimed at showing that science taken by itself can supply man with no basis for religion; unmarried; buried at Wincanton; see *The New Republic* (1877), *Is Life Worth Living?* (1879) ("Any supernatural religion that renounces its claim [to infallibility], it is clear can profess to be semi-revelation only. It is a hybrid thing, partly natural and partly supernatural, and it thus practically has all the qualities of a religion that is wholly natural …"); *Doctrine and Doctrinal Disruption* (1900) ("The history of the Church of Rome has never yet been attempted from what we may call the standpoint of the spiritual sociologist; and all that can here be done is to indicate, briefly and generally, the kind of aspect which, when thus examined, it will present to us. We shall find at the beginning the small and seemingly undifferentiated aggregate, with no definite nucleus, no acknowledged or permanent headship. Little by little we shall see a permanent headship, evolving itself; and along with this headship, and leading from it and up to it, an increasing variety of parts, whose differentiations become permanent also, each fulfilling some function complementary to the functions of the others, and all unified by their connection with some common brain or sensorium. This common brain or sensorium with which all other parts are connected, is, of all Churches, possessed by the Church of Rome alone; and this fact itself is sufficient, when viewed from the sociological standpoint, to place that Church at the head of the organic scale, and to separate it, scientifically, from all other Christian bodies by an interval like that which, in the sphere of biology, separates the highest from the lowest orders of life.

The result which its possession of this complete, organic character has on the Church of Rome as a teaching body is obvious. Being thus endowed, as we have seen, with a single brain, the Church is endowed also with a continuous historic memory; is constantly able to explain and to re-state doctrine, and to attest, as though from personal experience, the facts of its earliest history. Is doubt thrown on the Resurrection and Ascension of Christ? The Church of Rome replies, 'I was at the door of the sepulchre myself. My eyes saw the Lord come forth. My eyes saw the cloud receive Him.' Is doubt thrown on Christ's miraculous birth? The Church of Rome replies, 'I can attest the fact, even if no other witness can; for the angel said Hail! in my ear as well as Mary's'"); *Memoirs of Life and Literature* (1920) ("Without some authority at the back of it, unified by a coherent logic, no religion can guide or curb mankind, or provide them with any hopes that the enlightened intellect can accept. It is precisely this sort of authority which, for those who can accept its doctrines, the Church of Rome possesses, and is possessed by that Church alone"); Russell Kirk, "The Mind of W. H. Mallock," *The Month*, February 1953, p.69; Robert Lee Wolff, *Gains and Losses: Novels of Faith and Doubt in Victorian England* (1977), pp.475–505; Maurice Cowling, *Religion and Public Doctrine in England Vol. III: Accommodations* (2002), pp.296–308; *DNB* ("Mallock berated positivists, a term he used for both Comtists and scientific naturalists, for failing to provide a persuasive secular morality to counteract the skepticism unleashed by their scientific criticisms of revealed religion. He argued that the attempt to draw ethical rules from essentially materialist phenomena was doomed, because such phenomena gave equally compelling reasons for cynicism and hedonism. Only supernatural religion could guarantee adherence to moral sanctions").

Manby, Peter – religious controversialist; c. 1687 (made converts, e.g., his brother, Robert, also a clergyman of the Established Church, became a Catholic and then a Franciscan friar; both Robert's sons joined the Society of Jesus); d. 1697, London; unknown parents and background; educated at Trinity College, Dublin and took orders in Church of Ireland; minor canon at St. Patrick's, Dublin in 1660; chancellor there in 1666; chaplain to Archbishop of Dublin in 1670; Dean of Kerry in 1672; on converting he published *The Considerations which Obliged Peter Manby, Dean of Derry, to Embrace the Catholique Religion*, which caused a stir; given much support by James II; fled to France with James' forces after the Battle of the Boyne in 1690; see *DNB* ("His stated reasons for converting included concerns about the lack of authority of the reformers at the English Reformation, a commitment to confession which he saw as a shocking

omission in Protestantism, and, finally, an insistence that Catholicism was not to be reviled as idolatrous since it was the origin of the Anglican religion. Manby declared that there was much to be admired in Catholic writings and credited the mass as the ultimate inspiration for his conversion").

Mann, Theodore Augustus (name in religion Augustus William Mann and commonly called the Abbé Mann) – priest, scientist and antiquary; b. 22 June 1735, Yorkshire; c. 4 May 1756; d. 23 February 1809, Prague; son of Protestant; exhibited much ability in science; became Deist when fifteen; ran away to Paris in 1794, where greatly influenced by Bossuet's *Discours sur l'Histoire Universelle* and devoted himself to religious meditation, resulting in being received into the Church by the Archbishop of Paris, Christophe de Beaumont; joined English Carthusians at Nieuwpoort in Netherlands in 1758; regularly studied for thirteen hours a day; ordained priest 20 September 1760; prior 1764–1777; elected to Imperial and Royal Academy in Austrian Emperor's service at Brussels; obtained release from monastic vows so that he might write more freely; published prolific number of books, on science, history, textbooks for schools, and traveled much, including to England, on scientific projects; in April 1787 called to deathbed of Anthony Joseph Browne, seventh Viscount Montagu, then resident in Brussels, to reconcile him to the Catholic Church, which he did; elected Fellow of Royal Society in 1788; much disrupted by French Revolution; see *Gillow*, Vol. IV, p.402; *Catholic Encyclopedia*; *DNB*.

Manning, His Eminence Henry Edward, Cardinal – Cardinal priest, philanthropist and author; b. 15 July 1808,

Copped Hall, Totteridge, Hertfordshire; c. 6 April 1851 (received on the same occasion as James Hope-Scott (see above): "With the fullest conviction, both of reason and conscience, we have sought admittance into what we alike believe to be the one true fold and Church of God on earth"; his sister-in-law, Sophia Ryder (see below) and her husband, George Ryder (see below), had converted in 1846; his brother, Charles John Manning ((1797–1880), and his family, also became Catholics); d. 14 January 1892, Archbishop House, Carlisle Place, London; tenth child of William Manning (1763–1835), Governor of the Bank of England; unmoved by High Church upbringing and developed as Evangelical; first in Greats at Balliol College, Oxford; husband of Caroline Sargent (d. 1837); close bonds through marriage to Wilberforce family; Fellow of Merton College, Oxford; post in Colonial Office for two years; Anglican curate and then rector of Lavington-cum-Graffham, Sussex; Archdeacon of Chichester and Select Preacher to Oxford University; influenced by Tractarianism; conversion especially influenced by Newman's *Development of Doctrine* and by Erastianism of Church of England; another factor was the Gorham judgment (see entry for Thomas Minster); ordained Catholic priest 14 June 1851; DD of Rome; founder in England and first Superior of Oblates of St. Charles Borromeo (to work with the poor); Pronotary Apostolic and Domestic Prelate to Pope Pius IX; Canon of Westminster and then Archbishop of Westminster (from 1865) and Cardinal Priest of SS. Andrew and Gregory on the Coelian Hill (from 1875); leading Ultramontane; between 1851 and 1865 his converts numbered 346; did great work for education, Ireland, and the poor (his eloquent pleas on behalf of the poor prompted the secretary of the royal Commission on the Housing of the Working Classes to remark that "if there had been some half dozen Mannings England would have run some risk of being converted to Christianity"); he broke the deadlock in the London Dock strike in 1889; fought to curb the evils of intemperance; buried at Kensal Green cemetery (huge crowds at his funeral), but reinterred at Westminster Cathedral; see *Why I Became a Catholic* (n.d.); *England and Christendom* (1867); *Caesarism and Ultramontanism* (1874); *The True Story of the Vatican Council* (1877); *Confidence in God* (1891); *The Grounds of Faith* (1890); E. S. Purcell, *Life of Cardinal Manning,* 2 Vols. (1896) (letter by Manning to Robert Wilberforce, 22 January 1851, cited at pp.601–602: "1. The plain words of Scripture prove to me that the Church is One, Visible, and Perpetual. What is perpetuity in Faith but indefectibility, or, if you will, infallibility? There never has been or ever will be a moment when the Church of Faith shall cease to be One, visible and ascertainable. *Ephes.* iv. 4–16 seems to me, as Bull says, *luce meridiana clarius....* It seems that to be Scriptural is to be Roman...

2. Next, Historical Tradition is even more plain. The Universal Church of the first 700 years believed in divine, infallible guidance in its office. The Greek Church after the schism claims this as much as the Roman Catholic Church. No Christian denied it till Luther, after he was condemned by the Church. Again, mere human history would suffice – Schlegel says that 'the Catholic Church is the highest historical authority upon earth.' What is this but the *maximum of evidence* as to what Our Lord and the Holy Spirit revealed? This alone would convince me.

3. Lastly, what does Reason say, but that the *certitude* of revelation to succeeding ages demands a perpetual provision secure from error? How else can I be certain of what was revealed 1800

years ago or even that there was revelation at all? What is infallibility, but revelation perpetuated and inspiration produced by illumination – the extraordinary by the ordinary – the immediate by the mediate action of the Holy Spirit?"); Aimée Sewell, *The Conversion of Cardinal Manning* (1901); Shane Leslie, *Henry Edward Manning: His Life and Labours* (1921) (letter by Manning to Miss Maurice, 5 August 1850, cited at p.91: "I always felt that the Low Church had no objective Truths, the High Church little subjective religion. Now I see that in the Catholic system the objective and subjective are the concave and the convex. I do not say that the body and the soul, because these are two, and the objective and subjective become one. God and man are one by Incarnation. A Theology of 300 years is in conflict with a Faith of 1,800 years. I was born in the 300. My mature thoughts transplant me into the 1,800. This is the real balance, but people will not so look at it. I believe a man might hold what he likes in the English Church if he would be quiet and uphold the Church. The dishonesty is to be honest"); Vincent Alan McClelland, *Cardinal Manning: His Public Life and Influence 1865–1892)* (1962); David Newsome, *The Parting of Friends: A Study of the Wilberforces and Henry Manning* (1966) (letter by Manning to Samuel Wilberforce: "I admit at once that my teaching has been and is nearer to the Roman Church than to the Church of England as it teaches now. And why? Forgive me if I speak without reserve. It is because the Church of England is betrayed by the majority of its pastors to the public opinion of the day. Its voice contradicts its formularies. The manifest faithlessness of the living Church of England to its own recorded Faith, even more than its miserable contradictions is driving multitudes into mistrust, unbelief or secession.... But every year has brought out fresh proofs that what I believed to be the Theology of the English Church is only the opinion of a school, early, learned, and devout, beginning with the end of Q. Elizabeth and neutralized at the Revolution. I am as fully persuaded as I can be that your opinions are and that mine are not tenable now in the Church of England. I could as soon doubt of the Holy Trinity as that the Church of Christ is One, Visible and Infallible. Holy Scripture seems to me clear as the Sun.

In the Church of England there exists a protestant and a catholic element. Between these an unintelligible and as it seems to me false hearted compromise. The protestant element I have believed to be the disease of the English Church; the catholic to be its only life and substance. In that catholic element I have lived and labored with an unchanging and uniform perseverance: as I believe both our agreements and our opposition will prove"); Robert Gray, *Cardinal Manning* (1985) ("Ultimately, it is not in the success or failure of this or that endeavor, however admirable or misconceived, that Manning's claim to our respect and attention lies. It is rather in the witness to the beneficent power of Christianity that his whole life affords. His faith was far removed from the temper of the present age, which seems prepared to extend its credulity to almost anything but Christian dogma. The enemies of Christian dogma like to imagine that reason has triumphed over superstition. In fact the new orthodoxies are as blindly supported as the old.... The search is on for creeds that demand nothing and excuse everything. The faith by which Manning lived, on the contrary, demanded everything and excused nothing.

When the last sneer has been sneered at his careerist instincts, and the last *frisson* of intellectual superiority extracted from consideration of his theological extravagances, consider the bare fact that remains. A man of rare ability, ruthless will, dominating temperament and high ambition began his life as the slave of secular glory and ended it as the hero of the poor, the weak, the outcast and the despised. That is a noble progress to be achieved by devotion to ... to what, a chimera? Would that many more great men had been similarly deceived.

And if the chimera were, after all, reality? Then, if Henry Manning is not saved seventy times seven times, God help the rest of us"); Christopher O'Gorman, "A History of Henry Manning's Religious Opinions, 1808–1832," *Recusant History*, October 1992, p.152 (whole issue devoted to Manning); Gilley, "Manning and Chesterton," *Chesterton Review*, November 1992, p.485 (Manning special issue); David Newsome, *The Convert Cardinals: John Henry Newman and Henry Edward Manning* (1993); Madeleine Beard, *Faith and Fortune* (1997), pp.160–165; James Pereiro, *Cardinal Manning: An Intellectual Biography* (1998); Robert Gray, "Cardinal Henry Manning," in John Joliffe *(ed), English Catholic Heroes* (2008), p.168; "Newman, Manning and Their Age," *Saint Austin Review*, September/October 2008 (special issue devoted to Newman, Manning and Hopkins); Robert Gray, "Manning and the Upper Ten Thousand," *Catholic Herald*, 7 November 2008, p.8; *Gillow*, Vol. IV, p.409; *Catholic Encyclopedia*; *DNB* ("The scenes at his funeral on 21 January and the crowds that thronged the streets for the four miles between the Brompton Oratory and Kensal Green cemetery (where he was buried) had no precedent ... since the death of the first Duke of Wellington").

Markievicz, Constance Georgine (*née* **Gore-Booth) (Countess Markievicz in the Polish nobility)** – Irish republican; b.

4 February 1868, 7 Buckingham Gate, Pimlico, London; c. 1917; d. 15 July 1927, Dublin; daughter of Sir Henry William Gore-Booth (1843–1900), philanthropist and Arctic explorer; sister of Eva Gore-Booth (1870–1926), campaigner for women's suffrage; family prominent Anglo-Irish landowners; brought up in Church of Ireland; childhood friend of W. B. Yeats, the poet; educated by governesses, then at Slade School of Art, London; married Count Casimir Dunin-Markievicz, a Polish widower; part of the literary and cultural scene of Dublin; became Irish nationalist and member of Sinn Fein and Daughters of Ireland, a revolutionary women's movement; associate of Maud Gonne (see above); supporter of socialism and trade unionism (e.g., Irish Women Workers' Union); supported armed rebellion against the British and took part in the Easter rising of 1916; sentenced to death, but commuted to penal servitude for life because of her sex (released in general amnesty in 1917); imprisoned in 1918 for her alleged involvement in a "German plot"; elected as Sinn Fein candidate for Dublin in general election of 1918 (first woman elected to the British parliament), but refused to take her seat; opponent of Anglo-Irish treaty and fought for republican cause in Irish civil war; elected to Free State parliament in 1923, but refused to take the oath of allegiance to the king; joined Fianna Fáil on its establishment in 1926 and elected in general election of 1927; influence waned and poor health; buried in Glasnevin cemetery, Dublin; see *DNB* ("She claimed to have experienced an epiphany during the Easter rising, took instruction from a priest while in prison, and converted to Catholicism shortly after her release").

Marlborough, ninth Duke of (Charles Richard John Spencer-Churchill) – Catholic layman; b. 13 November 1871;

c. 1 February 1927 (received by Cardinal Bourne); d. 30 June 1934; first cousin of Winston Churchill; became ninth Duke on death of father in 1892; in 1895 married American heiress, Consuelo Vanderbilt; divorce in 1921 (causing a scandal); married shortly afterwards (in Presbyterian church) another American heiress, Gladys Marie Deacon, a lapsed Catholic; Consuelo Vanderbilt started annulment proceedings; annulment granted in 1926; these proceedings caused Duke to become increasingly interested in teachings of the Catholic Church and he took instruction from Fr. Martindale (see below); after conversion Duke withdrew from his second marriage and society and oversaw revival of Blenheim Palace; during last illness he refused medication, telling the priest, "I have joined the religion of which the centre is the crucifixion"; see Sir Shane Leslie, "The Marlborough Case: Last Words," *The Month*, March 1953, p.197; Madeleine Beard *Faith and Fortune* (1997), pp.175–178 ("When in 1934 the Duke was buried at Blenheim and his son and heir spoke without appreciation of his father's spiritual qualities, he was rebuked and enlightened by [Winston] Churchill, who perceived clearly in the late Duke the 'strong strain of the spiritual and the mystic in his being.' Churchill observed of the late Duke: 'The need of contact with the sublime and the supernatural of which he was profoundly conscious, led him to the Church of Rome. He asked for sanctuary within that august and seemingly indestructible communion, against which his ancestor had warred with formidable strength. The shelter and protections were accorded, and the last years of his life were lived in a religious calm which fortified him against the troubles of the world and the errors we all make in traveling through it'…

The priest was helped in his task [of instruction] by the Duke's innate sense of 'Authority and of Hierarchy and of Discipline, and, indeed, of the pageantry with which our human instinct always surrounds these things.' For him a name, a palace and a rank were not instruments for self-indulgence but 'earthly reflections of the spiritual hierarchy of the Church, through which God revealed infallibly to man immutable truth and unchanging moral law'").

Marryat (married names Church and Lean), Florence – novelist and actress; b. 9 July 1837, Brighton, Sussex; c. considerable period before her death; d. 22 October 1899, St. John's Wood, London; youngest daughter of eleven children of Captain Frederick Marryat RN (1792–1848), the novelist and naval officer; grand-daughter of Dr. Thomas Marryat (1730–1792), the physician and wit; educated at home; much traveling in India with army officer husband; published over seventy-five novels, primarily popular romances for women (many translated into other languages); frequent contributor to newspapers and magazines, and edited (1872–1876) *London Society*, a monthly publication; also playwright, comedy actress, operatic singer, lecturer, and entertainer; wrote a life of her father; attracted to spiritualism, an interest sanctioned by her spiritual director, Fr. Dalgairns (see above) of the London Oratory; buried at Kensal Green cemetery, London; see *Catholic Encyclopedia*; *DNB*.

Marshall, Arthur Featherstone – author; b. 1832; c. 1859 (brothers, Frederick and Thomas (see below) also converted); d. 1897; formerly Anglican curate; one time attaché to Japanese legation in Paris, widely known as author of *The Comedy of Convocation in the English Church*, a satire exposing the inconsistencies invoked in all three of the Anglican views: High, Low, and Broad

Church; his *Old Catholics at Cologne* also popular during the period immediately following First Vatican Council and defection of Döllinger; see *Catholic Encyclopedia*.

Marshall, (Claude Cunningham) Bruce – writer; b. 24 June 1899, 8 East Fettes Avenue, Edinburgh; c. 1924; d. 18 June 1987, Biot, France; educated at Universities of St. Andrews and Edinburgh; lost leg in World War I; degree in Commerce; worked as chartered accountant; World War II intelligence work; after war worked with displaced persons in Rome and then Vienna; lived in south of France from 1948; many popular novels on Catholic themes using his own experiences; ashes scattered in the garden of the crematorium at Nice; see *Father Malachy's Miracle* (1931), *All Glorious Within* (1944) ("'The universality of the Church of God is a fact for which Catholics ought never cease to give thanks. It is perhaps hard for us in this rusty, ramshackle fruit market in sorry, separated Scotland to realize that in our worship, faith and doctrine we are at one with the great congregations in the cathedrals of Europe. No bishop in Chartres, no Cardinal in Burgos or Warsaw, nay, my dear brethren, no Pontiff in Rome, no, not even the Holy Father himself, consecrates more surely bread to Christ's Body and wine to Christ's Blood than do I, your unworthy parish priest. It is a thought which ought to make us both proud and humble: proud because we alone among our fellow countrymen are in step with European tradition and speak the good same grammar of God; humble because we of ourselves have done nothing to deserve so glorious a privilege.'

Looking out over the faces at which he was preaching, Fr. Smith saw that they were looking neither proud nor humble, although here and there a mouth gaped and an eye peered...

'Yet it is not the universality of the Church that makes its doctrine true. If only one person in the whole world accepted the teaching of the Church that doctrine would still be true. If nobody at all believed the teaching of the Church the mathematic of faith would still be as true as was the law of gravity before Newton discovered it. For faith is not a sort of competition in a magazine, to which the various sects send in their doctrinal guesses and hope for the best; it is belief in revelation on the authority of God Himself'"); *The Fair Bride* (1953); *Girl in May* (1956); *A Thread of Scarlet* (1959); *The Bishop* (1970); Walter Romig (ed), *The Book of Catholic Authors*, Fourth Series (1948); *DNB*.

Marshall, Francis Albert – playwright and theatre critic; b. 18 November 1840, London; d. 28 December 1889, Bloomsbury Square, London; son of William Marshall, Liberal MP; married Imogene Fitzinman Marshall, opera singer, and on her death in 1885, Ada Cavendish (1839–1895), well-known actress; drama critic for the *London Figaro* and devoted two years to journalism; plays included farces, comic operas, comedies, and dramas; friend of Henry Irving and editor of the "Henry Irving Edition" of Shakespeare; devout Catholic; see *Gillow*, Vol. IV, p.470; *DNB*.

Marshall, Sir James – colonial judge; b. 19 December 1829, Edinburgh; c. 21 November 1857 (received by Fr. Robert Coffin (see above)); d. 9 August 1889, Margate; son of Anglican vicar; brought up strict Evangelical; loss of right arm through gun accident at age of sixteen; High Anglican curate before his conversion; his disability disbarred him from the priesthood; later classics teacher at Birmingham Oratory School and friend of Newman; moved to law at suggestion of Serjeant Edward Bellasis (see above);

barrister and senior puisne judge and then Chief Justice of Supreme Court of the Gold Coast, Africa; later Chief Justice of new Niger Territories; knighted by Queen Victoria in June 1882; Hon. Treasurer of the Catholic Truth Society; Knight Commander of St. Gregory the Great; see William R. Brownlow, *Memoir of Sir James Marshall* (1890) (originally published in The Month, September 1889, p.23) ("Some other young London clergymen were in the same difficulties. The mutual discussion of their misgivings deepened instead of dissipating them. 'We were at it till past midnight,' he wrote, 'and all I could see at the end was, that if the Pope is not the Vicar of Jesus Christ, he must be Antichrist, and that I must be either a Roman or a Protestant"); *Gillow*, Vol. IV, p.473; *DNB*.

Marshall, Thomas William – Catholic controversialist and journalist; b. 1818; c. November 1845 (received at Wardour together with his wife, Harriet; his brothers, Frederick and Arthur (see above), also converted); d. 14 December 1877, Surbiton, Surrey; son of John Marshall, government agent for colonizing New South Wales; parents Protestant; formerly Anglican vicar; greatly influenced by the Tractarian movement; in writing book on the *Episcopal Government of the Church, Notes on the Episcopal Polity of the Catholic Church* (1844) was led by his researches to abandon Anglican position as untenable; after conversion at first he and his wife in great poverty; appointed first inspector of Catholic schools with responsibility for southern counties of England and Wales; rendered great service to Catholic poor-school education; Knight of St. Gregory the Great; in 1870 made very successful lecturing tour in United States, speaking on subjects connected with the interests of the Church and in defense of her

doctrines; LLD of Jesuit College of Georgetown, Washington; author of *Christianity in China* (1855), *Christian Missions*, 3 Vols. (1862), and several other controversial works, attacking Church of England in combative style; sincere and devout Catholic; buried at Mortlake; see *Twenty Two Reasons for entering the Catholic Church* (1846); *Gillow*, Vol. IV, p.479 ("In this most important testimony to the Catholic faith, [*Christian Missions*], he contrasted the methods and results of Catholic and Protestant missions. On the one hand he showed the marvels and triumphs of the Church, and on the other, exposed the failure of Protestant missionaries, and the humbug by which they induced the British public to support them"); *Catholic Encyclopedia*; *DNB*.

Martelli, George Ansley – journalist and writer; b. 1903; wife, Ann, also a convert; Foreign Office official; worked in intelligence in World War II; head of Political Wartime Executive's Italian section; at one time *Daily Telegraph* special correspondent in Congo and Angola; wrote on politics and historical subjects; see "Neo-Reformation and Counter-Reformation in the Roman Catholic Church," *The Salisbury Review*, July 1984, p.32 ("A tree, as Our Lord said, is judged by its fruits; and the fruits of Catholicism are the saints, the martyrs, the theologians, the great Popes; and the painters, sculptors, architects, musicians, poets, novelists, film makers even (e.g., Bunuel), whose masterpieces are unimaginable without their Catholic background, so little understood in Britain since she cut herself off from this, the main stream of western culture").

Martindale, Cyril Charlie, SJ – priest and scholar; b. 25 May 1879, Kensington, London; c. 1897; d. 18 March 1963, Petworth, Sussex; brought up by Low

Church Anglicans; son of Sir Arthur Henry Temple Martindale of Indian Civil Service; mother died five months after his birth and he was brought up by aunts; at school influenced by Yellow Book culture and agnosticism; outstanding scholar at Oxford (firsts in honour moderations (1903) and *literae humaniores* (1905), plus several scholarships); entered the Society of Jesus in 1897; ordained priest in 1911; conducted a world-wide apostolate from Farm Street, London; published over eighty books, about sixty pamphlets and hundreds of articles; author and contributor to *The Month, American Catholic Encyclopedia*, etc; in great demand for sermons, lectures, discussions, speeches, retreats, and broadcast talks; very effective as a broadcaster; see *Catholic Thought and Thinkers* (1920); *The Creative Words of Christ* (1929); *What Are Saints?* (1932); essay in Maurice Leahy (ed), *Conversions to the Catholic Church: A Symposium* (1933) ("When will men understand that between what is Catholic and what is anything else, there is a great gulf fixed? You have to have your bridge. Perhaps God drags you, squealing and squirming, across it. It isn't history, nor psychology, nor philosophy, nor the need for authority, nor the love for symbolism, nor any other thing created, that does it, but God does it, Christ does it, Grace does it"); *Christianity is Christ* (1936); *Letters From Their Aunts* (1939) (fictitious letters on Christianity); *Bernadette of Lourdes* (1943); *Can Christ Help Me?* (1950); *The Faith of the Roman Church* (1951) ("[Christ] chose twelve – 'The Twelve' – whom He called Apostles, and sent them 'as' His Father had sent Him, to teach the whole world, and to do so under a guarantee, so that those who should hear them, would be hearing Him, as those who heard Him, were hearing God. Similarly, to 'despise' an Apostle, would be to despise God. The

series is exact: God, Christ, the Apostles, the latter being mouthpiece and representative of the former. Moreover, they were to govern under a like guarantee: what they should 'loose', allow, or 'bind', forbid, on earth, should be ratified in heaven, by God. Here indeed is a good implicit statement of what the Catholic means by infallibility. The Apostles would *not* be able to teach a lie or command in Christ's name a sin, else they would involve God himself. But since no man can thus exempt himself from the fate of human frailty, they were safeguarded by God Himself from failing in their office. The favor belonged to the office, not to the person. And so the Apostles conceived of themselves. 'It has been decided by the Holy Ghost and by Us' is the astounding preface to their first decree. And without a break the Church thought of herself as continuing this teaching office and function: her very name was 'The Teaching', and was opposed to that Gnostic theory which was, that special and private illumination gave to an elite the true knowledge of God. Christianity is not a gnosis, but a Didache. The Church has always been a Teaching Body, under the full guarantee of Christ, and not a mere assembly of persons experiencing emotions however noble or hatching ideas however valuable and, in the last resort, governing themselves by these"); *Jesus Christ and his Gospel* (1968); "C. C. Martindale, SJ – A Symposium," *The Month*, August 1963, p.19; Philip Caraman, *C. C. Martindale: A Biography* (1967); Francis Bywater, "*In Diebus Illis*: Father Cyril Martindale, SJ (1879–1963)," *Chesterton Review*, May 1991, p.205 ("His conversion was not the result of any intellectual process. At the age of eighteen, he felt an irresistible compulsion to join the Roman Catholic Church. He afterwards claimed that he had been 'pitchforked' into it by Our Lady. A no less compulsive force led him to join the Society of Jesus. This decision he attributed to the intervention of St. Aloysius. Thus, through no natural agency, he acquired that overwhelming sense of the supernatural that was the mainspring of his life. Hence his constant reference to the Saints. His whole life was dedicated to proclaiming, first through his writings and later through his broadcasts, the ever present, if invisible, existence of the Saints"); Walter Romig (ed), *The Book of Catholic Authors*, Fourth Series (1948); *DNB*.

Maskell, William – ecclesiastical historian; b. 1814, Shepton Mallet, Somerset; c. 22 June 1850 (received at Spanish Place, London); d. 12 April 1890, Penzance; formerly Anglican vicar; greatly influenced by the Tractarian movement; examining chaplain to Henry Phillpotts (1778–1869), Anglican Bishop of Exeter who opposed Catholic emancipation, and who refused to institute George Cornelius Gorham (1787–1857), to the living of Brampford Speke, when the Crown presented him, on account of his opposition to the view that baptism, as a Sacrament, conferred spiritual regeneration or sanctifying grace (Gorham appealed to Judicial Committee of Privy Council, a purely secular body, which ruled against the bishop, who then caved in and installed Gorham); Maskell carried out the examination in the Gorham case, finding Gorham unsound, leading to his own conversion; much correspondence with Newman before conversion; man of private fortune who was a substantial benefactor to Catholic institutions; father of Alfred Ogle Maskell, Fellow of Society of Antiquaries and author; buried at Penzance; see Stanley L. Jaki, *Newman to Converts: An Existential Ecclesiology* (2001), Ch. 11; *Gillow*, Vol. IV, p.504 ("[He] devoted himself to learned researches into the history of the

ancient ritual of the Church of England and cognate matters … the bent of his mind is clearly displayed in his first great work, *The Ancient Liturgy of the Church of England*, published in 1844, which was followed by the companion work, *Monumenta Ritualia Ecclesia Anglicanae*, in 1846–1847. It was but natural that the author of such works should be perplexed by subsequent decisions as to the doctrinal teachings of an establishment which claimed to represent the ancient Church in England"); *DNB*.

Mason, James Austin – priest and author; b. 1785; c. 21 March 1819 (mother and sister received in 1825 together with sister's husband, a Methodist preacher); d. 16 October 1844; born of Methodist parents and brought up in their principles, which he espoused with great zeal; became Methodist minister; formal religious discussion with local Catholic priest, Fr. Francis Martyn (recounted in *The Triumph of Truth*) led to his conversion; death of wife in 1818 and only son in 1820 left him at liberty to study for the priesthood; ordained priest at Advent 1825; worked in several parishes; most of his writings aimed at exposing and refuting the errors of Methodism; see *The Triumph of Truth, in the Conversion of the Rev. J. A. Mason from the Errors of Methodism to the Catholic Faith* (1827); *Gillow*, Vol. IV, p.512.

Mason, Philip (*pseud*. Philip Woodruff) – writer and administrator; b. 19 March 1906, Finchley, London; c. 25 February 1979 (received with his wife, (Eileen) Mary, *née* Hayes (1912–26 April 2000)); d. 25 January 1999, 97 Glebe Road, Cambridge; educated at Balliol College, Oxford (first in PPE); passed first into the Indian civil service in 1927; administrator in India; returned to England in 1947; smallholder; director of Royal Institute of International Affairs; work on issues of race relations; late in life he and his wife converted to the Catholic Church from High Church Anglicanism; author of stories, novels, studies of India, and of Catholic issues; he and his wife were married for sixty-three years; buried at city cemetery, Newmarket Road, Cambridge; see *A Shaft of Sunlight* (1978), especially pp.161–162 ("I was looking for the reconciliation between two vivid aspects of reality – to me the two most vivid – human love, suffering and endurance and the frightening silence of eternity. The Christian answer to that is the Incarnation, the incredible statement that Almighty Power and Love became flesh.... There was one aspect of the events presented in the gospels which I had picked as for me decisive.... It was a difficulty about humility, a mark of all the great saints. The figure at the centre of the gospels had lived, had healed, had taught; his teaching, but far more his death and continued presence with his followers, had transformed the Western world. Was it possible that he had been a good man and humble and a saint until the last weeks of his life, when he had fallen into the sin of pride and supposed himself to be something more than a man?... Now ... I became entirely convinced that it was not so, that the power, the certainty of a dual nature, the understanding of the purpose of his life and death – and of all life and death – had been there throughout. It was impossible to think him a deluded saint; he was either not a saint at all or much more. This was truly the reconciliation of power with love that I had hoped to find"); *A Thread of Silk* (1984), especially pp.191–197 ("Now, as I pondered on the sacramental principle, and as more and more I came to see it as the key to all understanding, I began to perceive that the Incarnation, the sacramental fact at the core of reality, led by its very nature to

one Church, the body of Christ, the continuing expression of the divine in material human form. The Holy Spirit had come and had continued to express itself in this ramshackle vehicle. The Church and the Spirit had grown together and had joyously and triumphantly overcome the heresies that had everywhere started up...

I fell back half-heartedly on the Anglican argument of the nineteenth century that – to take one example – the Assumption of the Mother of God into Heaven was not to be found in the New Testament. Half-heartedly, I write, because to argue that everything you believe must be proved from Holy Writ seems to imply that the Holy Spirit stopped work with the last word of the Book of Revelation.... That particular sand-castle about the Assumption fell with a splash in Venice. One morning we sat a long time in the Church of the Frari before Titian's great altarpiece of the Assumption. It is a painting of which reproductions can never give any idea. It is not only the glow and glory of the coloring but the sheer size of it, the sweep and flow and splendor of the whole superb achievement that make such an impression. We sat and soaked ourselves in the joy of it. When we came away I said to Mary: 'I believe in that picture.' I did not mean that I pictured the mother of Christ standing on the corner of a cloud which she used as a ski-lift to Heaven, but that I did believe in the essential truth of what the picture expressed in visual terms. The central, the poetic, truth of that picture is joy, the joy that the Mother of Jesus felt when she put off her earthly body. She went straight to Heaven and there she was blissfully united with her son. As we looked at that hymn of joy, the sandcastle of one excuse crumbled in the tide. What need was there to prove *that* from Holy Writ?

...[S]oon after we came back from

Venice, the words suddenly formed in my mind one morning before breakfast: 'Why not now?' I told Mary of these words as soon as I saw her and she said: 'Why indeed? I was thinking just the same'"); *Since I Last Wrote* (1996) ("When, very late, after more than seventy years as an Anglican, I was received into the Catholic Church, one of my reasons was that the Church is universal, world-wide; it was the main tide and I know that by nature I was one to swim with the tide, not a protester who by definition swims against it.... Before I left school for Oxford, I had begun to regard myself as a Catholic though still formally Anglican.... I was a loose Anglo-Catholic. It seems to me now that this is an illogical position. How can you say that you belong to the Catholic Church, an organized world-wide body, if you disown its Head and its local branches and give your adherence (when it suits you) to a body that it regards as schismatic?"); *DNB* ("Hitherto they had been devout, high-church Anglicans, always finding enough people round them who shared their outlook. But as they moved deeper into the English countryside, among Anglicans of every degree of belief or none, they began to feel themselves to be 'schismatics within a schismatic church'").

Massey, John – priest; b. 1650/1, Wedhampton, Wiltshire; c. March 1687; d. 11 August 1715, convent of the Blue Nuns at rue de Charenton, Faubourg St Antoine, Paris; son of Puritan minister; whilst at University College, Oxford, friend of Obadiah Walker (see below); whilst Fellow at Merton College, Oxford, and Anglican minister, his faith in the Established Church was shaken; supported James II who appointed him to post of Dean of Christ Church, but dispensed him from usual oaths or attendance at Protestant worship, whereupon

he renounced Protestantism and publicly declared himself Catholic; conversion influenced by John Leyburn, the vicar apostolic of all England; opened chapel at Christ Church for use of Catholics; when William of Orange landed in England in 1688, he secretly left Oxford and escaped to the Continent; stayed at royal court at St. Germain before going to English College, Douai, in 1692 then to Oratorian seminary at St. Magloire, where supported by Mary of Modena, wife of James II; ordained priest in August 1695; in 1699 chaplain to the famous English Blue Nuns, or Conceptionists, in Paris; spent rest of life in piety; fine classical scholar; buried in the church of the convent; see *Gillow*, Vol. IV, p.522; *DNB*.

Massinger, Philip – playwright; b. November 1583, Salisbury; d. March 1640, Bankside, London; son of Arthur Massinger, general-agent at Wilton for the second and third Earls of Pembroke and examiner to the council in the Marches of Wales; from a family originally Catholic, but his father was a Protestant; brought up as a page at Wilton; supported at Oxford University by Henry Herbert, second Earl of Pembroke; has been suggested he lost his patronage when he became a Catholic whilst at the university; produced some thirty-seven plays, often in collaboration with Fletcher or Beaumont or Dekker; all his works have deep religious feeling and strong Catholic sympathies; buried in Southwark Cathedral; see *The Virgin Martyr* (1621); *The Renegado* (1624); *The Maid of Honour* (1628); Edward Hutton, *Catholicism and English Literature* (1942), pp.79–84; *Gillow*, Vol. IV, p.525; *DNB*.

Matthew, Sir Toby (Tobie) – priest, courtier and writer; b. 3 October 1577, Salisbury; c. March 1606 (church of the

Annunciata, Rome); d. 13 October 1655, Ghent; eldest son of Dr. Tobie Matthew, later Archbishop of York; mother strong Puritan; very talented student; barrister and MP for Newport, Cornwall and then St. Albans; close friend of Francis Bacon (1561–1626); traveled in France and Italy 1605–1606, when he became friendly with Fr. Robert Persons, SJ, (see below) who convinced him he had erroneous ideas upon many doctrines; also often met Cardinal Pinelli, the grand-inquisitor; Lenten sermons in Florence made deep impression and he examined works of the Fathers, began to take instruction, and conversion followed; returned to England in 1606 after Bacon and other friends had approached Cecil, but Archbishop of Canterbury committed him to Fleet prison; refused to take the oath of allegiance; went abroad again in 1608, but not allowed by king to return; went to Rome and admitted into Roman College to study for priesthood; ordained priest 20 May 1614 by Cardinal Bellarmine; allowed to return to England in 1617; in and out of favor with the king, but from 1621 esteemed figure at court; disliked by Puritans and arrested in 1640; later retired to the house of the English Jesuits at Ghent and buried in a vault under their church; author of many devotional books and translations; see *Gillow*, Vol. IV, p.531; *Catholic Encyclopedia*; *DNB*.

Maturin, Basil William – priest and writer; b. 15 February 1847, All Saints' vicarage, Grangegorman, Dublin; c. 5 March 1897 (received at Beaumont College); d. 7 May 1915; one of ten children of William Maturin, (1806–1887), Church of Ireland clergyman; brought up in devout family of Tractarian persuasion; later took Anglican orders; member of Anglo-Catholic Society of St. John the Evangelist, and worked at times in United States and South Africa; lived in Philadelphia for ten years before conversion; ordained priest in 1898; lived with Archbishop Vaughan and did missionary work in London; then worked as a writer and itinerant preacher; Catholic chaplain at Oxford University 1914–1915 (interrupted by outbreak of World War I); victim of torpedoing of the *Lusitania* when returning home from a Lenten series of lectures in New York (during sinking he was seen "pale but calm" and giving absolution to several people; then seen handing a child into a lifeboat with request, "Find its mother"; body washed ashore without a lifebelt); author of devotional and pastoral works; buried in the family grave at Brompton cemetery, Fulham; see *Self-Knowledge and Self-Discipline* (1905); *Laws of the Spiritual Life* (1907); *The Price of Unity* (1912) (description of his conversion) ("It is impossible to hold, or to expect that any man's religion should require him to hold, two doctrines that are directly opposed and mutually exclusive of one another. It is, for instance, impossible to believe that our Lord instituted the Papacy as an integral part of the Divine constitution of the Church, and, at the same time that anything could justify a breach with the Papacy. That a man may believe, as a matter of faith, the divine authority of the Holy See, and at the same time the right of the English Church, which categorically denies it; or, while denying with the English Church the claims of the Holy See, may still assert that the Roman and Anglican bodies are each of them living parts of the same Catholic Church. If the English Church is right in this matter, the Roman Church is wrong, and in teaching such a doctrine as a Truth of Revelation, and insisting upon its acceptance as a condition of Communion, she is in heresy, and has ceased to be any part of the Body of Christ.

For it must be borne in mind that

Rome does not allow, in this matter, a distinction between what is of the *esse*, and what is of the *bene esse* of the Church. Some Anglicans maintain that the Papacy is indeed of the *bene esse* of the Church, and that it is their prayer and hope that one day they may be restored to their true allegiance to it. But this is not what Rome teaches, nor what she could accept as a condition of reconciliation. She does not recognize such distinctions in a matter which she believes to be divine, and if an Anglican holds this view, that Union with and submission to the Holy See is desirable, but not necessary, he is really no nearer to clearing Rome from the charge of teaching, as Truth, what is not true, than one who denies the authority of the See of Rome altogether.

It is therefore a direct contradiction – a holding of two things as true, which are mutually exclusive of one another – to assert that the Roman Church teaches as an article of faith that which is untrue, and insists upon it as one of the conditions of Communion, and at the same time to maintain towards her the attitude that most High Churchmen do maintain"); Wilfrid Philip Ward (ed), *Sermons and Sermon Notes* (1916) ("Our Lord Himself prescribed one and only one form of worship in which all the great doctrines of our faith were taught. To that he bid men come to be taught almost unconsciously. Two great doctrines sum up Christian faith and life: God becomes man and gives us His nature. I can't doubt the meaning when I hear *This is My Body*. Other religions profess to satisfy the religious instinct: Christianity to give a gift to heal us – this is the life of Christ. Therefore the Altar has always protected the supernatural teaching of Christianity"); Maisie Ward, *Father Maturin: A Memoir* (1920); *DNB*.

May, Herbert H. – c. 1891 (his wife was received earlier in the same year); brought up for seventeen years in Evangelical section of Church of England; then took Anglican orders as High Church curate; influenced by reading Milner's *End of Controversy* and Faà di Bruno's *Catholic Belief*; see J. G. F. Raupert (ed), *Roads to Rome* (1901), p.159 ("I need hardly say that to me my faith is the pearl of great price. Though, after my conversion, I experienced many temptations against faith, yet they were never logical; nothing could ever break the syllogism – All things taught by the Church are true. This is taught by the Church. This is true. As links in the chain of my conversion, I remember when a boy being much struck by my brother's explaining to me the verse 'Thou art Peter'; that Catholics think their Church the voice of God or something to that effect.... I remember a sermon preached by a Protestant clergyman, in which he said that the words 'Do this in remembrance of Me' meant 'Offer this sacrifice.' When I was convinced of the necessity of confession and the truth of the Real Presence, it seemed to me that the Church which taught these doctrines always and everywhere was the true Church, rather than a Church which, like the Church of England, taught them recently and partially").

Mayne, Saint Cuthbert – priest and proto-martyr of English colleges on the Continent; b. 1548, Youlston, near Barnstaple, North Devon; d. 30 November 1577, Launceston; Fellow of St. John's College, Oxford; became minister of the Established Church; gentle and kindly disposition; leaned towards the old faith, but continued as he was for several years; former close friends, e.g., Fr. Edmund Campion (see above), wrote to him and urged him to join them at Douai; one of the letters fell into the hands of the Archbishop of Canterbury, who sent a pursuivant to Oxford to arrest him, but he was away; went straight to Douai and was admitted in 1573; reconciled to the Church; ordained priest in 1575; left for the English mission in 1576; worked in Cornwall, being resident at Francis Tregian's estate, at Valveden or Golden, five miles from Truro; apprehended in June 1577 and imprisoned at Launceston; sentenced to death for high treason to which he answered "Deo gratias"; matter referred to Privy Council, which decided he should be executed as a terror to papists; hanged, drawn and quartered in Launceston market-place; see *Gillow*, Vol. IV, p.553.

Mayo, Arthur, VC – sailor; b. 18 May 1840; c. 5 November 1867 (received with his wife, Ellen); d. 18 May 1920; joined Royal Navy and later sailed to India; served in the Indian Navy and when aged seventeen took part in the fighting during the Indian Mutiny, his conduct being alluded to in Edward Fraser's *Romance of the King's Navy*, as follows: "A Victoria Cross was awarded to Midshipman Arthur Mayo, for having very gallantly headed a charge on November 22, 1857 in an action between the Indian Naval Brigade and the mutineer Sepoys of the 73rd Native Infantry and the Bengal Artillery. The Naval Brigade on the occasion were ordered to charge two six-pounders with which the mutineers were keeping up a destructive fire. They did so and captured both guns. Midshipman Mayo led all the way, a clear twenty yards in advance of everybody"; invalided home in 1860, he took a degree at Oxford University; later took Anglican orders and served as a curate before conversion to the Catholic Church; father of Fr. Edward Mayo, Fr. Francis Mayo, and Fr. Raymund Mayo, all priests of the Society of Jesus.

Menteith, Robert – author; bap. 25

January 1603, Edinburgh; fl. 1621; d. on or before 13 September 1660, probably in Paris; educated at University of Edinburgh; inclined to the Arminian doctrine and so supported episcopacy; Professor of Philosophy at the Protestant academy of Saumur (Calvinist establishment); returned to Scotland some time before 1629; presented by Charles I as a minister and took Anglican orders; had contact with the Catholic Abercorn family, who were often persecuted, and this may have inclined him to the Catholic faith; had an affair with Anna Hepburn, wife of Sir James Hamilton of Priestfield, as a result of which she became pregnant; he fled the country and went to Paris; converted to the Catholic Church and obtained the favor of Cardinal Richelieu; appointed secretary to De la Porle, grand prior of France, and later to the Cardinal de Retz, coadjutor of Paris, who made him a canon of Notre Dame; fled Paris on the imprisonment of Retz for his part in the Fronde, and spent over a year in the abbey of Baugerais; see *Histoire des Troubles de la Grand Bretagne* (1661) (on British history 1633–1646); *DNB*.

Meredith, Edward, SJ – priest and controversialist; b. 1648, Landulph, Cornwall; c. 1671, (received in Spain; his brother, Amos (1658/9–1687), also converted and entered the Society of Jesus); d. 1715, Rome; son of Anglican rector; after Oxford University accompanied Sir William Godolphin (see above) as secretary to the embassy in Madrid, where both were received into the Church; returned to England and worked on literary pursuits; left England at time of Popish Plot; joined the Society of Jesus in 1684 at Watten in Flanders as a scholastic (never ordained); returned to England in 1686; active controversialist during James II's reign; banished after Revolution of 1688; lived at court at St. Germain for some years; much travel in Italy and France; see *Gillow*, Vol. IV, p.563; *Catholic Encyclopedia*; *DNB*.

Merivale, Herman Charles (also used the pseudonym Felix Dale) – barrister, playwright and novelist; b. 27 January 1839, London; c. a few years before his death; d. 14 January 1906, Acton, Middlesex; son of Herman Merivale (1806– 1874), barrister, writer (historian) and one time Permanent Under Secretary of the India Office; grandson of John Herman Merivale, the poet; nephew of Charles Merivale, the historian; long-standing friends included Lord Salisbury, William Makepeace Thackeray, Matthew Arnold, Anthony Trollope, W. S. Gilbert, and many others; practiced at the bar, but after his father's death he devoted himself to literature and drama; wrote many dramas, farces and burlesques; collaborated with John Palgrave Simpson (see below); liberal in politics; lost whole of his fortune through default of his solicitor; occasional mental and physical breakdowns throughout his life; buried in Brompton cemetery; see H. C. Merivale, *Bar, Stage and Platform: Autobiographic Memoirs* (1902); *DNB*.

Messenger, Ernest Charles – priest and writer; b. 1888; c. 1908; d. 25 December 1952; former journalist; ordained priest in 1914; lecturer in philosophy; writer of religious works; translator; see *Why Roman Catholic?* (1917); *Evolution and Theology* (1931); *A Philosophy of Comparative Religion* (1935); *The Reformation, the Mass and the Priesthood*, 2 Vols. (1936 and 1937); *The Apostolate of the Sunday Mass* (1946); *Two in One Flesh*, 3 Vols. (1949); (ed) *Theology and Evolution* (1952); *The True Religion* (1963) ("Protestants say that Christ left His revelation in a book – the Bible – which each man is to read and interpret for himself, guided by the Holy Spirit. Catholics say that Christ instituted a

teaching body – the Church – to teach mankind in His name. It is possible that Christ should have done as Protestants say. It is conceivable and possible, but very improbable.

In the first place it assumes that every one can read and possess a Bible without difficulty. But this was impossible until quite lately. Previous to the nineteenth century comparatively few people could read, and books were scarce and expensive, still more so before the invention of printing in the sixteenth century.

The theory provides no means of knowing what books are inspired and canonical and which are not. As a matter of fact, it was the Church which testified as to which were the books of Holy Scripture. How could the Church do this if she had no authority?

The Bible is a very difficult book to understand. To understand it properly one ought to know Eastern languages, idioms, rites, and customs.

Finally, the theory is proved false by its results. The Protestant theory was invented in the sixteenth century – it was unknown before then – and the history of Protestantism has been a long series of divisions and sub-divisions, until there are now some two hundred religious bodies rejoicing in the name of Protestant. This is only natural, for if one had to interpret the Bible for oneself, one will very probably interpret it differently from one's neighbor.... The present multitude of warring sects and different interpretations proves, then, that the theory of which it is the result cannot be the one meant by our Lord").

Meynell, Alice Christiana Gertrude (*née* Thompson) – poet, essayist and journalist; b. 22 September 1847; c. 20 July 1868 (her mother, Christiana, received some time before and father received shortly before his death; her later to be husband, Wilfrid (see below) received in 1870); d. 27 November 1922; younger daughter of Thomas James Thompson (d. 1881); sister of Lady Elizabeth Butler, celebrated artist (see above); brought up in fairly wealthy family, but one with relatively Bohemian lifestyle; educated entirely by father; as Anglican she was religious from childhood; much ill health and depression during life; several volumes of verse (see especially *My Heart Shall Be Thy Garden, Regrets, Thoughts on Separation, After a Parting* and *Summer in England*) and essays (including *The Spirit of the Place, Hearts of Controversy* and *The Rhythm of Life*) and biographies of Holman Hunt (1893) and John Ruskin (1900); during her instruction with Fr. Dignam, a young Jesuit priest, the two became friends, but this later developed into hopeless love; Dignam asked to be sent abroad and communication between them ceased (her deep sorrow the subject of several fine poems, e.g., "Renouncement"); later wife of Wilfrid Meynell (1852–1948) (see below) who was smitten by *My Heart Shall Be Thy Garden*; co-edited with her husband several magazines, e.g., *The Weekly Register* and *Merry England*; mother of Everard Meynell, artist and art critic (and author of *The Life of Francis Thompson* (1913)), of Viola Mary Gertrude Meynell (1885–1956), writer, and of Frances Meredith Wilfrid Meynell (1891–1975), typographer and publisher (founder of *Nonesuch Press* in 1922 with David Garnett); charity worker and active suffragette; close friend of Coventry Patmore (see below) (though disagreed with his politics), and Francis Thompson (latter of whom was discovered and rescued by her husband and remained as an adopted son in the Meynell household for nineteen years); friend of G. K. Chesterton ("If I had been a man and fat, I would have been Chesterton"); in later life returned to poetry; see Rev. Geoffrey Bliss, "The Poetry of Alice Meynell," *The Month*, April 1923, p.315; Viola Meynell, *Alice Meynell* (1929) (letter to her daughter Olivia: "I don't at all allow that we have 'liberty' to think what we happen to choose as to right and wrong. I saw, when I was very young, that a guide in morals was even more necessary than a guide in faith. It was for this I joined the Church. Other Christian societies may legislate, but the Church *administers* legislation. Thus she is practically indispensable. I may say that I hold the administration of morals to be of such vital importance that for its sake I accepted, and now accept, dogma in matters of faith – to the last letter. To make my preachment clearer: Right and Wrong (morals) are the most important, or the only important, things men know or can know. Everything depends on them. Christian morality is infinitely the greatest of moralities. This we know by our own sense and intellect, without other guidance. The Church administers that morality, as no other sect does or can do, by means of moral theology. The world is far from living up to that ideal, but it is the only ideal worth living up to.... As to the 'divine' teachings of the Genesis allegory, I cannot withdraw that word. I have to remember that all the morality worth having – the morality that led on to Christianity – had its origin in that parable"); Bernard Delaney, "Alice Meynell," *Blackfriars*, November 1929, p.1446; Sr. M. Laurence, O.P, "Alice Meynell: A Message from the Sun," *Chesterton Review*, Spring-Summer 1979, p.207; June Badeni, *The Slender Tree: A Life of Alice Meynell* (1981) ("The early discovery of the need for discipline grew out of an early awareness of evil, a very real sense of sin, and a clear perception of her own nature.... Her passionate nature and the violence of her emotions frightened her, and she had no confident feeling of strength – only the realization that somehow she must find a way to shape that nature to what she believed was its ultimate destiny. She chose discipline and control, exercised over her by the Catholic Church, and by her over body and brain; this was henceforward the keynote of her whole life.... She saw no kind of bondage in her unconditional surrender to the Church as the arbiter of dogma and moral law. Many years later ... she expressed her philosophy in a single sentence. She would like, she said, to see the Statue of Liberty in New York harbor renamed, for it is not so much liberty as voluntary obedience that is the antithesis of slavery, and gives the truest freedom. This submission, this voluntary obedience, was for her not a fettering but a setting free; and again and again in her prose and in her verse she gave expression to her conviction that the only true freedom is that which lies on the further side of law, and can be reached by no other path"); David Jones, "Alice Meynell: A Catholic Suffragette Poet," *Catholic Life*, August 2004, p.34; *DNB*.

Meynell, Wilfrid – journalist and author; b. 1852; c. 1870; d. 1948; seventh son of Newcastle colliery owner; brought up as Quaker; came to London to make a living in journalism; editor of *The Weekly Register* (subtitled *A Catholic Family Newspaper*) and *Merry England* (an intended medium for Catholic authors); husband of Alice Meynell (see above); at one time literary adviser to *Burns and Oates*, publishers; contributor to *The Tablet, Daily Chronicle, The Lamp, Athenaeum, Academy, Saturday Review, Illustrated London News, Nineteenth Century*, and *Contemporary Review*, etc; discovered and rescued Francis Thompson, the poet, who remained as an adopted son in the Meynell household for nineteen years; great admirer and confidant of Cardinal

Manning; see Shane Leslie, "Wilfrid Meynell: 1852–1948," *The Tablet*, 30 October 1948, p.282; Viola Meynell, *Francis Thompson and Wilfrid Meynell* (1952).

Middlemass, Jean (real name Mary Jane Middlemass) – novelist; b. 1834, Regent's Park, London; d. 7 November 1919, Eaton Terrace, London; member of a wealthy Scottish family; well educated at home; in her thirties, after the death of her parents, wrote sentimental and melodramatic novels for young women; often set in France or London; also wrote stories for periodicals; later handicapped by poor eyesight; published forty novels between 1872 and 1906; final work *At the Altar Steps* (1910); her writing fell out of favor; see (most popular) *Dandy* (1881); *Sackcloth and Broadcloth* (1881); *Vaia's Lord* (1888); Sandra Kemp, Charlotte Mitchell, and David Trotter (ed), *Edwardian Fiction: An Oxford Companion* (1997).

Middleton, Charles (styled second Earl of Middleton and Jacobite first Earl of Monmouth) – politician; b. 1649/50, Scotland; c. 20 August 1702 (son converted shortly before); d. 9 August 1719; brought up at the exiled court of Charles II; after the Restoration returned to Scotland, then on to London; attached to the English embassy to France, began a military career; favorite of the king's brother, the Duke of York, and the Duchess of York; at this time skeptical about religion, but conformed to Church of England; secretary of state for the northern department in 1684, then transferring to the southern department in 1688; loyal to James II throughout the 1688 crisis; retired to his house in Winchester 1688–1691; secretary of state to James II in exile, then a member of the regency council to assist Mary of Modena during the minority of James III

(James Francis Edward Stuart); tried *in absentia* for treason, outlawed and attainted; secretary of state to James III; Lord Chamberlain to Mary of Modena until her death in 1718; saddened by the failure of the Jacobite rising in 1715; buried at the parish church of St. Germain; see D. Middleton, *The Life of Charles, Second Earl of Middleton* (1957); George Hilton Jones, *Charles Middleton: the Life and Times of a Restoration Politician* (1967); *DNB* ("Middleton experienced an important crisis in his private life during the summer of 1702. On his deathbed James II had urged him to become a Catholic. In the months which followed, a number of apparently miraculous cures took place which were believed to have been through the intercession of the late king. Middleton seems to have been troubled by this, particularly when his close friend Archbishop Noailles of Paris commissioned the curé of St. Sulpice to institute proceedings towards the canonization of the king in June 1702.... Shortly afterwards Lord Clermont [his son] fell ill and, seemingly at the point of death, was converted to Catholicism by Dr. Thomas Witham, the superior of the English College of St. Gregory at Paris. When his son quickly recovered his health, Middleton felt that James II had interceded again and on 20 August, while in Paris, he asked Dr. Witham to receive him into the Catholic Church as well").

Middleton, Blessed Robert, SJ – priest and martyr; b. 1569 or 1570, York; d. about 3 April 1601, Lancaster; father, Thomas Middleton, the brother of St. Margaret Clitherow, crushed to death on account of her faith in 1586, but he at least outwardly conformed to Anglican Establishment, and brought up his children in like manner; reading made him cease to conform to the state religion; in late 1593 or early 1594 went to Douai

and admitted into English College, and in 1597 sent to English College, Rome; ordained priest in 1598; went to the English mission; landed on south coast and traveled to Lancashire, where apprehended near Preston; together with another priest, Bl. Thurstan Hunt, alias Greenlow, was taken to Lancaster gaol (admitted into the Society of Jesus whilst there); they were sentenced to death, as in cases of high treason, for being priests ordained by authority of the Holy See and coming into this country; they were hanged, drawn and quartered at Lancaster; his sister was present at his execution and offered £100 for his life and for him to talk to a minister in hope of re-converting him; he reproached her and refused all attempts to sway him from his faith; see *Gillow*, Vol. V, p.12.

Millard, Christopher Sclater – bibliographer, bookseller, author, and socialist; b. 1872; c. 1897; d. November 1927; son of an Anglican canon; for a time student for Anglican ministry but converted to Catholicism; later teacher; then assistant editor for *Burlington Magazine*; helped Robert Ross edit Oscar Wilde's collected works; his 600–page bibliography of Oscar Wilde appeared in two volumes in 1914; of eccentric appearance and behavior; unmarried; see A. J. A. Symons, *The Quest for Corvo* (1934).

Milner, Blessed Ralph – layman and martyr; b. in Flackstead, Hampshire; d. 7 July 1591, Winchester; brought up in State religion; worked as laborer, maintaining his wife and eight children; struck by contrast between lives of Catholics and Protestants of his acquaintance, determined to embrace the old religion, and, after usual course of instruction, received into the Church; arrested on the very day of his first communion and committed to Winchester gaol for changing his religion; remained a prisoner of conscience for many years, though his good behavior caused gaoler to allow him out often on parole and entrust him with keys of prison!; brought alms and priests to Catholic recusant prisoners, and conducted priests to neighboring villages to administer the sacraments and preach; unlettered, but of high morality; cause of many conversions; apprehended in company of Fr. Roger Dickenson (Dicconson), a Catholic priest, and both imprisoned at Winchester; they were condemned and hanged, drawn and quartered; see *Gillow*, Vol. V, p.53 ("The judge, as if out of compassion, advised the old man to consent to go even but once to the Protestant Church, that he might so escape the ignominious death of the gallows, and live for the benefit of his family. But Milner answered with true Christian fortitude: 'Would your lordship then advise me, for the perishable trifles of this world, or for a wife and children, to lose my God? No, my lord, I cannot approve or embrace a counsel so disagreeable to the maxims of the Gospel'"); *Catholic Encyclopedia*.

Milton, Ernest Gianello Sebastian Clement Joseph – actor; b. 10 January 1890, San Francisco; c. 1942 (received with his wife); d. 24 July 1974; classical actor (notably Shakespeare), brought up a Jew though with Catholic ancestors; husband of Naomi Royde Smith, writer (see below); at most critical point of his conversion his friend Robert Speaight (see below), the actor and writer, intervened and introduced him to Fr. R. H. J. Steuart, SJ, who gave him his final instruction and received him; also actor manager; spent most of his life in England and was British citizen; influence on conversion of Alec Guinness (see above); see Matthew Hoehn, OSB (ed), *Catholic Authors* (1952).

Minster, Thomas – Catholic layman; b. 1813; c. 3 April 1851; d. 2 June 1852;

educated at St. Catherine's College, Cambridge; Anglican curate to Dr. Hook (1798–1875); member of the Tractarian movement; in 1848 selected by Dr. Pusey, its founder, as vicar of St. Saviour's, Leeds, built to put Tractarian principles into practice in the poorest area of the city; great work in Leeds cholera epidemic in 1849; carried on Catholic practices at St. Saviour's (e.g., use of intercessory prayer to the saints and auricular confession) to the annoyance of Dr. Hook (by then vicar of Leeds and lapsing into ultra-Protestantism) and resulting in censure issued by the bishop of Ripon; he, plus the previous vicar, three curates there, two other clergymen and thirty of the laity addressed themselves to Newman for reception into the Catholic Church; after conversion began to study for the Catholic priesthood, but ill-health soon led to his death; see *Gillow*, Vol. V, p.55.

Mitton, Arthur Tennant – b. 1840; c. 1899; formerly Anglican vicar; see essay in J. G. F. Raupert (ed), *Roads to Rome* (1901), p.165 ("Using my reason and judgment in weighing evidence as I felt bound to do, I came to the conclusion that the Church of England is the creation of the State, and so is a department of the State; that she had no existence prior to the Reformation, at which time she separated herself from the rest of Catholic Christendom. Believing this, I could not possibly remain longer in a communion which, I was convinced, was not the Church founded by Christ and His Apostles, – not the venerable and historic Church of this country, but a mere creation of yesterday. I had been from childhood brought up in the belief that the Church of England of the present day is identically the same (only purified and reformed) as the Church which had existed in this country from the earliest times. I tried, and tried honestly, to discover any points of similarity in things essential between the Ante-Reformation and the Post-Reformation Church, but in vain. I saw, not a reform of the ancient Faith, but the raising up on its ruins of a religious system, entirely alien to it in doctrine and practice. I saw that the Church of England, as she is now, and has been for more than three hundred years, has cut herself off from the communion of the Catholic Church by rejecting her teaching and authority; for surely there is abundant evidence to prove that, prior to the Reformation, the Catholic Church in England held and taught doctrines, such as the Real Presence of our Lord in the Blessed Sacrament, devotion to our Lady and the Saints, Purgatory, Prayers for the Faithful departed, and other doctrines which the Established Church repudiates and denies.

Then as to the question of discipline and authority. A visible and infallible body, such as the Catholic Church is, must have a visible and infallible Head. According to our Lord's promise, His Church was to be kept for all time from holding and teaching error, and the way in which she was thus to be preserved was by having as her Head an infallible Guide, from whose decisions, in questions of faith and morals, there should be no appeal. The Church of England asks her bishops for authoritative decisions in matters of faith, and she receives, in response to her appeal, a judgment or 'opinion' which no Episcopal or other authority can enforce. The Church of England, as a department of the State, can have no authority except such as the State may see fit to concede to it, and her bishops and archbishops have no power by which they can enforce their decisions or opinions without the consent of King and Parliament. And in this State-made body, there is disunion, discord, and strife amongst her members. It is hard for plain men like myself to see how she, any more than the sects which have come out of her loins, can claim to have received authority to make disciples of all nations and to win the world for Christ, seeing that she is herself a house divided against itself").

Mivart, St. George Jackson – zoologist; b. 30 November 1827, Brook Street, Grosvenor Square, London; c. 2 June 1844 (received at St. Chad's Cathedral, Birmingham; his wife converted in 1856, his mother and brother both in 1846); d. 1 April 1900, 77 Inverness Terrace, London; as adolescent the vision of a romanticized medieval past (evoked in Pugin's Gothic revival architecture) and a popular medievalized literature appealed to him; his conversion blocked his anticipated entry to Oxford University; self-made natural scientist; major interest in and contributions to implications to be drawn from Darwinian evolution theory for questions of human origins and mankind's place in nature; under influence of T. H. Huxley flirted with Darwinism; later argued against the sufficiency of Darwinian answer to question of organic diversity; accepted naturalness of organic change but ultimately referred the process as a whole to the continuing plan of a creator, the primary cause of it all; in relation to human origins argued that natural selection only a part of what was generally a more teleological evolutionary process, and that this evolutionary process as a whole explained only physical body of man but not his moral and intellectual capacities; argued that there was even hope for those condemned to hell; attacked papal encyclical on Scripture, *Providentissimus Deus*; criticized anti-semitism of French Catholic press during second Dreyfus trial and strongly condemned whole of the Church hierarchy for its implicit support of anti-semites; later he adopted an avowedly modernist stance and advocated an evolving faith in conformity to knowledge and reason, instead of what he referred to as "stultifying dogma"; refused to sign an orthodox profession of faith and was excommunicated in 1900; buried in Kensal Green cemetery, London; see *On the Genesis of Species* 9187I); *Man and Apes* (1873); *Contemporary Evolution* (1876); Jacob W. Gruber, *A Conscience in Conflict: The Life of St. George Jackson Mivart* (1960); Michael Clifton, *A Victorian Convert Quintet* (1998); Dom Paschal Scotti, "Happiness in Hell: The Case of Dr. Mivart," *Downside Review*, July 2001, p.177; Patrick Allitt, *Catholic Converts: British and American Intellectuals Turn to Rome* (1997), pp.107–118; *DNB*.

Monckton, Gilbert, second Viscount Monckton of Brenchley (Major General Gilbert Walter Riversdale Monckton) – army officer; b. 3 November 1915, Ightham Mote, a manor house near Sevenoaks, Kent; c. whilst at Cambridge University (his sister, Valerie Goulding (1918–2003) (see above) also converted); d. 22 June 2006; son of Sir Walter Monckton (1891–1965) (first Viscount Monckton of Brenchley), advisor to Edward VIII during the abdication crisis and later Conservative minister; educated at Harrow and Trinity College, Cambridge, graduating 1939; immediately joined army; part of British Expeditionary Force; evacuated from Dunkirk in 1940; at staff colleges before fighting in Italy and Germany; took part in Korean War; served in the British Army 1939–1976; army director of public relations in the 1960s; conversion influenced partly by Fr. Thomas Edward Flynn, later Catholic Bishop of Lancaster, and then by Mgr. Alfred Gilbey; President of the British Association of the Sovereign Order of Malta; much work for the shrine

at Lourdes; father of Hon. Christopher Walter Monckton, third Viscount; see obituary, *The Times* 27 June 2006 ("While at Harrow, his headmaster, Paul Vellacott, had said to him: 'You have thought so deeply I think that the only path for you is the road to Rome'").

Monsell, William (first Baron Emly) – politician; b. 21 September 1812, Tervoe, County Limerick, Ireland; c. 1850, at Grace Dieu, in presence of Ambrose Phillipps de Lisle and his family and household; d. 20 April 1894, Tervoe; at Oriel College, Oxford; grew up as a Protestant landlord in Ireland; Liberal MP for County Limerick 1847–1874; advocated tenant rights, civil and religious liberty; his experience in the Irish famine gave him an empathy with the Catholic peasants; member of the Tractarian movement, and in late 1840s took spiritual guidance from Manning; when Manning's Anglicanism was weakening, Newman took over and became close friend; joined the Catholic Church over the Gorham judgment (see entry for William Maskell); also very much influenced in conversion by Newman; wife, Lady Anna Marie Monsell, never became a Catholic, though she sympathized with him; under-secretary for Colonies and Post-Master General during Gladstone's administrations; lost much popularity in Ireland through opposition to Land League and to Home Rule movement; Lord Lieutenant and Custos Rotulorum for County Limerick; see Matthew Potter, *A Catholic Unionist: The Life and Times of William Monsell, First Baron Emly of Tervoe (1812–1894)* (1994); *Catholic Encyclopedia*; *DNB*.

Montagu, Walter, OSB – abbot and courtier; b. 1604/5, Aldgate, London; d. 5 February 1677, the Hospital of the Incurables, Paris; second son of Henry Montagu, first Earl of Manchester; after

Cambridge University he traveled on the Continent, visiting France and Italy; on his return he entered service of the Duke of Buckingham; sent to France in 1624 in relation to the planned marriage of the future Charles I and the French princess Henrietta Maria, which he negotiated successfully; began a devoted service to Henrietta Maria which ended only when she died; sent on several diplomatic missions abroad; resided for a time at the British embassy in Paris, when out of curiosity he visited Loudun to witness the exorcisms of some Ursuline nuns, which he believed to be supernatural and an experience which resulted in his spiritual conversion; he became a Catholic (possibly reconciled to the Church by Père Surin, who was in charge of the exorcisms); in 1635 went to Rome; secretly ordained priest whilst abroad; campaigned for a papal agency to England; returned to England in 1637 and was appointed chamberlain to the queen at Somerset House, her residence; in 1641 he was, with several recusants, banished and went again to France; returned to England in 1643, but was arrested and detained in the Tower until 1647; banished again and returned to France; created abbot of the Benedictine monastery of Nanteuil; later became abbot of St. Martin, near Pontoise; supported Mazarin and was Anne of Austria's almoner; in 1654 Henrietta Maria entrusted him with the care of her son Henry, Duke of Gloucester, whom he attempted to convert to the Catholic faith; some literary works, mainly verses; officiated at funeral of Henrietta Maria in 1669; used his income to relieve many English exiles, both Catholic and Protestant, who had suffered greatly under the Commonwealth; retired to Paris; probably buried at Pontoise; see *Exposition of the Doctrine of the Catholic Church* (1672) (translation from Bossuet); *Gillow*, Vol. V, p.73; *DNB*.

Monteith, Robert – politician and philanthropist; b. 23 December 1811, Glasgow; c. 1846 (received by Newman; his wife Wilhelmina (d. 1884) was received shortly afterwards); d. 31 March 1884, Carstairs House, Lanarkshire; one of fourteen children of Henry Monteith (1765–1848), a merchant landowner and MP; studied at Trinity College, Cambridge; member of the Apostles and a close friend of Alfred Tennyson; traveled the Continent and spent many winters in Rome with Catholic aristocratic friends; his godfather was Ignatius Spencer (see below); influenced by Kenelm Digby (see above), Bishop Gillis and David Urquhart; also consulted Newman; worked on political issues with Thomas Anstey (see above); worked to promote the re-assertion of international law; supported the apostolate of Don Bosco; member of the Catholic Poor Schools Committee and the Catholic Defence Association; encouraged and supported financially the return of religious orders to Scotland; large benefactions to the Church in Scotland and to charitable causes; see Bernard Aspinwall, "Robert Monteith, 1812–84," *Clergy Review*, 1978, p.265; Bernard Aspinwall, "The Scottish dimension: Robert Monteith and the Origins of Modern Catholic Social Thought," *Downside Review*, 1979, p.46; Bernard Aspinwall, "David Urquhart, Robert Montieth and the Catholic Church: a Search for Justice and Peace," *Innes Review*, 1980, p.57; *DNB*.

Montgomery, George – priest and author; b. 1818, Dublin; c. 1845; d. 7 March 1871; from staunch protestant family; at Trinity College, Dublin; formerly Church of Ireland curate and known in Ireland as "Protestant of the Protestants"; a visit to Newman's community at Littlemore led to his conversion; studied for the priesthood at Oscott

College; ordained Catholic priest 7 April 1849; worked on the mission in the Midlands; *Gillow*, Vol. V, p.87.

Moody, Robert Sadleir – teacher; b. 1823; c. 1854 (in Rome; his wife, Ellen (d. 1908) received also); d. 1907, Little Malvern; studied at Eton and Christ Church College, Oxford; attracted to the Oxford Movement whilst at university 1840–1843; took Anglican orders 1846 and worked as curate; was disgusted by the Gorham case (see entry for William Maskell); conversion also influenced by Robert Isaac Wilberforce's *Doctrine of the Incarnation* and by T. W. Allies, *Per Crucem et Lucem*; in 1859 became one of first masters at Birmingham Oratory School; Newman believed that he and still more his wife were undermining his position; left Oratory School in 1861; taught at Oscott for some years; in 1873 retired into private life at Malvern; see essay in J. G. F. Raupert (ed), *Roads to Rome* (1901), p.162 ("What, then, led me to take the step? It was a belief in the Visible Church, in the absolute necessity for that Church having a Visible Head, and in the irresistible evidence in favor of the supremacy of the Pope. This is all. All other questions seemed to me to depend entirely upon this one").

Moore, Charles Hilary – journalist and author; b. 31 October 1956; c. 1994 (his wife, Caroline, remained an Anglican, stating, "It shot in upon me, with terrible force, that I could not join a Church that taught that George Herbert was no true priest"); educated at Eton and Trinity College, Cambridge; editor *The Spectator* 1984–1990, deputy editor *Daily Telegraph* 1990–1992; editor *Sunday Telegraph* 1992–1995; editor *Daily Telegraph* 1995–2003; consulting editor the Telegraph Group from 2004; became a Catholic after Church of England ordained women; see essay in Joanna

Bogle (ed), *Come On In ... It's Awful* (1994) ("The key question to ask about the Church was not: 'What does it say about x and y?' but 'Is it what it says it is?' If you could accept that it was the true Church, everything else followed.... No doctrine is impossible in itself ... if the authority of the Church to teach it is allowed. The Papacy is the necessary instrument and historical expression of that authority"; essay in Rowanne Pasco (ed), *Why I Am a Catholic* (1995) ("I am strongly attracted by the fact that the Catholic Church is so much a church for sinners and that absolutely anyone might be in it. I have always liked that aspect of going to Mass, really the whole of human creation is there. It's almost an attraction of Catholicism that so many Catholics are often so bad. On the other hand the Church of England tends to have a slightly goody goody quality, though of course there are lots of Anglicans who are very serious about their religion"); "RC v CofE," *The Tablet*, 31 October 2009 (with Caroline Moore).

More (or Moore), Blessed Hugh – priest and martyr; b. about 1563, Grantham; c. 1584; d. 28 August 1588, London; brought up in new religion; soon after his majority he was reconciled to the Church by Fr. Thomas Stephenson, SJ, and disinherited by his father; admitted to English College, Rheims, in 1585; intention to become a priest, but became ill and had to return to England; on arrival taken into custody under charge of being reconciled to the Church and going abroad to a Catholic seminary; declined to appear in a Protestant church; tried at the Old Bailey and condemned to death with three others; drawn from Newgate with Bl. Robert Morton to a pair of gallows specially erected in Lincoln's Inn Field, and hanged; see *Gillow*, Vol. V, p.88.

Morgan, Venerable Edward – priest and martyr; b. 1584 or 1586, Bettisfield, Hanmer, Flintshire, Wales; d. 26 April 1642; parents had been reconciled to the Church and he himself received (by Fr. John Bennett, "the apostle of North Wales"); at age of sixteen sent to St. Omer's College and thence to the English College in Rome in 1606 to study Philosophy and Theology; went on to English College, Valladolid and then Madrid; in 1621 ordained priest at Salamanca and sent to the English mission; apprehended in 1627 and committed to the Fleet prison, where he was detained for fifteen or sixteen years; brought to trial and condemned in 1642; hanged, drawn and quartered at Tyburn; many conversions attributed to his holy example; see *Gillow*, Vol. V, p.118; *Catholic Encyclopedia*.

Morgan, William, SJ – priest; b. February or March 1623, Cilcain, Flintshire; d. 28 September 1689, St. Omer; brought up as Protestant by parents from minor gentry; ejected from Cambridge University at start of Civil War and joined king's army; captured at Naseby; after six months' imprisonment he entered the Spanish service and fought in the Low Countries; converted there; gave up soldiering and went to the English Jesuit establishments at Ghent and Liège; entered English College, Rome, in 1648; joined the Society of Jesus in 1651; worked in Rome as Professor of Philosophy; ordained priest in about 1657; taught at Liège 1661–1670; sent on the mission to North Wales; named by Titus Oates in 1678 as one of the popish plotters; escaped abroad in 1679 and was named as assistant to the new Jesuit provincial, John Warner; sent back to England in 1680, but arrested on arrival; imprisoned, but released in 1683; returned to Rome and was rector of English College until 1686; made provincial of the English mission in 1689; see *DNB*.

Morison, Stanley Arthur – typographer; b. 6 March 1889, Kent Villa, Tavistock Road, Wanstead, Essex; c. 28 December 1908 (received by Fr. Charles Nicholson, SJ, at the Church of Our Lady of the Assumption, Warwick Street, London); d. 11 October 1967, 2 Whitehall Court, Westminster; father a commercial traveler who deserted the family in 1903; mother a militant agnostic and freethinker with radical political opinions; grew up very similar to his mother, but did not reject all authority; conversion influenced by Fr. Herbert Thurston, SJ (1856–1939); concentrated on letter forms, printed and written; taken onto staff of Burns and Oates Catholic publishers by Wilfrid Meynell, managing director; conscientious objector during World War I; first marriage resulted in separation; then close, but chaste, relationship until his death with Beatrice Warde, American historian of typography; became Britain's greatest authority on letter-design and a great influence on book printing; closely involved with *The Times* (designer of Times New Roman typeface) and *Encyclopedia Britannica*; editor of *Times Literary Supplement* 1945–1948; declined three offers of knighthood; played key role in the acquisition by British Museum of *Codex Sinaiticus* in 1934; friend in later life of E. I. Watkin (see below); buried at Paddington new cemetery, Mill Hill; see N. Barker, *Stanley Morison* (1972) ("[H]e came to look for authority, some framework in which to control his own strength of personality. He was convinced that, without such a framework, he would have been a very wicked man indeed. On the other hand, he had as well an almost uncontrollable longing and compassion, which contrasted so oddly with his strong rationality.... A phrase from the psalms – ['Like the deer that yearns for running streams, so my soul is yearning for you, my God'] – used often to recur to him in after life.

But, with all these considerations, it is still difficult to imagine how he came to look for the solution – the complete solution for him – in the Roman Catholic Church. He made it sound so simple: 'bred a Victorian agnostic who found Huxley, Spenser and Haeckel insufficient guides to the kind of life he decided to live [he] submitted to the Roman Church.... This act on the part of a man who was aware of his own constitutional lack of humility profoundly affected his subsequent thought and action.' So indeed it did; but his 'constitutional lack of humility' was only part of the story. What brought him to 'hang around Farm Street,' to argue with a priest there,... and to take up with the London Jesuit community at all?... Perhaps the most likely cause is the simplest: Father Thurston, his first and closest friend at Farm Street, was the leading Catholic apologist of the time.... [H]e was a person of such calm resolution, such omniscient solidity, that he could well provide the answer to the problems that occupied Morison's mind.

It was not to be supposed that the answer came at once, nor without long trial and argument. Chance and emotion had their part in the process.... He found his way to the Benedictine Abbey of St. André [in Bruges]. There he first heard plain-song chanted. It was an experience for which he was quite unprepared by anything he had come across. It had an immediate influence on his spiritual indecision, and he remained addicted to it for the rest of his life – it was the only sort of music he really cared for. So, by such indirections, as well as the more direct path of argument, Morison came to accept religious belief and the Catholic Church"); David McKitterick (ed), *Stanley Morison*

and D. B. Updike: Selected Correspondence (1980) (letter by Morison, 30 October 1923: "The impact of modern knowledge upon ancient faith could have been differently dealt with had Christendom been united. Your splitting up the unity of the West has occasioned centuries of rubbishy controversy which does not help us an atom today. The result is that we all suffer – you from disintegration and we from centralization. Not that I mean to blame your theological forebears for the evils which led them to break into schism. But at least they might have had the sense if not the grace to realize that their action led to religious disruption"); Alan Pryce-Jones, *The Bonus of Laughter* (1987), pp.148–151; *DNB* ("Apart from the breviary, which he always carried, he read only for information, increasingly about liturgy and ecclesiology; in music he eventually cared only for plainchant").

Morrill, John – historian; b. 1946; educated at Trinity College, Oxford; elected Fellow of Selwyn College, Cambridge 1975 (Vice-Master from 1994); Professor of British and Irish History 1998; much work on the period 1500–1750 on cultural, political and social issues, and on religious dynamics and psychology of early modern British history; also on the historical relationship between the peoples of England, Scotland, Ireland and Wales; delivered the Ford Lectures in Oxford in 2005, entitled *Living with Revolution: The Peoples of Britain and Ireland and the Wars of the Three Kingdoms*; part of the revisionist movement in history; projects on electronic publications on history, e.g., founding editor of the Royal Historical Society Bibliography Online; consultant editor for seventeenth century lives in the *Oxford Dictionary of National Biography*; after conversion to the Catholic Church, ordained to the diaconate; see *The Na-*

ture of the English Revolution (1994); *The British Problem 1534–1707* (1996); (ed) *The Oxford Illustrated History of Tudor and Stuart Britain* (1996); *Christopher Dawson and the Catholic Idea of History* (1997) (with Stratford Caldecott); *Revolt in the Provinces: The English People and the Tragedies of War* (1998); *Stuart Britain: A Very Short Introduction* (2005); *Uneasy Lies the Head that Wears a Crown: Dynastic Crises in Tudor and Stuart Britain 1504–1746* (2005); *Oliver Cromwell* (2007).

Morris, John, SJ – priest and writer; b. 4 July 1826, Ootacamund, in the Nilgiri Hills, Southern India; c. 20 May 1846; d. 22 October 1893, Sacred Heart Church, Wimbledon; eldest of fifteen children of John Carnac Morris (1798–1858), director of East India Company and ecclesiastical historian; brought up mainly in London; no religion at Harrow, but became sympathetic with the Oxford movement; doubts regarding Anglicanism began in October 1845 when he went up to Trinity College, Cambridge, at the same time as Newman converted; also great interest in revival of Gothic architecture; correspondence with Ambrose Phillipps de Lisle (see above) influenced his conversion, which caused some sensation and led to the submission of his former tutor, Frederick Paley (see below); studied at English College, Rome; ordained Catholic priest on 22 September 1849; vice-rector of the English College, Rome; then canon of Westminster and secretary to Wiseman and to Manning; entered the Society of Jesus in 1867; several times at St. Beuno's College, North Wales; his works of ecclesiastical history inspired by his devotion to English heroes of the Catholic faith, e.g., St. Thomas Beckett; acted as postulator for the cause of the English martyrs; many books and contributions, mainly on Catholic history, to such as *The Month*, the *Dublin Review* and *The Tablet*; buried in the Catholic part of Wimbledon cemetery; see *The Life of Father John Gerard* (1881); *The Life and Martyrdom of St. Thomas Becket* (1885); *The Venerable Sir Adrian Fortescue, Martyr* (1887); *Catholic England in Modern Times* (1892); Richard Frederick Clarke, "Father John Morris," *The Month*, November 1893, p.305; Richard Frederick Clarke, "Some Further Recollections of Father John Morris," *The Month*, December 1893, p.457; J. H. Pollen, "The Conversion of Father John Morris," *The Month*, September 1894, p.167; J. H. Pollen, *The Life and Letters of Father John Morris* (1896); *Gillow*, Vol. V, p.122; *DNB* ("Morris was one of a circle of late nineteenth-century Catholic historians who devoted themselves to correcting protestant historical inaccuracies and misconceptions, and to documenting the English recusant experience").

Morris, John Brande – priest and mystical and devotional writer; b. 4 September 1812, Brentford, Middlesex; c. 16 January 1846; d. 9 April 1880, Queen Caroline Street, Hammersmith, London; son of Anglican minister; brother, Thomas Edward Morris (1814–1885) a committed Tractarian; Fellow of Exeter College, Oxford; lectured on Hebrew (assistant to Pusey) and Syriac; devoted himself to Eastern and patristic theology; member of the Tractarian movement; briefly with Newman at Maryvale; ordained Catholic priest 8 April 1849; Professor at Prior Park College, Bath; ministered in several parishes; a life-long friend was Frederick Faber (see above); had many chaplaincies, but too restless to settle anywhere for long; delicate health; several books on Catholic themes; buried at Mortlake Catholic cemetery; see *Jesus the Son of Mary, or the doctrine of the Catholic Church upon* *the Incarnation of God the Son, considered in its bearings upon the reverence shewn by Catholics to His Blessed Mother*, 2 Vols. (1851); *Gillow*, Vol. V, p.130; *Catholic Encyclopedia*; *DNB*.

Morse (or Mowse) (aliases Claxton, Ward, Shepperd), Saint Henry, SJ – priest and martyr; b. 1595, Broome, Suffolk; c. 5 June 1614 ("Having learnt the certain truth of the Catholic faith, upon full conviction I renounced my former errors and was received into the Roman Catholic Church, the mistress of all Churches"; his fifth brother, William (1591–1649) was received in April 1613, became a Jesuit and worked on the mission; third brother may have converted earlier on marriage into Catholic Bedingfield family); d. 1 February 1645, Tyburn; sixth of nine sons; parents Protestants; studied at Cambridge and Inns of Court, but traveled to Douai, where received into the Church; studied at English College, Rome; ordained priest and set out for the English mission in 1624; served in Newcastle area, but apprehended and taken to Newgate prison, then to York Castle (entered the Society of Jesus whilst there); banished in 1630 and went to Watten and then Liège; sent again to the English mission in 1633; worked in London heroically during the plague 1636–1637, three times being infected himself, and making many conversions; apprehended twice and convicted of being a priest; both times Queen Henrietta Maria obtained a respite releasing him on sureties; voluntarily went into exile in 1641; landed in the north in 1643 and worked in Durham area; apprehended and taken to Newgate; condemned to death upon his previous conviction; hanged, drawn and quartered at Tyburn; French and Portuguese ambassadors attended execution (footmen dipped their handkerchiefs in the martyr's blood); see

Philip Caraman, *Henry Morse: Priest of the Plague* (1957) ("Gentlemen, take notice, the kingdom of England will never be truly blessed until it returns to the Catholic and apostolic faith, and until its subjects are all united in one belief and live in obedience to one head, the Bishop of Rome"); *Gillow*, Vol. V, *p.133; Catholic Encyclopedia*; *DNB*.

Morton, Major Sir Desmond John Falkiner MC – army officer and intelligence officer; b. 13 November 1891, 9 Hyde Park Gate, London; c. 1916; d. 31 July 1971, Hammersmith Postgraduate Hospital, London; educated at Eton and the Royal Military Academy, Woolwich; Military Cross in World War I ("While he was commanding a forward battery at Arras a bullet lodged in his heart, but with characteristic resilience he survived to be awarded the MC" (*DNB*)); ADC to Field Marshal Earl Haig in 1917; after war various government posts, including at Foreign Office as an intelligence officer; great friendship with Winston Churchill whom he kept fully briefed during 1930s; assisted Churchill in his literary pursuits; personal assistant to Churchill when he became Prime Minister in 1940; Under Secretary, Treasury Office 1950; awarded many honors; relished theological discussion; unmarried; *DNB*.

Morton, John Cameron Andrieu Bingham Michael ("Johnny") (*pseud.* **"Beachcomber"**) – journalist and author; b. 7 June 1893, Park Lodge, Mitcham Road, Tooting, London; c. 1922; d. 10 May 1979; fought in World War I; wrote mainly humorous and satirical books (many under name "Beachcomber" for the *Daily Express*, which column he wrote 1924–1975); also novels, biography and French history; great friendship with Hilaire Belloc who influenced his conversion and of whom he wrote a fine memoir; also close friend of D. B. Wyndham Lewis (see above) from whom he inherited the Beachcomber column; Evelyn Waugh (see below) said of him that he showed the greatest comic fertility of any Englishman; see *Sobieski, King of Poland* (1932); *The Bastille Falls, and Other Studies of the French Revolution* (1936); *The Dauphin: A biography of Louis XVII* (1936); *Saint-Just* (1939); *Brumaire: The Rise of Bonaparte* (1948); *Camille Desmoulins and Other Studies of the French Revolution* (1950); *St Thérèse of Lisieux: the Making of a Saint* (1954); *Hilaire Belloc: A Memoir* (1955); *Marshal Ney* (1958); Richard Ingrams, *Beachcomber: The Works of J. B. Morton* (1974); *DNB* ("His humor was based on a strong dislike of the twentieth century, which he thought of as godless, noisy, and unpleasant. (Personally he would have no truck with it and refused to use a typewriter or even ride a bicycle).... He was well known for his practical jokes and once assembled a large and indignant crowd round a pillar box on the pretext that a small boy had been trapped inside").

Mossman, Thomas Wimberley – Catholic layman; b. 1826, Skipton, Yorkshire; c. 1885; d. 6 July 1885, West Torrington, Lincolnshire; Anglican vicar; became Tractarian and eventually leader of extreme Ritualist party (close associate of Frederick G. Lee (see above)); defended Anglican orders against Newman; author of various controversial works; having concluded that the Church of England was in schism, he and Lee formed the Order of Corporate Reunion in 1877 with the aim of establishing an English Orthodox Church on Uniate lines (both received Episcopal consecration in Italy in that year, possibly by the Archbishop of Milan or his suffragan); styled himself bishop of Selby; during his last illness received into the Catholic Church by his old friend, Cardinal Manning; see H. R. T. Brandreth, *Dr. Lee of Lambeth* (1951); *DNB*.

Mould, Daphne Desirée Charlotte Pochin – writer; b. 15 November 1920, Salisbury, Wiltshire; c. 11 November 1950; brought up as Anglican in High Church family; became agnostic; doctorate in geology from Edinburgh; wrote on geology, geography, and the saints of Scotland and Ireland; influenced in her conversion by the Benedictines of Fort Augustus; tertiary of St. Dominic from 1952; see *Scotland of the Saints* (1952); *Ireland of the Saints* (1953); *The Rock of Truth* (1953) ("By all ordinary tests the Church ought to have come to an end a dozen or more times. She ought to have been stamped out by the early persecutions; she ought to have been overwhelmed by every vigorous heresy – at the very least she ought to have been destroyed by the wickedness of her own members. But the odd thing is that the Church has not only survived, with that same exultant buoyancy that a curragh rides a choppy sea, but survived intact. She has been tangled up with politics, with intrigue, with heresy, and at the end ridden clear with her doctrines intact and unaltered.... One would expect that some of the more notorious Popes might have made some alteration in her dogmas – that the sinner would try to use his official position as head of the Church to put himself in the right and justify wrongdoing. Yet that has never happened. There have been plenty of wicked Catholics in high places, but – and this is the point to strike the outsider – they have preserved and stood condemned by Catholic doctrine. When you begin to make a proper study of the history of the Church the infallibility of the Pope is no longer a rather silly and audacious claim; it is something that you see actually working in time, in history. I began to feel that the survival of the Catholic Church was itself something of a miracle; that on the plain facts of her past there was every indication that she had some sort of supernatural support which kept her alive when she ought to he been made an end of"); *Irish Pilgrimage* (1955); *The Celtic Saints: Our Inheritance* (1956); *The Lord is Risen: The Liturgy of Paschal Time* (1959); *Peter's Boat: A Convert's Experience of Catholic Living* (1959); *The Angels of God: Their Rightful Place in the Modern World* (1960); *Saint Brigid* (1964); *The Irish Saints* (1964); *The Monasteries of Ireland* (1976); Walter Romig (ed), *The Book of Catholic Authors*, Fifth Series (1952); Matthew Hoehn, OSB (ed), *Catholic Authors* (1952).

Muggeridge, Katherine Rosalind ("Kitty") (*née* **Dobbs**) – writer; c. 27 November 1982 (received with her husband (see below)); d. June 1994, Welland, Ontario, Canada; wife of Malcolm Muggeridge (see below); author of biography of her aunt, Beatrice Webb (1858–1943); translator, e.g., of Jean Pierre de Caussade's *The Sacrament of the Present Moment*; interest in mysticism; see *Gazing on Truth: Meditations on Reality* (1985) ("It is easy to find historical evidence that the founder of Christianity lived and died on earth about two thousand years ago. But what is astonishing is that since his death not one week has passed when the Mass has not been celebrated and the Blessed Sacrament not been administered to someone by someone in the world, somewhere in the world. This is a unique fact in the history of mankind. It can only be interpreted as mystical evidence of the incarnation"); Joseph Pearce, *Literary Converts* (1999) *passim.*

Muggeridge, (Thomas) Malcolm – journalist, broadcaster and writer; b. 24 March 1903, Croydon, Surrey; c. 27 November 1982 (received with his wife (see above) at chapel of Our Lady, Help of Christians, Hurst Green, East Sussex; son, John (b. 1933), husband of Anne Roche, Catholic writer, received in 1962); d. 14 November 1990, Ledsham Court, The Ridge, Hastings; brought up by socialist parents; journalist with *The Guardian*, *Evening Standard*, and then editor of *Punch*; deputy editor of *Daily Telegraph*; wrote indictment of Soviet Union (*Winter in Moscow* (1934)) after visit in early thirties; television and radio broadcaster; strong apologist for Christianity; greatly influenced in his conversion by Mother Teresa of Calcutta and Fr. Paul Bidone; conversion influenced also by the Church's teaching on moral questions ("It was the Catholic Church's firm stand against contraception and abortion which finally made me decide to become a Catholic"); buried in Whatlington churchyard; see *Jesus Rediscovered* (1969); *Jesus the Man Who Lives* (1975) ("If God chose to become incarnate as Jesus, then his birth, whatever marvels may have accompanied it, must have had the same characteristics as any other; just as, on the Cross, the suffering of the man into whom the Bethlehem child grew must have been of the same nature as that of the two delinquents crucified beside him. Otherwise, Jesus's humanity would have been a fraud; in which case, his divinity would have been fraudulent, too. The perfection of Jesus's divinity was expressed in the perfection of his humanity, and vice-versa. He was God because he was so sublimely a man, and Man because, in all his sayings and doings, in the grace of his person and words, in the love and compassion that shone out of him, he walked so closely with God. As Man alone, Jesus could not have saved us; as God alone, he would not; Incarnate, he could and did"); "Why I am Becoming a Catholic," *The Times*,

27 November 1982 ("First, then is the Church's sheer survival. Through the turbulent history of 2,000 years, despite lapses and confused purposes every day, perhaps every hour, someone somewhere will have been handing out the Body and Blood of Christ in sacramental form at the altar rail. Then there are the saintly, from the Apostle Paul to Mother Teresa, all of whom in one way or other have contributed towards reanimating the faith which is the Church's mainstay from generation to generation"); *The Third Testament* (1977); *Conversion: A Spiritual Journey* (1988) ("As Hilaire Belloc truly remarked, The Church must be in God's hands because, seeing the people who have run it, it couldn't possibly have gone on existing if there weren't some help from above.... Mother Teresa is, in herself, a living conversion; it is impossible to be with her, to listen to her, to observe what she is doing and how she is doing it, without being in some degree converted"); John Bright-Holmes (ed), *Like It Was: The Diaries of Malcolm Muggeridge* (1981) ("[Liberalism's] great fallacy ... was the perfectibility of Man.... My experience has been the exact opposite – namely, that, left to himself, Man was brutish, lustful, idle and murderous, and that the only hope of keeping his vile nature within any sort of bound was to instill in him fear of God or his fellow men. Of these two alternatives, I preferred fear of God.... And, as a matter of fact, more potent and wonderful is fear of being cut off from the light of God's countenance and living in darkness – this fear the only deterrent which is, at once, effective and ennobling"); Anne Roche, *The Desolate City: The Catholic Church in Ruins* (1986) ("As the moral and cultural revolution in the West quickened, Mr. Muggeridge increasingly found himself defending unpopular Catholic positions. Ironically, in the case of *Humanae Vitae*,

he was opposed by Catholic spokesmen. 'I do not doubt,' he wrote to the *London Times*, at the beginning of the uproar about the encyclical on human life, 'that in the history books when our squalid moral decline is recounted, with the final breakdown in law and order that must follow (for without a moral order there can be no social, political, or any other order), the Pope's courageous and just, though I fear ... largely ineffectual stand will be accorded the respect and admiration it deserves.... He said, and I was hard put not to agree with him, that what we were experiencing was the collapse of western civilization into a new dark age, and the Church, being the western institution par excellence, was perishing with the world it created. I reaffirmed, as orthodox Catholics always do, the Petrine Promise, Christ's assurance to Peter that He would be with the Church unto the consummation of the world; which perhaps, we agreed, is upon us"); John Richard Ingrams, *Muggeridge: The Biography* (1995); Gregory Wolfe, *Malcolm Muggeridge: A Biography* (1995); William F. Buckley, *Nearer, My God* (1997), pp.200–216; Roger Kimball, "Malcolm Muggeridge's Journey," *The New Criterion*, June 2003; Cecil Kuhne (ed), *Seeing Through the Eye: Malcolm Muggeridge on Faith* (2005); Gerry Burns, "Converts to Catholicism: Malcolm Muggeridge," *Catholic Life*, February 2009, p.54; Joseph Pearce, *Literary Converts* (1999) *passim*; Fr. Charles P. Connor, *Classic Catholic Converts* (2001), pp.183–195; Lorene Hanley Duquin, *A Century of Catholic Converts* (2003), p.192; *DNB*.

Murray, (George) Gilbert Aimé, OM – classical scholar and internationalist; b. 2 January 1866, Sydney, Australia; c. 17 April 1957 (a deathbed reconciliation to the Catholic Church; much controversy about what actually happened; see references given below); d. 20 May 1957, Yatscombe on Boars Hill outside Oxford; baptized as Catholic in the Catholic College at Sydney University; father Catholic, but only partially accepted the Church's doctrines and disciplines and only wanted to impress broad principles of Christianity on his children's minds; mother Protestant; taken to England by mother in 1873 to complete his education; first class honors at Oxford in both classical moderations and *literae humaniores*; as young man President of Rationalist Press Association; married Lady Mary Henrietta Howard (d. 1956) of Castle Howard; chair in Greek at Glasgow University in 1889; a liberal influenced particularly by the writings of John Stuart Mill; many translations of classical works; Regius Professor of Greek at Oxford from 1908–1936; at this time agnostic and rationalist who was skeptical about religion; refused two offers of a knighthood; great supporter of the League of Nations and international relations; much illness in the family (premature death of three of his five children); in 1925 Lady Mary joined the Quakers, for whom she worked devotedly; his daughter Rosalind (see below) converted to Catholicism in 1933 (in 1939 she published *The Good Pagan's Failure*, a criticism of her father's secular humanism); one of the most distinguished academics of his time; after his death story came out that during his last illness a Catholic priest administered extreme unction and the apostolic blessing; cremated and ashes interred in Westminster Abbey; see *Unfinished Autobiography* (1960); John Crozier, "The Faith and Dr. Gilbert Murray," *New Blackfriars*, April 1991, p.188 ("Towards the end of his life Rosalind heard her father say: 'We radicals, I think, were much too drastic and made mistakes. We used to think we could keep the essence of Christianity while discarding the dogma.

Now I think we are mistaken'"); Francis West, *Gilbert Murray, A Life* (1984); Duncan Wilson, *Gilbert Murray OM, 1866–1957* (1987); Christopher Stray (ed), *Gilbert Murray Reassessed: Hellenism, Theatre, and International Politics* (2007); *DNB*.

Murray, Rosalind – b. 1890; c. 1932; d. 1967; novelist and writer on metaphysics and religious topics; daughter of Dr. Gilbert Murray (see above); wife of Arnold Toynbee (1889–1975), the historian; mother of Philip Toynbee (1916–1981), writer; see *The Good Pagan's Failure* (1939) (a criticism of her father's secular humanism) ("We have ascribed the failure of the Good Pagan civilization, through all its varying and degenerating phases, to the one primal fault from which it sprang, the denial of God and all that went with God, the rejection of the Supernatural Order in all its bearings, inner and outer, both in the human soul and in the world.

We have traced it through its different forms and phases, its failure to deal with actual human nature, to recognize sin and pain and loss and the needs of an immortal soul; we have seen it as a gigantic effort of idolatry and rebellion, an attempt to replace the Divine by the Human, the Supernatural by the Natural, the Spiritual by the Material, the Eternal by the Temporal, an effort to compress our whole existence into a moderate and twilight Limbo – a passionate limitation of all life.

We have seen that this gigantic attempt is failing, that by excluding Heaven we have not abolished Hell, that by denying redemption we have not been redeemed, the sinner is still there, in the sinner and in ourselves. 'Unhappy man that I am,' he is still crying, 'who shall deliver me from the body of this death?'

The Good Pagan has not delivered him and he cannot, he has told him that no deliverance is needed, that it will all come right, he need not worry. But he does worry, and will always worry, because, though he may not know it, he has a soul; because his soul was made by God for Himself, and cannot rest until it rests in Him"); *The Life of Faith* (1943); "Finding Life and Light" in John A. O'Brien (ed), *The Road to Damascus* (1949); *The Further Journey: In My End is My Beginning* (1953) ("All, whatever our beliefs, are moving, forward or backward as the case may be, upward or downward, and in all growth and development depend in fact and at the deepest level on grace, however little some may recognize it. The Pagan and complete agnostic does in fact depend as wholly as the Christian on the activity of God for all he does and is, and may achieve, for his existence; the natural human good on which he concentrates is no more truly his, apart from God, than is the supernatural grace in whose reality he disbelieves. He can deny, but he cannot escape the immensity of God: 'If I ascend into Heaven, thou art there: If I descend into Hell, thou art present' (Ps. Cxxxviii, 8)").

Muskett (*vere* Fisher) (alias Ashton), George (often referred to as "Gregory Muskett") – priest; b. about 1580; c. 1596; d. 24 December 1645, Douai; he and his brother, Thomas, went to Wisbeach Castle, where the imprisoned priests secretly instructed a number of youths, who, ostensibly as servants, were allowed to reside there; escaped to Douai in 1596, where formally received into the Church; sent to English College, Rome in 1601; ordained priest 11 March 1606; went on the English mission and worked mostly in London; imprisoned in Newgate from 1610 for some years, then released; said to have made more converts than any missioner; apprehended again in 1628 at the house of Lord Stourton in Clerkenwell; confined in the Clink prison under condemnation of death for several years; with hurdle waiting at the prison gate, a reprieve, obtained by queen, arrived; in 1641 appointed President of Douai College; known in Rome as "Flos Cleri Anglicani"; buried in the Our Lady chapel in parish church of St. James, Douai; brother Thomas also ordained priest (at Douai in 1603) and came on the English mission (possibly in Staffordshire in 1620); another brother, Richard, also converted and went to English College, Rome, but his health broke down; see *Gillow*, Vol. V, p.145.

Napier, Michael Scott – priest; b. 15 February 1929, India; c. 1952 (instructed at Cambridge University by Mgr. Alfred Gilbey; received by Canon Alfonso de Zulueta at the Holy Redeemer, Chelsea); d. 22 August 1996; baptized into Church of Scotland of which his father was a member (his mother later converted to the Catholic faith); devout Anglo-Catholic at Cambridge University; joined the London Oratory in 1953; ordained Catholic priest 1959; provost of London Oratory 1969–1981 and 1991–1996; Visitor of the Apostolic See 1981–1993; chaplain to the Knights of Malta and chaplain of the Constantinian Order of St. George; largely responsible for shaping the London Oratory with great taste in music and architecture; see "Holland Visited," *Salisbury Review*, July 1986, p.96.

Nelson, Lady Theophila – b. 1654; c. about 1685 (converted by Cardinal Philip Howard, who received her into the Church); d. 26 January 1706, Ormond Street, London; second daughter of George, Earl of Berkeley; married, first, Sir Kingsmill Lucy, Baronet; after his death she traveled abroad and met in Rome her second husband, Robert Nelson, philanthropist and noted religious writer (believed in hereditary right of James II and became a nonjuror; he founded Society for Promoting Christian Knowledge (SPCK)); she corresponded with Bossuet, Bishop of Meaux; much controversy about her conversion, which she defended in print; husband remained Anglican (their religious differences did not disturb their affection); after the Revolution of 1688 they traveled abroad much before settling in London; see *A Discourse concerning a Judge of Controversies in Matters of Religion* (1686); *Gillow*, Vol. V, p.161; *DNB* (entry for Robert Nelson).

Nelson, Thomas Horatio – Catholic layman; b. 1857; c. Easter Day 1878 (an older brother, Charles Horatio (1856–1900) received earlier and a younger brother, Edward Agar Horatio, received in 1888; his mother, converted in 1896, as did Charles Horatio's wife, Ellen); d. 1947; brought up as High Church Anglican; son of the third Earl Nelson; a great-grandson of Admiral Horatio Nelson (1758–1805); visited Newman in 1878 for advice as to possible conversion and was received into the Church (by Newman) shortly afterwards; prominent and devout Catholic layman rest of his life; succeeded his father in 1913; see Stanley L. Jaki, *Newman to Converts: An Existential Ecclesiology* (2001), pp.353–354.

Nesbit, Edith (married name Bland) – writer; b. 15 August 1858, 38 Lower Kensington Lane, London; c. 1902; d. 4 May 1924, Jesson St. Marys, Dymchurch; father (1818–1862), the owner of an agricultural college and prominent chemist and educationist, died early; brought up in Brighton, France, the North Downs, then London; raised as an Anglican; met her husband, Hubert Bland (1855–1914) (see above) in 1877; wrote poems and short stories; followed her husband into the Fabian Society and

wrote two novels about the early days of the socialist movement under the name of Fabian Bland; the Blands had a ménage a trois with Alice Hoatson, their housekeeper, who had children by her husband; she had many admirers, including George Bernard Shaw; had bohemian social circle; friend of Mgr. Robert Hugh Benson (see above), Cecil Chesterton (see above) and Frederick Rolfe ("Baron Corvo") (see below); wrote many very successful children's stories, notably *The Treasure Seekers* (1899) and *The Railway Children* (1906); first modern writer for children; criticized Pope Benedict XV for his neutrality during World War I; irregular in belief and habit; had lifelong credulity about ghosts; believed that Bacon wrote Shakespeare; some have doubted whether she formally converted, but after her husband's death she re-married in 1917 according to Catholic rites, although her funeral service was Anglican; buried in the churchyard of St. Mary's in the Marsh, Dymchurch; see Doris Langley Moore, *E. Nesbit: A Biography* (1967); Julia Briggs, *A Woman of Passion: The Life of E. Nesbit 1858–1824* (1987) (letter to her mother, written as a child from her convent school in France, pleading to be allowed to become a Catholic: "You say that you do not believe that our Lord is body and soul in the Holy Communion? Well, at the last supper when our Lord took the bread and wine He did not say This is the figure of My body this is the figure of My blood. He said this is my body this is my blood. Do this in remembrance of me. What are you to do in remembrance of Him? What had he just done? He had changed bread and wine into his body and blood. The priests being the descendants of the apostles operate the change"); *DNB*.

Neville, William Payne – priest; b. 1824; c. 3 April 1851 (received at Leeds by Newman); d. 1905; after Oxford University, where he came under the influence of Newman, he went as a lay-helper to St. Saviour's, Leeds (see entry for Thomas Minster), acting as almoner and opened a night school; his changing views prevented him from taking Anglican orders; after conversion went to stay at the Birmingham Oratory, then entered Oratorian Order there and remained for rest of his life; ordained priest in 1861; after death of Ambrose St. John in 1875, he increasingly attended on Newman and became his secretary and nurse; present when Newman died (Newman's last recorded words were a whispered "William, William"); as chief literary executor to Newman, collected and copied Newman's letters and papers; always hesitant and undecided.; buried at Rednal.

Newcastle, Dowager Duchess of (Henrietta Adela) (*née* **Hope**) – b. 1843, Surrey; c. 1879 (received by Fr. Bernard Vaughan); d. 1913; daughter and heiress of Henry Thomas Hope, original owner of the Hope Diamond; wife of the sixth Duke of Newcastle, Henry Pelham, Alexander Pelham-Clinton (d. 1879), whose enormous gambling debts she repaid; re-married in 1880 Thomas Theobald-Hobart (d. 1892), Anglican rector; member of Franciscan Third Order; great benefactor of the poor, especially in London (supported by Cardinal Vaughan); built complete Catholic complex at Woodford Green, Essex, with a Franciscan Friary, parish church of St. Thomas of Canterbury and St. Anthony's school for young ladies, established in the convent of the Sisters of the Holy Family of Bordeaux; buried in the church of St. Thomas of Canterbury at Woodford Green; see Madeleine Beard, *Faith and Fortune* (1997), pp.169–170; Ann Farmer, "Dowager Duchess of Newcastle: Friend of the Poor," *Catholic Life*, April 2002, p.10.

Newdigate, Alfred – bookseller and printer; b. 14 July 1829, Astley Castle, Warwickshire; c. 1875 (his wife, Selina Charlotte (d. 13 August 1920), was received earlier, on 20 November 1873; their older children received in due course); d. 20 April 1923; educated at Eton and Christ Church, Oxford; took Anglican orders and became a convinced Tractarian; wrote to Newman about the question of Anglican orders; he and his wife also corresponded with Newman regarding when one would have an obligation to convert; after his conversion he opened a bookshop and Catholic repository and developed others under the name of the Art and Book Company; also a notable printer; cooperated with James Britten (see above) and the Catholic Truth Society; much charitable work; father of Fr. Charles Alfred Newdigate, priest of the Society of Jesus and vice-postulator of the cause of the English martyrs beatified in 1929; three daughters, Gertrude (d. May 1888), Agnes (d. 1953), and Edith (d. 1965), became nuns in the Society of the Sacred Heart of Jesus; all of their children remained active in the Catholic faith; cousin of Charles Newdigate Newdegate (1816–1887) the anti-Catholic politician; buried with his wife in the cemetery attached to the church of St. Charles Borromeo, Hampton-on-the-Hill, near Warwick; see Stanley L. Jaki, *Newman to Converts: An Existential Ecclesiology* (2001), pp.349–351 ("As to Newdigate's question of why the Roman Church would deny the Catholic character of the Anglican Church, Newman's answer was as straightforward and brief as possible: 'There is but one Catholic Church, viz. the Roman and … the Church of England is separated from it…

…Of course, unless … in her heart she [Mrs. Newdigate] believes the Roman Church to be the minister and Prophet of God, I should be the last to wish her to

become a Catholic.... But if she does, O my dear Sir, will it be a thought welcome on a death bed to recollect that you have hindered her?'...
Newman wrote in a similar vein to Mrs. Newdigate, coupling gentleness with firmness. She had the duty to convert and only the priest to whom she was to go to be received could advise any further delay: 'If your mind has been clear for some time that the Church we call Catholic is the one true fold of Christ, and if you can acknowledge all her teaching, what she teaches and shall teach, it is your simple duty to ask for admittance into her communion, and you cannot delay your actual reconciliation, except the priest to whom you go tells you to delay'"); Rev. John Sharp, "Parson to Printer: A Victorian Convert's Story," *Recusant History*, October 2009, p.509.

Newman, Venerable John Henry – Cardinal priest, theologian, philosopher, man of letters; b. 21 February 1801, 80 Old Broad Street, London; c. 9 October 1845 (received by Bl. Dominic Barberi at Littlemore ("It was like coming into port after a rough sea")); d. 11 August 1890, Birmingham Oratory; son of John Newman, banker, of London; Evangelical conversion in 1816; educated at Trinity College, Oxford; Fellow of Oriel College, Oxford; ordained to the Anglican ministry; vicar of St. Mary's, Oxford, the university church; broke with earlier Evangelical position in 1830 and deprived of his tutorship at Oriel; was for a considerable time, in conjunction with Pusey, the recognized leader of the High Church Party; took prominent part in publication of *Tracts for the Times*, being the author of the famous *Tract 90*, a Catholic interpretation of the Thirty-nine Articles; resigned his parish of St. Mary's and retired to Littlemore in 1843, where he remained until his conversion

in 1845 ("The secession of Dr. Newman dealt a blow to the Church of England under which it still reels" wrote Disraeli in his preface to *Lothair* (1870)); ordained Catholic priest 1 June 1847 (Trinity Sunday) by Cardinal Fransoni at Propaganda, Rome (same occasion as Ambrose St. John (see below)); founder and superior of Birmingham Oratory and school; pastoral ministry to the poor in Birmingham; founder and first rector of Catholic University, Dublin; replied to attack on him by Charles Kingsley with autobiographical *Apologia Pro Vita Sua* (1864) (Kingsley's youngest daughter, the novelist Mary St. Leger Harrison (*pseud.* Lucas Malet) (see above) later became a Catholic); proclaimed Cardinal-deacon of San Georgio in Velabro in 1879; enormous output of books, articles and letters; his influence in the Church was said by Fr. R. Addington, another Oratorian priest, to have been like that of "a very powerful depth-charge going down and exploding every so often with ever greater force"; made many converts (Pusey said of him, "He has won more souls to Christ than any beside"); fought against liberalism, being the belief that teaches that "One creed is as good as another"; buried in the grave of Ambrose St. John at the Oratory country house at Rednal, outside Birmingham (his epitaph: *ex umbris et imaginibus in veritatem*); see *Letters and Diaries of John Henry Newman* (letter by Newman to Maria Giberne, 8 January 1845: "This I am sure of, that nothing but a simple direct call of duty is a warrant for any one leaving our Church [Newman being then an Anglican]; no preference of another Church, no delight in its services, no hope of greater religious advancement in it, no indignation, no disgust, at the persons and things, among which he may find ourselves in the Church of England. The simple question is, Can *I* (it is personal, not whether another, but can *I*) be saved in the English Church? Am I in safety, were I to die tonight? Is it a mortal sin in me, not joining another Communion?").

An Essay on the Development of Doctrine (1845) ("The common sense of mankind.... feels that the very idea of revelation implies a present informant and guide, and that an infallible one; not a mere abstract declaration of Truths unknown before to man, or a record of history, or the result of an antiquarian research, but a message and a lesson speaking to this man and that.... We are told that God has spoken. Where? In a book? We have tried it and it disappoints; it disappoints us, that holy and most blessed gift, not from any fault of its own, but because it is used for a purpose for which it was not given. The Ethiopian's reply, when St. Philip asked him if he understood what he was reading, is the voice of nature: 'How can I, unless some man shall guide me?' The Church undertakes that office...

...The most obvious answer, then, to the question, why we yield to the authority of the Church in the questions and developments of faith, is that some authority there must be if there is a revelation given, and other authority there is none but she. A revelation is not given, if there be no authority to decide what it is that is given. In the words of St. Peter to her Divine Master and Lord, 'To whom shall we go?' Nor must it be forgotten that Scripture expressly calls the Church 'the pillar and ground of the truth'.... The absolute need of a spiritual supremacy is at present the strongest of arguments in favor of its supply. Surely, either an objective revelation has not been given, or it has been provided with means of impressing its objectiveness on the world").

Loss and Gain (1848) ("'Many a man ... finds himself unable, though wishing to believe, for he has not evidence

enough to subdue his reason. What is to make him believe?' His fellow-traveler had for some time shown signs of uneasiness; when Charles stopped, he said, shortly but quietly, 'What is to make him believe? The will, his will ... the evidence is not in fault ... there is quite evidence enough for a *moral conviction* that the Catholic or Roman Church, and none other, is the voice of God.' 'Do you mean,' said Charles, with a beating heart, 'that before conversion one can attain to a present abiding actual conviction of this truth?' 'I do not know,' answered the other; 'but at least he may have habitual *moral certainty*; I mean, a conviction, and only one, steady, without rival conviction, or even reasonable doubt, present to him when he is most composed and in his hours of solitude, and flashing on him from time to time, as through clouds, when he is in the world – a conviction to this effect, "The Roman Catholic Church is the one only voice of God, the only way of salvation."' 'Then you mean to say,' said Charles, while his heart beat faster, 'that such a person is under no duty to wait for clearer light.' 'He will not have, he cannot expect, clearer light before conversion. Certainty in its highest sense is the reward of those who, by an act of the will, embrace the truth, when nature, like a coward, shrinks. You must make a venture; faith is a venture before a man is a Catholic; it is a grace after it. You approach the Church in the way of reason, you live in it in the light of the Spirit'").

Sermons Addressed to Mixed Congregations (1849) ("Turn away from the Catholic Church, and to whom will you go? It is your only chance of peace and assurance in this turbulent, changing world. There is nothing between it and skepticism, when men exert their reason freely. Private creeds, fancy religions, may be showy and imposing to the many in their day; national religions may lie huge and lifeless, and cumber the ground for centuries, and distract the intention or confuse the judgment of the learned; but on the long run it will be found that either the Catholic Religion is verily and indeed the coming in of the unseen world into this, or that there is nothing positive, nothing dogmatic, nothing real in any one of our notions as to whence we come and whither we are going. Unlearn Catholicism, and you become Protestant, Unitarian, Deist, Pantheist, Skeptic, in a dreadful, but infallible succession").

Certain Difficulties felt by Anglicans in Catholic Teaching (1850) ("For us Catholics, my brethren, while we clearly recognize how things are going with our countrymen, and while we would not accelerate the march of infidelity if we could help it, yet we are more desirous that you [Anglicans] should leave a false church for the true, than that a false church should hold its ground. For if we are blessed in converting any of you, we are effecting a direct, unequivocal, and substantial benefit, which outweighs all points of expedience—the salvation of your souls").

Lecture on the Present Position of Catholics (1851) ("To my mind, certainly, it is incomparably more difficult to believe that the Divine Being should do one miracle and no more, than that He should do a thousand; that He should do one great miracle only, than that He should do a multitude of less besides.

This beautiful world of nature, His own work, He broke its harmony; He broke through His own laws which He had imposed on it; He worked out His purposes, not simply through it, but in violation of it.

If He did this only in the lifetime of the Apostles, if He did it but once, eighteen hundred years ago and more, that isolated infringement looks as the mere infringement of a rule:

If Divine Wisdom would not leave an infringement, an anomaly, a solecism on His work, He might be expected to introduce a series of miracles, and turn the apparent exception into an additional law of His providence").

The Idea of a University (1852–1859) ("In the midst of our difficulties I have one ground of hope, just one stay, but, as I think, a sufficient one, which serves me in the stead of all other argument whatever, which hardens me against criticism, which supports me if I begin to despond, and to which I ever come round, when the question of the possible and the expedient is brought into discussion. It is the decision of the Holy See; St. Peter has spoken, it is he who has enjoined that which seems to us so unpromising. He has spoken and has a claim on us to trust him. He is no recluse, no solitary student, no dreamer about the past, no doter upon the dead and gone, no projector of the visionary. He for eighteen hundred years has lived in the world; he has seen all fortunes, he has encountered all adversaries, he has shaped himself for all emergencies. If ever there was a power on earth who had an eye for the times, who has confined himself to the practicable, and has been happy in his anticipations, whose words have been facts, and whose commands prophecies, such is he in the history of ages, who sits from generation to generation in the Chair of the Apostles, as the Vicar of Christ, and the Doctor of his Church. These are not words of rhetoric, gentlemen, but of history. All who take part with the Apostle are on the winning side. He has long since given warrant for the confidence which he claims. From the first he has looked through the wide world of which he has the burden; and, according to the need of the day and the inspiration of his Lord, he has set himself now to one thing, now to another; but to all in season, and to nothing in vain" (for a more expansive version of this theme, see *Cathedra Sempiterna* (1853), reprinted in Stanley L. Jaki, *Newman's Challenge* (2000), p.307)).

Letters and Diaries of John Henry Newman (letter by Newman to Lady Chatterton (see above), 10 June 1863: "There are three momentous questions, and only one answer to each of them.... By the three questions I mean, 1. Is there a God? 2. Has He spoken to us? 3. Through whom has He spoken? For myself, I think these three questions equally easy and equally difficult; and I trust and pray that He, through whose grace you have ever held the truth as regards the first, and have arrived at a clear conviction upon the second, and in His own time lead you on to the one true answer to be given to the third.

That answer seems to me most direct and easy, by means of the line of thought which you have yourself suggested in your letter: viz. Our Lord and His Apostles founded a Church to remain for all time; and the Catholic Roman Church is in matter of fact the continuation, and therefore the present representative of that Apostolic Church. It is here that your difficulty comes in: Why the present Catholic Church should be in many respects so unlike what we should expect and wish it to be? – So large a subject can hardly be treated in the compass of a letter: but I would have you give full weight to the following considerations:

1. Doubtless the face of the Visible Church is very disappointing to an earnest mind, nay, in a certain sense, a scandal. I assert, rather than grant, this grave and remarkable fact.

2. Another remarkable fact is this, – that it has ever been so. I do not believe there ever was a time when the gravest scandals did not exist in the Church, and act as impediments to the success of its mission. Those scandals have been the occasion of momentous secessions and schisms; in the earlier times, of the Novatian, the Donatist, the Luciferian; in latter of Protestantism and Jansenism.

3. It is also a fact, that, in spite of them still, the Church has ever got on and made way, to the surprise of the world; as an army may fight a series of bloody battles, and lose men, and yet go forward from victory to victory. On the other hand the seceding bodies have sooner or later come to nought. At this very time we are witnessing the beginning of the end of Protestantism, the breaking of that bubble of 'Bible-Christianity' which has been its life.

4. And it is a further fact, that our Lord distinctly predicted these scandals as inevitable; nay further, He spoke of His Church as in its very constitution made up of good and bad, of wheat and weeds, of the precious and the vile. One out of His twelve Apostles fell, and one of the original seven deacons. Thus, a Church, such as we behold, is bound up with the very idea of Christianity.

5. Lastly, at least from St. Augustine's day, the fact has been so fully recognized in the Church, as to become a doctrine, and almost a dogma, admitted by all; and never considered in consequence at all to interfere with that Sanctity which is one of her four Notes").

Apologia Pro Vita Sua (1864) ("From the time that I became a Catholic, of course I have no further history of my religious opinions to narrate.... I have been in perfect peace and contentment. I never have had one doubt.... I am far of course from denying that every article of the Christian Creed ... is beset with intellectual difficulties; and it is simple fact, that, for myself, I cannot answer those difficulties. Many persons are very sensitive of the difficulties of religion; I am as sensitive as any one; but I have never been able to see a connection between apprehending those difficulties, however keenly, and multiplying them to any extent, and doubting the doctrines to which they are attached. Ten thousand difficulties do not make one doubt, as I understand the subject; difficulty and doubt are incommensurate").

Letter to Pusey on Occasion of His Eirenicon (1866) "A convert comes to learn, and not to pick and choose. He comes in simplicity and confidence, and it does not occur to him to weigh and measure every proceeding, every practice which he meets with among those whom he has joined. He comes to Catholicism as to a living system, with a living teaching, and not to a mere collection of decrees and canons, which by themselves are of course the framework, not the body and substance of the Church!").

The Letters and Diaries of John Henry Newman (letter by Newman to S. S. Shiel, 25 January 1870: "In Scripture, we are told that to become interested in the promises, we must *join* the Church. The first Christians are represented as continuing in the *fellowship* of the Apostles – and those who were to be saved are said to have been added by Almighty God to His *Church*. The apostles were visible men – the Church was a visible body, St. Paul speaks of the Church as 'the pillar and ground of the Truth,' thereupon it was a visible teaching body. If a man commit a fault against another, that other is directed by our Lord to 'tell it to the Church,' – therefore the Church was a visible body (1 Timothy, 3:15. Matthew, 18:17). And the earliest Fathers as the Martyrs St. Ignatius and St. Cyprian, both of them in the clearest way speak of the Church as a visible body. Therefore the Church is the Ark of salvation, and it is necessary to join a visible body. I can understand a man doubting, *which* is the Church, at first sight, but not his doubting that it is a duty to join the Church, if he can find it. As to the question 'Which is the Church

of *Christ?*' Of course it would puzzle anyone – but there *is* a question which would puzzle no one. In the Creed we profess belief in 'the *Catholic* Church' – Now then go into any town, and ask for 'the Catholic Church,' and you know whither you would be directed. This is no accident – the early Fathers insist on it – they say that no sect *can* take the title of 'the Catholic Church.' Fourteen hundred years ago St. Cyril of Jerusalem says to his Catholic hearers 'When you go into a strange place do not ask for 'the Church,' for you will be sent to some sect – but ask for 'the Catholic Church,' and you will be directed right' (Catecheses, XVIII, 26)").

An Essay in Aid of a Grammar of Assent (1870) ("By Religion I mean the knowledge of God, of His Will, and of our duties towards Him; and there are three main channels which Nature furnishes for our acquiring this knowledge, viz. our own minds, the voice of mankind, and the course of the world, that is, of human life and human affairs. The informations which these three convey to us teach us the Being and Attributes of God, our responsibility to Him, our dependence on Him, our prospect of reward or punishment, to be somehow brought about, according as we obey or disobey Him. And the most authoritative of these three means of knowledge, as being specially our own, is our own mind, whose informations give us the rule by which we test, interpret, and correct what is presented to us for belief, whether by the universal testimony of mankind, or by the history of society and of the world.

Our great internal teacher of religion is … our Conscience. Conscience is a personal guide, and I use it because I must use myself; I am as little able to think by any mind but my own as to breathe with another's lungs. Conscience is nearer to me than any other means of knowledge. And as it is given to me, so also is it given to others; and being carried about by every individual in his own breast, and requiring nothing besides itself, it is thus adapted for the communication to each separately of that knowledge which is most momentous to him individually, – adapted for the use of all classes and conditions of men, for high and low, young and old, men and women, independently of books, of educated reasoning, of physical knowledge, or of philosophy. Conscience, too, teaches us, not only that God is, but what He is; it provides for the mind a real image of Him, as a medium of worship; it gives us a rule of right and wrong, as being His rule, and a code of moral duties. Moreover, it is so constituted that, if obeyed, it becomes clearer in its injunctions, and wider in their range, and corrects and completes the accidental feebleness of its initial teachings. Conscience, then, considered as our guide, is fully furnished for its office...

...One of the most important effects of Natural Religion on the mind, in preparation for Revealed, is the anticipation which it creates, that a Revelation will be given. That earnest desire of it, which religious minds cherish, leads the way to the expectation of it. Those who know nothing of the wounds of the soul, are not led to deal with the question, or to consider its circumstances; but when our attention is roused, then the more steadily we dwell upon it, the more probable does it seem that a revelation has been or will be given to us. This presentiment is founded on our sense, on the one hand, of the infinite goodness of God, and, on the other, of our own extreme misery and need – two doctrines which are the primary constituents of Natural Religion").

A Letter to the Duke of Norfolk on the Occasion of Mr. Gladstone's Expostulation (1875); C. Kegan Paul, *Biographical*

Sketches (1883), p.171; Richard Holt Hutton, *Cardinal Newman* (1905); J. D. Folghera, *Newman's Apologetic* (1928); H. John Chapman, OSB, "Newman and the Fathers," *Blackfriars*, July 1933 (whole issue is devoted to Newman) ("The Fathers had been to [Newman] a delight, an inspiration. They had been a far-off model to imitate in remodeling the English Establishment. But now he realized that he himself could belong to the Church of the Fathers, that there was but One Universal Church, one and the same in the days of Ignatius or Athanasius or Leo and of Pope Pius IX. And when he had been received into that Church by Father Dominic, he kissed the leather backs of the Patristic tomes around his room, because he was now their brother, not merely an ardent student, not *hospes et advena*, but *domesticus Dei et civis sanctorum*"); Edward Hutton, *Catholicism and English Literature* (1942), pp.191–202; John A. O'Brien, *Giants of the Faith: Conversions Which Changed the World* (1957), p.145; A. Martin, "Autobiography in Newman's Novels," *The Month*, May 1960, p.290; C. S. Dessain, *John Henry Newman* (1966); Christopher Hollis, *Newman and the Modern World* (1967); Robert Lee Wolff, *Gains and Losses: Novels of Faith and Doubt in Victorian England* (1977), pp.41–71; J. Murray Elwood, *Kindly Light: The Spiritual Vision of John Henry Newman* (1979); Ian Ker, *John Henry Newman: A Biography* (1988); Stanley L. Jaki (ed), *Newman Today* (1989); Ian Ker, *Newman on Being a Christian* (1990); Sheridan Gilley, *Newman and His Age* (1990); David Newsome, *The Convert Cardinals: John Henry Newman and Henry Edward Manning* (1993); Joyce Sugg, *Ever Yours Affly: John Henry Newman and His Female Circle* (1996); Ian Ker (ed), *Newman and Conversion* (1997); Stanley L. Jaki, *Newman's Challenge*

(2000), Vincent Ferrer Blehl, SJ, *Pilgrim Journey: John Henry Newman 1801–1845* (2001); Stanley L. Jaki, *Newman to Converts: An Existential Ecclesiology* (2001), Ian Ker, *The Catholic Revival in English Literature, 1845–1961* (2003), Ch. 1 ("Reading and appreciating the beautiful prose of the Prayer Book requires education and taste. But as Willis, the Catholic convert in *Loss and Gain*, remarks, 'The idea of worship is different in the Catholic Church from the idea of it in your Church for, in truth, the religions are different.' Catholic worship does not essentially consist in reading out words: 'I could attend Masses for ever and not be tired. It is not a mere form of words – it is a great action, the greatest action that can be on earth. It is, not the invocation merely, but, if I dare use the word, the evocation of the Eternal. He becomes present on the altar in flesh and blood, before whom angels bow and devils tremble.' A verbal, cerebral religion requires education and intelligence; the Catholic mass, by contrast, is a drama centered on an event that is equally accessible to all the worshipers"); Stanley L. Jaki, *The Church of England as Viewed by Newman* (2004), Stanley L. Jaki, *Apologetics as Meant by Newman* (2005); Stanley L. Jaki, *Neo-Arianism as Foreseen by Newman* (2006); Walter E. Conn, "From Oxford to Rome: Newman's Ecclesial Conversion," *Theological Studies*, 2007, p.595; Stanley L. Jaki, *Justification as Argued by Newman* (2007); Philippe Lefebvre and Colin Mason (ed), *John Henry Newman: Doctor of the Church* (2007); Philippe Lefebvre and Colin Mason (ed), *John Henry Newman: In His Time* (2007); James Tolhurst, "Cardinal John Henry Newman," in John Joliffe (ed), *English Catholic Heroes* (2008), p.156; "Newman, Manning and Their Age," *Saint Austin Review*, September/October 2008 (special issue devoted to Newman,

Manning and Hopkins); Patrick Allitt, *Catholic Converts: British and American Intellectuals Turn to Rome* (1997) *passim*; Joseph Pearce, *Literary Converts* (1999) *passim*; *Gillow*, Vol. V. p.165; *Catholic Encyclopedia*; *DNB*.

Nicholl, Donald – historian and theologian; b. 23 July 1923, Claremount, Halifax, Yorkshire; c. 1946 (Blackfriars, Oxford; wife, Dorothy, also convert); d. 3 May 1997, Betley, Staffordshire; brought up as an Anglican in poor family; won Brackenbury scholarship to Oxford, but called up after one year; served in World War II in India, Ceylon and Hong Kong; returned to Oxford, where struggled over his vocation between medieval history and the intellectual issues of twentieth century, finally choosing the latter and Russia in particular; several university posts; wrote mainly on spiritual subjects; rector of Ecumenical Institute of Tantur, near Jerusalem; correspondent for *The Tablet*; influenced by Richard Southern, the medieval historian; buried in Keele churchyard; see *Holiness* (1981); *The Beatitude of Truth: Reflections of a Lifetime* (1997); *The Testing of Hearts: A Pilgrim's Journal* (1998); obituaries by Adrian Hastings and Fr. Gerard Hughes, *The Tablet*, 10 May 1997, p.612 ("These Asian years set his consciousness firmly within a world context and, while strengthening his Christian identity, turned him into a Catholic. In India it seemed obvious to him that nothing less made full sense if one was to be a Christian at all").

Nichols, (John Christopher) Aidan, OP – priest and theologian; b. 17 September 1948, Lytham St. Anne's, Lancashire; c. 7 April 1966 (Holy Thursday); brought up in the Church of England; educated at Christ Church, Oxford (first in Modern History); entered Dominican Order in 1970; ordained priest in 1976;

prior of Blackfriars, Cambridge 1998–2004; John Paul II Memorial Visiting Lecturer at Oxford University 2006–2008 (first lectureship of Catholic theology at Oxford since the Reformation); author of many books and articles on Catholic themes; see *From Newman to Congar: The Idea of Doctrinal Development from the Victorians to the Second Vatican Council* (1990); *A Grammar of Consent: The Existence of God in Christian Tradition* (1991); *Holy Order: The Apostolic Ministry from the New Testament to the Second Vatican Council* (1991) *The Shape of Catholic Theology: An Introduction to Its Sources, Principles, and History* (1991); *Rome and the Eastern Churches: A Study in Schism* (1992); *The Panther and the Hind: A Theological History of Anglicanism* (1993); "Prelude: A Dominican's Story" in *Scribe of the Kingdom*, Vol. I (1993) ("It took the death of my father, when I was fourteen, to stir me into seeking reception. I needed a Savior who could deal with death by triumphing over it, and so affirm the lastingness of what deserved, by its merits, to be for eternity...

...[M]y grounds for adhering to the communion in which I expect to die ... were: clarity and certitude of doctrine; a mystical depth in worship and devotion; and a spirituality which could give one guidance, courage and consolation not only in dying but in living as well: the whole being held together in a continuity over time which joined me to the centre of all history, Jesus Christ, the Pantokrator and man of sorrows, in whom the heights and depths of strength and weakness, joy and grief, are one"); *Epiphany: A Theological Introduction to Catholicism* (1996), *Looking at the Liturgy: A Critical View of Its Contemporary Form* (1996); *Dominican Gallery: Portrait of a Culture* (1997); *Catholic Thought Since the Enlightenment: A Survey* (1998); *Christendom Awake: On Re-*

Energising the Church in Culture (1999) (citing Bishop Peter Cule of Mostar: "The extent to which contemporary humanism feeds off contemporary atheism (and vice versa) has not been reckoned with. The former crowds out God, and the latter's denial of God encourages a kind of living in which the very question of God comes to seem without meaning. Yet the truth remains, as one of the fathers of the Second Vatican Council put it, that 'no one has a doctrine so sublime and consonant with human nature as does the Church'"); *Come to the Father: An Invitation to Share the Catholic Faith* (2000) ("The key belief of the Church, on which everything else turns, is the Incarnation. I call this 'the Great Assertion' because it is of world-shaking significance that Jesus is personally identical with the divine Son, who is himself very God, 'Light from Light.' Clearly, the question whether or not some human individual is thus identical with the uncreated Word through which the world was made cannot be a bagatelle. (It is, surely, the ultimate in 'gobsmackers'!) The claim that Jesus of Nazareth, not a figure of myth but someone whom historians can research, was personally united to the Godhead may be dismissed as false, but it can hardly be written off as trivial. Yet put in such terms it remains a question of theory, albeit one of vast speculative importance for our understanding both of God and of human dignity. The same question when put, as the Creeds do, in the context of salvation, becomes charged with practical import for my life and destiny. It now turns into the question, Do the deeds of Jesus Christ as found in the Gospels have only a morally inspirational value (this was another of the truly just men of history)? Or did those deeds actually change the terms of living? Did they change the terms on which the very gift of human life itself is received from

God? That would be the case if in those deeds One who was personally divine was active precisely so as to re-order the origin, life-resources and final destiny of human beings, in a word to *re-make* us. He can re-make us if he acts on us in a divine creative way, making us participate in his way of being and thus in God"); *Beyond the Blue Glass: Catholic Essays on Faith and Culture* (2002); *Discovering Aquinas: An Introduction to His Life, Work and Influence* (2002); *A Pope and a Council on the Sacred Liturgy* (2002); *A Spirituality for the Twenty-First Century* (2003); *Hopkins: Theologian's Poet* (2006); *Lovely, Like Jerusalem: The Fulfillment of the Old Testament in Christ and the Church* (2007); *The Thought of Pope Benedict XVI* (2007); *The Realm: An Unfashionable Essay on the Conversion of England* (2008); *Reason With Piety: Garrigou-Lagrange in the Service of Catholic Thought* (2008); *Redeeming Beauty: Soundings in Sacral Aesthetics* (2008); *From Hermes to Benedict XVI: Faith and Reason in Modern Catholic Thought* (2009); *G. K. Chesterton: Theologian* (2009); *Criticising the Critics* (2010).

Nicholson, Francis – Catholic controversialist; b. about 1650; c. about 1682; d. 13 August 1731, Lisbon; after Oxford University became Anglican rector; affected by the Oates Plot, a sermon of his being reported to the bishops; influenced by Obadiah Walker (see below); on the accession of James II he declared himself a Catholic; after his conversion he engaged in several controversies; after the Revolution of 1688 he entered the English Carthusian monastery at Nieuwpoort, Flanders, but austerities too great for his constitution and he returned to England in about 1692; later resided in Portuguese court at Lisbon in the service of Dowager-Queen Catherine of Braganza, widow of Charles II; in 1706 purchased an estate at Pera, which he made over to the English College at Lisbon in 1721; buried at the college; see *Gillow*, Vol. V, p.178 ("At Oxford Nicholson was a pupil of Obadiah Walker, and hence was regarded by the Low Church party in the university as having 'the Pope in his belly'"); *Catholic Encyclopedia*; *DNB*.

Nicolson (Nicholson), Thomas Joseph – vicar apostolic of Scotland; b. 1644/6, Birkenbog, Banffshire, Scotland; c. 1682; d. 12 October 1718, Preshome; studied at Aberdeen University; in 1666 made Professor at Glasgow University (taught Greek, Mathematics and Philosophy); in 1681 he refused to take the Test Act oath and resigned; after conversion he entered the Scots College, Douai, then went on to Padua where he taught in the episcopal seminary; ordained priest 9 March 1686; returned to Scotland in 1687 and worked in Edinburgh and Glasgow; at the Revolution he was imprisoned, then banished; in 1694 appointed vicar apostolic of Scotland; consecrated bishop 27 February 1695 in Paris secretly; in Scotland he acted with authority and united lowlands and highlands; in 1704 he ordained a priest (the first ordination in Scotland since the Reformation); in 1714 he set up a small seminary at Loch Morar; imprisoned for a time after the Jacobite rising in 1715; buried in St Ninian's churchyard, Tynet, Banffshire; see *Gillow*, Vol. V, p.200; *Catholic Encyclopedia*; *DNB*.

Norfolk, Duchess of (Hon. Augusta Mary Minna Catherine) (*née* **Lyons**) – benefactress; b. 1821; c. 27 January 1850 (received by Fr. Frederick Faber (see above); her brother, Richard Lyons, first Earl Lyons (1817–1887), diplomat, received November 1887; the first wife of the fifteenth Duke of Norfolk, Lady Flora Paulyna Hetty Barbara Abney

Hastings (1854–1887) converted in 1875); d. 22 March 1886; daughter of Admiral the first Baron Lyons; wife of the Earl of Arundel, later the fourteenth Duke of Norfolk (1815–1860) (see below); after her husband's death, she became a generous benefactress to Catholic causes.

Norfolk, fourteenth Duke of (Henry Granville Fitzalan-Howard) – Catholic layman and politician; b. 7 November 1815; c. 1840s, in Paris (although baptized a Catholic as an infant), his wife, Augusta (see above) also converted); d. 25 November 1860; eldest son of Henry Charles Howard, thirteenth Duke (1791–1856); captain in the Life Guards; Whig MP for Arundel 1837–1851; after his conversion he spoke infrequently in the Commons, but invariably on Catholic themes, on which he also wrote; with his wife he devoted much of his time and wealth to charity on a vast scale; see Madeleine Beard, *Faith and Fortune* (1997), pp.140–141 ("[He] became a Member of Parliament in order to defend the Irish peasantry, and plead for Catholics who were in workhouses, in hospitals and in the army, none of whom had chaplains at the time. As fourteenth Duke he sought to turn Arundel into a Catholic paradise where the Angelus would ring again and estate workers would be given time for choir practice"); *Gillow*, Vol. V, p.186; *DNB* ("Soon after his marriage Fitzalan met the Catholic writer and politician Count de Montalembert in Paris. The friendship that resulted was the most important of his early life. Until then he had been only nominally Catholic; now he threw himself into the French Catholic revival of the 1840s, attending mass at Notre Dame, and listening to the sermons of Père Lacordaire and Père de Ravignon. 'You must look upon me as a convert,' he told Montalembert. For his part

Montalembert considered Fitzalan 'the most pious layman of our times,' This 'conversion' determined Fitzalan's life's work...

Norfolk's faith had two wellsprings. One was the early intimacy with Montalembert, from whom he derived an acute sense of Europe's Catholic past. The vanished simplicity of master and servant holding a common faith greatly appealed to him. In later years greater influence was exerted by John Henry Newman and Frederick Faber. Faber – who acted as his confessor – considered him a near saint").

Northcote, James Spencer – priest, college head and historian; b. 26 May 1821, Feniton Court, near Honiton, Devon; c. 7 January 1846 (at Prior Park; wife, Susannah, *née* Poole, a cousin (d. 1853), received in November 1845, plus three of her sisters, Maria (later Mother Mary Imelda Poole, see below), Elizabeth and Lucy, in September 1845); d. 3 March 1907, Stoke-on-Trent; educated at Corpus Christi College, Oxford (first in Classics) where he came under the influence of Newman and Pusey; later Anglican curate, but resigned when his wife was received into the Catholic Church; lifetime study of the Roman catacombs, culminated in his great work *Roma Sotterranea*, written in conjunction with William R. Brownlow (see above); acting editor of *The Rambler* 1852–1854; after wife's death studied for the priesthood; ordained priest 29 July 1855; DD of Rome; worked on several missions; very successful President of Oscott College 1860–1876, then Provost of Cathedral Chapter of Birmingham from 1885; his three sons and three daughters all predeceased him (the only one who survived into adulthood became a Dominican nun); buried at Oscott cemetery; see *The Fourfold Difficulty of Anglicanism* (1846) ("I have thus endeavored, with all fairness and truth, to test the English communion by those four notes of the true Church, which are set before us in the Nicene Creed; and I think I have proved that to neither of them can she successfully lay claim; that so far from being one, either with the rest of Christendom, or with herself, her alienation from every other communion and her internal discord are proverbial; that the spiritual life in its higher forms, in which alone it deserves the name of Sanctity, is unknown to her; that so far from being Catholic, it is her very boast that she is national; and that, instead of ruling with an Apostolically derived authority, she has professedly received her jurisdiction from the English crown. I have also endeavored to express my own undoubting conviction, that there is a Church, and one only, to which all these notes apply; whose Unity is the marvel of the world; which teems in every age with multitudes walking in the varied paths of Christian perfection; which embraces in her wide bosom all nations, peoples and languages, countless in numbers and unrivalled in extent; and whose sway, transmitted from hand to hand, is derived from no earthly potentate, but from the Prince of the Apostles, who received it from Jesus Christ Himself"); *A Pilgrimage to La Salette* (1852); *Celebrated Sanctuaries of the Madonna* (1868); *Roma Sotterranea: or some account of the Roman Catacombs especially of the Cemetery of San Callisto* (1869); *A Visit to the Roman Catacombs* (1877); *Epitaphs of the Catacombs, or Christian Inscriptions in Rome during the First Four Centuries* (1878); *Mary in the Gospels* (1906); *DNB*.

Northcote, Philip Mary – priest and author; formerly Scottish Episcopalian; ordained Catholic (Servite) priest and worked on the missions in England, Scotland, and South Africa; see *The Way*

of Truth (1906) ("The paths by which persons approach the true fold are as numerous as there are individuals, since it matters not to the great Enlightener by what channel He casts His heaven sent ray into the dark recesses of the human soul, and thus many are brought to a knowledge of the truth by means which the skeptic calls unreasonable. As a matter of fact, there is no such thing as an unreasonable conversion, for faith so utterly transcends reason that it is really immaterial how it is conveyed to the mind, so that God makes use of the most diverse way for imparting the Divine illumination in accordance with the varying characteristics of each individual soul. Thus we often see that the utterance of a child, the example of simple servant girl, or some such trivial matter, will bring conviction to a cultured understanding which has remained for years invulnerable to the keenest weapons of logic"); *God Made Man* (1912); *The Catholic Faith* (1914); *The Bulwarks of Faith: A Book of Apologetics* (1925); *Is Faith Credulity?* (1938).

Norton, Mabel – teacher; b. in England; c. 1936; went to live in Lisbon, Portugal in 1910; was a Protestant when taken by a friend, a Portuguese marchioness, her husband, and their family, to Fatima on 13 October 1917, where she witnessed the miracle of the sun; moved back to England in 1933; visited Portugal in 1943 and joined the British pilgrimage there the next Summer; returned in 1947, becoming enthralled by Fatima and especially the story of one of the seers, Jacinta; in 1948 she wrote a book on Fatima (published in 1950), giving a very accurate eyewitness account of what the sun appeared to do there (no other major student of Fatima, who wrote a book or several on that subject, was an eyewitness); see *Eyewitness at Fatima* (1950) ("After the 'dancing' the people began to disperse. We had risen from our knees but were still in the same place close to the road when someone said, "Look! The children!" They passed quite close to us at the tail of an ox-cart decorated with wild cane and green boughs, and as they passed little Jacinta turned her dark eyes in our direction. Jacinta, did you know that I, the Protestant, who hardly believed there *had* been a miracle, would one day do all I could to bear witness to the truth, and become one of your firmest lovers?").

Norton, Matthew, OP (name in religion Thomas) – priest; b. 1732, Roundhay, near Leeds; c. about 1750; d. 7 August 1800, Hinkley, Leicestershire; converted to the Catholic faith during a visit to Flanders; in 1751 enrolled as student in English Dominican college at Bornhem, near Antwerp; entered the Order and studied at English Dominican College at Louvain; ordained priest 1757; brilliant scholar; worked on the English mission, mainly in Leicestershire, 1759–1767, including chaplain at Aston Flamville, seat of the Turville family; elected prior of Bornhem in 1769 and rebuilt priory and college; returned to Leicestershire, working around Hinkley, but also for a time rector of college at Louvain and vicar provincial in the Low Countries; great interest in farming and methods of cultivation, for which his writings won awards; buried in Aston Flamville churchyard; see *Gillow*, Vol. V, p.198; *DNB*.

Nourse, Timothy – agricultural and religious writer; b. about 1636, The Place, Newent, Gloucestershire; c. 1672 (wife, Lucy (d. 1732) also a convert); d. 21 July 1699; Fellow and Bursar of University College, Oxford; took Anglican orders and became a noted preacher; accused of consorting with Catholic clergy and hearing Mass in Queen Catherine of Braganza's chapel at Somerset House; after the Test Act he converted to Catholicism; deprived of his fellowship, he retired to his small country house at Newent; it is said that when taken ill on a visit to London in 1677, he reverted to Anglicanism, but regretted this and returned to the Catholic faith; suffered much during the Popish Plot persecutions in 1678; wrote several works on religion (arguing for natural religion and Catholic apologetics) and one on agricultural improvement; occasional conformist, but used Catholic forms in writing his will; buried at Newent; see *Gillow*, Vol. V, p.200; *DNB*.

Noyes, Alfred – poet and scholar; b. 16 September 1880, St Mark's Road, Wolverhampton; c. 1927; d. 28 June 1958, Ryde, Isle of Wight; brought up in an Anglican environment (father devout); entered Exeter College, Oxford, but left without taking a degree; wrote much poetry (popularly, *The Highwayman*), novels, biography, and books on religious topics; lecturer at several universities, notably Princeton; after death of his first wife, married Mary Angela Weld-Blundell, member of old Catholic family; idolized Tennyson; his biography, *Voltaire* (1936) sought to exculpate that philosopher from charges of atheism (but refuted by Kathleen O'Flaherty's *Voltaire: Myth and Reality* (1945)); buried at St. Saviour's Catholic church, Totland, Isle of Wight; see *The Unknown God* (1934); *Two Worlds For Memory* (1953) ("Algernon Cecil once remarked that when he became a Catholic he expected to feel a certain isolation in England, but to his great surprise he found himself a member of an immense army. That army is composed, of course, not only of the great company on earth, but of the much wider communion of the *Civitas Dei*. My experience was of the same kind. On earlier visits to Canada and the United States, for instance, I had spoken in many cities which apparently belonged to an almost exclusively contemporary world. When I visited these countries as a Catholic, I became aware for the first time of a great world behind the superficial scene, a world that belonged to the ages and held the keys to the treasure house of history...

In England it gave a new significance to the ruins of Glastonbury and Tintern, a new meaning to Westminster Abbey itself, and even to Christmas, for modern England has forgotten that the Abbey once implied an Abbot, and that Christmas was once the Mass of Christ. It was a renaissance of the mind, in which the literature and philosophy of all the ages acquired a new and vital beauty.... There is a sun around which the whole universe moves. It does not try to be original, for it is itself the origin. It does not need to be modern, for it is older than time, and new every morning"); Derek Stanford, "Alfred Noyes (1880–1958)," *The Irish Ecclesiastical Record*, September 1958, p.190; Patrick Allitt, *Catholic Converts: British and American Intellectuals Turn to Rome* (1997) *passim*; Joseph Pearce, *Literary Converts* (1999) *passim*; *DNB*.

Oakeley, Frederick – priest and author; b. 5 September 1802, Abbey House, Shrewsbury; c. 29 October 1845 (chapel of St. Clement's over Magdalen Bridge, Oxford); d. 29 January 1880, 39 Duncan Terrace, Islington; eleventh and youngest child of Sir Charles Oakeley, first Baronet (1751–1826); formerly chaplain Fellow of Balliol College, Oxford; Anglican clergyman and Prebendary of Lichfield; appointed preacher for University of Oxford; period of Evangelicalism 1830–1835; growing attraction to the Oxford Movement partly due to friendship with William George Ward (see below); minister at Margaret Street in London 1839–1845, making it a

centre of musical and liturgical excellence, becoming thereby the introducer of Ritualism (among the congregation were Gladstone, Edward Bellasis (see above) and Alexander Beresford Hope); made English translation of *Adeste fidelis* ("Ye faithful approach ye" changed without his permission to "O come all ye faithful"); in 1845 on W. G. Ward's condemnation by the University of Oxford, declared his adhesion to *Tract 90* and became most prominent member of "Romeward" section of the Oxford Movement; suspended by his bishop; joined Newman's community at Littlemore prior to his conversion; ordained priest 14 November 1847 (by Wiseman); Canon of Westminster; for many years worked among the poor of Westminster; author of many works on aspects of liturgy, devotion and apologetics, notably *The Ceremonies of the Mass* (1855); short-sighted, small of stature, lame, he exercised a wide influence by personality, writings and charm of conversation; remained always Newman's friend and defender; Newman referred to him as "a man of elegant genius, of classical mind, of rare talent in literary composition"; buried at Kensal Green cemetery, London; see *A Letter on Submitting to the Catholic Church* (1845); Michael Clifton, *A Victorian Convert Quintet* (1998); P. J. Galloway, *A Passionate Humility: Frederick Oakeley and the Oxford Movement* (1999) ("Oakeley gave the following reasons for leaving the Church of England. Firstly, the interpretation of Holy Scripture was, in the Church of England, left to private judgment. 'This, I believe to be the very straight road to heresy; and which in the Anglican Communion, actually issues in a countless variety of discordant and even contradictory exhibitions of the truth'.... Secondly, the Church of England had 'no recognized system of moral theology, according to which, those who undertake

... the direction of souls, are bound to shape their instructions. All is accidental, capricious and vague.' Additionally, there was no recognized system of practical sacramental confession. Thirdly, the Roman Catholic Church 'plainly corresponds with that type of the Catholic Church which is deeply and habitually impressed upon my whole moral and spiritual nature'"); *Gillow*, Vol. V, p.204; *Catholic Encyclopedia*; *DNB*.

Oates, William – publisher; b. 28 February 1828, Horsforth, near Leeds; c. April 1851 (received by Fr. Nicholas Darnell (see above) at St. Anne's Cathedral, Leeds; his brother Thomas (b. 1835) was also received into the Catholic Church in 1851); educated at St. Saviour's, Leeds and York Training College; when the clergy of St. Saviour's converted in a body (see entry for Thomas Minster) he also converted; later a school teacher; in 1857 became managing partner of the Catholic publishers Austin and Oates in Bristol; in 1863 he joined the firm of Burns and Lambert, London, which then changed its name to Burns, Lambert and Oates, and finally to Burns and Oates; gentle and unassuming character; his son Wilfrid succeeded him in the business; another son became secretary to Cardinal Vaughan; one of his daughters, Mother Mary Salome, of the Bar Convent, York, became well known for her books for children; see *Gillow*, Vol. V, p.210.

O'Brien, Charlotte Grace – author and social reformer; b. 23 November 1845, Cahirmoyle, County Limerick, Ireland; c. 1887; d. 3 June 1909, Ardanoir, Foynes, Ireland; from family of seven children; daughter of William Smith O'Brien (1803–1864), the Irish Nationalist and MP for Ennis and Limerick; committed Irish nationalist herself; through her efforts the Mission of Our Lady of the Rosary for the protection of Irish immigrant girls was founded in New York in 1881, to exercise a moral influence over steamship companies to protect girls on board their vessels, and watch over and assist girls at landing depot; wrote fiction, drama and poetry; articles in *Nineteenth Century* and *Pall Mall Gazette*; unmarried; buried at Knockpatrick; see *DNB*.

O'Brien, Sophie (*née* Raffalovich) – author and Irish nationalist; b. 16 January 1860, Odessa; c. June 1890; d. early January 1960, Paris, a week before her hundredth birthday; brought up within Judaism; daughter of Herman Raffalovich (d. 1893) of Paris, wealthy Russian Jewish banker to the Tsar; spent her first thirty years in Paris; interested in Catholicism since the age of ten; sister of André Raffalovich (see below), poet, and lifelong friend of fellow poet John Gray (see above); wife of William O'Brien MP (1852–1928), Irish nationalist and founder of *United Ireland* and *The Irish People*; converted before her marriage; published eight books reflecting on her life, marriage, and friends in Ireland; buried at Neuilly-St Front, near Soissons, France; see *DNB* ("She became very committed to her new church, and many of her close friends were nuns; the Catholic influence was pronounced in her writings, especially on the image of women. She believed that women should receive higher education and follow careers (albeit within accepted female occupations such as teaching), but she was not a supporter of women's rights, and, contrary to her husband's views, never agreed with female suffrage, refusing to vote when women were enfranchised").

O'Connor, (Lucy) Violet (*née* Bullock-Webster) – writer; b. 25 April 1867, Devon; c. 1897; d. October 1946; studied in Paris and Cheltenham; tried vocation with the Dominicans, then taught in infants' school; married poet and musician, Armel O'Connor, in 1908; designed house in Ludlow, named Mary's Meadow, where they lived (entrance porch arranged with seat and table where Christ, in the person of the poor, could always be given welcome and meal); the house was woven into many of her books (e.g., *The Idea of Mary's Meadow*, *The Songs of Mary's Meadow*, *Mary's Meadow Papers* and *Thoughts for Betty from the Holy Land*; books on, *inter alia*, flowers, women's suffrage, field sports and the saints; "There is not a single word – deliberately or not – in any of my books which could offend the eye of a contemplative nun"; contributor to articles in *The Pall Mall Gazette*, *The Pilot* and *The Ladies Pictorial*; see *My Dear Mommy – Mrs. Armel O'Connor. By Michael* (1943) (in fact an autobiography).

Oddie, William John Muir – writer, journalist, and broadcaster; b. 1 June 1939; c. Easter 1991 (received with his wife, Cornelia, a lapsed Catholic who had become an Anglican in 1974, and their three children); brought up in family with no religious beliefs; went to Congregationalist school; studied at Trinity College, Dublin; PhD from Leicester University 1970; varied between agnosticism and atheism, then became Anglican in 1974, influenced greatly by C. S. Lewis, in particular his *aut deus aut malus homo* argument; later Anglo-Catholic clergyman and Fellow of St. Cross College, Oxford, 1981–1985; converted after Church of England ordained women ("I saw that if Anglicanism did this, what it was saying was, 'We take to ourselves the power, apart from the universal Church, to do something the rest of the universal Church will not do. In other words, we declare unilateral

independence from the Catholic faith … we are no longer even claiming to be part of universal Christendom'"); editor of *Catholic Herald* 1998–2004; freelance journalist with *Sunday Telegraph*, *Daily Telegraph*, *Daily Mail*, *Sunday Times*; chairman of Chesterton Society; writings on religious matters; see *What Will Happen to God: Feminism and the Reconstruction of Christian Belief* (1984); (ed) *After the Deluge: Essays towards the Desecularisation of the Church* (1987); *The Crockford's File: Gareth Bennett and the Death of the Anglican Mind* (1989); "Edifice without support," *Daily Telegraph*, 21 January 1991; essay in Joanna Bogle (ed), *Come On In … It's Awful* (1994) ("Becoming a Catholic does bring about a real personal conversion – a *metanoia* or turning again – not because Catholic beliefs are not possible outside the Roman Catholic Church, but because in most non-Roman churches where they are permitted, they are optional rather than normative: what is different is the sense of being part of something which knows what it is, and what it is for. An Anglo-Catholic is one who has decided that Catholicism is true and that it is possible to practice it in the Church of England; a Roman Catholic believes, not only that Catholicism is true, but that an essential part of being a Catholic is to be in full communion with a Church which is built unambiguously on Catholic belief"); *The Roman Option: Crisis and the Realignment of English-Speaking Christianity* (1997); *EWTN Audio Library* (16 June 2003) ("I remember going into [York Minster] … and standing in the middle of the nave, with the majestic Norman arches towering above me and I simply found myself saying to myself, 'Either this is based on the truth, or it's based on a lie. If it's a lie, how come it is so sublime; What's the sublimity of all this mean'"); (ed) *John Paul the Great: Maker of the Post-*

Conciliar Church (2003); Joanna Bogle, "Obedience to the Pope Was What He Wanted," *This Rock*, September 2005, p.38 ("He had written to the Anglican Bishop of Oxford to explain his position, and the bishop issued a press statement saying that Oddie was 'moving into another room in the same house.' 'But when I went to see him, I told him that was simply untrue. The truth was that I had been camping out in a garden shed, some distance from the main house, and one night when the rain was pouring in and the roof leaking, I went to the main house and begged for some shelter. And they opened the door and said 'But of course! A room has always been ready and prepared for you. Welcome home!' That was the reality'"); *Chesterton and the Romance of Orthodoxy: The Making of GKC, 1874–1908* (2008); *EWTN Audio Library* (16 June 2008) ("We [the Church of England] had been told by the Pope that he had no authority to ordain women. We were saying we did. I think that was the Church of England defining itself in a way that I hadn't heard before'").

Oldmeadow, Ernest James – writer and music critic; b. 31 October 1867, Chester; c. 1900 (wife, Annie Cecilia, writer (novelist, lives of the saints) received in 1907); d. 11 September 1949; former Methodist minister; writer of fiction and biography; editor of *The Dome* 1897–1900; musical critic of *The Outlook* 1900–1904; contributor to *The Standard, Westminster Gazette, Nineteenth Century and After, Saturday Review, Morning Post*, etc.; editor of *The Tablet* 1923–1936; *bon vivant* with wide interests and zest for controversy (e.g., his accusations of blasphemy and obscenity in Evelyn Waugh's *Black Mischief*); Knight Commander of the Order of St. Gregory the Great 1934; see *Great English Painters* (1908); *Great Musicians* (1908); *A Layman's Christian Year* (1938); *Francis Cardinal Bourne*, 2 Vols. (1940 and 1944).

Oliver, Edward James ("Jimmy") – novelist, essayist and journalist; b. April 1911, London; c. about 1931 (received by Fr. Martin D'Arcy, SJ); d. December 1992; from a solid middle-class family; read History at Christ Church College, Oxford; became a Catholic during his first term at Oxford; worked for the Catholic publishers, Sheed and Ward, reading and reporting on French, Spanish and German manuscripts; later sub-editor of *The Tablet*; worked in field security, the Intelligence Corps 1940–1942; worked for the BBC European Service 1944–1948; wrote novels, then later biographies; wrote many articles on Catholic themes including several on Chesterton; close friend of Fr. Bryan Houghton (see above); expert on G. K. Chesterton; see *Honeymoonshine* (1936); *Not Long to Wait* (1948); *The Clown* (1951); *Coventry Patmore* (1956); *Gibbon and Rome* (1958); *Balzac the European* (1959); *Hypocrisy and Humour* (1960); Barbara Wall, "*In Diebus Illis*: E. J. Oliver," *Chesterton Review*, May 1993, p.201.

Orchard, William Edwin – priest; b. 20 November 1877, Wing Road, Linslade, Buckinghamshire; c. 2 June 1932, Rome; d. 12 June 1955, Brownshill, near Stroud, Gloucestershire; former Presbyterian minister; rose to national fame by his ministrations at the Congregational King's Weigh House Chapel, London where he leaned towards Catholic ritual and doctrine and pioneered the "Free Catholic" movement; attempts to construct a "bridge church" in the search for Christian unity failed; he resigned from the Weigh house and was received into the Catholic Church; ordained Catholic priest in 1935; much writing, conducting of missions and retreats, and personal counseling; buried in cemetery attached to the Dominican priory, Woodchester; see *From Faith to Faith: An Autobiography of Religious Development* (1933) ("There does not seem in these three objections of exclusiveness, corruption or obscurantism anything that justifies schism, or should hinder individual submission. Even if scriptural texts by which Rome justifies her claims are too disputed to be trusted…, there remains the impressive fact that it is difficult to see how the faith could have been preserved through the dark ages, or how it can survive the centuries of confusion now threatening, without the Papacy. Like everything else in Christianity, that this has undergone development is no argument against it; its germs can be discovered in earliest times, and go back to seeds sown by Christ Himself…. The theory that the Catholic development of Christianity is false to the original faith leaves the whole idea of the Church in ruins, and exposes Christianity to the charge of being, however pure in essence, inevitably corruptible. Apart from the Papacy, no other means of attaining unity has been elsewhere discovered; it was once universally allowed by East as well as West; it was so readily recognized to be the fulfillment of Christ's promise to Peter that it continued so long unchallenged; it has risen again to power when men thought it was about to collapse…. In the future, everything seems to show it will still be needed to guide and protect His Church and to keep it pure in faith and united in fellowship"); *The Cult of Our Lady* (1937); *The Necessity for the Church* (1940); Elaine Kaye and Ross Mackenzie, *W. E. Orchard: A Study in Christian Exploration* (1990); *DNB*.

Ornsby, Robert – classical scholar and biographer; b. 1820, Lanchester, Durham;

c. May 1847 (wife, Elizabeth, sister of Fr. John Dalgairns (see above), received in 1848); d. 21 April 1889, Earlsfort Terrace, Dublin; brother of George Ornsby (1809–1886), antiquarian and Anglican Prebendary of York; educated at Lincoln College, Oxford (first in Classics); Fellow of Trinity College, Oxford; became Anglican curate; wrote biographies; for some years assistant editor of *The Tablet*; Professor of Greek and Latin Literature at the Catholic University College, Dublin; private tutor to the future fifteenth Duke of Norfolk and his brother; Fellow of the Royal University of Ireland; see *Life of St. Francis de Sales, Bishop and Prince of Geneva* (1860); *Memoirs of James Robert Hope-Scott of Abbotsford, D.C.L., Q.C.*, 2 Vols. (1884); *DNB*.

Oxenford, John – dramatist, critic, translator, and song writer; b. 12 August 1812, Camberwell, Surrey; c. September 1875; d. 21 February 1877, Southwark, London; voluminous knowledge (mainly self-taught, plus some private tuition from a brilliant and erratic scholar, S. T. Friend); formerly, and for many years, a Deist; married, though unhappily; qualified as solicitor, but turned to literature; dramatist (some say well over a hundred plays) and translator of many plays from French, Spanish, Italian, and, most successfully, German; many review articles on a wide variety of subjects for a long list of periodicals; poet and for more than twenty-five years theatre critic to *The Times*; buried at Kensal Green cemetery, London; see *Gillow*, Vol. V, p.225; *Catholic Encyclopedia*; *DNB*.

Oxenham, Henry Nutcombe – controversialist and poet; b. 15 November 1829, Harrow, Middlesex; c. 31 October 1857 (received by Manning); d. 23 March 1888, Kensington; son of Anglican clergyman; Anglican curate himself;

published works on his Tractarian views and practice; was at the inaugural meeting of the Association for the Promotion of the Unity of Christendom (APUC) in September 1857 with the then Anglican, F. G. Lee (see above), and the Catholic, Ambrose Phillipps De Lisle (see above); disliked excesses of Ultramontanism; started to train for priesthood and received the four Minor Orders; attacked the Catholic seminary system; Cardinal Wiseman refused to confer on him Major Orders; taught successively at St. Edmund's College, Ware and the Birmingham Oratory school; translator of Döllinger, a close friend; unwilling to accept the doctrine of papal infallibility after Vatican I, but never outwardly severed his connection with the Catholic Church, and before death received all the sacraments; in 1874 attended at Bonn the meeting of 'Old Catholics' but later disapproved of that movement; buried at Chislehurst, Kent; see *The Catholic Doctrine of the Atonement* (1865); *Catholic Eschatology and Universalism* (1876); *Gillow*, Vol. V, p.228; *Catholic Encyclopedia*; *DNB*.

Page, Blessed Francis, SJ – priest and martyr; b. in Antwerp; d. 20 April 1602, Tyburn; brought up in Protestant family; educated in the practice of the law; converted by Fr. John Gerard; went to Douai and ordained priest 1 April 1600, returning to England in the same year; condemned for priesthood in 1602; received into the Society of Jesus whilst in Newgate; hanged, drawn and quartered at Tyburn; little information about him; relative of Bl. Anthony Page (d. 1593), a priest, executed at York solely for being a priest; see *Gillow*, Vol. V, p.231.

Paget, Commander Claude – officer in the Royal Navy; b. 3 October 1851; c. 19 March 1887; d. 30 January 1917; brought up in the Church of England by a very pious mother; took part in the Abyssinian Expedition in 1868; died by accidental drowning; see essay in J. G. F. Raupert (ed), *Roads to Rome* (1901), p.178 ("My conversion, through the grace of God, came about in this way. I made the acquaintance of a man whose brother I had previously known. I discovered that he was a Catholic, while I knew his brother to be a Protestant, and in the course of conversation I asked him one day how he explained the circumstance. His answer was simply this: 'Because the Catholic is the only safe religion to die in.' I said to myself: Good God! Can this be true? I had thought that one religion was as good as another, and that it was merely a question of birth. I had very little conversation with my friend, but I remember asking him: Were there not some very wicked Popes? To which he replied, 'There may have been some in the long list of Roman Pontiffs. One of our Saviour's chosen disciples turned out to be a traitor'...

I was also struck by the contrast between the clear fulfillment in the Catholic Church of the Savior's promise: 'the gates of Hell shall not prevail against it.' And the statement in the Homily of the Church of England, that 'all Christendom, old and young, ecclesiastics and lay people, had been drowned in damnable idolatry for the space of eight hundred years or more.' Where, I asked myself, was our Savior's promise?...

It is often said that we Catholics are such 'priest-ridden' people. I answer: If this is because we honor and obey our priests, and because we ask their advice in things spiritual and temporal, we certainly are priest-ridden, and are proud of it. We obey our priests in things spiritual because Jesus Christ said, 'He that heareth you heareth Me, and he that despiseth you despiseth Me' (St. Luke x. 16); and 'If he will not hear the Church, let him be to thee as the heathen and publican' (St. Matt. xviii. 15–17). We honor priests, because they are the anointed of the Lord, who daily offer the Body of our Lord in the Holy Sacrifice of the Mass. I know that it is difficult for the non-Catholic to grasp the exalted position which a priest must ever occupy in the eyes of a good Catholic. He is honored, not because of any good qualities which he may personally possess, but because of his holy office and of the position which he holds in the one Church of the Redeemer").

Pakenham, Hon. and Rev. Charles Reginald (name in religion Fr. Paul Mary Pakenham, CP) – priest and soldier; b. 21 September 1821, Dublin; c. 15 August 1850 (received by Wiseman); d. 1 March 1857, Mount Argus; born into a family of Irish Protestant aristocracy; fourth son of Thomas, second Earl of Longford, and of Lady Georgiana Lygon, daughter of first Earl Beauchamp; educated at Royal Military College, Sandhurst; captain in Grenadier Guards and ADC to Queen Victoria; gave up a brilliant career in the army; conversion attributed to reading the works of Newman; joined Passionist Order in 1852; ordained priest 29 September 1855; founded Irish Passionist Order at Mount Argus of which he was the first rector; indifferent health; nephew of the first Duke of Wellington who is reputed to have said, "Well, Charles, you've been a good soldier, now strive to be a good monk"; funeral in Dublin attended by thousands; when his coffin was moved thirty years later the body was found perfectly intact and incorrupt; buried in a corner of the Chapel to Blessed Paul of the Cross, Mount Argus; see Rev. Joseph Smith CP, *Paul Mary Pakenham* (1930); Madeleine Beard, *Faith and Fortune* (1997), pp.123–126; *Gillow*, Vol. V, p.233.

Palairet, Sir (Charles) Michael – diplomat; b. 29 September 1892, Berkeley, Gloucestershire; c. 1916 (received with his wife, Mary, in Paris); d. 5 August 1956, Lynch Mead, Allerford, Minehead, Somerset; educated at Eton College; joined the diplomatic service in 1905; posted to Rome in 1906; transferred to Vienna in 1908 and to Paris in 1913; various postings until made minister to Romania in 1929; in Vienna during the build-up to the Anschluss in 1938; minister, then ambassador in Greece 1939–1943; worked in the Foreign Office 1943–1948; translated German religious books; father of Anne Mary Celestine Asquith, countess of Oxford and Asquith (1916–1998); see *DNB* ("They were to remain staunch Catholics for the rest of their lives").

Paley, Frederick Apthorp – classical scholar and writer; b. 14 January 1815, Easingwold, York; c. 1846; d. 9 December 1888, Boscombe Spa, Bournemouth, Hampshire; son of Anglican rector; grandson of William Paley (1743–1805), Anglican Archdeacon of Carlisle and author of *The Evidences of Christianity*; educated at St. John's College, Cambridge where greatly influenced by the Oxford Movement; in residence at Cambridge 1838–1846 teaching a number of pupils and studying and publishing in classics and ecclesiastical architecture; in 1846 suspected of having encouraged one of his pupils, John Morris, later a Jesuit (see above), to join the Catholic Church; he was ordered to give up his rooms in college; this ruined his prospects of further advancement at Cambridge; employed 1847–1856 as private tutor in Catholic families, successively those of the Talbots (Earls of Shrewsbury), Throckmortons and Kenelm Digbys; Professor of Classical Literature at Catholic University College, Kensington, London; many articles, papers, and commentaries on classics and religion; buried in Bos-combe cemetery; see *Gillow*, Vol. V, p.234; *DNB*.

Palgrave, William Gifford – traveler, diplomat, and author; b. 24 January 1826, Parliament Street, Westminster, London; c. 1849; d. 1888, Montevideo, Uruguay; son of Sir Francis Palgrave (1788–1861), founder of the Public Record Office and convert to the Church of England from Judaism; brother of Frank Palgrave (1824–1897), anthologist, poet and art critic, Robert Palgrave (1827–1919), banker and economist, and Sir Reginald Palgrave (1829–1904), clerk of House of Commons; army officer in India; studied at Trinity College, Oxford; in the army in India; after his conversion he was for a time member of the Society of Jesus (never ordained) and missionary in Syria and Arabia, making many converts and founding numerous schools; a leading explorer and scholar of the Middle East; many publications, mainly on travel; at one time a French agent with permission of the Vatican; then several British diplomatic posts; later renounced Catholicism and came under the influence of various Eastern religious systems, especially Shintoism; minister-resident in Uruguay 1884–1888, where he became reconciled to the Catholic Church in 1884; buried in St. Thomas's cemetery, Fulham, London; see M. Allan, *Palgrave of Arabia: The Life of William Gifford Palgrave, 1826–88* (1972); *DNB*.

Palmer, Charles Ferrars (name in religion Raymund) – priest, physician and historian; b. 9 September 1819, Tamworth; c. 1842; d. 27 October 1900; son of Shirley Palmer (1786–1852), physician and writer on medicine; studied medicine at Queen's College, Birmingham; practiced as a surgeon in Tamworth and wrote the first history of the town;

joined Dominican Order in 1855; ordained priest in 1859; at Woodchester, Gloucestershire 1853–1866; then to St. Dominic's Priory. London; most of his very many publications concerned the history of the Dominican Order in England; see *DNB*.

Palmer, John Bernard, O Cist – priest; b. 15 October 1782, Dorset; d. 10 November 1852; son of small farmer; brought up Protestant; received into the Church by Fr. Leonard Brooke, SJ, chaplain to Thomas Weld, of Lulworth Castle, Dorset, where he was a valet; joined Cistercian monastery at Lulworth in 1808; ordained priest 15 August 1838; appointed prior of the small community established in Charnwood Forest in 1835; community took possession of the new monastery, Mount St. Bernard, in 1844; elected its first abbot; consecrated 18 February 1849 (first mitred abbot in England since the Reformation); long and painful final illness; see *Gillow*, Vol. V, p.239.

Palmer, William – author, theologian, and archaeologist; b. 12 July 1811, Mixbury, Oxfordshire; c. 28 February 1855, chapel of the Roman College; d. 5 April 1879, piazza Campitelli 3, Rome; son of Anglican rector, greatest influence on his life; elder brother of Sir Roundell Palmer (1812–1895), twice Lord High Chancellor of England and first Earl of Selborne; Fellow of Magdalen College, Oxford (expert in classics) 1832–1855; adherent of the Oxford Movement (drawn by personality of Newman); ordained deacon in the Church of England in 1836; anticipated Newman's argument in Tract 90; before conversion to Rome, traveled much in the east with the object of drawing together the bonds of union between English and Oriental Churches in order to facilitate inter-communion (no success); made attempts (rebuffed) to join Greek and Russian Orthodox Churches; after conversion remained devout Catholic living in Rome, devoting himself to archaeology and writing, *inter alia*, *An Introduction to Early Christian Symbolism* (1859); buried in cemetery of San Lorenzo in Campo Verano, Rome; see Robin Wheeler, "Orthodox or Catholic?: The Choice of William Palmer," *Downside Review*, January 2006, p.33 ("Palmer was all too aware that he was cut off from the Sacraments of any church; that he could not spend the rest of his life 'in studying, and even to some extent *judging*, all Churches, without belonging in God's sight to any one of them.' He could see the great happiness of his English friends who had converted, and was moved by the warmth and touching zeal they showed for the souls of others'"); *Gillow*, Vol. V, p.240; *DNB*.

Parkes (married name Belloc), Elizabeth Rayner ("Bessie") – campaigner for women's rights and journalist; b. 16 June 1829, Birmingham; c. 1864; d. 29 March 1925; both parents Unitarians and mother's background one of radical dissent; granddaughter of Dr. Joseph Priestley (1733–1804), theologian, philos- opher and discoverer of oxygen; wife of Louis Swanton Belloc, French barrister; mother of Mrs. Mary Adelaide Belloc-Lowndes, authoress, and of Hilaire Belloc (1870–1953), author, Catholic apologist, and journalist; significant friendship with Barbara Leigh Smith, later Bodichon, the two being a source of mutual education; also friend of Marian Evans, the future George Eliot; campaigned for more equality of opportunity for women and extension of women's education; founder of *English Woman's Journal*; from early 1860s attracted to the Catholic faith, encouraged by friendships with Adelaide Proctor (see below) and Cardinal Manning;

buried in churchyard of the Catholic church at Slindon; see *DNB*.

Parr, Harriet (*pseud.* Holme Lee) – novelist; b. 31 January 1828, York; d. 18 February 1900, Whittle Mead, Shanklin, Isle of Wight; one of six children; father, a traveling merchant, died when she was a child, leaving the family destitute; a governess for twelve years; helped by Charles Dickens to find a publisher for her second novel, *Gilbert Messenger* (1855), which was a great success; able to retire from teaching, move to the Isle of Wight, and concentrate on writing; published thirty or more novels and had considerable popularity, especially with Catholic readers; all her novels somewhat sentimental, but written in a refined tone and straightforward style; published four non-fiction works under her own name; unmarried (lived alone with her cats and her servant of forty years); see *The Life and Death of Jeanne d'Arc, Called the Maid*, 2 Vols. (1866); *DNB* ("She taught Sunday school and acted as a ministering angel to the local population. In fact, she was often mistaken for a Sister of Mercy").

Parsons, Gertrude (*née* Hext) – novelist; b. 19 March 1812, Restormel, Cornwall; c. 1844 (husband, Daniel Parsons (1811–1887), High Anglican curate who was taught by Newman at Oxford, converted in 1843), d. 12 February 1891, Teignmouth, Devon; deeply religious woman, who was charitable to the poor and a leading benefactor of the mission at Little Malvern; many of her books were on Catholic themes (e.g., *Thornberry Abbey* (1846), a semi-autobiographical conversion story, *Edith Mortimer* (1857) and *The Sisters of Ladywell* (1881)); edited *The Workman or Life and Leisure* to provide suitable reading material for working-class Catholics; contributor to *The Lamp, Once a Week*,

Notes and Queries, London Society, etc.; buried at priory church, Little Malvern; see *Gillow*, Vol. V, p.245; *DNB*.

Patmore, Coventry Kersey Dighton – poet and essayist; b. 23 July 1823, Woodford, Essex; c. 1864, in Rome (son by first wife, Emily August Andrews, received in 1865; second wife, Marianne Caroline Byles (d. 1880), a convert already (in 1853)); d. 26 November 1896, The Lodge, Walhampton, near Lymington, Hampshire; son of Peter George Patmore (1786–1855), writer and man of letters who was agnostic if not atheist; his mother was puritanical; educated privately; at a finishing school in Paris where he fell in love with a Miss Gore; she spurned him, leading to his romantic obsession with lost love reflected in his poetry; more than two hundred literary essays; worked as assistant in British Museum 1846–1865; agnostic in youth, later seen as liberal Protestant writer; acquainted with members of the Pre-Raphaelite Brotherhood; contributor to *The Germ*, the Pre-Raphaelite organ, and to *The St. James' Gazette*; championed causes of love, marriage and religious devotion, his most famous work being *The Angel in the House* (1854–1863) about the spirit of love in a Christian marriage; converted through the influence of Aubrey de Vere, the poet (see below), and his later to be second wife, Marianne Caroline Byles, a wealthy Catholic convert; explored the Catholic faith through a study of Aquinas and other saints; close friend of Gerard Manley Hopkins (see above) and Alice and Wilfrid Meynell (see above); culmination of his meditations was *The Rod, the Root and the Flower* (1895), reconciling earthly and heavenly love in nuptial passion; regarded the inequality of the sexes as preordained; father of Henry John Patmore (1860–1883), the poet, and Emily Honoria, a poet and mystic, who became a nun; buried in cemetery in Lymington (Catholic section); see *Autobiography* (1900); Basil Champneys, *Memoirs and Correspondence of Coventry Patmore*, 2 Vols. (1901); Shane Leslie, *Studies in Sublime Failure* (1932), pp.113–178; Derek Patmore, *The Life and Times of Coventry Patmore* (1949); W. H. Gardner, "The Achievement of Coventry Patmore I and II," *The Month*, February 1952, p.89 and April 1952, p.220; E. J. Oliver, *Coventry Patmore* (1956) "His thoughts and his beliefs had become wholly Catholic, but he was still reluctant to take the final step. The prejudices of generations, so strong that conversion at that period had almost the air of treachery to England, an argument to which he was peculiarly sensitive, the horror with which his mother's relations at Edinburgh had spoken of popery at the very outset of his religious life, and the opposition of his dead wife, all these things kept him outside the Church. Then suddenly he realized that these accumulated antipathies were not arguments but shadows which could only be dispersed by a decisive act of the will"); W. H. Gardner, "The Status of Coventry Patmore," *The Month*, October 1958, p.205; Sister M. A. Weinig, *Coventry Patmore* (1981); Antony Matthew (ed), *The Bow set in the Cloud* (1996) ("The only evidence to which the Church appeals is *self-evidence*. To the sane and simple mind all serviceable truth is self-evidence, on being simply asserted. The Gospel of Christ is merely 'good news'"); David Jones, "Coventry Patmore: Catholic 'Angel in the House' Poet," *Catholic Life*, April 2002, p.30; *Gillow*, Vol. V, p.247; *Catholic Encyclopedia*; *DNB*.

Patterson, George Hare – c. 1898 (received with his daughter, Gwendoline); formerly Unitarian minister in Ireland; see essay in J. G. F. Raupert (ed), *Roads* *to Rome* (1901), p.183 ("I looked with inquiring eyes at all the Churches, and although I found good and earnest men in all, helpful agencies here and there, I found only one Church whose news had a clear and certain sound, an unequivocal claim.... I did not trouble over mere side issues, but went straight for the main point: Authority and Divineness of commission. My investigations were primarily directed to the credentials of the Church, seeing that if they proved sound, all else must follow in logical sequence. Granting the reality of the Church's claim, no matter how great the difficulties involved, there could be no longer room for doubt regarding anything contained in the deposit of Faith. I came to view the Church as a living organism, following the natural laws of development and of assimilation, yet ever preserving its identity unchanged, by virtue, as I afterwards discovered, of the perpetual indwelling of the Holy Ghost. In no other way could its marvelous vitality be explained or accounted for...

The book ... that above all others helped to clear away my intellectual difficulties, and that showed me the soundness of the Church's position, together with the Divine nature of its mission was Newman's *Grammar of Assent*. The grace of God did the rest").

Patterson, Bishop James Laird – bishop; b. 16 November 1822; c. 1850 (received at Jerusalem; brother, Major-General William Thomas Laird Patterson (1839–1889), who had a great appreciation of Newman, received in 1866; and mother also converted); d. 3 December 1901; brought up in ordinary Protestantism of the period on the "Bible only"; studied at Trinity College, Oxford; became Anglo-Catholic curate under the influence of Pusey; after conversion ordained Catholic priest; at one time President of St. Edmund's College,

Ware, Hertfordshire 1870–1880; then Auxiliary Bishop of Westminster and titular Bishop of Emmaus; see essay in J. G. F. Raupert (ed), *Roads to Rome* (1901), p.192 ("In the set to which I belonged (the scholars of Trinity) I heard for the first time of the principle of authority as the basis of religious belief, and I immediately, as by a sort of instinct, adhered to it as a philosophy of belief and a rule of life, never for an instant doubting that the exponent of this principle was 'the Church' – that is, the Church of England as by law established.... At the end of that time a course of lectures on ecclesiastical history ... and a good deal of reading on cognate subjects, medieval architecture, archaeology, and especially the study of our ancient Churches in frequent excursions, brought home to me the perception of the great difference which there is between the medieval religion and that of the existing Church of England; it especially struck me as extraordinary that the outcome of the changes of the sixteenth century, which we were told to esteem as excellent and admirable, should evidently have been an immense decrease of religious belief and religious practice throughout the land.... [T]he more I read and reflected, and also (in visits to the Continent) saw and heard of the working of the Catholic Church, of its absolute unity in faith and discipline, the more I perceived the absence of those characteristics in the Anglican Communion.... [I] found [in Egypt and Palestine] a great variety of ancient local churches and representing some of the earliest heresies, often mutually contradictory, but all agreeing in rejecting the supremacy of the Pope. On the other hand, the Catholic Churches, whether following the Latin or the Greek, the Armenian, the Syrian, the Coptic, the Abyssinian, Maronite, or any other rite, were absolutely one in doctrine and in obedience to the Pope as

Vicar of Christ and Supreme Head of the Catholic Church").

Paul, Charles Kegan – publisher and author; b. 8 March 1828, White Lackington, near Ilminster, Somerset; c. 12 August 1890 (the day after Newman's death; he attended Newman's funeral; received at the church of the Servites, Fulham); d. 19 July 1902, 9 Avonmore Road, West Kensington, London; at Eton and Exeter College, Oxford; eldest of ten children of Anglican vicar; at Oxford regarded himself as "a very broad High Churchman"; then Anglican curate with Christian socialist views gained through his friendship with Charles Kingsley; later abandoned his living and moved on to Comtist positivism; friendships with George Eliot and Thomas Hardy; managed and purchased publishing firm, which became C. Kegan Paul & Co.; Newman greatly influenced his conversion and the re-reading of *A Grammar of Assent* "proved to be the crowning gift of the many I received from that great teacher"; also influenced by Cardinal Manning's *Religio Viatoris*; essayist and translator; friend of Wilfrid Meynell (see above); buried at Kensal Green cemetery, London; see *Faith and Unfaith, and Other Essays* (1891); "Miracle," *The Month*, October 1892, p.217; *God* (1893); *Confessio Viatoris* (1898); *Memories* (1899); *On The Way Side: Verses and Translations* (1899) (from "Freedom": "Ah Christ, if there were no hereafter/ It still were best to follow Thee"); essay in J. G. F. Raupert (ed), *Roads to Rome* (1901), p.196 (contains the concluding chapter of *Memories*) "In the training of my intellect and literary faculty, such as it is, one man had always held predominant sway. Those young men who entered on their Oxford careers towards the end of the decade, 1840–1850, found that one prophet at least had gained honor in his own country, even if

he had experienced also scorn and rejection. John Henry Newman was a moving intellectual force along with Ruskin and Carlyle…. [They] delivered their message and passed on, but Newman abode, and his intellectual influence developed into one that was moral and spiritual, preparing my soul for the great grace and revelation God had yet in store. Like Thomas à Kempis, so Newman studied day by day, sank into my soul and changed it. Since Pascal none has put so plainly as he the dread alternative – all or nothing, faith or unfaith, God or the denial of God…

But, apart from the direct leadings of God's grace and the general effect of the *Imitation* and Newman's writings, it may be well to specify more closely some of the arguments which weighed with me to accept the faith I had so long set at nought. First, and above all, was the overwhelming evidence for modern miracles, and the conclusions from their occurrence. A study in Pascal's life, when I was engaged in translating the *Pensées*, directed my special attention to the cure of Pascal's niece, of a lachrymal fistula, by the touch of the Holy Thorn, preserved at Port Royal. It is impossible to find anything of the kind better attested, and readers may judge for themselves in the narrative written by Racine, and the searching investigations by unprejudiced, and certainly not too credulous, critics, Saint-Beuve and the late Charles Bread.

Next in importance were the miracles of Lourdes, one of which, as wrought on a friend of my own, came under my notice. I do not mean, especially in the former case, that these facts proved any doctrines … but rather, that the Thorn must, from its effects, have been one that had touched the Sacred Head, that the spring at Lourdes could only have had its healing powers by the gift of God, through our Lady. It was not that miracles having been declared in the Bible made these latter occurrences possible, but that these, and in times so near our own, made the Bible miracles more credible than they were before, adding their testimony to that which the Church bears to Holy Scripture. And it was on the testimony of a living Church that I would accept the Scripture, if I accepted it at all; for surely, of all absurd figments, that of a closed revelation to be its own interpreter is the most absurd.

At Beaulieu, near Loches, the end came.... I remained in conversation with the *curé*, who was superintending some change in the arrangements of the altar. We spoke of Tours and St. Martin, of the revived cult of the Holy Face...., and at last he said, after a word about English Protestantism, 'Mais Monsieur est sans doute Catholique?' I was tempted to answer, 'A peu près?' but the thought came with overwhelming force that this was a matter in which there was 'no lore of nicely calculated less or more'; we were Catholics or not. My interlocutor was within the fold and I without; and if without, then against knowledge, against warning, for I recognized that my full conviction had at last gone where my heart had gone before. The call of God sounded in my ears, and I must perforce obey"); *DNB*.

Pearce, Joseph – writer; b. 1961, Barking, London; c. 19 March 1989; brought up in nominally Protestant and anti-Catholic family; grew to be agnostic in a Protestant culture, and involved in the National Front party's neo-nazi politics from 1976 (served two prison sentences for publishing material likely to incite racial hatred); was editor of *Nationalism Today*; had regular contact with Ulster Defence Association in Northern Ireland and became a member of the Orange Order; opposed Pope John Paul II's visit to Britain; conversion influenced by

Chesterton's "Reflections on a Rotten Apple" in *The Well and the Shallows*, by his *The Outline of Sanity*, and by distributism; also influenced by Newman, Tolkien (see below) and Belloc; after conversion co-editor of *Saint Austin Review*; Associate Professor of Literature, Ave Maria University, Florida; writer of many mainly Catholic studies; see *Wisdom and Innocence: A Life of G. K. Chesterton* (1996); *Tolkien: Man and Myth* (1998); "The Catholic Literary Revival," in V. Alan McClelland and Michael Hodgetts, *From Without the Flaminian Gate* (1999), p.295; *Flowers of Heaven: One Thousand Years of Christian Verse* (1999); *Literary Converts: Spiritual Inspiration in an Age of Unbelief* (1999); "Me and My Faith" *The Tablet*, 1 May 1999, p.609; *Solzhenitsyn: A Soul in Exile* (1999); *The Unmasking of Oscar Wilde* (1997); *Bloomsbury and Beyond: The Friends and Enemies of Roy Campbell* (2001); *Small is Still Beautiful* (2001); *Old Thunder: A Life of Hilaire Belloc* (2002); *C. S. Lewis and the Catholic Church* (2003); "Race With the Devil: From the Hell of Hate to the Well of Mercy," *This Rock*, May-June 2003; *Literary Giants, Literary Catholics* (2005); "Tradition and Conversion," in Sheridan Gilley (ed), *Victorian Churches and Churchmen* (2005), p.183; *The Quest for Shakespeare: The Bard of Avon and the Church of Rome* (2008); *Through Shakespeare's Eyes: Seeing the Catholic Presence in the Plays* (2010); "The National Front Member" in Greg Watts, *Catholic Lives* (2001) ("If you look at the history of the Church over the last 2000 years there have been major crises in every decade, major scandals, major issues of members of the Church getting it wrong and society being barbaric. Five hundred years ago the Reformation would have been seen as the end, and before that some might have thought the same in the Dark Ages. Yet the

Church has always emerged as the voice of sanity. The fact that those of us today who are trying to be saints are in a minority shouldn't surprise us. Events of the world are transient and pass, Truth is eternal"); *EWTN Audio Library* (19 November 2001; 3 March 2003); Ed West, "Rescued from racism by the love of GK," *Catholic Herald*, 5 February 2010, p.7.

Pearsall, Robert Lucas – musician, composer and antiquary; b. 14 March 1795, Clifton, Bristol; c. 2 August 1856 (on his deathbed; received by his friend the Bishop of St. Gallen); d. 5 August 1856, castle of Wartensee on Lake Constance, Switzerland; privately educated; practiced as barrister; then pursued his passions for music, history, heraldry, and genealogy on the Continent, mainly in Germany; composer chiefly of vocal music: madrigals in sixteenth century style, part-songs and church music; buried in the chapel of Wartensee Castle; staunch Anglican until shortly before his death; see E. Hunt and H. W. Hunt, *Robert Lucas Pearsall: the 'Compleat Gentleman' and his Music, 1795–1856* (1971); *Grove Music Online*; *DNB*.

Pepler, Conrad, OP (formerly Stephen Pepler) – priest and writer; b. 5 May 1908, Hammersmith, West London; c. 1919; d. 10 November 1993; Quaker background; son of Hilary Pepler (see below); worked in the print shop at Ditchling; entered the Dominican Order in 1927; ordained priest in 1933; editor of *Blackfriars*; developed a new periodical, *Life in the Spirit*, and also Blackfriars Publications; warden of Dominican conference centre, Spode House, 1953–1981; archivist; theologian of mysticism; had special love for the ancient Dominican rite; formulated an ecological theology; gave conditional absolution to Ludwig Wittgenstein at the latter's death;

see *Riches Despised: A Study of the Roots of Religion* (1957) ("The problem to be faced by the modern Christian for himself or for the millions of possible Christians around him arises simply from the fact that his religion is a wholesome religion making perfect all the good natural things that God has made, whereas the society in which he lives is a vast impersonal organization of men who at heart despise the good natural things, and treat them purely as utilities for their own benefit. The modern industrial man is out of tune with the hymn of nature, and out of time with her rhythm. Being out of tune and out of time with the rest of the divine orchestra of the universe, he is necessarily unable to appreciate the value of the Conductor, who beats out a regular pulse of which the modern industrial man is quite unaware. That makes it difficult, though not of course impossible, for the divine operation of grace to seize man and make his very heart to beat with the divine pulse of supernatural love. The barriers of a false imagination and a false culture are immense – but not insuperable"); Owen Dudley Edwards, "Four For Chesterton," *Chesterton Review*, February and May 1995, p.89; Aidan Nichols, *Dominican Gallery: Portrait of a Culture* (1997), pp.342–400.

Pepler, Harry Douglas Clark ("Hilary") – writer and printer; b. 14 January 1878, Eastbourne, Sussex; c. 1916; d. 20 September 1951, Hopkins Crank, Ditchling Common, Sussex; Quaker influences in childhood; collaborated with Eric Gill (see above), though they later disagreed; influenced by Chesterton (see above) and Belloc; converted after conversations with Fr. Vincent McNabb; writer on arts and crafts and distributism; pioneer for social improvement and the family; author of books to encourage rural Catholic self-sufficiency; later interest in puppetry; father of Fr. Conrad Pepler OP (see above); buried in churchyard of St. Margaret's, Ditchling; see A. Sheep [Pepler himself], *Missions, or Sheepfolds and Shambles* (1922) ("I submit the story of Our Blessed Lord Who chose the country for His dwelling place, a country Maid for Mother, and the hills in which to pray. Whose gospel lives with images of country life – lambs (O Lamb of God), swine, oxen, asses, hens, seed-sowing, harvests, corn and barns. Who chose His first disciples, men with country crafts, and taught them in the country. But even they wavered in the town caught in the net of disbelief and doubt which was Jerusalem. And He who spent His life by farm and lake wept over the city which had killed her prophets. It is most strange that the lovers of Our Blessed Lord should think they can succeed where He Himself has failed. The modern Baptist stands by the city cesspool, but the Jordan flows between unpopulated hills – a pure baptismal water given by God to cleanse men of their lusts and usuries"); Brocard Sewell, *Like Black Swans: Some People and Themes* (1982), Ch. 8; *DNB*.

Pepper, John Henry – illusionist and educationist; b. 17 June 1821, Westminster, London; c. 1890s; d. 25 March 1900, Leytonstone, Essex; "Professor" of Chemistry, later director at Royal Polytechnic, London; gave many displays of popular experiments, illusions, and magic-lantern displays; illusion popularly known as "Pepper's ghost" (an apparatus for producing "spectral optical illusions") had an enormous vogue; displays took him to America, Canada and Australia; also issued a series of manuals of popular science, which had a wide circulation, e.g., *The Boy's Playbook of Science* (manual of experiments which could be carried out at home); buried in Norwood cemetery; see *DNB*.

Percy (alias Fisher and Fairfax), John, SJ – priest; b. 27 September 1569, Holmside, County Durham; c. 1583; d. 3 December 1641, London; both parents Protestants; at fourteen sent to live with a Catholic woman; under her influence and that of a local Catholic priest he converted; sent to English College, Rheims, and then on to Rome in 1589; on 13 March 1593, by papal dispensation, was ordained a priest before full canonical age; entered the Society of Jesus in 1594; came to the English mission in 1595, but at once arrested in London and sent to the Bridewell; escaped and went to Yorkshire where he worked 1596–1598 (reconciled his mother and sister to the Catholic faith); joined John Gerard as a chaplain in Vaux household at Harrowden; converted members of the Digby family, including Sir Everard Digby, his wife, Mary, and John Digby of Rutland; Digbys' household chaplain in 1599; not involved in Gunpowder Plot of 1605, but considered by government officials to be guilty by association with the Digby and Vaux families; remained hidden at Harrowden until arrested there in 1610 with Fr. Nicholas Hart; tried and sentenced to death, but after a year in Gatehouse prison, commuted to exile by James I; Professor of Holy Scripture at Louvain; went back to England, but arrested immediately and imprisoned for three years; held conferences in prison (and on furlough) and reconciled many Protestants to the Church (notably countess of Buckingham, mother of George Villiers, Duke of Buckingham and the king's favorite); reputation of "Fisher the Jesuit" as a controversialist grew between 1622 and 1624 (even debated with James I himself); pardoned but again apprehended and sent to Gatehouse until 1635, when released at the intercession of Queen; writer of many works of apologetics; see *The Treatise of Faith* (1605); Timothy H. Wadkins, "King

James I meets John Percy, SJ (26 May 1622)," *Recusant History*, October 1988, p.146; *Gillow*, Vol. V, p.261; *Catholic Encyclopedia*; *DNB* ("*The Treatise* was primarily a *reductio ad absurdum* negation of Protestantism. 'There must be one true faith which has existed visibly in all ages,' Percy's argument went. Since Catholics could show a visible apostolic pedigree and Protestants only a church since Luther, the Catholic faith must be true while Protestantism was novel and therefore false. Answering Percy's question 'where was your church before Luther?' became a provocative challenge for protestants …").

Percy, Thomas – conspirator; b. 1560, Beverley, Yorkshire; c. in his youth; d. 8 November 1605, Holbeach House, Staffordshire; after Cambridge University he made career in service of his cousin, ninth Earl of Northumberland; pugnacious character; in 1602 carried a letter to James VI of Scotland, petitioning tolerance for Catholics should he succeed to the English crown; great disappointment at James' subsequent reluctance to act in this way; in May 1604 sworn into Gunpowder Plot and hired in his own name the house next to the parliament house, and later a ground-floor vault under Lords' chamber itself; died after his capture of wounds received in the struggle at Holbeach House (shot by the same bullet as Catesby); his wife a sister of John Wright, another conspirator; one of his daughters later married the son of the instigator of the plot, Robert Catesby, also named Robert; see *Gillow*, Vol. V, p.267; *DNB*.

Perrot (*vere* Barnesley), John – priest; b. 1631, Worcestershire; c. about 1647; d. 27 May 1714; after converting went over to English College, Lisbon, in 1647; Vice-President of the college in 1659 and President 1662–1670; Archdeacon of Northamptonshire, Hants, and Cambridgeshire in 1672 and Dean in 1676; at the time of the Popish Plot in 1678 he continued to exercise his pastoral charge; continued in office until his death; see *Gillow*, Vol. V, p.268.

Persons (Parsons), Robert, SJ – priest and controversialist; b. 24 June 1546, Nether Stowey, Somerset; c. about 1574 (received in Louvain; father received sometime after 1579; mother later became part of the underground Catholic network; at least two brothers, George and Richard, also converted); d. 15 April 1610, English College, Rome; sixth of eleven children of a yeoman; studied at Balliol College, Oxford (later Fellow, Bursar and Dean there); twice he subscribed to oaths of supremacy, but never ordained in the Established Church; forced to resign fellowship, partly because of his Catholic leanings; set out for Padua to study medicine, but stopped at Louvain and was reconciled to the Catholic Church, probably by Fr. William Good, SJ; walked the road from Venice to Rome as act of penance; entered the Society of Jesus in Rome in 1575; ordained priest in July 1578; sent with St. Edmund Campion, SJ (see above) to England by Pope Gregory XIII and landed in 1580; firmly opposed church papism, i.e., occasional conformity by Catholics; made many converts on tour through London, Midlands, West country; set up a printing press and produced pamphlets; after Campion's arrest, he retired to the Continent (for the rest of his life he wore the rope that had bound Campion's hands to the hurdle tightly round his waist as an act of mortification); took part in plans for a Spanish invasion of England; opened schools, seminaries and priests' residences; rector of English College, Rome; prefect of the English mission; taken as supporting claim to the English throne of Isabella,

Infanta of Spain, as being a descendant of John of Gaunt; played a major part in contention between Jesuits and Seculars; lifelong collaboration with William Allen; unequalled as a controversialist; reputation suffered from what came to be known as the "black legend," the long English tradition of anti-Jesuit propaganda; buried next to Cardinal Allen before high altar of chapel at English College, Rome; see *The First Booke of the Christian Exercise, Appertayning to Resolution* (1582) (revised editions of 1585 and 1607 known as *The Christian Directory*); Victor Houliston, "The Fabrication of the Myth of Father Parsons," *Recusant History*, October 1994, p.141; Victor Houliston, "The Polemical *Gravitas* of Robert Persons," *Recusant History*, May 1995, p. 291; Francis Edwards, *Robert Persons: The Biography of an Elizabethan Jesuit, 1546–1610* (1995); *Gillow*, Vol. V, p.273; *Catholic Encyclopedia*; *DNB*.

Phillimore, John Swinnerton – classical scholar and poet; b. 26 February 1873, Boconnoc, Cornwall; c. 24 August 1905; d. 16 November 1926, Cam Cottage, Shedfield, Hampshire; educated at Christ Church, Oxford (best classical scholar of his time, gaining first classes in classical moderations (1893) and in *literae humaniores* (1895); Professor of Greek and Latin, Glasgow; many articles on classical subjects; wrote much poetry (*Things New and Old* (1918) reflects the effect of his conversion); friend of Hilaire Belloc; see "Blessed Thomas More and the Arrest of Humanism in England," *Dublin Review*, July 1913, p.1; S. N. D., "John Swinnerton Phillimore," *The Month*, February 1927, p.97 ("The simplicity of his faith was a very beautiful thing. He loved the Church with all the ardor of his strong nature; he identified himself with her interests; he obeyed her laws with docility and

loyalty, and he never ceased thanking God for His great mercy in leading him onto the true fold"); *DNB*.

Phillips, Arthur – composer and university professor; b. 1605; c. 1656; d. 27 March 1695; studied at New College, Oxford; organist of Magdalen College, Oxford; Choragus or Professor of Music at Oxford 1639–1656; "wrote settings of royalist verse, a set of keyboard variations, and some instrumental ensemble music" (*DNB*); after becoming a Catholic he resigned his position at Oxford and went to France as organist to Queen Henrietta Maria; returned to England after the Restoration and became steward of a Catholic gentleman (usually thought to be John Caryll) in Harting, Sussex; see *Grove Music Online*; *DNB*.

Phillips, Lucy Agnes – c. 15 August 1851 (received by Newman; her son and two daughters were received, also by Newman, 22 August 1851); d. 3 March 1857; daughter of Charles John Vaughan (1816–1897), headmaster of Harrow school and later Anglican Dean of Llandaff; several of her brothers attained good positions in the Church of England; widow of George Peregrine Phillips (d. 1847, aged thirty-five), an Evangelical clergyman; a chance remark made to her dying husband by his doctor, William Duke (1805–1864), a friend of Newman, who had converted with his wife and eight children in August 1864, awakened her interest in Catholicism; her conversion was greatly influenced by Fr. Joseph Gordon (see above) of the Birmingham Oratory; much correspondence also with Newman before her conversion; she and her children had to escape to Malines in Belgium to prevent her family, who resented her conversion, from seizing the children; later they returned to live near the Oratory; she gave herself up to works of charity until her health broke down;

after her death an uncle and aunt of her children tried to reclaim them to Protestantism, but after legal action two Catholics were appointed as sole guardians; she established a small hospital in Birmingham with the help of the Oratorians; her son George E. Phillips (1843–1918) subsequently became a Catholic priest in 1869, rector of the Junior House at Ushaw 1884–1914, and author of *The Extinction of the Ancient Hierarchy* (1905); her daughter Elizabeth Agnes married Richard Pope (see below); see Fr. George E. Phillips, *Early Reminiscences of Cardinal Newman and of His First Fellow Oratorians*, Ushaw College Yearbook, March 1916 (note by her son on being taken at the age of eight, at the time of his mother's conversion, to the convent chapel of the Sisters of the Holy Childhood, St. Leonards, where his mother stayed after she became a widow: "At the altar a priest was saying Mass; and, though, I understood nothing of what he was doing, there was something in the grave and silent way in which he moved about, joined to the respectful recollection of the people present, which made me feel that there was a mysterious sacredness about the place very different from anything I had elsewhere experienced. I did not then know that Our Blessed Lord himself was there, and that His grace was working in my heart"); Stanley L. Jaki, *Newman to Converts: An Existential Ecclesiology* (2001), Ch. 12 ("About the Notes of the Church, which he now called to Mrs. Phillips' attention, [Newman] said: 'The more obvious reasons for believing the Church to come from God are its great notes, as they are called – such as its antiquity, universality, its unchangeableness through so many revolutions and controversies, its adaptation to our wants.' From pondering the Notes one could recognize the nature of the Church as a guide given by heaven to man.

Being a guide it had to be a living guide, different from mere written texts, unable to settle matters

What Newman now said was aimed at a typical evangelical, bent on the Bible and uneasy about a Church. And Newman aimed with extremely sharp contrasts that may sound almost blasphemous in this age of a Catholic return to the Bible: 'The more you think on these subjects, the more, under God's grace, will you be led to see that the Catholic Church is God's *guide* to you! How ignorant we are! Do we not *want* a guide? Is the structure of Scripture such as to answer the purposes of a guide? How can a bare letter written 2000 years ago, though inspired, *guide* an individual now? Every thing has its use – God uses it according to its use – Is it the use of a written Word to answer doctrinal questions starting up to the end of time? As little surely, as it is the use of a spade to saw with, or a plough to reap with.' The question to ponder was the connection between the fact of a Revelation and the channels through which it was given so that it might function clearly: 'If then Divine Mercy has given individuals, you and me, a revelation, *how*, in what *channel*, does he bring it home to us?' The channel was the visible Church: 'Even the Jews, whose doctrinal system was so simple, had a visible church'").

Pickles, Wilfred – actor-comedian and broadcaster; b. 13 October 1904, 24 Conway Street, Halifax; c. 1930 (marriage convert); d. 27 March 1978, 19 Courcels, Brighton; errand boy at twelve and shop assistant at thirteen; then worked for his father in building trade; got involved in amateur dramatics; became BBC news reader and program announcer (first one to speak with a northern accent); fund raiser for children's charities after early death of his son; later career as a variety artist in comedy and pantomime; fronted (with his wife, Mabel) first British quiz show, *Have a Go*, to give away prizes; later a character actor; see *DNB*.

Piggins, J – brought up as an Anglican; former Anglo-Catholic minister; converted at time of South India question; see "More Converts Explain," The Month, November 1956, p.279 ("I saw quite clearly for the first time that, whatever casuistry one employed, it was impossible for any normally intelligent person to believe that Cranmer and his associates had not deliberately intended to do away with the sacrifice of the Mass, the unchanging Christian sacrifice of the previous fifteen hundred years").

Pike, Blessed William – layman and martyr; b. in Dorsetshire; c. 1586; d. December 1591, Dorchester; joiner who lived at Moors, West Parley; converted by Ven. Thomas Pilcher (b. 1557) who was executed at Dorchester on 21 March 1587; tried for high treason for being reconciled to the Church of Rome and denying the Queen's supremacy; confessed that he maintained the authority of the Roman See; asked at his death what had brought him to that resolution, he was still able to say, "Nothing but the smell of a pilchard," this being a pun on the name of the martyr who converted him, which was sometimes spelt Pilchard, his own name also being that of a fish; hanged, cut down alive, bowelled, and quartered; see Challoner, *Memoirs of Missionary Priests* ("Being cut down all alive and being a very able, strong man, when the executioner came to throw him on the block to quarter him, he stood upon his feet, whereupon the Sheriff's men, overmastering him, threw him down, and pinned his hands fast to the ground with their halberds, and so the butchery was perfected"); L. E. Whatmore, "The Venerable William

Pike, Layman," *Recusant History*, April 1968, p.258; *Catholic Encyclopedia*.

Pittar, Fanny Maria – b. 1813, Scotland; c. 1842 (received with three of her children, among whom was Fr. John Pittar, SJ (1837–1889); d. 24 December 1889, "Refuge de Marie," Ghent; moved to London at age of sixteen; brought up as High Church Anglican; later went to India with her husband, John; her husband gave up any religious practice and she went to live with her parents in Dublin; renewed a friendship begun in India with a Mrs. Gray, now in Edinburgh, who had subsequently become a Catholic; she visited Mrs. Gray in order to convert her to Protestantism, but was converted by her to the Catholic faith; succeeded in having her children baptized, but her parents wanted them brought up Protestant; escaped with her children to Brittany; both of her sons became priests of the Society of Jesus, though both predeceased her; see *A Protestant Converted to Catholicity by Her Bible and Prayer-Book* (1895) ("The [Catholic] preacher, the Right Rev. Dr. Gillis, commenced by calling the attention of his congregation to the Protestant and Catholic calendars.... He then showed how every day in the Catholic calendar is dedicated to God by some pious and holy remembrance; every day the Catholic Church is open, and every day she invites her faithful children to join her, in offering to the offended majesty of heaven the all-meritorious acceptable and satisfactory sacrifice and atonement of Jesus Christ crucified for our redemption...

He then turned ... to the Protestant calendar: '*The fisheries north of the Tweed open.*' An announcement purely material, and interesting only to fishermen and lovers of salmon. Next, '*Partridge and pheasant shooting ends.*' Sorrowful tidings to the sportsman and the *gourmand*!

Then, '*The Purification of the Blessed Virgin!*' Why announce a religious ceremony or feast in no way observed by their church? And why call the Virgin *Blessed*, when they so openly abuse the Catholics for so doing?'").

Plunkett-Greene, Olivia – socialite; b. 1907; c. 1930 (under the influence of St. Teresa of Avila and St. John of the Cross; her mother, Gwen Plunkett-Greene (1878–1957), daughter of Sir Hubert Parry, the composer, and niece by marriage of Baron Friedrich von Hügel (1852–1925), whose letters she edited in 1928, received in 1926) d. 1955; influence on Evelyn Waugh's conversion; she had, according to Fr. Martin D'Arcy, "a peculiar and inimitable cast of faith of her own"; in later life a recluse.

Pollard, Margaret Steuart (*née* Gladstone) ("Peggy") – poet; b. 1 March 1904, 2 Whitehall Court, London; c. 1947; d. 13 November 1996, Truro, Cornwall; great granddaughter of William Gladstone; first-class honors in both parts of oriental languages tripos at Cambridge, first woman to do so; initial interest in Hinduism, but became interested in the Eastern Orthodox church; translator of church Slavonic; Sanskrit scholar; worked to protect Cornwall's countryside; Cornish secretary for Council for the Preservation of Rural England 1935–1945; helped to revive Cornish language, chiefly by writing "mystery plays"; involved with Cornish bardic gathering, the Gorsedd, and became a bard in 1938; writer on Cornwall; after her conversion many Catholic initiatives and charitable activities; helped to revive in 1965 fifteenth-century guild of Our Lady of the Portal, supported building of a Catholic church in Truro, Our Lady of the Portal and St. Piran (the Cornish national saint), which was opened in 1973 on presumed site of a medieval chapel; see *DNB*.

Pollen, John Hungerford – writer, architect and decorative artist; b. 19 November 1820, 6 New Burlington Street, London; c. 20 October 1852 (Rouen, France; daughter-in-law, Mrs. Maud Beatrice Pollen, received in 1898); d. 2 December 1902, 11 Pembridge Crescent, London; great great nephew of Samuel Pepys; educated at Eton and Christ Church, Oxford; Fellow of Merton College, Oxford and influenced by the Tractarian movement; in summer 1847 traveled to France with two Oxford friends, Thomas William Allies (see above) and John Wynne, to discover how the Catholic Church succeeded in bringing faith and hope to the poorest parts of the community; Anglican curate at St. Saviour's, Leeds, (see entry for Thomas Minster), working with the poor (did not convert to Rome when the other clergy there did, but two years later); husband of Maria Margaret Pollen (1838–1919) (see below); sometime Professor of Fine Arts at Catholic University College, Dublin; associated with Pre-Raphaelite Brotherhood; many architectural commissions, including University Church in Dublin and ceiling of chapel of Merton College, Oxford); at one time private secretary to George Robinson, Marquess of Ripon (see below); one of Newman's most devoted friends; buried in family vault at Kensal Green cemetery, London; see *Narrative of Five Years at St. Saviour's* (1851), Anne Pollen, *John Hungerford Pollen, 1820–1902* (1912) ("Every doubt is at rest, and I have found that kind of calm which one needs repose and reflection to enjoy in full. I cannot tell you how great an advantage I think it to have been able to do this out of England"); *DNB* ("During the time he spent in Rome immediately after his conversion, Pollen was introduced to William Thackeray, who described Pollen as 'the most interesting man I have met here … and I try to understand from him what can be the secret of the religion for which he has given up rank, chances and all the good things in life'").

Pollen (*née* La Primaudaye), Maria Margaret ("Minnie") – expert in antique textiles; b. 10 April 1838, Leyton, Essex; c. 1851; d. 1919; daughter of Charles James La Primaudaye (1807–1859) (see above); wife of John Hungerford Pollen (see above); from a Huguenot family; brought up as an Anglican; lectured on textiles and exhibited her collection of lace (published *Seven Centuries of Lace* (1908)); mother of Fr. John Hungerford Pollen, SJ, priest of the Society of Jesus; of Lieutenant Walter Hungerford Pollen (1860–1889) of the Royal Engineers; of Fr. Anthony Cecil Hungerford Pollen (1860–1940), priest of the Birmingham Oratory, who as a naval chaplain won the Distinguished Service Cross at the Battle of Jutland for a work of rescue in which he was severely burned; of Commander Francis Gabriel Hungerford Pollen of the Royal Navy, who served in the Gordon Relief Expedition and in Burma; of Fr. George Hungerford Pollen, SJ (1863–1930), also a priest of the Society of Jesus; of Arthur Joseph Hungerford Pollen (1866–1937), barrister, businessman, expert on gunnery, and chairman of *The Tablet*; of Captain Stephen Hungerford Pollen, at one time of Duke of Edinburgh's (Wiltshire) Regiment, ADC to Viceroy of India, 1894–1898, served in South Africa; of Clement Hungerford Pollen (1869–1934), assistant private secretary to Sir Ambrose Shea, when governor of the Bahamas; of Anne Mary Hungerford Pollen, a nun; and of Margaret Pollen.

Poole, Maria Spencer Ruscombe (known as Minnie in her family) (name in religion Sister Mary Imelda) – b. 1815; c. 1845 (received with her sisters, Elizabeth and Lucy; another sister,

Susannah and her husband, James Spencer Northcote (see above) were received shortly afterwards); d. 1881; daughter of a solicitor; both parents died early; she and her sisters, Elizabeth (widowed early) and Lucy, were greatly influenced by the Tractarian movement and by Newman's sermons; they had Pusey as a spiritual director; they were greatly affected by the conversion of J. M. Capes (see above); they went out to Rome 1846–1848 where they met Newman who became a great friend; in 1849 she and Lucy (Sr. Mary Columba, d. 1850) entered St. Catherine's Convent at Clifton, Mother Margaret Hallahan's Dominican community; acted as Mother Margaret's right hand; became provincial in 1868; died suddenly; see "The Modern Pilgrim's Progress or the History of Puseyism in a Dream," *The Rambler*, 11 February 1853, p.122; Sugg, *Ever Yours Affly: John Henry Newman and His Female Circle* (1996).

Pope, Richard Vercoe (known as "Pa Dick") – teacher; b. 1830; d. 1903; brother of Thomas Alder Pope (see below); both parents Methodists and he was brought up in this faith; attended London University and became an Anglican; worked for several years as a missionary in the Society for the Propa- gation of the Gospel in south-east India; example of Indian Catholics led to his conversion; afterwards cut off completely by his own people, notably his two brothers, both Protestant ministers, one Anglican and one Methodist (but later reconciliation with the latter); came to the Oratory School, Edgbaston as second master at start of 1862; taught wide range of subjects; kind and sympathetic teacher; wife died in June 1862, leaving him with four young children; in 1867 married Elizabeth Agnes, daughter of Mrs. Lucy Phillips (see above) and had four more children, eldest of whom was Fr. Hugh Pope, OP

(1869–1946); she died giving birth to her fourth child; after his wife's death he became a mild, quiet and very pious man. see Paul Shrimpton, *A Catholic Eton?: Newman's Oratory School* (2005).

Pope, Thomas Alder – priest, teacher, writer and translator; b. 1819, Bedeque, Prince Edward Island, Nova Scotia; c. 1853; d. 1904; brother of Richard Vercoe Pope (see above); brought up as a Methodist; at school in Cornwall; at Jesus College, Cambridge, where he came under the influence of Tractarianism; Anglican curate whose effigy was burned in 1850 by his parishioners who objected to his High Church views; on his becoming a Catholic he was completely cut off by his own people; after his wife's death he was left a widower with two small children; he went to France, his daughter being educated in a convent, whilst he and his son lived at Monsieur Labbé's school; taught at the Birmingham Oratory school for three years; both children having died, he joined the Oratory in 1867; ordained priest in 1869; in 1879 accompanied Newman to Rome when he received the Cardinalate; see *An Introduction to the History of France* (1860).

Poskitt, Bishop Henry John – bishop; b. 6 September 1888, Birkin, near Pontefract, Yorkshire; c. 1915; d. 19 February 1950; born into Anglican family, but had recusant forebears and was related to Bl. Nicholas Postgate; former Anglican minister; ordained Catholic priest in 1917; Doctor of Divinity and canon lawyer; fourth Bishop of Leeds 1936–1950; much work in developing Catholic education and child welfare in diocese; buried in the cemetery at St. Edward's, Clifford, near Leeds; see Robert Finnigan and James Hagerty (ed), *The Bishops of Leeds, 1878–1985: Essays in Honour of David Konstant* (2005), p.95.

Potter, Thomas Joseph – priest, poet, and novelist; b. 9 June 1828, Scarborough, Yorkshire; c. 24 February 1847; d. 31 August 1873, All Hallows' College, Dublin; parents intended him to take orders in the Church of England, but he was received into the Catholic Church at the age of eighteen and joined Stonyhurst College; entered All Hallows' College in 1854; ordained priest 28 June 1857; Professor of *Belles Lettres and Sacred Eloquence* (later Director) at All Hallows' College; many poems (mainly religious), several novels and short stories; wrote guidebook drawing on his experience at All Hallows', *Sacred Eloquence, or, The Theory of Preaching* (1868) (which became a standard text for seminarians); provided companion volume in *The Spoken Word, or, The Art of Extempore Preaching* (1872). see *Gillow*, Vol. V, p.349; *DNB*.

Poulton (Pulton), Ferdinando – jurist; b. 1535, Desborough, Northamptonshire; c. 1598; d. 20 January 1617/8, Bourton, Buckinghamshire; Fellow of Christ's College, Cambridge, commoner of Brasenose College, Oxford, and member of Lincoln's Inn; always a student of philosophy, jurisprudence and theology; writings mainly on law; two of his sons, Thomas and Ferdinando, became Jesuits; one of his daughters, Eugenia (b. 1580) became one of the foundresses of the English Benedictine convent at Ghent and its second abbess; buried in the parish church of Desborough; see *Gillow*, Vol. V, p.352.

Pounde (*alias* Duke, Harrington, Gallop, Wallop), Thomas, SJ – Jesuit lay brother; b. 29 May 1539, Belmont, Hampshire; c. 1570; d. 5 March 1615/6, Belmont; son of a wealthy gentleman; studied law; was for a long time in favor with Elizabeth I; conformed to the Established Church; after his conversion to

Catholicism he was inwardly determined to become a priest; wrote several controversial works; committed to various prisons between 1574 and 1584; in 1579, whilst in prison, admitted to the Society of Jesus; obtained his final release in 1604; died in the room in which he was born; see Stefanio Tutino, "Makynge Recusancy Death Outrighte?" *Recusant History*, May 2004, p.31 ("In 1574, as he was about to leave the country to go 'beyond the seas', his plan was uncovered and he was imprisoned by Elizabeth's agents; he would not be released until thirty years later, in 1604, upon pardon by James I"); *Gillow*, Vol. V, p.354.

Poyer, Very Rev. Mgr. Charles – priest; b. 1860, Windermere; c. 1880; educated at Haileybury; successively Professor at the Institut Goin-Lambert, Rouen; Vicaire of St. Romain and Aumonier de l'Assomption, minor canon of Rouen; joined the English mission; private secretary to Cardinal Vaughan; private chamberlain to Pope Leo XIII; chaplain of Tyburn Convent, Marble Arch, London; see essay in J. G. F. Raupert (ed), *Roads to Rome* (1901), p.206 ("I joined the Church from two motives only: the first the *authority* of the Catholic Church, and the second her *unity of doctrine*.

These two facts seemed to me to require explanation, and after trying to discover authoritative teaching and unity of faith amongst Low Churchmen, Broad Churchmen, and lastly with the High Church party, I finally turned my attention to the Catechism of the Council of Trent. This gave me, what for many years I had been seeking for – a clear and logical reason for submitting my private judgment, in matters of faith and morals, to that Divine Institution which was founded by Jesus Christ to 'teach all nations.'

Where that Institution was to be found, the unity of its doctrine, its infallibility, its power, its sanctity, and other prerogatives, were truths which, by the grace of God, became to my mind logical conclusions from following step by step those marvelous explanations of the teaching of the Holy Roman Catholic and Apostolic Church which are contained in the Catechism of the Council of Trent.

The mind was convinced, but that was not sufficient. The heart had to be converted. How this miracle was effected only those will understand who have, in prayer, sought for that peace which the world cannot give").

Prestage, Edgar – historian and Portuguese scholar; b. 20 July 1869, Manchester; c. 1886 (received with his mother, Elizabeth Rose (1843/4–1917)); d. 10 March 1951, 16 Holland Street, Kensington, London; permanent bond with the Portuguese ("Religion", he said, "proved a closer tie than nationality"); first Professor of Portuguese at King's College, London University; Knight of St. Thiago; editor and translator of various Portuguese works; member of Portuguese Royal Academy and of Lisbon Geographical Society; son-in-law of Goncalves Crespo, the Portuguese poet, through marriage to Maria Cristina, his daughter; his wife committed suicide in 1918; traditionalist and monarchist; many publications, mainly concerned with Portuguese restoration of 1640; supporter of Salazar; in later years more concerned with his lifelong commitment to Catholicism than with his further research; see *Portugal: a Pioneer of Christianity* (1933); *DNB*.

Preston, John – priest; b. 29 October 1712, London; son of an ironmonger; the most promising student at Merchant Taylors' school at time of his conversion and forced to leave; left to cope for himself and obtained a post as corrector of the Greek press; entered English College,

Lisbon, in 1732; ordained priest in 1736; discharged duties of President and Vice-President of the college, but never given those offices; introduced into Portugal the new Newtonian philosophy (on which he wrote a treatise); writer of other philosophical works; held in high esteem by the Portuguese court; in 1775 tutor to the prince of Brazil; see *Gillow*, Vol. V, p.362.

Price, Theodore – clergyman; b. c.1570; Bron-y-Foel, Merioneth, Wales; d. 15 December 1631, Westminster; educated at Jesus College, Oxford; took Anglican orders; principal of Hart Hall, Oxford, 1604–1622; fellow of Jesus College; allied himself with the ceremonialism of William Laud; appointed a prebendary at Westminster Abbey, but no further preferment; friend of Hugh Holland (see above); good evidence for his reputed conversion; see *DNB* ("Following unsuccessful surgery for 'the Torment of the Stone', Price told Roman Catholic visitors of his 'Affection and Devotion' for their church, and received Roman rites. In addition, he emphatically refused to be attended by any Church of England clergyman. The conversion became a *cause célèbre*, with Price's burial at Westminster Abbey on 21 December seemingly delayed by the reluctance of the prebendaries to conduct a burial service").

Price, William Benedict, OSB (otherwise known as Jones, possibly his real name) – priest; b. in London; d. 19 October 1639; after his conversion went over to Douai College; ordained priest 1598; entered the Benedictine Order; procurator for the English Benedictines of the Spanish congregation; went on the English mission and became superior; elected President-General in 1629; great sufferings in prison during his many years on the mission; see *Gillow*, Vol. V, p.368.

Procter, Miss Adelaide Anne (sometimes used pseudonym Mary Berwick) – poet and women's activist; b. 30 October 1825, Bedford Square, London; c. 1851 (received with her two younger sisters); d. 2 February 1864; daughter of Bryan Walter Procter (1787–1874), better known as "Barry Cornwall," the poet, playwright, song writer, and biographer of Charles Lamb; regular contributor to the weekly journal *Household Words*, edited by Charles Dickens; principal poetic work, *Legends and Lyrics* (1858) and her religious poems, *A Chaplet of Verses* (1862); her poetry was more popular than that of any other living writer except for Alfred Lord Tennyson; tireless social reformer and philanthropist, who worked with the disadvantaged; one of the founders of *The English Woman's Journal* to further the cause of women entering the workforce; health never very robust; buried in Kensal Green cemetery, London; see David Jones, "Adelaide Anne Proctor: Poet and Reformer," *Catholic Life*, February 2005, p.38 ("Why shouldst thou fear the beautiful angel, Death, Who waits thee at the portals of the skies, Ready to kiss away thy struggling breath, Ready with gentle hand to close thine eyes?... Oh what were life if life were all? Thine eyes were blinded by their tears, or thou wouldst see, Thy treasures wait thee in the far-off skies, And Death, thy friend, will give them all to thee"); *Gillow*, Vol. V, p.370; *DNB*.

Prout, Elizabeth (name in religion Mother Mary Joseph of Jesus) – nun; b. 2 September 1820, Coleham Head, Shrewsbury; c. between late 1843 and 1846, possibly on 25 March 1844 (strong oral tradition that she was received by Bl. Dominic Barberi; her mother became a Catholic before her death in 1862); d. 11 January 1864, Holy Cross Convent, Sutton, St. Helens, Lancashire; father, a cooper, was a baptized Catholic who no longer practiced, mother a devout Anglican; converted under the influence of Fr. Barberi who opened the first Passionist monastery in England at Aston Hall, two miles from her home; entered novitiate of the Sisters of the Infant Jesus, but withdrew because of ill-health; ran a school for the poor in Manchester; foundress in Manchester in 1852 of the Sisters of the Cross and Passion, set up to offer contemplative consecrated life to women who could not afford the dowries required by existing Orders; aim of the Order a radical identification with Our Lord in His Passion, partly through a life of personal austerity and partly through a commitment to serve Him in the poor; set up many schools in poor areas to safeguard the Catholic faith, plus several convents; worked with Fr. Ignatius Spencer, CP (see below) to rewrite the original rule making it more obviously a version of the Passionist Rule of St. Paul of the Cross; always in delicate health; buried in St. Anne's cemetery, Sutton, but her remains re-interred (like those of Fr. Ignatius Spencer) in Bl. Dominic Barberi's shrine in the church of St. Anne and Blessed Dominic; see Dr. Edna Hamer (Sister Dominic Savio), *Elizabeth Prout (1820–1864): A Religious Life for Industrial England* (1994); Sr. Dominic Savio CP, "Elizabeth Prout," *Catholic Life*, April 2005, p.47; Sr. Dominic Savio Hamer, CP, *With Christ to His Passion* (2008); Dominic Savio Hamer, "M. Elizabeth Prout, CP," in Joanna Bogle (ed), *English Catholic Heroines* (2009), p.237; *DNB*.

Pryce-Jones, Alan Payan – book critic, author and journalist; b. 18 November 1908, 17 South Street, Mayfair, London; c. before his move to the United States (converted by Fr. Martin D'Arcy); d. 22 January 2000, Galveston, Texas, United States; son of Colonel Henry Morris Pryce-Jones of the Coldstream Guards; maternal great grandfather was Lord Grey of the Reform Bill; educated at Eton and Magdalen College, Oxford; aesthete at Oxford forming many life-long friendships, e.g., with Harold Acton, John Betjeman, Anthony Powell; sent down without a degree in 1928 after being gated but slipping out to a dance and being caught; assistant editor of the *London Mercury* 1928–1932; in 1934 married Thérèse Carmen May ("Poppy") Fould Springer (1914–1953) whose French-born Jewish family owned extensive property in Austria and the Palais Abbatial at Royaumont in France; lived the Viennese high life until the Anschluss; in World War II served in France with the 4th Hussars and then an intelligence staff officer at Bletchley Park; then in northern Italy becoming a lieutenant-colonel, and finally in Vienna as a liaison officer with the Soviet army; very successful editor of the *Times Literary Supplement* 1948–1959 (proposed by Stanley Morison (see above), the previous editor); widened the scope of the *TLS* and introduced a Catholic tendency; great raconteur; Old Vic and National Portrait Gallery trustee; on the Royal College of Music council; major influence on the early development of the Third Programme at the BBC; librettist of Lennox Berkeley's 1954 opera, *Nelson*; many lectures for the British Council; moved to United States in 1960 to be a Ford Foundation advisor; worked as a book critic for the *New York Herald Tribune*, the *World Journal Tribune* and *Newsday* 1963–1971; settled in Newport, Rhode Island; father of David Pryce-Jones (b. 1936), journalist and author, expert on Middle East, Eastern Europe and intelligence matters; buried at Viarmes, near Chantilly, Oise, France; see (ed), *An Outline of Modern Knowledge* (1956); *The Bonus of Laughter* (1987) (memoirs) ("My feeling for

Catholicism was much like that of Evelyn Waugh. I needed it as a force of order. I needed the Petrine rock to sustain me. And in those days Catholic observance was a delight. Benediction, Tenebrae, the music of Palestrina or Victoria, a numinous presence carefully evoked, spread glory over the liturgical year. It still took me a decade to convert a predisposition to a way of life…

I needed order, I needed logic, and in the Church of England I found neither.… I concluded that there are two reasons for becoming, or remaining, a Catholic. One is the unquestioning unintellectual confidence of the Sicilian or Irish peasant; one is the need of a strong and disciplined structure of belief, unaffected in its essentials by time or circumstances: a Rock of Ages…

I was not to foresee, in 1951, what would happen only a few years later. I could not guess that an excellent old man would be so feckless, so inane indeed, as to dismantle nearly two thousand years of Christian experience in pursuit of an aggiornamento; to set aside the grace and dignity bestowed by the human imagination on liturgical music and words for the sake of cheap pieties sung to an electric guitar; to attenuate whatever in Catholic life requires effort or skill in order to tempt other denominations into the fold; and above all to vulgarize, to pare down; to show largeness of mind by appointing to distribute the communion wafer a middle-aged lady in sensible tweeds.

By now, attendance in a Catholic Church is often an affliction to the minority who resent the transformation of God the Father into God the Pop, while the majority look elsewhere for what the Church once had to offer"); *DNB*.

Pryor, Alfred Reginald – botanist and author; b. 24 April 1839, Hatfield, Hertfordshire; c. 1858; d. 18 February 1881, Baldock, Hertfordshire; father a brewer; converted whilst at University College, Oxford; by 1873 was interested in botany; worked on *A Flora of Hertfordshire* for several years (published posthumously in 1887); bequeathed to Cardinal Manning a large sum of money for Catholic educational purposes; unmarried; see *Gillow*, Vol. V, p.371; *DNB*.

Pugin, Augustus Welby Northmore – architect, ecclesiologist, writer and designer; b. 1 March 1812, 39 Keppel Street, Russell Square, London; c. 1835 (his second wife, Anne, was received in 1839); d. 14 September 1852, St. Augustine's (now The Grange), Ramsgate, Kent; only son of Auguste Charles Pugin (1768/9–1832), a French architect, archaeologist and architectural artist; precocious child with fascination for medieval architecture and drawing; father nominal Catholic, but brought up by his English mother as Protestant; drawn to Catholicism originally by the beauty of medieval architecture, but also wrote: "I have long seen the fallacy of the new sects, and trust ere long I shall be united in the original true and apostolic church, which suffers no variation" (letter to his principal human influence, E. J. Willson (1787–1854) a Catholic architect); after conversion he devoted himself to the furtherance of his faith and of Gothic architecture; his central idea was the equation of Christianity with Gothic, or pointed, architecture and his influence on the course of the Gothic revival was great; most important commissions were the Catholic cathedrals at Birmingham, Southwark, Nottingham, Newcastle upon Tyne; Mount St. Bernard's Abbey, Leicestershire (first monastery in England since the Reformation); Maynooth College, Ireland; the new Houses of Parliament; St. Augustine, Ramsgate, Kent; St. Giles, Cheadle, Staffordshire; St. Edmund's College, Ware, Hertfordshire;

Wiseman and Newman questioned his exclusive attachment to Gothic architecture and to rood screens in particular; his health broke down at end of his life and he was certified insane; his first two wives died early (the first in childbirth); his third, Jane, survived him; eight children from the three marriages; his son, Edward Welby (1834–1875, also important architect; buried in the Pugin chantry in St. Augustine's Church (tomb designed by his son); see *Contrasts* (1836); *The True Principles of Pointed or Christian Architecture* (1841); *An Apology for the Revival of Christian Architecture in England* (1843); *Glossary of Ecclesiastical Ornament* (1844); *A Treatise on Chancel Screens and Rood Lofts* (1851); Michael Trappes-Lomax, *Pugin: A Medieval Victorian* (1932) ("The real reason [why Pugin became a Catholic was] that he was 'perfectly convinced that the Roman Catholic Church is the only true one.' 'I learned the truths of the Catholic religion,' he afterwards said, 'in the crypts of the old cathedrals of Europe. I sought for these truths in the modern Church of England, and found that since her separation from the centre of Catholic unity she had little truth, and no life; so, without being acquainted with a single Priest, through God's mercy, I resolved to enter His Church'.... 'With what delight did I trace the fitness of each portion of those glorious edifices to the rites for whose celebration they had been erected. Then did I discover that the service I had been accustomed to attend and admire was but a cold and heartless remnant of past glories, and that those prayers which in my ignorance I had ascribed to reforming piety, were in reality only scraps plucked from the solemn and perfect offices of the ancient Church. Pursuing my researches among the faithful pages of the old chronicles I discovered the tyranny, apostasy and bloodshed by which the

new religion [Protestantism] had been established, the endless strifes, dissensions, and discords that existed among its propagators, and the devastation and ruin that attended its progress: opposed to all this, I considered the Catholic Church, existing with uninterrupted apostolical succession, handing down the same faith, Sacraments, and ceremonies unchanged, unaltered through every clime, language, and nation. For upwards of three years did I earnestly pursue the study of this all-important subject; and the irresistible force of truth penetrating my own heart, I gladly surrendered my own infallible judgment to the unerring decisions of the Church, and embracing with heart and soul its faith and discipline, became an humble, but I trust faithful member'"); Denis Gwynn, *Lord Shrewsbury, Pugin and the Catholic Revival* (1946); Phoebe Stanton, *Pugin* (1971); A. Wedgwood, *A .W. N. Pugin and the Pugin Family* (1985); Patrick Allitt, *Catholic Converts: British and American Intellectuals Turn to Rome* (1997); Michael Fisher, *Pugin-Land: A. W. N. Pugin, Lord Shrewsbury and the Gothic Revival in Staffordshire* (2002); Roderick O'Donnell, *The Pugins and the Catholic Midlands* (2002); Rosemary Hill, *God's Architect: Pugin and the Building of Romantic Britain* (2007) (On the announcement of his third marriage: "By the enclosed card you will perceive that I am married and have got a first rate Gothic woman at last who perfectly understands and delights in spires chancels screens stained windows Brasses vestments etc"); Roderick O'Donnell, "Augustus Welby Northmore Pugin," in John Joliffe *(ed), English Catholic Heroes* (2008), p.137; *Gillow*, Vol. V, p.375; *DNB*; also *True Principles*, The Journal of the Pugin Society.

Purbrick, Edward Ignatius, SJ – priest and author; b. 22 June 1830; c. 1850 (his elder brother, James (d. 1900), was received in the same year, also became a Jesuit, and was at Stonyhurst for many years; his father was received on his death bed in 1872); d. 1914; educated at Christ Church College, Oxford; became a Catholic when an undergraduate; joined the Society of Jesus in 1851; ordained in 1864; rector of Stonyhurst College 1869–1879; English provincial 1880–1888; provincial of the Maryland Province 1897–1900; in 1872 argued for the establishment of a Catholic college at Oxford; promoted the opening of the halls, which became Campion Hall and St. Benet's Hall; close friend of Fr. Thomas Byles (see above); see *Sermons* (1869); *May Papers; or, Thoughts on the Litanies of Loreto* (1874); C. C. Martindale, "Edward Ignatius Purbrick, SJ: A Sketch," *The Month*, August 1926, p.116, September 1926, p.203, October 1926, p.299.

Queensberry, ninth Marquess of (John Sholto Douglas) – sportsman and controversialist; b. 20 July 1844, Florence; c. 31 January 1900 (nursed in his last days by his brother Archie, a Catholic priest, who claimed that Queensberry had been received into the Catholic Church on his deathbed, though no corroborative evidence of this; his mother, Sybil, wife of the eighth Marquess, converted in 1922; her daughter, Lady Fox-Pitt, became a Catholic in 1925); d. 31 January 1900; brother of the author and traveler, Florence Dixie (1855–1905); brought up a high-churchman; naval career before becoming Marquess; father, the eighth Marquess, committed suicide in 1858; then to Magdalene College, Cambridge where he was fine sportsman, but left without taking a degree; promoted the sport of boxing; lent his name to the Marquess of Queensberry rules that formed basis of modern boxing; became estranged from

his wife and took several mistresses; affected by premature death of his father, two brothers, and his eldest son, three of them probably by suicide; adopted an agnostic and secularist position; President of the British Secularist Union on its formation in 1877; unable to sit in the House of Lords because of his refusal to take religious oath of allegiance to the Sovereign; reverted to life of private pleasure and was divorced by his wife for adultery; his second marriage was quickly annulled; angered by the relationship of Oscar Wilde (see below) with his son, Lord Alfred Douglas (see above); was sued for libel in 1895 by Wilde whom he had accused of posing as a sodomite; the libel case was later withdrawn; his ashes were buried at the family burial-ground at Kinmount, Scotland; see Brian Roberts, *The Mad, Bad Line: The Family of Lord Alfred Douglas* (1981).

Quinn, David – journalist; b. 1963, Dublin; c. (revert) 1993; father journalist; brought up as nominally Catholic; after university went to Australia; stopped going to Mass in 1986; was inclined towards evangelical Protestantism, having doubts regarding Catholic approach to the doctrine of justification; married in a Baptist church (his wife, Rachel, a Baptist) with dispensation from the Catholic Church; influenced to return to the Catholic Church by reading Karl Adam, G. K. Chesterton (see above) and C. S. Lewis; returned to Ireland in 1993; became journalist; defended the Catholic cause; editor of *The Irish Catholic* 1997–2003; then columnist with *Irish Independent*; see "The God Delusion: David Quinn and Richard Dawkins Debate," Catholiceducation.org website ("The theory of evolution explains how matter – which we are all made from – organized itself into for example highly complex beings like

Richard Dawkins and other human beings but what it doesn't explain just to give one example is how matter came into being in the first place. That, in scientific terms, is a question that cannot be answered and can only be answered, if it can be answered fully at all, by philosophers and theologians. But it certainly cannot be answered by science and the question of whether God exists or not cannot be answered fully by science either and a common mistake that people can believe is the scientist who speaks about evolution with all the authority of science can also speak about the existence of God with all the authority of science and of course he can't. The scientist speaking about the existence of God is actually engaging in philosophy or theology but he certainly isn't bringing to it the authority of science *per se...*

If you're an atheist logically speaking you cannot believe in objective morality. You cannot believe in free will. These are two things that the vast majority of humankind implicitly believe in. We believe for example that if a person carries out a bad action, we can call that person bad because we believe that they are freely choosing those actions...

It's quite a different category to say 'Look, we will study matter and we will ask how matter organizes itself into particular forms,' and come up with the answer 'evolution.' It is quite another question to ask 'Where does matter come from to begin with?' And if you like you must go outside of matter to answer that question. And then you're into philosophical categories.... You must have an uncaused cause for anything at all to exist"); *EWTN Audio Library* (21 November 2005).

Raffalovich, Marc-André (usually known as André, then as André-Sebastian after his conversion) – author; b. 11 September 1864, Paris; c. 3 February

1896 (received by Fr. J. M. Bampton, SJ, at Farm Street, London); d. 14 February 1934, 9 Whitehouse Terrace, Edinburgh; son of Herman Raffalovich (d. 1893) of Paris, wealthy Russian Jewish banker to the Tsar; younger brother of Arthur, diplomat and economist; brother of Sophie O'Brien (see above); wealthy Russian-Jewish émigré; part of the decadent movement; generous benefactor to Aubrey Beardsley (see above) in his last illness, and association with Oscar Wilde (see below); provided his close friend, John Gray (1866–1934) (see above), with whom he collaborated in writing a play, *The Blackmailers*, with financial and emotive support; naturalized as British subject in 1891; also influenced by J-K. Huysmans, the French novelist; wrote five volumes of poetry and two novels; buried in Mount Vernon cemetery outside Edinburgh; see Brocard Sewell, *Footnote to the Nineties: A Memoir of John Gray and André Raffalovich* (1968); Robert Whelan, "Why did so many Victorian decadents become Catholics?" *Catholic Herald*, 5 January 2001; *DNB*.

Raine, Kathleen Jessie – poet and literary scholar; b. 1908, 6 Gordon Road, Ilford, Essex; c. late 1940s (later withdrew from the Church); d. 6 July 2003; brought up in a Methodist family (father a lay preacher); educated at Girton College, Cambridge; "regarded as the great beauty of her generation at Cambridge" (*DNB*); specialized on subject of William Blake by whom she was greatly influenced; also influenced by Eastern traditions and Platonism; rebelled against the rationalism and materialism of the European Enlightenment; close relationship with the writer Gavin Maxwell; see *Collected Poems* (1956); *Blake and Tradition* (1968); *Defending Ancient Springs* (1969); *Autobiographies* (1991); Stratford and Leonie Caldecott,

"Kathleen Raine: A Challenge to Catholics," *Catholic Herald*, 18 July 2003 ("In a way she represents a host of intelligent, imaginative people lost to the Church because we have forgotten the importance of symbolism and gutted the liturgy. Love is reduced to sentiment and the Gospel to moralism"); see Maggie Parham, "Obituary," *The Tablet*, 19 July 2003, p.30 ("Last spring, when it appeared that she might be dying, she asked for a visit from a Catholic priest whom she loved and respected and requested Communion and the Last Rites. There was no re-conversion – she still had serious problems with dogma and doctrine – but there was reconciliation. He was moved when she told him that she had never ceased to believe in, and to pray to, Our Father"); *DNB*.

Rainolds (Reynolds), William – priest and author; b. about 1544, Pinhoe, Devon; c. 1575; 24 August 1594, Antwerp; elder brother of the Puritan theologian, John Reynolds (1549–1607); Fellow of New College, Oxford, then an Anglican rector; in 1572 resigned his fellowship; conversion to the Catholic Church influenced by the famous controversy between Thomas Harding and John Jewel; also influenced by Cardinal Allen; went to Rome and made a public recantation of Protestantism; in 1577 entered English College, Douai; in next two years traveled to Rheims (new location of English College), Louvain, and Paris; ordained priest 31 March 1580 at Chalons; appointed Professor of Scriptures and Hebrew at the English College at Rheims by Cardinal Allen, but became seriously ill and gave up most of his teaching; solemnly promised that, on recovery, he would devote rest of his life to writing in defense of the Catholic Church, and that became his main occupation in life; involved in translation of the Rheims Bible and answering controversial works of opponents in England (including his brother); see *Gillow*, Vol. V, p.409; *DNB*.

Ramsay, Andrew Michael (Jacobite Sir Andrew Ramsay, baronet) (known in France as the Chevalier de Ramsay) – philosopher and Jacobite sympathizer; b. 29 May 1686, Ayr, Scotland; c. 1710; d. 16 May 1743, St. Germain-en-Laye; father a staunch Calvinist, mother an Anglican; soon rejected doctrine of predestination; at one time intent on studying for the Episcopalian ministry; later drawn to Deism; then an interest in the mysticism of Madame Bourignon and later of Madame Guyon; came closer to the Jacobin nobility; went to Cambrai in August 1710 and took part in six months of spiritual debate and confession with Archbishop Fénelon, during which he was received by Fénelon into the Catholic Church; secretary to Madame Guyon in Blois until her death; wrote several books; found permanent employment with the Jacobite court and became tutor to the young prince, Charles Edward, in 1623 in Rome; later moved to Paris and continued his literary career ("Attempted to reconcile the philosophy of Descartes with that of Newton in a mystical Christian context" (*DNB*)); went to England where he was elected Fellow of the Royal Society and awarded degree of DCL from Oxford University; prominent figure in French freemasonry; buried in the parish church of St. Germain-en-Laye (his heart was entombed at the convent of the Sisters of the Holy Sacrament, rue Casette, Paris); see *Life of Fénelon* (1723) (includes an account of Madame Guyon and the story of his own conversion); *The Philosophical Principles of Natural and Revealed Religion*, 2 Vols. (1748–1749); George David Henderson, *Chevalier Ramsay* (1952); *DNB* ("On his deathbed he recalled that his deep sense of piety [in his youth] manifested itself in hours spent at prayer in a ruined Roman Catholic church").

Ramsay, James – artist; b. 1786; c. 1825; d. 23 June 1854; best known as a portrait painter (many of Catholic subjects), but also exhibited scriptural and historical subjects; painted several altarpieces; *Gillow*, Vol. V, p.386.

Randall, Sir Alec Walter George, KCMG – diplomat and writer; b. 27 July 1892; d. 24 January 1974; studied at London University; entered Foreign Office in 1920; second secretary HM Legation to Holy See 1925–1930; first secretary HM Legation, Bucharest 1930–1933; served in Foreign Office 1933–1935; first secretary HM Legation Copenhagen 1935–1938; counselor in Foreign Office 1938–1945; ambassador to Denmark 1947–1952; retired from Foreign Service 1953; alternate delegate to UN Assembly and Economic and Social Council, New York and Geneva 1953–1957; see *Vatican Assignment* (1956); *Discovering Rome* (1960); *The Pope, the Jews and the Nazis* (1963); "How it all began," *The Tablet*, 8 February 1969, p.132 ("There was taking place in Westminster Cathedral what I recognized as the Three Hours devotions. The bareness and desolation of the cathedral impressed me more than the words from the pulpit; but what struck me most was the unself-conscious behavior of so many people, of all social conditions, devoutly making the 'Way of the Cross.' For me it was in striking contrast to the rationalism and prosperous congregation I had seen at the City Temple…

For a time I was attracted to Anglo-Catholicism, but did not find it the final or sufficient answer to my enquiries. Perhaps Chesterton's *Orthodoxy* proved with me, as I know it did with many others, an

important stage in my progress to the Catholic Church").

Ranken, George Elliot – journalist and lawyer; b. 1828; c. 1849 (his wife and family were received in 1847); d. 1889; captain of the Royal Glamorgan Artillery; forfeited his fortune on his reception into the Church; worked in the War Office; Private Chamberlain to Popes Pius IX and Leo XIII; for fifteen years editor of *The Tablet* (long-standing friend of its proprietor, Cardinal Vaughan).

Raupert, (John) Godfrey Ferdinand (sometimes used the pseudonyms of "Scrutator" or "Viator") – author and lecturer; b. 29 September 1859, Stettin, North Germany; c. 1894 (received by Cardinal Vaughan); d. 4 January 1929, Wiesbaden, Germany; came to England at age of nineteen to study journalism; became staunch Evangelical Anglican; took Anglican orders in 1887 and worked as curate; became deeply interested in spiritualism, which as a Catholic he combated with lectures and books; made Knight of St. Gregory by Pope Pius X; especially fond of the *Memorare*; great devotion to the saints; father of Fr. (Eric) Gregory Raupert, OP (1892–1976); see *Ten Years in Anglican Orders* (1898); *Roads to Rome: Being personal records of some of the more recent converts to the Catholic faith* (1901); *Back to Rome: Being a Series of Private Letters etc. Addressed to an Anglican Clergyman* (1903), *Modern Spiritism* (1909), *The Supreme Problem: An Examination of Historical Christianity from the Standpoint of Human Life* (1910) ("The following striking statement, attributed to Napoleon at St. Helena … will be seen to contain weighty and significant thoughts …: 'The conception of Christ as a mere Jewish peasant, endowed with fine spiritual instincts, fired by high enthusiasms and laboring unsuccessfully as a religious, ethical and political reformer of his country is, to my judgment, wholly inadequate to the facts of human life and of that record of human life which we call history.

Consider what Christ has been for nineteen hundred years to the foremost people of the world, and to their noblest men and women. Is it possible to believe that the martyrs who counted it all joy to die for Him, the virgins, His mystical spouses, who discerned in Him, the fairest among ten thousand, the altogether lovely, and found their life in losing it for Him; the confessors, the doctors, the ascetics, to whom His very name was as a sweet song in the ear, as wondrous honey in the mouth, as heavenly nectar in the heart – *in aure dulce canticum; in ore mel mirificum; in corde nectrar coelicum* – is it possible to believe that all the generations of these holy souls were walking in a vain shadow, were given over to a strong delusion to believe a lie?

Nay, though nineteen hundred years have passed away since He was uplifted on the Cross, still His name has Its hold on the human mind.... Amid the most vicious nations, under the most diversified circumstances, in the most cultivated, in the rudest races and intellects, the Owner of that great Name reigns. High and low, rich and poor, acknowledge Him, are venturing at His word – are looking for His presence. Palaces, sumptuous, innumerable, are raised to His honor. His image, in its deepest humiliation, is triumphantly displayed in the proud cities, at the corners of the street, on the tops of mountains; ... it is worn next the heart in life; it is held before the failing eyes in death. Here, then, is One Who is not a mere name: He is not a mere fiction. He is a substance. He is dead and gone, but still He lives as the living energetic power of a thousand generations. Can He be less than divine?"; *Spiritistic Phenomena*

and Their Interpretation (1913) (a summary of all his work on this subject); *The Dangers of Spiritualism* (1920); Rev. Gregory Raupert, OP, *A Convert From Spiritualism: J. Godfrey Raupert, K.S.G.* (1932).

Ravenscroft, James – bibliophile; d. 1710–11; from ancient family with large estate in Wickham, Lincolnshire; member of the Inner Temple; great interest in books of controversy and much impressed by St. Francis de Sales' *Introduction to the Devout Life* and Fr. Person's *Booke of Resolution*; married with large family; during Civil War suffered greatly for his support of the royalist cause; when ill at past middle age, he was received into the Church; subsequently gave himself to study and piety and put together finest library of Catholic books in England; arrested during the Oates Plot; at his trial allowed to defend himself in Latin and was acquitted; died at a great age; see *The Theatre of Catholique and Protestant Religion* (1690); *Gillow*, Vol. V, p.393.

Rawes, Henry Augustus – priest, poet, author, and hymn-writer; b. 11 December 1826, Easington, near Durham; c. March 1856; d. 24 April 1885, Brighton; son of Anglican clergyman; formerly Anglican curate himself; one of the original members of English Congregation of Oblates of St. Charles founded by Manning; ordained priest in November 1857; DD of Rome; superior of Oblate Fathers from 1879; Ultramontane; well-known preacher and author of many devotional works and religious poems; buried at Mortlake Catholic cemetery, Surrey; see *Gillow*, Vol. V, p.394; *Catholic Encyclopedia*; *DNB*.

Reade (Read), Thomas – army officer and lawyer; b. 1606/7, Linkenholt, Hampshire; c. 1648; d. early March

1669; Fellow of New College; turned to civil law; staunch royalist during the Civil War; enlisted in the royalist army at Oxford; made Principal of Magdalen Hall; after Oxford had surrendered to the parliamentary forces a warrant was issued for his arrest; Reade went to Paris and was received into the Catholic Church; he entered Douai College; probably entered the Carthusian monastery of Nieuwpoort intending to join the order; some say he was ordained priest at Douai 6 March 1649, others that he was never ordained; in 1659 he wrote a work in defense of Catholicism, but no copy seems extant; at the Restoration returned to London; died in poverty; probably buried in the church attached to the Savoy hospital; see *Gillow*, Vol. V, p.399; *DNB*.

Redford, John Meredith – priest and writer; b. 1936; c. 1960; brought up as an Anglican, but lapsed as teenager; came back to Anglicanism (influenced by writings of St. Paul and C. S. Lewis); became deacon in the Church of England; after conversion studied for the priesthood; ordained Catholic priest in 1967; lecturer in Scripture and Revelation Theology; director of first distance learning theology degree course in Britain based at Maryvale Institute, Birmingham; see *Catholicism: Hard Questions* (1997); *What Catholics Believe* (1998); "How I saw the light with Paul," *The Universe*, 3 June 2001, p.20 ("As I was mentally and spiritually wrestling wondering whether I ought to become a Catholic, I opened the Bible at random. I had always been warned against this, remembering the story of the old lady who had opened the Bible at random and had read 'Judas went and hanged himself,' then turned over again and read, 'Go, do thou likewise'! But then, in my room alone with God, I read Paul again: 'There is one body and one

Spirit, just as you were called to the one hope of your calling, one Lord, one faith, one baptism … one God and Father of all, who is above all and through all and in all' (Ephesians 4:4–6). Paul was leading me towards the fullness of visible unity in the Catholic Church"); *Are the Gospels Anti-Semitic?* (2004); *Bad, Mad or God?: Proving the Divinity of Christ from St. John's Gospel* (2004); "Bad, Mad, or God?" *The Pastoral Review*, January 2006, p.46 ("Newman spoke in his philosophy of the principle of Antecedent Probability. If A were to be true, then it would probably happen like B. If God were to come to earth as Man, then he would probably perform extraordinary miracles like walking on the water and feeding five thousand people with five loaves and two fishes. He would probably have to declare that he was who he claimed to be, to make sure that there could be no doubt of the matter. And, if he did declare himself, he would probably use terms from his own culture, like 'Before Abraham was, I AM' in Hebrew *'ani hu'* (Jn. 8.38), rather than say that he was *homoousios* ('of one being') with the Father, from the Hellenistic culture. It would certainly be likely that, having claimed to be God, his contemporaries would think that he was blaspheming, and would want to put him to death as a blasphemer. And finally, if he were to convince people that he was truly whom he claimed to be, he would have to rise from the dead and appear to his disciples bodily, continuing to be with him in his Spirit.

Of course, Antecedent Probability would not expect that this God become man should die the excruciating death of a criminal. But the unexpected elements in the Gospel story, such as the crucifixion, make it more credible than of a Greek god descending to earth and destroying all and sundry. But there are elements which to me are necessary as a *sine qua non* for one claiming to be God; particularly his claims to be divine, his miracles and above all his resurrection ..."); *The Truth About Jesus* (2006) ("What persuaded [C. S. Lewis] about the truth of Christian faith was the following argument, which he called 'Bad, Mad or God?' Jesus claimed to be God Lewis said.... If he did so claim, you could not understand that he was just a good man. If he made such a stupendous claim, he had either to be bad, a deceiver; or he had to be mad, like those unfortunate patients in a psychiatric hospital who have delusions of grandeur.

But, argues Lewis, the Gospels show us a man who is neither bad nor mad. On the contrary, all agree that Jesus of Nazareth was wise and sane. Furthermore, Lewis said, if God wishes to give us a revelation to believe, a God become man, that person would have to do mighty deeds to prove his credentials; like walk on the water and feed five thousand people with five loaves and two fishes; as well as being morally good. This is precisely what we find in the Gospel accounts.

After a lifetime's study of the four Gospels, I buy into that argument. The Gospels are not tape-recordings of Jesus' life. They do not often contain the actual words he said (the *ipsissima verba*). The Catholic Church never requires us to believe that. Sometimes the Gospels give us the reported speech of Jesus. But the Gospels contain substantially what Jesus said and did. A recent study has shown that the Gospels are in the form of a classical biography, where history is important. And what the Gospels say is credible, if we, unlike Reimarus and the *Jesus Seminar* at least allow ourselves the possibility at first to believe that it might be true. They make sense"); *Born of a Virgin: Proving the Miracle from the Gospels (2007); Who Was John?: The Fourth Gospel Debate After*

Pope Benedict XVI's Jesus of Nazareth (2008); *Catholicism: The Basics* (2009).

Reeve, Richard, OSB (name in religion Wilfrid) – monk; b. 22 June 1642, Gloucester; c. 1667; d. 31 October 1693, Berkeley Street, Piccadilly, London; early attack of palsy made him incurably lame; after Oxford, converted at George Napier's chapel in Holywell; master of Magdalen College school 1670, but resigned in 1673 after being warned that he would be ejected unless he adhered to the Anglican Church; in 1674 went to Douai; in 1675 became a monk, but, on account of his lameness, was never ordained; instructed English students in classics, poetry, rhetoric, and Greek; best known for his work, 1677–1681, copying the mystical writings of the English Benedictine, Augustine Baker; his name was mentioned in 1678 in relation to the Popish Plot in view of his Stuart sympathies; taught in France 1685–1687, where admired by his friend Bossuet; recalled to England in 1688 to be reinstated, by authority of James II, as master of Magdalen College school, but declined the appointment and was nominated master of Bluecoats school; on outbreak of 1688 Revolution was apprehended, but released in 1689; great classicist and grammarian; buried in the church of St. Martin-in-the-Fields; see *Gillow*, Vol. V, p.403; *DNB*.

Renouf, Sir Peter Le Page – Egyptologist, oriental scholar, and theologian; b. 23 August 1822, St. Peter Port, Guernsey; c. March 1842 (Easter); d. 14 October 1897, 46 Rowland Gardens, South Kensington, London; educated at Pembroke College, Oxford, where he read 14 to 16 hours a day and was much influenced by Newman whose sermons he attended; drawn into the Tractarian movement; he studied the Catholic question and in October 1841 he published anonymously a pamphlet on the Real Presence; after his conversion, Wiseman employed him as Professor at Oscott; tutor for a French noble family and traveled on the Continent 1846–1854; at one time Professor of Ancient History and Oriental Languages at Catholic University College, Dublin; husband of Ludovica Brentano (1836–1921), daughter of Christian Brentano, niece of the poets Achim von Arnim and Clemens Brentano, and sister of philosopher Franz Brentano (1838–1916) and economist Lujo Brentano; Government Inspector of Catholic Schools in England 1864–1886; tendency to liberalism; opposed the promulgation of the dogma of papal infallibility; his pamphlet on the condemnation of Pope Honorius was put on the Index; sought reconciliation of Döllinger to the Church; turned more to Egyptology; keeper of Egyptian and Assyrian Antiquities in British Museum from 1886, but obliged to retire in 1891; buried in crypt of St. Joseph's Church, St Peter Port, Guernsey; see Kevin J. Cathcart, *The Letters of Peter Le Page Renouf*, 4 Vols. (2002–2004); *Gillow*, Vol. V, p.405; *DNB*.

Rhodes, Anthony Richard Ewart – writer; b. 24 September 1916, Plymouth, Devon; c. 1992; d. 23 August 2004, London; studied Mechanical Sciences at Trinity College, Cambridge; entered army and fought in World War II; lecturer in English Literature at University of Geneva and then at Eton College; turned to writing; some journalism; wrote histories, biography, travel books, novels, poetry, and a best-selling war memoir of Dunkirk, *Sword of Bone* (1942); reporter for *Daily Telegraph* at Hungarian uprising in 1956; translator; research for his trilogy on the relation between religion and temporal authority so impressed him that he converted from an open-minded Anglicanism to Catholicism; wrote first major defense of Pope Pius XII against charges that he had betrayed the Jews; one of the last of England's gentleman scholars; see *A Sabine Journey: To Rome in Holy Year* (1952); *The Dalmatian Coast* (1955); *Art Treasures of Eastern Europe* (1972); *The Vatican in the Age of the Dictators* (1973) ("For every Alexander VI there were a hundred good and pious Popes, whose names no one bothers to recall…. The goals of the Vatican are not those of a lay State; they are transcendental, not immanent. Its aim is to 'save souls', which includes the making of converts regardless of race or nationality. The care of souls, liberty to celebrate Mass and administer the Sacraments, above all to impart religious education to the young – this is what the Church aspires to – in short, to prepare man for the after-life. To obtain the best conditions for achieving this in the various nation States, of whatever political color, is its aim"); *Propaganda* (1976); *The Power of Rome in the Twentieth Century: The Vatican in the Age of Liberal Democracies* (1983*)* ("Today, when over a century has passed since 1870, the history of the Papacy has not followed the course the liberals and atheists anticipated: gradual erosion of the Church under her unceasing attacks, finally lapsing into total disintegration. In the period from 1870 to 1922, the Church lived through one of the bitterest, and yet most subtle, attacks on the realm of the Spirit which has ever been known. How did the papacy defeat this and retrieve its fortunes, which had sunk so low in 1870 – so that today under Pope John Paul II, its prestige in the world is as high as, if not higher than, that of any lay state? And with prestige goes power. Napoleon understood this well when he said at the end of his career to the Marquise de Fontanes, 'There are only two powers in this world – the sword and the spirit. In the long run, the sword is always defeated by the spirit.'

Some Catholic apologists have seen a parallel between the Goths, Huns and Vandals who destroyed the Roman Empire in the Dark Ages, and the liberals, socialists and freethinkers of the nineteenth and twentieth centuries. But this is inexact. There is far greater recuperative power in the Church of Rome today than there was in the effete Empire of Honorius. To quote Cardinal Manning ...: 'In the course of history, some forty Popes have at one time or another been expelled from Rome – nine times by Roman factions, seven times by foreign invaders. Six times the city of Rome has been held to ransom by usurpers. Twice it has been nearly destroyed. Once, it was so utterly desolate that for fifty days nothing human breathed in it, and no cry was heard but that of the foxes on the Aventine. Warfare, suffering, exile – that has been the lot of many Popes. Yet with imperishable vitality and invincible power they persist, they remain ...'"); *Flanders in 1940 and Other Poems* (1989); *The Vatican in the Age of The Cold War* (1992) ("There can be no doubt that there has been a considerable improvement in the international standing of the Holy See since the Second World War, particularly in the Protestant lands. But this does not mean that the Holy See will yield an inch to Protestant ecumenical suggestions as far as doctrine is concerned. It is convinced that it alone is in possession of the mission confided by Christ, the founder of the Church, to the man named by the Evangiles as 'the first of the Apostles,' Peter, who was martyred and buried in Rome. The claim of the Roman Catholic Church is to be the true body of Christ"); Alan Rush, obituary, *The Independent*, 25 August 2004 ("The universal aptness of the Roman Church for all conditions of men and nations well befits her claim to divine origin. And here is her strength – not in the vaudeville of her services and the politics of her princes").

Rich, Edward Charles – theologian; b. 15 July 1895, London; c. 19 May 1956; d. 26 May 1959; brought up in strict Evangelical home; educated at Christ Church, Oxford; former Anglican minister and Prebendary of St. Paul's Cathedral, London; see "Recent convert clergy tell how and why," *The Tablet*, September 1956, p. 141 ("I found in the lives of the saints the strongest and most convincing argument for the truth of Catholicism, a quality of heroic sanctity to be found nowhere else and with an unfailing supply. From this I was led to enquire into the reasons for this. Step by step I came to see that such fruits of holiness find their source in a faith that in turn depends upon a supernatural authority.

...I set to work to enquire into the basis of Anglican authority for myself.... I came to the conclusion that Newman was right in his main conclusions that the Development of Doctrine is an inevitable process. But also that if the original deposit is to remain true as its implications are drawn out down the ages, then the Church must be preserved from error in pronouncing upon them. Infallibility was therefore a Divine endowment bestowed up on the Church"); *Seeking the City* (1959) ("Newman had put his finger unerringly on the ultimate issue. Expressed in its simplest form, the problem is this. Because development is a law of life, whether in nature or grace, the original Divine Revelation given once for all in Jesus Christ must be subject to its workings. Therefore if the original deposit is true, the subsequent developments must also be true, if the promise of Christ is to be fulfilled. In other words, the Church must be preserved from error when she pronounces upon the implications of the Faith. Development and infallibility must go hand in hand. Unless this is acknowledged, later generations would have no guarantee of the implications of the truths of Revelation outside the pages of Holy Scripture").

Richardson, Nicholas James – classical scholar; b. 4 February 1940, Winchester, Hampshire; c. 2003; read Classics at Magdalen College, Oxford; awarded first in Mods and Greats, followed by BPhil and DPhil in Classics; Fellow and Tutor in Classics, then Sub-Warden, at Merton College, Oxford 1968–2004 (Emeritus Fellow 2004–); Warden of Greyfriars Hall, Oxford 2004–2007, first layperson to hold that post; visiting fellow at several universities; main research interests in Greek and Latin literature with wide range of publications on these subjects; see (ed), *The Homeric 'Hymn to Demeter'* (1974); *The Iliad: A Commentary* (1993); The Homeric Hymns (contrib, 2003).

Richardson, Thomas – publisher; b. 1797, Derby; c. 1853 (received by Fr. Faber (see above)); d. 20 February 1875, White Cross Fields, Derby; began to publish Catholic books early in second quarter of nineteenth century; publisher of largest proportion of Catholic books in England for many years; published *Dublin Review* 1844–1863; see *Gillow*, Vol. V, p.414.

Ricketts, Ralph Robert – writer; b. 12 October 1902, Simla, India; c. 1940; d. 1998; father a Bengal Lancer; family either civil servants or army officers in India; childhood in England with relatives; later at Magdalen College, Oxford; formerly nominal Anglican, but ignorant of theology; with a friend, Martin Cooper, later *Daily Telegraph* music critic, began spiritual journey that led to his conversion; sub-editor and contributor on the *London Mercury* under Sir John Squire; from 1934 a novelist and short story writer; leading theme in his novels was the conflict between the worldly and the spiritual life (some comparisons made with Graham Greene (see above)); in later years he focused more on religion, his inner life strengthened, and he found his greatest joy in silence; his spiritual director was Bishop Christopher Butler (see above); see *A Lady Leaves Home* (1934); *Camilla* (1937); *The Manikin* (1956), *Love in Four Flats* (1959); (ed) *We Are Happy* (1960), *Henry's Wife* (1961), (ed), *Bid The World Goodnight* (1981) (a symposium on old age and death).

Rigby, Saint John – layman and martyr; b. at Harrock Hall, near Wigan, Lancashire; d. 21 June 1600, London; conformed at times to Protestant Church to avoid penalties; repented of this and was reconciled to the Catholic Church by St. John Godfrey Jones (alias Buckley), OSF, then a prisoner in London; represented Mrs. Fortescue, daughter of Sir Edmund Huddleston, for whom he was in service as steward, on a charge of recusancy; in cross-examination it came out that he himself was also Catholic, and he was committed to prison 14 February 1600; tried and was offered his freedom if he would go to church, which he refused to do; then charged with being reconciled to the "Romish religion," and condemned to death; reprieved and retained in prison until next assizes, when again condemned; hanged, drawn and quartered at St. Thomas' Waterings, Southwark; see *Gillow*, Vol. V, p.420.

Riley, Harold – priest; b. 24 December 1903; c. 1995, at the age of 91; d. 7 March 2003; ordained to Anglican ministry in 1928; wrote, lectured and preached widely; also held administrative posts in the Church of England; onetime member of King's Weigh House Chapel (Anglo-Catholic) with W. E. Orchard (see above); after retirement from full-time ministry became recognized as a fine Anglo-Catholic scripture scholar; ordained Catholic priest at the age of 91;

lived as a Catholic priest and hermit for last eight years of his life; see *The Order of the Synoptics: Why Three Synoptic Gospels?* (1987) (with Dom Bernard Orchard)); *The Making of Mark: An Exploration* (1989); *The First Gospel* (1992); *Preface to Luke* (1993); "The Brothers of the Lord," *Downside Review*, January 1998, p.45; Fr. Michael Seed, *Thinking of Becoming a Catholic?* (2007) ("He entered the Church in the morning and was ordained a deacon in the afternoon. Cardinal Basil Hume ordained him a priest at the Church of Our Lady, Lisson Grove, London a few days later. We think he was probably the oldest candidate for ordination in the world. But when I first approached Cardinal Hume about the possibility of reception and ordination he thought I was crazy. 'You're asking me to ordain a man of 91?' he asked with a raised eyebrow. 'The Vatican will think I've gone mad.' 'Well, Father, they think you are insane anyway,' I replied rather naughtily").

Riley-Smith, Jonathan Simon Christopher – historian, specializing in the Crusades; b. 27 June 1938; c. 13 October 1959 (instructed and received by Mgr. Alfred Gilbey); brought up as Anglican; at school age was attracted to Anglo-Catholicism; educated at Eton and Trinity College, Cambridge; converted to the Catholic faith whilst at Cambridge; teaching posts at University of St. Andrews 1964–1972; Cambridge University 1972–1978; London University 1978–1994; Dixie Emeritus Professor of Ecclesiastical History, Cambridge University 1994–2005; Fellow of Emmanuel College 1994–2005; see "My Conversion," an unpublished memoir written privately for his children ("It is possible that I am a Catholic because I was brainwashed by my grandmother, to whom I was very close. My conversion to the Church of Rome was certainly not the result of any spiritual experience or independent intellectual conviction, although I have acquired a philosophical armory since then. Although my grandmother died an Anglican, she brought me up to believe that the Protestant Reformation had been gravely sinful, that the Church of Rome was the one authentic church proclaiming true doctrine and that the Church of England was a poor, illegitimate shadow of the real thing"); *What were the Crusades?* (1977) (4th edition, 2009) (with L. Riley-Smith); *The Crusades: Idea and Reality* (1981); *The Crusades: A Short History* (1987) (2nd edition, 2005); *The Atlas of the Crusades* (1991); *The Oxford Illustrated History of the Crusades* (1995) (with N. Coureas); *Hospitallers: The History of the Order of St. John* (1999); "Rethinking the Crusades," *First Things*, March 2000; *The Crusades* (2006); "How the crusades helped to purify the Church," *Catholic Herald*, 5 May 2006; *The Crusades, Christianity, and Islam* (2008).

Ripon, first Marquess of (George Frederic Samuel Robinson) – politician; b. 24 October 1827, 10 Downing Street, London; c. 4 September 1874 (he and Lady Ripon remained separated by religion, but devoted to one another during fifty-five years of marriage); d. 9 July 1909, Studley Royal; son of Frederick John Robinson (1782–1859), Viscount Goderich, Whig Prime Minister 1827–1828; cousin of Lady Amabel Kerr (see above) who was influential in his conversion; known as Lord Goderich from 1853 to 1859; educated at home; deeply influenced by his mother's strict evangelical beliefs; at the age of seventeen he found in a bookshop a Roman breviary and began reciting the Office, but when this was objected to he grew indifferent to religion; associated with the Christian Socialist movement from 1848 (Thomas Hughes a lifelong friend);

espoused radical ideals, which he developed as an MP; Secretary of State for War in Palmerston's government where he achieved army reforms; later Secretary of State for India; on several occasions Minister of State during Gladstone's administrations; only in 1870, when his brother-in-law was assassinated by brigands in Greece, did he turn to religion again; became Grand Master of English Freemasons in 1870 after twenty years in the craft (resigned before his conversion, as he did from Gladstone's cabinet); wrote to Newman that his works "have tended more than any other human cause to bring me to the Catholic Church"; on his conversion *The Times* wrote that "a statesman who becomes a convert to Roman Catholicism forfeits at once the confidence of the English people"; much work for the Catholic Union of Great Britain; returned to politics when Viceroy of India 1880–1884 (attempted to initiate local self-government reforms and was very popular there for his attempts to improve the lives of Indians); supporter of Home Rule for Ireland; First Lord of the Admiralty in 1886; Colonial Secretary under Gladstone and Rosebery 1892–1895 (opposed South African War); Lord Privy Seal and Leader of the House of Lords 1905–1908; finally resigned from politics in 1908 in protest against rescinding of permission for a procession with the Blessed Sacrament through London streets by the papal legate; many educational and charitable works (visited the poor as a brother of St. Vincent de Paul); as Catholic his spiritual life was devout; buried in St. Mary's Church in Studley Park; see Lucien Wolf, *Life of the First Marquess of Ripon*, 2 Vols. (1921), especially supplementary chapter to Vol. 1., compiled by Fr. Sebastian Bowden, at pp.321–355; Anthony F. Denholm, "The Conversion of Lord Ripon in 1874," *Recusant History*, April 1969, p.111;

John P. Rossi, Lord Ripon's Resumption of Political Activity," *Recusant History*, April 1971, p.61; John Rossi, "The Ripon Diary, 1878–80, Parts I, II and III," *Recusant History*, January 1973, p.8, October 1973, p.120, and October 1974, p.261; Fr. John Parsons, "Lord Ripon (1827–1909): How to Base Political Life on Christian Principles," Parts I and II, *AD2000*, October and November 1995; Madeleine Beard, *Faith and Fortune* (1997), pp.192–196; *Catholic Encyclopedia*; *DNB* ("[H]e argued that the Christian nation, while pursuing the highest well-being of the people, should be distinguished 'by its scrupulous respect for the rights of its neighbors, and a just consideration of their interests.' A Christian's patriotism, he insisted, was wider than that of the pagan, and to put considerations of policy and force before considerations of right was not only wrong but folly, for 'higher wisdom' has it that in the long run material force is the weakest, and that solid foundations can only be laid on 'justice alone'").

Rist, John Michael – philosopher; b. 6 July 1936, Romford, Essex; c. June 1980 (wife, Anna Thérèse, née Vogler, converted earlier); parents Anglican; at school confirmed into the Anglican Church, but later humanist; educated at Trinity College, Cambridge; became immersed in the classical world and later philosophy; Professor of Classics and Philosophy at University of Toronto; see *On the Independence of Matthew and Mark* (1978); "Where Else" in Kelly J. Clarke (ed), *Philosophers Who Believe* (1993), pp.83–103 ("Christianity is above all others the religion that speaks of God's presence in history, not only in the past, as in creation and in the incarnation, but continuously into the present and, according to a theory of the development of doctrine akin to that of Newman, through the Church into the future.

Of course that does not mean that all religious and ethical advances will be made by Christians, let alone by theologians or bishops; God needs no such limitations. What it means is that Christians must claim that the Church will, at least eventually, be able to accept all that is best among such advances, whatever their origin. Thus Christianity began to look not only coherent but plausible. Yet if Christianity, why Roman Catholicism rather than Protestantism, Anglicanism or (perhaps better) Orthodoxy, which might appear to have a better claim than these? Essentially because though half a loaf is better than no bread, and three-quarters is better still, a whole loaf is best – best not least because the most coherent both philosophically and historically. To be coherent and plausible, however, is not necessarily to be true. God, I concluded, must have revealed himself to us if we are to know much about him. This is what Christians had always claimed. But earlier I had supposed that the historical origins of Christianity were so obscure, so liable to misrepresentation by various interested parties right back to the beginning, that we could not accept even as a reasonable hypothesis that the Gospel accounts are true. In the seventies I picked up again the problem of Christian origins.... I knew enough Patristic scholarship to be aware that our Gospel canon was not, and could not have been, authenticated and stabilized by its authors, but only by acceptance by the Church, as happened in the second century. Examination of the early evidence and of the gospels themselves convinced me that Matthew's Gospel could not depend on Mark's and was more or less equally early (certainly before A.D. 70). Thus the full range of Christian claims must go back to the very earliest followers of Jesus, and in all probability to Jesus himself. The solution that either Jesus was a lunatic or that

his earliest followers were all blatant liars again seemed the only alternative possibility if their claims were false. I could no longer delude myself that 'real' scholarship told us that we have no evidence that Jesus himself, as well as the earliest generation of his followers, made claims for his divinity. The attempt of the biblical critics to show that such claims grew up (or were fabricated) within the Church seemed to be a tissue of bad argument, unhistorical treatment of the sources and wishful thinking: the wish being to make Christianity acceptable to the conventional 'liberal' orthodoxy, with its characteristic bad faith, of the nineteenth and twentieth centuries. The resulting 'scholarship' was defective to a degree that would not be acceptable in other philological disciplines. When I saw this clearly, biblical scholarship no longer stood in the way of my return to Christianity. I had to decide only whether the totality of Jesus' recorded behavior looked like that of a madman; it was not difficult to see that it did *not"); Augustine* (1994); *On Inoculating Moral Philosophy Against God* (2000); *Real Ethics: Reconsidering the Foundations of Morality* (2002) ("In the world of realist morality, the 'determination' that this *ought* to be done is not something secured by a human will reacting to human inclinations, but something to be first recognized by the human mind *de facto*, simply because the world is as it is. Though human reason may give the command that X should be done (in the belief that X 'morally' ought to be done), that 'ought to be done' – rather than the mere 'would be rationally done' – implies further authorization – and that not merely because of the inability of the human reason to determine correctly even when it determines sincerely. In justifying itself as moral rather than prudential or at best constructively rational in the Kantian sense, fallible human rea son requires …some sort of external warranting…. That external can only be God, whose 'nature' – and therefore *ex hypothesi* our 'original' nature – is communicated by way of non-arbitrary commands. Insofar as practical morality provides us with *obligations* rather than simple appeals to our (limited) reason, it requires the justification not of an impersonal and inactive Form but of an omniscient, providential and perceptive deity…

We are forced to concede that moral obligation – the only obligation clearly separable from prudence or enlightened self-interest – remains a utopian dream in a non-theistic … universe, and vain are the attempts of theists to deny this in the hope of persuading secular moralists that the debate between them can be resolved in purely this-worldly terms. As they should have foreseen, philosophers who … attempt to argue that God need not be invoked in such debates are no more able to avoid him than was Kant, who, attempting to show that morality needs no metaphysical foundations (in his understanding of metaphysical), had to allow that without the ultimate sanction of God, his moral universe would collapse: a side of Kant, as we have seen, well appreciated by Nietzsche, who held that after the 'death' of God there could be no foundations for morality"); *What is Truth?: From the Academy to the Vatican (2009)*.

Rivers, Charles Edmund – priest; b. 1863, South Africa; c. 17 December 1883; brought up in High, Broad and Low Church Anglicanism at different times; had High Church leanings and later espoused Ritualism; ordained Catholic priest; see essay in J. G. F. Raupert (ed), *Roads to Rome* (1901), p.206 ("It was very soon brought home to me that there must be absolute truth somewhere; that there must be an unvarying moral standard; that we must know what we are to believe, and how we are to act. I began to wonder if, after all, the Roman Church might offer some security as regards these matters…

I was certain that the Christian Revelation was Divine, but it was clear that the Church of England was only a human institution. There was no definiteness and certainty in her message. God was clearly calling me to come out of her…

What we should seek to point out to inquirers in the present day is that the Catholic Church has all the good that is contained in the various sects outside her pale. We are High Church in the sense that our ceremonial observances are sublime and elevating, that the teaching of our spiritual writers and mystics is lofty beyond words – 'so high, who can attain unto it?' Yet we care not for ritual for its own sake, but as the necessary attendant upon the Heavenly Mysteries, and their expression and accompaniment. We are Low Church in the sense that we can descend to the level of the humblest intelligences. We give missions to the poor and the unlettered; we have plain low Mass and devotions in the vernacular. The great founder of the Friars Preachers is himself styled 'Evangelicus Pater Dominicus' – a true teacher of the humble words of God. We are Broad Church in the sense that there is nothing provincial or insular in our gospel – 'latum mandatum tuum nimis,' within the bounds of the Church's dogmatic definitions all is free and wide; 'controvertitur' is the summing up of many a discussion of the schools – the theologians differ; but not concerning the Real Presence or Real Absence in the Blessed Eucharist, or as to whether there are two Sacraments or seven, or if the Christian ministry implies a sacrificial priesthood or just the reverse. These are matters which are vital and essential; they mean life or death, not only to the Oxford student and undergraduate, but to the servant and tradesman; not only to the refined and educated, but also to the coarse and rough; either there is one Church, infallible, eternal, or Christ has been a false prophet – the gates of hell have already prevailed against her.

The Church has her conservative side, in that she cannot change; she is radical, in that she goes to the root of all questions, social, political, scientific, and moral. She appeals to all classes of society, and chooses her clergy from every rank and station of life.

However long the Anglican compromise may still continue to exist, it is surely clear that it has the seeds of decay and death within it. Its testimony does not agree; it is of the earth, earthy: a mere State creation, doomed to failure and catastrophe. Unbelief, official and authoritative, is taught unrebuked by many of its clergy. The Incarnation, Eternal Punishment, the Blessed Trinity, the very existence of sin and virtue as such are denied. May its best children leave it, and may they soon learn to know with Catholics throughout the world, of every nation and people and tongue, what is the length, and breadth, and depth, and height of the all-embracing love of Christ; may they receive that unction from the Holy one which shall enable them to know all things, being made wise unto salvation!").

Rivington, Luke – priest and author; b. May 1838, London; c. 1888, Rome; d. 30 May 1899, London; son of Francis Rivington (1805–1885), well-known publisher; formerly as Anglican was curate at All Saints, Margaret Street, London, Superior of the Society of the Holy Ghost, Stoke, member of the Society of St. John the Evangelist at Cowley, Oxford, and missionary in India and Africa; ordained Catholic priest 21 September 1889; did not undertake any parochial work, but devoted himself to preaching, hearing confessions and writing controversial works; DD of Rome; see *Dependence: Or the Insecurity of the Anglican Position* (1889); *The English Martyrs: Or Where is Continuity?* (1892); *The Primitive Church and the See of Peter* (1894); *Anglican Fallacies: Or Lord Halifax on Reunion* (1895); *Rome and England: Or Ecclesiastical Continuity* (1896) ("The thesis of this book may be put in the following syllogism:

1. There can be no real continuity between two religious bodies, one of which has persistently held that the government of the Church was committed by our Lord to St. Peter and his successors, whilst the other maintains that 'the Church of Rome hath no jurisdiction in this realm.'

2. (a) The Church of England as now by law established, maintains the latter position, and has maintained it since the middle of the sixteenth century; whereas (b) the Church of England, from the days of St. Augustine of Canterbury onwards, held that the government of the Church lay with the Bishops of Rome as successors of St. Peter by Divine appointment.

3. Therefore the Church of England as now by law established, is not continuous or identical with the *Ecclesia Anglicana* or Church of England founded by St. Augustine or St. Gregory the Great. *That* Church of England must be looked for elsewhere; it will be found only where the doctrine is held that St. Peter and his successors, the Bishops of Rome, are regarded as the rulers of the Universal Church"); *Tekel, or the Anglican Archbishops Arraigned at the Bar of Logic and Convicted of 75 Flaws* (1897); *The Roman Primacy, A.D. 430–451* (1899); *Authority: Or a Plain Reason for Joining the Church of Rome* (1906) ("The sum and substance of my argument is that our

Lord provided for His Church an authority to which men submitted themselves in the first days of Christian faith. 'Now therefore are we all here present before God, to hear all things that are commanded thee of God,' were the words of the first Gentile convert addressed to Peter; and the attitude of Cornelius to the Prince of the Apostles in person is the attitude of after ages to his successor. As St. Francis of Sales says, 'nobody has authority to change the form of administration, save our Lord who established it'...

But the 'form of administration' committed to the Church was changed in England in the sixteenth century according to the verdict of impartial historians.... The question arises, which of the two, if either, is the form appointed by our Lord, and this resolves itself into the question of the place of Peter in the Gospel history and the early Church. Carlyle put the matter pithily when he said, speaking of the Protestant dismissal of the principle of authority in religion, that if St. Peter came to him that night, he should say, 'Peter, my good Peter, you may go: we have done with you.' This is the whole question in a nutshell. Take the entire religious literature of England since the days of Elizabeth and compare it with the religious literature of England from the days of St. Bede until the sixteenth century, and one salient feature will be seen to mark the latter, which is absent from the former. From the days of St. Augustine to that sixteenth century the name of Peter fills our literature; it disappears, except for hostile criticism, from the middle of that century onwards. And the name of Peter is the symbol of authority. Even those portions of the Canon of the Mass which are with much probability traced to the Prince of the Apostles disappear, and Cranmer and Henry and Elizabeth succeed in ousting Peter from the affections of the English

people. The seat of authority was displaced, as an adulterer first, and then his illegitimate and godless daughter, said in effect, 'My good Peter, you may go: we have done with you.'

Authority is, therefore, the question which in good logic we have to keep before us. The ills of its displacement are before us in the confusion and disorder which have ensued. They raise the question which must ever ... be supreme in religious matters – the answer to which alone can, and assuredly can, settle our difficulties. The question of Anglican orders, for instance, is quite secondary. For myself I was most careful to make it plain that it was not on the ground of their invalidity that I made my submission. I wrote thus to the only person whom I considered to have a right to know my reason, in the following words: 'I have come to the conclusion that we have no jurisdiction and therefore, even if I have valid orders, it would be a sin to exercise them.' One might, indeed, disbelieve in Anglican orders without believing in the Supremacy of the See of Peter as of divine institution, and in that case a person would be no nearer the Church; and, on the other hand, one might, at that time, have believed in the Petrine Supremacy and have thought that Anglican orders were possibly valid. Of course, this is not possible now, since Leo XIII has had the charity, and ... the courage, to define our position in regard to these orders"); *Gillow*, Vol. V, p.429; *Catholic Encyclopedia*.

Roberts, Saint John, OSB (name in religion Augustine) – priest and martyr; b. 1576, Trawsfynydd, Merioneth, Wales; c. June 1598 (received by Louis Godibert, Canon of Notre Dame); d. 10 December 1610, Tyburn; a descendant of ancient princes of North Wales; studied law at one of the inns of court; visited Paris, where received into the Church in Notre

Dame; in 1598 admitted into English College, Valladolid; entered the Benedictine Order in 1599; ordained priest at Salamanca in 1602 and reached England in April 1603; worked mostly in England; arrested, imprisoned and banished four times; founded St. Gregory's monastery at Douai, first post-Reformation English Benedictine house for men, in 1606–7; back in England in 1610; arrested in his mass vestments, having finished celebrating mass; tried and condemned to death for exercising his function in England; hanged, drawn and quartered at Tyburn; see Dom Bede Camm, *Nine Martyr Monks* (1931); *Gillow*, Vol. V, p.431; *DNB* ("He admitted he was a priest and a monk adding that if he, as he was accused, had deceived the people, 'then were our ancestors deceived by Blessed St. Augustine, the Apostle of the English, who was sent here by the Pope of Rome, St. Gregory the Great'").

Robinson, Blessed Christopher – priest and martyr; b. 1565–1570, Woodside, near Carlisle, Cumberland; d. late March 1597, Carlisle; family were temporizers in matters of religion; probably brought up as Protestant; entered English College, Rheims, in 1589; ordained priest 24 February 1592; set out for the English mission in September 1592; worked in Cumberland and Westmoreland; wrote an account of the trial and death of St. John Boste (see above) at Durham in 1594, which he witnessed; arrested 4 March 1597 at Johnby Hall, near Penrith, home of the Musgrave family; probably imprisoned at Carlisle Castle; tried at Carlisle Assizes; condemned for priesthood; hanged, drawn and quartered, probably at Harraby, Carlisle; see J. E. Bamber, "The Venerable Christopher Robinson," *Recusant History*, January 1957, p.18; Rt. Rev. B. Foley, *Bl. Christopher Robinson* (1987) ("The earliest

reference to his death is contained in a postscript to a letter to Rome from the Superior of the few Jesuits in England at the time, Fr. Henry Garnett, SJ…. 'One Robinson, a seminary priest, was lately in a purchased gaol-delivery hanged at Carlisle. The rope broke twice and the third time he rebuked the sheriff for cruelty saying that, although he meant no way to yield but was glad of the combat, yet flesh and blood were weak, and therefore he showed little humanity to torment a man so long. And when they took order to put two ropes, then, said he, by this means I shall be longer a-dying; but it is no matter, I am willing to suffer all'…

Champney wrote in his brief account: 'By his weakness, his sweet speech, and humble demeanor, his constancy and eagerness to embrace death, he caused many to lament his condemnation and to honor the Catholic religion'"); *Catholic Encyclopedia*.

Robinson, Right Rev. Mgr. Walter Croke – priest and author; b. 4 June 1839; c. 8 April 1872; d. 17 April 1914, Brighton; son of an Anglican rector; brought up as Low Church Anglican, but became Tractarian; later Anglican curate; ordained Catholic priest in 1875; Fellow of New College, Oxford (first Catholic fellow of an Oxford college since James II's reign); Domestic Prelate to Pope Leo XIII; for three years vice-rector of Catholic University College, Kensington, London; was chaplain of Kensington workhouse and infirmary; then preacher and lecturer of the Archdiocese of Westminster; see essay in J. G. F. Raupert (ed), *Roads to Rome* (1901), p.219 (later re-published as a pamphlet under the titles of *From Darkness to Light* (1904)) ("It was not very long before it dawned upon me that every Anglican, of whatever school, was in reality a law to himself, and that he acted on his own authority; and then it was that the question of *authority* became to me the 'articulus stantis vel cadentis ecclesiae,' and ever afterwards. I asked every one I met, 'By what authority dost thou believe, and doest thou these things?' Sometimes, on my inquiry of this or that divine, I was referred to the Prayer-book as my authority, sometimes to the Fathers of the Church, sometimes to the Primitive Church...

For any practical purpose, what is wanted is the living voice of authority to determine infallibly what the book means or does not mean in the case of Holy Writ; and what is true or false doctrine in the pages of all other writers, even those of the Fathers of the Church, all of whom – with the solitary exception of Saint Gregory Nazianzen – we as Catholics know have more or less committed themselves, here and there, to false doctrine...

By Private Judgment ... a man must find out the Catholic Church. When he finds it, it is a huge *objective fact*. All men must be agreed about it as a gigantic organization, which has existed these nineteen hundred years. For all that time – the name and date of every Pope being historical facts – it has been a chief factor in the history of Europe. All that time it has taught with the living voice, and ruled with an incomparable discipline. There it is today as of old, independent altogether of what men may think about it; a stubborn, undeniable, unmistakable fact. Whether it be true or false in its doctrine is besides the mark: there it is, and there it will be; that is all we are maintaining. Well, then, a man discovers this Church; he makes his allegiance to it, and is formally accepted by it. Henceforth he rests upon the authority of the Catholic Church, not upon his mental apprehension of it. He is a Catholic, not because he thinks he is, but because of the fact of his formal reception into the Catholic Church...

Bad Popes and bad priests never troubled me for a moment. The office and the man are so obviously distinct, that the mind must be addled that does not see it at a glance. A policeman may be an immoral man, but the bus-drivers and cabmen will obey him, and rein in their horses at his bidding, because he is a policeman. The sentence of an immoral judge will avail to hang a guilty murderer, because it is the official act of a judge; it is not invalid because the judge is a bad man...

I come, then, finally to the five conclusions ... which point unmistakably – in the reputed language of Lord Macaulay after one of Cardinal Wiseman's famous lectures – to 'either the Catholic Church or Babel.'

Point I. – *If my soul is to be saved, God must show me the way. It is not for me to choose my own way, and offer that to God....* The Ritualist, the High Churchman, the Broad Churchman, the Evangelical, the Nonconformist, all alike formulate their own views of religion, and offer them for God's acceptance as their account of salvation. The Catholic Church calls that putting the cart before the horse. The Catholic standpoint is this: that it is for God to reveal His own way of salvation, and all that man has to do, is to find out where that is, and to obey it. Further, that God *has* revealed it, and has committed this revelation to a competent authority upon earth, to guard it from error, and to enforce its observance. It is the duty of man to find out where this oracle of truth is, and submit mind and heart to it.

Point II. – *When God does reveal the way of salvation, it will and must be ONE* – (1) One in *number*. (2) One in *unity*.

(1) One in number; i.e. "ONE LORD, ONE FAITH, ONE BAPTISM" (Eph. iv. 5). Nowhere does Scripture give a hint as to more than one Church...

(2) Next, if the revelation is one in number, it will be one in unity too; that is to say, the earthly teachers of it will be one, and the taught will be one. Why? Because it is the truth. Truth is one: one in the teachers, and one in the taught of its very nature...

Point III. – If God does make a revelation of the way by which the soul is to be saved, that revelation will be infallible.

A. Infallible in its SUBJECT-MATTER –

(1) Because Almighty God delivers it. How can it be otherwise?

(2) Because my soul wants nothing else. I cannot trifle with eternity. I cannot afford to make a mistake about it, which it is impossible to put right after death.

B. Infallible in its EARTHLY MOUTH-PIECE –

(1) For of what practical use would be infallible truth with a fallible mouth-piece?

(2) How can Almighty God punish me for ever, if I refuse to believe a teacher who may mislead me? It is my solemn duty to refuse belief in such a one. Remember, we have to give an account of our faith as well as of our morals, and of faith before morals. 'He that believeth and is baptized shall be saved: he that believeth not shall be condemned' (St. Mark xvi. 16). How can God punish me eternally for want of faith, unless He gives me an infallible teacher, whereby I can secure infallible truth? An infallible teacher of salvation is the most pressing of all the needs of the soul, and yet the very mention of an infallible teacher makes the average Englishman shiver in his shoes. This is indeed astounding. Well, then, somewhere on earth, and in some authoritative body of men, or in the office of one man, must be placed by Almighty God the infallible oracle of truth. The way of salvation, then, is reduced to great simplicity by this time. All a man has to do, is to find out where

the oracle is, and then believe what it teaches, and do what it commands.

Point IV. – *This way of salvation will be exclusive.* That is to say, it will be the only one; and every other way of salvation will be false. This means that the true Church, wherever it is, will not only be the best of all Churches, but the *only* one...

Point V. – *To accept when once seen or willfully to reject this way of salvation is a matter of life or death eternal.* This seems obvious from the words of Scripture already quoted. To see it not, by a man's own fault, is likewise to be lost. Once the solid conviction has crossed a man's brain, that if he inquired honestly into the credentials of the Catholic Church he would be convinced of the truth of it, and bound to submit to it in mind and will, – that man must go on in his inquiry, otherwise he will be lost. To see it not, not by a man's fault – that is to say, in a case where it has never occurred to a man's mind that his own religion is false or that any other religion can be true – then, not to believe in the Catholic Church will not, of course, entail eternal loss on that account...

Let the religious inquirer examine any system of religion other than that of the Catholic Church, he will find that it breaks down on one or more of these five points").

Rockstro, William Smith (baptized in the name of Rackstraw) – pianist, composer, and writer on music; b. 5 January 1823, North Cheam, Surrey; c. 1876; d. 2 July 1895, West Kensington, London; friend and piano pupil of Mendelssohn; wrote a number of successful songs; composer of piano fantasias, transcriptions, and drawing-room pieces; successful pianist and teacher of singing and the piano; wrote books on early music, especially Palestrina, and biographies of musicians (e.g., Handel and Mendelssohn); Professor of counterpoint and plain-song at the Royal College of Music, London; see *History of Music for the Use of Young Students* (1879); *A General History of Music* (1886); *Grove Music Online*; *DNB*.

Roe, Saint (Bartholomew) Alban, OSB – priest and martyr; b. 1583, Suffolk; d. 31 January 1642; brought up Protestant; when at Cambridge went to St. Albans gaol to argue with a poor man confined for recusancy, but was shaken in his religious opinions, and subsequent reading and conversations with priests led him to convert; went over to Flanders and was admitted into English College, Douai; then went to English Benedictine monastery at Dieulouard in 1613; ordained priest and came on the English mission in 1615; apprehended by pursuivants in 1618 and committed to the New Prison, Maiden Lane, London; there for five years, then perpetual banishment in 1623; came back to England four months later; in 1625 apprehended again and committed to gaol at St. Albans, where he had begun his conversion; after two months transferred to Fleet prison in London where he spent seventeen years (though some periods of parole); committed to Newgate and tried at the Old Bailey; condemned to death for being a priest and exercising his functions in this country; his brother, James (d. 1657) also became a Benedictine; a sister became a nun abroad; see Dom Bede Camm, *Nine Martyr Monks* (1931); *Gillow*, Vol. V, p.437.

Rolfe, Frederick William (styled Baron Corvo, one of many pseudonyms he assumed) – author; b. 22 July 1860, 61 Cheapside, London; c. 1886; d. 26 October 1913, Albergo Cavaletto, Venice; brought up in a dissenting family by parents who both suffered from depression; precociously religious as a child; made up an aristocratic ancestry; discovered early a passion for writing, painting and photography; became a teacher; invited by third Marquess of Bute (see above) to be headmaster of his cathedral choir school in Oban, but left after an acrimonious two months; began religious studies at St. Mary's College, Oscott, near Birmingham, and at the Scots College, Rome, but was expelled from both; produced several paintings and published several books and stories (most successful his novel *Hadrian the Seventh* (1904)); influenced by *fin-de-siecle* decadent school of writers; lived degenerate life in Venice from 1898 to his death; unmarried; buried in a pauper's grave in San Michele cemetery, Venice, where he was re-interred in 1924; see A. J. A. Symons, *The Quest for Corvo: An Experiment in Biography* (1934) ("His becoming Catholic I could easily understand. The attraction of the Catholic Faith for the artistic temperament is a phenomenon which has been the subject of many novels, and is one of the facts of psychology.... Rolfe, as his books showed, was a medievalist, an artist, and a scholar in temperament; so that to him the tradition of the Catholic Church, with its championship of learning and beauty, must have been a real and living thing"); Donald Weeks, *Corvo* (1971); M. J. Benkovitz, *Frederick Rolfe: Baron Corvo* (1977); Brocard Sewell, *Like Black Swans: Some People and Themes* (1982), Ch. 4; Robert Whelan, "Why did so many Victorian decadents become Catholics?" *Catholic Herald*, 5 January 2001; Philip Waller, "Roman Candles: Catholic Converts among Authors in Late-Victorian and Edwardian England," in Peter Ghosh and Lawrence Goldman (ed), *Politics and Culture in Victorian Britain: Essays in Memory of Colin Matthews* (2006), p.192 ("Notwithstanding fierce competition from other literary converts, Rolfe must be ranked indisputable champion of paranoid peculiarity. Resembling a weasel with a monk's tonsure, he wore across his chest a crucifix that burnished his skin, and on one finger a ring with a spur to gouge the eyes of Jesuits who, he believed, were plotting to assassinate him. Equally fiercely, he venerated the Catholic faith and abominated most Catholic institutions, clergy, and communicants"); Ralph McInerny, *Some Catholic Writers* (2007); *DNB*.

Romanes, Ethel (*née* Duncan) – writer and religious activist; b. 15 August 1856, Ashfield Wavertree, Lancashire; c. 1919 (her son, Norman Hugh, was received in 1927 and became the head of the Chiswick Press); d. 30 March 1927, Santa Margherita, Italy; educated privately; wife of George John Romanes (1848–1894), a wealthy evolutionary biologist, who was a disciple of Darwin, though he kept open to the Christian faith; wrote a successful biography of her husband after his early death; moved in "intellectual, scientific, and Anglo-Catholic circles" (*DNB*); wrote a number of short devotional works; had six children; one son died in 1910, another was killed in World War I in 1915, and her daughter, an Anglican sister, died in 1918 after a painful illness; converted to the Catholic Church in the wake of these griefs; on the committee of the Catholic Truth Society, and active in the Converts' Aid Society; see *The Story of Port Royal* (1907); *A Great Mistake* (1921); *Anne Chichester* (1925) (last two are novels published as a Catholic); *DNB*.

Rope, Henry Edward George – priest; b. 23 October 1880, Shrewsbury; c. 6 January 1907, Breslau (for information on the conversion of other members of his family, see entry for his sister, Margaret Agnes Rope, below); d. 1 March 1978; cousin of Margaret Edith Rope (see below); father a devout High Anglican;

brought up in the Church of England; lapsed into infidelity at Oxford; lector in English at the University of Breslau 1905; went to English College, Rome; ordained Catholic priest 27 February 1915; lover of English Gothic architecture and the faith and civilization that created it; writer of history, biography and poetry; distributist; archivist to English College in Rome; editor of *Catholic Gazette* and *The Ransomer*; see "Tolerance," *The Month*, August 1920, p.125 ("As the late Monsignor Benson shrewdly put it, the average British family will hear with equanimity of its members becoming Quakers or Buddhists or even atheists, but should any of them think of becoming Catholics, henceforward the two thieves are the only fit companions for them!"); "Compromise No Charity," *The Month*, November 1926, p.442; *Forgotten England* (1931) ("In the north transept aisle [of Hereford Cathedral] the shrine of St. Thomas, carefully pieced together again in the last century, is still standing.... But where now are the saint's relics, and where the pilgrims to his tomb? Let the continuity-mongers tell us! And where and when was the last Mass said in the great cathedral?"); *Matthew Parker's Witness Against Continuity* (1931) (" Be it noted, Anglican continuitarians never vouchsafe to explain when and where Blessed Thomas More, by turning Papist, changed his religion, which, in view of the fact that he was put to death for refusing to change it, is not altogether astonishing"); "Catholic Intolerance," *The Month*, September 1931, p.203 ("To return to the question of religion. Here especially it is our duty to mark very definitely the limits of tolerance, if we are to be loyal to the Faith entrusted to us. We are surrounded by religious bodies whose rule of faith is ultimately their own private judgment, for none of them, not even the 'highest' Anglican, admits a living and infallible Authority in religion. Consequently it would be the height of intellectual arrogance for any member of these sects to say that he alone possessed the truth and that all who differed from him were in error: common politeness enjoins mutual tolerance. But Catholics basing their belief on God's living Oracle, the Church, must denounce as wrong and harmful everything contrary to her teaching. They must be as intolerant towards false beliefs as was their Master Christ. Their breadth of mind is shown by a ready admission that multitudes of non-Catholics, who have had no real chance of learning the truth, are in good faith, and that even 'Anglo-Catholics,' who have had the grace to see the more patent errors of Protestantism may yet be blind to the claims of the true Church. But it is not 'broad-mindedness' to tolerate their pretensions, still less to foster and flatter their delusions, on the plea that they are leavening the Protestant mass around them and preparing England to return to the Faith. Such a policy savors of doing evil that good may result, even if there were real evidence that it would be successful. On the contrary, speaking objectively, 'Anglo-Catholics' are more to blame than their Protestant fellows, because, having seen the need of Authority in religion, they will not recognize it where alone it exists"); essay in Maurice Leahy (ed), *Conversions to the Catholic Church: A Symposium* (1933) ("I learned [from Ruskin] that it was precisely Catholicism that made Europe beautiful and noble, just as natural religion had built the Parthenon before it.... 'He can't be wrong whose life is in the right.' It was very easy to quote, but how the dickens was one's life to be in the right without an infallible compass?... What I did find [in a Catholic book] was clear uncompromising assertion of the Church's teaching, very unlike the ever-

shifting utterances of Anglican writers, utterly independent of fashions of thought or 'public opinion'"); *Pugin* (1935); *Benedict XV: The Pope of Peace* (1940); *Gregory XVI and England* (1948); Matthew Hoehn, OSB (ed), *Catholic Authors* (1952); *Evolution and the Lunatic Fringe* (1964); Ronald Warwick, "Father H. E. G. Rope: Witness for Continuity," *Christian Order*, October 1978, p.452 ("Father Rope's distributism, as well as his robust and devotional Catholicism led him into the company of Chesterton and Belloc, and into the latter's friendship. He paid many happy visits to Kings Land and was often a guest at Christmas – those Christmases so memorably described by Belloc in *A Remaining Christmas*. Father Rope would offer the Holy Sacrifice of the Mass in Belloc's private oratory as the focal point of those Gargantuan festivities...

...In his latter years, Father Rope, himself became a witness *for* continuity, the continuity between those who today defend the traditional and unchanging. He belonged to that rapidly diminishing number who can remember the time when men reverenced tradition and were skeptical of novelty. Father Rope never capitulated before the inversion that took place in his own lifetime; 'Fashion contradicts tradition. *Modus locutus est. Causa finita est.* Tradition obligingly dies. Only – it doesn't'").

Rope, Margaret Agnes ("Marga") – nun and artist in stained glass; b. 20 June 1882, Shrewsbury, Shropshire; c. 1901; d. 6 December 1953, Quidenham Convent, Norfolk; brought up as an Anglican in an urban professional family with several doctors; after the early death of her father, her mother, an Anglican, and five of her six children (including Margaret and Henry, later Fr. Henry Rope (see above)) converted to Catholicism; family experienced some poverty, since the will of her father, who was High Anglican and very anti-Catholic, denied them money as Catholics; educated at home until going to Birmingham Muncipal School of Art in 1900, where she studied stained glass under Henry Payne; worked from home 1909–1923; influenced by the arts and crafts movement of William Morris and his followers; became a Carmelite nun in 1923 and took the name of Sr. Margaret of the Mother of God; able to continue her work until increasing illness after the war meant she could only help her first cousin, Margaret Edith (see below); specialized in the English martyrs, the Annunciation and the lives of the Saints, all done with great skill and conveying individual personality; seven windows of hers are in Shrewsbury Cathedral; buried in the monastery enclosure at Quidenham; see Emma Clancy, "Shrewsbury's Shining Light: Stained Glass Artist Margaret Rope," *Catholic Life*, November 2008, p.18; www.arthur.rope.clara.net.

Rope, Margaret Edith ("Tor") – artist in stained glass; b. 29 July 1891, Leiston, Suffolk; d. 9 March 1988; born into a farming family with several artistic relatives; educated at Chelsea School of Art and LCC Central School of Arts & Crafts, where she specialized in stained glass; worked much with her first cousin, Margaret Agnes Rope (see above); lived in London for many years; became a Catholic after joining a pilgrimage to Lourdes; career of over fifty years, producing well over one hundred windows; frequent subjects were the Annunciation, the Crucifixion, the Virgin and Child, lives of the Saints, daily life and children, and the question of nature; see website for Margaret Rope (above).

Rose, George (*pseud*. Arthur Sketchley) – writer; b. 19 May 1817, London; c. 1 November 1855 (received by Cardinal Manning); d. 11 November 1882, 96 Gloucester Place, Portman Square, London; nephew of Right Hon. Sir George Rose (1782–1873), Master in Chancery; was evangelical Anglican; at Oxford became Newmanite; according to his friend Francis Burnand (see above), "he was too hard-headed and logical to have ever been, or to have remained, a Puseyite"; briefly Anglican curate; lost his faith in the Church of England; after his conversion to the Catholic faith was tutor to Lord Arundel, later the fifteenth Duke of Norfolk; turned to drawing-room dramas, two novels, and very successful humorous sketches featuring his creation "Mrs. Brown" (a character despising everything not English), both written and performed as monologues (toured the world giving readings from these); unmarried; buried in Catholic cemetery of St. Thomas, Fulham; see *Gillow*, Vol. V, p.448; *DNB*.

Ross, Eva Jeany – social scientist; b. 2 June 1903, Northern Ireland; c. 1930; d. June 1969; father professed no particular religious affiliation; mother member of Church of England; after a Unitarian sunday-school, sent to Catholic school; worked in business as executive secretary; emigrated to United States after conversion; taught Economics, Sociology and Anthropology at several American universities and in Britain; saw the need for a Catholic textbook in sociology and published *A Survey of Sociology* (1932); studies of Catholic social movement in several countries; author of a standard sociology textbook; a founding member of the American Catholic Sociological Association and its President in 1943; see *Social Origins* (1936): "The study of social origins enables us better to understand the fundamental operations behind our major culture patterns. It enables us to meet on their own ground those sociologists who still propound unilinear evolution. These theorists take scanty account of history, and they will not listen to philosophical disquisition, or to religious revelation. They ignore the existence of a Creator, and of an intelligently created and planned world, whose inhabitants have a destiny beyond the grave. If, however, we can show them the obviously false inferences which they have drawn from the culture of those very primitives whom they have professed to study scientifically and with an unbiased mind, surely then they can hardly fail to take at least some cognizance of our claims"); *Basic Sociology* (1953); *Introducing Sociology* (1967); Anon "Eva Jeany Ross," *Catholic Life*, April 2003, p.23; Walter Romig (ed), *The Book of Catholic Authors*, First Series (1942); Matthew Hoehn, OSB (ed), *Catholic Authors* (1948); Patrick Allitt, *Catholic Converts: British and American Intellectuals Turn to Rome* (1997) *passim*.

Ross, (Ian) Anthony, OP – priest, writer and historian; b. 1917, near Beauly, Inverness-shire, Scotland; c. 10 February 1937; d. 24 May 1993, Blairgowrie, near Perth; brought up as Scottish Free Presbyterian; after conversion was cut off financially by his family; entered the Dominican Order in 1939; ordained priest 29 September 1945; prior of Woodchester in 1951; did much teaching; founder of *The Innes Review* and of the Scottish Catholic Historical Association; deputy chairman of the Parole Board for Scotland in 1979; rector of Edinburgh University 1979–1982; in 1982 elected provincial of the Dominican Order in Britain, but six months later suffered a stroke; Scottish nationalist and researcher on Scottish Catholic history; active peace campaigner; broadcaster; magistrate and prison visitor; close friend of the poet, Hugh MacDiarmid; articles in Dominican and Scottish periodicals; see *The*

Root of the Matter (his autobiography) (1989) ("'H'm-m!' [a Free Presbyterian cousin] said thoughtfully, 'but how can you stomach the Roman Church's scandalous history?' By then I had learned much more about its scandalous history than he had ever done. I had read the historian Edward Gibbon, and also Lord Macaulay's famous account of a New Zealander standing amid the ruins of London far in the future and musing on the phenomenon of papal survival. I drew comparisons between the Old Testament Church and the Catholic Church, between patriarchs, prophets and high priests on the one hand, and kings, visionaries and Popes on the other. I analyzed the genealogies of Christ offered in the gospels of Matthew and Luke, with their record of murder, incest, adultery and infidelity among the People of God as it moved towards its messianic fulfillment. The trouble with the Protestant churches, I declared, was that they had turned to schism in a perfectionist zeal, subtly asserting their own righteousness in place of Christ's. One of the best reasons for joining the Catholic Church, I maintained with a sudden feeling of fresh understanding, was precisely the obvious fact that above any other it is the Church of sinners, dependent upon Christ alone as the source of that holiness exemplified in its saints, in people like Francis of Assisi or Father Damien of Molokai, or in Mary and Joseph. The fruits of the Spirit, and the scandals, are always there, as Christ said they would be"); Owen Dudley Edwards, "Four For Chesterton," *Chesterton Review*, February and May 1995, p.89.

Ross, Robert Baldwin ("Robbie") – writer, critic, art dealer, journalist and gallery owner; b. 25 May 1869, Tours, France, of Ulster parents who had moved to Canada before settling in France; c. 1894; d. 5 October 1918, 40 Half Moon

Street, Mayfair, London; son of Hon. John Ross, QC, Solicitor-General of Canada; brought up as Anglican, but developed distinctly Catholic bias; part of the decadent movement and a major figure on the London literary and art scene from mid-1890s; most constant and loyal friend of Oscar Wilde (see below) and his literary executor; left instructions in his will that his ashes be taken to Père Lachaise cemetery in Paris and placed within Oscar Wilde's tomb, which was done, but not until 30 November 1950, fiftieth anniversary of Wilde's death; see essay in J. G. F. Raupert (ed), *Roads to Rome* (1901), p.234 ("Being rather a precocious reader as a child, I noticed that the saints, historical and legendary, whose lives I only knew through Protestant sources, were always spoken of with benevolent contempt or apology, and reading somewhere that 'the English Church has never produced saints but good practical citizens,' any lingering belief in Anglicanism, either as an interpretation of Scripture, a rule of life, or as a form of faith entirely disappeared from my mind…

If … reason enters into the conversion of ordinary converts such as myself, it is rather the absence of reason on the other side which renders the Anglican and Protestant position so unsatisfactory. The Anglican position seems to me to break down on its defense. The Protestant position breaks down in its attack on Catholicism"); Maureen Borland, *Wilde's Devoted Friend: A Life of Robert Ross* (1990); Jonathan Fryer, *Robbie Ross: Oscar Wilde's Devoted Friend* (2000); Robert Whelan, "Why did so many Victorian decadents become Catholics?" *Catholic Herald*, 5 January 2001; *DNB*.

Ross of Bladensburg, Lieutenant-Colonel Sir John Foster George – army officer; b. 27 July 1848; c. 1878 (wife,

Blanche, received in 1874; mother, Harriet, received in 1863; older brother, Robert Skeffington (1847–1892), later priest of the Society of Jesus, received in 1875; younger brother, Edmund James Thomas, received in 1876; sister, Harriet Margaret, later a nun, received in 1863; sister-in-law, Alexina Frances (1859–1896), also converted); d. 10 July 1926; son of David Ross of Bladensburg, County Down, Ireland; of the Coldstream Guards, with whom he served in the Suakim Campaign of 1885; then Chief Commissioner of the Dublin Police; JP for County Down, Ireland; author (historian of the Coldstream Guards).

Rothenstein, Sir John Knewstub Maurice – art historian and administrator; b. 11 July 1901, 1 Pembroke Cottages, Kensington, London; c. 1926 (his wife, Elizabeth, and his daughter, Lucy, also became Catholics); d. 27 February 1992, Beauforest House, Oxfordshire; son of the artist Sir William Rothenstein (1872–1945); brother of the printmaker Sir Michael Rothenstein (1908–1993); read Modern History at Oxford; contributed articles on art to newspapers and periodicals; taught Fine Art at American universities; director of Leeds, then Sheffield, art galleries; Director of the Tate Gallery 1938–1964; knighted in 1952; great supporter of contemporary British art; many honors; interested in contemporary art in the Church; see *Summer's Lease: Autobiography, 1901–38* (1965) ("My interest in religion up to this time [school at Bedales] was casual and intermittent, and vitiated by a suspicion that it was an unexciting subject. [Bernard Shaw's] *Preface to Androcles and the Lion* killed that suspicion with a single flashing stroke: before I had read more than a few pages I knew that the relation of man to his Creator – supposing there to be a Creator – ought to be man's ultimate preoccupation. Although its immediate effect was to cause me to reject the notion of the divinity of Christ, this essay brought his personality before me with thrilling vividness. After reading Shaw, Christ was never again for me an archaic or a legendary figure, still less the Pale Galilean: but a complex, enigmatic, an overwhelming, endlessly surprising personality.... I fell to comparing Shakespeare with the Four Evangelists. Shakespeare's utterance is so god-like that there are times when it is difficult to remember that he was a man. The Four Evangelists in comparison with Shakespeare were quite ordinary men.... Yet the supreme creation of a unique poetic genius does not compare, in subtlety, in consistency, in majesty, even in poetic quality, with the figure which emerges from the attempts at biography of an imaginative fisherman with a sense of metaphysics, of a cultured and sympathetic doctor, of a publican and a terse and competent reporter. The same transcendency marks the central figure in all four Gospels.... Him I therefore began to regard with a new reverence; and presently with something more than reverence. Eventually the time came when I was no longer able – Shaw's persuasive arguments notwithstanding – to believe that a Being of such transcendent wisdom could be subject to a delusion, or that a Being of such transcendent moral force could mislead his disciples and, through them, a great part of mankind. Jesus' claim to be God is stated in terms so specific that they must be rejected or accepted: it cannot be ignored...

Once I was convinced that Christ, in claiming to be the Son of God, was neither deceived nor deceiving, the rest followed. The Church of Rome – whatever the shortcomings of many of its servants – was manifestly the Church of the Apostles, and all others in schism, in disregard of Christ's prayer that those who

believed in him should be of one fold"); *Brave Day, Hideous Night: Autobiography, 1939–65* (1966) ("It was [Newman] who had been the principal human agent in making me a Catholic, and, what was, perhaps more difficult, in keeping me a Catholic through recurrent periods of skepticism"); *Time's Thievish Progress: Autobiography III* (1970); *DNB*.

Rowe, Miss – c. 1873; brought up as Anglican; isolated and poorly instructed Catholic; much correspondence with Newman after her conversion about her realization that as a Catholic she could not continue going with her family to Anglican services and about the relationship between the Anglican communion and the Catholic Church; see Newman's letter to Miss Rowe, 23 October 1873 ("It is strange and sad to think how many converts like you are solitary, – doubtless it is intended to throw their thoughts directly on their Lord and Savior to increase their faith, and to try their constancy"); Stanley L. Jaki, *Newman to Converts: An Existential Ecclesiology* (2001), Ch. 20 ("Newman ... had to spell out bluntly ... that 'The prime, I may say the only reason for becoming a Catholic, is that the Roman Communion is the only True Church, the Ark of Salvation. This does not mean that no one is saved who is not within that Church, but that there is no other Communion or Polity which has the promises, and that those who are saved, though not in the One Church, are saved, not by virtue of the Law or Sect which they profess, as the 39 Articles say, but because they do not know better, and earnestly desire to know the truth, and in consequence are visited by the superabundant mercy of God which He has not promised or covenanted'...

In the presence of plain truth regarding eternal salvation Newman became animated. '*What* is the true Church?' he challenged Miss Rowe to ponder and answer. And he helped her to do both by posing three questions, all of which called for a plain consent. They were to bring out in her eyes the catholicity of the Roman Church: 'Is it not to extend one and the same over all the world? And do we not see the Roman Church, knit together and fighting together, all over Europe and America, not to speak of Asia, militant against the great powers of the earth? It ought to be one and the same in every age – and is not the very taunt and the accusation brought against the Roman Church, that she is continuing all the doctrines and practices of the medieval times?' The Catholic Newman felt strongly for medieval Catholic times. Newman then referred to the unity, the single voice which a truly Catholic Church had to display. Newman did this by portraying the single voice of that unity against the background of the three different voices – high, broad, and low – of the Anglican Church: 'As the Prophet of God, [the Catholic Church] ought to speak with one voice; and does she not everywhere speak one faith, whereas, the Anglican has this decided mark of error, that it has and ever has had three doctrines different from each other, energetically preached from its pulpits, a broad, a high, and a low?'").

Rowsham, Blessed Stephen – priest and martyr; b. in Oxfordshire; d. March 1587, Gloucester; minister of parish of St. Mary's, Oxford, the university church; on conversion he went to English College, Rheims in 1581; ordained priest at Soissons in September 1581; went to England in 1582 and was arrested almost at once; thrown into a dungeon known as the "Little Ease"; transferred to the Marshalsea in 1584 and then into exile; went on the English mission again in 1586; arrested in 1587 in Gloucester and committed to Gloucester gaol; tried and condemned to death for receiving orders abroad and returning into this country; hanged, drawn and quartered at Gloucester; see *Gillow*, Vol. V, p.450.

Royde-Smith, Naomi Gwladys (Mrs. Ernest Milton) – literary editor and writer; b. 30 April 1875, Llanwrst, Wales; c. 1942 (received with her husband); d. 28 July 1964, Marylebone, London; eldest of eight children; childhood spent in Halifax, Yorkshire; then educated in London and private school in Geneva; wife of Ernest Milton, actor (see above); brought up Congregationalist and eclectic; became a reviewer and writer for the *Saturday Westminster Gazette*, both reviewing and writing (literary editor by 1912); hostess at many literary functions involving eminent writers; turned to fiction and wrote nearly forty novels; several biographies and four plays; popular writer between the wars; lecturer to non-political societies; buried in Hampstead cemetery; see *Children In the Wood* (1928) (heavily autobiographical of childhood); *The Delicate Situation* (1931); *For Us in the Dark* (1937); *The Altar-Piece: An Edwardian Mystery* (1939); Matthew Hoehn, OSB (ed), *Catholic Authors* (1952); *DNB*.

Rubbra, (Charles) Edmund Duncan – composer, critic, pianist, and teacher; b. 23 May 1901, 57 Cambridge Street, Northampton; c. 4 August 1947 (feast of St. Dominic); d. 14 February 1986, Lindens, Bull Lane, Gerrards Cross; brought up in poor working class family; parents had love of music; left school at fourteen; studied with Vaughan Williams and Gustave Holst; freelance pianist for a time; served in the army in World War II; lecturer in Music at Oxford University; prolific output (over 160 works); allegiance to the symphony (wrote eleven); two Mass settings; wide ranging musical interests; fine vocal and choral music; influence of both Christianity and Buddhism on his music; music reviewer for *The Month* and *The Listener*; see Ralph Scott Grover, *The Music of Edmund Rubbra* (1993); Antony Bye, "Rescuing Edmund Rubbra," *Catholic Herald*, 21 December 2001; *Grove Music Online*; *DNB* ("His deeply religious nature shines through much of his music: the canto movement of the sixth symphony (1954), for example, and the eighth, subtitled 'Hommage à Teilhard de Chardin'").

Rudkin, Miss P. – c. 29 December 1919; brought up in old-fashioned Protestant family, but early on developed a love for Catholicism; went to Broad Church school, where she lost her faith; became High Church Anglican before converting to the Catholic Church; see *The Road Home* (1920) ("Now history was my *forte*. I knew that the ancient Church in this land was Catholic, *in communion with the Pope*. I knew what took place at the Reformation, and I did not believe the High Church version of that event. I believed in Anglican orders for the simple reason that I *felt* they were valid – true Anglican reasoning – and I had not given them much thought.... However, there was no getting away from the Papal decision. High Churchmen brought up their case before the great tribunal for adjudication, but when that case was given against them, rebelliously refused to abide by the issue…

In the course of instructions I met with no doctrinal difficulties. *If* the Church was Christ's very own, He would see it did not err. It must be infallible, as He dwelt therein. Indulgences presented no obstacle; they seemed but right and kind and wise, so like the merciful tenderness of God. The Immaculate Conception of Our Lady? No other belief was possible in connection with her…

And she always *knows* – for she has the mandate from Our Lord Himself through the long unbroken line down from Peter the Apostle, the Rock on which foundation she is so solidly and beautifully built. She holds the keys. She was born before the New Testament was written. She was the earliest, sole form of Christianity. From her sprang every sect and denomination mutilating Divine truths, every religion professing Christ. Hers is no uncertain voice, no stammering utterance, no whittling away at doctrines to please the popular taste. Inside her churches kneel all nations, all classes side by side, with missal, rosary, or simple prayer book, holding the same faith").

Rugeley (alias Burgess), John Baptist, OCD – priest; b. 17 April 1587, Shenston, Staffordshire; c. 1603; d. 1 March 1669/70, London; from ancient family; father Protestant, mother Catholic; sent by his guardian to St. Omer's College, where he was received into the Church; went to English College, Rome; ordained priest 6 April 1612; went to the English mission in 1614; arrested soon after arriving and imprisoned for three or more years in Wisbeach Castle, then banished; returned twice more, but arrested each time and put in prison; bribed warders and gained release; escaped to Ireland, where he entered the Carmelite Order at Dublin; went back to the English mission in 1634, working for long period in Wells, Somerset; moved to London, but imprisoned in 1657; freed under bond; see *Gillow*, Vol. V, p.452.

Rumbold, Colonel Sir Arthur Carlos Henry – army officer and colonial administrator; b. 25 September 1820; d. 12 June 1869; fifth Baronet; grandson of Sir George Berriman Rumbold (1764–1807), second Baronet and diplomat; entered army in 1837 as an ensign; in 1848 appointed stipendiary magistrate in Jamaica; in 1855 joined the allied army in the Crimea; fought with the imperial Ottoman army; on 4 March 1857 appointed President of Nevis in the Leeward Islands, and on 17 November 1865 of the Virgin Islands; in 1867 administrator of St. Kitts and Anguilla; see *DNB*.

Russell, Conrad – diplomatic service; b. 3 April 1878; c. April 1947 (on his death bed; "When Diana [Russell] saw her brother she asked him why he had acted as he had done. 'I wanted to know', he answered, 'if there was anyone at the other end of the telephone.'"); d. 27 April 1947; son of Lord Arthur Russell; educated at home; parents agnostic but took their children to morning service and sometimes to a Catholic Mass; worked in the Colonial Office for Joseph Chamberlain; service in World War I; gentleman and letter writer; lifelong agnostic until final conversion, though frequently discussed religion, especially with Maurice Baring (see above); see Georgiana Blakiston (ed), *Letters of Conrad Russell, 1897–1947* (1987).

Russell, Henry Kenneth Alfred ("Ken") – film director; b. 3 July 1927, Southampton; c. 1957; served in both the Royal Air Force and the Merchant Navy; freelance photographer; filmmaker with BBC; several adaptations of composers' lives, e.g., Elgar, Debussy, Delius, and Richard Strauss; work has direct or indirect religious themes, often focusing on sacrifice and resurrection, e.g., *Lourdes* (1958), *The Devils* (1971); nominated for Oscar for best director for *Women in Love* (1969); biopics on Tchaikovsky. and Liszt; see Iain Fisher, "Ken Russell Savage Messiah Themes Religion," www.iainfisher.com ("His conversion to Catholicism has similarities with that of novelist Graham Greene. Like Greene it occurred just as Russell's life changed:

meeting his wife and starting his career. And like Greene his belief changed over the years, but always influenced his work. There are three overlapping phases: the devout Catholic, the Catholic testing faith to its limits, and the irreverence of later years as organized religion fails to live up to expectations").

Russell, Henry Patrick – author; c. 1896 (received with his wife and family); son of Alexander Wood Russell of the Bengal Civil Service; for sometime Sub-Lieutenant 18th Royal Irish Regiment; Anglican vicar before conversion; see essay in J. G. F. Raupert (ed), *Roads to Rome* (1901), p.237 ("If I must give a reason in few words I will say that, starting with the belief that our Lord has established an ecclesiastical kingdom here on earth, Visible and Catholic, I came to see that it cannot be as a house divided against itself, with antagonistic forms of government; but that it is indivisible, and that its unity consists, not in identity of institutions such as an Episcopal hierarchy and Sacraments (else would Donatists and others have been parts of the Church, which Anglicans themselves do not allow), but that it consists in an unity of polity and government – in a word, in the unity of a *kingdom*…

Now, it should surely be obvious to every one that there is but one ecclesiastical body politic, which interpenetrates every part of the world, and unites men of every nation and race in a religion which is everywhere one and the same in faith and obedience; that there is but one ecclesiastical kingdom which can with any truth be described as the Visible Church Catholic.

So true is this that Anglicans admit (and I presume, Easterns also) that they depend upon Rome for the Catholic note; that they would not, even though united with the Eastern Churches, form without Rome, a Catholic Church in any true sense of the word, since such combination would still be confined as to locality and race. Rome, however, does not depend upon them for the Catholic note. She, without them, is a (the) Catholic Church. And herein do we see the necessity to Anglicans of their contention that the Roman, Greek, and Anglican communions form one and the same visible Church. But if the unity of the Church is the unity of a kingdom, we see also the absurdity of the contention").

Russell, John Leonard, SJ ("Doc") – priest; b. 22 June 1906; c. 1936; d. 2 February 2006 (achieved the distinction of becoming the oldest British Jesuit ever); obtained MA, PhD and Diploma of Agriculture at Cambridge University; entered the Society of Jesus in 1937; ordained priest 12 September 1945; between 1947 and 1986 lectured in Cosmology, Chemistry, Physics, Mathematics and the Philosophy of Science at Heythrop College; wrote technical and popular scientific articles in various journals; also regularly contributed articles and reviews to the Jesuit publications, *The Month* and the *Heythrop Journal*; see *Science and Metaphysics* (1958); *Is Humanism Enough?* (1970); Joseph A. Munitiz, "The Writings of John L. Russell: A Tribute to his Academic Work," *Heythrop Journal*, July 2008, p.668.

Rutt, Rev. Mgr. Canon (Cecil) Richard – priest; b. 27 August 1925; c. 1994; educated at Pembroke College, Cambridge; Japanese translator in the navy in World War II; went to Korea as Anglican missionary in 1954; Anglican Bishop of Taejon in 1966; later Anglican Bishop of Leicester; returned to England in 1974; ordained Catholic priest in 1995; see "Provincial or Universal" in Dwight Longenecker (ed), *The Path to Rome* (1999) ("The more I thought about it the

more I realized that from its inception the whole Anglican communion had been built on the shifting sands of political expediency, theological compromise and spiritual relativity.... I shall never lose my grateful affection for my Anglican guides and friends; but what they could not give was a life in the Catholic Church – a house founded on the rock").

Ryder, George Dudley – Catholic layman; b. 1810; c. 5 May 1846 (received in Rome with his sister, Sophia ("Sophy") Ryder (see below); his three eldest children, Henry Ignatius Dudley (9) (see below), George Lisle (7) and (Caroline) Alice (5) following (for later details, see under entry for his wife, below); his wife, Sophia Lucy (see below), was received two days after himself (note: his mother was also called Sophia); another relative, Lady Edith Ryder, was received in 1882); d. June 1880; son of Henry Ryder (1777–1836), England's first Evangelical bishop, successively bishop of Gloucester, Lichfield and Coventry; his mother was aunt of Ambrose Phillipps de Lisle (see above); grandson of first Earl of Harrowby; had Newman for his tutor at Oxford, plus Richard Hurrell Froude (he was known as Froude's protégé); became Anglican rector; as Anglican he was one of Newman's disciples; brother-in-law of Cardinal Manning, Henry Wilberforce (see below), a lifelong friend, and Dr. Samuel Wilberforce (1805–1873), successively Anglican Bishop of Oxford and Winchester; widowed with seven children in 1850; after his conversion he worked for several Catholic causes; Newman acted as his spiritual director; interred with his wife in the burial ground of Mount St. Bernard Abbey ("The prayer carved on his tombstone was as follows: 'Oh my God, I thank Thee for what Thou givest, I thank Thee for what Thou witholdest, I thank Thee for what Thou withdrawest,

May thy holy and most Blessed Will be done in and by me and mine for ever in all circumstances at all times forever'"); see Penelope Hunting, "The Conversion of the Reverend George Dudley Ryder, 1846," *Recusant History*, May 2003, p.500.

Ryder, Henry Ignatius Dudley – priest and controversialist; b. 3 January 1837; c. 1846 (child convert); d. 7 October 1907, Edgbaston, Birmingham; eldest son of George Dudley Ryder (see above) and his wife, Sophia (see below); nephew of Cardinal Manning; pupil at the Birmingham Oratory school; joined the Oratorian Order, taking the name of Ignatius; ordained priest in 1862; much pastoral work, e.g., in the Birmingham workhouse and prison; wrote against the views of W. G. Ward (see below) on papal infallibility and an influential book on apologetics, *Catholic Controversy*; superior of the Birmingham Oratory after Newman's death in 1890 until 1905; buried at Rednal; see *Idealism in Theology, A Review of Dr. Ward's Scheme of Dogmatic Authority* (1867); *A Letter to W. G. Ward on his Theory of Infallible Instruction* (1868); *Postscriptum to Letter, etc* (1868); *Catholic Controversy* (1882) (a reply to R. F. Littledale's *Plain Reasons Against Joining the Church of Rome*); *Outside the Church There is No Salvation* (1891); *Essays* (1911).

Ryder, Sophia ("Sophy") (name in religion Sister Mary of the Sacred Heart) – nun; b. 1817; c. 5 May 1846 (received in Rome with her brother, George Dudley Ryder (see above); d. 1901; youngest daughter of Dr. Henry Ryder (1777–1836) Evangelical bishop of Gloucester, Lichfield and Coventry; in 1849 she became a Good Shepherd nun (first English novice of the Order to be received and trained in England); see *A Conversion and a Vocation* (1908).

Ryder, Sophia Lucy (*née* Sargent) – b. 1814; c. 5 May 1846; d. 1850; daughter of Anglican rector; wife of George Dudley Ryder (see above); sister of Mary Wilberforce (1810–1878), daughter-in-law of William Wilberforce (1759–1833), the philanthropist and slave emancipator; mother of Fr. Henry Ignatius Dudley Ryder (1837–1907), Catholic priest (see above); of Sir George Lisle Ryder (1838–1905), Newman's first Catholic godson and chairman of the Board of Customs; of Fr. Charles Edward Ryder (1842–1912), Catholic priest; of Fr. Cyril Ryder (1844–1931), Catholic priest of the Redemptorist Order and author of a life of Fr. T. E. Bridgett (see above); of (Caroline) Alice (1841–1934), wife of the architect Henry Clutton (see above) (who had converted to Catholicism in 1857); of Beatrice Mary (1849/50–1877), wife of Richard Hurrell Froude (see above); of Cecilia, later a nun; interred with her husband in the burial ground of Mount St. Bernard Abbey.

Ryder of Warsaw and Cavendish, Baroness (Margaret) Susan ("Sue") – charity founder and social worker; b. 3 July 1924, Leeds; d. 2 November 2000, Bury St. Edmunds, Suffolk; brought up by devout and well off Anglican parents; mother's social work with the poor showed her poverty at first hand; served in Europe, especially in Poland, with the Special Operations Executive in World War II; lived life of rigorous frugality; formed Sue Ryder Foundation to provide homes and help for sick and disabled; wife of Leonard Cheshire (see above) with whom she worked to raise money for their foundations; see essay in Rowanne Pasco (ed), *Why I Am a Catholic* (1995) ("When innocent children were deliberately injured or starved to death, it caused some people to question their own faith, but I saw them as sharing in the sufferings of Christ. That is the only way I can answer it"); *And the Morrow is Theirs* (1976); *Child of My Love* (1986; revised 1998); Richard Morris, *Cheshire: The Biography of Leonard Cheshire, VC, OM* (2000); *DNB*.

Sackville, Thomas (first Baron Buckhurst and first Earl of Dorset) – administrator and poet; b. 1536, Buckhurst, Withyham; d. 19 April 1608; son of Sir Richard Sackville (1507–1566), MP and Privy Councillor; educated at Oxford University; friend of Robert Persons (see above) at Oxford; became barrister and MP; made a reputation as a poet; in the 1560s in Rome he discussed with Pope Pius IV possible ways of reconciling England and the papacy; sent by Queen Elizabeth I in 1586 to inform Mary Stuart of her sentence of death (Mary was moved by his consideration); he was one of the officers of state who administered the country after the queen's death and proclaimed James I king; reconciled to the Church (by Fr. Richard Blount, the Jesuit superior in England) near the end of his life, having been previously a church papist; buried at Withyham, Sussex; see Anthony Charles Ryan, "The Sackvilles at the Reformation," *Catholic Life*, October 2003, p.20; *DNB*.

Sackville-West, Hon. Edward Charles, fifth Baron Sackville ("Eddy") – novelist and music critic; b. 13 November 1901, 105 Cadogan Gardens, London; c. 17 August 1949; d. 4 July 1965, Cooleville House, Clogheen, County Tipperary, Ireland; descended from Thomas, first Earl of Dorset, Lord High Treasurer and cousin of Queen Elizabeth I; cousin of Vita Sackville-West; as a boy a pious Anglo-Catholic, then lost his Christian faith in 1924; at Eton and Christ Church College, Oxford, but left without taking a degree; five autobio-

graphical novels; also biography; fine music critic for *New Statesman* 1935–1955; producer at BBC in World War II; with Desmond Shaw-Taylor compiled a famous record guide in 1951, revised several times; several homosexual relationships in his life; became a Knight of Malta; spent last and happiest years in Ireland; unmarried; buried at St Mary's Church, Clogheen; see *A Flame in Sunlight: the Life and Work of Thomas De Quincey* (1936); *The Rescue: a Melodrama for Broadcasting* (1943 (for which Benjamin Britten produced a score); Jocelyn Brooke, "The Novels of Edward Sackville-West: An Appreciation," *The Month*, August 1951, p.99; Michael de-la-Noy, *Eddy: The Life of Edward Sackville-West* (1988) ("Apparently it was while reading George Orwell's novel *1984*, published in 1949, that Eddy became convinced that 'the devil's agents, recently associated with the conquered Nazis, were still very much with us' and that it was 'high time to declare myself – to take the side of Christ against the gospel of materialism.'"); Matthew Hoehn, OSB (ed), *Catholic Authors* (1952); Joseph Pearce, *Literary Converts* (1999), pp.258–260, 350–351; *DNB*.

Sadler, Dom. Thomas, OSB (name in religion Vincent Faustus) – priest; b. 1604, Warwickshire; d. 19 January 1681, Dieulouard; converted by Fr. Augustine Baker through his Benedictine uncle, Dom Walter Sadler (see below); entered the Benedictine Order at St. Lawrence's Priory, Dieulouard in Lorraine; came to the English mission in the south province before 1637; chaplain to Sir Henry Tichborne and to William Sheldon and worked for many years in London; superior of Kent 1649; assisted in founding of the Confraternity of the Rosary, members of which were primarily "pious Rosarists" of aristocratic background (dean for many years); many spiritual writings and translations for the confraternity; elected to titular position of cathedral prior of Chester; became definitor of province of Canterbury in 1661; see *Gillow*, Vol. V, p.463; *Catholic Encyclopedia*; *DNB*.

Sadler, Dom. Walter Vincent Faustus, OSB (alias Robert Walter) – priest; d. 21 June 1621, Barbican, London; after his conversion went over to English College, Rheims in 1590; ordained priest in December 1592; came to the English mission in 1593; worked in Berkshire; imprisoned and exiled at one point; entered the Benedictine Order whilst in the Gatehouse prison, London; elected first provincial of Canterbury in 1619; made many converts, his last being his nephew, Thomas Sadler (see above); see *Gillow*, Vol. V, p.463.

St. John, Ambrose Maria – priest and author; b. 29 June 1815, Islington, London; c. about 3 October 1845 (his nephew, Edward St. John (1855–1934), also converted and was later a priest and canon of Southwark diocese); d. 24 May 1875, Ravenshurst Farm, Edgbaston; grandson of St. Andrew St. John, Anglican Dean of Worcester; educated at Christ Church, Oxford, where he was a pupil of Pusey; later Fellow of Christ Church 1838–1845; Anglican curate (1841–1843) to Henry Wilberforce (see below); close friend of Newman; after his conversion he joined the Oratorian Order; ordained Catholic priest 1 June 1847 (Trinity Sunday) by Cardinal Fransoni at Propaganda, Rome (same occasion as Newman); one of the original members of the Birmingham Oratory where he spent the rest of his life; many labors on the missions; for several years headmaster of the Oratory School; editor of *Raccolta* of Indulgences; fine orientalist and classicist; buried in private cemetery belonging to Birmingham Or-

atory; see Newman, dedication in *Apologia Pro Vita Sua* (1864) ("And to you especially, dear Ambrose St. John; whom God gave me, when He took every one else away; who are the link between my old life and my new; who have now for twenty-one years been so devoted to me, so patient, so zealous, so tender; who have let me lean so hard upon you; who have watched me so narrowly; who have never thought of yourself, if I was in question"); *Gillow*, Vol. V, p.466; *Catholic Encyclopedia*; *DNB* ("Shortly after his [St. John's] death, Newman acknowledged that 'As far as this world was concerned I was his first and last' (*Letters and Diaries*, Vol. 27, p.305). In recognition of this deep spiritual friendship and absolute loyalty, Newman asked to be buried in the same grave").

Sala, George Augustus Henry – author and journalist; b. 24 November 1828, 12 New Street, Dorset Square, London; c. November 1895; d. 8 December 1895, Hove, Sussex; in law son of dancing master of Italian descent, but natural father almost certainly Captain Charles Fairfield, army officer; successively clerk, scene painter at the Princess and Lyceum Theatres, London; then (1857–1895) on staff of *Daily Telegraph* as a leader writer and special correspondent; contributor to *Chat, Household Words, All The Year Round, Illustrated London News, Sunday Times, Temple Bar*, etc.; wrote five novels; flamboyant life style led to frequent financial crises; buried in Hove cemetery; see *Gillow*, Vol. V, p.466; *DNB*.

Salvo, Marquise de (*née* Lucy Anne Mary Caroline Claxton) – benefactress; b. 29 May 1813, Bristol; c. February 1846 (received in Paris); d. 14 November 1892, Paris; brought up as a Protestant; her parents left England in 1820, so she was brought up chiefly in

Italy; cousin of William Anderdon (see above); niece of Manning; widow of the Marquis de Salvo, a Sicilian nobleman in Neapolitan service at the court of Louis Philippe in Paris; correspondence with Newman before and after her conversion; lifelong friend of Lady Georgiana Fullerton (see above); lived in Paris until her death and did so with great regularity in her devotions and good works; main foundress of the Institute of Notre Dame de France in London; painter whose pictures were often sold for charity; buried at Montmorency in the same grave as her husband; see M. E. H., "The Late Marquise de Salvo," *The Month*, June 1893, p.228; Stanley L. Jaki, *Newman to Converts: An Existential Ecclesiology* (2001), Ch. 8 ("Newman diagnosed her predicament without hesitation: 'It is not possible that I should be able to give more than *one* answer to the very serious question on which your letter turns. I seriously think it unsafe for anyone to remain out of the Catholic Church who is aware of the fact that he is without it – and if you believe that the English Church is one Church and the Catholic Church another Church, I do not see what is to be done but to join the Catholic Church.... You may suppose that *I* have no doubt on the point, considering how much I have given up for it. I never could think it right to change my religion on any ground short of the *absolute necessity* of the act, as a condition of *everlasting salvation*'").

Sandford, John Douglas – barrister and civil servant; b. 1832; d. 1892; son of Anglican rector; grandson of Anglican Bishop Sandford of Edinburgh; student at Trinity College, Oxford, then at the Inner Temple; became a barrister in 1870; worked as civil servant in India 1856–1884; had some correspondence 1876–1878 with Newman before his conversion; see Stanley L. Jaki, *Newman*

to Converts: An Existential Ecclesiology (2001), pp.360–363 ("Newman ... insists that devotion to Our Lady need not, and generally does not obscure devotion to her Son, and he appeals to this broad fact the other way, namely, 'if we look through Europe, we shall find, on the whole, that just those nations and countries have lost their faith in the divinity of Christ, who have given up devotion to His Mother...'

Newman's next letter to Sandford was written six months later.... Newman now dealt entirely with Mary's status: 'As to your question nothing seems to me more unnatural than the ordinary Protestant interpretation of the text in question. A girl of thirteen asking a physical question! And if she did, would not she incur the same guilt as Zacharias, and deserve the same punishment for unbelief? But it is all plain, if it is a moral difficulty which the Blessed Virgin expresses. All Jewish women are said to have been hoping to be the Mother of the Messiah – therefore marriage was in such special honor. Mary had given up that hope, and devoted herself to a single life – and she says, 'How is this consistent with my purpose? I have no husband – I am not to be married and the Messias cannot be born of me – Do you mean I am to relinquish what I have so solemnly accepted?'

It would have indeed been difficult to put it better. The same holds for Newman's explanation of Joseph's role: 'That she was betrothed to Joseph as a protector (and for no other reason) seems to have been a matter of necessity, as Protestants generally allow. She could not live as a single woman, and her celibacy required the outward defense of a husband'").

Santley, Sir Charles – singer; b. 28 February 1834, Liverpool; c. 1880; d. 22 September 1922, 13 Blenheim Road, St.

John's Wood, London; brought up as Unitarian; keen singer (baritone), pianist and violin player; studied singing in Italy; long and versatile career as opera singer (baritone); after 1876 only sang in concerts; at the top for last forty years of 19th century; many musical honors; Knight-Commander of the Order of St. Gregory the Great 1887; first singer ever to be knighted (1907); wrote two books on singing and a memoir; composed some works for Catholic liturgy; see *Reminiscences of My Life* (1909); J. M. Levien, *Sir Charles Santley* (1930); *Grove Music Online*; DNB.

Sassoon, Siegfried Loraine, MC – poet and prose writer; b. 8 September 1886, Weirleigh, Brenchley, near Paddock Wood, Kent; c. 14 August 1957 (his wife's niece, Jessica Gatty, who later became a nun, was received in October 1961); d. 1 September 1967, Heytesbury House, near Warminster, Wiltshire; son of Alfred Ezra Sassoon (1861–1895), financier and sculptor; brought up entirely by his mother; descended on father's side from a Jewish family, though he was brought up as an Anglican; studied at Clare College, Cambridge, but left without taking a degree; lived as a gentleman; Military Cross in World War I; poet of First World War (becoming a pacifist); his public protest against the war led to a psychiatric hospital; encouraged and helped Wilfred Owen; later also prose writer, much autobiographical; several homosexual relationships, but later marriage and family; influenced by nuns of Stanbrook Abbey and, regarding his conversion, by Mgr. Ronald Knox (see above), the Asquiths, and Mother Margaret Mary McFarlin (1905–2001); Catholic faith gave him great comfort and joys in his last years; honorary degree of DLitt from Oxford University in 1965; buried in Mells churchyard, Somerset; see *Memoirs of a*

Foxhunting Man (1928); *Memoirs of an Infantry Officer* (1930); *Sherston's Progress* (1937); *The Old Century and Seven More Years* (1938); *The Weald of Youth* (1942); "Lenten Illuminations," *Downside Review*, Summer 1958, p.219 (poem containing an account of his conversion); *Collected Poems* (enlarged edition 1960); *Siegfried's Journey* (1945); *The Path to Peace* (1960) (a spiritual anthology of his poetry); Dame Felicitas Corrigan (ed), *Siegfried Sassoon: Poet's Pilgrimage* (1973) ("When I was in the vortex of struggling towards submission … I came upon the following passage in Speaight's biography [of Hilaire Belloc], from a letter to Katharine Asquith: 'The Faith, the Catholic Church, is discovered, is recognized, triumphantly enters reality like a landfall at sea which first was thought a cloud. The nearer it is seen, the more it is real, the less imaginary: the more direct and external its voice, the more indubitable its representative character, its "persona", its voice. The metaphor is not that men fall in love with it: the metaphor is that they discover home. "This was what I sought. This was my need." It is the very mould of the mind, the matrix to which it corresponds in every outline the outcast and unprotected contour of the soul. It is Verlaine's "Oh! Rome – oh! Mere" And that not only to those who had it in childhood and have returned, but much more – and what a proof! – to those who come upon it from the hills of life and say to themselves, "Here is the town"'); Rupert Hart-Davies (ed), *Siegfried Sassoon Diaries (1915–1925)*, 3 Vols. (1983–1985); Paul Moeyes, *Siegfried Sassoon: Scorched Glory* (1997); Jean Moorcroft Wilson, *Siegfried Sassoon: The Making of a War Poet, !886–1918* (1998); John Stuart Roberts, *Siegfried Sassoon, 1886–1967* (1999) ("As to what happens at conversion nobody can explain – except that there is a before and after; the crossing of a border: a moving between states – darkness to light; chaos to order and everything made new. Sassoon in the spring of 1957 was aware of an 'instant release'. His puzzlement was why he had taken so long to understand that it was not an intellectual argument but just unconditional surrender"); Jean Moorcroft Wilson, *Siegfried Sassoon: The Journey From the Trenches, 1918–1967* (2003) ("One of the powerful attractions of the Catholic Church for Sassoon appears to have been the notion of confession and absolution. 'Could I but be absolved of what my years have wrought,' he had written in an unpublished poem of 1947; and two years later had argued, in a letter to [H. M.] Tomlinson, that the whole point of life was 'to try to rise above one's waistline.' There is no doubting the sense of guilt he carried with him up to his entry into the Church…

A more complex question is why Sassoon chose to become a Catholic rather than simply returning to the Anglican faith of his upbringing…. In responding to Tomlinson, who sympathized with his spiritual needs but found his choice of Church puzzling, he told him that the Catholic Church gave him a 'sustenance' the Church of England could not; it seemed 'so real' and its followers so different from the 'inhibiting reticence' which characterized the average Anglican…

Dennis Silk believed that a decisive factor in Sassoon's turning to Rome was his despair at world events, Korea and Suez in particular. He also maintained that Sassoon 'wanted to be told what to do' in his old age, and that the Catholic Church, with its claim to be the 'One True Church' and belief in the infallibility of its leader, the Pope, provided that authority. Sassoon himself, in his attempt to explain his decision, had written: 'My faith needs authority to sustain it, I suppose. And this great edifice of Catholicism makes Anglicanism seem unreal and ineffective. The faith I am now blessed with came to me through Catholic influence …' In becoming a Catholic he had found similar relief to the kind he had experienced in joining the army: he was once more 'under orders'. And as Maurice Wiggin, who met him towards the end of his life, suggested, his 'instinct for order' was very important to him"); Max Egremont, *Siegfried Sassoon* (2005) ("Authority was what he wanted, not the soft, apologetic Church of England. The Abbot of Downside surely would 'put the fear of God into me.' And Sassoon longed to be 'put in my place.' 'Be ye as little children': he yearned for those reassuring words and 'never to be lonely and forsaken again'…

Siegfried Sassoon's conversion was not, like that of J. H. Newman, the result of long intellectual reasoning. Nor did the light come in a sudden burst, as experienced by St. Paul. What happened had come slowly, encouraged by a slow falling away of much that had seemed worth while in his life, a process that began as far back as what he saw as the betrayal of his sacrificial idealism during the First World War…

Roman Catholicism brought authority – an end to questioning, the return of a certainty…. It brought an understanding, and forgiveness, of everything about him that was wrong. In the Church, he belonged, at last, to a definable and (to him) an admirable world, an elect drawn together by religious mystery, by the idea of the unknowable which he believed was at the core of the most important part of his life: his poetry. The search for utopia – recreated in his prose books – ended with monks, nuns and priests, the holy Catholics of his last years. Sassoon's Catholicism also had beauty and history, even glamour, exemplified by what he saw and loved at Mells, the

Roman Catholicism of *Brideshead Revisited*. When his new faith began to manifest itself in inexplicable visions and mysticism as well, his joy in it became an ecstasy greater than anything that he had ever known...

All his life had been a searching for religion – 'for a faith that I could accept.' The aspect he liked most was 'the complete authority of the Church,' and this was odd ... after his rebellious record in the First World War"); Joseph Pearce, *Literary Converts* (1999), *passim*; *DNB*.

Saward, John – priest and writer; b. 1947, Middlesex; c. 1 October 1979 (received at Campion Hall, Oxford with his wife and their three children, Catherine, Helena, and Anna); brought up as a practicing Anglo-Catholic (later became Anglo-Papalist); religious doubts at school, but studied the Protestant Reformation and saw its destructive impact on English culture; at age of 16 or 17 concluded that if Christianity was true, then Roman Catholicism was Christianity in its complete form; fell away from all religion in mid-1960s, but returned; became Church of England clergyman; influenced by the Blessed Virgin in the sense that she and the Church always bound up together; also influenced in his conversion by the writings of Fr. Philip Hughes and Dom David Knowles; also by Newman's phrase "the one true fold of the redeemer"; lecturer in Dogmatic Theology, Ushaw College 1980–1992 (helped by Bishop Gordon Wheeler (see below) to find this position); Professor of Systematic Theology at St. Charles Borromeo Seminary, Philadelphia 1992–1998; then Professor of Dogmatic Theology at the International Papal Theological Institute in Gaming, Austria; then associate lecturer at Blackfriars in the University of Oxford; ordained Catholic priest in 2003; Fellow of Greyfriars College, Oxford, 2003; author

of many books and articles on Catholic themes; consulting editor of *Communio*; see *The Case Against the Ordination of Women* (1978); *Perfect Fools: Folly for Christ's Sake in Catholic and Orthodox Spirituality* (1980); *The Beggar Saint: Benedict-Joseph Labre* (1984); *The Mysteries of March: Hans Urs von Balthasar on the Incarnation and Easter* (1990); *This Great Sacrament Revere* (1992); *Redeemer in the Womb: Christ Living in Mary* (1993); *Christ is the Answer: The Christ-Centred Teaching of Pope John Paul II* (1994) ("Jesus Christ is the centre, but not dead centre. Having descended into Hell in His soul, He rose again in His body, and ascended into heaven in both. The Cross is the still point of the turning world, but its pivotal power comes from the Resurrection.... If Christ is not risen, says St. Paul, our faith is in vain (cf. 1 Cor. 15.14). No Easter, no Christianity. The Pope quotes Romano Guardini: 'With Jesus' Resurrection stands or falls Christian faith.' It is the supreme confirmation and crowning of all that Jesus did and taught 'from His birth to His Passion and Death, by His deeds, miracles, teaching, example of perfect holiness and especially by His transfiguration.' Above all, it confirms the truth of His divine identity as consubstantial Son of the Father: 'The Resurrection of the Crucified proved that He really was "I am" (cf. John 8.59), the Son of God.'

Against all the demythologizing and etherealizing interpretations 'from Valentinus to Bultmann,' the Pope reaffirms the historicity and bodiliness of the Resurrection. The preaching of the Apostles is based on a 'real event,' not a 'myth or conception.' Of course, though truly historical, it is not just one event among many, it is the Event of events, in a certain sense 'transcending and standing above history.' The Apostles did not invent the Resurrection. When Our Lord, after the Transfiguration, foretold His coming Resurrection, the disciples did not know what He was talking about (cf. Mark 9.9f). They had been brought up to look forward to a general resurrection at the end of history, but they knew nothing of an anticipated resurrection. No Jew would be predisposed to fabricate such a belief, least of all eleven frightened Jews shattered by the 'extreme test' of their Master's execution.

The Resurrection was bodily, the raising up of Jesus' body from the tomb. The empty tomb by itself was not a direct proof of the Resurrection. Mary Magdalene thought the emptiness meant that someone had taken the body. Nonetheless, for those of good will it was a first step towards recognizing the fact of the Resurrection. The tomb was empty, they realized, because Jesus had Himself emptied it – by rising again in the flesh. When He appears to the disciples, the Lord reassures them that He is no ghost, but gloriously alive in body, with flesh and bones (cf. Luke 25.36f)…

…Christ's Resurrection confirms not only His full and complete divinity, but also His full and complete humanity. A Jesus 'risen' only in spirit would be a dead man, a departed soul, not a complete human being …"); *The Beauty of Holiness and the Holiness of Beauty: Art, Sanctity and the Truth of Catholicism* (1997); *The Way of the Lamb: The Spirit of Childhood and the End of the Age* (1999); *Re-Awakening the Catholic Memory* (2001) ("'And I hold in veneration, for the love of Him alone, Holy Church as His creation and her teachings as His own.' In these words from his poem *The Dream of Gerontius*, Cardinal Newman sets out the reasons why he and you and I are Catholics. We believe that the Catholic Church was not invented by man, but instituted by God-made-man, and her teachings are not humanly devised whimsy, but divinely declared

wisdom. The Church is the Bride and Body of Christ, alive with His life, teaching by His authority. For this belief, Newman sacrificed nearly everything on earth that was dear to him, and for this belief, we too must be ready to give our all"); *Cradle of Redeeming Love: The Theology of the Christmas Mystery* (2002) ("[T]he Catholic Church, the undeceiving Mother of Christ's faithful, commemorates the evangelists on their feast days as named men who were either disciples or disciples of disciples of the Lord, and at every celebration of the Holy Sacrifice she solemnly proclaims the Gospel 'according to' one or other of the four named evangelists. Since the Holy Spirit leads the Church into all the truth, we can trust the Church's daily assertions of the authorship and authenticity of the Gospels. It is Holy Mother Church, the Bride of the Word, 'to whom it belongs to judge of the true sense and interpretation of Holy Scripture.' The Bible is the Church's book. It is she who made the canon of Scripture, she who discerned, with the Holy Spirit's assistance, the inspiration He once gave to the sacred writers. In the person of Mary, the Church meditated on the mysteries of Jesus long before any of the evangelists had lifted his pen (cf. Lk 2:51). It is therefore to the Church, both to her Tradition and to her Magisterium, that we should turn for enlightenment concerning the identity and mission of the evangelists, the servants of the mysteries"); *Sweet and Blessed Country: The Christian Hope For Heaven* (2005) ("A merely 'spiritual' resurrection is no resurrection at all, and of no use to anyone for anything. Were the risen Christ no more than a soul separated from His body, He would be a dead man (cf. *S.T.* a. 4), not a living man, and therefore indistinguishable from John Brown and all those other mere men whose poor bodies lie a-mouldering in the grave. His claim to be the only-begotten Son of the Father would be, as Scottish law has it, 'not proven' (cf *S.T.* 3a q. 50, a. 4). The prayer on the Cross, 'Father, into thy hands I commend my spirit' (cf. Luke 23:46) would have received no response from Heaven. 'Resurrection' means the rising again of what has fallen, that is, of the body in death"); *EWTN Audio Library* (22 September 2008) ("There is a contradiction in believing Christianity to be a divinely revealed religion, that God has revealed himself fully and completely in his Son made man and then has just simply, as it were, left us to get on with it without an infallible teaching office to enable us faithfully to adhere to that revelation and understand it more deeply; and of course that we believe to be the living magisterium of the Catholic Church.... Without that living magisterium which teaches with the authority that Christ has given to it we are thrown back on private judgment").

Scanlan, Olive Mary – teacher and lecturer on literary and artistic subjects; b. at Broomfield, near Taunton, Somerset; both parents practicing Anglicans; brought up in Anglicanism; at twelve learned from a Catholic governess a notion of what the Catholic religion was about and how great a part it played in lives of its members; married a lapsed Catholic who died two years later reconciled to the Church; see *Memories of a Convert* (1944) ("It seemed to me quite clear, from the teaching of the New Testament, that Our Lord had come down to earth for a threefold purpose – to redeem us, through His Passion and Death upon the Cross, to show us how to live and to found a Church. This Church was to be (as the Nicene Creed tells us) *One, Holy, Catholic and Apostolic.* She was to be one – that is to say, within her fold there was to be found perfect unity of dogma, of Sacraments and of Ritual. Where was this perfect unity to be found, outside the Catholic Church? The Eastern Church, which since her schism from Rome I had always believed had guarded the ancient doctrines of the faith, and differed from the Roman Church only in her denial of the fact that the Pope was Supreme Pontiff, had I learnt, from the date of her severance from the Catholic Church – gradually split up into almost as many divisions as the Church of England.

In the English Church, many of the clergy were teaching and preaching doctrines which their own bishops flatly denied. The High Church believed itself to be the unique possessor of the truth. The Low Church accused the High Church of idolatry, and the Broad Church had reached the point of teaching hardly any doctrine at all!").

Schumacher, Ernst Friedrich ("Fritz" or "E.F.") – economist; b. 16 August 1911, Bonn, Germany; c. 29 September 1971 (second wife, Verena Rosenberger ("Vreni") (b. 1941) and daughter, Barbara, received in 1968); d. 4 September 1977, Switzerland; came to England as Rhodes Scholar 1930; at first influenced by Marxist ideas; absorbed Keynes' ideas on employment; economic adviser to British Control Commission in Germany 1946–1950; economic adviser to the National Coal Board 1950–1970; became a Buddhist in 1950s; after becoming a Catholic he made distributist ideas much more influential with his idea of intermediate technology and books *Small is Beautiful* (1973) and *A Guide for the Perplexed* (1977); took British nationality; buried in Caterham, Surrey; see Barbara Wood, *Alias Papa: A Life of Fritz Schumacher* (1984) ("It is when we come to politics that we can no longer postpone or avoid the question regarding man's ultimate aim and purpose. If one believes in God one will pursue politics mindful of the eternal destiny of man and of the truths of the Gospel. However if one believes that there are no higher obligations it becomes impossible to resist the appeal of Machiavellianism – politics as the art of gaining and maintaining power so that you and your friends can order the world as *they like it*"); Joseph Pearce, *Small is Still Beautiful* (2001); Joseph Pearce, *Literary Converts* (1999), *passim*; *DNB*.

Scott, Clement William – theatre critic; b. 6 October 1841, London; c. 1865 (influenced by his Tractarian father, a fervent admirer of Newman); d. 25 June 1904, 15 Woburn Square, London; son of Anglican curate; brother-in-law of George du Maurier (1834–1896), the artist and author of *Trilby*; at one time at the War Office; very influential drama critic for *Daily Telegraph* 1871–1897, throughout the 1880s editor of *The Theatre*, then drama critic of *New York Daily Herald*; founder and editor of short-lived *The Free Lance*; saw himself as preserver of popular taste and Victorian values (denounced Ibsen's work); also plays, travel essays, poetry and short stories; father of Eric Clement Scott, drama critic; buried in chapel of Sisters of Nazareth, Southend; see *DNB*.

Scott, George Gilbert – architect and scholar; b. 8 October 1839, 20 Spring Gardens, London; c. 1880 (received with his wife, Ellen); d. 6 May 1897, London; educated at Jesus College, Cambridge (later Fellow of the college); eldest son of Sir George Gilbert Scott (1811–1878), architect and author; great grandson of Thomas Scott who influenced Newman; principal influence on his architecture was George Frederick Bodley, his father's former pupil; helped to change direction of English church design in 1870s by using English and late styles of Gothic instead of thirteenth-century and continental models; also de-

signed wallpaper and furniture; High Churchman whose conversion shocked his family; finally decided to become a Catholic after attending Newman's mass in his private chapel in Birmingham; mental instability in later years; father of Giles Gilbert Scott (1880–1960), the architect and designer of the Anglican Liverpool Cathedral; another son, Adrian Gilbert, also distinguished architect; buried in Hampstead additional burial-ground, London; see *Essay on the History of English Church Architecture prior to the Separation from the Roman Obedience* (1881); *Gillow*, Vol. V, p.485; *DNB*.

Scott (alias Craford), Blessed William Maurus, OSB – priest and martyr; b. about 1579, Chigwell, Essex; d. 30 May 1612, Tyburn; brought up in the Church of England; studied Civil Law at Cambridge; spent two years studying the Catholic religion; conversion influenced by St. John Roberts, OSB (see above), who received him into the Church; went to Spain to English College, Seville; then to Benedictine Abbey of St. Facundus, Sahagun; ordained priest in 1610 and went to the English mission; worked in the London district; present at the execution of St. John Roberts and helped to recover some of his body parts; arrested, detained a year, and banished; the same happened several times; shortly after his final return to England, he was arrested and imprisoned in the Gatehouse and Newgate; condemned to death for priesthood (to which he responded "Deo Gratias"); hanged, drawn and quartered at Tyburn; see Bede Camm, *Nine Martyr Monks* (1931), p.180; *Gillow*, Vol. V, p.486.

Scott-Moncrieff, Ann (*née* Agnes Millar Shearer) – writer; b. 1914, Kirkwall, Orkney Islands; c. Easter 1940 (received with her husband George [see below]);

d. 17 February 1943; daughter of Major John Shearer; at seventeen worked on the local paper, *The Orcadian*; went to London to pursue a literary career; returned to Scotland and was married in 1934; wrote two children's stories and a volume of short stories; articles on Scottish nationalist issues; was planning a book of Scottish saints for children at the time of her death; her tragic death inspired a poem by Edwin Muir (he also said that "she had great gifts, and if she had lived might have been one of the best Scottish writers of her time"); see Joseph Kelly, "Catholic Authors," *Catholic Life*, February 2004.

Scott-Moncrieff, Charles Kenneth Michael – translator; b. 25 September 1889, Weedingshall, Polmont, near Falkirk, Stirlingshire, Scotland; c. during World War I; d. 28 February 1930, Rome; Scottish Presbyterian background; uncle of George Scott-Moncrieff (see below); wrote poetry from early age; degrees in Law, then English Language and Literature; served in France in World War I, when seriously injured and won MC; great friend of Wilfrid Owen; private secretary to Lord Northcliffe and journalist on *The Times*; from 1923 worked entirely as a translator; the most celebrated translator into English (along with Constance Garnett); between 1922 and 1930 published translations of almost all of Proust's *A La Recherche du Temps Perdu* and many other works; lived in Italy from 1923 until his death; after his conversion he practiced his faith "assiduously and fervently" (*DNB*); unmarried; buried in Verano cemetery; see *Memories and Letters* (1931); *DNB*.

Scott-Moncrieff, George Irving – journalist, playwright and novelist; b. 1910, Edinburgh; c. 1940 (received with his wife, Ann (see above)); d. 1974; second son of C. W. Scott-Moncrieff, Episcopalian minister; grandparents were Presbyterians and ancestors Covenanters; nephew of Charles Scott-Moncrieff (see above); editorial and journalistic work in London 1929–1932; after first novel, *Café Bar*, returned to Scotland; joint editor of the *New Alliance* 1939–1941, a Scottish cultural journal with Irish sympathies; active supporter of Scottish nationalism; published another novel, some verse, and books on the land and buildings of Scotland; his writings influenced the conversion of Russell Kirk, the American conservative writer; see Joseph Kelly, "Catholic Authors," *Catholic Life*, February 2004.

Seager, Charles – orientalist; b. 1808, Welsh Bicknor, Monmouthshire, Wales; c. 12 October 1843 (wife, Anna (d. 27 March 1893) converted in 1844); d. 18 September 1878, Florence; son of an Anglican rector and classicist; pupil of Pusey at Oxford; became Anglican curate; one of the earliest Tractarian converts to the Catholic Church (Newman, then still an Anglican, tried to restrain him); Professor of Hebrew and of Comparative Philology at Catholic University College, Kensington, London; member of council of Society of Biblical Archaeology (many contributions to *Transactions* of the society); published eleven works on philology, liturgy, apologetics, and politics, as well as a book of travels in the Rhineland, *The Female Jesuit Abroad* (1853); one of his sons, Ignatius (d. 1870) ordained Catholic priest in 1869; left several bequests to Catholic societies and missions; buried in Oxford; see *Gillow*, Vol. V, p.488; *DNB*.

Selle, Edward Augustine OSA – priest; c. 1863 (brother received in 1861); born of Church of England parents and brought up in Low Church, remaining practicing member until he was twenty;

after conversion to the Catholic faith he studied for the priesthood and became a professing member of the Society of Mary; ordained priest; worked in Ireland, America and England; joined the Augustinian Friars in 1878; received many converts into the Church; see T. H. Shaw, "The History of the Conversion of the Rev. Father Selle, OSA," in T. H. Shaw, *The McPhersons; or Is the Church of Rome Making Progress in England* (1879), p.184 ("Strange as it may seem, though quite natural according to the rule of Protestants, my own Bible was the occasion of my conversion. Reading the 6th chapter of St. John's Gospel, and comparing it with the words of Our Blessed Lord, at the Last Supper, and then, again applying the words of St. Paul to the 1 Corinthians, xi. 29, I could not reconcile the Divine Word with the rejection of the doctrine of the Real Presence. My next step was to find out that the Church – the Catholic Church – which I had so despised and hated, held the doctrine of Transubstantiation. A doubt of my religion being the true one, then, *for the first time*, flashed across my mind. It was the moment of grace; and, thanks be ever due to God, I corresponded to the grace.... Like a late noteworthy convert, Mr. Orby Shipley [see below], I felt bound to change 'the principles of private judgment for the revealed basis of faith, which is *authority*'").

Sergeant, (Emily Frances) Adeline (*pseud*. Adeline Hall) – novelist; b. 4 July 1851, Ashbourne, Derbyshire; c. 23 October 1899; d. 4 December 1904, Agincourt, Albert Road, Bournemouth; daughter of Wesleyan Methodist minister; mother, Jane Hall, also daughter of Wesleyan Methodist minister, was well known in religious circles as writer of various evangelical short stories under pseudonym Adeline Hall; brought up as Nonconformist, then became Anglican, from which she lapsed for some time into religious indifference and unbelief; joined Fabian Society and worked on women's issues, especially suffrage; in 1893 her religious impulses reasserted themselves and she associated herself with the Ritualist section of the Church of England; wrote over ninety novels and tales; contributor for many years to *People's Friend*; unmarried; see *Esther Denison* (1889); essay in J. G. F. Raupert (ed), *Roads to Rome* (1901), p.239 ("It was not long before I began to ask what right I had to use the prayers of the Saints – prayers written by St. Thomas Aquinas and St. Bernard, which I found in my Anglican books of devotion – when, as I gradually learned, these Saints themselves would have utterly repudiated the Church to which I belonged. It was a great step forward when I realized that the Church of St. Augustine, of Aquinas, of Thomas of Canterbury, and of More was the Church of Rome as it exists at the present time, and that the Saints whom I venerated would pronounce me excommunicate if they were living now! It was hard to feel that I did not belong to them! The words of Flaubert, I think, used to re-echo in my ears: 'It is safest in religion to believe like the Saints.' And it was my love for them that first seemed to turn my face in the direction of the Church...

...I had learned to disavow the principles of the Reformation and to believe in a divinely instituted Church; also in the doctrine of obedience to authority. I asked, therefore, why we perpetuated the errors of the Reformation by remaining in a Church without a head, cut off from the main body of Christendom? Would not the quickest way to reunion be that of individual submission, if the whole body could not be moved to submit? Why not go over at once to the Holy Catholic and Roman Church?...

And more and more, as time goes on, I am permeated with reverence for the Catholic Church, and filled with joy that I am no longer a wanderer from that blessed Fold. For, when I consider the infinite scope of the Church's manifestation, the inspired wisdom of her counsels, the multitude of her devotions, the care and tenderness lavished on the smallest and weakest of her children – equally dear to her with the mightiest upon earth; when I look at the roll of her saints, evangelists, and martyrs, extending in unbroken line from the days of the Apostles to our own, and thence to the end of time; when I think upon the prayers which ascend continually from the lips of her saints, living and dead, crowned by the intercession of the great Mother of God; last of all, when I adore upon the Church's Altars the Sacred Body and Blood in which God's Presence remains with us until the end of the world; – then indeed I humbly say with St. Augustine, 'Too late have I known Thee, O Ancient Beauty!' while, at the same moment, my soul re-echoes the Psalmist's exultant cry – 'Beati qui habitant in domo tua, Domine: in saecula saeculorum laudabunt Te'"); *DNB*.

Sergeant (aliases Holland, Smith), John – priest, controversialist, and philosopher; b. 2 February 1623, Barrow upon Humber, Lincolnshire; d. 1707; after Cambridge University he became secretary to Thomas Morton, bishop of Durham; his perception of devious misuse of texts and quotations in theological arguments, and his research on the Fathers, resulted in his conversion; influenced in that by Fr. George Gage (1602–1652); admitted into English College, Lisbon, in 1643; ordained priest 24 February 1649; went to England where he had great success, converting his parents and many others; went back to Lisbon in 1654 and became Professor of Philosophy; returned to England in 1655, where encouraged to write in defense of the Catholic cause, which he did for about fifty years; also wrote about internal Church matters; friend of John Austin (see above); traveled on the Continent; for two years after the Revolution of 1688 he had to use other aliases and pretend to be a doctor; at the end of his life illness affected quality of his writing; reputation suffered as result of conflicts with the Jesuits; see *Schism Disarm'd* (1655); *Schism Dispatcht* (1657); *Sure-Footing in Christianity* (1665); *Faith Vindicated from Possibility of Falsehood* (1667); *Six Catholick Letters* (1687); *Literary Life* (dated 1700, published 1816) (autobiographical apologia); D. Krook, *John Sergeant and His Circle* (1993); *Gillow*, Vol. V, p.491; *DNB* ("Sergeant continued with the vehemence of a convert to urge the superiority of an oral and practical Catholic tradition over protestant resort to the scriptures as a certain ground of faith").

Sewell, Brocard (real name Michael Seymour Sewell) – priest and writer; b. 30 July 1912, Bangkok; c. 3 September 1930, St. Peter's in Chains, Stroud Green; d. 2 April 2000; father employed as teacher by King of Siam; mother died shortly after giving birth; brought up by maternal grandparents in Launceston, Cornwall; raised in a family which produced many Anglican clerics, some linked with the Oxford Movement; at evangelical public school; worked on *G.K.'s Weekly* (edited by Chesterton, (see above), and influenced also by Belloc); active in distributist movement; spent some time with the Dominican Order and with the Canons Regular, but in 1952 entered the Carmelite Order; ordained in July 1954; founded *St. Albert Press*; began *Aylesford Review*; wrote to *The Times* in 1968 attacking the encyclical *Humanae Vitae* and calling on Pope

Paul VI to resign, resulting in his being sent by his Order to Canada; began *Antigonish Review*; writer of biographical cameos of, e.g., Olive Custance, Cecil Chesterton, and the poet-divine John Gray; encouraged many young writers; see *My Dear Time's Waste* (1966); *The Vatican Oracle* (1970) (plea for conciliar theology with the Council of Constance (1414–1418) as an ideal); *The Habit of a Lifetime* (1992) ("From God to Church is quite a step; but it is a logical step. The Church on earth is made up of sinful human beings – redeemed humanity is not a sinless humanity – so she does not always appear as immediately attractive. I saw that less clearly sixty or so years ago, when I identified the 'true' church with ultramontane Roman Catholicism. When, much later, I had to make a serious study of church history, I saw that this would not quite do; but I still believe that the right notion of church order is that of a visible society, with a ministry of bishops, priests, and deacons, standing in the apostolic succession, affirming the historic creeds, and administering the sacraments. And I believe that the bishops of the church, and their flocks, should be in communion with the chief bishop, the Bishop of Rome, who inherits the primacy of blessed Peter in the apostolic college"); Donald Carlus, "The Lost Club: A Weird and Marvellous Pursuit" (A Tribute to Father Brocard Sewell) http://freepages.pavilion.net/users/tartarus/brocard.html; Wilfred McGreal, O Carm, "Brocard Sewell, Carmelite Friar: An English Eccentric," *Catholic Life*, May 2008, p.32 ("Vatican II was for Brocard the proverbial curate's egg: while he welcomed much of the teaching he was not happy with the liturgical reform. He bewailed the English of the liturgical translations and would refer to the temporary altars that appeared in many churches as 'Cranmer's tables' while the

great tenor of the liturgy turned churches into 'Anabaptist Conventicles'"); Joseph Pearce, *Literary Converts* (1999), pp.168–170.

Seymour, John – writer, broadcaster, and self-sufficient farmer; b. 12 June 1914, London; c. 1981; d. 14 September 2004; many years working at a variety of jobs in South Africa; fought in World War II against the Italians in Ethiopia, then fought in Burma; moved into self-sufficiency; influenced by G. K. Chesterton (see above) and E. F. Schumacher (see above); found fame with *The Complete Book of Self-Sufficiency* (1976); see letter, Spring 1997, reproduced in Joseph Pearce, *Literary Converts* (1999), p.441 ("I tried to be, in my youth, a happy atheist, or agnostic, but never for a moment did it work for me no matter how hard I tried. I was actually a paid-up member of the H. G. Wells Society when I was a teenager, long before Wells got to the end of his tether I had got to mine.... I was immediately [when moving to County Wexford in Ireland in 1981], although a heathen, drawn into the community, and expected and required to take my part in it, and I could immediately see that it was the Church that held it all together, and kept it healthy and good.... At last I worked my way to the humility to admit that I do not know everything – and who am I to despise and reject the wisdom of Christendom during the last two thousand years? Have I anything better to offer? The answer is I have not. I have seen ... the beastly mess that modern atheism has led the world of humans into during our lifetime"); Joseph Pearce, *Literary Converts* (1999), pp.439–443.

Shand Kydd, Frances Ruth Burke (*née* Frances Ruth Roche; other married name Frances Ruth Spencer) – voluntary worker; b. 20 January 1936, Park

House, Sandringham, Norfolk; c. 1994; d. 3 June 2004, Callanish, Clachan Seil, near Oban, Scotland; father was fourth Baron Fermoy (1885–1955); mother of Diana, Princess of Wales (1961–1997); first wife of Earl Spencer (1924–1992); lady in waiting to the Queen Mother in 1960; married Peter Shand Kydd (d. 2006), but they divorced; affected by the disintegration of her daughter's marriage to Charles, Prince of Wales; turned to the Catholic Church; involved in Catholic causes and charity work; buried in Pennyfuir cemetery, Oban; see *DNB*.

Sharpe, Alfred Boyer – priest and author; c. 1898; formerly Anglican vicar in England and United States; ordained Catholic priest; see essay in J. G. F. Raupert (ed), *Roads to Rome* (1901), p.246 ("Finally, I came – I could scarcely say how – to see the Church in a new light. I perceived that there was no need to go to history, or to disputed points of theology. The Church, if it existed at all, was a living body, and must be sought for and tested as such. It could not, on its own principles, be subject to decay; it claimed perpetual youth in virtue of our Lord's promises; it must stand or fall by what it is today. Our Lord had intended the Church to be recognizable by all, learned and ignorant alike; it was to be a city placed upon a mountain, a light shining in the darkness. It might, indeed, need practical reform on its human side from time to time, but it could never forget, or deny, or obscure the truth into which it was guided by the Holy Ghost, and of which it claimed to be the divinely appointed witness and teacher. Thus a Church which depended for evidence of its genuineness solely or mainly on historical research and learned argument was proved by that very fact to be no Church; and a Church which was uncertain as to the extent of the revelation committed to it, or which failed to teach what it held to be Divine truth, by positive declaration on the one hand and by condemnation of error on the other, must equally forfeit all claim to be considered.

It is obvious that these considerations must be fatal to any form of Anglicanism; and equally obvious that they point unequivocally to the Catholic Church as the only divinely accredited authority in religion. If theory is set aside, and regard is had only to contemporary facts, it is obvious again that the Catholic Church alone among all Christian societies bears the four notes of the Church visibly impressed upon her. She alone is everywhere, and goes into the whole world, preaching the gospel to every creature, as exercising her certain right and duty; she alone can claim continuous solidarity with the Church of the Apostles; she alone has an ideal of sanctity, and holds it up before the world in the multitude of her canonized members. And as to doctrine, the question as to the true Church must be decided before doctrine can be brought to any test. The Church is the pillar and ground of the truth, and the true doctrine must be that of the true Church, not *vice versa*. To test the claims of the Church by the truth or falsehood of her teaching is to prejudge the whole matter, and would imply that revelation is either non-existent or superfluous.

Further, I saw that the Catholic Church was an institution that would work as no other would. It alone had authority which sufficed for the guidance of its members and for the due combination of its various forces. I perceived that though the possession of this authority was not of itself a sufficient evidence of the validity of the claims of the Catholic Church, yet its absence sufficed to rule all other claimants out of court. The one was a living organism, whose every part gave evidence of its common life; the others were mechanical engines, more or less skillfully put together, which were unable, and scarcely even pretended to show anything of that organic development and progressive adaptation to environment which is the surest evidence of life, and without which decay and impotence, such as has already overtaken all non-Catholic religious bodies is inevitable.

In a word, I saw clearly that the Catholic and Roman Church was not merely *a* Church, or the best Church, but the only Church").

Sharp (Sharpe), James, SJ (alias Francis Pollard) – priest; b. 26 September 1576, Bradford, West Yorkshire; d. 11 November 1630, Lincoln; parents Protestants (Puritans); after conversion at Oxford, entered St. Alban's College at Valladolid in 1602; ordained priest 14 April 1604; taught at the English College, Douai, then came on the English mission and worked in Yorkshire (for some time he was at Everingham); joined the Society of Jesus in 1607/8; Professor of Holy Scripture and Hebrew at Louvain; returned to England in 1611; tried to convert his parents, but they delivered him over to the Archbishop of York; detained for some time, then banished; returned to England again and worked in Yorkshire, Lincolnshire and Leicestershire until his death; see *Gillow*, Vol. V, p.499; *DNB*.

Shaw, T. H. – religious writer; came from a Ritualist background; compiled a list of Catholic converts; did much work in seeking to bring others into the Church; see *Holy Church the Centre of Unity; or, Ritualism compared with Catholicism* (1877) ("We should call a man insane who endeavored to roof in his house before he had laid the foundation or measured its dimensions; just so it is in fact when people seeking the true Church begin by attacking and trying to understand every dogma. These can

never be fully understood. It is only as the house becomes built up that the roofing begins; so it is in the spiritual house of the soul. Faith leads us to the Church. Faith is, then, the foundation. As the soul grows in grace and humility, so the mysteries of godliness expand before the eye of the soul, revealing that which at one time appeared most obscure.... The great thing needed is Divine faith, and this is never found by mere arguing and reading; it is the free gift of God, to be obtained only by earnest prayer.... Get this, and then search whether Jesus Christ did establish a visible Church"); *Which Is It? Or, War in the Heavens* (1878); *The McPhersons; or, Is The Church of Rome Making Progress in England?* (1879).

Shewring, Walter Hayward – poet and classicist; b. 1 January 1907; c. June 1926 (received by Mgr. Moyes); d. 1990; background Protestant, partly Low Church, partly Nonconformist; later High Anglicanism; influenced by Eric Gill; contributor to Catholic journals; Classics teacher at Ampleforth School for sixty years; did best-selling and more literary translation of Homer's *Odyssey*; see *Notes on Greek Literature* (1936); *Topics: Ten Essays* (1940); *Art in Christian Philosophy* (1946); *Making and Thinking* (1957); *Homer's Odyssey* (1980); Matthew Hoehn, OSB (ed), *Catholic Authors* (1952) ("The two points of unity and authority proved decisive").

Shipley, Orby – liturgical scholar; b. 1 July 1832; c. 24 October 1878 (received by Manning, his wife, Zoe (d. 1923) having been received three days before); d. 5 July 1916, Colway House, Lyme Regis; son of Anglican clergyman; educated at Jesus College, Cambridge; Anglican clergyman himself for twenty-two years and extreme High-Churchman; as

Catholic published articles and reviews on religious, literary, and historical subjects for over thirty years; editor of the *Weekly Register* after it had been bought by Cardinal Manning in 1881; editor of many old Catholic works ("These editions include devotional manuals, spiritual exercises, lives of saints, prayers, invocations, meditations, sermons, homilies, and hymns dating from the patristic age to the eighteenth century, most translated from Greek, Latin, Spanish, Italian, or French sources" (*DNB*)); venerated tradition and authority; for a time editor of *The Weekly Register*; bequests to Catholic causes; special interest in the Virgin Mary and in sin, confession, and penance; see *Six Short Sermons on Sin* (1867); *A Theory about Sin* (1875); *Principles of Faith in Relation to Sin* (1879); *Carmina Mariana* (1893, second series, 1902); *DNB*.

Shirley (or Sherley), James – poet and dramatist; b. September 1596, London; c. about 1625 (accepted by the majority of sources, but revised *DNB* doubts his conversion); d. October 1666, London; at Oxford (where esteemed by Laud) and Cambridge; took Anglican orders in 1619 and assigned to a curacy; after conversion he was a fervent Catholic for the rest of his life; became a teacher and then a playwright; several works of a Catholic nature; close to Charles I and encouraged in his work by Queen Henrietta Maria; very successful dramatist; when the long parliament closed the theatres in 1642 he reverted to teaching and writing textbooks on the rules of grammar and verse; returned later to writing; last of the great Elizabethan dramatists; buried with his wife in the Church of St. Giles-in-the-Fields; see, in particular, *The Grateful Servant* (1629) and *St. Patrick for Ireland* (1640); *The Contention of Ajax and Ulysses* (1659); *Catholic Encyclopedia*; *DNB*.

Sibthorp, Richard Waldo (also known as Sibthorpe) – b. 4 October 1792, Canwick Hall, near Lincoln; c. 27 October 1841 (the first Anglican clergyman to convert since 1830); d. 10 April 1879, Nottingham; fifth son of Colonel Humphrey Waldo Sibthorp, MP for Lincoln; nephew of John Sibthorp (1758–1796), the botanist; brother of Colonel Charles de Lact Waldo Sibthorp (1783–1855), MP for Lincoln, the opposer of Catholic Emancipation, Parliamentary Reform and Free Trade (one of the fiercest anti-Catholics in parliament); Wesleyan influences won him away from a boyhood infatuation with Catholicism under his French tutor, the émigré priest, Abbé Beaumont; attracted at Oxford by the Catholic faith, he went to Bishop John Milner with intention of entering the Catholic Church, but was brought back, under police surveillance and chancery order, by an elder brother; took Anglican orders and became noted Evangelical preacher; in 1827 Anglican secretary of the Religious Tract Society, a body pledged to fight Catholicism; later Fellow of Magdalen College, Oxford; ordained Catholic priest 21 May 1842 at St. Chad's Cathedral, Birmingham; left the Church in 1843 (never gave up his Bible to the Church and recurrently saw the "man of sin" in 2 Thessalonians as the papacy) and returned to the Church of England and was reinstated as a clergyman; returned to the Catholic Church in January 1865, when he became attached to St. Barnabas Cathedral, Nottingham; great benefactor to the Catholic Church and to the poor; author of apologetical and devotional works (e.g., *Daily Bread* (devotional readings for each day of the year)); always had a burning desire for sanctity; when he died he had first a Catholic and then an Anglican funeral (cf. Thomas More's words to his son-in-law, William Roper, in Robert Bolt's *A Man for all*

Seasons: "Listen, Roper. Two years ago you were a passionate Churchman; now you are a passionate Lutheran. We must just pray, that when your head's finished turning your face is to the front again"); buried in Lincoln cemetery; see*Some Answer to the Inquiry Why are you become a Catholic?* (1842); Gertrude Donald, "The Spoilt Convert," *Dublin Review*, April-June 1938, p.291 and July-September 1938, p.153; Michael Clifton, *A Victorian Convert Quintet* (1998); Michael Trott, "'I Want to be a Saint': The Troubled Life of Richard Waldo Sibthorp," *Catholic Life*, September 2004, p.52; Michael J. Trott, "A Recurring Grief, The Rankling of a Thorn," *Recusant History*, May 2003, p.488 ("Despite everything, Rome could make saints and, as he grew older, Richard Sibthorp longed to be a saint"); Michael Trott, *The Life of Richard Waldo Sibthorp: Evangelical, Catholic and Ritual Revivalism in the Nineteenth-Century Church* (2005); *DNB*.

Sidney, Marlow – gentleman; b. 9 January 1752, Soho, London; c. about 1773, with his wife Mary (1753–1844) (both received by Fr. James Horne, alias Green, chaplain at the Venetian embassy in London); d. 12 July 1839, Cowpen Hall, Northumberland; mother from a Huguenot family; brought up as an Anglican; whilst he was at Cambridge University a first cousin, Mary Mangaar, came to stay with his widowed mother; he and Mary became secretly engaged and soon married; he had doubts over the meaning of John vi in relation to the Anglican Eucharist; meetings with Dom Lewis John Barnes, OSB, chaplain to the fifteenth Baron Stourton, impressed him in favor of the Catholic faith and led to his conversion; admitted to the sacraments by Bishop Challoner (see above); fervent Catholic who worked hard for the interests of the Church; housed a group of nuns expelled from France during the Revolution; inherited his uncle's estate in Northumberland; see Henrietta Barnewall, *A Hundred Years Ago: or a Narrative of Events leading to the marriage and conversion to the Catholic Faith of Mr. and Mrs. Marlow Sidney* (1877); Rt. Rev. B. C. Foley, *Some People of the Penal Times* (1991), p.5; *Gillow*, Vol. V, p.505.

Simeon, Sir John Barrington – politician and author; b. 5 February 1815; c. 1851 (received by Fr. James Brownbill; his first wife, Lady Jane Maria, received in 1851; his second wife, Hon. Lady Catherine (d. 1904) received in 1861; daughter-in-law, Mrs. Laura Jane Simeon, received in 1883); d. 21 May 1870, Fribourg, Switzerland; educated at Christ Church, Oxford; Liberal MP for the Isle of Wight 1847–1851; resigned the seat after becoming a Catholic; re-elected in 1865 despite opposition from William George Ward (see below) who supported the Conservative candidate; remained the MP until his death; a friend of Newman who advised him; supporter of the Oratory school and of Newman's attempts to found an oratory in Oxford; his house was a political and literary centre in the 1860s; friend of Jowett, Manning, Aubrey de Vere (see below), Leslie Stephen, and Tennyson; editor of poetry and letters; succeeded his father as third Baronet in 1854; great mourning on the Isle of Wight on his death; funeral attended by Tennyson who wrote the poem "To Sir John Simeon" on the same day; *Gillow*, Vol. V, p.507.

Simpson, John Palgrave – playwright and novelist; b. 13 June 1807, Norwich; c. 1842; d. 19 August 1887, 9 Alfred Place West, Thurloe Square, South Kensington, London; after Cambridge University, declined to take holy orders in the Church of England, despite his parents' wishes, but traveled about central Europe, especially Germany; while at Munich he became a Catholic (Pope Gregory XVI, to mark approval of the step, enrolled him as a Knight of the Order of St. Gregory); contributor to *The Times*, *Blackwood's Magazine*, *Bentley's Miscellany*; he wrote, singly or in collaboration (notably with Arthur À'Beckett and Herman Merivale, see both above), sixty plays 1850–1885, including comedies, melodramas, farces, operettas, and extravaganzas; published four novels and wrote on travel and history; secretary of Dramatic Authors' Society 1868–1887; popular and striking figure in society; unmarried; buried in St. Thomas's cemetery, Fulham; see *DNB*.

Simpson Richard – controversialist, linguist, literary scholar, and musical composer; b. 16 September 1820, Beddington, Surrey; c. 1 August 1846 (received with wife, Elizabeth Mary, by Fr. Brownbill; his brothers William received in 1843; his brother Robert received in 1846 (later became a priest, but became mentally ill in 1859 and was cared for by Richard); sister, Emily, received in 1848); d. 5 April 1876, Villa Sciarra, Rome; studied at Oriel College, Oxford; became Anglican vicar; early enthusiast for Pugin and Gothic architecture; editor of *The Rambler* (leading liberal Catholic journal of mid-nineteenth century) and its successor, *The Home and Foreign Review*; came into conflict with the hierarchy over his irreverence towards authority (Newman stated about Simpson that "He will always be flicking his whip at Bishops, cutting them in tender places, throwing stones at Sacred Congregations, and as he rides along the road, discharging pea shooters at Cardinals who happen by bad luck to look out of the window"); made intensive study of Shakespeare (one of the first to advance the theory that Shakespeare was a

Catholic); buried in Rome; see Henry Bowden, *The Religion of Shakespeare: Chiefly from the Writings of the Late Mr. Richard Simpson, MA* (1899); Damian McElrath, OFM, *Richard Simpson, 1820–1876: A Study in XIXth Century Liberal Catholicism* (1972) ("Simpson's reasons [for converting] revolve principally about the Sacramental idea, that the soul is acted upon by external means, that God can convey spiritual blessings through outward material instruments. The Eucharist is just such a material sign. The Real Presence of Christ depends upon the data of revelation and not upon its conformity with common sense or reason"); Michael Clifton, *A Victorian Convert Quintet* (1998); Patrick Allitt, *Catholic Converts: British and American Intellectuals Turn to Rome* (1997), pp.88–106; *DNB*.

Sitwell, Dame Edith Louis – poet and biographer; b. 7 September 1887, Scarborough; c. 4 August 1955 ("swathed in black like a sixteenth century infanta" (Evelyn Waugh)); d. 9 February 1964, London; eldest of three children of Sir George Reresby Sitwell, fourth Baronet (1860–1943); Sir (Francis) Osbert Sacheverell Sitwell (1892–1969), and Sir Sacheverell Sitwell (1897–1988), were her younger brothers; public reading of *Façade* in 1923 made her the most talked about poet in the country; also novels and biographies; influenced in her conversion by T. S. Eliot (1888–1965), Roy Campbell (1901–1957) and Evelyn Waugh (see below); unmarried; buried in graveyard at Weedon Lois, near Weston, Northamptonshire; see *Alexander Pope* (1930); *Aspects of Modern Poetry* (1934); *Fanfare for Elizabeth* (1946); *A Notebook on William Shakespeare* (1948); *Victoria of England* (1949); *Collected Poems* (1957); *English Eccentrics* (1958); *The Queens and the Hive* (1962); *Taken Care Of* (1965) (autobiography);

Victoria Glendinning, *Edith Sitwell: A Unicorn Among Lions* (1981) ("She wanted peace of mind above all things. She said once that 'it was the serenity in the faces of the peasant women praying in the churches in Italy that drew me to the Church'"); Gerard Meath, OP, "The Poetry of Dame Edith Sitwell," *The Tablet*, 13 August 1955, p.153; Richard Greene (ed) *Selected Letters of Edith Sitwell* (1998); David Jones, "A 'Hopelessly Unworthy' Catholic Poet," *Catholic Life*, January 2005; Joseph Pearce, *Literary Converts* (1999), *passim*; *Edith Sitwell: The Spoken Word* (British Library CD); *DNB*.

Slack, Aidan – priest; b. 1895; c. 1916 (on his twenty-first birthday, after four years study); brought up and lived as a Protestant; after conversion studied for the priesthood and was ordained priest; worked in the County Durham area; see "A Convert's Reasons," *Catholic Truth*, May–June, 1932 (the author's own account of his conversion written in the third party) ("Indeed the claims of this Church, the Catholic Church, were so gigantic and staggering that he thought either this Church is all that she claims to be or else she is the greatest fraud and apostasy the world has ever known. Now he knew that she had been peopled with thousands of Saints and today she is commanding the respect of all but the prejudiced so that she cannot be the greatest of frauds and so this forced him back to the conclusion that she is all that she claims to be, in other words God's infallible Church...

...Looking round Westminster Cathedral one day he bought a Catholic Truth Society pamphlet and began to read. It was a pamphlet entitled 'The Protestant Rule of Faith an Impossible One' by Bishop Vaughan. The author points out in the tract that the Bible was never intended to be the sole rule of Faith and to be a substitute for a living Church because the reading of the Bible by the general public only became possible in the 16th Century after the two human inventions of paper and printing. Also the Bible needs an infallible Church to interpret it. For each to interpret the Bible for himself has produced no less than 300 non-conformist sects, each contradicting the other. Again it was not as if the Bible has dropped down from Heaven ready bound and printed, as a kind of rival to the Church. On the contrary, it was the Catholic Church who put the Bible together as it stands today. It was the Catholic Church who with her infallible authority accepted the inspired books of the Old and New Testaments and rejected the uninspired ones. It was the Catholic Church who preserved the Bible for us in the days before printing when it had to be laboriously copied out by hand. Monks spent their whole lives in that work of love. Finally it is the Catholic Church today who alone can guarantee for us the inspired character of Holy Writ and who encourages her children to read it and who claims to be its sole interpreter").

Slesser (formerly Schloesser), Sir Henry Herman (Thomas) – judge; b. 12 July 1883, 29 Hamilton Terrace, St John's Wood, London; c. 1946; d. 3 December 1979, Holcombe House, Moretonhampstead, Devon; of Jewish descent, but brought up as Evangelical; later agnostic; Fabian Society involvement (brought him into contact with important left wing political figures); in 1912 standing counsel to the Labour party; changed name by deed poll at outbreak of World War I; became Anglo-Catholic; Labour MP; Solicitor-General in first Labour Government 1924–1929; strongly conservative views on social issues such as birth control and the law governing marriage and divorce; specialist in trade union law; Lord Justice of Appeal 1929; liable to cite views of St. Thomas Aquinas in a judgment; verses etc, and other publications on historical subjects; see *Judgment Reserved* (1941) (reminiscences written before his conversion); *Through Anglicanism to the Church: The Steps to a Conversion* (1949) ("Whatever may have been the case with Henry VIII (who may not have intended to go further in his repudiation of papal spiritual authority than did the Gallicans of his time), by the reign of Edward VI the King and Court were genuinely and aggressively Protestant, and … Elizabeth, though in some ways more accommodating to Catholic sentiment, in reality took up the same position; that it was impossible not to admit a breach of continuity; that the clergy were no longer ordained as sacrificing priests – the ground of their subsequent repudiation by the Papacy as not being in valid orders; that the sacraments were reduced to two alone necessary for salvation; and that many other indications were not lacking illustrative of the complete rejection of Catholicism, by no one accepted more readily than by the Anglican prelates themselves who, for the most part, gloried in the breach"); *The Anglican Dilemma* (1952); *Anglo-Catholicism* (1955); *The Art of Judgment and Other Studies* (1962); Matthew Hoehn, OSB (ed), *Catholic Authors* (1952); *DNB*.

Smith, Sir Andrew – army medical officer and naturalist; b. 3 December 1797, Kirktoun parish, Roxburghshire, Scotland; c. 6 March 1844 (on marriage to his housekeeper, Ellen Henderson (1802–1864), and conversion to her Catholic faith); d. 11 August 1872, 16 Alexander Square, Brompton, London; made his reputation through his enquiries into zoology, ethnography, and geography of Cape Colony 1820–1837; author of *Illustrations of the Zoology of South Africa*, 4 Vols. (1849); rose to become director-general of army and ordnance medical departments; blamed by the press for poor state of medical care for British troops in Crimean campaign (Florence Nightingale sought his dismissal, but parliamentary select committees exonerated him); buried at Kensal Green cemetery, London; see *DNB*.

Smith, Delia – cookery writer and television presenter; b. 18 June 1941, Woking, Surrey; c. 1963; wrote column for *Daily Mirror* and *Evening Standard*; books on cookery have sold millions of copies; many television series; formerly attended many different non-Catholic churches; profound effect on her of St. Thérèse of Lisieux's autobiography; see "A Spiritual Journey," *The Tablet* 11 August 1984, p.763; *Journey Into Prayer* (1986); *Journey Into God* (1988); essay in Rowanne Pasco (ed), *Why I Am a Catholic* (1995) ("I became a Catholic … because I suppose I fell in love. It was love for the Church and especially for the Mass").

Smith, Lady Eleanor Furneaux – writer; b. 1903, Birkenhead, Lancashire; c. 1931 (received with her sister, Lady Pamela Smith); d. 20 October 1945; daughter of F. E. Smith (1872–1930), first Earl of Birkenhead (Lord Chancellor); lived for much of her youth in Belgium; wrote newspaper gossip and film columns; worked for a traveling circus; wrote several successful novels; see *Ballerina* (1932); *Life's A Circus* (1939) (reminiscences); *British Circus Life* (1948); *The Etiquette of Letter Writing* (1950); Frederick Winston Furneaux Smith, *Lady Eleanor Smith: A Memoir* (1953); Anon, "Lady Eleanor Furneaux Smith (1903–1945)," *Catholic Life*, June 2002, p.7.

Smith, Bishop Richard – bishop and controversialist; b. November 1567, Hanworth, Lincolnshire; d. 18 March

1655, apartment adjacent to English Augustinian Convent, rue des Fosses St. Victor, Paris; at Oxford unable to accept the new religion; converted and moved to Rome, where received into English College in 1586; ordained priest May 1592; then went to English College, Valladolid, in 1593 to teach Philosophy; then to English College, Seville, where he was Professor of Controversy; went to England in 1603; in 1606 went to Rome and discussed the question of the Jesuits and the regulars; served the mission in England from 1609 for several years; appointed vicar apostolic of English Church with title of Bishop of Chalcedon *in partibus infidelium* in November 1624; came to England in 1626 and claimed to be the ordinary of both England and Scotland, causing controversy; Pope found against him and he retired to France in 1631; his resignation accepted by Holy See; warmly received by Cardinal Richelieu; buried in chapel of English Augustinian Convent, Paris; see *Of the Fundamental and not Fundamental Points of the Faith* (1645); *Gillow*, Vol. V, p.511; *DNB*.

Smith, Sydney Fenn, SJ – priest; b. 1843; c. 1864; d. 1922; son of Anglican vicar; entered the Society of Jesus in 1866; ordained priest; Master at Stonyhurst and Beaumont Colleges, and Professor of Theology and Holy Scripture at St. Beuno's College; editor of *The Month* 1897–1901; editor of *Scripture Manuals for Catholic Schools*; attached to Writers' Staff, Farm Street, London; prolific author on Catholic topics; see *Papal Supremacy and Infallibility* (1890); *The Great Schism of the West* (1893); *Rome's Witness Against Anglican Orders* (1893); *Reasons for Rejecting Anglican Orders* (1895); *The Landing of St. Augustine* (1897); *Jesuit Obedience* (1901); "The Problem of Evil," *The Month*, July 1905, p.1 and September 1905, p.225; *The Use*

of Holy Images (1913); *Wayside Crosses and Holy Images* (1917); *The Spanish Inquisition* (1936); *The Suppression of the Society of Jesus* (2004) (first published in *The Month*, February 1902 to August 1903 as a series in nineteen installments).

Somerset, Henry, fifth Earl and first Marquis of Worcester – b. 1577; d. December 1646; entered Magdalen College, Oxford in 1591; subsequently traveled on the Continent where he was received into the Church; he succeeded as Earl of Worcester in 1627/8; created Marquis by Charles I for his great aid to the royalist cause; defended Raglan Castle, but was last garrison holding out for the king and surrendered on honorable terms; betrayed and taken to Westminster and put in the custody of the black rod, Covent Garden, where he died; father of nine sons and four daughters; see *Gillow*, Vol. V, p.515.

Spark, Dame Muriel Sarah (*née* Camberg) – writer; b. 1 February 1918, Edinburgh, Scotland; c. 1 May 1954 ("The reason I became a Roman Catholic was because it explained me" (interview with Malcolm Muggeridge)); d. 13 April 2006; born to a Jewish father and Anglican mother, but not brought up in any church-going environment; between her schooldays and 1952 was almost indifferent to religion; flirted with Anglo-Catholicism; her writing supported by Graham Greene (see above) and Evelyn Waugh (see below); wartime post in political intelligence at MI6; poet and short story writer, later prolific author of twenty-two novels (establishing her reputation with *The Prime of Miss Jean Brodie* (1961)) and editor of literary letters; made Dame Commander of Order of British Empire in 1993 in recognition of her services to literature; she said that it was not until she became a Catholic that she was able to see human existence as a whole, as a novelist needs to do ("I write as a Scot and I write as a Catholic, I don't even have to think about it. That's there like your freckles you know"; "It's the only religion I view as rational – it helps you get rid of all the other problems in your life. There really is such a thing as beauty of morals"); a recurrent theme in her novels is the question why evil exists in a world made by a good God (e.g., *The Mandelbaum Gate* (1965); *The Only Problem* (1984)); a preoccupation with the *Book of Job*; lived later years in Rome and then in Tuscany; see *The Comforters* (1957) (conversion story novel); "My Conversion," *Twentieth Century*, Autumn 1961, p.58; *Curriculum Vitae* (1992) (autobiography) ("In 1953 I was absorbed by the theological writings of John Henry Newman through whose influence I finally became a Roman Catholic. I tried the Church of England first, as being more 'natural' and near to home. But I felt uneasy. It was historically too new for me to take to. When I am asked about my conversion, why I became a Catholic, I can only say that the answer is both too easy and too difficult. The simple explanation is that I felt the Roman Catholic faith corresponded to what I had always felt and known and believed. There was no blinding revelation in my case. The more difficult explanation would involve the step by step building up of a conviction; as Newman himself pointed out, when asked about his conversion, it was not a thing one could propound 'between the soup and the fish' at a dinner party. 'Let them be to the trouble that I have been to,' said Newman"); Ruth Whittaker, *The Faith and Fiction of Muriel Spark* (1982); Norman Page, *Muriel Spark* (1990); Jennifer Lynne Randisi, *On Her Way Rejoicing: The Fiction of Muriel Spark* (1991); Judy Sproxton, "The Women of Muriel Spark: Narrative

and Faith," *New Blackfriars*, September 1992, p.432; Joseph Bottum, "Lectio Divina: The Prime of Miss Muriel Spark," *Crisis*, March 2000; Bryan Cheyette, *Muriel Spark* (2000); Robin Baird-Smith, "Keeping the Devil at Bay with Laughter," *The Tablet*, 22 April 2006, p.23 ("I once asked Muriel Spark why she had become a Catholic. Her answer fascinated me. She said: 'Because it is the one thing that has stopped me going mad'"); Ralph McInerny, *Some Catholic Writers* (2007); Martin Stannard, *Muriel Spark: The Biography* (2009); Joseph Pearce, *Literary Converts* (1999), pp.161, 292–294; *DNB*.

Speaight, Robert William ("Bobby") – actor and literary scholar; b. 14 January 1904, Corner Cottage, St Margaret's Bay, Kent; c. 31 October 1930 (received by Fr. Martin D'Arcy at Farm Street, London); d. 4 November 1976, Campion House, near Benenden, Kent; both parents fervent Protestants and both his godfathers were Anglican clergymen; brought up in the Tractarian tradition; read English at Lincoln College, Oxford; noted actor at Oxford; after visit to Bavaria and Oberammergau passion play, "I suddenly felt with quite overwhelming force that I wanted to become a Catholic"; contacts with G. K. Chesterton, Christopher Hollis, Compton Mackenzie (see all above), Belloc, etc., but he most admired Maurice Baring (see above); very fine actor; creator of Thomas à Becket in first production of T. S. Eliot's *Murder in the Cathedral*; principal character in Dorothy L. Sayers' sequence of radio plays on the life of Christ, *A Man Born to be King*; writer on theatre and biographer; see essay in Maurice Leahy (ed), *Conversions to the Catholic Church: A Symposium* (1933) ("[The Catholic Church's] body was one; her voice was clear; her dogmas were immutable; her testimony was consistent; her teaching was harmonious.... The choice of the modern world, as it seemed to me, lay between Catholic transcendentalism and a purely Pragmatic materialism of which Communism was the most serious and intelligent example. To these the ecstasies of art, the quest of science, and the fastidious delights of humanism were no proper alternatives; and the Papal claims seemed strictly necessary to ensure the maintenance of true theological belief and the preservation of moral order"); *The Life of Hilaire Belloc* (1957); *The Christian Theatre* (1960); *The Property Basket: Recollections of a Divided Life* (1970) ("I could not see why a dogma which was thought credible yesterday should suddenly be dismissed as incredible today. Either the Resurrection was a fact of history, or it was not. If it happened, it interested me very much; if it did not happen, I was not in the least comforted to regard it as a significant myth...

...If Christ's promise meant anything should there not be an authority to decide them for me? Either the Church was divided and effective authority was in abeyance; or, as Catholics believed, the Church of Rome was the repository of revealed truth and its divinely inspired interpreter. The claim was a gigantic one, and only the Church of Rome was bold enough to make it. The question therefore was this: Did the Church of Rome, by the coherence of its doctrine, the witness of its saints, the continuity of its tradition and its international character, substantiate this claim?...

...That in basic matters of doctrine the Church must be regarded as infallible seems to me now, and even seemed to me then, incontestable.... I was not shocked that a body which prided itself on 'proceeding confidently in the doctrine of God' should do so with a certain manifestation of self-confidence...

...Once the Incarnation was admitted,

I could see no reason to stop short of the Papal claims if these were sensibly interpreted. The Incarnation was the crux – was it conceivable, and was it necessary? The doctrine of original sin might be difficult to explain, and the explanations did not bother me. But it was plainer than the midday sun that Newman was right in seeing mankind involved in some 'aboriginal calamity'; and that Baudelaire was right in refusing to recognize progress as anything else but a 'diminution of the results of original sin'; and that T. E. Hulme was right in dismissing the aesthetic attractions of Catholicism, such as they were, and in declaring that he could swallow the décor for the sake of the dogma, not the other way about. The idea that you could have a religion without dogma was as silly as the idea that you could have a car without a carburettor. You could not run your life any more than you could run your car without knowing how the gears worked, and how or when to put on the brakes. Anything that worked was dogmatic. And so the Incarnation, improbable as it might appear and strictly unimaginable as it undoubtedly was, came as the realistic answer to man's infirmity; and in so far as man responded he was cured. This, at least, I did not have to take on trust; it was manifest in history, and in the lives of many I had known"); *George Bernanos: A Study of the Man and the Writer* (1973); Walter Romig (ed), *The Book of Catholic Authors*, Fourth Series (1948); Joseph Pearce, *Literary Converts* (1999), *passim*; *DNB* ("Speaight was a Catholic intellectual in the great European tradition").

Spencer, Hon. and Rev. George, CP (name in religion Ignatius of St. Paul) – priest; b. 21 December 1799, Admiralty House, London; c. 30 January 1830; d. 1 October 1864, Monteith

House, Carstairs, Lanarkshire, Scotland; youngest of the eight children of George John Spencer, second Earl Spencer (1758–1834), First Lord of the Admiralty at the time; mother was Lavinia (1762–1831), daughter of Charles Bingham, first Earl of Lucan; from a very wealthy family, that of the late Diana, Princess of Wales (he was her great-great-great uncle); always delicate in health; developed an Evangelical piety in his youth; then Anglican rector and chaplain to Dr. Charles James Blomfield (1786–1857), Anglican Bishop of London; vacillated between High Church leanings and Evangelical beliefs; greatly influenced in his conversion by Ambrose Phillipps de Lisle (1809–1878) (see above), then seventeen years old and a recent convert; ordained Catholic priest 28 May 1832; much work with the poor; his life's work was his Crusade of Prayer for Unity in the Truth, aimed at the conversion of England, for which intention Mass would be said every Thursday; joined Passionist Congregation of St. Paul of the Cross in 1847; instrumental, in cooperation with Elizabeth Prout (see above), in founding Sisters of the Cross and Passion, a new religious congregation with no dowry requirements for admission and no class distinctions; in 1849 he became Superior of the Passionists in England; interred in crypt of St. Anne's Passionist Retreat, Sutton, St. Helens, but in 1973 his remains removed to a side chapel in the new church of St. Anne and Blessed Dominic in Sutton, where they lie beside those of Bl. Dominic Barberi and Elizabeth Prout; see *A Short Account of the Conversion of the Hon. and Rev. G. Spencer to the Catholic Faith* (1831); *The True Method of Making Converts to the Church of Christ* (1839); Rev. Father Pius, *Life of Father Ignatius of St. Paul, Passionist (The Hon. And Rev. George Spencer), Compiled chiefly from his Autobiography, Journal*

and Letters (1866) ("There is a mystery to Protestants who see Catholic rites for the first time. They are taught to look upon true worship as consisting in the meaning of some well-written sentences, pronounced with emphatic unction, and responded to some degree with fervor. The service, the fine old psalms, anthems and collects of the Prayer Book, issuing forth in melodious accents from the lips of a God-fearing man, is about the highest kind of public worship they can have any notion of…. But service and sermon must be heard, and listened to, and understood. With this idea in their minds, and accustomed to see the minister assume a manner and mien calculated to produce prayerful thoughts in his congregation, they are surprised, if not shocked, at the Catholic Mass. They find the priest hurrying off through Latin prayers and producing breathless attention by his own silence; they see him arrayed in unintelligible attire, moving one way and another, bowing, genuflecting, standing still or blessing…. It is not our object to explain Catholic mysteries, but it may be as well to hint that if a stranger to Jerusalem happened to wander to Calvary on the great day of the Crucifixion, and believed in the divinity of the Victim who hung upon the Cross, he would find more devotion in kneeling in silence at His feet than in listening in the most eloquent declamation he could hear about it. Such is the case with the Catholic now as then; he knows the same Victim is offered up still, and when the great moment arrives in the middle of the Mass, he would have everything to be hushed and silent, except the little bell that gives him notice of the awful moment"); Cecilia Dawson Oldmeadow, "A Hail Mary from Everyone," *Catholic Fireside*, 1954 ("In 1848 he wrote: 'I only ask now for one Hail Mary a day to be said by everybody throughout the world for the conversion of England. Why not take up this object, and in every letter you write try to make people promise to do this? We should have great results if millions did this'"); J. V. Bussche, *Ignatius (George) Spencer, Passionist (1799–1864)* (1991); Jerome Vereb, CP, *Ignatius Spencer: Apostle of Christian Unity* (1992); Sr. Dominic Savio (Hamer) CP, "Unity in the Truth: Fr. Ignatius Spencer's Crusade of Prayer, 1839–1864," *North West Catholic History*, Vol. XXIII (1996), p.5; Madeleine Beard, *Faith and Fortune* (1997) ("About to set off for the Isle of Wight he looked for a book to take with him in the library at Althorp. 'I hit upon a copy, in Greek, of St. John Chrysostom on the Priesthood.... I read, and read it again. Is it possible? I thought to myself. Why, this is manifest popery. He certainly must have believed in the Real Presence. I had no idea that popish errors had commenced so soon; yes, and gained deep root, too; for I saw that he wrote as of a doctrine about which he expected no contradiction'"); Fr. Ben Lodge, CP, *Ignatius Spencer* (2005); *DNB*.

Spencer (Spenser), John, SJ (alias Tyrwhitt) – priest and religious controversialist; b. 10 August 1600, Lincolnshire; converted when at Cambridge University; d. 17 January 1671, Grafton Manor, seat of the Earl of Shrewsbury; entered the Society of Jesus in Watten in 1626; ordained priest 18 March 1632; missioner at Watten and then on the English mission in Lincolnshire; Professor of Moral Theology or convener of discussions on controversial theology at Liège in 1641; military chaplain to the English troops in Flanders; in May 1657 involved in a disputation with Anglican divines; much work from then on concerning controversial theology; working in England (Worcestershire and London) from 1669 until his death; see *Scripture Mistaken* (1655); *Schisme Unmask't* (1658);

Gillow, Vol. V, p.520; *DNB* ("Protestants, according to Spencer, conceded that they could not withstand Catholic arguments based on historical succession, tradition, patristics, and so on. But scripture, the word of God, was a more powerful weapon and it was firmly held in protestant hands. However, Spencer argued that protestants tortured scripture to support their arguments which, upon detailed examination, rested on nothing but errors, mistakes, and faulty translations. His work was intended to demonstrate the veracity of traditional Catholic teaching on justification by faith, good works, purgatory, and real presence").

Spenser, Blessed William – priest and martyr; b. Gisburn, Yorkshire; c. 7 November 1582; d. 24 September 1589, York; brought up Anglican; Fellow of Trinity College, Oxford, in 1579; became convinced of the truth of the Catholic faith and influenced students to convert, though he delayed doing so; sailed from the Isle of Wight to near Cherbourg with four other Trinity men; they went on to Rheims; received into the Church five days later; ordained priest 24 September 1583 by the Cardinal Archbishop of Guise; sent on the English mission in 1584; reconciled to the Catholic faith his parents and his uncle (the latter became a Catholic priest); voluntarily immured himself in York Castle to help the prisoners there; condemned for priesthood; executed together with Robert Hardesty, a layman who had given him shelter; see *Catholic Encyclopedia*.

Spurrier, Alfred Henry – physician; b. 1866; c. 1887; before conversion had short correspondence with Newman about faith and the Church; began studying for the priesthood at the Gregorian in Rome; shifted to London Hospital before serving as a health officer in Zanzibar;

physician-in-extraordinary to H. H. Sultan of Zanzibar; editor of Government of Zanzibar *Gazette*; see Stanley L. Jaki, *Newman to Converts: An Existential Ecclesiology* (2001), pp.371–372 ("[Newman explained: 'I believe [the Church] to be a human institution as well as divine, and so far as it is human it is open to the faults of human nature; but if, because I think, with others, that its rulers have sometimes erred as fallible men, I think it had failed, such logic won't hold; indeed, it is the wonderful anticipation in Our Lord's and St. Paul's teaching, of apparent failure [and real] success in the times after them which has ever been one of my strong arguments for believing them divine messengers'").

Squire, Dom Aelred (real name Kenneth Squire) – priest; b. 6 December 1920, Streatham, London; c. 1943 (instructed and received by Fr. Conrad Pepler, OP at St. Peter's, Eynsham); d. 1 May 1997, New Camaldoli Hermitage, Big Sur, California; brought up as an Anglican; his reading as a schoolboy made him a convinced Catholic in his heart during his teens; by then he said daily the Little Office of Our Lady in Latin; postulant at Prinknash Abbey, but joined the Dominican Order in 1946; ordained 1952; taught at Blackfriars, Oxford, until 1965; moved to Belgium to live as a hermit; returned to London to teach at a study centre conducted by Dominican Sisters in London; migrated to Norway in 1972 to serve as a mission priest at Lillehammer; finally yielded to monasticism in 1980, first with the Benedictines at Christ in the Desert, New Mexico, transferring his vows from the Dominicans in 1982, and at last, from December 1983, with the Camaldolese Benedictines at Big Sur, California; spiritual director, writer on spirituality, and patristic scholar; periods of semi-eremitical life; see *Asking the Fathers* (1973)

(introduction to patristic spirituality and theology); *Summer in the Seed* (1980).

Stanfield, Francis – priest and musical composer; b. 1835; his mother and younger brother, who also became a priest, also converted; d. 1914; son of George Clarkson Stanfield (1828–1878), the painter; ordained Catholic priest; composer of many popular Catholic hymns, e.g., *Sweet Sacrament Divine*.

Stanley, Bishop Algernon Charles – bishop; b. 16 September 1843; c. 1879; d. 23 April 1928; fourth son of second Baron Stanley of Alderley, PC, President of the Board of Trade, and Post Master General; grandson of the thirteenth Viscount Dillon; formerly High Anglican clergyman; ordained Catholic priest; coadjutor to Cardinal Vaughan; later Auxiliary Bishop of Westminster 1903–1928.

Stanley, Mary – nurse and philanthropist; b. 1813; c. 1855 (received before her return to England from Crimea by Fr. William Ronan, an Irish Jesuit army chaplain); d. 26 November 1879; eldest daughter of Edward Stanley (1779–1849), Anglican Bishop of Norwich; sister of Arthur Penrhyn Stanley (1815–1881), Anglican Dean of Westminster; Henry Manning was her spiritual mentor as an Anglican; friendship with Florence Nightingale, but this was eventually broken; before her reception into the Church she established a Military Hospital at Koulali during Crimean War and nursed the wounded with Frances Margaret Taylor (see below); eventually her health was broken; much philanthropic work, especially in the Lancashire cotton famine of 1861; writer on the topic of nursing; unmarried; see *Gillow*, Vol. V, p.524; *DNB*.

Stanton, A. J. Francis – writer; c. 10 June 1921 (followed by son, Lawrence);

born into Anglican atmosphere; former Anglican clergyman followed by some time as Non-Conformist; then High Anglicanism before conversion to the Catholic faith; see "A Convert's Reflections," *The Month*, May 1928, p.396; *Catholic Mysticism* (1929); *Impressions of a Pilgrim* (1930) ("In the last analysis there is but one question for an enquiring Protestant – the question of Authority. No special dogma presents any difficulty if one can believe and accept an authority on which all Christian dogmas rest. The real issue between Catholics and Protestants is Authority or Private Judgment. If the Catholic Church is the living voice of God in its authoritative teaching, and the very will of God in its legislation, then difficulties of belief are at an end. The doctrines of the Church may appeal, for this or that reason, but one can only become a Catholic if these doctrines are accepted as revealed doctrines, proclaimed infallibly, though the Church advanced no other proof. All arguments advanced against Catholic doctrine are without pertinence unless it is possible to prove that God has not appointed this one Holy Catholic Church to teach. 'A thousand difficulties do not make one doubt,' if one's authority speaks with the voice of God. To submit to Catholic doctrine on rational grounds, and not to submit to Catholic authority, is to remain a Protestant, for the court of appeal is still a private judgment which any day might find itself in disagreement").

Stanton, Richard Mary – priest; b. 1820; c. 9 October 1845 (received on the same occasion as Newman); d. 1 January 1901; educated at Brasenose College, Oxford; ordained Anglican deacon, the Anglican Bishop of London refusing to promote him further on account of his advanced views; accompanied Newman to Littlemore in 1843; one of Newman's seven companions in the novitiate of the Oratorians at Sta. Croce, Rome; ordained Catholic priest 15 August 1847 in Rome; returned to England at the end of 1847, being the first of the Oratorians to set foot in England; he joined the new Oratory at Maryvale under Newman; in 1849 he joined with Faber (see above) and Dalgairns (see above) in the foundation of the London Oratory and remained there until his death, only survivor of the original founders, and twice superior; specially noted for his liturgical learning and his knowledge of Canon Law; see *Gillow*, Vol. V, p.525.

Steele, Francesca Maria Fanny (*pseud.* Darley Dale) – novelist; b. 1848, Dalston, London; c. 1887; d. 16 August 1931; daughter of an insurance company official; educated at London University; lived in Jersey, 1874–1884, then in Gloucestershire; supported her mother and her sister after her father's death in 1884, since her father had lost most of his money in a bank failure; published children's books and adult fiction, e.g., *The Daughters of Job* (1902) and *Brother Francis* (1904); published under her own name religious history and biography, e.g., *The Life and Visions of St. Hildegarde* (1914) and *The Convents of Great Britain and Ireland* (1924); contributor to the *Catholic Encyclopedia*, *American Catholic Quarterly*, etc.; see Sandra Kemp, Charlotte Mitchell, and David Trotter (ed), *Edwardian Fiction: An Oxford Companion* (1997).

Stern, Bertha Gladys (known as Bronwen and wrote under the name G. B. Stern; called Peter by her friends, but Tynx by Rebecca West) – novelist and film script writer; b. 17 June 1890, 99 St. Mark's Road, North Kensington, London; c. 1947; d. 18 September 1973, Wallingford, Berkshire; brought up in a liberal German-Jewish family ("We ate ham without a qualm, and never went to the synagogue except for an occasional wedding"); wrote from age of eight (nearly fifty novels, plus short stories and plays, two biographies and much journalism); lived in England, Italy, and United States; wrote a trilogy on Jewish life which sold widely: *Children of No Man's Land* (1919), *Tents of Israel* (1924) and *A Deputy Was King* (1926); influenced by St. Thérèse of Lisieux and Baron von Hügel (1852–1925); friend of Sheila Kaye-Smith (see above); buried in cemetery at Blewbury, Berkshire; see *All In Good Time* (1954) (story of her conversion); *The Way It Worked Out* (1956) ([responding to a young woman who mocked religion] "I should like … to have achieved a twist in space, and included our young realist among a crowd heckling Frank Sheed at the Catholic Evidence Guild one wet and windy Sunday evening on a street-corner in Liverpool; 'If I couldn't make a better world than God, I'd be ashamed!' shouted a burly opponent. And Mr. Sheed turned to him and said, oh so winningly, on such a coaxing note: 'Make us a rabbit now, just to establish confidence!' And the heckler oozed away"); "This Makes Sense," in John A. O'Brien (ed), *The Road to Damascus, Vol. V: Where Dwellest Thou* (1956), p.73 ; *DNB*.

Stevenson, Joseph, SJ – historian, and archivist; b. 27 November 1806, Berwick-upon-Tweed; c. 24 June 1863 (received by Fr. Gallwey, SJ, at Farm Street, London; his wife, Mary Ann (d. 11 July 1869) was received in 1865); d. 8 February 1895, Farm Street, London; son of Robert Stevenson, surgeon; generally a poor student; originally member of the Church of Scotland, later joining the Church of England; worked for the Manuscript Department of the British Museum, sub-commissioner of Public Records; took Anglican orders and worked as a curate; librarian and keeper of Durham Records; fascinated by the life of St. Cuthbert; father of eleven children; after the death of his wife, entered Oscott College and was ordained priest in 1872; joined the Society of Jesus in 1877; main contribution to British scholarship lay in the transcription of documents dealing with medieval and early modern English and Scottish history; also published some forty articles in *The Month*; see J. H. Pollen, "Converted by History," *The Month*, March 1895, p.331; David Hunter Blair, *John Patrick, Third Marquess of Bute, KT (1847–1900): A Memoir* (1921) ("The late Jesuit historian, Father Joseph Stevenson, who spent a great number of years in laborious study (for his work in the Record Office) of the original documents and papers of the Reformation period, frankly avowed that it was what he learned in these researches, and no other considerations whatever, which convinced him – an elderly clergyman of the old school – that the Catholic Church was the Church of God, and the so-called Reformation the work of His enemies"); *Catholic Encyclopedia*; *Gillow*, Vol. V, p.529; *DNB*.

Stocken (James) Frederick – classical composer and musicologist; b. 1967, Birmingham; c. 1996; father British, but mother a Jewish refugee from Nazi Germany; brought up as an Anglican (only discovered his Jewish roots on his mother's side in his early twenties); organ scholar of St. Catharine's College, Cambridge; doctorate in music from the University of Manchester; best-known composition is his *Lament for Bosnia* (19940; also a violin concerto, a Mass, *Missa Pacis*; a ballet (*Alice*), and two symphonies; a great admirer of J. S. Bach and Anton Bruckner; see "Ruin or Renewal: The Future of Music," *Salisbury Review*, March 1991, p.34; "Bully Boy Boulez," *New Statesman*, 20 March 2000; "Music as a Christian Art," *Second*

Spring, Vol. 5, 2004, p.55 ("Is it mere co-incidence that in the very year, 1907, that Schoenberg began ripping the intestines out of music in his first atonal compositions, Pope St. Pius X was issuing his encyclical *Pascendi Gregis* against Modernism? To the casual historical observer the activities of an atonal composer and a Pope shoring up the theological purity of the Catholic faith would seem entirely separate. But with hindsight we can discern a relationship between the decline in Catholic, and indeed in all Christian, belief in the West and the collapse of music. Many of those who rejected religious faith at that time still believed that the common-sense moral assumptions of their culture would remain in place, and they were proved wrong during the twentieth century. In a similar way, the commonly accepted musical laws of Western culture could not survive the loss of the faith which provided a context in which they made sense.

There are parallels between bad music and false doctrine. Heresy is the distortion of an aspect of truth so that it becomes out of proportion. (The most famous example in Christian history is the misunderstanding of Christ's humanity versus his divinity.) It seems that a similar failure to keep melody, harmony and rhythm in balance and in proportion has been the case with music over the last century. Percussion instruments, for instance, which are so magical in their effects, seem to swamp so many modern scores at the expense of melody. Indeed the reliance on instrumental timbre, which is so vital in any music, has grown out of proportion so that musical form itself has been all but abandoned. Indeed Modernism in all its forms could be said to be an exaggeration of things that are vital to all great art, whether it be color in art or rhythm in music. Certain elements are isolated and then blown into nightmarish proportions, just as in heresy an aspect of the truth is taken out of its context and placed in a false perspective.

I am not here advocating any sort of timidity in musical creation. Indeed the music of Bach, Mozart and Beethoven shows a kind of radical extremism in its attention to the balance and proportion of rhythm, harmony and melody. What these composers accepted was that there were timeless laws of music that could be adapted to every age, in the same way that Catholic dogma remains the same but may be subject to new insights through time. The whole background of a culture steeped in the Catholic faith allowed composers to accept both the order and freedom that tonality brings with a 'religious' faith, even if they never stopped to think of it in those terms"); www.frederickstocken.com.

Stockley, William Frederick Paul – literary scholar; b. 1859, Templeogue, County Dublin, Ireland; c. 1894, Montreal ("As Brownson says for me, 'This is the most rational act a thinking man can perform'"; his sister, Alice Josephine Stockley, later a nun, received in 1897); d. 1943; influenced by the Irish critic and poet, Edward Dowden (1843–1913), to whom he attributed his interest in religious and literary history; Professor of English at University of New Brunswick, Canada, then at University of Ottawa; then Professor of English Literature and History at University College, Cork 1905–1930; friend of William James; member of De Valera's first government, but later a critic of De Valera, supported Army council of IRA as *de jure* government of Ireland, and left politics; author of over five hundred articles on mainly literary subjects, including Shakespeare and a commentary on Newman's *Dream of Gerontius*; see *Essays in Irish Biography* (1933); *Newman,*

Education and Ireland (1933); Joseph Kelly, "William F. P. Stockley, 1859–1943," *Catholic Life*, March 2004, p.43.

Stokes, Elizabeth Scott – c. 1898; brought up as a strict Anglican; had doubts between the ages of twenty and thirty and converted to Rome; see essay in J. G. F. Raupert (ed), *Roads to Rome* (1901), p.253 ("The need of a trustworthy and authoritative guide for oneself and for one's children, in facing the daily problems of life in all its relations, led me ... to the following conclusions:

I. The Catholic Church has the longest and the widest experience in philosophical and practical dealing with every problem of human life, public and private. To briefly substantiate this assertion, it needs only to point out that the theologians of the Church have for centuries been occupied with the philosophical aspects of faith and unbelief, of holiness and sin, as they affect the intellect and as they influence the heart. The Catholic clergy, regular and secular, undergo a severe training, based on the teachings of these centuries, for their duties in the confessional – a training without parallel elsewhere. These duties bring them in contact with all the so-called most modern problems of the day: the innumerable difficulties, for instance, that beset the married life, the celibate life, and the much trodden yet unmapped country that lies between.

II. The uncompromising morality of the Catholic Church, encompassed and pervaded at all costs by the broadest and humblest charity, appears, in my judgment, to be nearer to the spirit and teaching of Christ in the Gospel than that of any other Christian communion.

The truceless war with sin, the lifelong endurance, shown perhaps more often in sustaining a dreary siege against temptation from without and within, than in the pitched and eager battle against the invigorating foe – this on the one hand, and the meekness of charity to sinners, well-nigh beyond and against all reason, on the other – these are characteristics of the men who have the care of Catholic morals which can hardly be known till the convert has spent some time under their rule.

Many among us who are not Catholics cling, thank God! no less firmly than ourselves to Christ's doctrine. But they cannot make a lasting and effectual stand (neither can any save the infallible Church) against such infringements of God's law as man by custom or enactment chooses to sanction. For the children's sake and for our own, it is good to embrace and to hold fast by that religion which ennobles and sanctifies love in every relation, and which raises aloft the standard of modesty, simplicity, and charity. The Catholic Church holds the estate of virginity to be holier and higher than the estate of marriage; but none the less she holds the estate of marriage higher and holier than do any outside her communion who profess and call themselves Christians, or who aim at ethical perfection.

III. The authority of the Pope and of the Councils of the Church, that authority to give dogmatic definition of the truth concerning God and His purposes, past, present, and to come, of which we speak when we call the Church infallible, seemed to me to be in no degree illogical or spiritually improbable. The definitions themselves may, being spiritually discerned, seem strange or even foolish, or again over-wise, to the natural man. But that the revelation of God, instead of ceasing should be expanded and developed, albeit in language no longer actually inspired, is no monstrous or incredible thing in a Church to which the gift of the abiding presence of the Holy Ghost Himself was emphatically assured. And once this presence, this revelation, be granted, there is no question of hesitancy to accept this or that point of doctrine. What God shows us we believe, as though we saw it. And having this faith, it is not hard to trust one's self for guidance to those servants of God of whom Christ said, 'He that receiveth whomsoever I send, receiveth Me.'

One more point regarding the Papal authority.... It seems an obvious one, but in my limited reading I have never seen it discussed. It is a single prerogative, but so far as I am aware it has never been either disputed or usurped, and this seems to me not a little remarkable. I refer to the canonization of the saints. The Holy Father alone can give this honor, and his power so to do seems often to be tacitly admitted by many who else would scorn his claims. Let those who unconsciously have been illumined with this one flame from the searching fire of Rome, take heart of grace and stand in its full radiance").

Stone, Jean Mary – historian; b. 1854/6, Brighton; c. whilst being educated in Germany (received by Bishop Kettler of Mainz); d. 3 May 1908, 77 High Street, Battle, Sussex; educated at a Calvinist school in Paris and Aschaffenburg in Germany; on her return to England, her historical studies were encouraged by the Society of Jesus, in particular by Fr. Joseph Stevenson (see above) to write *Faithful unto Death* (1892), a study of the sufferings of the English Franciscans during the sixteenth and seventeenth centuries; several later influential published works; some of her work anticipated recent scholarship on the Reformation, in particular that in England it was achieved against the tide of popular conviction; contributor to the *Dublin Review* and *The Month*; spent her last years in Sussex, some of them in the village of Storrington; unmarried; see *Eleanor Leslie: A Memoir* (1898); *The*

History of Mary I, Queen of England (1901) (revised the "old traditional, but generally spurious portraits" of the queen); *Reformation and Renaissance* (1904) (study of the two great revolutionary movements of the fifteenth and sixteenth centuries from the standpoint of the old religion) ("If truth has no independent existence, but is simply what it appears to each individual mind, one set of doctrines is as worthy of credence as another that may be diametrically opposed to them; and if there is no divinely appointed judge of what constitutes revealed truth, it is clear that any one is free to preach and teach whatever may seem good to him. What is merely a matter of individual opinion can by no interpretation be made binding on any conscience. But the Church has always considered herself the guardian of a divinely bestowed Revelation which it behoves her to defend at all costs...

The Church ..., as time went on, suffered from the dual nature of her composition. Although divinely founded, and secured by Christ's own words from every error of doctrine, built upon a Rock against which the waves of chance and change might beat in vain, her treasure was yet held in fragile earthen vessels, and her teaching conveyed through men, not angels. In the very nature of things prosperity must breed corruption. But so long as the watchman on the high tower was duly vigilant all was still well"); *Studies from Court and Cloister* (1905) ("Even before England was England, she was the Isle of Saints, and throughout the Middle Ages religion was her chief care, in a manner almost incredible in this secular and materialistic age. She not only covered the land with magnificent churches and cathedrals, to the architecture of which we cannot in these days approach, even by imitation, distantly, but she also built huge monasteries, and these monasteries were the cradles, the homes of vast stores of ever-accumulating knowledge. A system of philosophy, to which the world is even now returning, recognizing that there is no better training for the human intellect, is so distinctly medieval, that all that savored even remotely of St. Thomas Aquinas or Duns Scotus in the University was utterly destroyed in a great bonfire made at Oxford in 1549. At the dissolution of the monasteries by Henry VIII, the labor, the learning, the genius of centuries were as nought. Exquisitely written and illuminated Bibles, missals and other choice manuscripts, displaying a wealth of paleographic art to which we have lost the key, were torn from their jeweled bindings, and were either thrown aside to spoil and rot, or to become the prey of any who needed wrappers for small merchandise"); *The Church in English History* (1907) (manual for teachers and older students); *Catholic Encyclopedia* ("In Germany Miss Stone was brought into touch with the Catholic religion, and exchanged Protestantism for the 'free atmosphere,' as she expressed it, of the Catholic Church"); *DNB*.

Strauss, Eric Benjamin – physician for psychological medicine; b. 18 November 1894; c. 1917; d. January 1961; head of Psychiatric Department at St. Bartholomew's Hospital, London; Doctor of Medicine of Oxford University; elected a Fellow of the royal College of Physicians in 1939; Graham Greene's psychoanalyst; books both written and translated on neurology; neuropsychiatry, and medical psychology; adopted a neo-Thomist approach to psychiatric problems; friend of Caryll Houselander (see above) to whom he referred some of his cases; see *Reason and Unreason in Psychological Medicine* (1953); "The Church and Sex," in Elizabeth Pakenham (ed), *Catholic Approaches* (1955), p.81;

"Magic and Scruple," *The Month*, January 1956, p.14; *Psychiatry in the Modern World* (1958); *Recent Advances in Neurology and Neuropsychiatry* (1962) (with Walter Russell Brain)

Strugnell, John – biblical scholar; b. 25 May 1930, Barnet, Hertfordshire; d. 30 November 2007, Cambridge Massachusetts; recognized as a child prodigy; raised in the Church of England, but later converted to the Catholic faith; studied at Jesus College, Oxford (double first in Greats and Oriental Languages); prodigious mastery of ancient texts; in 1954 joined the international team of elite scholars entrusted with editing the Dead Sea Scrolls; position at the Oriental Institute at the University of Chicago 1956–1957; in 1958 married Cécile Pierlot, whose father was prime minister of Belgium during World War II; position at Duke University Divinity School 1960–1966; Professor of Christian Origins at Harvard Divinity School 1966–1991 (later Emeritus Professor); in 1970s he devoted himself to study of the Apocrypha and Pseudepigrapha; read, wrote and spoke nine languages; suffered from manic depression and alcohol problems; editor-in-chief of the Scrolls project 1984–1990; first general editor to invite Israeli and other Jewish scholars to join the Scrolls project; in 1990, when he was inebriated and off medication (and by now divorced), he was quoted as saying that Judaism was "a horrible religion" which "should not exist" and "It's Christian heresy, and we deal with our heretics in different ways. You are a phenomenon that we haven't managed to convert – and we should have managed"; accused of anti-semitism and removed from his position as editor; insisted that his remarks were taken out of context and he only meant "horrible" in the Miltonian sense of "deplored in antiquity"; defended by Frank Moore Cross, a colleague at Harvard who said that the comments were based on a theological argument of the early Church Fathers that Christianity superseded Judaism; maintained good relations with several Jewish colleagues and students; enormous influence in his field, partly through students he trained; regarded teaching and supervising as his life's work.

Stuart, (Henry) Francis Montgomery – novelist and poet; b. 29 April 1902, Townsville, Queensland, Australia; c. 1920, on marriage to Iseult Gonne; d. 2 February 2000; Ennis, County Clare; parents both Irish; father committed suicide in 1902; came to Ireland to live as infant; raised a Protestant; poor academic record; deeply influenced by visiting Lourdes; met the beautiful Iseult Gonne (1894–1954), daughter of Maud Gonne (see above) and they eloped; married 4 April 1920 after he converted; tempestuous relationship; imprisoned for republican activities during the civil war; successful first collection of poetry, but several novels failed; left family in 1940 to teach in Germany; broadcast anti-British talks; novels about his wartime experiences praised by critics; *Black List Section H* (1971) (autobiographical) seen as his best book but several periods of inferior work; buried in St. Patrick's churchyard, Fanore, Clare; see Geoffrey Elborn, *Francis Stuart: A Life* (1991); Anon, "Francis Stuart, 1902–1999," *Catholic Life*, June 2003.

Stuart, Mother Janet Erskine – nun; b. 11 November 1857, the rectory, Cottesmore, Rutland; c. 6 March 1879, Farm Street, London; d. 21 October 1914, Roehampton; last of six children of Low Church Anglican rector; influenced by the devout Catholic household of her cousins, daughters of the convert second Earl of Gainsborough, Charles George Noel (see above), and his wife; for three years spent her days hunting and fishing, her evenings in prayer and study; influenced in her conversion and future vocation by Fr. Peter Gallwey, SJ; joined the Society of the Sacred Heart in 1882; a born teacher, she taught her teachers that to educate was "to fit citizens for the Kingdom of Heaven"; Superior of convent at Roehampton from 1894; developed Sacred Heart schools and colleges; from 1911 Mother General of the Society in which capacity she visited Sacred Heart convents throughout world; spiritual daughter of her predecessor, Mother Mabel Digby (see above); buried at Roehampton; see Maude Monaghan, *Life and Letters of Janet Erskine Stuart* (1922); C. C. Martindale, SJ, *Mother Stuart* (1933); P. Smith-Steinmetz, *Life of Mother Janet Stuart* (1948); Madeleine Beard, *Faith and Fortune* (1997), pp.93–98 ("One evening when Janet Stuart was thirteen she and her brother Douglas were working in silence in the school room at Cottesmore. Douglas looked up from the book he was reading and said 'Aristotle says every rational being must have a last end. What is yours?' Janet said she did not know. 'I made up my mind that it must be found. The search lasted seven years and was one of the happiest times of my life. It began by my examining the grounds of my faith, and they all melted away'.... That night was spent reading the Penny Catechism. The first question and answer ('Who made me? God made me') impressed her with a conviction she never lost. She then read Manning's *Grounds for Faith*. She wrote to a friend that her devotion to the Blessed Virgin Mary began with a recitation of the *Memorare*, which 'took me off my feet at once, for it was so daring a statement that I thought it would not have lived if it had been a lie.' She said it constantly and clung to it as 'the first definite something that seemed to come automatically after my seven years of groping in the dark'"); *DNB*.

Sullivan, John, SJ – priest; b. 1861, Ireland; c. 21 December 1896, Farm Street, London; d. 1933; born into a wealthy Protestant family, youngest of four boys and one girl; son of Edward Sullivan, barrister and Lord Chancellor of Ireland; his mother was a devout Catholic; following a common practice then, it was agreed before marriage that any sons would be brought up Protestant, any girls Catholic; went to London and was called to the bar in 1888; traveled extensively in his late twenties; spent much time visiting the poor, the sick and the dying; shy, remote figure and little known about his reasons for conversion except letter in which he wrote, "I owe everything in the world to my mother's prayers" and his great devotion to St. Augustine and St. Monica; entered the Society of Jesus in 1902; ordained priest in 1907; reputation for holiness and powers of healing; buried in community cemetery in Clongowes Wood, but moved in 1960 to Gardner Street Church, Dublin; declared a Servant of God in 1960; see Rev. Fergal McGrath, SJ, *Father John Sullivan, SJ* (1942, pamphlet); Fergal McGrath, SJ, *Father John Sullivan, SJ* (1945, full biography) ("It is quite certain ... that the prayers and example of his mother played a powerful part in his conversion. [In a preface which he wrote he says]: 'But the story of the conversion of the writer of this preface ... may be summed up in the words of St. Augustine ...: 'I believe that to the faithful and daily tears of my mother it was granted that I should not perish'"); Rev. Morgan Costello, SJ, *The Saintly Father John: John Sullivan, SJ* (1963); Susan Gately, "Father John Sullivan SJ: A Life that Spanned Two Worlds – From Nobleman to Ascetic and Healer," *Catholic Life*, July 2003, p.22.

Summers, (Augustus) Montague (name in religion Alphonsus Joseph-Mary) – literary scholar, occultist, and eccentric; b. 10 April 1880, Pembroke Lodge, Clifton, near Bristol; c. 19 July 1909; d. 10 August 1948, 4 Dynevor Road, Richmond; youngest of seven children of a wealthy banker; brought up in the evangelical Anglican faith of his parents; at Trinity College, Oxford, where he had reputation for dandyism, intelligence and wit; ordained as deacon in the Church of England and given a curacy; at that time rumored to be studying Satanism and acquitted of a charge of pederasty; after his conversion he may have received minor orders as a deacon, but no record of ordination to the priesthood has ever been found; yet always addressed as a cleric, and adopted Catholic priestly attire, and purported to offer Mass in his private chapel (his religious devotion never denied); became increasingly eccentric; schoolmaster and great scholar of Restoration drama; wrote several books on demonology, witchcraft, vampires, and werewolves, plus a history of the gothic novel; many rumors about him, both good and bad; buried in Richmond cemetery; see Joseph Jerome (Fr. Brocard Sewell), *Montague Summers* (1965); *DNB*.

Sutcliffe, Joseph George – c. 1880 (received with his wife, Katherine (1853–1890), daughter of an Anglican rector); formerly Anglican curate; brother of William Ormond Sutcliffe (see below); see essay in J. G. F. Raupert (ed), *Roads to Rome* (1901), p.257 ("I found the Catholic Church the Church of the New Testament:

1. She alone truly reverences it. She alone, sole heiress of the Jewish Church, chose out and arranged the books of the New Law. She alone preserved them down the ages. She alone today combats fearlessly for the preservation of their

meaning and integrity; alone, as her Divine Master, unmoved by the passing ideas of the world, and by fear of results. The 'Reformers' came not to Holy Writ as disciples, but as judges; and would reject all that gainsaid their new religion. The judgment of Solomon must again decide between the two claimants – the one prepared to suffer all, if only the object of her love be safe; the other prepared at once to sacrifice the object of pretended love, if only her enemy be spited.

2. Our Lord and His Apostles taught Catholic principles. The early Christians were Catholics heart and soul. I found that the 'Church of England' was not in earnest when it claimed to restore primitive Christianity. Its true aim was, if possible, to satisfy both sides.

I found that the presentment of the Protestant 'Reformation,' taken on trust by pious Protestants, is a myth; that its agents and its methods were not marked by the seal of sanctity; the seal of Divine approval.

I remarked a general parallel between the refusal of the Jews to consider the credentials offered by our Lord, and the refusal of Protestants to listen to those presented by the Catholic Church. The objections raised by the Jews against our Lord and His mission are those thrown at the Church by Protestants. I noted the same contemptuous certainty, and the same *a priori* prejudices.

I remarked that Protestantism has not applied its dissolving principles to the affairs of this world – e.g., commerce, politics, the army or the navy – and has, a few sectaries excepted, only pretended to do so in matters of religion.

To prefer to the Church certain chief aids of the 'Reformation' and their work is to cry again with the Jews – 'Not this man, but Barabbas'").

Sutcliffe, William Ormond – priest; b. 1856; c. 1881; brought up as Evangeli-

cal; educated at Shrewsbury School and St. John's College, Cambridge (first class Classical Tripos 1880); gradually became more High Church; ordained Catholic priest 1888; Canon of Westminster; first Master of St. Edmund's House, Cambridge (established for the university residence of secular clerics) 1897–1904; chief religious inspector for the Archdiocese of Westminster 1906; on council of Catholic College for Women at Cambridge; brother of Joseph George Sutcliffe (see above); see essay in J. G. F. Raupert (ed), *Roads to Rome* (1901), p.264 ("I was now struck by the great chain of passages bearing on the Petrine claims: John i. 42; Matt. x. 2; Matt. xvi. 18, 19; Luke xxii. 31, 32; John xxi. 15–17. It seems to me now striking, but I do not know that I noticed it then, that the Key-bearer of the House of David gave the keys to St. Peter; He Who is the foundation, than which no other can be laid, made St. Peter to share in the work of supporting the Church when He called him Rock; and the Good Shepherd committed His whole flock, lambs and sheep, to the care of St. Peter...

In course of time other reasons appeared to help to convince me of the claims of the Catholic Church; for instance, the great argument that the New Testament teaches that the Christian religion is to be preached to men *with authority*, and that they are bound to receive it under pain of eternal condemnation ... Mark. xvi. 15, 16; Matt. xxviii. 19, 20.... But the Apostles to whom these words were said were soon to die, whereas the promise was to endure to the consummation or end of the world; hence, I argued, the command and the promise were made, not only to the Apostles then living, but to their successors. Again it is written, 'The gates of hell shall not prevail against it [the Church]' (Matt. xvi. 18); and, 'The

Church of the living God, the pillar and ground of the truth' (I Tim. iii. 15).

From these passages and others … it seemed clear that our Lord intended to found a Church with authority to teach and the promise of His perpetual assistance, and I could find this Church nowhere but in the Catholic Church. Those Churches of the East which are separated from Western Christianity could not appeal to me as representing the universal Church; and other Christian bodies did not even profess to do so, Anglicans admitting that Roman Catholics and Eastern Orthodox are part of the Church, and other bodies, such as Wesleyans, Baptists, and Congregationalists, claiming the right of private judgment for the individual, as indeed do many Anglicans.

Again, it followed from the above passages that the Protestant principle that the Church had erred was untrue. But following the history of the Catholic Church back into the past, I found no break in its continuity from the beginning; I found no point at which it could be said to commence except the Day of Pentecost; it seemed clearly the continuation of the Church of the first centuries. Therefore as the Church cannot fail, but is the pillar and ground of the truth, the Catholic Church today had the same authority as the Church of the lifetime of St. Peter and St. Paul").

Sutherland, Graham Vivian – painter and printmaker; b. 24 August 1903, 8 Pendle Road, Streatham, London; c. 1926; d. 17 February 1980, Hampstead, London; began as etcher and engraver and painted little before 1935; under influence of the painter Samuel Palmer (1805–1881); primarily painter of landscapes; official war artist, producing semi-abstract pictures of desolation after bombing which exactly expressed atmosphere of such a scene; later religious works and portraits (e.g., large-scale crucifixion for St. Matthew's Church in Northampton, inspired by photographs of liberated concentration camps and Mathias Grünewald's Isenheim altarpiece; also the huge tapestry Christ in Glory for new Coventry Cathedral); elder brother of Humphrey Sutherland (1908–1986), classical scholar and numismatist; buried near his home in Trottiscliffe, Kent; see Roger Berthoud, *Graham Sutherland: A Biography* (1982) ("We were all interested in religions of all kinds at that time, in much the same way as people at Cambridge were later interested in communism.… Chesterton and Belloc were an influence in a way. Then, of course, there was the Oxford Movement: Cardinal Manning, Newman – all, of course, starting as Church of England"); *DNB*.

Sutherland, Halliday Gibson – doctor and writer; b. 24 June 1882, Glasgow, Scotland; c. 1919; d. 19 April 1960, St. Marylebone, London; brought up in Scottish Free Church; studied medicine at Edinburgh University; conversion influenced strongly by Belloc's *The Path to Rome*; medical consultant; discovered how germs of cerebro-spinal fever are transmitted; authority on the management of tuberculosis; trenchant critic of birth control; co-founder in 1926, with Laetitia Fairfield (see above) of the League of National Life, set up to fight against promotion of birth control as an instrument of social control; controversy with Marie Stopes culminating in her suing him for defamation, his defense being upheld by the House of Lords; author of medical books, notably on tuberculosis, travel writing, plus several autobiographies; made Knight Commander of Order of Isabel the Catholic in 1954; see *Birth Control: A Statement of Christian Doctrine against the Neo-Malthusians* (1922); *Birth Control*

Exposed (1925); *Arches of the Years* (1933) (autobiography); *A Time to Keep* (1934), pp.200–286 (autobiographical reminiscences) ("Apart from the unique and tremendous claim that this was the One True Infallible Church of God, I discovered that most of what I had hitherto heard or thought about the Church was false. I discovered that this Church, accredited with superstition and idolatry, was apparently engaged in upholding the dignity of human reason in a world of chaos. Nay, more, it seemed as if my own Protestantism, and the weakness thereof, had been based on sentiment and emotion, two attributes of mind on which Rome held a tight rein. It was also apparent that God could not have approved a hundred different sects, each declaring the others to be wrong. There could only be one Truth and one true Church"); *In My Path* (1936) (autobiographical reminiscences); *Lapland Journey* (1938); *Hebridean Journey* (1939); *Birth Control: Ethical, Social, and Medical Objections* (1944); "Communists and Spain," *The Month*, February 1947, p.77; *Southward Journey* (1947); *Spanish Journey* (1948); *Control of Life* (1951); *Irish Journey* (1956); Ann Farmer, *Prophets and Priests: The Hidden Face of the Birth Control Movement* (2002); Walter Romig, *Book of Catholic Authors*, Second Series (1943); *DNB*.

Symondson, Anthony, SJ – priest, writer and architectural historian; b. 1940, London; c. 1985; former Anglican minister; secretary of Converts Aid Society; entered the Society of Jesus 1989; ordained priest; teacher at Stonyhurst College for a time; writer on architecture; *Catholic Herald* columnist; on Westminster Cathedral art committee; on Catholic Southern Historic Churches Committee; see (ed) *The Victorian Crisis of Faith* (1970); "Are Anglo-Catholics Catholic?" in Dwight Longenecker (ed),

The Path to Rome (1999) ("It was the acceptance of the office of the Pope as the centre of the unity of the Church, the system of centralized government expressed by him and the claim that by Divine appointment he has universal authority over Christendom that made me realize that I could no longer stay in the Church of England. An invisible, spiritual union was absurd because it was not recognized by Rome"); *Sir Ninian Comper: An Introduction to His Life and Work* (2006) (with Stephen Bucknall); *Peter Favre* (2006); *Paul VI* (2008).

Symons, William Christian – decorative designer and painter of portraits, landscape and genre; b. 28 November 1845, Vauxhall, Surrey; c. 1870; d. 4 September 1911, Stocks House, Udimore, near Rye, Sussex; friend of James Abbott McNeill Whistler; also influenced by John Singer Sargent; paintings included seascapes, landscapes, and genre subjects in impressionistic style; also accomplished portraitist; designed and executed a number of decorations for John Francis Bentley's (see above) Westminster Cathedral; not well known to wider public during his lifetime, since then his work re-assessed favorably; buried at Udimore; see *DNB*.

Talbot, Hon. and Very Rev. George – priest and papal official; b. 1816, Evercreech, near Wells, Somerset; c. June 1843 (received by Cardinal Wiseman); d. 16 October 1886, Bon Secours convent at Passy, Paris; fifth son of third Baron Talbot of Malahide; became Anglican vicar; doubts about Church of England in 1842; consulted Newman; ordained Catholic priest 6 June 1846; applied to join Newman's Oratory, but was refused; Canon of St. Peter's, Rome; Chamberlain to Pope Pius IX; very influential with Pope Pius IX and supported the Ultramontanism of Wiseman and Manning;

lacking in judgment; described Newman as "the most dangerous man in England"; in 1868 removed to an asylum at Passy, near Paris; buried in cemetery of Père Lachaise, Paris; see *DNB* ("Today he is best remembered for his view that the laity should be restricted to hunting, shooting, and entertaining").

Talbot, Hon. Admiral Sir John – naval officer; b. c.1769, Malahide, near Dublin; c. 1849; d. 7 July 1851, Rhode Hill, near Lyme Regis, Dorset; third son of the first Baron Talbot de Malahide; son-in-law of the ninth Baron Arundell of Wardour; served in the French Revolutionary and the Napoleonic Wars; served under Nelson; saw much service; engaged in several prominent single ship actions; captured the *Ville de Milan* and her prize, the *Cleopatra*, in 1805; as captain of the *Victorious* took the French 74–gun ship, *Rivoli*, after a severe engagement; blockaded the Connecticut coast during the war of 1812; *DNB*.

Taylor, Frances ("Fanny") Margaret (name in religion Rev. Mother Mary Magdalen) – nun and journalist; b. 20 January 1832, Stoke Rochford, Lincolnshire; c. 14 April 1855 (received at Easter at the camp hospital near Scutari in the Crimea; her sister, Charlotte, received in 1857); d. 9 June 1900, Soho Square convent, London; daughter of Anglican clergyman; youngest of ten surviving children; educated at home; became attracted to Tractarianism; joined the volunteers organized by Florence Nightingale to go out to nurse in the Crimea; nursed the wounded there, admiring the Irish nuns and the ladies' first superintendent, Mary Stanley (see above); her conversion largely due to the example of wounded and dying Irish Catholic soldiers; back home did much charitable work; author of *Tyborne and Who Went Thither* (1857), a novel about Elizabethan Catholic martyrs, and of several stories and biographies; 1862–1871 proprietor and editor of *The Lamp*, a Catholic periodical for middle and lower classes; helped to found *The Month* and *The Messenger of the Sacred Heart*; friend of Lady Georgiana Fullerton (see above), who acted as a guide; foundress and Mother-General of the Congregation of the Poor Servants of the Mother of God (set up to work among the poor); very active in spreading devotion to the Sacred Heart and Apostleship of Prayer; her last years were ones of pain and suffering; buried in Maryfield convent, Roehampton; see F. C. Devas, *Mother Mary Magdalen of the Sacred Heart* (1927) ("She herself always attributed the grace of her conversion mainly, under God, to the example given her by the faith, resignation, and patience in suffering, of the Irish soldiers whom she had nursed, and to the prayers they continued to offer for her after their death. The contrast between these fervent, well-instructed Catholic men, and their kind-hearted, but ignorant English Protestant comrades, struck her…. One set of men had a well-grounded faith; it was everything to them that they should die in the Grace of God, strengthened with the Sacraments for which they longed. The other set, knowing nothing of grace or Sacraments, if they thought about the matter at all, cherished a vague hope that God would not be too hard on them. The one set loved Jesus and Mary and Joseph and St. Patrick, as real and very living persons. The other set had only an abstract God, whose name they had used most frequently as a meaningless expletive"); R. G. Wells, *A Woman of Her Time and Ours: Mary Magdalen Taylor, SMG* (1988); Joyce Sugg, *Ever Yours Affly: John Henry Newman and His Female Circle* (1996); *Gillow*, Vol. V, p.538; *Catholic Encyclopedia*; *DNB*.

Taylor, Frank Sherwood – chemist and historian of science; b. 26 November 1897, Bickley, Bromley, Kent; c. 15 November 1941; d. 5 January 1956, St Denis, The Avenue, Crowthorne, Berkshire; father was a "non-militant Huxleyan agnostic"; childhood enthusiasm for practical science; seriously wounded at Passchendaele in 1917; studied Chemistry at Oxford; teacher and lecturer in Chemistry; writer of numerous books and articles on chemistry, general science, history of science, and relationship between science and religion, often writing for non-specialist reader; also studies on alchemy, especially Greek alchemy; editor of *Journal of Alchemy and Early Chemistry (Ambix)* from its inception in 1937 until his death; commissioned by Rationalist Press to write *Galileo and the Freedom of Thought* (1938) to promote the rationalist cause, but writing of it brought him into the Catholic Church; in 1940 elected curator of Museum of the History of Science at Oxford; in 1950 appointed Director of the Science Museum in London; deeply sincere and loyal to friends; see *The World of Science* (1936) ("Science, while not denying the existence of God, concerns itself with things it can understand and test and experiment with. For the rest it minds its own business and leaves everyone to decide on his own religious views"); *The Attitude of St. Thomas to Natural Science* (1944); "The Church and Science," *The Month*, March-April 1944, p.89 ("I traveled to Glasgow to give a lecture on *Galileo and the Freedom of Thought* to the Rationalist Press Association. I was not an expert on Galileo, and I got up the subject for the occasion. When I came to go further into the matter and to consult such original records as have survived, I found to my surprise that most of the Protestant and Rationalist accounts were full of mis-statements which could hardly be less than intentional, and that

the Catholic accounts, if not entirely uncolored, were far more accurate. Moreover it seemed to me, as it seemed to T. H. Huxley when he read up the same subject, that 'the Pope and the cardinals had on the whole the best of it'.... But unlike Huxley, I did not remain in my former opinions, for the small insight I gained into the operations and the doctrines of the Church led by a seven years' progression to the step I took some eighteen months ago. It is not my purpose to relate my personal history, nor, as I might, to point out the singular providence of God who used the Rationalist Press Association as an agent for my conversion; but rather to point out the disservice which the anti-Catholic factions did themselves by telling lies or suppressing truth about matters of history. What is sauce for the goose is sauce for the gander; and the moral of my tale is that we shall do our cause a great deal of harm if we falsify, suppress, or refuse to discuss, any matters that appear to raise difficulties between the Church and the man of science"); *The Fourfold Vision: A Study of the Relations of Science and Religion* (1945); *The Attitude of the Church to Science* (1946); "On the Excellence of Things," *The Wind and the Rain*, Vol. 3 (1946), p.116; *Two Ways of Life: Christian and Materialist* (1947); *Concerning Science* (1949); *St. Albert: Patron of Scientists* (1950); *Man and Matter: Essays Scientific and Christian* (1951); *An Illustrated History of Science* (1955); A. V. Simcock, "Alchemy and the World of Science," *Ambix*, November 1987, p.121; Matthew Hoehn, OSB (ed), *Catholic Authors* (1952); *DNB*.

Temple, Dom George Frederick James, OSB – priest and mathematician; b. 2 September 1901, 134 Wornington Road, North Kensington, London; c. 1919; d. 30 January 1992, Wotton Bridge, Isle of Wight; parents were English country folk from Oxfordshire; left school early owing to death of his father; enrolled at Birkbeck College, London, in 1918; became part-time research assistant and wrote several papers on general relativity; worked under Sir Arthur Eddington at Cambridge; Professor at King's College, London 1932–1953; research on wide range of subjects, e.g., on aerodynamics; Sedleian Professor of Natural Philosophy, Oxford 1953–1968; books on quantum theory and history of mathematics; close friendships with the Dominicans and Benedictines and great love for the theology of Aquinas; following the death of his wife in 1979, he joined the Benedictine Order 1980, being admitted to Quarr Abbey, Ryde, Isle of Wight; ordained Catholic priest in 1983 at the age of eighty-two; see *An Introduction to Quantum Theory* (1931); *The General Principles of Quantum Theory* (1934); *The Classic and Romantic in Natural Philosophy* (1954); "Physics and Philosophy," in Elizabeth Pakenham (ed), *Catholic Approaches* (1955), p.51; *The Finite, the Infinite and the Absolute* (1964); *Religion and Modern Scientific Thought* (1964); *100 Years of Mathematics* (1981); *DNB* ("All his life he was a man of unfailing courtesy, wit, and kindness, though capable of trenchant criticism").

Terry, Sir Richard Runciman – organist, choirmaster and musical scholar; b. 3 January 1864, Ellington, Northumberland; c. 1896; d. 18 April 1938, Kensington, England; nephew of Sir Walter Runciman, first Baronet; founder of Cambridge University Musical Club; musical critic for *Cambridge Review*; successively organist and choirmaster at St. John's Cathedral, Antigua, West Indies; after conversion was at Downside Abbey 1896–1901 (taught music and revived school choir); passion for the music of William Byrd and other pre-

Reformation English composers and revival of Renaissance polyphony, especially Latin liturgical music by English composers; greatly inspired by the revival of Gregorian chant by Dom Prosper Guéranger at Solesmes; later organist and director of the choir at Westminster Cathedral; compiled the influential *Westminster Hymnal* (1912) and wrote on Catholic church music; knighted in 1922; see Hilda Andrews, *Westminster Retrospective: A Memoir of Sir Richard Terry* (1948); *DNB*.

Thompson, Edward Healy – physician, author, and translator; b. 1813?, Oakham, Rutland; c. 1846 (received with his wife, Harriet (1811–1896), writer of novels, biography and history; his brother, Charles (1819–1896), physician specializing in homoeopathic medicine and greatly influenced by the Oxford Movement, received in 1853 with his wife, Mary (1822–1880)); d. 21 May 1891, Cheltenham, Gloucestershire; studied at Emmanuel College, Cambridge; became Anglican curate; friend of J. R. Hope-Scott (see above) and Edward Badeley (see above); became a keen Tractarian; after conversion devoted his powers chiefly to literature and controversy; writer of books of apologetics and Catholic biography; uncle of Francis Thompson (1860–1907), the poet and author; conservative in politics, but in 1886 supporter of Home Rule; see *Remarks on Certain Anglican Theories of Unity* (1846); *A few earnest thoughts on the duty of communion with the Catholic Church by a recent convert* (1847); *The Unity of the Episcopate Considered* (1847); *The Life and Glories of St. Joseph* (1888); *Before and After the Gunpowder Plot* (1890); *Gillow*, Vol. V, p.540; *Catholic Encyclopedia*.

Thompson, James Eyre – barrister; d. 30 August 1914; brought up amidst narrowest of Evangelical surroundings; formerly on reporting staff of *The Times* in Houses of Parliament; then *Times* Law Reporter in House of Lords and Law Journal Reporter in House of Lords and Privy Council; member of North Kensington Catholic Association; see essay in J. G. F. Raupert (ed), *Roads to Rome* (1901), p.270 ("I used to go and hear Monsignor Capel sometimes and was much taken by the argument that the Church was a ... living organism; not a ... mere aggregation of particles or individuals.... [T]he statement in Newman's 'Anglican Difficulties' ... that the Catholic Church deemed the smallest venial sin as incomparably a greater evil than any physical catastrophe, immensely affected me. Certainly I owe more to Newman than to any one else...

...[E]ven in boyhood, the often quoted remarks of Macaulay (in his essay on 'Ranke's Popes') on the Church's power of utilizing every form of enthusiasm whereby what in the Church of England degenerates into a Joanna Southcote, is elevated in the Catholic Church to a St. Teresa, had their effect.

I have dealt here merely with what I read and thought before I entered the Church. But for myself, then as now, the alternative in the world of thought is the Church *versus* Agnosticism or rather Nihilism, with its inevitable Pessimism and Materialism; and, in the moral and practical sphere, between the presence *versus* the absence of a perpetual witness for righteousness against brute force, and individual as well as national selfishness. If the Church were not what she claims to be, she must have been swept away long ago as a ridiculous anachronism. I remember marking, in one of Goldwin Smith's lectures, the prophecy that the end of the century would see the disappearance of the Papacy. But the Papacy has not yet vanished").

Thorold, Algar Labouchere – author and politician; b. 1866; c. 1884 (wife, Theresa Mary, daughter of an Anglican vicar, received in 1898); d. 30 May 1936; only son of Anthony Wilson Thorold (1825–1895), Anglican Bishop of Rochester and Winchester; educated at Eton and Christ Church, Oxford; joined Foreign Office (Information Department) 1917; in charge of a propaganda mission to Italy, where he remained until the end of 1918; member of the British Peace Delegation in Paris, 1919; first press attaché at British embassy, Paris, 1920; proprietor of *Truth* and editor of the *Dublin Review* 1926–1934; supported particularly the writings of Christopher Dawson (see above) in his journals; translator of works by St. Catherine of Siena, Jean Pierre de Caussade, especially on prayer; expert on the work of Anthony Trollope; see *An Essay in Aid of the Better Appreciation of Catholic Mysticism* (1900);

Thorold, Thomas, SJ (alias Carwell) – priest; b. c.1600, Lincolnshire; c. 1622; d. 9 August 1664; brought up in Protestant family; studied at St. Omer, then entered English College, Rome, in 1629; ordained in Rome 2 February 1633, then joined the Society of Jesus; served on the English mission from 1646; rector of the London district by 1654; later served as vice-provincial of England; he may have been the Thomas Thurrall appointed chaplain to Queen Catherine of Braganza by warrant of 13 May 1663; see *DNB*.

Thwaites, Hugh Simon, SJ – priest and author; b. 21 July 1917, near London; c. 21 December 1941; baptized Church of England; mother and father became Christian Scientists; confirmed as an Anglican, but at eighteen followed Christian Science for a while; returned to Anglicanism; about to study for the

Anglican ministry, but World War II broke out; joined the army; became friends with a Catholic family and was introduced to Frank Sheed's *A Map of Life*, Joseph Faà di Bruno's *Catholic Belief*, and Vernon Johnson's *One Lord, One Faith* (especially influenced by the latter); received into the Church on an American troopship in the Indian Ocean; taken prisoner by the Japanese on the fall of Singapore; in prison camps for over three years; after the war joined the Society of Jesus; ordained Catholic priest in 1954; great supporter of the traditional Latin Mass; said about the Anglican Church: "Their church is like whisky with three parts water. We are straight out of the bottle"; see *Our Glorious Faith and How to Lose It* (1995); *War Memoirs of an Amateur* (1997); *EWTN Audio Library* (18 August 2003) ("The heart of the faith is that Jesus is God and the Catholic Church is the one true Church. If you've got that you've got everything that matters. The rest will come bit by bit...

...What I hold onto is something St. Augustine said, that in this life we're in the womb of Mary, in the darkness of faith. When we die she gives birth to us to the light of eternity. So in this life, just like an unborn baby the mother is carrying, everything the baby has need for its growth can only come through its mother, so everything that we need for our growth in Christ can only come through Mary. That's why the Church calls her the mediatrix of all graces").

Thynne, Lord Charles – priest and author; b. 9 February 1813; c. 1852 (received with wife, Lady Harriet Frances (1816–1881); daughter, Gertrude Thynne, Countess of Kenmare, was received in 1853); d. 11 August 1894, Ditton Park; seventh and youngest son of second Marquess of Bath; son-in-law of Richard Bagot (1782–1854), Anglican

Bishop of Oxford, who denounced effort of Newman to give in *Tract 90* a Catholic interpretation of the Thirty-nine Articles; brother of Charlotte Montague-Douglas-Scott, Duchess of Buccleuch (see above); was Anglican rector and canon of Canterbury; much correspondence with Newman before his conversion (Newman wrote to him regarding Anglicanism: "Two different bodies cannot form a single body: one or other is not the Church, or, to use your language, one or the other is in schism.... The question is, whether, were you dying, you would be satisfied in your not having joined Rome"); after death of his wife, he was ordained a Catholic priest in 1886 (in Rome by Cardinal Manning) and served at Ditton Park, residence of his sister; see *A Letter to his Late Parishioners* (1853); Stanley L. Jaki, *Newman to Converts: An Existential Ecclesiology* (2001), Ch. 15 ("Newman easily disposed of Thynne's claim that Romans, Greeks, and Anglicans made up one kingdom. Newman would see no problem in the fact that Catholics exist in insignificant numbers in many places. The problem lay with Thynne's claim, because the alleged unity of Greeks, Anglicans, and Romans was not visible at all. Nor could the problem be circumvented by a reference to race. Americans and the English were one race, but surely two very different kingdoms. And since Thynne used the idea of race as indicating a common descent, this, whatever their common Christian origin, still would not make Greeks, Anglicans, and Romans '*one kingdom* (i.e., visible)'"); *Gillow*, Vol. V, p.543.

Titterton, William Richard – writer and journalist; b. 1876; c. 1931; d. 22 November 1964; journalist on many newspapers; writer (of verse and on issues of modern thought); assistant to G. K. Chesterton (see above) on the *Eye*

Witness, New Witness, and on *G.K.'s Weekly*; became distributist; owed his conversion largely to Chesterton; also on the staff of *The Universe* Catholic weekly; see *Have We Lost God?* (1933); *Chesterton: A Portrait* (1936); Anon, "William Richard Titterton," *Catholic Life*, November 2003, p.27.

Tolkien, John Ronald Reuel – writer and philologist; b. 3 January 1892, Bloemfontein, Orange Free State, South Africa; c. 1900 (child convert) (received with his younger brother Hilary; his wife, Edith, *née* Bratt (d. 1971) converted before their wedding in 1916); d. 2 September 1973, Bournemouth; father (d. 1896) a bank manager; his mother (see below) also died young, leaving her sons as wards of Fr. Francis Morgan of the Birmingham Oratory; educated at Exeter College, Oxford; fought in World War I until invalided home with trench fever; Professor of English Literature at Leeds University in 1924; Professor of Anglo-Saxon, Oxford, in 1925; Fellow of Merton College; turned from philology to fiction and constructed a story cycle, notably in *The Hobbit* (1937) and *The Lord of the Rings* (1954–1955); both were enormously successful, the latter also as a film; many honors; buried in Wolvercote cemetery, near Oxford; posthumous publication of many other works; see Humphrey Carpenter, *J. R. R. Tolkien: A Biography* (1977); Humphrey Carpenter (ed), *The Letters of J. R. R. Tolkien* (1981) (Letter to his son, Michael, 1 November 1963: "If [Christ] is a fraud and the Gospels fraudulent – that is: garbled accounts of a demented megalomaniac (which is the only alternative), then of course the spectacle exhibited by the Church (in the sense of clergy) in history and today is simply evidence of a gigantic fraud. If not, however, then this spectacle is alas! Only what was to be expected: it began before

the first Easter, and it does not affect faith at all – except that we may and should be deeply grieved. But we should grieve on Our Lord's behalf and for Him, associating ourselves with the scandalizers not with the saints, not crying out that we cannot 'take' Judas Iscariot, or even the absurd & cowardly Simon Peter, or the silly women like James' mother, trying to push her sons.... It takes a fantastic will to unbelief to suppose that Jesus never really 'happened', and more to suppose that he did not say the things recorded of him – so incapable of being 'invented' by anyone in the world at that time: such as 'before Abraham came to be I am' (John viii); 'He that hath seen me hath seen the Father' (John ix); or the promulgation of the Blessed Sacrament in John vi: 'He that eateth my flesh and drinketh my blood hath eternal life.' We must therefore either believe in Him and in what he said and take the consequences; or reject him and take the consequences.... The only cure for sagging or fainting faith is Communion...

I myself am convinced by the Petrine claims, nor looking around the world does there seem much doubt which (if Christianity is true) is the true Church, the temple of the Spirit dying but living, corrupt but holy, self-reforming and rearising. But for me that Church of which the Pope is the acknowledged head on earth has as chief claim that it is the one that has (and still does) ever defend the Blessed Sacrament, and given it most honor, and put it (as Christ plainly intended) in the prime place. 'Feed my sheep' was His last charge to St. Peter; and since His words are always first to be understood literally, I suppose them to refer primarily to the Bread of Life. It was against this that the W. European revolt (or Reformation) was really launched – 'the blasphemous fable of the Mass' – and faith/works a mere red herring"); Joseph Pearce, *Tolkien: Man and*

Myth (1998); John Beaumont, "The Catholic Witness of J. R. R. Tolkien," *Downside Review*, April 1999, p.115; Joseph Pearce, (ed), *Tolkien: A Celebration* (1999), p.102; Michael Coren, *J. R. R. Tolkien: The Man Who Created The Lord of The Rings* (2001); *Tolkien Special Issue, Chesterton Review*, February-May 2002; Stratford Caldecott, *Secret Fire: The Spiritual Vision of J. R. R. Tolkien* (2003); Special Issue on "The Catholic Genius of J. R. R. Tolkien," *Saint Austin Review*, July/August 2008; Joseph Pearce, *Literary Converts* (1999), *passim*; Lorene Hanley Duquin, *A Century of Catholic Converts* (2003), p.23; *DNB* ("Tolkien ... remained a devout Catholic to the end of his life, going so far as to insist, in a letter of 2 December 1953 to a Jesuit friend, Robert Murray, that although *The Lord of the Rings* contains no overt reference to Christianity at any point, and very little to religion, it nevertheless remains 'a fundamentally religious and Catholic work'.... He also created a mythological mediation between the Catholic Christianity in which he was a devout believer and the motifs of pre-Christian Germanic story").

Tolkien, Mabel (née Incledon) – b. 1870; c. June 1900 (received with her sister, May); d. 14 November 1904; mother of J. R. R. Tolkien (see above); brought up with Methodist and Unitarian influences; then High Anglican; after conversion financial support cut off by her family; worked as a private tutor; emotional strain and additional financial hardship led to early death; see Humphrey Carpenter, *J. R. R. Tolkien: A Biography* (1977) ("My own dear mother was a martyr indeed, and it was not to everybody that God grants so easy a way to his great gifts as he did to Hilary and myself, giving us a mother who killed herself with labor and trouble to ensure us keeping the faith"); *Humphrey*

Carpenter (ed), The Letters of J. R. R. Tolkien (1981) ("When I think of my mother's death ... worn out with persecution, pov-erty, and, largely consequent, disease, in the effort to hand on to us small boys the Faith, and remember the tiny bedroom she shared with us in rented rooms ... where she died alone, too ill for viaticum, I find it very hard and bitter, when my children stray away").

Toynbee, Jocelyn Mary Catherine – archaeologist and art historian; b. 3 March 1897, 12 Upper Westbourne Terrace, Paddington, London; c. 1930; d. 31 December 1985, 4 Marston Ferry Road, Oxford; sister of historian Arnold Toynbee (1889–1975), who grew closer to Catholicism in his later years; devoted to learning, especially classical learning; director of studies in Classics at Newnham College, Cambridge; Professor of Classical Archaeology, Cambridge; many books and articles on classics and archaeology; unmarried; see "On a Firm Foundation," in John A. O'Brien (ed), *The Road to Damascus: Vol. II: Where I Found Christ* (1950), p.98 ("What, then, after twenty years in the Catholic Church, would I say to Anglicans and Anglo-Catholics? I would assure them that, if they believe (as they surely do) that Christianity is the infallible Revelation to man of Him who is Truth Itself, their faces are already set toward the Catholic Church: barriers which they seem to see erected between themselves and her are really imaginary. In our eyes, indeed, they are already, if validly baptized, one with us in virtue of their baptism. Since there is only one Church and one baptism, they were all members of the Catholic Church until such time as they formally adhered to Anglican denials of Catholic doctrine and forms of worship conducted outside Catholic unity. Thus an Anglican, in becoming a

Catholic, does not, as is so often thought, repudiate his baptism: he returns to that to which it admitted him"); *The Shrine of St. Peter and the Vatican Excavations* (1956) (with J. B. Ward Perkins); *Art in Britain under the Romans* (1964); *The Art of the Romans* (1965); *Death and Burial in the Roman World* (1971); *Roman Historical Portraits* (1978); *DNB*.

Trail, Ann Agnes (name in religion Agnes Xavier) – nun and artist; b. 16 February 1798, Panbride, Forfarshire, Scotland; c. 16 June 1828; d. 3 December 1872, Edinburgh; second of eleven children of Scottish Presbyterian minister and brought up in that belief; trained as artist from 1822 to 1824; traveled through Italy before being received into the Church in Rome ("Artistic yearning and religious enquiry had come to a common conclusion" (*DNB*)); in 1833 entered the Order of the Ursulines of Jesus; founded St. Margaret's, Greenhill, Edinburgh, first post-Reformation convent in Scotland, and spent the rest of her life at the convent; always influenced by Ambrose Phillipps de Lisle (see above) and Ignatius Spencer (see above) and their scheme for the conversion of England; wrote a spiritual autobiography and instructed many substantial and generous converts; buried in the chapel of St. Margarets Convent, Edinburgh and subsequently in Grange cemetery; see Rev. T. E. Bridgett (ed), *Conversion of Miss Trail, A Scotch Presbyterian (written by herself)* (1897); *DNB*.

Trapp, (Hubert) Thornton – c. 1956; brought up as an Anglo-Catholic; former Anglo-Catholic minister; in 1954 he challenged the Archbishop of Canterbury to come "out into the open" about Freemasonry, declaring in his parish magazine that "the Christians' God and the Masons' God are not one and the same ... the two loyalties are in conflict," but no reply; converted at the time of the South India question; see "More Converts Explain," *The Month*, February 1957, p.74 ("Why should the people of my [Anglo-Catholic] parish be taught to go to Mass on the feast of the Assumption, while the people of my neighbor's parish were taught to deny the very existence of the Mass and the Assumption? After all, the Catholic Church did exist in England. Was it right of me to try to turn another body into a feeble copy of it against the will of the founders of this body, against the will of most of its members, violating its very constitutions and raison d'être?").

Trevor, (Lucy) Meriol – writer; b. 15 April 1919, London; c. 1950; d. 12 January 2000; daughter of an Indian army lieutenant-colonel; Welsh extraction; spent her early years in Kent, Hampshire, Cambridge, and Persia, where her father was consul general; Oxford graduate in Greats; pacifist in World War II; early on repudiated Christianity, but reading C. S. Lewis moved her from agnosticism; novelist, (nineteen novels for children, eighteen for adults; all with themes of moral struggle) and biographer; much of her fiction has a Catholic theme; Fellow of Royal Society for Literature 1967; later in life became concerned at the banal nature of the new liturgy and increasing apostasy of the West; much Catholic apologetics; unmarried; see *Sun Slower, Sun Faster* (1955) (includes a description of a recusant Mass: "The shadowy bare attic, the kneeling people, the two candles with their steady flames, the crucifix gleaming up there ... all seemed to loosen her mind from herself and she thought of Calvary.... She was aware only of the priest's gestures and whispers, preparing the way of the mystery.... A strange feeling invaded her as if all around them were crowds upon crowds of martyrs and angels, people from all times and all places, spirits from all heavenly spheres, now bowing down with the few poor earthly Christians, bowing down in a silence intense with adoration as old Thomas rang the little sanctus bell and the priest raised the Host high above his head.... The priest turned and made the sign of the cross and all signed themselves; then he came forward and moved along the line, placing the Hosts in the mouths of the people. Cecil had a very strange feeling: she felt that this was at the same time the most natural and the most unnatural thing she had ever seen. They were like little birds being fed by their mother: and yet it was grown people who knelt to receive what looked like a paper penny of bread on their tongues. She knew at once why the Mass provoked such love and such hate. Either what they believe is true, or else it is a dreadful delusion, she thought"); *The Sparrow Child* (1958); *A Narrow Place* (1958); *Shadows and Images* (1960) (fictional account of a conversion at the time of the Oxford *Movement); Newman: The Pillar of the Cloud* (1962); *Newman: Light in Winter* (1962); *The Rose-Round* (1963); *Lights in a Dark Town* (1964); *Apostle of Rome: A Life of Philip Neri* (1515–1595) (1966); *Pope John* (1967); *Prophets and Guardians: Renewal and Tradition in the Church* (1969); *The Shadow of the Crown* (1988) (novel in defense of James II); "Why so much wrong within our Church?" *The Universe*, 26 July 1992 ("Historical records provide all too many instances of religious oppression and aggression. But because God created humankind with free will, 'what is wrong with the Church' in any age is the result of human fallibility, not a failure of Divine providence, which has always maintained it within the Way, the Truth and the Life. Catholics have always known this and

have never seen any bad policies of Popes, corrupt practices of clerics, disciplinary injustices or devotional aberrations as invalidating the apostolic authority of the faith, or as interrupting the communication of Divine life through the sacraments. The Way is always there for all to follow.

If the Church were merely a human institution it would have collapsed long ago, as one earthly empire after another has collapsed during the 2,000 years of history. But it has not merely survived external disasters and internal dissensions, it has developed, in understanding and in action, always holding to the revelation of God in Christ and ministering His forgiveness and saving love to anxious and sick humanity.

For the Holy Spirit continually purifies, unifies and revivifies the Church, working through all its members and principally through those we call saints. Anyone and everyone has been, and can be, thus inspired. Whatever is wrong with the Church comes about because not enough Christians are committed to following Christ first, and self last"); Pat Pinsent, "Two Catholic Writers for Children: Cecily Hallack and Meriol Trevor," in Pat Pinsent (ed), *Out of the Attic: Some Neglected Children's Authors of the Twentieth Century* (2006), Ch. 7.

Tristram, Ernest William – painter and art historian; b. 27 December 1882, Carmarthen, Wales; c. 1914 (brother, Fr. Henry Tristram (see below) received; also sister and both parents); d. 11 January 1952, Newton Abbot; brought up in a family of lapsed Catholics; studied under the arts and crafts architect and designer, W. R. Lethaby; expert in medieval painting; made many fine watercolor copies of medieval wall and panel paintings; great skill in preservation of paintings led to saving of many works; responsible for the cleaning and decoration on the

Coronation Chair and the great retable at Westminster Abbey; Professor of Design at the Royal College of Art 1925–1948; his great work was *English Medieval Wall Painting*, 2 Vols. (1944 and 1950, a third volume being published posthumously by his second wife, Eileen, in 1955); see Hubert Wellington, "E. W. Tristram," *The Month*, May 1952, p.305 ("He relished Ananda Coomaraswamy's verdict that one might as well attempt the study of a mathematical papyrus without a knowledge of mathematics as to study Christian or Buddhist art without a knowledge of their accompanying philosophies and liturgical signs"); *DNB*.

Tristram, Henry Trevor – priest and writer; b. 1881, Camarthen; d. 8 February 1955; brother of Ernest Tristram (see above); read Classics at Jesus College, Oxford, and simultaneously achieved a first in the London University external degree course; joined the Oratorians; ordained to the priesthood in 1911; classics master at the Oratory School, Caversham, Reading (1922–1941) (sometime rector); specialist on Cardinal Newman; worked on a life of Newman which was never completed; edited several editions of Newman's works; gave much help to other Newman scholars; see *Christopher Columbus* (1915); *Newman and His Friends* (1933); *The Living Thoughts of Cardinal Newman* (1949).

Trouncer, Margaret (*née* Lahey) – writer; b. 1906, near the Parc Monceau, Paris; c. 1930; d. 1982; father American of Scottish/Irish descent, mother Russian singer; one uncle was aide-de-camp to the last Tsar; childhood in Paris; brought up in the Greek Orthodox Church; family came to live in Derby, England in 1914; at St. Hilda's College, Oxford; took a degree in English Literature and Language; became a devout Anglican; influenced in her conversion to the Catholic faith by the Dominicans at Oxford and historical discussions with them; attended retreats under the great theologian, Père Garrigou-Lagrange; great passion for modern French novelists and a number of mystics; friend of Shane Leslie (see above), T. S. Eliot, Henri Ghéon; several biographies, mainly of French subjects, plus novels on spiritual themes; articles in Catholic journals; her husband, Tom, an RAF pilot, was killed in a crash in October 1940; see *St. Margaret Mary Alacoque,1647–1690* (1956); *A Grain of Wheat: The Story of St. Bernadette of Lourdes,1844–1879* (1958); *Miser of Souls: The Life of St. John-Marie-Beptiste Vianney, Curé of Ars, 1786–1859* (1959); *The Gentleman Saint: St. François de Sales and his Times,1567–1622* (1963); *Charles de Foucauld* (1972); Walter Romig (ed), *The Book of Catholic Authors*, Second Series (1942); Matthew Hoehn, OSB (ed), *Catholic Authors* (1952).

Trower, Philip – writer on Catholic affairs and novelist; b. 16 May 1923; c. March 1953; fought in the Italian campaign in World War II and worked in political intelligence; reviewer for *Spectator* and *Times Literary Supplement* 1948–1954; lectured and had articles published on both sides of the Atlantic; for ten years covered the postconciliar Synods of Bishops in Rome; see *The Church Learned and the Revolt of the Scholars* (1979); *A Danger to the State* (1998) (novel on the suppression of the Jesuits); *Turmoil and Truth: The Historical Roots of the Modern Crisis in the Catholic Church* (2003) ("A word about Catholics who adopt or promote heresies, and about why fully believing Catholics are bound, not only to continue loving them, but also, out of love, to oppose them. Not to oppose them would be equivalent to saying that the revelation of God is a matter of opinion, is not to be found fully in the teaching of the Catholic Church, or that in handing it on the Church has got parts of it wrong.

These may be acceptable opinions for anyone else, but neither can be a tenable position for a Catholic, since the converse – God has made a revelation that can be certainly known and the Church is its guardian and interpreter – is the very heart of our religion. Loving, as even the most closely knit families know, has never excluded resisting or speaking out about what one believes to be seriously wrong. What counts is the spirit in which it is done"); *The Catholic Church and the Counter-Faith* (2006); letter to John Beaumont: "A major factor in my conversion was in discovering that miracles did not stop in New Testament times but had continued in the Church right down to the present. The passage in the Gospels where Our Lord says that his followers would perform even more amazing wonders than He had Himself had always puzzled me. Now I found his words had been fulfilled and where. Catholics who play down miracles do not realize what a disservice they are doing to the Church. After all if God thinks it worthwhile to confirm our faith with miracles from time to time, why should we be embarrassed by them."

Trusted, Charles F. – c. 1918; former Anglican clergyman; see *Where Does Christ Rule and Teach: A Letter to his Parishioners* (1918) ("I have been convinced that the Catholic Church in communion with Rome, and this Church alone, answers to the description in the Gospels of the visible Church, or Kingdom, which our Lord promised to set up here upon earth, to last to the end; and that she therefore possesses Divine authority both to rule and to teach, and rightly claims our obedience. Our Lord did not choose to make a book His

commissioned Teacher of mankind, for a book needs an interpreter. Mere written words are capable of various interpretations, and what we want is not the mere letter but the sense, the true meaning, of our Lord's words. As Cardinal Newman has remarked, 'a revelation is not given, if there be no authority to decide what it is that is given.' Our Lord chose therefore to form a society of men to be the home, the instrument, the guardian, and the interpreter, of His saving message. He chose to form a visible kingdom, in accordance with the prophecies which went before Him. He constituted the Apostles to be His representatives and the first rulers and teachers of that Kingdom; and He promised to them His enabling Presence all the days unto the consummation of the age. Thus He implied that the Apostles should have successors, and that as He would be with the Apostles so should He be with their successors, as members and officers of an organized body, for the same object" (St. Matt. XXVIII 18–20)).

Tylden (Tilden; alias Godden), Thomas – priest and controversialist; b. December 1622, Addington, Kent; d. November 1688, Somerset House, London; at Cambridge he befriended John Sergeant (see above) who later became a Catholic and influenced his own conversion; went to English College, Lisbon, in 1643; ordained priest; occupied chairs of Philosophy and Divinity there and elected President of College in 1656; after Restoration returned to England and chaplain and preacher to Queen Catherine of Braganza at Somerset House; treasurer of queen's household; at Oates Plot in 1678 his apartments searched and servant killed, but he escaped and retired to Paris; returned to Somerset House on accession of James II; learned theologian and able controversialist; probably buried in vault under chapel at Somerset House; see *Catholicks No Idolators* (1672); *Gillow*, Vol. II, p.503; *Catholic Encyclopedia*; *DNB*.

Tyler, Antony (*pseud.* Antony Matthew) – diplomat, civil servant, and banker; b. 1936, London; c. 31 May 1985 (received by Fr. Hugh Thwaites (see above); wife received later); parents Anglican; brought up as an Anglican in Sarawak and Australia; at university in Australia (less practice of his religion there) and then Cambridge; worked in diplomatic service in Foreign Office 1962–1970; merchant banker; rejoined British civil service; conversion influenced by Newman, Kenelm Digby, Chesterton (see all above), Belloc, and Fr. Thwaites); founded Fisher Press in order to re-publish important Catholic books; master of Catholic Writers Guild; chairman of trustees of Catholic Central Library; author of guide for potential converts; see *Pearl of Great Price: Becoming a Catholic – A Practical Guide* (1991) ("Much of my life has been spent traveling in one way or another.... Looking back on all this to-ing and fro-ing, I now see that there was one recurring theme which was significant for my spiritual journey; wherever I traveled I visited churches, private chapels, cathedrals and monasteries. As it happened, most of these belonged to the great Catholic tradition of Christendom. For many years I was just a tourist, looking at what was beautiful to my eye or of historical interest. Somehow I did not associate what I saw with religion at all.... Nor ... do I consciously remember noticing my fellow human beings, or reflecting on the reasons why they might also be there.... Then, gradually, I began to notice them too. And there they were, as they always had been: kneeling on the imported Italian marble pavement of an Australian cathedral in an old gold mining town, or on rush matting in a wooden church in the Casamance in Senegal, or before the tabernacle in the ambulatory chapel of some baroque monastic church: praying quietly, or lighting candles, saying their rosary, or making the Stations of the Cross. Some were sitting patiently on benches waiting their turn to enter the confessional box. I began to be aware of something mysterious, yet powerfully attractive; and then to envy this strong assurance of Faith. For unlike me, these worshippers were in harmony with the purpose for which the buildings, and all that was in them, had been made"); *EWTN Audio Library* (22 September 2003).

Tyrrell, George, SJ – priest and writer; b. 6 February 1861, 91 Dorset Street, Dublin; c. 1879; d. 15 July 1909, Mulberry House, Storrington; brought up in poor but genteel Irish evangelical Anglican family; early religious formation in moderate Anglicanism, but also much influenced by High Church beliefs and Christian socialism; after conversion joined the Society of Jesus; ordained priest in September 1891; hectic round as author, counselor, confessor, and preacher with reputation as liberal Catholic; close friend of Baron Friedrich von Hügel (1852–1925), Maude Petre, Wilfrid Ward and Henri Bremond; heavily influenced by modernist thought of Loisy, Blondel and Laberthonnière; a combative personality; dismissed from the Jesuits in 1906 and excommunicated in 1907; did not recant his then views; buried in the Anglican churchyard at Storrington; see David G. Schultenhover, SJ, *George Tyrrell: In Search of Catholicism* (1981); Nicholas Sagovsky, *On God's Side: A Life of George Tyrrell* (1990); Marvyn R. O'-Connell, *Critics on Trial: An Introduction to the Catholic Modernist Crisis* (1994); *DNB* ("All hope of reconciliation ended with the publication, in July 1907, of the decree *Lamentabili* and, in September 1907, of the papal encyclical *Pascendi*, which named and characterized, and thereby created 'modernism'. The encyclical was a carefully constructed synthetic attack on positions espoused by Tyrrell and Loisy, accusing the modernist of agnosticism and immanentism, that is, of failing to do justice to the cognitive, supernatural content of revelation, and of propounding the 'synthesis of all heresies'").

Vallance, (William Howard) Aymer – artist, designer and writer; b. 1862; c. 1889; d. 16 July 1943; son of Captain T. W. Vallance, of the 5th Lancers; brought up in affluent family in Kent; educated at Harrow and Oriel College, Oxford; took Anglican orders; settled in London and studied ecclesiastical art; had a fascination for the medieval generally, with a great love for the art and architecture of the Middle Ages; lecturer on Gothic architecture for the Architectural Association; worked for *The Art Journal* and *The Studio*; fifty year connection with Batsford Ltd, the publishers; a scholarly antiquarian who was elected a Fellow of the Society of Antiquaries in 1895; lover of the arts and crafts movement; friend of William Morris, about whom he wrote the first biography; influential in success of Aubrey Beardsley (see above); reconstructed a derelict hall-house, Stoneacre, at Otham (handed over to the National Trust in 1929); see *The Art of William Morris* (1897); *William Morris: His Art, His Writings and His Public Life* (1897); *The Old Colleges of Oxford: Their Architectural History Illustrated and Described* (1913); *Old Crosses and Lych- gates* (1933); *English Church Screens* (1936); *Greater English Church Screens* (1947).

Vane (Fane), Thomas – physician; b. 1599/1600, Kent; d. about 1692; studied divinity at Cambridge; took Anglican orders in 1621; became chaplain extraordinary to Charles I, and Anglican rector; resigned these preferments and became a Catholic (likely that from 1630s he was exhibiting Arminian sacramental preferences); traveled in France and Italy with his wife; took a degree in medicine and practiced as a doctor; see *A Lost Sheep Returns Home: or the Motives of the Conversion to the Catholike Faith of Thomas Vane* (1643) (dedicated to Charles I's Catholic queen, Henrietta Maria); *Gillow*, Vol. V, p.563.

Vassall (later Phillips), (William) John Christopher – admiralty official and spy; b. 20 September 1924, London; c. 1953; d. 18 November 1996, Westminster, London; father an Anglican chaplain at St. Bartholomew's Hospital, London; mother a practicing Catholic, but did not overtly influence him to follow her; brought up in Somerset; disappointed in his ambition to enter Keble College, Oxford; conscripted into the Royal Air Force and trained as RAF photographer; joined the civil service and gained posting with the admiralty; in 1952 sent to Moscow on staff of naval attaché; homosexual entrapment by KGB; supplied documents (some with critical information) to his Soviet controllers 1954–1962; convicted of espionage in 1962 and sentenced to eighteen years imprisonment; befriended by Lord Longford (see above) in prison; released in 1972; spent some time in a monastery; changed his name to Phillips, worked as clerk with British Records Association, and lived in obscurity in St. John's Wood, North London; see *Vassall: The Autobiography of a Spy* (1975); *DNB*.

Vassall-Phillips, Oliver Rodie, CSSR (originally Oliver Vassall) – priest and author; b. 1857; c. 18 March 1878 (received by Fr. Parkinson at St. Aloysius, Oxford); d. 8 May 1932 (at sea while returning from a lecturing tour of South Africa); eldest son of Robert Lowe Grant Vassall, of Oldbury Court, Bristol; educated at Eton and Balliol College, Oxford; converted when an undergraduate at Oxford; influenced most by Newman, whose *Apologia* and *Development of Christian Doctrine* he "devoured" as a boy of sixteen ("To Cardinal Newman I always feel that, under God, I owe my very soul"); joined the Redemptorist Order in 1880; ordained priest 1884; assumed maternal grandfather's name in 1901; successively rector of Mount Alphonsus, Limerick; Bishop Eton, Wavertree, Liverpool; Bishop's Stortford, Essex; and of Kingswood, Bristol; well-known preacher and controversialist; author of several books; great apologist for the Catholic faith; see essay in J. G. F. Raupert (ed), *Roads to Rome* (1901), p.273 (reprint of a paper written in 1878) ("But why should I not accept the testimony of the Catholic and Roman Church? The fathers at the Council of Chalcedon cried out, '*Petrus per Leonem locutus est.*' Why am I to be forbidden to believe them? Why am I to be forbidden to believe St. Ambrose when he says, '*Ubi Petrus, ibi Ecclesia*'? Why am I to be forbidden to submit myself to the Shepherd to whom our Blessed Lord when about to leave this world committed all His sheep and all His lambs; for whom He prayed specially that his faith should not fail, and to whom alone He gave a new name, and the keys of the kingdom of heaven?

I profess in the Creed that I believe the Church of God to be One, and to be Catholic; as a matter of plain fact, is there any Christian body which is one and which is universal, save the Roman Church? It was probably at the first Eucharist that Christ prayed that His Church on earth should be by its visible unity a plain sign to men of the unity of the Godhead (St. John xvii). Am I seri-

ously to believe that the prayer of my dying Lord has been unanswered? If there is one thing on which the great Apostle St. Paul insists, it is the absolute necessity of unity. '*Corpus unum, sicut unus est Dominus, una fides, unum baptisma.*' 'Is Christ then divided?' he asks indignantly, when speaking of the deadly sin of schism, almost as if he could foresee the time when 'the divisions of Christendom' should be a trite commonplace of discussion. But can any one, on the one hand, pretend that the '*unum ovile sub uno pastore*' is to be found apart from the unity of Rome? On the other, dare any one deny the supernatural unity of faith, of worship, of discipline, among the children of the mighty Mother? As in the Apostles' days, so it is now; Roman Catholics, so far as their creed goes, are undeniably of one heart and one mind.

Next, can any one deny the Catholicity of the Roman Communion? There is no other Church in the world which is not merely national. The Roman Catholic priest alone dares grapple with his Savior's command to teach *all* nations.

I also profess my belief in the Creed that the Church of God is Holy, and that she is Apostolic. Now, with regard to sanctity as a simple matter of fact, *who* is the Mother of the Saints? To look merely at the purely *modern* Roman Church – where, out of her fold, can you find the like of St. Ignatius Loyola and St. Francis Xavier, St. Teresa and St. Catherine, St. Francis de Sales and St. Vincent de Paul, St. Alphonsus Liguori, St. Paul of the Cross, and St. Philip Neri? You will, I think, search in vain outside the Roman Church for sanctity such as that of the three Jesuits – St. Aloysius, St. Stanislaus, and the Blessed John Berchmanns – as you will search in vain for examples of heroism that may be compared with the martyrs of Japan and of China. Many good and kindly men as the Church of

England has in these latter days possessed, who would think of comparing even the best evidences of her highest type of character with, for instance, the saintly Curé d'Ars? With regard to Apostolicity, I am not going now to compare the claim of the Anglican Establishment to that note of the Church; but I presume, at least, that no one would think of denying it to the Church of Rome.

If I apply St. Augustine's test as to the true Church, and ask which Church is called 'Catholic' in popular parlance, what answer do I receive? If I ask 'the British Church' what I am to do, shall I not be told, in the words of the Council of Sardica (AD. 347), 'to refer to the head, that is to say, to the See of Blessed Peter'?

If the Church is, as St. Paul teaches, the '*columen et firmamentum veritatis*,' and *if* the doctrines of the Real Presence and the Sacrifice of the Altar be truths, which, as a matter of historical fact, is the Church that has been 'the pillar and ground' of these verities, and which is the Church that has by an almost consistent tradition rejected them?

Has any *adequate* explanation from the non-Catholic point of view ever been so much as offered, of the growth, perpetuity, and ever-vigorous life of the Roman Catholic Church – of that organic Society which Lord Macaulay admitted to be, in his judgment, the most remarkable phenomenon presented by the history of the world? Are not the vicissitudes of her fortunes, and her constantly recurring and unparalleled triumphs over every difficulty which has temporarily threatened to bar her way, the very strongest proof that she alone it is to whom it was promised that the gates of hell should never prevail against her; as also the most magnificent witness to the Divinity of Him Who (at a time when she existed only potentially) promised her that Divine aid which should enable her to perfectly accomplish her supernatural mission, even unto the end of the world?"); *Catholic Christianity: or The Reasonableness of Our Religion* (1920); *The Mother of Christ: or The Blessed Virgin Mary in Catholic Tradition, Theology, and Devotion* (1922); *The Mustard Tree: An Argument on Behalf of the Godhead of Christ* (1923); *Tom Smith's Conversion* (1925) ("As for the Reformed Church of England as a whole, we know too well the names of the men responsible for her separation from the Holy See – they are among the most horrible in all history. Lord Macaulay, no lover of Catholicism, has summed them up – Henry, the murderer of his wives; the Protector Somerset, the murderer of his brother; Elizabeth, the murderer of her guest, and the like. With regard to the separated Churches of the East, we know the exact dates when they separated from Catholic Unity, and the names of the men who effected the separation – the Nestorians were made a separate body by Nestorius, the Eutychians by Eutyches, the Greeks first by Photius, and then – after they had been reconciled to Catholic Christendom – again by Michael Cerularius.

It has often been asked: 'Where was Protestantism before Martin Luther?' The answer is 'Nowhere. It did not exist.' And if it should be asked: Where was the Church of England before Henry the Eighth, or the Greek Church before Photius?' the only answer that can be given is: 'In union with the Catholic and Roman Church.' The Catholic Church alone goes back straight, without break, to the Holy Apostles Peter and Paul: but it was not founded by St. Peter and St. Paul. It was founded by Jesus Christ, the Apostles' Lord"); *After Fifty Years* (1928) ("Christ is the one great Fact in the world's history without measure or parallel with which it may be compared. No other life that has ever been lived in the story of humanity may be placed in the same category as His; and closely dependent upon Christ, from the hour that He sent His Holy Spirit to dwell with us, on the first Whit Sunday, is the other great outstanding Fact – the Fact of the Catholic Church, visible to all who will open their eyes to see, unique, standing alone as Christ stands alone, refusing to be ignored, whether throughout the history of Christendom since Christendom was, or throughout the world today, peremptory in its claims – in this again like to Christ and representing His attitude – teaching 'with authority and not as the scribes.' These were solid certainties, external to myself, to which I could appeal, independently altogether of the needs of my own nature, which might be peculiar to myself, and therefore untrustworthy as motives on which one might be content to rest the whole conduct of one's life and know that one was acting reasonably and rightly...

...With the history of faith in Christ standing out in the pages of history with all its achievements – the faith of saints and martyrs – I did not feel it necessary to examine its evidences closely on my own account, even if it had been possible at that time to do so. After all, I was becoming a Catholic in the final determination, not in consequence of any 'proofs' or 'evidences,' but because of Christ Himself. For all those who have read the Gospels, as I am thankful to say I had been made to do regularly week by week at school, our Lord should be His own evidence – completely sufficient in His own divine Personality. He stands alone amongst all the sons of men. There is none who has ever lived that can be placed alongside of Him, His equal, or in the same category as He. This, in itself, when duly pondered, ought to be enough. No unbeliever in Christianity has ever been able to account for Christ. In the effort to do so he will break down

at the first stage of the investigation. In fact, the task has never been seriously attempted...

I am assuming that the divine Author of Christianity has left a Church behind Him to Represent Himself until He return again to judge the world. And, frankly, once we believe without reserve in Our Lord Jesus Christ and in the trustworthiness of the four Gospels, there is no room for reasonable argument with regard to this fact upon which so much – indeed, everything – hinges as on an essential pivot...

...[E]very form of Protestantism – every form of the appeal to private judgment in religion leveled against the considered verdict of the Teaching Church – is impossible – impossible, that is, to reconcile with the declared purposes of Christ. From the earliest days of Protestantism, 'Where was your Church before Luther?' was a deadly question. Equally deadly is the question: 'If your theory be true as to the old Church having become corrupt in her teaching – the theory on which, admittedly, alone can your history and actions be defended or justified – what has become of the promises of Christ?'"); *Apostolic Christianity: or the Witness of the Apostles to Christ* (1932) ("[F]ew people seem to me to consider with sufficient seriousness all that is involved in the way of intellectual difficulty by the rejection of Christianity. Those who actually do reject it, fail, at least so far as we can discover from their writings, to see what necessarily follows from this rejection. I will give three examples, which should, I think, make clear what it is that I have it in mind to say:

(1) It has been recorded in a narrative worthy of credit – no one will suggest that it has been invented – that before her Son was born the Mother of Christ declared publicly that, in consequence of her Motherhood, all generations should

call her Blessed. This is a declaration which has been fulfilled ever since she spoke the strange words; it is being fulfilled before our eyes today. Mary of Nazareth was an unsophisticated Jewish maiden; in social condition, although the descendant of a long line of Jewish kings, she was the espoused wife of a carpenter living in Syria. When, then, she made this prediction, who will deny that either she was mad or inspired by God? The undeniable fact, for such it is, that her words have been verified – that they have come to pass – goes to prove that they came to her from heaven. There seems to be no alternative in reason.... How then, we may ask, do unbelievers in Christ attempt to account for his Mother's words? Such an attempt is never made. The facts are simply left alone; if they remain unchallenged, it can only be because the conclusion is seen to be unchallengeable. To anyone who does not believe in Christ, the prophecy of his Mother defies reasonable explanation.

(2) It is also recorded in the Gospels that our Lord Jesus Christ permitted a woman who had led a sinful life, on her repentance, to pour a vase of very precious ointment over his feet and wipe them with her flowing hair. This is an astonishing fact – it is described as an act of homage and gratitude and love for his person. Moreover, not only did he permit this, but he actually declared that wherever what he alluded to as his 'Gospel' should be preached throughout the world, there that which the Magdalen had done should be made known for her praise as a memorial of her. What could have seemed at the time to be more extravagantly unlikely of accomplishment, if Christ were as other men? Yet that it has been accomplished is beyond a doubt. Throughout the world the Gospel of Christ has as a fact been preached, and throughout the world, as a direct result of this preaching, the name of the Mag-

dalen is known, loved and venerated.... If Christ be what the Catholic Church believes him to be, it is easily understood and follows inevitably from his Godhead, but if he were not, how explain the fulfillment of those words of his?...

(3) Again, it is recorded that on the night before he suffered, Jesus Christ observed the ceremony of the Jewish Passover together with his Apostles, that he then declared that his body should be broken for them as bread is wont to be broken, that his blood should be shed for them and for many for the forgiveness of sins – and that he then commanded them to 'do this' (using sacrificial words) in commemoration of him. In consequence of this action of his and of this command, at the present time more than three hundred thousand Christian priests offer each morning a Sacrifice for the living and dead which they believe to have been instituted by him, to continue until he should come again in majesty to judge the world.

Not very long ago I was endeavoring to say Mass in the face of some difficulty, and I asked myself *why* I was taking so much trouble to do this thing to which I had, alas, not been brought up by the traditions of my family. Without hesitation I answered my question: Because of what Christ had done nearly two thousand years ago. I desire each day to be mindful of his passion and death in the manner which he commanded. Then it came over me with overwhelming force – something which I need hardly say I knew already – how unthinkable it was that this holy rite should have lasted through all the ages, that such vast importance should have been attached to it in all parts of the world, unless Christ were in truth what he claimed to be. It is offered 'in memory' – as a memorial of him. But of whom? Is there another 'memorial' of any other who has passed away with which we may compare or liken it? If not, once again the conclusion seems inevitable; he is not as other men").

Vaughan, Eliza (*née* Rolls) – b. 1810; c. 1830, four months after her marriage; d. 1853; first wife of Lieutenant-Colonel John Francis Vaughan (1808–1880) of Courtfield, Ross, Herefordshire; mother of thirteen children; of Herbert Cardinal Vaughan (1832–1903), second Bishop of Salford, then Archbishop of Westminster and founder of St. Joseph's College for Foreign Missions at Mill Hill, London; of Most Rev. Roger William Bede Vaughan (1834–1883), Benedictine monk of Downside and Archbishop of Sydney, New South Wales; of Fr. Joseph Vaughan (1841–1896), Benedictine monk (Dom Jerome) and founder of St. Benedict's Abbey, Fort Augustus, Scotland; of Fr. Kenelm Vaughan (1840–1908); priest of Archdiocese of Westminster; of Colonel Francis Baynham Vaughan, Private Chamberlain to Pope Pius X; of Fr. Bernard Vaughan, SJ (1847–1922), priest of Society of Jesus and renowned preacher; of Reginald Vaughan, JP for Monmouthshire; and of Right Rev. John S. Vaughan, Bishop of Sebastopolis and Auxiliary of Salford; four of her five daughters became nuns: Gwladys (1838–1880) joined the Visitation Order in Boulogne; Helen (1839–1861) entered the Sisters of Charity in London and died shortly afterwards; Clare (1843–1862) became a Poor Clare in Amiens and died after nine months there; and Mary (1845–1884) became prioress of the Augustinian convent in Newton Abbot; grandmother of Fr. Herbert Vaughan, Catholic priest and DD of Rome; of Fr. Francis Vaughan, Catholic priest; and of Rev. William Vaughan, lay-brother of the Society of Jesus; see J. G. Snead-Cox, *The Life of Cardinal Vaughan,* 2 Vols. (1910); Madeleine Beard, *Faith and Fortune* (1997),

pp.170–171 ("For an hour a day she had prayed in front of the Blessed Sacrament at Courtfield, pleading that her children spend their lives serving God. Six of her sons became priests, of whom three became bishops, and four daughters became nuns. After breakfast she went into the chapel, knelt at the prie dieu, and fixed her eyes on the Tabernacle, reminding all her children that in the Tabernacle 'One who loved us more than even she did was always abiding, ever ready to greet us when we want to see Him'.... 'She made Heaven such a reality to us that we felt that we knew more about it, and liked it in a way far better than our home, where, until she died, her children were wildly, supremely happy. Religion under her teaching was made so attractive, and all the treasured items she gathered from the lives of the Saints made them so fascinating to us, that we loved them as our most intimate friends, which she assured us they most certainly were'"); Robert J. O'Neil, *Cardinal Herbert Vaughan: Archbishop of Westminster, Bishop of Salford, Founder of the Mill Hill Missionaries* (1997).

Vere, Aubrey Thomas Hunt de – poet, critic, and essayist; b. 10 January 1814, Curragh Chase, Adare, County Limerick, Ireland; c. 15 November 1851, Avignon (received by Manning; his eldest brother, Edmond de Vere (1808–1880) and his wife, Mary Lucy, became Catholics also in 1851); d. 21 January 1902, Curragh Chase; son of Sir Aubrey de Vere, second Baronet (1788–1846), accomplished poet and friend of Wordsworth; brother of Sir Stephen de Vere (see below); educated privately; member of Anglo-Irish ascendancy; much of early life spent in traveling; friendly with Wordsworth, Tennyson, Patmore, Newman and Manning; Manning a particular influence on his conversion; aim of his verse to illustrate the supernatural in the form of supernatural truth by recording the conversion to Christianity of Ireland and England; at the request of Pope Pius IX, he composed some hymns in honor of the Virgin Mary, entitled *May Carols,* or, *Ancilla Domini* (which celebrate Mary as the mediatrix between the material and spiritual worlds, the means whereby the incarnation took place in human flesh; he sees her animating all beauty); organized famine relief schemes during the great Irish famine; unmarried; buried in the churchyard at Askeaton, County Limerick; see *Essays, Chiefly Literary and Ethical* (1889); *Recollections* (1897); W. Ward, *Aubrey de Vere: A Memoir* (1904) (quoting De Vere: "Religio [means] *to bind again* ... and how can you bind except by Doctrines reduced to their orthodox form and Duties explained, applied, and enforced?"); Patrick J. Cronin, *Aubrey de Vere: the Bard of the Curragh Chase* (1997); Sean Ua Cearnaigh, "The Religious Poems of Aubrey de Vere," *Catholic Life,* December 2002; *DNB.*

Vere, Sir Stephen Edward de, fourth Baronet – poet, philanthropist, classical scholar, and barrister; b. 26 July 1812, Curragh Chase, Adare, County Limerick; c. 1848 (received in Canada); d. 10 November 1904, Foynes, County Limerick, an island in the River Shannon; son of Sir Aubrey de Vere, second Baronet (1788–1846); brother of Aubrey de Vere, the poet (see above); translator of Horace; life dedicated to improvement of conditions, social and political, of the Irish people and emigrants (went himself as a steerage passenger to Canada and reported to parliament on the terrible conditions, leading to legislation); High Sheriff and Liberal MP for County Limerick 1854–1859; supported tenant rights and Gladstone's land legislation, but opposed to Home Rule; unmarried; buried at Foynes by the door of the Catholic church that he built; see *Catholic Encyclopedia* ("Sir Stephen de Vere became a Catholic from his observation of the peasantry whom he had taught, fed, and nursed in his own house"); *DNB* ("De Vere's admiration of the Irish Catholic people led him to embrace the Roman Catholic religion, and his reception into that church took place during his visit to Canada in 1848").

Walford, Edward – writer and compiler of reference works; b. 3 February 1823, Hatfield Place, near Chelmsford, Essex; c. January 1851 (brother, John Berry, received in 1847; another brother, John Thomas (1834–1894), later a priest of the Society of Jesus, who taught at Beaumont College and St. Beuno's College, received in March 1866; a third brother, Frederick, received in 1867; mother and sister, Frances, also converted); d. 20 November 1897, Ventnor, Isle of Wight; son of an Anglican rector; educated at Balliol College, Oxford; became Anglican curate; wrote, edited, and compiled biographical, topographical, and antiquarian books (eighty-seven in total) and articles for a range of magazines and newspapers; produced several biographies at short notice; returned to the Church of England in 1860, but in 1870/1 reverted to the Catholic faith; buried at Holy Trinity, Ventnor; see *DNB* ("Although it was reported that he had finally returned to the Church of England, his grave is in the Catholic area of the churchyard").

Walker, John – lexicographer and elocutionist; b. 18 March 1732, Colney Heath, Middlesex; c. about 1758 (shortly after his marriage); d. 1 August 1807, Tottenham Court Road, London; parents died when he was young; decided on a career on the stage and joined several provincial theatre companies; in 1757 joined Garrick's company at Drury

Lane; in 1758 married Miss Sybilla Minors (1723–1802), a well-known comic actress at Drury Lane; they worked successfully, notably in Dublin and London; retired from the stage in 1768; in 1769 started a school in Kensington with Fr. James Usher, under whose influence he had converted to Catholicism (adhered to the faith for the rest of his life); became a very successful teacher of elocution; writer and lecturer on the subject (leader of the "mechanical," as opposed to the "natural" school of elocution); wrote the most successful and authoritative pronouncing and rhyming dictionaries of his time; friends and patrons included Samuel Johnson, Edmund Burke, and Bishop Milner; buried at St. Pancras; see *Gillow*, Vol. V, p.569; *DNB*.

Walker, Obadiah – college head and author; b. 1616, Darfield, near Barnsley, Yorkshire; c. about 1686; d. 21 January 1699, London; fine student and teacher at University College, Oxford; lifelong friendship with Abraham Woodhead (see below); took Anglican orders; supported royalists during the Civil War and when Oxford surrendered to the rebels, he was expelled from his fellowship; visited Paris and Rome and "encountered the splendors and challenges of Counter-Reformation Catholicism" (*DNB*); following the Restoration, restored to his fellowship; elected master of University College in 1676; some concern within Oxford authorities at his Catholic sentiments; not until 1686 did he avow himself a Catholic; James II issued a dispensation, allowing the converts to retain their posts, and permitted free access to the royal court; a license authorized him to print, reprint, publish, and sell many Catholic apologetic works; had a Catholic altar erected in his lodgings and public Masses celebrated (the king attended Vespers); appointed Catholics to high positions in the university; on the

1688 Revolution, arrested and detained in the Tower; mastership declared vacant; charged with being reconciled to Rome, but finally allowed to live privately in London; buried in St. Pancras churchyard; see *DNB*.

Walls, Ronald – priest and writer; b. 1920, Edinburgh; c. 1948 (received with his wife, Helen, and three sons); formerly Scottish Presbyterian minister; after his wife's tragic death in 1974 in a road accident in which he was badly injured, he fought through his grief and found himself called to the priesthood; ordained priest in 1977; see *The One True Kirk* (1960) ("With the Catholic Church it was different. Put at its lowest, where else could one go to find a body of clear, unchanging doctrine covering the whole field of human life? There might well be imperfection in the members of this Church, but never could it be said that the Bread of Life was lost.... Yes – the revelation of the Son of God had to do with seeing and hearing and handling and passing on; and that dogmatic solidity which was claimed only by the Church whose visible head is the Bishop of Rome was neither an arrogant scandal nor an optional extra for those who are temperamentally addicted. It was an utter necessity for spiritual health"); *Love Strong as Death* (2002) (autobiography).

Walpole, Saint Henry, SJ – priest and martyr; b. 1558, Docking, Norfolk; c. 1581 (according to some by witnessing Edmund Campion's execution; others say his interest in controversy at Cambridge University led to his conversion, others that he was nurtured from childhood in Catholic tenets); d. 7 April 1595, York; eldest of ten children of a gentleman; studied at Cambridge and Gray's Inn; suspected of being a Catholic and driven into exile; went to Rouen and

Paris and arrived in 1582 at English College, Rheims, where enrolled as a theological student; accepted by the English College, Rome, in 1583; in 1584 applied for admission to the Society of Jesus and completed two years' probation; ordained priest in Paris 17 December 1588; three of his brothers and a cousin became Jesuit priests; arrested in 1589 at Flushing, but ransom paid and he was released in 1590; worked most of next two years on the Continent; returned to the English mission in 1593 and landed with others at Bridlington, Yorkshire; apprehended and confined at York Castle; sent to the Tower where examined and racked by Topcliffe; he admitted being a Jesuit priest and gave information on the seminaries in Spain and names of students, but did not compromise anyone in England whose life would have been in peril as a result; tortured further; tried at York on indictment for abjuring the realm without license, for receiving holy orders overseas, and for returning to England as a Jesuit priest to exercise his priestly functions; hanged, drawn and quartered at York; England's first Prime Minister, Sir Robert Walpole, was descended from the same family; see A. Jessopp, *One Generation of a Norfolk House* (1913); *Catholic Encyclopedia*; *DNB* ("It was Henry Walpole's attendance at Campion's execution at Tyburn on 1 December 1581 that changed his life. Some blood from the martyr splashed onto Walpole, who had earlier attended Campion's disputation in the Tower of London, and also his trial. Walpole accepted this as a call to take up the work of Campion").

Walsh, Thomas – vicar apostolic of the London district; b. 3 October 1776, London; d. 18 February 1849, 35 Golden Square, London; father a Catholic merchant died very early; mother a Protestant; not baptized a Catholic as an infant; went to St. Omers College at Liège in 1792; students and staff imprisoned by the French revolutionaries in 1793; released in 1795 and went to St. Edmund's College, Ware; conditionally baptized; as a deacon went as secretary to the new bishop and vicar apostolic of the midland district, Dr. Gregory Stapleton; ordained priest 19 December 1801; President of Oscott College 1818–1825; consecrated co-adjutor bishop to John Milner in 1825 and, on Milner's death in 1826, succeeded him as vicar apostolic of the Midland district; developed Catholic revival and big building program with help of John Talbot, sixteenth earl of Shrewsbury (1791–1852); supported Pugin's designs both for churches and vestments; promoted public prayers for the conversion of England; made Wiseman his co-adjutor and encouraged religious orders; transferred to London as senior vicar apostolic in 1848; buried in the crypt of St. Chad's Cathedral, Birmingham; see *Catholic Encyclopedia*; *DNB*.

Ward, Catherine – Catholic laywoman; b. 1813; c. early 1849 (her husband Major-General George Tylee (1807–1865), whom she married in 1857, had become a Catholic in 1847, influenced by Fr. John Joseph Gordon (see above); her brother-in-law, Samuel Wayte, converted in 1850; her niece, Susan Du Boulay (1826–1906) (see under entry for Augusta Drane above) became a Catholic and a nun); d. 1897; daughter of Seth Stephen Ward of Camberwell; her nephew, Samuel William Wayte (1819–1898), was a Fellow and later President of Trinity College, Oxford; brought up a "half churchwoman, half dissenter"; became Anglo-Catholic; after conversion of Newman she put herself under the spiritual direction of Dr. Pusey; much correspondence with Newman before her own conversion; see

Stanley L. Jaki, *Newman to Converts: An Existential Ecclesiology* (2001), Ch. 10 ("[Catholics] should find much food for thought in Newman's advice to Miss Ward about the manner in which one was to cope with grave shortcomings in the Catholic Church. The presence of these shortcomings, Newman argued, was logical since 'where there is the greatest light, the shadows are strongest'.... He now turned the topic to the poor as the ones who had not yet lost their vision of reality. He was not suggesting that the poor must first be made affluent so that they may be tuned to the truths of Revelation. He rather asserted to Miss Ward, a product of upper-class English society, that it was to the poor that the Notes of the Church alone remained obvious: 'To the poor is the Gospel preached. Accordingly the notes of the Church are simple and easy, and obvious to all capacities. Let a poor man look at the Church of Rome, and he will see that it has *that* which no other Church has'...

...'The Roman Church, whether corrupted, whether perverted, (which is a question of *opinions*) yet in matter of fact is the continuation of that old Church, called Catholic, which has been in the world from time immemorial, which has been in the world so long that you cannot say when it was *not* in the world, to which you can assign no date short of the Apostles'").

Ward, Thomas – controversialist; b. 13 April 1652, Danby Castle, near Guisborough, Yorkshire; d. 1708, St. Germain; brought up as Presbyterian or Calvinist; became tutor to children of a gentleman of fortune; became interested in religious controversy, church history, the Fathers, and Scripture; on conversion his father cut him out of his will, but after father's death, his mother and the rest of his family converted; married Catholic wife and with her permission served in the papal

guards for several years; in Rome researched the important documents on the history of the Church in England; returned to England in 1685 and wrote several works on controversy; on the Revolution of 1688 he fled to the royal court at St. Germain; had one son, the secular priest Lawrence Ward, alias Green, and one of his three daughters was a nun in Brussels; buried at St. Germain; see *Some Queries to Protestants* (1687); *The Tree of Life* (1688); *Errata to the Protestant Bible* (1688); *The Pope's Supremacy* (1700); *England's Reformation* (1710); *The Controversy of Ordination* (1719); *Gillow*, Vol. V, p.570; *Catholic Encyclopedia*; *DNB*.

Ward, William George – theologian, philosopher, and controversialist; b. 21 March 1812, London; c. 5 September 1845 (received by Fr. Brownbill, SJ, at Farm Street, London, together with his wife, Frances Mary (1818–1898), daughter of John Wingfield, the Anglican Prebendary of Worcester; sister and her husband, William Frederick Wingfield (1813–1874), formerly Anglican curate, then barrister, received in 1845); d. 6 July 1882, Netherhall House, Fitzjohn Avenue, Hampstead, London; son of William Ward (1787–1849), MP for London and director of the Bank of England; studied at Christ Church and at Lincoln College, Oxford; Fellow of Balliol College, Oxford; follower of Newman and the High Church movement; from 1838 chief of a Romanizing party among the Tractarians; leader of the Oxford Movement after Newman's departure to Littlemore; his *Ideal of a Christian Church* (1844) was condemned by Oxford University Convocation as inconsistent with the Thirty-nine Articles and his MA was removed from him; PhD of Rome; editor of *Dublin Review* 1863–1878; a fiery controversialist (many books and articles), and leading

Ultramontane (during First Vatican Council he said that he "would like a new papal Bull every morning with my *Times* at breakfast"); defended infallibility of the encyclical *Quanta Cura* and the accompanying *Syllabus of Errors* of 1864; great supporter of Cardinal Manning; campaigned against liberalizing party among the English Catholics; in later life repudiated Newman, fearing he might be a crypto-liberal; friendly correspondence with John Stuart Mill; father of nine children, including Wilfrid Ward (1856–1916), historian, biographer, and editor of *Dublin Review* (husband of Josephine Mary Ward (1864–1932), the Catholic novelist, and father of Maisie Ward (1889–1975), Catholic writer and publisher); Right Rev. Mgr. Bernard Ward (1857–1920), priest, historian, canon of Westminster, and for several years President of St. Edmund's College, Ware, Hertfordshire; and Margaret (b. 1860), later a nun; buried in Catholic churchyard of Weston Manor, Freshwater, Isle of Wight; see Wilfrid Ward, *William George Ward and the Oxford Movement* (1893); Maisie Ward, *The Wilfrid Wards and the Transition* (1934); *Gillow*, Vol. V, p.572; *Catholic Encyclopedia*; *DNB*.

Wardell, William Wilkinson – architect and engineer; b. 27 September 1823, Poplar, London; c. 1846 (received in London; adopted as a motto at the time of his reception "Inveni Quod Quaesivi" ("I have found that which I sought")); d. 19 November 1899, Upton Grange, Sydney, Australia; parents ran a workhouse; brought up as an Anglican; spent time at sea; worked in the offices of a surveyor and an architect; while surveying land, he began measuring and drawing medieval buildings; conversion influenced by his friend and mentor, A. W. N. Pugin (see above); designed about thirty Catholic churches, most in London and

the south-east, in a Gothic revival style very similar to that of Pugin (though also did Italianate designs); also presbyteries, convents, and schools; emigrated with his family to Australia in 1858 owing to tuberculosis; many designs there, notably St. Patrick's Cathedral, Melbourne and St. Mary's Cathedral, Sydney; buried in Gore Hill cemetery, Sydney; see obituary, *The Tablet*, 6 January 1900, p.27; Ursula M. De Jong, *William Wilkinson Wardell: his Life and Work, 1823–1899* (1983); T. A. Hazell, "A Quest for Perfection," www.stpatrickscathedral.org ("The attraction to the Catholic Church, initially through its art and architecture, became after study and enquiry a return to origins, to the spirituality and tradition of England's Catholic faith. His new life, and for family reasons there was an abrupt break with his past, from then onwards was one of praising God through perfection in architecture and the erection of worthy and timeless buildings in his honor.

Spirituality is, for most of us, an intensely personal matter and it was certainly so for William Wardell. But we can gain an insight into what he thought, by what we know of his personal life and the few mementos which he has left. We know that in each of his homes, both in England and in Australia, there was a room set aside, for use as a chapel for private prayers, and that it was to this room that he withdrew for several periods of the day and night. Its central feature was a beautifully carved crucifix in wood, which he had acquired in France in the 1840s, but it is obviously much older than that.... One of [his] prayer books, the *Hortus Animae* or *Garden of the Soul*, was the traditional spiritual manual used by English-speaking Catholics throughout the 19th century. But its main interest lies in two prayers to the Blessed Virgin, composed by Wardell himself and transcribed into blank pages in the book. Here, Mary is invoked as 'my patroness, my mother, and my advocate with God' and further, Wardell writes, 'I consecrate myself for ever, with all that belongs to me, to thy service.' The Blessed Virgin seems truly to have been the guide and comfort of his life. We also know that periods of prayer preceded periods of drafting plans of church buildings"); *DNB*.

Watkin, David John – architectural historian; b. 7 April 1941; c. 22 May 1963; Professor of History of Architecture, Cambridge University; head of the department of Art History at Cambridge; influenced in his conversion by Mgr. Alfred Gilbey; champion of classical and traditional architecture against modernist architecture; see *Morality and Architecture* (1977); *A History of Western Architecture* (2000); *Morality and Architecture Revisited* (2001); David Watkin (ed), *Alfred Gilbey: A Memoir by Some Friends* (2002) ("I was captivated by the notion that the magnificent architectural and decorative Baroque style, the one by which I was most excited, was embodied in the forms and ritual of an institution which survived to the present day as a continuation of the Roman Empire in the form of an absolute monarchy, the papacy. Always attracted by splendor and hierarchy, I disapproved of socialism, egalitarianism, and Protestantism which I saw as dominated by the singing of sentimentally worded Victorian hymns which I had sung daily at school. The Catholic Church, then, its pomp as 'one with Nineveh and Tyre,' was what I wanted to be part of").

Watkin, Edward Ingram ("Edda") – writer and translator; b. 27 September 1888, Stand, Cheshire; c. 1908 (received at Downside Abbey; Ronald Chapman (1917–1996), the husband of his daughter Teresa and biographer of Fr. Faber

and G. F. Watts, was received in 1940); d. 2 March 1981, Torbay, Devon; brought up in a nominally Protestant family; went through Anglo-Catholic period; educated at New College, Oxford (first class honors in Greats); converted whilst at Oxford; prolific author, writing many books and essays, mainly on culture and religion; lifelong friend of Christopher Dawson (see above); introduced English Catholics to several continental theologians later influential at the Second Vatican Council; later regretted some of the consequences of the Council, especially the dismantling of the liturgy, and refused to go to any Mass not celebrated in the old rite; friend in later life of Stanley Morison (see above); father of Dom Aelred Watkin (1918–1997) titular abbot of Downside; buried in Torquay cemetery; see *Some Thoughts on Catholic Apologetics: A Plea for Interpretation* (1913); *The Catholic Centre* (1932) (argued that Catholic Christianity was the true *via media*); *Theism, Agnosticism, and Atheism* (1936); *The Balance of Truth* (1943); *Catholic Art and Culture* (1947); *Neglected Saints* (1955); *Roman Catholicism in England from the Reformation to 1950* (1957); *The Church in Council* (1960); Magdalen Goffin, "Fighting Under the Lash," *Downside Review*, July 1995, p.203; Magdalen Goffin, *The Watkin Path, An Approach to Belief: The Life of E. I. Watkin* (2006) ("[At Oxford] Watkin's Anglo-Catholicism was soon smelt out and he proved to be easy game. The Roman Catholic faith, he was swiftly reminded, was the faith that had created and sustained Europe. All the other Christian churches in the West depended upon it for their creeds, liturgy and architecture. How ludicrous it was to think of St. Patrick as any sort of Protestant! How absurd to imagine that such a thin and narrow an interpretation of Christianity as Protestantism – the mere *disjecta membra* of Catholicism – could ever have founded and built such a glorious place as Oxford! Great Britain had been Roman Catholic, that is to say in communion in faith and worship with the successor of St. Peter, for well over a thousand years. Protestants could justify their position only by vilifying their predecessors and calling them superstitious and idolatrous. It was obvious that they believed in Christianity on the authority of the Church of Rome, the very church they reviled. What could be more ridiculous than to have a Sovereign as Head of the Church and allow Parliament to decide what one should think about almighty God? No wonder Anglicanism was falling apart.... There was only one Church in the West capable of standing firm, The Roman Catholic Church, the single organization that had safeguarded Christian doctrine and religious experience down the ages"); Patrick Allitt, *Catholic Converts: British and American Intellectuals Turn to Rome* (1997) *passim*; Joseph Pearce, *Literary Converts* (1999), *passim*; *DNB*.

Watson, Right Rev. Mgr. Edward J. – priest; c. 1876 (received by Newman); Protestant upbringing; developed into High Anglicanism; barrister, then Anglican curate; after conversion ordained Catholic priest; Professor at St. Edmund's College, Ware, Hertfordshire; Domestic Prelate to Pope Pius X; see essay in J. G. F. Raupert (ed), *Roads to Rome* (1901), p.283 ("I had long suspected that the Roman theory (as we called it) of unity was the only logical one, and I had arrived at that suspicion by the somewhat circuitous route of the British colonies. If the present Church of England could justify her opposition to Rome as heiress of the medieval Church, still how in the world could she have jurisdiction in South Africa, New Zealand, Australia, India, Canada? It was futile to talk of the missionary spirit. Missionary

spirit for England was missionary spirit for France and missionary spirit for Russia. Priority of occupation or diocesan limitation had never been regarded, nor could they be; and even if they could be sufficient as laws, they would still need an administrator and arbiter. The evangelization of the world brought home to me very forcibly the necessity of, to say the least, a central executive – another road that seemed to lead to Rome...

In [Newman's] *Loss and Gain* I found my fears drawn out and marshaled in dire array; they pressed me close and pierced me through and through. And then I saw my old bugbear, Catholic subscription to the Thirty-nine Articles, in a light new to me indeed, but true beyond dispute.... Let it be granted that Catholic subscription is no quibble; let it be supposed that men who really hold Catholic doctrines can sign without a qualm. Yet surely all the world of sense and honesty allows that those same articles do at least admit of the opposite interpretation.... I had agreed to let the Councils of God's Church be called fallible; to let the Mass and the Sacraments be shamefully blasphemed, and the most pernicious falsehoods about grace and works be taught with my unfeigned assent and consent. There was no doubt about it. I came in personal contact with clergymen who did such things; their religion was entirely different from mine, and so for that matter was the religion of many persons in the congregation, and the Church of England gave me no authority to teach them otherwise").

Watts, C. J. – c. 21 June 1890 ("after forty years' wandering in the wilderness of religious doubt and uncertainty, I at last found rest in the certainty of the Divine unity of the one Church"); formerly Baptist preacher; see essay in J. G. F. Raupert (ed), *Roads to Rome* (1901), p.296 ("It has often occurred to me since

I have become a Catholic, that if non-Catholics who are in earnest, and who are disposed to inquire concerning the claims of the Church, would but ask themselves the question …: What has any one of the many religious sects outside the Catholic Church got to offer that the Catholic Church does not fully and perfectly supply, and in a far more lasting and definite manner? Such a question pondered over and thoughtfully answered would lead, I think, to very excellent results.

I will now quote a passage from Dr. James Martineau's *Seats of Authority in Religion* (p.169), seeing that it is the testimony of one who is not only a non-Catholic, but also a non-Protestant in the ordinary sense of the term. He says – 'If somewhere among the communities of Christendom there is a sovereign prescription for securing salvation, the Roman Catholic Church has obvious advantages over its competing claimants for possession of the secret. Regarded merely as an agent for the transmission of an historical treasure, she has, at least, a ready answer for all her Western rivals and a *prima facie* case of her own. They have to all appearance quite a recent genesis, their whole tradition and literature lying within the last three centuries and a half; and, in order to make good their title deeds as servitors of Christ, they must carry it over a period of four times as long during which it was lost, and identify it at the other end with the original instrument of bequest. Her plea, on the other hand, is that she has been there all through; that there has been no suspension of her life, no break in her history, no term of silence in her teaching; and that, having been always in possession, she is the vehicle of every claim and must be presumed, until conclusive evidence of forfeiture is produced, to be the rightful holder of what has rested in her custody. If you would trace a divine legacy from the age of the Caesars, would you set out to meet it on the Protestant tracks, which soon lose themselves in the forests of Germany or on the Alps of Switzerland, or on the great Roman road of history, which runs through all the centuries and sets you down in Greece and Asia Minor at the very doors of the Churches to which the Apostles wrote? But it is not only to its superiority as a human carrier of a divine tradition that Catholicism successfully appeals. It is not content to hide away its signs and wonders in the past, and merely tell them to the present, but it will take you to see them now and here. It speaks to you not as the repeater of an old message, but as the bearer of a living inspiration; not as the archaeological rebuilder of a vanished sacred scene, but as an apostolic age prolonged with unabated powers. It tells you, indeed, whence it comes; but for the evidence even of this it chiefly asks you to look at what it is, and undertakes to show you as you pass through its interior all the divine gifts, be they miraculous gifts or heavenly graces, by which the primitive Church was distinguished from the unconsecrated world. This quiet confidence in its own divine commission and interior sanctity simplifies the problem which it presents to inquirers, and, dispensing with the precarious pleas of learning, carries it into the court of sentiment and conscience, addressing to each candidate for discipleship only such preliminaries as Peter or Philip might have addressed to their converts – as if there had been no history between. No Protestant can assume this position; yet he can hardly assail the Roman Catholic without resorting to weapons of argument which may wound himself. Does he slight and deny the supernatural pretensions of today – the visions, the healings, the saintly gifts of insight and guidance more than human? It is difficult to do so except on grounds more or less applicable to the reports of like phenomena in the first ages. Does he insist on the evident growth, age after age, of Catholic dogmas as evidence of human corruption tainting the divine evidence of truth? The rule tells with equal force against the scheme of belief retained by the Churches of the Reformation; there is a history no less explicit and prolonged of the doctrine of the Trinity and of the Atonement, than the belief in Purgatory and Transubstantiation. Does he show that there are missing links in the chain of Church tradition, especially at its upper end, where verification ceases to be possible? He destroys his own credentials along with his opponent's, for his criticism touches the very sources of Christian history. The answer of the Catholic Church to the question, 'Where is the holy ground of the world, where is the Real Presence of the living God?' 'Here within my precincts, here alone,' has, at least, the merit of simplicity, and is easier to test than the Protestant reply, which points to a field of divine revelation discoverable only by the telescope halfway towards the horizon of history.... It carries its supernatural character within it; it has brought its authority down with it through time; it is the living organism of the Holy Spirit, the Pentecostal dispensation among us still; and if you ask about its evidence, it offers the spectacle of itself.'

This testimony from such a source had a great effect in helping me to make up my mind when I was inquiring into the claims of the Catholic Church, and, together with [the writings of Wiseman, Newman and Manning], secured for me not only a ready and implicit assurance that it was God's Church built upon the impregnable foundation of apostolic truth, which I was about to enter, but also furnished me with very explicit groundwork on which my mind could feel and know that the step taken was both a reasonable and a right one. I had long felt that there was no via media between the negations of doubt and the certain assurance of authority. The difficulty had hitherto been to find out this one abiding authority for Divine teaching, and I was forced to the conclusion that, if the concurrent testimony of history, together with the inherent vitality of a Church of nineteen centuries, did not prove the Church of Rome to be that authority, then there was no Church at all in the world, and God had left us all orphans indeed, piteously feeling about in the darkness, 'with no language but a cry.' Thank God that to me, too, there came the Divine guidance, and that the kindly light of faith dawned on my soul").

Waugh, (Arthur) Evelyn St John – novelist, essayist, and journalist; b. 28 October 1903, 11 Hillfield Road, West Hampstead, London; c. 29 September 1930 (received by Fr. Martin D'Arcy ("to whom, under God, I owe my faith") at Farm Street, London; "Conversion is like stepping across the chimney piece out of a Looking Glass world, where everything is an absurd caricature, into the real world God made; and then begins the delicious process of exploring it limitlessly"); d. 10 April 1966, Combe Florey, Somerset; brought up as an Anglican; at Hertford College, Oxford; period as skeptic; socialite; one of the finest novelists of the twentieth century; his first marriage to Evelyn Gardner (1903–1994) annulled in 1936 and he married Laura Herbert (1916–1973) from a staunch Catholic family; served in World War II in Royal Marines, No.8 Commando and the Blues; lived the life of a country gentleman on the considerable earnings from his books; after his conversion devoted himself to defending Christian civilization and contemplating the meaninglessness of human existence without God; critic of the liturgical changes made after the Second Vatican Council; see "Converted to Rome: Why it has happened to me," *Daily Express*, 20 October 1930 ("It seems to me that in the present phase of European history the essential issue is no longer between Catholicism, on the one side, and Protestantism, on the other, but between Christianity and Chaos.... Christianity exists in its most complete and vital form in the Roman Catholic Church"); *Edmund Campion* (1935); *Brideshead Revisited* (1945) ("Something quite remote from anything the builders intended, has come out of their work, and out of the fierce little human tragedy in which I played; something none of us thought about at the time; a small red flame – a beaten-copper lamp of deplorable design relit before the beaten-copper doors of a tabernacle; the flame which the old knights saw from their tombs, which they saw put out; that flame burns again for other soldiers, far from home, farther, in heart, than Acre or Jerusalem. It could not have been lit but for the builders and the tragedians, and there I found it this morning, burning anew among the old stones"); "Come Inside" in John A. O'Brien (ed), *The Road to Damascus* (1949) ("England was Catholic for nine hundred years, then Protestant for three hundred, then agnostic for a century. The Catholic structure still lies lightly buried beneath every phase of English life; history, topography, law, archaeology everywhere reveal Catholic origins. Foreign travel anywhere reveals the local, temporary character of the heresies and schisms and the universal eternal character of the Church. It was self-evident to me that no heresy or schism could be right and the Church wrong. It was possible that all were wrong, that the whole Christian revelation was an imposture or a misconception. But if the Christian revelation was true, then the Church was the society founded by Christ and all other bodies were only good so far as they had salvaged something from the wrecks of the Great Schism and the Reformation"); *Helena* (1950) ("Tell me, Lactantius, this god of yours. If I asked you when and where he could be seen, what would you say?' 'I should say that as a man he died two hundred and seventy-eight years ago in the town now called Aelia Capitolina in Palestine.' 'Well, that's a straight answer anyway. How do you know?' 'We have the accounts written by witnesses. Besides that there is the living memory of the Church ...' 'Well, that's all most interesting"); *The Sword of Honour Trilogy* (1952–1961) ("The Mystical Body doesn't strike attitudes and stand on its dignity. It accepts suffering and injustice.... When you spoke of the Lateran Treaty did you consider how many souls may have been reconciled and have died at peace as the result of it? How many children may have been brought up in the faith who might have lived in ignorance? Quantitative judgments don't apply. If only one soul was saved, that is full compensation for any amount of loss of 'face'"); *Ronald Knox* (1959); *Face to Face with John Freeman*, BBC Television interview, 18 June 1960 ("Well, I think I'd always, I say always, from the age of sixteen or so, realized that Catholicism was Christianity, that all other forms of Christianity were only good so far as they chipped little bits off the main block. It is a conversion to Christianity rather than a conversion to Catholicism as such"); "Changes in the Church: Questions for the 'Progressives,'" *Catholic Herald*, 7 August 1964 ("The function of the Church in every age has been conservative – to transmit undiminished and uncontaminated the creed inherited from its predecessors. Not 'is this fashionable notion one that we should accept?' but 'is this dogma (a subject on which we agree) the Faith as we received it?' has been the question (as far as I know) at all General Councils ... Conservatism is not a new influence in the Church.... Throughout her entire life the Church has been at active war with enemies from without and traitors from within...

Finally, a word about liturgy. 'Participation' in the Mass does not mean hearing our own voices. It means God hearing our voices. Only He knows who is 'participating' at Mass. I believe, to compare small things with great, that I 'participate' in a work of art when I study it and love it silently. No need to shout...

I am now old but I was young when I was received into the Church. I was not at all attracted by the splendor of her great ceremonies – which the Protestants could well counterfeit. Of the extraneous attractions of the Church which most drew me was the spectacle of the priest and his server at low Mass, stumping up to the altar without a glance to discover how many or how few he had in his congregation; a craftsman and his apprentice; a man with a job which he alone was qualified to do. That is the Mass I have grown to know and love"); Christopher Hollis, *Evelyn Waugh* (1954); David Pryce-Jones (ed), *Evelyn Waugh and His World* (1973), especially Ch. 6, "The Religion of Evelyn Waugh" by Fr. Martin D'Arcy, pp.59–79 ("All converts have to listen while the teaching of the Church is explained to them – first to make sure that they do in fact know the essentials of the faith and secondly to save future misunderstandings, for it can easily happen that mere likings or impressions, which fade, may have hidden disagreements with undiscovered doctrines. Another writer came to me at the same time as Evelyn Waugh and tested what was being told him by how far it corresponded with his experience. With such

a criterion, it was no wonder that he did not persevere. Evelyn, on the other hand, never spoke of experience or feelings. He had come to learn and understand what he believed to be God's revelation, and this made talking with him an interesting discussion based primarily on reason. I have never myself met a convert who so strongly based his assents on truth.... Nor, though he writes about 'little emotion', was his conversion so very matter of fact, because it proved to be an illumination and an inspiration. Hard, clear thinking had with the help of grace given him the answer for which he had been searching, and one can see its effect in his subsequent writings"); Christopher Sykes, *Evelyn Waugh: A Biography* (1975) ("His dislike of the reform-movement was not merely an expression of his conservatism, nor of aesthetic preferences. It was based on deeper things. He believed that in its long history the Church had developed a liturgy which enabled an ordinary, sensual man (as opposed to a saint who is outside generalization) to approach God and be aware of sanctity and the divine. To abolish all this for the sake of up-to-dateness seemed to him not only silly but dangerous.... He could not bear the thought of modernized liturgy. 'Untune that string' he felt, and loss of faith would follow.... Whether his fears were justified or not only 'the unerring sentence of time' can show"); Michael Davie (ed), *The Diaries of Evelyn Waugh* (1976) ("Easter 1965: A year in which the process of transforming the liturgy has followed a planned course. Protests avail nothing. A minority of cranks, for and against the innovations, mind enormously. I don't think the main congregation cares a hoot. More than the aesthetic changes which rob the Church of poetry, mystery and dignity, there are suggested changes in Faith and morals which alarm me. A kind of anti-clericalism is abroad which seeks to reduce the priest's unique sacramental position. The Mass is written of as a 'social meal' in which the 'people of God' perform the consecration. Pray God I will never apostatize but I can only now go to church as an act of duty and obedience.... Cardinal Heenan has been double-faced in the matter. I had dinner with him *a deux* in which he expressed complete sympathy with the conservatives and, as I understood him, promised resistance to the innovations which he is now pressing forward. How does he suppose the cause of participation is furthered by the prohibition of kneeling at the incarnatus in the creed? The Catholic press has made no opposition. I shall not live to see things righted"); Mark Amory (ed), *The Letters of Evelyn Waugh* (1980) (letter to Lady Diana Cooper, 17 September 1964: "Prayer is not asking but giving. Giving your love to God, asking for nothing in return. Accepting whatever he sends as his will for you. Not 'Please God give me a happy day' but 'Please God accept all my sufferings today in your honor.' He doesn't want sugar-babies.... Do you believe in the Incarnation and Redemption in the full historical sense in which you believe in the battle of El Alamein? That's important. Faith is not a mood"); Martin Stannard, *Evelyn Waugh: The Early Years 1903–1939* (1986); Noel Annan, *Our Age: Portrait of a Generation* (1990), Ch. 11, "The Deviants – Evelyn Waugh"; William Myers, *Evelyn Waugh and the Problem of Evil* (1991); Martin Stannard, *Evelyn Waugh: No Abiding City 1939–1966* (1992); Selina Hastings, *Evelyn Waugh: A Biography* (1994); Douglas Lane Patey, *The Life of Evelyn Waugh* (1998); Michael G. Brennan, "Damnation and Divine Providence: the Consolations of Catholicism for Graham Greene and Evelyn Waugh," in William Thomas Hill (ed), *Perceptions of Religious Faith in the Work of Graham*

Greene (2002), p.255; Eric Hester, "Brideshead Revisited by Evelyn Waugh," *Catholic Life*, January 2003, p.30; Ian Ker, "Waugh the Catholic," *The Tablet*, 18 October 2003; Ian Ker, *The Catholic Revival in English Literature, 1845–1961* (2003), Ch. 6, "Evelyn Waugh: The Priest as Craftsman"; Geoffrey Wheatcroft, "A Prophet Without Honour," *Times Literary Supplement*, 24 October 2003. p.13; R. J. Stove, "Casualties of Waugh," *The American Conservative*, 26 September 2005, p.22; Ralph McInerny, *Some Catholic Writers* (2007); Patrick Allitt, *Catholic Converts: British and American Intellectuals Turn to Rome* (1997) *passim*; Joseph Pearce, *Literary Converts* (1999), *passim*; Lorene Hanley Duquin, *A Century of Catholic Converts* (2003), p.90; *Evelyn Waugh: The Spoken Word* (British Library CD); *DNB*.

Waugh, F. J. Norman – priest and author; c. 1888; son of Congregationalist minister; brought up as Nonconformist; ordained Catholic priest; director of the Society for the Prevention of Cruelty to Children; see essay in J. G. F. Raupert (ed), *Roads to Rome* (1901), p.305 ("I had always been taught what I still believe to be sound sense and good logic, viz. that if the Pope is not the Head of the Church, neither is the King or the Queen of this realm. Under God, I believe that I owed my conversion to the Catholic Faith to the startling originality of certain sections of modern Nonconformity. The idea gradually grew within me that if the doctrines, or rather the views, adopted by a number of the more advanced thinkers among educated and more thoughtful Nonconformists were indeed the reflected rays of Divine Truth, that then not until the nineteenth century had the Word of God been made manifest – and that to the few, and not to the many. It was this impossible thought which first led me to examine the claims of the

Catholic Church to be the divinely appointed guardian of and witness to the truths of revelation. It was then I began to see that Holy Scripture cannot be made to witness for and against the same doctrines; and that, as its inspiration is known only through the testimony and teaching of the Christian Church, so the Book and its truths are for ever sealed, unless rightly interpreted by some time-lasting and divinely appointed authority").

Weale, William Henry James – art historian; b. 8 March 1832, 19 York Buildings, Marylebone, Middlesex; c. 1849; d. 26 April 1917, 29 Crescent Grove, Clapham Common; converted under influence of writings of Pugin (see above) and Newman; inheritance in 1855, on death of his mother, gave him financial independence; moved to Bruges with his family and began lifelong study of early Flemish arts and crafts; Knight of Belgian Order of Leopold; returned to London in 1878; for seven years keeper of National Art Library, South Kensington (dismissed for being "too active a reformer … and has done too much for the benefit of his readers and the public"); writer on lives of Flemish artists; organizer of Bruges Exhibition of Flemish Masters in 1902; many honors, especially in Belgium; father of eleven children including Miss Frances Clara Weale, authoress, and Fr. Francis Lawrence Weale, Catholic priest; buried at St. Mary Magdalene, Mortlake, near Richmond; see *DNB*.

Wegg-Prosser (born Haggitt), Francis Richard – Catholic layman; b. 19 June 1824, Newnham Courtney, Oxfordshire; c. December 1852 (received by Bishop Grant); d. 16 August 1911, near Hereford; only son of Anglican rector and Prebendary of Durham; first in Mathematics at Oxford; took name of Wegg-Prosser in 1847 on succeeding to Belmont, the property of his great-uncle Richard Prosser, Anglican Prebendary of Durham; MP for Herefordshire 1847–1852 (resigning on his conversion); correspondence with Newman about difficulties regarding papal infallibility; built on his estate the Benedictine monastery and Cathedral Church of Belmont Abbey; member of Superior Council of Society of St. Vincent de Paul; served on Council of the Catholic Union; in his secular life devoted to mathematical science and particularly to astronomy (wrote a book, *Galileo and his Judges* (1889)); friend of Robert Campbell (see above); see Stanley L. Jaki, *Newman to Converts: An Existential Ecclesiology* (2001), Ch. 13 ("Newman merely demanded of Wegg-Prosser to consider that one did not have to prove more effectively the divine origin of the Church than the divinity of Christ. This was a matter of sheer logic. And so was the priority of the Church over the primacy of Peter. Only if the Church was divine did that primacy make sense. Therefore the order of investigation was this: the continuation of the primitive Church in the Roman Church 'can be proved overpoweringly (without any reference to or assumption at all of Papal Supremacy) to those who admit that a Church, one and the same, from first to last there ever will be'"); *Catholic Encyclopedia*.

Wesley, Mary (real name Mary Aline Siepmann, *née* Farmar) – novelist; b. 24 June 1912, Red Gables, Englefield Green, Egham, Surrey; c. 26 August 1956 (received with her second husband, Eric Siepmann (1903–1970), journalist and reviewer); d. 30 December 2002, Bogan Cottage, North Street, Totnes; isolated upper-class childhood; looked after by a succession of sixteen governesses; presented at court in 1930; worked as volunteer in London soup kitchens and attended Communist party meetings; in 1937 married the wealthy Charles Swinfen Eady, second Baron Swinfen (1904–1977); during World War II worked for the War Office at Bletchley Park; financial difficulties until sudden success as a novelist at the age of seventy (e.g., *Jumping the Queue* (1983), *The Camomile Lawn* (1984), *Not That Sort of Girl* (1987)); friends included Graham Greene (see above), Nancy Mitford, Malcolm Muggeridge (see above), and Antonia White (see below); towards the end of her life she confessed to being in a state of rage "because they've rewritten the Bible and done away with Latin"; buried beside her second husband, in graveyard of Buckfast Abbey; see Patrick Marnham, *Wild Mary: A Life of Mary Wesley* (2006) ("It was in the city churches of Tuscany that Mary acquired a lifelong love of the theatre of the old Roman Catholic Mass. When she was sure that her mother was not looking she would disobey her instructions, dip her fingers into the holy water font and cross herself…

…Any comfort or guidance she or Eric might have received from their Catholicism seems to have waned after the Vatican Council's decision to abandon the Tridentine Rite in 1965. To a large extent they were both victims of the Council. It had been the beauty and certainty supplied by the old Mass that had originally attracted Mary to the Church and that nourished her faith"); *DNB*.

West, Charles – physician; b. 8 August 1816, London; c. 1874; d. 19 March 1898, Hotel Terminus, Paris; son of Baptist minister and educated in a school opened by his father; trained at St. Bartholomew's Hospital, London and Universities of Bonn, Paris and Berlin; his lectures and book on the diseases of children made him famous as father of British pediatrics; founder of, and chief physician at, the Children's Hospital, Great Ormond Street, London; elected Fellow of the College of Physicians in 1848; member of Academy of Medicine, Paris; prolific writer on medical subjects and very fine public speaker; regarded the profession of medicine as a sacred duty and had a strict moral code; buried at St. Mary's Catholic Church, Chislehurst, Kent; see *DNB*.

Westall, A. St. Leger – son of Anglican clergyman of High Church opinions; was Anglican curate himself and adherent of the most advanced High Church school before his conversion to the Catholic Church; see essay in J. G. F. Raupert (ed), *Roads to Rome* (1901), p.309 ("[F]rom the beginnings of Christianity until the Reformation, it was universally believed that the Church was one, in the sense that she was made by God to be One Visible Body or Corporation, incapable of division into warring fragments, and that this was her first or chief mark. One Church, One Faith, One Voice; that was the undoubted and undoubting testimony of all the ages. To teach or to allow two faiths was as impossible as to believe in two Gods; to be divided into two antagonistic 'branches,' each with its own belief, was as impossible as to divide Christ into various antagonistic personalities. That our Lord founded one Society which was to remain one; that He deposited in her one Faith, and endowed her with the gift of infallibility in order that she might ever teach this and no other; that such a Society still existed, and made these claims, and carried them into effect, and that no other Society so much as claimed the allegiance of the whole world; that this Society was the Catholic and Roman Church, and that her claims were those of the Primitive and Medieval Church, while the Anglican position was diametrically opposed to both; – all this gradually took possession of me as indubitable truth. How else could we know what the Faith was that He delivered to His Apostles? When I had begun to grasp this as the crucial fact, other difficulties began to disappear. A Church, a visible organization, was the vehicle of God's revelation to man. From her I must learn it. Whether or not bishops are essential to the Church, whether there is a priesthood or not, whether Saints may be invoked or not, whether the Mass is a Propitiatory Sacrifice or not, whether the Pope is supreme or not, – all these questions can be answered for certain by the Church and by nobody else, for none but the Church has Christ's authority to declare them. A case may be made out for and against any one of these, or indeed any other Christian doctrines; study might lead one to form an opinion, and on many points the more careful the study the more difficult it is to decide between conflicting opinions. To give a decisive answer is the *raison d'être* of the Church in all ages and for all nations, and the Church in communion with Rome alone claims to do so, and acts on the claim.

Another feature in her seemed to me to point the same way. The Roman Church never stirred from her position. The separated Easterns, or many of them, had three or four times surrendered to Rome, most notably at Florence; never had Rome surrendered to them. If the Anglican Church were in continuity with the pre-Reformation Church, then, on her own confession, she had agreed with Rome for a thousand years of her existence. The efforts of Church Defence lecturers to prove that the early English Church was anti-papal or non-papal, I regarded with unmitigated contempt. The popular Anglican falsification of early Church history led me to question very seriously the theory that 'continuity,' in any but an Act-of-Parliament

sense, was preserved at the Reformation.... To put in a few words what took me many months, if not years, to grasp, I came to the conclusion that the State destroyed the old Church, and erected a brand-new one on its ruins"); see "The Fathers Gave Rome the Primacy," *Dublin Review*, January-April 1903, p.101.

Westlake, Nathaniel Hubert John – painter, designer and writer; b. 1833; c. 1857 (his wife, Frances, *née* Lloyd, also a convert); d. 1921; protégé of the architect William Burges; partner from 1868 in the firm of stained glass manufacturers, Lavers, Barraud and Westlake (sole partner from 1880); many works, including design of windows for St. Paul's, Worcester and Peterborough Cathedral; painted the roof and the Stations of the Cross for the chapel at Maynooth; late in life executed drawings for the mosaics in Newman's memorial church at the Birmingham Oratory; writer on Christian archaeology and art; see *A History of Design in Painted Glass*, 4 Vols. (1881–1894); *On the Authentic Portraiture of St. Francis of Assisi* (1897); *History of Design in Mural Painting* (1902).

Wetherell, Thomas Frederick – writer and editor; b. 1830; c. 1855; d. 1908; studied at Brasenose College, Oxford; after becoming a Catholic was cut out of an inheritance by an uncle; clerk at the War Office; wrote against Corporate Reunion; helped Henry Wilberforce (see below) with the *Weekly Register*; co-editor of the *Rambler* with Acton; co-editor of the *Home and Foreign Review*; editor of the *Chronicle* 1867–1868; editor of the *North Berwick Review* 1869–1871; private secretary to Lord Granville at the Foreign Office 1869–1872; prepared a bibliography of Acton's writings; supporter of Home Rule for Ireland; see "The Latest Phenomena of Anglicanism,"

Dublin Review, March 1857, p.95; "Catholic Unity and English Parties," *Dublin Review*, September 1857, p.172.

Wheeler, Bishop (William) Gordon – bishop; b. 5 May 1910, Hilcrest, Dobcross, Saddleworth, Yorkshire; c. 18 September 1936 (received at Downside Abbey); d. 20 February 1998, Mount St Joseph's Home, Shire Oak Road, Leeds; brought up in a family with deep Anglican faith; educated at University College, Oxford; former Anglo-Catholic minister with admiration for Newman; after conversion went to Beda College, Rome; ordained priest 31 March 1940; administrator of Westminster Cathedral; co-adjutor Bishop of Middlesbrough in 1964; Bishop of Leeds 1966–1985; writer of two books of reminiscence; buried in crypt of St. Edward's Church, Clifford, near Boston Spa, Yorkshire; see *Let's Get this Straight* (1969); *In Truth and Love* (1990) ("With regard to the Roman Catholic Church, yes there was a special attraction in those days regarding liturgy but also regarding Unity, Holiness, Apostolicity, Universality, and Authority. Fundamentally the call to me was to be one with the Universal Church. I had never really thought of the Anglican Church as a Universal Church in the sense that the Catholic Church is. Nor have I ever regarded any authority in the Church of England as measuring up to that authority which Our Lord gave to St. Peter and consequently to his successors"); *More Truth and Love* (1994) ("It is important to realize that those who are turning to us these days are in no way misogynists. And neither are we. On the contrary. For we see a woman, the Blessed Virgin Mary, as God's choice for the most supreme of all vocations: that of being called to be the vehicle of incarnation and ultimately therefore of our salvation through Jesus Christ Our Lord. We see, too, that God made us male and

female; and we have differing roles to fulfill. He chose to be made a Man. That same Man, Jesus, chose other **men**, to be welded into His great High Priesthood as **men** like Himself. His feminine followers had other roles to fulfill in all the great Orders of Womanhood, but also as outstanding individuals and notable examples of human motherhood. Today women are playing a fuller and greater part in the life of the Catholic Church than ever before. That is an enrichment when it gives us the charisma of true femininity. But it does not demand the addendum of the priesthood of the women of today any more than it did for Our Lady two thousand years ago. From the very start of the Church's life the icon of ministerial priesthood was manhood, and so to the thinking of the Catholic and Orthodox Churches of today, it will ever remain…

I have heard some people bring up the plea of 'the Development of Doctrine' in regard to women priests. But, as Newman made abundantly clear, there could be no development of any doctrine which was not inherent already in some degree in Scripture or in the Apostolic era. The briefest study of Newman's 'Essay on the Development of Christian Doctrine' will convey a deeper understanding of his meaning when he wrote: 'I wish to hold that there is nothing which the Church has defined or shall define but what an Apostle, if asked, would have been fully able to answer and would have answered, as the Church has answered; the one answering by inspiration, the other from its gift of infallibility'"); *DNB*.

White, Antonia (real name Eirene Adeline Hopkinson, *née* Botting) – writer; b. 31 March 1899, 22 Perham Road, West Kensington, London; c. 8 December 1906 (child convert received with her father, Cecil (1871–1929),

Anglican who became atheist at university and was senior Classics master at St. Paul's School, London, and with her mother, Christine (1871–1939)); d. 10 April 1980, Danehill, Sussex; childhood dominated by her father; educated as boarder at the Sacred Heart Convent, Roehampton 1908–1914, on which she based her novel, *Frost in May*; worked as governess, clerk, freelance copy writer, and actress; wrote novels, short stories and children's books and translated over thirty novels from French; always plagued with doubts and mental breakdowns, she lapsed from the faith 1926–1940; worked for the BBC and SOE during World War II; came back to the faith though unsettled; buried in Catholic cemetery at West Grinstead, Sussex; see *Frost in May* (1933); *The Lost Traveller* (1950); *The Hound and the Falcon: The Story of a Reconversion to the Catholic Faith* (1965) (letters, 1940–41, to the Catholic intellectual Peter Thorp) ("If the Church is what she claims to be, she should be full of the most mixed, incongruous and mutually antipathetic human beings. One of the most important practical aspects of the Church is just this necessity for breaking down one's fastidiousness. It isn't hard, of course, to feel an 'even-Christian' with whores and homosexuals, with the poor, the dirty, the ignorant and the stupid. But it is far harder to feel the same bond with the spiritual fascists, the sour old devotees, the cocksure apologists, the hearty tankard-thumping Bellocians, the pilers up of indulgences, the prurient defenders of 'holy purity,' the complacent and the snobbish. Nearly all the intelligent, the witty, the tolerant seem to be on the other side and one looks rather wistfully over the walls sometimes, longing for them to come in; sometimes longing to go back to them"); *As Once in May* (1983) (autobiography, edited by Susan Chitty and published posthumously); Susan Chitty, *Now To My Mother: A Very Personal Memoir of Antonia White* (1985): Susan Chitty (ed), *Antonia White Diaries, 1926–1957* (1991); Susan Chitty (ed), *Antonia White Diaries, 1958–1979* (1992); Julietta Benson, "Varieties of Disbelief: Antonia White and the Discourses of Faith and Skepticism," *Literature and Theology*, September 1993, p.284; Jane Dunn, *Antonia White: A Life* (1998); Walter Romig (ed), *The Book of Catholic Authors*, Fifth Series (1952); Matthew Hoehn, OSB (ed), *Catholic Authors* (1952); *DNB*.

White, Victor, OP (born Henry Gordon White) – priest, theologian, and philosopher; b. 1902, Croydon; c. 1921; d. 22 May 1960 (his last words being "Dear God, take me"); brought up as an Anglican; his father and several other relatives were Anglican clergymen; entered the Dominican Order 1924; ordained priest in 1928; based at Oxford 1929–1956; taught dogmatic theology, moral theology, and church history; generally a scholastic approach to theology, but much correspondence with Carl Jung (though they disagreed about evil as *privatio boni*); eventually their friendship broke down; see *God The Unknown* (1956) ("If the Christ-fact is to be lived – just because it is fact, and historic fact – it must be communicated to us, and accurately communicated. It is not enough for our salvation that God should have dealt in such or such wise with his people; it is necessary that those historic dealings should be related to me if they are to have for me any redemptive value. It is not enough that Christ should have lived and died and risen; if I am to realize all that in myself I must know it and who he is. Nor can I do the will of God unless his will in my regard be made known to me; I cannot receive his grace unless I be told what means he has appointed for its reception.... The Church is the Body of Christ; in Bossuet's phrase, it is Jesus Christ himself, but Jesus Christ extended in space and continued in time.... Hence the office of teaching, and of teaching in his name and indeed in his place, belongs to the very essence and purpose of the Church"); Aidan Nichols, *Dominican Gallery: Portrait of a Culture* (1997), Ch. 3 ("[Fr. Victor] was a distinctly apophatic theologian: emphasizing God's infinite exceeding of all man's concepts and images, he could echo Thomas in repeating Denys the Areopagite's axioms in the *Mystical Theology* that the most perfect union with God is union with the utterly Unknown. It is not enough to say that our knowledge of God is inadequate and indistinct.... God lies outside all categories and classes of being, just as he is beyond any possibility of being imagined or conceived.

This does not of course imply that Fr. Victor – or Thomas Aquinas, or Denys – was agnostic about the fact *that* God is. It is *what* he is, not that he is, which is the mystery. Through the existence of other things – a rather multifarious collection of other things, 'all sorts of happenings, changes, productions, things, values, strivings,' we can prove that there *is* that which human beings call 'God' or 'the Divine.' The famous 'Five Ways' to the existence of God, in Fr. Victor's careful formulation: 'enable us to know that the being or existence of God (*Dei esse*), but only that what men call God is, or exists (*Deum esse*). They show that *unless* there is some unknown ground or source ... on which everything ultimately depends, then nothing could ever exist or happen at all. This is not to say ... that God is an 'explanation' of the universe, for we cannot 'explain' what is to some extent known by what is unknown. But we do claim that if there were no God, there could not be anything else,'
...The *quinque viae* lead to a 'learned

ignorance,' whereby we can affirm 'there is an Unknown'.... As we have seen, Fr. Victor is even reluctant to use the phrase 'the existence of God' in this context, for 'existence' means having a place in reality's domain, whereas God both transcends and includes all reality"); Clodagh Brett, *Fr. Victor White, OP: The Story of Jung's 'White Raven'* (2007); Ann Conrad Lammers and Adrian Cunningham, *The Jung-White Letters* (2007); Fergus Kerr, OP, "Comment: Remembering Victor White," *New Blackfriars*, January 2008, p.1 ("In Thomistic theology, evil is regarded as absence of good, *privatio boni*, a doctrine never easy to accept. On the other hand, what is the alternative? Are we caught up in a cosmic struggle between two evenly matched principles, one good and one evil? Should we settle for some Gnostic dualism? Or stick to faith in the goodness of divinely created reality, accepting the corollary that evil is not something positive?").

Whittaker, Sir Edmund Taylor – mathematician and astronomer; b. 24 October 1873, 7 Virginia Street, Southport, Lancashire; c. June 1930; d. 24 March 1956, 48 George Square, Edinburgh; educated at Trinity College, Cambridge; Fellow of Trinity and taught there until 1906; Professor of Astronomy, Trinity College, Dublin, 1906–1911; Professor of Mathematics at Edinburgh University 1912–1946; brilliant historian of physics and first-rate mathematical physicist; member of Pontifical Academy of Sciences from 1936; many scientific, philosophical and historical papers; in 1954 elected by fellows of the Royal Society to receive the Copley Medal, the highest award granted by the scientific Royal Society of London, "for his distinguished contributions to both pure and applied mathematics and to theoretical physics"; father of the mathematician

John Macnaughten Whittaker (1905–1984); see *The Beginning and End of the World* (1942); *Space and Spirit: Theories of the Universe and the Arguments for the Existence of God* (1946); *The Calculus of Observations* (1949); *From Euclid to Eddington* (1949); *A Course of Modern Analysis* (1950); Matthew Hoehn, OSB (ed), *Catholic Authors* (1952); Joseph Pearce, *Literary Converts* (1999), p.170; *DNB*.

Wicklow, eighth Earl of (Rt. Hon. William Cecil James Philip John Paul Howard) (known at Oxford as Billy Clonmore) – journalist, author, translator; b. 30 October 1902; c. 1931 (received by Fr. Martin D'Arcy); d. 8 February 1978; only child of Ralph Howard, seventh Earl of Wicklow; known as Viscount Clonmore until succeeding to the Earldom in 1946; brought up in the Church of Ireland and taught an old-fashioned Protestantism as a child; educated at Eton and Merton College, Oxford; friend of Evelyn Waugh and John Betjeman at Oxford; took Anglican orders; enthusiastic Anglo-Catholic; after his conversion he lived as a layman; "disinherited by his father and banished from the family home on Sundays because he was thought to be an embarrassment on account of his attending Mass with the servants, who were Catholics"; sometime editor of the *Dublin Review*; served as Captain in the Royal Fusiliers during World War II; founder with Patrick Reynolds of the publishers Clonmore and Reynolds, Dublin; translator of Dr. Pierre Barbet, *The Passion of Our Lord Jesus Christ* (1954) and of R. P. H. Perroy, *The Mass Explained to Children* (1956); compiler of anthologies; husband of Eleanor, *née* Butler, architect and member of the Irish Senate 1948–1951; see *More About Dom Marmion* (1950); (ed) *The Glory of Mary* (1952); *Fireside Fusilier* (1958);

(ed) *Life After Death* (1959); (ed), *Rome is Home: The Experience of Converts* (1959) ("[I] was amazed – no weaker word would suffice – by the overwhelming evidence in the Fathers to the truth of the Petrine claims, both as to Papal Supremacy and, more important still, the necessity of being in communion with the See of Peter…

As regards the claims of the Church of England, and the Anglican theories of the Church, the more I read, the more the Elizabethan settlement showed itself as a *coup d'état*. The martyrs, the behavior of most of the Bishops, the previous history of the Church in England, said one thing and spoke with one voice…

Traveling, more than anything else, showed me the universality of the Catholic Church – how, unlike every other religious body, it moulds nations, and is only to a limited extent molded by them, and how it is the Church of every race, not merely a product of the Mediterranean").

Widdecombe, Ann Noreen Hugh – politician and novelist; b. 4 October 1947, Bath, Somerset; c. 21 April 1993 (received by Fr. Michael Seed (see above)); brought up in evangelical Low Church family; attended a Catholic convent school; read PPE at Oxford University; later active Anglican laywoman; in her thirties was for some years an agnostic ("I did actually take the position that we have no knowledge beyond material phenomena"); Conservative MP; converted when the Anglican Church voted to ordain women; opposed the abolition of section 28 of the Local Government Act which banned the promotion of homosexuality by local authorities; in 1994 became minister of state in the Department of Employment; in 1995 minister of state at the Home Office; also a novelist and television presenter; see Valerie Grove, "The minister, a priest and the road to Rome," *The Times*, 23 April 1993 ("I give thanks to Almighty God for the authoritarian element. To have a Church which calls a sin a sin and has done with it, is a blessed relief. What the Church of England has done is to confuse sinners and sins. It has always been the job of the Church to accommodate sinners, but what you don't do is accommodate sin. You don't say, 'If this standard is difficult for human beings to reach, we will reduce the standard to that which they are most likely to reach.' You should say, 'Here is the standard, and we understand if you can't reach it, but this is the standard.' That is so lacking in the Church of England now"); essay in Rowanne Pasco (ed), *Why I Am a Catholic* (1995); essay in Joanna Bogle (ed), *Come On In ... It's Awful* (1994); foreword to Dwight Longenecker (ed), *The Path to Rome* (1999) ("In finding the Catholic Church I have found Peter. I have always had Christ but now I have Peter as well. If the Church is founded upon the Apostolic succession then at the foundation of that line of authority is Peter, the rock upon which Christ founded His Church, the direct link with Jesus Christ who binds and looses on earth and Heaven. No one but the Pope claims to be the successor to Peter and none but the Catholic Church can trace its line and its teaching without fail right back to the first Apostles"); "The Politician" in Greg Watts, *Catholic Lives* (2001) ("I had admired the Roman Catholic Church from afar for a long time as it seemed to stand alone in being ready to promulgate teaching which was at odds with the permissive weave of society in general. Rome stood for Christian morality with no regard to what might or might not be fashionable or popular or easy to achieve.... Many other Christians have difficulty with the exclusive nature of the Church; its interdict on inter-communion, its insistence that it alone possesses the fullness of truth. This, however, is a reflection of our times when it is unfashionable to be sure of anything, when anything is tolerated except intolerance and when every individual is infallible except the Pope. It cannot be a serious objection though it is one which is often put forward"); interview, *New Statesman*, 4 February 2008, p.33 ("Where would we be without God? We wouldn't").

Widdrington, Roger – recusant; b. c.1572, Swinburne Castle, near Hexham; c. July 1594; d. 10 February 1641/2; his parents conformed to the new religion and he was brought up a Protestant; his conversion was as a result of witnessing the execution of a seminary priest, St. John Boste (a similar account is related by another witness, the priest and future martyr Christopher Robinson (see above)); had studied at Cambridge, but was prevented by reason of his religion from taking a degree; in 1599 appointed bailiff and steward of the Regality of Hexham; over the next several years he was proceeded against many times for recusancy, but remained steadfast; see Challoner, *Memoirs of Missionary Priests* ("When the hangman pulled out Mr. Boste's heart, showed it to the crowd, with a 'Behold the heart of a traitor,' a voice was heard to the effect: 'No, the heart of a servant of God.' At which Mr. Widdrington of Cartington, who heard the voice, was so struck, that he was thereupon reconciled to the Church'"); Ann M. C. Forster, "The Real Roger Widdrington," *Recusant History*, January 1972, p.196.

Wilberforce, Henry William – journalist and writer; b. 22 September 1807, Clapham, Surrey; c. 15 September 1850 (wife, Mary (see below) received 22 June 1850; eldest brother, William (1798–1879), MP for Hull, received in January 1863 (latter's wife, Mary

Frances (1800–1880) in 1852 and his son, William (1821–1900), proprietor for a time of the *Weekly Register*, in 1864, whose own wife, Rosa Elizabeth (1830–1878) was received in 1851)); d. 23 April 1873, Chester House, Stroud, Gloucestershire; fourth and youngest son of William Wilberforce (1759–1833), the statesman, philanthropist and slave emancipator; brilliant student at Oxford where he had Newman for his private tutor and to guide his reading (he was Newman's dearest friend from his Tractarian days); became Anglican vicar; four of his children had died by 1851 (one, Caroline (1849–1915) became a nun; two of his three brothers, Robert (see below) and Samuel (1805–1873), later Anglican Bishop of Oxford and Winchester, also took Anglican orders and all three men married daughters of John Sargent (1780–1833) (Sargent's other daughter married Henry Edward Manning, later Cardinal Manning); much correspondence with Newman before his conversion; influenced by the Gorham judgment ((see entry for William Maskell); after his conversion, which caused great shock, devoted himself to journalism and writing (proprietor and editor of *The Weekly Register*); often in financial difficulties, but spirit never failed; secretary of Catholic Defence Association in Ireland; close friend of Manning; vested in the Dominican habit as he died, having received the last rites from a son of his, Fr. Arthur Henry Bertrand Wilberforce, OP; Newman preached at the funeral; buried in the Dominican churchyard at Woodchester; see *Reasons for Submitting to the Catholic Church: A Farewell Letter to his Parishioners* (1851) (republished under the title *Why I Became a Catholic* (2001)) ("You see I have mentioned thirteen different marks which prove that the Catholic Church is the true Church, to which we all ought to submit. They are these: 1. It is the Church set up by Christ and the Apostles, and the Protestant Churches are new. 2. The Church is infallible: that is, it cannot teach error; and this is the old Church which has never changed, but has always taught the same things she now teaches. 3. This Church is founded upon St. Peter, the first Pope, on whom Christ built His Church. 4. It is spread all over the world, not in any one country. 5. It teaches the same thing in all places and at all times. 6. It is a kingdom by itself separate from all the kingdoms of the world – the kingdom of Heaven: as our Lord called His Church. 7. It forgives sins by the hands of its priests, and by the authority of Jesus Christ. 8. It keeps up the custom of the Apostles by anointing the sick with oil. 9. It offers the daily sacrifice to God. 10. It keeps to, and shows the meaning of, all parts of Scripture, not only some parts. 11. It honors and practices the 'Counsels of Perfect,' virginity, poverty, and obedience. 12. Miracles continue to be worked in it, and not among Protestants. 13. It is hated by the world. Scripture shows that these are all signs of the true Church, and these things, and many others of like sort have convinced me, my dear friends, that the Catholic Church is the one only Church of Jesus Christ upon earth; the one Ark of Salvation from the fearful flood of fire which is coming upon the world"); J. H, Newman, *Memoir of Henry William Wilberforce* (1873) ("Viewed on its human side, Mr. Wilberforce's conversion may be attributed, on the one hand, to the straightforward logic of a clear mind; on the other, to his intimate profound perception of the unseen world, and of his responsibilities in relation to it. While he was resolute in pursuing its principles to their legitimate issues, he was undaunted in facing those issues, whatever they might be. Religion was to him not knowledge, so much as obedience. The simple question was, as he felt it, not to rid himself of the thousand difficulties speculative and practical, which hem in and confuse our intellect here below, but what was the word and what was the will of Him who gave him a work to do on earth. If that was plain, it was nothing to the purpose, it was nothing to him, that 'clouds and darkness' closed it in on every side. 'What must I do to be saved?' that was the whole matter with him, as with all serious minds. That there had been a Revelation given from above to man, in order to our eternal salvation, was undeniable; the only point was, what was it? What were its gifts, its promises, its teaching? Where were these to be found? How were they to be obtained? His intellect made answer – the more clearly and distinctly the longer he thought upon it – in the Church universally called Catholic, and nowhere else. It, and it alone, carried with it the tokens and notes, the continuity, succession, and claims, of that divine polity which had been founded and formed by the Apostles in the beginning. This, then, was the fold of Christ, the Ark of Salvation, the Oracle of Truth, and the Anglican communion was no part of it. To this Church he was in consequence bound to betake himself without hesitation or delay, as soon as he had in his intellect a distinct recognition of it"); *The Church and the Empires* (1874); David Newsome, *The Parting of Friends: A Study of the Wilberforces and Henry Manning* (1966) ("Do what he could for the dying Irish Catholics [in the cholera epidemic of 1849], Henry could not bring them the Sacraments"); Stanley L. Jaki, *Newman to Converts: An Existential Ecclesiology* (2001), Ch. 2; *Gillow*, Vol. V, p.583; *Catholic Encyclopedia*; *DNB*.

Wilberforce, Mary – b. 1811; c. 22 June 1850; d. 1878; wife of Henry William Wilberforce (see above); daughter of John Sargent (1780–1833), Anglican rector; sister-in-law of Cardinal Manning; of Samuel Wilberforce (1805–1873), Anglican Bishop of Oxford and Winchester; and of George Dudley Ryder (see above); mother of Fr. (Arthur Henry) Bertrand Wilberforce (1839–1904), a Dominican friar with a fine reputation as a giver of missions and spiritual guide; of Henry Edward Wilberforce, secretary to the Earl Marshall, who married Emily (d. 1951), daughter of Robert Sadleir Moody (see above); of Wilfrid Ignatius Wilberforce (1850–1910) author; of Caroline Mary Wilberforce, a nun of the Order of St. Francis; and of Agnes Everilda Mary (1845–1890), second wife of Richard Hurrell Froude (1842–1932) (see above); see David Newsome, *The Parting of Friends: A Study of the Wilberforces and Henry Manning* (1966).

Wilberforce, Robert Isaac – author; b. 19 December 1802; c. 31 October 1854 (received in Paris); d. 3 February 1857, Albano, near Rome; second son of William Wilberforce (1759–1833), the statesman, philanthropist and slave emancipator; educated at Oriel College, Oxford (gained double first in Classics and Mathematics); later Fellow and Sub-Dean of Oriel (colleague of Newman there); became Anglican vicar, canon of York and Archdeacon of the East Riding of Yorkshire; able advocate of the Tractarian movement; widowed twice; subsequently studied for the priesthood, but died in minor orders; see *An Inquiry into the Principles of Church Authority, or Reasons for Recalling my Subscription to the Royal Supremacy* (1854) ("The Church's authority … depends on that presence of the Spirit, which gives it life. This authority had resided first in its completeness in the Person of Our Lord, when He was manifest in the Flesh. He was pleased to bestow it in a plenary manner on the College of His Apostles. From them it has descended to their successors, the Bishops throughout the world. But to preserve the unity of this wide-spread commission, Our Lord was pleased to give an especial promise to one of His Apostles, and to bestow upon him a name and office derived from Himself.... The Primacy of St. Peter ripened into the Supremacy of the Pope. But then comes a change. There arises a powerful monarch in a remote land, who resolves to separate the Church of his nation from the unity of Christendom. He effects his purpose by force or fraud, and bids it recognize a new principle of unity in himself. He passes to his account, and his children rule after him. But this new principle of unity is found in time to be insufficient. No sooner is the grasp of the civil ruler relaxed, than a host of parties divide the land. The very thought of unity, and hope of concord, is gradually lost. The national Church is surrounded by sects, and torn by dissensions. *Intra muros peccatur ab extra*. And can it be doubted what advice would be given to its children by the great Saint, who looked forth on a somewhat similar spectacle in his native land; and whose life was expended in winning back his brethren one by one to the unity of Christendom? He did not think that the national unity of Africa was any pledge of safety to the Donatists; or that the number and succession of their Bishops entitled them to respect. 'Come, brethren, if you wish to be inserted in the vine; for we grieve, when we see you lie thus cut off from it. Number the bishops from the very seat of Peter, and in that list of Fathers see what has been the succession; this is the rock against which the proud gates of Hell do not prevail'"); David Newsome, *The Parting of Friends: A Study of the Wilberforces and Henry Manning* (1966); *Catholic Encyclopedia*.

Wilberforce, William – b. 1798; c. January 1863 (his wife, Mary Frances, 1800–1880, daughter of Rev. John Owen, Anglican vicar and one of the founders of the Bible Society, was received in 1852; his son, William (1821–1900) was received in 1864, his first wife, Rosa Elizabeth (1830–1878) having converted in 1851); d. 1879; eldest son of William Wilberforce, 1759–1833, the statesman, philanthropist and slave emancipator; JP for Yorkshire, Middlesex and Gloucestershire; Lord of the Manor of Markington, Yorkshire; MP for Hull; see David Newsome, *The Parting of Friends: A Study of the Wilberforces and Henry Manning* (1966).

Wilde, Oscar Fingal O'Flahertie Wills – writer; aesthete, and socialite; b. 16 October 1854, 21 Westland Row, Dublin; c. 30 November 1900 (death bed conversion; Fr. Cuthbert Dunne, CP, an Irish priest, brought by Robert Ross (see above), had conditionally baptized him, and given him extreme unction and absolution, being satisfied that Wilde, although now speechless, understood and approved; his younger son, Vyvyan, converted one month before); d. 30 November 1900, Hôtel d'Alsace, rue des Beaux-Arts, Paris ("Catholicism is the only religion to die in"); brought up in a family influenced by the (established) Church of Ireland and Irish Evangelicanism; baptized into Church of Ireland, but at age of six baptized in the Catholic Church at his mother's instance, by Rev. L. C. Prideaux Fox (1820–1905); educated at Magdalen College, Oxford (double first in Classical Moderations and Greats); spent much of his time at Oxford deliberating upon possible conversion to Rome; paganism and Catholicism always warring attractions for him; married Constance Mary Lloyd (1858–1898), a Protestant Dublin girl (two children of marriage); dandyesque social figure and great literary success as writer (poet, playwright, essays, children's stories, and one novel); homosexual associations with, *inter alia*, Robert Ross (see above) and Alfred, Lord Douglas (see above); accused of sodomy by ninth Marquess of Queensberry (see above), the father of Lord Alfred Douglas; took out a warrant for criminal libel against Queensberry, but prosecution failed; charged with gross indecency; convicted and sentenced to two years penal servitude with hard labor; declared bankrupt; great suffering for his wife and family; on release from jail in May 1897 his request to the Jesuits of Farm Street, London, for a six-month retreat was refused (he wept at the news); exile in France 1897–1900; received the blessing of Pope Leo XIII in April 1900 in Rome; buried at Bagneux, but in 1909 his uncorrupted body was moved to Père Lachaise cemetery, Paris; see *The Picture of Dorian Gray* (1890); *Salome* (1891); *Lady Windermere's Fan* (1892); *An Ideal Husband* (1895); *The Importance of Being Earnest* (1895); *De Profundis* (1897*); The Ballad of Reading Gaol* (1897); Rt Rev. Abbot Hunter Blair, OSB, "Oscar Wilde as I Knew Him," *Dublin Review*, July-September 1938, p.90; Merlin Holland and Rupert Hart-Davis (ed), *The Complete Letters of Oscar Wilde* (2000); Vyvyan Holland, *Son of Oscar Wilde* (1954); Rev. Edmund Burke, CP, "Oscar Wilde: The Final Scene," *The London Magazine*, May 1961, p.37; H. Montgomery Hyde, *The Trials of Oscar Wilde* (1973); H. Montgomery Hyde, *Oscar Wilde: A Biography* (1976); Richard Ellmann, *Oscar Wilde* (1988); Gary H. Paterson, "Oscar and the Scarlet Woman," *Antigonish Review*, Spring/Summer 1991, p.241 ("Shortly after his release from prison, Wilde remarked to Reginald Turner, 'The Catholic Church is for saints and sinners alone. For respectable people the Anglican Church will do'…

…Wilde went to Rome in Passion Week of 1900. There he was more than ever before impressed by the outward splendor of the Easter celebrations. Particularly, he was struck by the figure of the Pope whom he thought was wonderful 'as he was carried past me on his throne, not of flesh and blood, but a white soul robed in white, and an artist as well as a saint.' It would seem that Wilde's attraction to the Papacy was a form of hero-worship, the same kind of admiration that he felt toward royalty.... Wilde, in being drawn toward the ancient institution of the Church, with all its pageantry and tradition, was quite naturally impressed by the successor of St. Peter and Vicar of Christ"); Kevin Morris, "The Other Oscar Wilde," *The Tablet*, 2 December 1995, p.1545; Ellis Hanson, *Decadence and Catholicism* (1997); Joseph Pearce, *The Unmasking of Oscar Wilde* (1997) ("Much of my moral obliquity is due to the fact that my father would not allow me to become a Catholic. The artistic side of the Church and the fragrance of its teaching would have cured my degeneracies"); Andrew McCracken, "The Long Conversion of Oscar Wilde," *New Oxford Review*, September 1998; William Oddie, "Chesterton Versus Wilde: the Culture Wars of the Fin de Siecle," *Catholic Herald*, 11 December 1998; Robert Whelan, "Why did so many Victorian decadents become Catholics?" *Catholic Herald*, 5 January 2001; Jeffery A. Tucker, "Oscar Wilde – Roman Catholic," *Crisis*, April 2001; Horst Schroeder, *Additions and Corrections to Richard Ellmann's Oscar Wilde* (2002); Merlin Holland, *Irish Peacock and Scarlet Marquess: The Real Trial of Oscar Wilde* (2004); Joseph Pearce, *Literary Converts* (1999), *passim*; *DNB* ("*De Profundis* is … an extraordinary record of a man hurled from the pinnacle of literary success to the uttermost public degradation, and of the spiritual means by which he turned away from despair. Wilde fixed his mind on Christ, first as a person, then (in *The Ballad of Reading Gaol*) as a redeeming god").

Wilkinson, Bishop Thomas William – bishop; b. 5 April 1825; c. 1846 (sister, later a nun, received in 1848); d. 17 April 1909; second son of George Hutton Wilkinson, first County Court Judge and Recorder of Newcastle; formerly an Anglican curate (two brothers were Anglican vicars); ordained Catholic priest in 1848; became the fifth Bishop of Hexham and Newcastle in 1889; President of St. Cuthbert's College, Ushaw, Durham; see essay in J. G. F. Raupert (ed), *Roads to Rome* (1901), p.316 ("I simply owe everything to Newman, the *Tracts for the Times*, and generally the Puseyite movement").

Williams, Christopher John Fardo – philosopher; b. 1930; d. 1997; brought up as an Anglican; entered the Benedictine novitiate, leaving later; Professor of Philosophy, Bristol University; see "Knowing Good and Evil," *Philosophy* (1991), p.235; "Not by Confounding the Persons nor Dividing the Substance," in A. G. Padgett (ed), *Reason and the Christian Religion: Essays in Honour of Richard Swinburne* (1994), p.227 ("Following St. Thomas, I would say that we affirm the existence of God because we need an explanation of certain facts about the world, the fact of its changeableness, the fact of its contingency, the fact of its limited perfection, the fact of its order. The first of the five ways starts from the premiss that what is in the process of change must be caused to change by something else. Where we are prompted to look for explanations, it is not too difficult to know where to begin; but it is not so easy to know where to stop. Every atheistic philosopher who puts pen to paper (or switches on his word processor) recycles the Schopenhauer canard that those who use the principle of causality to prove the existence of God are like people who hire a cab and dismiss it when they have reached their destination. I start with the present state of the world, and trace that back and back through a vast number of previous states until I reach, perhaps, a big bang. What, I ask, produced the big bang? The only explanation is that the big bang was made by God. Ah, says Schopenhauer, but who made God? As though a philosopher as considerable as St. Thomas would have left himself open to the charge that he had used the premiss 'Everything has a cause' to obtain the conclusion 'There is an uncaused cause.' But of course, he did *not* use that premiss. He used the qualified premiss 'everything that is in the process of change has a cause,' or 'Everything that has a beginning of existence has a cause.' If we reach a cause which is not itself in process of change, which had no beginning of existence, and whose existence is necessary, the pressure to take the series of explanantia further and further back comes to an end. The same principle applies where an explanation is sought for something having a 'perfection' to a limited degree: why just so much and no more? But possession of unlimited perfection does not cry out for explanation. How could there be an *explanation* of someone's possessing all knowledge? One could hardly say 'How did you come to know *all that*?'").

Williams, Paul M. – philosopher; b. 12 September 1950; c. Easter 2000; formerly Anglican; became Buddhist; Professor of Indian and Tibetan Philosophy and Head of Department of Theology and Religious Studies, Bristol University; see "Out of my head," *The Tablet*, 5 August 2000, p.1046 ("I was not (thank God) converted by a strange experience.

I was converted by Cardinal Ratzinger of the Congregation for the Doctrine of the Faith. Oh yes, I remember it well. I was picked up from the station on my way to a Buddhist meeting. Had I heard that outrageous comment of Ratzinger? The comment about Buddhism being a form of spiritual auto-eroticism? I had not, but Ratzinger (I explained) is a reactionary. No need to worry. That's not really what Catholics think of Buddhism.... The trouble was (unlike just about everyone else) I knew exactly what Ratzinger was talking about. He had put into words The Difference. And the difference worried me.

Consider the following: 'Catholicism is all about the mind. It is all a series of strategies for transforming the mind from mental states considered to be negative, to those considered to be positive.' Right or wrong? As a Buddhist I regularly began talks by saying just this about Buddhism. Few Buddhists would disagree. Buddhism is all about the mind. Mental states are essentially subjective. Buddhism takes as its starting point *states of consciousness*.... But wait. That may be true of Buddhism, but Catholicism is not all about the mind at all. The Christian religion is all about *God*, and the salvific actions of God through Christ. Instead of reducing everything to forms of subjectivity – my experiences – everything, but everything, reduces to God. And to the family of God"); "The Philosopher" in Greg Watts, *Catholic Lives* (2001) ("It is my conviction of the *truth* of Christianity, precisely expressed in its dogmas, that has converted me from Buddhism to Catholicism.

A. For I have come to believe that God exists. The God I hold to exist is God as a necessary being, Creator of all things out of nothing. All other things are created, and as such are of a totally unimaginably different order from God. This God is the sort of God that would be rec-ognizable to Christian orthodoxy as represented by the Catholic tradition of Aquinas. Buddhists do not hold that such a God exists. Thus I could no longer be a Buddhist.

B. I have also come to believe that Jesus was indeed bodily resurrected from the dead. That is, I believe Jesus genuinely died, the tomb was empty, and Jesus was subsequently, after his real death, physically alive. He had been physically resurrected from the dead. I repeat the word 'physically' because I gather there are those who accept the resurrection yet interpret it differently from what I would call a literal, physical resurrection. Perhaps they take the resurrection as a vision, or as a myth, or as a way of speaking about an understanding that the disciples gained concerning the significance of Jesus's life and death. They do not take it as a literal, physical, bodily resurrection. I understand that scholars working on the resurrection sometimes referred to the sort of literalist approach that I have come to accept by saying that it entails that if someone had possessed a working camera they would have photographed Jesus after the resurrection. Fine. That is what I mean.

Since I believe the resurrection took place, in the sense in which I have defined it, I do not feel I can be any sort of theist apart from a Christian. I cannot be a Muslim, or a mainstream Jew, or a dualist Saivite or Vaisnavite. None of these, as I understand it, accepts the literal physical resurrection of Jesus from the dead...

C. If I am to be a Christian, what sort of Christian? I want to argue that priority has to be given to the Roman Catholic Church. In other words, I need a strong argument *not* to be a Catholic. Since I failed to be convinced by arguments not to be a Catholic I shall be a Catholic. One of my principles here is that on some things – indeed, some very important things – we cannot know what God has actually done short of him telling us. His telling us is a revelation. One form of revelation is Scripture. But God cannot be constrained, and that is only one form of revelation. Another major form of revelation is through the tradition and teaching authority (*magisterium*) of an authoritarian Church.

A recurrent theme running through much of my thought on these things has been the philosophical and spiritual dangers of basing religion on what I shall term 'subjectivism,' or 'subjectivity.' Subjectivism occurs in systems that give overwhelming primacy to certain sorts of private experiences, sensations, intuitions, or emotions, and seek to base all that is ultimately most valuable in the religious (or other ideological) system on those. It is ultimately in those intuitions or experiences, such as the emotion of feeling saved, feeling one with the universe, seeing God, or the experience of *nirvana*, enlightenment, that the rest of the religion concerned is validated. Thus ultimate authority, or validation, or the goal, is essentially *private*. This can be contrasted with the authority of an external body, revelation through the public words of Scripture (literally understood, if that is possible), or the public pronouncements of an authoritative Church. It seems to me that subjectivism is prone to losing all sense of objectivity of truth. It has a genuine problem in escaping the privacy of experience, and hence solipsism (*the* world itself as nothing more than the world of the flow of *my own* experiences). It thus provides an insufficient base for grounding not only a common world of objective being but also (and therefore) any genuine morality and any spiritual practice apart from self interest. I now think that only in Being Itself, i.e. necessary being, in other words God, can the objectivity of the everyday world be grounded. And

correspondingly only in a divinely authorized and hence infallible Church founded on Being Itself cam morality and a spiritual liberation which transcends individual self interest be also grounded"); *The Unexpected Way: On Converting from Buddhism to Catholicism* (2002) ("There must be a Church with the authority to reveal meaning. Which? With the exception of the Eastern Orthodox Churches, all Churches viable for me exist as derivatives from or in opposition to the Roman Catholic Church. They all gain their distinctive features from their relationship to Rome.... Finally, there has to be one arbiter of orthodoxy, and this is what Christ intended in his declaration in the Gospels that upon Peter the Church would be founded. The alternative would be endless problems in establishing Church unity.... Of the ancient pre-eminent sees of Rome, Constantinople, Alexandria, Antioch and Jerusalem, only that of Rome has flourished throughout the ages and is still flourishing as leader of a worldwide Christian movement, the largest in existence.... But what of Protestantism? Why not remain an Anglican?.... Was Protestantism so necessary to God? Can one really hold that, although the story is not very edifying nevertheless the Henrician Reformation in England was guided by the Holy Spirit? Can one really hold that the Elizabethan 'middle way' – carefully crafted to harmonize both moderate Protestant and Catholic wings of the Church of England (out of communion with the Pope and the Christian mainstream), and known only in Britain – was nearer the historical intentions of Christ and Christianity?... Could we really imagine that [the] Saints would look at the contemporary Christian world, study the history of the Reformation and decide that the reformers were right, breaking communion with Rome themselves? And how could I now follow a denomination that would be rejected by the Saints of the Church?"); "Face to Face: Paul Williams talks to Kieran Flanagan" *Saint Austin Review*, September 2002, p.26 ("Catholicism has what Buddhists call 'the lineage'. And as Chesterton says at one point, Catholicism really speaks as if it had the truth. So I argue that I need a very good argument not to be a Catholic. I looked but I did not find a sufficiently strong counter argument.... These three arguments made me a Catholic: God, resurrection, no convincing reason to reject Catholicism"); *EWTN Audio Library* (17 February 2003); "Aquinas Meets the Buddhists," in Jim Fodor and Frederick Christian Bauerschmidt (ed) *Aquinas in Dialogue: Thomas for the Twenty-First Century* (2004); Joanna Bogle, "An Unexpected Enlightenment," *Catholic Herald*, 2 December 2005, p.7; *Buddhism* (2006).

Williams, Shirley Vivien Teresa Brittain (Baroness Williams of Crosby) (*née* Catlin) – politician and writer; b. 27 July 1930; c. (baptized) 1948 ("I am often asked in Catholic circles whether I am a cradle Catholic or a convert, to which the only answer is that I am both"); father, Professor Sir George Catlin, a Catholic convert who later lapsed, but finally returned to the Church; mother, Vera Brittain, an Anglican, but one with considerable doubts about the practice of her Church; educated at Somerville College, Oxford; Fulbright Scholar at Columbia University; Labour politician and minister in 1964–1970 government and Cabinet Minister in 1974–1979 government; co-founder of the Social Democratic Party and its first elected MP in 1981; spearheaded merger of SDP and Liberals into Liberal Democrats 1988; Professor Emeritus at John F. Kennedy School of Government, Harvard University; see

God and Caesar (2003). ("I felt at one with the internationalism of Roman Catholics, so much at odds with the national ethos at that time of the Church of England. But I think the main reason I chose to be and remain a Catholic lay in the claims the Church made for herself, and in the demands she made on her adherents. 'I am the Way, the Truth and the Life'; 'You are Peter, and on this rock I shall build my Church, and the gates of Hell shall not prevail against it.' These are breathtaking claims. It seemed to me that, if I was to be a Christian, I should embrace Christianity in its strongest form. It was the huge claims and the huge demands made that drew me to the Church of Rome"); *Climbing the Bookshelves: The Autobiography* (2009); Vincent McKee, "Shirley Williams: Centrist politician with enduring Catholic conscience," *Catholic Life*, March 2003, p.8.

Williamson, Benedict (real name William Edward Williamson) – priest, architect and writer; b. 1868, London; c. 1896 (Farm Street, London); studied law for a time, then trained as an architect; following his conversion known as Benedict Williamson; practice as an architect 1896–1906; worked on Farnborough Abbey and responsible, e.g., for St. Ignatius Church, Tottenham, St. Boniface, Tooting, and Our Lady of Perpetual Help, Fulham; in 1906 entered Beda College, Rome, to study for the priesthood; ordained priest in 1909; attempted to revive the male wing of the Bridgettine Order, well known in England before the Reformation, but this came to a standstill in 1915, partly because of the effects of World War I; prolific author; see *The Straight Religion* (1917); *The Bridgettine Order: Its Foundress, History and Spirit, Etc.* (1922); *The Real Thing (The Claims and Teachings of the Catholic Church)* (1925); *The Book of Life, etc.* (Life of Jesus Christ) (1926);

The Sure Way of St. Thérèse of Lisieux (1928); *The Treaty of the Lateran* (1929); *The Story of Pope Pius XI* (1931); *Gemma of Lucca* (1932); *The Doctrinal Mission and Apostolate of St. Thérèse of Lisieux* (1933); *How to Build a Church: What to Do and What to Avoid* (1934); *St. Thérèse and the Faithful: A Book for Those Living in the World* (1935); *The Madonna According to the Teaching of St. Thérèse of Lisieux* (1937).

Williamson, Hugh Ross – writer; b. 1 January 1901; c. 15 October 1955 (received with his wife by Fr. Basil Fitzgibbon, SJ, at Farm Street, London); d. 13 January 1978; son of a Congregational Moderator; followed secular career 1925–1942 as journalist, editor, playwright, historian, politician, and broadcaster; then Anglo-Catholic minister; converted to the Catholic Church at the time of the South India crisis; influenced in his conversion by Chesterton (see above) and Mgr. Robert Hugh Benson (see above); writer of history, novels, plays, religion, theology, and children's books; broadcaster; anticipated in his writings some now generally accepted theses, e.g., that the Reformation in England was the "shipwreck of faith," that Robert Cecil acted as an agent provocateur in the Gunpowder Plot, and that Shakespeare was a Catholic; appalled by the liturgical changes brought in after Vatican II; see *The Poetry of T. S. Eliot* (1932) ("Protestantism is a half-way house where one takes refuge because of a disinclination to think the matter out to a conclusion. Only the Catholic and the agnostic dare to reach the end of their journeys"); *A.D. 33: A Tract for the Times* (1941); *Charles and Cromwell* (1946); "A Convert Explains," *The Month*, November 1955 ("What possible theory of Orders in the Catholic sense, can apply to such a body [the Church of South India], denying the full Christian

faith, denying the sacraments, denying the priesthood and denying the Apostolic Ministry? It is a *reductio ad absurdum* without parallel in Christian history that a "Bishop" who is officially not allowed to believe that he is a bishop should ordain a "Presbyter" who is officially not allowed to believe that he is a priest to administer a "sacrament" which he is officially not allowed to believe is a sacrament in the One Holy Catholic Apostolic Church in which he is officially allowed *not* to believe"); *The Gunpowder Plot* (1951); *The Great Prayer: Concerning the Canon of the Mass* (1955); Appendix IV to Anthony A. Stephenson, SJ, *Anglican Orders* (1956) ("For myself, preaching on 6 July, I said that 'yesterday the Church of England, as we have known it, came to an end.' Since that day the body which still calls itself the Church of England is, in fact, only the English branch of the undenominational 'Church of South India,' and in leaving it I cannot feel that I am deserting the body in which I was ordained priest twelve years ago in the belief that it was 'a branch of the Catholic Church.' There is no such body left to desert. And with gratitude for the light I see at last that the One Holy Catholic and Apostolic Church into which I, in common with all Christians, was baptized and in which I have, in the Creed, regularly professed my belief in what St. John Fisher called 'Christ's Catholic known church', the Church of Rome"); *The Walled Garden: An Autobiography* (1956) ("No one, I think, has been able to describe a conversion in terms which are objectively appropriate. As in the language of the mystics, analogies which give only a shadow of the substance have to be used. Chesterton, in his sonnet on his conversion, perhaps has suggested the reality of it most vividly when he speaks of the 'one moment when I bowed my head/And the whole world turned over and came upright' and how suddenly he found that the old controversies and arguments 'are less than dust to me/Because my name is Lazarus and I live.' But, for me, there is an earlier passage in his *Orthodoxy* which I find even more appropriate: 'Catholic doctrine and discipline may be walls; but they are the walls of a playground. Christianity is the only frame which has preserved the pleasure of Paganism. We might fancy some children playing on the flat grassy top of some tall island in the sea. So long as there was a wall round the cliff's edge they could fling themselves into every frantic game and make the place the noisiest of nurseries. But the walls were knocked down, leaving the naked peril of the precipice. They did not fall over; but when their friends returned to them they were all huddled in terror in the centre of the island; and their song had ceased.' So, inside the walls, I have found the freedom and the safety and happiness of the garden again"); *The Beginning of the English Reformation* (1957) ("From the vantage point of posterity we see that what is called the Reformation in England was accomplished within the span of a lifetime of seventy-five years.... By 1606, throughout the length and breadth of England, no monastery or nunnery or shrine or chantry existed; to say Mass or to attend Mass, to make a convert to Catholicism or to be a convert were all punishable by death; an Oath asserting that the Head of the Church in England was the successor of Henry VIII instead of the successor of St. Peter was obligatory on all persons of whatever rank under the penalty of exclusion from places of trust and from all the liberal professions; Catholics were required not only to attend Protestant churches but to take Communion there under pain of the confiscation of two-thirds of their property; they were debarred from the legal and medical professions, from the army

and the universities and, if they sent their children abroad to be educated as Catholics, their inheritance was taken away from them and given to their Protestant relations, who were encouraged by liberal bribes to inform against them. In England there was no crucifix to be seen or any statue of Christ's Mother in any public place and that none should remain as private relics in Catholic homes, Justices of the Peace were given indiscriminate right of search; if any crucifix were there discovered the figure was to be publicly defaced at the Quarter Sessions"); *The Day They Killed the King: On the Execution of King Charles I* (1957); *The Challenge of Bernadette* (1958); *A Children's Book of Saints* (1960); *The Day Shakespeare Died* (1962); *The Modern Mass* (1969); *The Great Betrayal* (1970) (both of these were critiques of the Novus Ordo Missae); *Kind Kit* (1972); *Catherine de Medici* (1973); *Letter to Julia* (1974) ("In April 1536, at the end of the twenty-seventh year of King Henry VIII, there were, scattered throughout England and Wales more than eight hundred religious houses, and in them lived close on 10,000 monks, canons, nuns and friars. Four years later, in April 1540, there were none...

The Oath which every Anglican bishop takes today when he does homage to the Sovereign on entering into his see runs: 'I declare that Your Majesty is the only Supreme Governor of this your realm in spiritual and ecclesiastical things, as well as in temporal, and that no foreign prelate or potentate has any jurisdiction within this realm, and I acknowledge I hold the said Bishopric as well the spiritualities as the temporalities thereof, only of Your Majesty.' The first part of this is the essential part of the Oath of Supremacy imposed by Henry VIII. Nothing has changed. The issue for which Fisher and More and the first Carthusian saints and martyrs died is, with exactitude, the issue which still separates Catholicism from Anglicanism. But now that the financial and political reasons have vanished, it is easier to discuss the matter in its correct and unemotional terms and ask your Anglican friends why they believe Queen Elizabeth II to be, as far as they are concerned, the successor of St. Peter"); *Who Was the Man in the Iron Mask? And Other Historical Mysteries* (2002); Joseph Pearce, *Literary Converts* (1999) *passim*.

Williamson, Richard Nelson – bishop of the Society of St. Pius X; b. 8 March 1940, Buckinghamshire; c. 1971; brought up as an Anglican; graduated in English Literature at Clare College, Cambridge; school teacher 1965–1970; novice with the Oratorians for a few months before joining the Society of St. Pius X and entering its seminary at Écône, Switzerland; ordained priest in 1976 by Archbishop Marcel Lefebvre; after ordination taught at the seminary at Weissbad in Germany and at Ecône; in 1983 rector of St. Thomas Aquinas seminary, Ridgefield, Connecticut, United States, which later moved to Winona, Minnesota; on 30 June 1988 he was consecrated (together with three other priests) a bishop by Archbishop Lefebvre, the latter not having a pontifical mandate for this; the Vatican issued a statement declaring them to be excommunicated; he denied the validity of the excommunication, arguing that the consecrations were necessary due to a moral and theological crisis in the Church; carried out confirmations and ordinations; in 2003 appointed rector of the seminary of Our Lady Co-Redemptrix in La Reja, Argentina; has been accused of anti-semitism and holocaust denial; by a decree signed on 21 January 2009 Pope Benedict XVI lifted the excommunications; removed as rector of the Argentine seminary.

Willis, Thomas Frederick – publisher; c. 1876 (wife, Alice Mary, received in 1883); formerly an Anglican curate; father of Ambrose Willis, publisher of *The Tablet*; see essay in J. G. F. Raupert (ed), *Roads to Rome* (1901), p.320 ("Submission of judgment in matters of faith, which is a primary necessity in, nay, a very test of, a true messenger of God, seems impossible in the Anglican Communion, because the Anglican Church does not claim infallibility. For to submit absolutely to, *i.e.* to credit with infallibility, one who declares himself fallible is surely unreasonable...

The most Catholic party in the English Church are now declaring distinctly that they ask for nothing more than toleration alongside of those who teach the exact contrary. Now, that is nothing less than a definite surrender of the proposition that 'the Church of England is the Body of Christ.' Can they who are commissioned to carry Divine truth to a world which is eternally opposed to God, and are commanded to seal their witness, if need be, with their blood – can they dare to ask for Divine truth to be *tolerated* side by side with its contradictory? Surely to do so is to deny that it is Divine truth. And if it is not Divine truth, it is not truth at all; it is blasphemy....

The principles on which the separated position of Anglicanism is defended by various adherents are all contrary to Christian doctrine as found in Scripture. *Nationalism*, which has been, all through, the theory of the High Church Tories, is plainly anti-Christian, because our Blessed Lord came to destroy all barriers of race, as far as religion was concerned, and to set up one world-wide heavenly kingdom. 'There is neither Greek nor Jew, Barbarian nor Scythian;' 'He hath redeemeth us *out of* every kindred and tongue and nation.' The very idea of a *National* religion as an excuse for schism, *i.e.* as superior and not subordinate to the oneness of the Church, is a return to the pre-Christian state of things.

Congregationalism, which is practically the Anglican system, is the same thing, only narrower. It makes every clergyman a Pope to his people, and throws to the winds the One Faith and One Body, even if it retain the One Spirit and One Lord and One Baptism...

Private Judgment in the individual as to the doctrines of faith is narrower still, and makes every one the whole Church to himself. It makes all faith impossible, except faith in oneself. And every defense of the Anglican position that can be given seems to rest ultimately upon one of these three principles...

The wording of the Thirty-nine Articles bears a most suspicious resemblance to the wording of heretical formulae in all ages by its adoption of equivocal expressions. Heretical formulae have always been designedly *inclusive*, Catholic formulae designedly *exclusive* – the object of Catholic formulae being to secure inward peace from doubt at whatever cost of outward; and the object of heretical formulae being to secure outward peace at whatever loss of spiritual peace and inward clearness of faith.

All through the Anglican system there is such a resting upon civilization, and worldly position, and respectability and public opinion, that it looks much more like a religion designed to make this world comfortable, than the religion of Him Who was born in a stable, and Whose kingdom is not of this world, and Whose maxim was, 'He that loveth his life shall lose it.'

Anglicans are separated from the main body of Christendom, and their connection with our own pre-Reformation Church is very slight and indirect. It does not appear from Scripture that Apostolic Succession *alone* constitutes a valid ministry. All the early schismatical bodies had that. The thing which is evident from Scripture is, that our Lord gave the Holy Ghost unalienably to a Society, not to individuals, and that he who separates from that Society loses the gift").

Wilson, Ian – author; b. 1941; c. 1972; brought up in South London in an anti-Catholic environment; received a nominally Anglican education, but agnostic from early age; graduated in Modern History from Magdalen College, Oxford; worked in marketing before writing a best-selling book on the Turin Shroud in 1978; his screenplay, *Silent Witness*, based on the book, won a BAFTA award; gave up his day job and concentrated on writing; converted from Anglicanism; author of many books on religious and scientific themes; lived in Bristol, England for many years before emigrating to Brisbane, Australia in 1995; see *The Turin Shroud: The Burial Cloth of Jesus Christ?* (1978); *The Bleeding mind: An Investigation into the Mysterious Phenomena of Stigmata* (1988); *Stigmata: An Investigation into the Mysterious Appearance of Christ's Wounds in Hundreds of People from Medieval Italy to Modern America* (1989); *Holy Faces, Secret Places: An Amazing Quest for the Face of Jesus* (1991); *The Blood and the Shroud: New Evidence That the World's Most Sacred Relic Is Real* (1998); *Jesus: The Evidence* (2000); *The Bible is History* (2000); *The Turin Shroud: Unshrouding the Mystery* (2000); *Murder at Golgotha: A Scientific Investigation Into the Last Days of Jesus's Life, His Death, and His Resurrection* (2007); correspondence with John Beaumont: "[My conversion] was no 'Damascus Road' – simply a very gradual and subtle process. It began when I was fourteen and first came across the Shroud image. That seriously jolted my then fierce and complacent agnosticism. Then when more than a decade later I began to research the Shroud, the Catholics who helped at that time, two of them converts themselves, impressed me deeply. They accepted my agnosticism without qualm, and never tried to push their faith on me. Then, in 1967 I married my wife Judith, a cradle Catholic, and on attending Mass with her heard for the first time the gospel in the Jerusalem Bible translation. Having received a nominally Anglican education I was used to the King James translation, in which the language, although beautiful, had never particularly 'reached' me. By contrast the Jerusalem Bible had a directness to it, as of Jesus talking across 2000 years. So in the early 1970s I began attending instruction and was received late in 1972."

Windle, Sir Bertram Coghill Alan – scientist, educationist, and apologist; b. 8 May 1858; c. 24 January 1883 (first wife, Madeline (1861–1900) was received in 1887; second wife, Edith Mary, also converted); d. 1929; son of an Anglican vicar; family moved to Ireland in 1862; had conventional Anglican education; worked at University of Birmingham leading up to posts of Dean of the Medical Faculty and Professor of Anatomy; conversion influenced by Newman's *Apologia Pro Vita Sua* and *Catholic Controversy* by Henry Ryder (see above); President of Queen's College, Cork (used his scholarship and administrative drive to transform the university); Senator of Royal University of Ireland and a Commissioner of Intermediate Education; steadfast friend of British connection with Ireland (supporter of Gaelic League, but no sympathy with wider aims of Sinn Fein); spent last ten years of his life writing, lecturing and traveling widely through United States and Canada, based at University of Toronto; President of the Canadian Catholic Truth Society; contributing editor of *Commonweal*, founded in 1924;

very learned in both humanities and science (twenty-one books in all); see "Some Debts Which Science Owes to Catholics," *The Month*, May 1908, p.449; "The Intellectual Claims of the Catholic Church," *Catholic World*, November 1909, p.234; *The Church and Science* (1924); "Scott and the Oxford Movement," *Commonweal*, 3 December 1924, p.101 ("The lovely things still remaining after the violence of Henry VIII, Cromwell, and other crowned and uncrowned ruffians cannot but turn the hearts of those who admire them to think kindly of those who constructed them"); *Who's Who of the Oxford Movement* (1926); *The Catholic Church and Its Relations with Science* (1927); essay in J. G. F. Raupert (ed), *Roads to Rome* (1901), p.326 (reprint of an article in the *Weekly Register* of 9 March 1900, entitled "Books that have influenced me"); Sr. Monica Taylor, *Sir Bertram Windle: A Memoir* (1932); E. J. McCorkell, "Bertram Coghill Alan Windle," CCHA, *Report*, 25 (1958), p.53; Patrick Allitt, *Catholic Converts: British and American Intellectuals Turn to Rome* (1997), *passim* ("Windle emphasized ... that the Church had made no dogmatic statement on the question of origins and that, contrary to popular prejudice, there were very few points where religion and science came into conflict. The Church, far from being the enemy of science, had been almost its only advocate throughout the medieval and early modern ages.... The Church had always pointed out that the province of science was limited, that only things susceptible to measurement could be included in it. Windle showed a little epistemological subtlety. He pointed out that scientists no less than Christians have to make an act of faith, first, that the material world really exists and, second, that it acts according to known or at least knowable and predictable laws. Not only an act of faith but also an act of abstraction, because in describing, categorizing, and measuring phenomena scientists are selecting and transforming their original qualities rather than duplicating them. The scientific account of a tree, for example, is a very different thing from the tree itself").

Windsor, Edward, Lord Downpatrick (Edward Edmund Maximilian George Louis Windsor) – member of the extended British Royal Family; b. 2 December 1988, London; only son of George Windsor, Earl of St. Andrews (who is the elder son of the Duke and Duchess of Kent) and his wife, Sylvana Windsor, the Countess of St. Andrews (also a Catholic); c. 2003 (permanently forfeiting his right of succession to the British throne; his grandmother, the Duchess of Kent (see above under Katharine, Duchess of Kent) received in 1994; his uncle, Lord Nicholas Windsor (see below) received in 2001); educated at Eton and Keble College, Oxford.

Windsor, Lord Nicholas (Nicholas Charles Edward Jonathan Windsor) – member of the extended British Royal Family; b. 25 July 1970, London; c. 2001 (permanently forfeiting his right of succession to the British throne; his mother was received in 1994); youngest child of Duke and Duchess of Kent (see above under Katharine, Duchess of Kent); great grandson of George V; married Paola Doimi di Delupis de Frankopan in 2006 in Church of Santo Stefano degli Abissini in the Vatican (first time a member of the extended British Royal Family has married in the Vatican since at least the Reformation).

Wingham, Thomas – musical teacher and composer; b. 5 January 1846, London; c. 1877; d. 24 March 1893, London; Professor of piano at Royal Academy of Music, London; choirmaster of the London Oratory; among his compositions were four symphonies, six overtures, several instrumental works in smaller form, two masses, and a "Te Deum"; see *Catholic Encyclopedia.*

Wolfe, William (alias Lacey) – priest and controversialist; b. 1584, Scarborough; d. 17 July 1673, Dolphin Hall, Oxford; poor family; sent to Oxford University by a Catholic uncle by whom he had been educated; reconciled to the Catholic Church at Oxford; joined the Society of Jesus at St. Omer in 1607/8; entered English College, Rome in 1608; ordained priest at Louvain in 1617; taught at St. Omer 1618–1622; worked on the English mission from 1623 until his death; worked in the Lancashire district and the Oxfordshire district, then in Worcestershire and Warwickshire; buried in the parish church of Somerton, Oxfordshire; see *Gillow*, Vol. IV, p.88; *DNB.*

Wolseley, Sir Charles, seventh Baronet – politician; b. 20 July 1769, Wolseley Hall, Staffordshire; c. October 1837; d. 3 October 1846, Wolseley Hall, Staffordshire; educated privately, went in late teens on a grand tour of the Continent, during which he made contact with the revolutionary forces and was present at the fall of the Bastille; one of original members of Union for Parliamentary Reform (1812); one of founders of Hampden Club; when the reform movement was becoming formidable, he identified himself with more extreme section of radicals; assisted victims of Peterloo massacre; sentenced to eighteen months' imprisonment himself for sedition and conspiracy; withdrew from forefront of political agitation, and from about 1826 took no public part in politics; in 1837 he presided at an anti-popery meeting, but was induced by Ambrose Phillipps de Lisle (see above) to return to his home with him, where, after much discussion, he was received into the Church; his conversion caused some astonishment; see *Gillow*, Vol. V, p.590; *DNB*.

Wood, Barbara – writer; c. 1968 (mother received earlier and father in 1971); daughter of E. F. Schumacher (see above); felt a strong attraction to the Catholic Church since her schooldays; see *Alias Papa: A Life of Fritz Schumacher* (1984); Joseph Pearce, *Literary Converts* (1999), pp. 372–373 ("For me, the encyclical [*Humanae Vitae*] was proof that I could trust the Church, that it wouldn't drift with the whims of society. It wouldn't be a slave to fashion").

Woodcock, Blessed John (alias Farington, Thompson) (name in religion Martin of St. Felix) – priest and martyr; b. 1603, Leyland, Lancashire; c. about 1622; d. 7 August 1646, Lancaster; middle class parents (mother a Catholic); brought up in the Church of England; studied at St. Omer in 1628, then at the English College, Rome, but did not complete his studies; instead he joined the Capuchins in Paris in 1630, but soon after transferred to the English Franciscans at Douai; received the habit from Bl. Henry Heath (see above) in 1631; ordained priest in 1634; worked in Flanders and then on the English mission from 1643; landed at Newcastle-on-Tyne, but soon worked in Lancashire; about to celebrate mass at the house of Mr. Burgess of Woodend, Clayton-le-Woods, when the house was raided by pursuivants; escaped but captured the following morning at nearby Bamber Bridge; imprisoned 1644–1646 in Lancaster Castle; condemned on his own confession for being a priest, together with two secular priests, Edward Bamber and Thomas Whittaker; hanged, drawn and quartered at Lancaster Castle (when

he was flung off the ladder the rope broke. Having been hanged a second time, he was cut down and disemboweled alive); the Poor Clare nuns at Arundel Sussex possess a relic of his arm bone; another relic (a piece of cloth) is treasured at Ladywell Shrine, near Preston, Lancashire, along with the altar and vestments that, by tradition, he used at Mr. Burgess's house; see *Catholic Encyclopedia*; *DNB*.

Woodhead, Abraham – controversialist; b. about 1609, Meltham, Yorkshire; c. about 1652; d. 4 May 1678, Hoxton, near London; student and then Fellow of University College, Oxford; took Anglican orders; from start of Civil War traveled abroad and began to have doubts about his Anglican faith; conversion influenced by reading the lives of the saints and writings of controversialists like Jewell and Harding; great interest in the life and work of St. Philip Neri; lifelong friendship with Obadiah Walker (see above); lost his fellowship; after conversion spent thirty years or so at Hoxton, near London, in a religious community of scholars, a sort of little oratory, devoting themselves to prayer and writing and inspired by the writings of St. Philip Neri; he wrote and translated many works of controversy and spirituality; King's Commissioners reinstated him in his fellowship in 1660; returned to Hoxton on finding residence in college inconsistent with his religious principles and being accused of "popery"; gentle and loving character; buried in St. Pancras's churchyard under a plain stone inscribed in Latin (English translation): "I have chosen to be an abject in the house of my God and I abode in the wilderness, not seeking that which is profitable to me but to many"; see *An Historical Narration of the Life and Death of Our Lord Jesus Christ* (1685); *Motives to Holy Living* (1688); *Catholic Theses on*

Several Chief Heads of Controversy (1689); *Ancient Church Government*, 5 Vols. (four published between 1662 and 1736); Anne Barbeau Gardiner, "Abraham Woodhead, 'The Invisible Man,'" *Recusant History*, October 2003, p.570; *Gillow*, Vol. V, p.591; *DNB*.

Woodruff, (John) Douglas – journalist, editor, and wit; b. 8 May 1897, Wimbledon; c. 1910; d. 9 March 1978, Marcham Priory, near Abingdon, Berkshire; parents of staunchly Protestant stock, but mother became a Catholic five years after her marriage; conversion influenced by writings of Mgr. Robert Hugh Benson (see above), e.g., *Come Rack, Come Rope* (1912); later influences were Chesterton (see above) and Belloc; joined foreign service; late to New College, Oxford where fine scholar and President of the Union; colonial editor *The Times* 1926–1936; editor *The Tablet* 1936–1967, which he developed greatly (regretting its liberal turn afterwards); involved in Catholic publishing; writer on Catholic and historical issues; husband of Marie Immaculée Antoinette (Mia) Acton (1905–1994), eldest daughter of Richard Maximilian, second Baron Acton, of the foreign service; see *Charlemagne* (1934); *European Civilisation: The Grand Tour* (1935); *Mirabeau* (1936); *Talking At Random* (1941); *More Talking At Random* (1944); *Still Talking At Random* (1948); "The Uncommitted Mind," in Elizabeth Pakenham (ed), *Catholic Approaches* (1955), p.35 ("[I]t remains curiously noteworthy that perhaps the biggest dissuasion keeping men from the Church is the low view they have formed of the characters which history reveals to them as having professed the Catholic Faith. This may be a natural reaction, but it is quite illogical, as though a man should deny himself something of great value because he had seen other people foolishly undervaluing

it. The scandals of the Church are on the surface, the actions of men in power; and power acts by a kind of Gresham's Law, the bad driving out the good. Political scandals become the subject matter of historians, just as the peccadilloes of humbler men become the subject of official and legal inquiry, and enter historical and legal record, where the vast company of private people who have lived in and through their religion finds, from the nature of the case, neither historians nor judges. And yet it is this great silent army that is the witness to what the Catholic religion has meant to so many millions of men and women, as the light by which they have lived, in all sorts of times and places and conditions: a religion out of the Roman Palestine of the first century which is everywhere so strangely and fully adequate and everywhere so completely at home, because it is not the work of men of any one time and place but has come into human history from outside"); Joseph Pearce, *Literary Converts* (1999) *passim*; *DNB*.

Wootten, Frances – matron; c. 1850 ; d. 9 January 1876; wife of Dr. John Wootten (1799–1847), a popular Oxford doctor; she and her husband were Tractarians and friends of the Puseys and of Newman; her husband's death left her childless but wealthy; after her conversion she came to live in Birmingham in the Oratory parish; great benefactress, giving a gift to the Oratory of £10,000; was the first and very successful matron (or Chief Dame) of the Oratory School from 1859 until her death; "She is more like a Saint than most people you come across" (Newman); buried at Rednal ("Fortis et Sapiens" is the epitaph, given by Newman, on her grave stone); see Dora Nash, "Frances Wootten," in Joanna Bogle (ed), *English Catholic Heroines* (2009), p.230 ("Wherein lies her heroism? Certainly she did not in any sense die for her faith, or convert the heathen as a missionary, or sacrifice herself to a life of enclosure as a holy nun. She will never be canonized. But I think she deserves inclusion amongst a roll-call of English Catholic heroines because she exemplifies a number of qualities which ordinary women can recognize and appreciate and which are taken for granted, or even scoffed at, by the world. Firstly, she is the archetypal 'helpmeet,' an idea which comes from that seminal text in Genesis 2, but is not only to be found in the married relationship. The complementarity of the sexes can work in other situations too, and here she was in effect a colleague of England's foremost Catholic educator, carrying out his principles and plainly understanding very well why he held them. How many priests have relied on the chaste friendship, loyal support and womanly wisdom of a female ally who is content to be in their shadow? Such women could adopt a worse 'patron saint' than Frances Wootten.

She could also be seen as a model for Catholic women who have no children of their own. Quite late in life ... she was called to take on a heavy responsibility, which involved mothering young and teenage boys not her own: her original brief had been to be 'Guardian of the children.' This was a remarkable 'second career' for a Victorian widow").

Wormald, (Thomas) Brian Harvey Goodwin – historian; b. 24 July 1912; c. 1955; d. 22 March 2005; brought up as an Anglican; educated at Harrow and Peterhouse College, Cambridge (firsts in both parts of the Historical tripos); took Anglican orders in 1943; adopted Tractarian socialism of Figgis and Tawney; specialized in 16th and 17th century English history; co-founder of Strafford Club in 1939; presided over Peterhouse, Cambridge History school for 25 years (Fellow of college for 66 years); influenced by Herbert Butterfield, the historian; made religion centre of his intellectual life; an eccentrically conservative figure; his son, Patrick (1947–2004) was a distinguished historian of Anglo-Saxon England; see obituary, *The Times*, 6 May 2005 ("In the 1950s he was alienated from Anglican compromise and backsliding and came to admire Pope Pius XII's definition of the Assumption of the Virgin Mary as an assertion of the authority which he missed in the Church of England. He renounced his orders to become a Roman Catholic layman and, despite uneasiness occasioned by Pope John XXIII, remained such for the rest of his life"); obituary, *The Independent*, 8 April 2005 ("His wardrobe ran to silver-buckled shoes and a monocle, and his loathing of pedantry, teetotalism and the creeping spread of lower-middle-class values could be expressed in the most forthright of Anglo-Saxon terms").

Worth, Henry George – c. 1895; formerly Anglican curate; member of the Pontifical Commission of 1904 for the Vatican Edition of the Gregorian Liturgical Books; see essay in J. G. F. Raupert (ed), *Roads to Rome* (1901), p.329 ("Some people seem to think that schism is an unimportant matter; such should study St. Augustine's writings against the Donatists. He shows that they might have Sacraments and the true doctrine, but being cut off from the Catholic Church by schism they could not have salvation.... 'Outside the Catholic Church you can have everything except salvation; you can have honor, the sacrament, you may sing Alleluia, and answer Amen; you may hold and preach the faith in the name of the Father, the Son, and the Holy Ghost; but nowhere except in the Catholic Church can you find salvation' (St. Aug. *Sermo ad Coes. Eccl.*

Plebem, vi.). If we consider this we see at once how absurd is the commonly received idea among Anglicans that it is wrong to attend Roman Catholic services in England, but right when we are abroad, because if the Roman Catholic Church is in schism in England, she is guilty of it everywhere, and it would therefore be a sin to communicate with her *anywhere*").

Wyatt, Harold E. – c. 5 August 1954 (received with his wife, also a Salvationist); when growing up, tried Church of England, atheism, and Quakerism; member of Salvation Army for twenty-seven years; later openness to other forms of Protestantism; finally converted to the Catholic Church; see *From the Salvation Army to the Catholic Church* (1960) ("Instead of the Epistles and Gospels of the first century being followed by a complete blank until the sixteenth century, classed roughly by Protestants as 'the Dark Ages', I found that God had His saints right through the whole Christian era, and also in every civilized country. I was surprised that there had been so many people in the world of such greatness of character, saintliness and profound humility, compared with whom most of our Protestant reformers were but well-meaning humanitarians and that those saints were fairly evenly spread throughout the whole Christian era.... It was not until I read of a Jewish conversion to the Catholic Faith that I realized that Christianity is the extension and completion of the Mosaic law of the Jews, and that Our Lord had ordained outward ceremonies and Sacraments in His Church").

Wycherley, William – dramatist; b. 1641, Wycherley Hall, Clive, near Shrewsbury, Shropshire; c. about 1658, but abjured the faith in about 1660; reverted to the Catholic faith later in life; d. 1 January 1716, Mrs. Armstrong's lodging house, Bow Street, London; father a royalist supporter of Charles I; well educated at home by his father, then sent to France to complete his education and there became a Catholic; then at Oxford where Thomas Barlow, provost of Queen's College, a hard-line Calvinist, persuaded him back to Protestantism; traveled much in Spain; several successful comic dramas and much progress at court; George Villiers, second Duke of Buckingham his patron; became a Jacobite with deep-rooted Catholic sympathies; friend of Charles II; unhappy marriage to the countess of Drogheda (d. 1685); led a dissolute life; imprisoned in the Fleet prison for debt; in later life friendship with the young Alexander Pope (1688–1744), the poet; ill and under pressure to repay debts he made a final marriage for money; buried in vault of St. Paul's Church, Covent Garden; the stereotype of "the wicked, attractive, brilliant Restoration wit, rake, and gallant" (*DNB*); see *Gillow*, Vol. V, p.598; *DNB* ("He seems always to have had Catholic sympathies and some years before had told Pope he was a Catholic; it was in this faith that he died. Wycherley's nurse testified that he had received the sacrament some time before his [final] marriage 'according to the Church of Rome as a Dying Man'").

Yeo, Margaret Routledge – writer; b. 1877, Canterbury, Kent; c. 1906; d. 13 May 1941, Uxbridge, near London; grand-daughter of an Anglican bishop; some say brought up as an Anglican, but Mgr. Ronald Knox says she boasted she was a converted pagan; husband a chronic invalid; novelist and short story writer, but true métier was biography; also many articles on the English martyrs; oblate of Prinknash Abbey; recovered from cancer of the throat; see *St. Francis Xavier* (1931), *Don John of*

Austria (1934), *The Greatest of the Borgias* (1936), *A Prince of Pastors: St. Charles Borromeo* (1938), *These Three Hearts* (1940); Anon, "Margaret Yeo (1877–1941)," *Catholic Life*, July 2002, p.7 ("After completing a motor tour through Italy in 1939, which took her to out of the way places 'where nothing has changed for many thousand years,' she wrote, 'it seemed that only two things last in this world, the Catholic Church and cultivating the earth. Perhaps the drift away from these two is the major cause for the decadence of our materialistic mechanistic civilization'"); Walter Romig, *Book of Catholic Authors*, First Series (1942).

Young, Francis, SJ – priest; b. 1570, Claines, near Worcester; d. 30 March 1633; studied at Eton and Trinity College, Oxford; owed his conversion to Bl. Edward Oldcorne, the martyr; entered English College, Rome, in 1598; ordained priest in 1599; entered the Society of Jesus at Louvain in 1600; spent some years on the English mission until imprisoned, first in the Clink and then in the Gatehouse prison, and banished in 1618; returned to England and served the Lincolnshire missions, and then in Suffolk and Worcestershire until his death; see *Gillow*, Vol. V, p.599.

Zaehner, Robert Charles (Andrew) (nicknames, "The Prof", "Robin", "Doc") – philosopher, orientalist, and intelligence officer; b. 8 April 1913, Oak Hill Lodge, Sevenoaks, Kent; c. 1946; d. 24 November 1974, Oxford; both parents Swiss; at school religion became for him "an incoherent farce"; first in Oriental Languages at Oxford University; worked for SOE in World War II and for MI6 afterwards; Spalding Professor of Eastern Religions and Ethics at All Souls College, Oxford in 1952; reader in Philosophy of Mathematics; erudite eccentric; admirer of Pope John XXIII; Gifford Lecturer 1967–1969; unmarried; buried in Wolvercote cemetery, Oxford; see "The Religious Instinct," in Alan Pryce-Jones (ed), *An Outline of Modern Knowledge* (1956), p.64; *The Catholic Church and World Religions* (1964); *Christianity and Other Religions* (1964); *Concordant Discord: The Interdependence of Faith* (1970) ("It cannot be sufficiently emphasized that Christianity is the religion of the Word made flesh. The Word's name is not only Jesus but Emmanuel, 'God with us,' not only in Palestine nearly two thousand years ago but here and now in the sacrament of the Eucharist. This is the essential difference between Christians and Muslims. For the Christians God becomes flesh and blood, and he leaves as a token of his abiding presence with us the sacrament not of his soul or of his godhead but of his flesh and blood: for the Muslims the Word is made Book, *Biblos*, Bible…

…Grace, for the Catholic, is really received not through sermons, however learned, however inspired, but through the sacraments which operate in silence"); *Drugs, Mysticism and Make-Believe* (1974); *Which God is Dead?* (1974); *The City Within the Heart* (1980) (published posthumously); Michael Dummett, "Eccentric extraordinary," *The Tablet*, 14 December 1974, p.1213 ("Zaehner's contention was that the various religions were so unalike in their objectives and their interpretations of the world that it was hard to see what justified our using the same word 'religion' of them all"); Maurice Cowling, *Religion and Public Doctrine in England Vol. III: Accommodations* (2002), pp.354–370; *DNB* ("Zaehner called the [function of bringing the great religious systems together in closer understanding, harmony and friendship] 'damnable', because such harmony would be only 'apparent, verbal and fictitious'…

In his last years he turned against Teilhard [de Chardin], calling his work
'pseudo-science, pseudo-theology and
pseudo-philosophy.' Instead, Zaehner
turned to Aristotle, admiring his rationalism, courage, and industry. Aristotle,
he declared, was 'the father of our rational civilization and stepfather of the
Catholic Church', and it was his God
who was that of the Christians and the
Hindus").

Appendix One

Introduction to John Beaumont, *Converts to Rome: A Guide to Notable Converts from Britain and Ireland during the Twentieth Century* (2005)

The purpose of the book is to revive a most praiseworthy enterprise which came to an end shortly before World War I. By then Mr. William Gordon Gorman (died 1932) had come out with four successive editions of his *Converts to Rome*, of which the first saw print in 1884 as a slender volume of 80 pages in double columns. According to its subtitle, it was "a list of over three thousand Protestants who have become Roman Catholics since the commencement of the nineteenth century." The next year Mr. Gorman published an enlarged edition which contained the names of more than four thousand converts, most of them, as in the former editions, coming from the British Isles.

To compile such a list was an avocation of not only Mr. Gorman but also of some others, because on the title page of the first edition he identified himself as the "editor of the last two editions of 'Rome's Recruit's.'" Gorman's list included only such who belonged to professional circles, such as physicians, writers, professors, members of the clergy as well as of aristocratic families. The fourth enlarged edition of *Converts to Rome* from 1910 ran to 89 pages in double columns. Mr. Gorman, himself a convert, could write with no small satisfaction that practically all leading English families had a Catholic convert within their ranks.

Unfortunately, by the time the centenary of the conversion of England's foremost convert, John Henry Newman, was celebrated, a visitor, himself a convert, from Australia, found little interest among English Catholics in converts. By then the once very active Converts Aid Society was hardly functioning. In fact in the most important festive commemorations of that centenary, only in the one delivered by Ronald A. Knox was reference made to the fact that in Newman's life and thought conversion occupied a central position and that his conversion catalyzed, so to speak, the rush of converts to Rome. Such and similar details were set forth in an unwittingly very original modern book on Newman, which appeared under the title *Newman to Converts: An Existential Ecclesiology* (2001). Its author, the present writer, unfolded in that book of well over 500 pages the message contained in about two hundred letters Newman wrote to prospective converts over a period of forty years, letters which previously had not been found noteworthy by leading Newmanists.

If one is to summarize Newman's message in those letters, it may be compressed into a single phrase which he included in six out of the eighteen letters he had written during the two days of his reception into the Catholic Church. In that phrase he stated that he was about to join the "One True Fold." Implied in that phrase was the message that joining the Catholic Church as that very Fold was not a luxury or a choice, but a duty, the supreme duty available for man on this earth. Such a message does not resonate well in our new-fangled ecumenical or often "ecumaniacal" atmosphere, which cannot be dissipated by arguments, however cogent. Against that atmosphere only that argument is effective which is personal witness, the witness of converting. It takes time and again special courage as well as resolve to face various forms of backlash. Not that a convert in today's England would face the same kind of social ostracism which was often the fate of those who, say, in Newman's time, "seceded" to Rome, to recall a designation then quite common in "good" society, as if one's civic loyalty was above suspicion only as long as one gave a wide birth to the Catholic Church.

Apart from social considerations the act of converting remains a daunting step for a reason which is tied only to the Catholic Church. The Catholic Church alone proposes its message as one to which an assent is to be given that is full and irrevocable, because it is an assent to a divine truth, though presented through human channels. All other Churches offer their wares as subject to one's private judgment. This was the point in which Newman found a compelling reason to speak of Protestantism and Catholicism as being two different religions. An evidence of this is the difference between the moral teaching of the Catholic Church and that of all other churches.

Moral precepts cut into human flesh far more sharply than do more or less abstract dogmas. Coming as they do today into the Church from a world which is awash in total permissiveness, converts feel doubly the burden which they take upon themselves by their step. In doing so they take comfort from Christ's assertion that his yoke is easy and his burden is light. This is so, because his yoke and burden are connected with an assurance which cannot fail, an assurance guaranteed also by the Church's infallibility, the only Church which claims such a privilege in its official teaching in faith and morals. Outside that Church shadows and images rule instead of truth. So did Newman sum up his own story in the phrase, "ex umbris et imaginibus in veritatem," he ordered to be put on his tombstone.

A perfect echo to that phrase was provided by Chesterton when he recalled that it was his wife who led him from the dreary land of Unitarianism into the Church of England. He then tried out "all the best kinds of Anglicanism," only to "find them to be pale imitations" (M. Ffinch, *G. K. Chesterton: A Biography* (1986), p.201. Tolkien achieved the almost impossible of going one better on Chesterton when he defined Anglicanism as "a pathetic and shadowy medley of half-remembered traditions and mutilated beliefs" (J. Pearce, *Tolkien: Man and Myth, A Literary Life* (1998), p.35). The Church of England, with its liturgical paraphernalia and the splendor of expropriated medieval cathedrals is, of course, even less than pale imitation and vague medley. That Church is the most deceptive fake of the original, a judgment which should not look unjust to anyone who in these very years witnessed that Church's warm welcome of the worst kind of moral and sacramental deviations, such as abortion, homosexuality, cloning, and women's ordination, including the latter's prospective elevation to the rank of bishop. Surely Newman was right when he labeled that Church as "a mere imposture" (for this and similar epithets used by Newman see my book *The Church of England as Seen by Newman* (2004), p.7).

Yet, instead of a mass exodus from the Church of England one witnesses only the most courageous in its ranks moving towards the One True Fold. Catholics, whom post-Vatican II theology taught to forget about original sin, would alone be surprised on seeing this surprisingly weak stream of converts. But if prospective converts find that Catholics, including some of their "leading" theologians, hold that other churches are partial realizations of the One True Fold, they would hardly feel encouraged to make the move. If the magnet is made intentionally weak, pieces of iron will not feel attracted to it as powerfully as they would be otherwise.

The list of converts presented here is largely limited to those who lived during the twentieth century and was compiled by one who has read almost everything that converts in Britain wrote about the reasons why one should join the Roman Catholic Church. The list is preliminary. Any one who knows of converts who belong to professional circles are urged to communicate to him their data (john.beaumont7@virgin.net). That he limited his list to such circles should not mean that conversions from the common ranks would be of less value. But living in an age in which publicity counts too much, plain laborers, ordinary housewives, college students and bus driver converts had to be left out, though often their cases count more in God's eyes than cases noteworthy to mere human eyes. At any rate, only those coming from professional circles provide plain refutation to the age-old fallacy that one must trample one's own intellect in order to become a Catholic.

May this guide serve as an antidote to the theological vagueness that has become a mark of discourse in recent decades with a heavy reliance on studiedly inaccurate figures about Catholics who prefer the new to the old. About those who converted one can certainly say that in view of the gravity of their step they are not so much to be numbered as to be weighed. Still their numbers exemplify those brave people who, as they escaped through the Berlin Wall, voted with their feet. Converts escape from the tyranny of private judgment in matters of religion, although more and more cradle-born Catholics are imbued with the notion that their private judgment is above the official teaching of the Church.

The act of conversion witnesses not to C. S. Lewis' claim, namely, that conversion is the choice of a new suite within a large building that houses all Christian Churches, but the acceptance of the tenet that only One Church speaks in the name of Christ. The one who took that "mere" apologist of a "mere Christianity" to task most firmly for that "mere" if not pseudo-ecclesiology was none other than a convert who held in religious awe his own heroic mother, who converted when he was merely eleven and then soon died of exhaustion as she had to work eighteen hours a day as a seamstress to provide education for her two sons. Mrs. Tolkien was not a professional, but professed her faith heroically after her relatives denied her all assistance simply because she had become a Catholic. So much about the pain felt over not including non-professionals in this list.

Mrs. Tolkien remains one of the *saintly* converts who would forever be known only to God and to a handful down here. As to her older son, he is not celebrated for his youthful conversion, not even for his remaining a staunch Catholic for the rest of his life, but for his literary achievement. Half a century after his death J. R. R. Tolkien stays at the top of the list of preferred authors, taken by opinion polls sponsored by most reputable editorial houses. Would that Catholics, for whom this booklet is primarily prepared, take courage in an age when so many in the Church's leadership, to say nothing of its numerous self-appointed "leaders," seem to be plagued by that most pernicious disease which is the failure of nerve. Let them note that converts still vote, if not with their feet, at least by their decision on behalf of eternal truths. These truths are not a matter of interpretations and reinterpretations, let alone a matter of the whims, fads, and fancies of ever gullible times, but a matter of truths guaranteed by Almighty God who cared so much for such truths as to have His own Son die on the cross in order to communicate them to us, failing men and women.

November 2005   Stanley L. Jaki

Appendix Two

Introduction to John Beaumont, *Converts from Britain and Ireland in the Nineteenth Century* (2007)

"The great conversions of the XIX century were not convictions of individual, but of social sin." So wrote Bernard Shaw in reference to the theme of Dickens' *Hard Times*, as if Mr. Gradgrind's sin, a ruthless climbing on the social ladder, had not been his own sin, apart from being the sin of others as well. Moreover, if the sin of others could be spoken of as the sin of a general entity, such as society, one's own sins could be glossed over even more readily as a matter that did not call for conversion, which includes plain repentance. Also, as a great master of style, Bernard Shaw could readily assume that he would never be taken to task by most of his readers as by his time it was not in style to speak of personal sin. Further, there is no evidence in Bernard Shaw's voluminous writings that he would have had remorse about anything he had said, written, or done.

A great contrast with the saints or even with those whom society at large viewed as saints when they died. An outstanding example of this can be found in the encomiums which came from non-Catholic and even secularist England when John Henry Newman, possibly the foremost convert of the nineteenth century, died in 1890, when Bernard Shaw was thirty-four and well on his way to literary fame. It is difficult to assume that Bernard Shaw's information about Newman did not include details about Newman's conversion on 7–8 October 1845. It hardly ever happens that one's conversion is marked with two days, but in Newman's case such was the case. The reason for this was the length of his confession, which is an integral part of the formal act of converting to the Catholic Church.

Newman began his confession at 11pm, shortly after he entered the room where the Passionist Father, Dominic Barberi (among the Blessed since 1963), had just sat down by the fire to dry his garments, soaked as he was to his skin by a rain that poured down as he walked for an hour from the stage coach station in Oxford to Littlemore. After a word of greeting, Newman, the pride of Oxford, fell on his knees before the missionary priest of peasant stock and an Italian to boot, and started reciting his sins. It was well after midnight that he stopped, though only to continue next morning.

A saintly man and among the Venerables since 1998, proved by that long confession that the more one had advanced in spiritual life, the more sins of which one was conscious. At any rate, the list of sins had to be long because it had to cover several decades. Newman gave only a glimpse of that list in the *Apologia*, where he spoke of some sins of his youth he was particularly ashamed of. As one who had been in the thick of debates, with spoken and printed words, on behalf of the Church of England for twenty or so years, he had to be all too aware of the temptations of vainglory, anger, and resentment that accompany such an activism.

Newman was not only of a logical mind, but logical or consistent to the point of being acutely sensitive to his own faults, which cannot be said of Bernard Shaw.

Newman was too good a logician not to know that the capitalist society as such could not sin. The bankruptcy of his father's banking business was not a societal sin, whatever miscalculations the elder Newman could have made as a banker. The elder Newman failed as a banker simply because he miscalculated in a business, steeped then as now in taking financial risks.

An industrialist society could not sin either, but its captains of industry surely could as they had little compunction about child labor. Nor could a parliamentary society as such sin, except its parliamentarians and those who through party zeal chose intellectual and moral misfits to serve as their representatives. Much greater was, of course, the sin of individual journalists, editors, and teachers, to say nothing of demagogues. Were not individuals alone the sinners, there would have been no justification to track down the last Nazi, although this logic was not heeded when it was the turn to indict Stalinists, Maoists, and other practitioners of genocide.

Just as sins are the acts of individuals, so are conversions. Those who prefer to ignore this, personify masses without being outraged over the injustice done to individuals by mass movements, or by ideologies about masses. Contrary to Ortega y Gasset, the revolt of the masses was the revolt of those who manipulated them. Precisely because the Catholic Church has always aimed at individuals, did she become the greatest uninterrupted mass movement of human history. This unrelenting focusing on individuals came, of course, from the Church's conviction that individuals alone, not masses, have a chance for an eternal life as their God-given destiny. Long before it became a fad to speak of mass movements Thomas Aquinas, and before him Saint Augustine, laid it down that nations would receive their rewards or punishment on this earth, a point which is indirectly acknowledged by gurus of political science.

To say this would have taken courage even in Newman's time, and surely takes heroism today when those gurus, pampered within the Ivy Towers of academia, know only of destinies on earth, and all too often only of short-term advantages. Thomas Aquinas was a member of the nascent Order of Friars Preachers who went to heroic lengths to carry the good news to individuals convinced as they were that for each individual there is in store the fearsome alternative, the one between eternal salvation or eternal damnation. The view of that alternative is the triggering force in each true conversion, notable or not. As Newman himself agonized during the winter of 1844–45 whether to convert or not, he was particularly beset with the specter of that alternative. The proof of this are letters he wrote at that time to his sister Jemima (Mrs. John Mozley). There he spoke of the possibility that eternal damnation might be his lot were he not to convert and hide thereby in his bosom the fact that there were compelling reasons for joining the Church of Rome, the One True Fold of salvation.

It is significant that Newman was received into the Catholic Church by a priest, who by then traveled up and down in England, and spoke to the English only of the cross of Christ. In doing so he followed in the footsteps of the Founder of Passionists, Saint Paul of the Cross, who in turn merely took a leaf from the missionary libretto of Paul of Tarsus. The music coming from such a libretto was not of this earth. To be receptive to it presupposed the work of grace in the soul. Some Englishmen, who came into contact with Dominic Barberi in Rome before he arrived finally in England in 1840, converted, some did not. After he came to England, it was simply by mere accident, to use the secularist term for Providence, that he met Newman for a second time, the time of Newman's conversion. Dominic Barberi did not proselytize. He preached to anyone who came in his way and the spiritual harvest he reaped was enormous.

Dominic Barberi never told Father George Spencer to become a Passionist. By the time the two first met, Father Spencer had made a stir as a Church of England clergyman, by devoting much of his time to the poor and the sick. As the youngest son of the second Earl Spencer, the First Lord of the Admiralty, and the brother of a Chancellor of the Exchequer, and the cousin of one who became Prime Minister, George Spencer was surely a member of the Establishment. Add to all this that Diana Spencer, or Princess Diana, had him as an ancestral relative.

George Spencer was supposed to live according to "high" standards that were at his disposal through his connections and the emoluments that were his through the resources of the Established Church. He was not disinherited when he became a Catholic priest in 1832, and used much of his income to build Catholic Churches, mostly in the Midlands. But no monetary mercy was shown to him when he became a Passionist, shortly after he had met Dominic Barberi in 1846. It was the conversion of a convert as the joining of a religious order had from the times of Saint Benedict been considered a conversion, a reform of one's mores.

Fr. Ignatius of Saint Paul, for this became George Spencer's name after he had joined the Passionists, died in 1864. His cause for beatification was formally introduced in 1992. His body lies buried in the Church of St Anne's (Sutton, Lancashire), next to Dominic Barberi's body which was found incorrupt when his casket was opened in 1886, thirty-seven years after his death. Next to them lies the body of Elizabeth Prout (1820–1864), a convert from Shrewsbury and the founder of a new branch of Passionist nuns, where she was known as Mother Mary Joseph of Jesus. Efforts on behalf of her beatification have been pursued for some time.

The literary production of those three was not small, but with their writings all three aimed at the heart of God's simple flock. Not that they were no good intellects. Father Dominic started his religious career as a lay brother. Nor did his superiors think him fit to the priesthood until they found him to possess an extraordinary memory. Eventually he was charged with the theological and philosophical instruction of his younger confreres. Some of them smiled at him behind his back for it was known that he had strange premonitions about becoming a missionary in England. Once in England, he did not write learned volumes as did Newman, but simply preached the cross of Christ to the poor and the rich. But he produced a priceless phrase which in its conciseness speaks volumes: "Men, O Englishmen, hear the voice of Littlemore. Those walls bear testimony that the Catholic Church is a *little more* than the Protestant Church, the soul a *little more* than the body, eternity a *little more* than the present time. Understand well this *little more*, and I am sure you will do a *little more* for your eternal salvation."

Newman did not know yet of Fr. Dominic, nor of the Passionists for that matter, when he jotted down the lines in a challenge to Rome, lines that eventually became his confutation: "If they want to convert England, let them go barefooted into our manufacturing towns; ... let them be pelted and trampled on, and I will own that they can do what we cannot. I will confess that they are our betters, far." In the case of Dominic Barberi this became true to the letter. He was pelted by Englishman unmindful of their reputation for fair play.

There is no place here to speak of Ignatius Spencer's heroic missionary work, nor of the humble achievements of Elizabeth Prout. They were just two of thousands of converts who thronged to within the narrow confines of small Catholic chapels before Newman and his associates added intellectual lustre to the Second Spring. This book is a roster of such converts who excelled in formulating in striking ways the reasons that prompted them to join the One True Fold.

Those reasons, varied as they are, have a role to play. But the Gospel will forever remain the message of the scandal of the cross, which is a scandal to the Jew and a laughing stock to the Greek, as Saint Paul reminded the first Christians in Corinth, the third most important city in the Roman Empire: "Consider your situation. Not many of you are wise, as men account wisdom; not many are influential, and surely not many are well-born. God . . . chose the world's lowborn and despised, those who count for nothing, to reduce to nothing those who were something" (1 Cor 1:26–28).

Let these words be a profitable guide for reading this most meritorious book, which comprises the testimonies of converts who excelled as intellectuals. The typical educated Catholic, whether in England or elsewhere, knows relatively little even of Dominic Barberi, George Spencer and Elizabeth Prout, and next to nothing of countless simple folks who converted. Most of the one-hundred-thousand who converted in America during the 1950s were such folks. Let them not be wholly forgotten while there is no end to the list of Newman Clubs and there is even a Newman University.

For this disparity Newman would be the first to protest, riveted as he was on the mystery of the cross, and on the need to be crucified with Christ, as the greatest treasure to possess. He kept telling prospective converts that it made more than good sense to sacrifice everything for the one great valuable pearl. All of Newman's converts had a full experience of this fact hardly ever spoken of. Nor had the vastness of his correspondence to prospective converts attracted his biographers and countless other Newmanists, who all too often tried to present him at times at an almost complete disregard of those letters' contents. Well, those letters contained not a whiff of progressive theology, which has become increasingly uneasy about conversions to the Catholic Church as the only safe way to salvation, to recall another favorite expression of Newman's. The evidence is in a vast volume, *Newman to Converts: An Existential Ecclesiology*, published in 2001, by the author of this introduction.

Among the pleasing, if not mind-boggling phrases of that "theology" one finds such assertions that Catholic ecclesiologists of the last few decades do not agree with Newman's all-or-nothing view of the Church of Rome as the God-given place of salvation. Such assertions would be largely forgotten when converts would still flock to the Roman Catholic Church. They vote with their feet on behalf of truth, which the more literate among them often put in striking phrases. The list given of them in this book was composed with that fact in view. It is a book that stands apart among books on converts, but is in line with the saying that facts prevail and one should be eager to find oneself on their side.

Nowadays many a theologian has become so comprehensive as to fail to comprehend the reality of hell as they preach the venomous news that all would go to heaven. They want to offer tasty meat at a total disregard of the fact that living meat comes from that marrow, the place of the formation of red blood cells, which can be housed only inside the bones that form that tangible skeleton which turns the Church into an organism, indeed into an organization. In such times, the need for a revitalization of our memory about a glorious list of nineteenth-century converts to Catholicism may be the best theological answer to a pernicious theological aberration which wants the idea of the Church but not its visible concrete reality.

While ideas, tenets, and notions can be given ever new spin, it is not so easy to twist and turn facts. And just as biographies can carry truth far more effectively than learned treatises, brief vignettes quoted from the writings of notable nineteenth-century converts may prove especially telling. But it takes well-tuned ears to hear their witness to Truth, writ large, the only Truth worth espousing.

The Feast of Saint Peter's Chair, 2007   Stanley L. Jaki

Appendix Three

Introduction to John Beaumont, *Early Converts* (2008)

The story of Christianity or rather of a Church, which if Christian can only be Catholic, has been from the start the story of conversions. The story opens with Saul whom the Lord himself converted. After Saul became Paul, he lived a life entirely devoted to making converts, from among Jews as well as Gentiles. The centuries that followed are highlighted by notable conversions. Justin Martyr, Cyprian of Carthage, Augustine of Hippo are major landmarks in that history. Later, entire nations became converted from paganism to Christianity, until Europe became Western Christendom.

One did not have to see the doctrinal fallacies of the Protestant Reform, it was enough to register the breakup of a previously solid cultural and often political unity of Christians in Europe, to look askance at what Luther initiated. Humanly speaking the outcome could not have happened in some cases, such as in England. Henry VIII might have nipped Lutheranism in the bud even on the Continent and given European history a direction wholly different from the one which historians, thriving often on clichés, take for a natural development.

Even in England the outcome would have been different had the Pilgrims of Peace not trusted a perfidious monarch. There followed the gradual suppression of Catholic England in the name of a pseudo-Catholicism. The reaction of English Catholics was heroic but also shortsighted. They hoped that England might be recaptured to its Catholic heritage. The "seminary priests" worked first for the reconciliation of individuals rather than for their conversion. Such is the reason why this book contains few entries on 16th-century converts in England.

The number is much larger from the 17th century, because by then it had become abundantly clear that the Church of England was thoroughly Protestant in character. It was therefore more proper from that century on to convert one to the Catholic Church rather than to have him reconciled with it. Even more pronounced was the case during the 18th century which witnessed Catholics in England diminish in number almost to the point of extinction. Bishop Challoner, a convert from his youth, registered this fact in somber words.

The present book offers a hitherto unmatched list of converts in England (and Ireland) during those three centuries.

Now that the decree, which the Office for the Doctrine of the Faith issued on June 29, 2007, dissipated the last misconceptions about ecumenism at least for those who are willing to read plain words, the role of conversions might regain its proper lustre. Further, with the beatification of John Henry Newman to be carried out soon, he may become the official patron saint of converts, whose theologian he was in an eminent degree, though not in eyes of some Newmanists who even today feel free to set him up as one not keen on conversions.

Converts have never petered out, only some progressive ecclesiologists thought it possible to downplay their importance. Although claiming to themselves an existential approach, mindful of facts above all, they failed to appraise in its true weight the fact that each conversion is a vote made with one's feet on behalf of a sound ec- clesiology. Their suggestion that the time has become ripe for a corporate reunion of Canterbury and Rome is refuted by the moral disorientation of the two Anglican Archbishops and most of their fellow bishops, some of whom view their "episco- pacy" as a form of civil service. At any rate, Newman did not fail to point out that for an individual to postpone his conversion until the moment of a corporate reunion is not only a betting on something most improbable, but also to play a hazardous game with one's conscience. May this book, with its plethora of data, strengthen some vacillating souls and enlighten some souls in the One True Fold.

The Feast of All Saints, 2008   Stanley L. Jaki

Appendix Four

POPERY AT THE PALACE
by Fr. Mark Elvins, OFM. Cap, and John Beaumont

Summertime is traditionally the time when good news stories are hard to come by and the papers and weekly journals are most likely to have to trawl for catchy items. Admittedly, the government is doing its best to help by reeling from one disaster to another almost on a weekly basis. But, it isn't generally like this and the press re-trenches to the staple fodder of Royal Ascot, Wimbledon strawberries and the latest fashion in boaters for Henley. Well, we can do better than that. We have a story of real significance, combining Royalty with an organization that is the bane of our liberal secular establishment, namely the Catholic Church. A few months ago, of course, the papers were full of the love travails of Prince William. It seemed that poor Kate Middleton just could not take the frenetic pace demanded of a future queen. The romance seems to be back on again, though doubts remain. A number of newspapers have suggested that in order for a person to be suitable in these days, she must, as it were, be bred for the job. Some analysts have even gone so far as to suggest that the most effective bride would come from the various Catholic princesses of Europe. Just one problem here, of course, which is that if William were to marry one of these beauties (assuming there is no latter day Anne of Cleves lurking amongst them), he would immediately lose his right of succession to the throne. As everyone knows, you can't be a Catholic, or marry one, and sit on the throne of England. Long gone are the days when Henry VIII was awarded the title Fidei Defensor (Defender of the Faith) by Pope Leo X in response to his treatise *Assertio Septem Sacramentorum* (*The Defence of the Seven Sacraments*), written to defend the seven sacraments of the Catholic Church, and the Sacrifice of the Mass, against the assertions of Martin Luther, and insistent upon the supremacy of the papacy. Henry, then, was defender of the Catholic faith as opposed to those later kings and queens, charged with the duty of defending the Protestant religion. All of this is a far cry from the present Prince of Wales, who appears to want to defend any old rag bag of ideas. We have to go back as far as King James II to find the last Catholic monarch to rule England.

Edward VII as a later defender of the faith?

Or do we? Recently evidence has come to light to cast doubt on this assumption. It is admittedly circumstantial and some of it might not stand up to cross-examination. But, it's worth looking at and even if presented somewhat tongue in cheek, has some merit. We start with King Edward VII and the coronation service. We know that Edward had major difficulties with the Protestant Declaration. In its original form this was simply the test which had been imposed on all Members of Parliament, and upon all officials in the time of the Titus Oates' Plot, and it required the person who took the test to denounce Transubstantiation with the idolatry of the sacrifice of the Mass, the invocation of the saints, as well as "the worship of the Virgin Mary." Even after the abolition of the Declaration in the case of subjects of the Sovereign, it still remained to be taken by the Sovereign at the time of Edward VII's coronation. It was reported in *The Tablet* at the time that the King was so ashamed of what he was required to do that he mumbled the Declaration so quietly that only the Lord Chancellor standing before the throne could hear what he was saying. Moreover the King had to pledge that he made this declaration "without any dispensation, or hope of dispensation, from the Pope or any other authority," just in case he was secretly thinking of becoming a Catholic.

One of the reasons for Edward VII's attitude was that he had strong Catholic sympathies. An indication of these is contained in an interesting article by Sir Shane Leslie, "Sidelight on King Edward VII" (*The Month*, January 1957, p.37). Leslie notes how his subject was brought up in the narrowest possible Anglicanism, but developed a broadness of mind which made him an Irish sympathizer, a friend of France, and a champion of Catholic equality. Leslie gives examples of the King's Catholic sympathies:

"The King never missed an excuse for attending Mass, but his position allowed him but few occasions. He always attended the Austrian emperor's birthday Mass if he was in the Austrian dominions. He attended the Requiem for the King of Portugal in St. James's Palace. His attitude was to stand within the Sanctuary, which was perfectly consistent with his deep reverence for Catholic belief."

The article also describes activities before the King's succession to the throne which throw light on his (and his wife's) great devotion even then to the Blessed Sacrament:

"The late Fr. Forster was Parish Priest at the Chapel of the Irish Guards, and used to recount that in old days he was sometimes summoned to bring the Blessed Sacrament to Marlborough House when any Catholic guest of the Prince was in need of his services. Fr. Forster on these occasions found the gates open before him and at the threshold of Marlborough House was always met by the Prince and Princess carrying lighted tapers and conducting him, without saying a word, to and from the bedroom of their ailing guest."

King Edward VII had no particular friends among the Anglican bishops, but he developed personal friendship with two priests, Fr. Bernard Vaughan and the Abbot of Tepl, the Premonstratensian abbey in the Archdiocese of Prague. Fr. Vaughan was a Jesuit, a famous preacher and public speaker, who resided from 1901 until his death in 1922 at Farm Street, London. In 1898 on the French Riviera Fr. Vaughan preached a Lenten course. His hearers at Cannes included Edward, then Prince of Wales, who asked for the manuscript of his sermon on St Mary Magdalen. As there was no manuscript, Vaughan wrote out the sermon, "The woman that was a sinner," from his notes and presented it to the Prince, with whom a close friendship developed. Another close friend of the King was the Portuguese Catholic, the Marquess de Soverall. As Prince of Wales, Edward had visited Pope Pius IX three times.

The Right Reverend David Hunter-Blair, the Benedictine monk, recounts (in *Memories and Musings* (1929)) other Catholic associations, for example the King's warm regard and esteem for Henry Duke of Norfolk, a notable Catholic. Also, his attendance at Mass was more than a mere formality, the King following "every detail, missal in hand, with attention, veneration, and respect." Further, he points out that Edward VII was the first English king since the Plantagenets to cross the threshold of the Papal Palace in Rome. Edward carried out his intention to visit Pope Leo XIII on this occasion (in 1903) in spite of the disapproval of the Prime minister, Arthur Balfour. Hunter-Blair also recounts the fact that, as Prince of Wales, the King attended two Nuptial Masses, one "in the Kensington pro-Cathedral, when his Premier, W. E. Gladstone, refused to attend ... 'lest there should be a popular outcry.'" The other was in 1889 at the London Oratory.

In *The Universe* Catholic newspaper of the 13th of May 1910 the editor recorded the King's "munificence to the Catholic Church at King's Lynn," not far from Sandringham and added that practically the last big religious function he attended was the Blessed Sacrament procession at Lourdes. On that occasion he entered the grotto and apparently prayed at La Roque church there. This is further evidence of at least a disposition to become a Catholic.

Sir Shane Leslie, another convert of course, confirms that after Edward VII's death there were many rumors of his conversion to the Church, but cites no specific authorities to support this. So, what evidence is there on this question?

An intriguing factor is that Paul Cambon (1843–1924), the French Ambassador at the time of the King's death (he was Ambassador from 1898 to 1920 in all), was summoned by Queen Alexandra to pay a final friendly visit to the King as he lay dying and noticed a Catholic priest leaving his bedside. According to the Catholic writer, Gerard Noel, writing in the Catholic Herald (28th June 1985), Paul Cambon noted in his memoirs that he knew the priest by sight, but not by name. Certainly, shortly after King Edward VII's death a full Catholic Requiem Mass was offered in Westminster Cathedral for the repose of his soul.

With regard to the identity of the priest, there is evidence that it may have been the one mentioned earlier, namely Fr. Cyril Forster. A member of the same family, Dr. Lavinia Braun-Davenport, was reported recently by Mary Kenny in her column in the *Catholic Herald* (25 September 2009) as saying that in her family tradition she was "brought up with the knowledge that my grandmother's great uncle, Fr. Cyril Forster, had converted the King of England to Catholicism on his deathbed." The king was Edward VII. The suggestion is that Fr. Forster was taken by Sir Ernest Cassel, a close friend of the King and a Catholic convert himself (from Judaism), to see the sovereign as he lay dying. It is claimed that Edward there accepted the Roman Catholic faith. Mary Kenny states that it was possible that Cassel brought along Fr. Forster. However, her further claim that all the standard biographies of Edward VII agree that Sir Ernest Cassel was the king's last visitor cannot be supported. It also seems to conflict with Cambon's account. Whatever may be the case here, Dr. Braun-Davenport's grandmother left a note saying that Edward's conversion was "a 'family secret' – the Old Rake's Repentance!" The matter was treated discreetly, but the lore was passed down through the Forster family just the same. Mary Kenny goes on to pose the question as to whether Fr. Forster was a reliable witness, if, without betraying the confessional secret, he did not deny it to his own family? Kenny writes as follows:

"Apparently he was a man of respected integrity. And he was already well known to the King, and trusted by him. Sir Shane Leslie ... described Fr. Forster, in 1964, as 'a gentleman of the old school, hating cant and advertisement ... courageous, old-fashioned and transparently honest ... The public never heard his name, but as the Royal residences lay in his parish, he had become a friend of King Edward VII, whom, it was supposed, he had at last received into the Catholic fold."

A further strand of evidence comes from Niall Diarmid Campbell, the tenth Duke of Argyll (1872–1949). The tenth Duke certainly told acquaintances of his that Edward VII died a Catholic. The tenth Duke succeeded his uncle, the ninth Duke, in 1914. The ninth Duke was married to Queen Victoria's daughter, Princess Louise, so there was a close court connection.

Finally, Philip Trower, the writer on Catholic issues, describes an account given by one of his great aunts, who back in the late 1880s married an Austrian professor in Innsbruck. She had two daughters, the eldest of whom married a doctor, Alfons Huber, who eventually became head of the great psychiatric hospital in Vienna, Am Steinhof. At some time, probably during the 1920s or 1930s, Mrs. Huber was staying with her daughter and son-in-law at Am Steinhof, when two German princesses paid a visit to the hospital and afterwards came to tea. It was during tea that, to everyone's surprise, they said, as if it were something quite well known, that Edward VII had died a Catholic. The identities of the two princesses is not known, and there must have been a considerable number of German princesses at that time, but Mr. Trower believes Mrs. Huber's account to have been that these ladies were connected with the English royal house. The account is not something that his great aunt would have invented. She was an old-fashioned Anglican and if anything had evidently been rather put out by what she had been told as witnessed by her tone of voice when asking her great nephew whether he had heard any story of the same sort.

Fr. James Martin Gillis, the famous Paulist preacher, writing in his column in the *New York News*, on the 13th of April 1936 declared that: "Edward VII had the decency to protest against the oath against Transubstantiation. In reward for his courage in that matter, he died a Catholic." He added that ... "I have direct, authentic reliable inside information on the matter which I could not as a journalist obtain permission to publish. But you may put it down as fact – Edward VII died a Catholic."

Fr. Gillis did not reveal the source of the evidence that he claimed to have. This is unfortunate. The conclusion of Shane Leslie, referred to above, in his review (see The Tablet, 21st March 1964, p.323) of Philip Magnus's biography of Edward VII, is much more nuanced. He sums things up in this way:

"There can be no doubt that Fr. Forster ... was one of the king's visitors on his last day but, though much gossip was exchanged, anyone knowing Fr. Forster would know that he would not have done more than assure the king he was dying in good faith. When questioned on the subject he always answered: "I wish I could tell you."

The position, then, is uncertain, though there is more than merely circumstantial evidence supporting the case for conversion. It is then interesting to speculate as to whether Sir David Hunter-Blair is giving us a hint in the course of his comments referred to earlier. In reviewing Sir Sidney Lee's two-volume biography of the king, he says this:

"His account of the King's death makes melancholy reading enough; but he, at least, does not know the whole and true history of those last hours."

George V and the Catholic faith

During the reign of Edward VII efforts were made in Parliament to change the wording of the Protestant Declaration, but these were frustrated by anti-Catholic pressure. However, after Edward's death on 6th May 1910 a new Bill was rushed through parliament. This modified the wording of the oath to read: "I am a faithful Protestant," and so it was King George V who was to derive the benefit. Like his predecessor, he too had Catholic sympathies and was tolerant of his wife, Queen Mary, attending the Catholic Church of the Assumption, Warwick Street. In a recent biography of Princess Margaret written by Noel Botham and entitled *Margaret - The Last Real Princess* (Blake Publishing Ltd., 2002), we read that Queen Mary herself was received into the Catholic Church with the approval of the King (see pp.364–367). In this it is claimed that she was guided by a senior Jesuit priest from Farm Street, who would subsequently visit Buckingham Palace each Sunday to say a private Mass for her. It is further claimed that not only had the King been present at his wife's instruction, but that he himself was also received into the Church. Hence, the same priest, with Queen Mary in attendance, gave King George V the last rites of the Catholic Church shortly before he died on 18th January 1936. However, we have to raise some possible doubts about this testimony. We know nothing regarding the credibility of Mr. Botham, but we do know that he also wrote a book entitled *The Murder of Princess Diana*, which promotes a conspiracy theory regarding this case. Now, this doesn't by itself render Botham unreliable on George V, but it does give some cause for concern.

However, there is further evidence from a better source, Canon Reginald Fuller, a priest of the diocese of Westminster and a notable scripture scholar, who was assistant at the Church of Assumption at one time. He stated that he had known a retired Catholic nurse who had been present at Buckingham Palace at the time of King George V's death, and that it was the Queen who had sent for the priest at the Church of the Assumption, knowing the King's attraction to the Catholic Church.

Thus, although largely unknown, two of our recent sovereigns may have indeed been hidden defenders of the faith. One cannot be sure and we would be grateful to those who can add further to this story. On a more serious note, the anomaly of bearing such a Catholic title as "Defender of the Faith" whilst making an oath to be "a faithful Protestant" indicates vividly the injustice of requiring the monarch to embrace a faith that may be at odds with his or her conscience.

This is a revised and expanded version of an article originally published in the January 2009 issue of *Catholic Life*.

Appendix Five

Newman, Conversion, and the One True Fold
by John Beaumont

On 8th January 1845 John Henry Newman, then still an Anglican, wrote to a friend, Miss Maria Giberne, as follows:

"The simple question is, Can *I* (it is personal, not whether another, but can *I*) be saved in the English Church? Am I in safety, were I to die to-night? Is it a mortal sin in me, not joining another Communion?"

This statement from one who was undoubtedly the greatest convert of the nineteenth century illustrates something that has been downplayed on occasions in recent years, the seriousness of the process of conversion. No better example of this crucial search for the truth can be found than that of Newman's last few days as a Protestant and his preparation for reception into the Catholic Church. This can be done primarily by reading Volumes X and XI of his *Letters and Diaries*, together with that classic text, written some twenty years later, *Apologia Pro Vita Sua*, in which he gave an account of his conversion. In those sources can be seen also the vital importance to Newman of the oneness of the Church, something he emphasizes again and again in his writings.

Newman was received into the Church over the period of the 8th and 9th October 1845. He began to make his confession to Fr. Dominic Barberi on the evening of the 8th, continued the next day and was received that same day. In the *Apologia* Newman explains how this came about:

"One of my friends at Littlemore [J. D. Dalgairns] had been received into the Church on Michaelmas Day, at the Passionist house at Aston, near Stone, by Father Dominic, the Superior. At the beginning of October, the latter was passing through London to Belgium; and, as I was in some perplexity what steps to take for being received myself, I assented to the proposition made to me that the good priest should take Littlemore in his way, with a view to his doing for me the same charitable service as he had done to my friend."

On 3rd October, Newman resigned his fellowship at Oriel College, Oxford. From then until 5th October he wrote to four persons, indicating what he might do, but only in terms of what was "possible", "likely", or "probable". The 5th October, a Sunday, he spent preparing for a general confession. Then, during the period from 7th October to the morning of 9th October, Newman wrote no fewer than twenty-nine letters to relatives and close friends, nineteen of which still survive, letters that were "not to go till all was over." In these letters he announced definitively that he was about to be received into the Church. There is in fact a thirtieth letter, also surviving, as he wrote twice during this time to his sister, Jemima (Mrs. John Mozley), having received a letter from her after sending the first one.

It is most enlightening (and, of course, moving) to read the texts of the nineteen extant letters. One of the most interesting aspects is the phraseology that Newman uses in order to express what was about to happen to him. In three of the letters he refers to his prospective "admission into the Catholic Church" and in one to admission into the "bosom of the Catholic Church." One of these letters refers also to his being "received," a term used on its own in three others. More significant, however, is the fact that in five of the other twelve letters (including those to luminaries such as Manning, Faber, and Henry Wilberforce) he uses the term "one true fold of Christ" or "one true fold of the Redeemer." In another three (including that to Pusey) the reference is to the "one and only fold of Christ" or the "one and only fold of the Redeemer." On one occasion it is the "one Church and one Communion of Saints"; and three times (notably to Jemima and to Newman's great friend, R. W. Church) he uses the term "one fold of Christ" or "one fold of the Redeemer". In addition, on many occasions, in later letters to prospective converts, Newman referred to the Catholic Church as "the one ark of salvation".

It is interesting to note that after Newman's death, R. W. Church claimed that Newman had become a Catholic because only the Catholic Church preserved in full strength the spirit of "devotion and sacrifice" of the Church of the Apostles. This evades the true issue by falling back on subjective phenomena (devotion and sacrifice) when Newman was interested above all, as can be seen in the last paragraph, in the evidence of objective truth (the One True Fold).

Now let us move on another 146 years and consider the following. In 1991 Dr. William Oddie was received into the Catholic Church. He was an Anglican clergyman and fellow of St. Cross College, Oxford. He had, of course, written to the Anglican Bishop of Oxford, Richard Harries, to explain his position. The bishop then issued a press statement, which was widely publicized at the time, in which he stated that Oddie was merely "moving into another room in the same house." What is less well-known is Oddie's response to this, which reads as follows:

"When I went to see him, I told him that was simply untrue. The truth was that I had been camping out in a garden shed, some distance from the main house, and one night when the rain was pouring in and the roof leaking, I went to the main house and begged for some shelter. And they opened the door and said 'But of course! A room has always been ready and prepared for you. Welcome home!' That was the reality."

There is a world of difference between the approach of John Henry Newman and that of Dr. Richard Harries. Was this Anglican cleric correct in his statement? And does this mean that the Catholic Church's teaching has changed on this most important issue?

Well, it is certainly clear what Newman would have thought about Richard Harries' press release in 1991. We know this because of a remarkably similar event. In a letter written by Newman, two months after his conversion, to Dalgairns, Newman describes a meeting with Dr. Pusey, who never of course converted, and states disapprovingly that Pusey expected them to act like vinedressers who had merely "transferred to another part of the vineyard."

Equally trenchant would have been Newman's attitude to those who today look forward to the eventual fusion of Rome and Canterbury. He had correspondence with such people, notably G. Dawson, an Anglican clergyman, in his own time, and left no doubt as to what was the authentic Catholic attitude. In a letter written in 1848 Newman expressed clearly and directly why there could be no fusion:

"The Anglican and the Catholic are two religions. I have professed both, and must know better than those who have professed one only. It is not a case, then, that one believes a little more, and the other a little less; and therefore that they could unite. The religions never could unite; they never could be reconciled together."

He goes on to expound on this by listing a large number of points where the two religions crucially differ, for example in respect to a living authority, one centre of jurisdiction, the sacraments, and the question of ordination, concluding as follows:

"It is a dream then to think of uniting the two religions; I speak from experience of both. And, in finding this to be the case, I am recording no disappointment on my part. I joined the Catholic Church to save my soul; I said so at the time. No inferior motive would have drawn me from the Anglican. And I came to it to learn, to receive what I should find, whatever it was. Never for an instant have I had since any misgiving I was right in doing so – never any misgiving that the Catholic religion was not the religion of the Apostles."

It is because Newman held that conversion was a vitally important matter and, as he put it to Mrs. Lucy Agnes Phillips, the widow of an evangelical clergyman, "the Catholic Church claims absolute submission to her in matters of faith," that he insisted that a decision must be made. On the one hand, as he wrote to many correspondents, and to Mrs. Phillips herself in 1851, "unless you believe her doctrines, as the word of God revealed to you through her, you can gain no good by professing to be a Catholic – you are not one really."

On the other hand, Newman emphasized the seriousness and urgency involved, and the danger of delaying beyond a certain point. He wrote as follows in 1873 to another prospective convert, Mrs. Newdigate:

"If your mind has been clear for some time that the Church we call Catholic is the one true fold of Christ, and if you can acknowledge all her teaching, what she teaches and shall teach, it is your simple duty to ask for admittance into her communion, and you cannot delay your actual reconciliation, except the priest to whom you go tells you to delay."

Newman kept preaching, especially to converts, that there was only One True Fold, that to belong to it was the key to one's eternal salvation, whereas to postpone endlessly one's conversion might inure one into the treacherous habit of living in sin, the sin of schism. He puts it in this way to Lord Charles Thynne, another prospective convert:

"Two different bodies cannot form a single body: one or other is not the Church, or, to use your language, one or the other is in schism.... The question is, whether, were you dying, you would be satisfied in your not having joined Rome."

So, to return to the question put earlier, has the Church changed its teaching on this issue? Not at all. One only needs to look at the teaching of the Second Vatican Council, especially the Constitution on the Church (*Lumen Gentium*) and the Decree on Ecumenism (*Unitatis Redintegratio*), together with a number of important postconciliar documents. These would include, in particular, the following texts issued by the Congregation for the Doctrine of the Faith: *Mysterium Ecclesiae* (1973); *Notification on the Book of Father Leonardo Boff, "The Church: Charism and Power"* (1985); *Dominus Jesus* (2000).

The latest summary and clarification of all of this is contained in the same Congregation's document, *Responses to Some Questions Regarding Certain Aspects of the Doctrine of the Church*, issued on 29th June 2007. The crucial passage is the following:

"Christ 'established here on earth' only one Church and instituted it as a 'visible and spiritual community,' that from its beginning and throughout the centuries has always existed and will always exist, and in which alone are found all the elements that Christ himself instituted. 'This one Church of Christ, which we confess in the Creed as one, holy, catholic and apostolic.... This Church, constituted and organized in this world as a society, subsists in the Catholic Church, governed by the successor of Peter and the Bishops in communion with him'."

In number 8 of the Dogmatic Constitution *Lumen Gentium* "subsistence" means this perduring, historical continuity and the permanence of all the elements instituted by Christ in the Catholic Church, in which the Church of Christ is concretely found on this earth.

It is possible, according to Catholic doctrine, to affirm correctly that the Church of Christ is present and operative in the churches and ecclesial Communities not yet fully in communion with the Catholic Church, on account of the elements of sanctification and truth that are present in them. Nevertheless, the word 'subsists' can only be attributed to the Catholic Church alone precisely because it refers to the mark of unity that we profess in the symbols of the faith (I believe ... in the 'one' Church); and this 'one' Church subsists in the Catholic Church.

In addition, in the Notification on Leonardo Boff, referred to above, the essential points are made very clearly indeed. In response to Boff's assertion that the one Church of Christ "is able to subsist in other Christian Churches," the Notification states that "the Council chose the word 'subsistit' specifically to clarify that the true Church has only one 'subsistence,' while outside her visible boundaries there are only 'elementa Ecclesiae' which – being elements of the same Church – tend and lead to the Catholic Church." This is all part of the connection between Christ and his Church. The real reason the Church is One is because Christ is One. The voice of Christ is not preserved by Churches that contradict one another.

In addition to all of the above teaching, there is now the *Doctrinal Note on Some Aspects of Evangelization* issued by the Congregation for the Doctrine of the Faith on 6th October 2007 and dealing with the implications for mission. This is completely in line with the documents referred to above.

So, when we look at Newman's reflections on conversion and its nature we can be confident that we are looking at the truth. In addition to the teaching of the Church on this question there is, of course, the force of logic. It was expressed by an expert on Newman, Fr. Stanley Jaki, as follows:

"Newman's words were so many reminders that the Son of God, in whom alone there is salvation, established only One Fold, which therefore had to be the sole True Fold. After all, if God was one, and the Son was Only begotten and took flesh in only one specific moment in space and time, then the uniqueness of that Fold had to appear a matter of elementary logic."

Finally, there is no better way to express the Catholic faith on this issue than was done by Newman himself in 1851 in a letter to an unnamed woman:

"Dear Madam, Of course, my only answer to you can be that the Catholic Church is the true fold of Christ, and that it is your duty to submit to it. You cannot do this without God's grace and therefore you ought to pray Him continually for it. All is well if God is on our side."

This is a revised and expanded version of an article originally published in the Septemeber/October 2008 issue of the *Saint Austin Review*.

About the Author

John Beaumont is a lawyer by training and was formerly Head of the School of Law at Leeds Metropolitan University, England. He is now working as a legal consultant and freelance writer on Catholic issues. He has written for leading Catholic journals in both the United States and Great Britain.